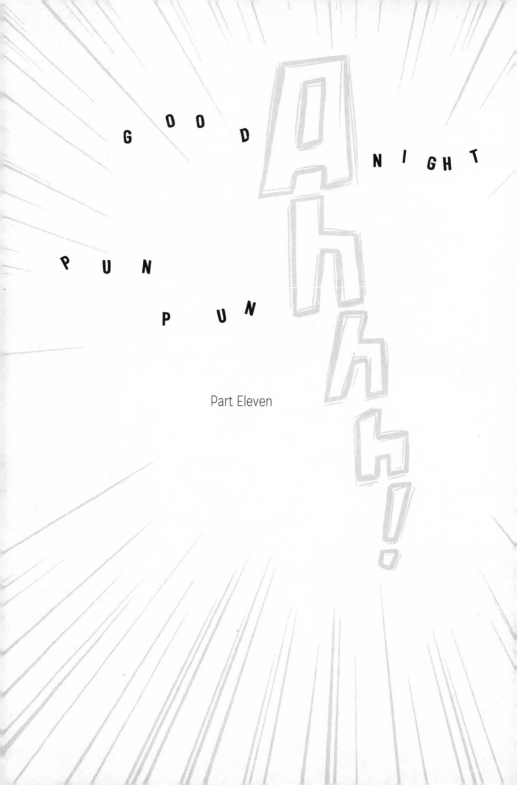

GOOD NIGHT PUN PUN

Part Eleven

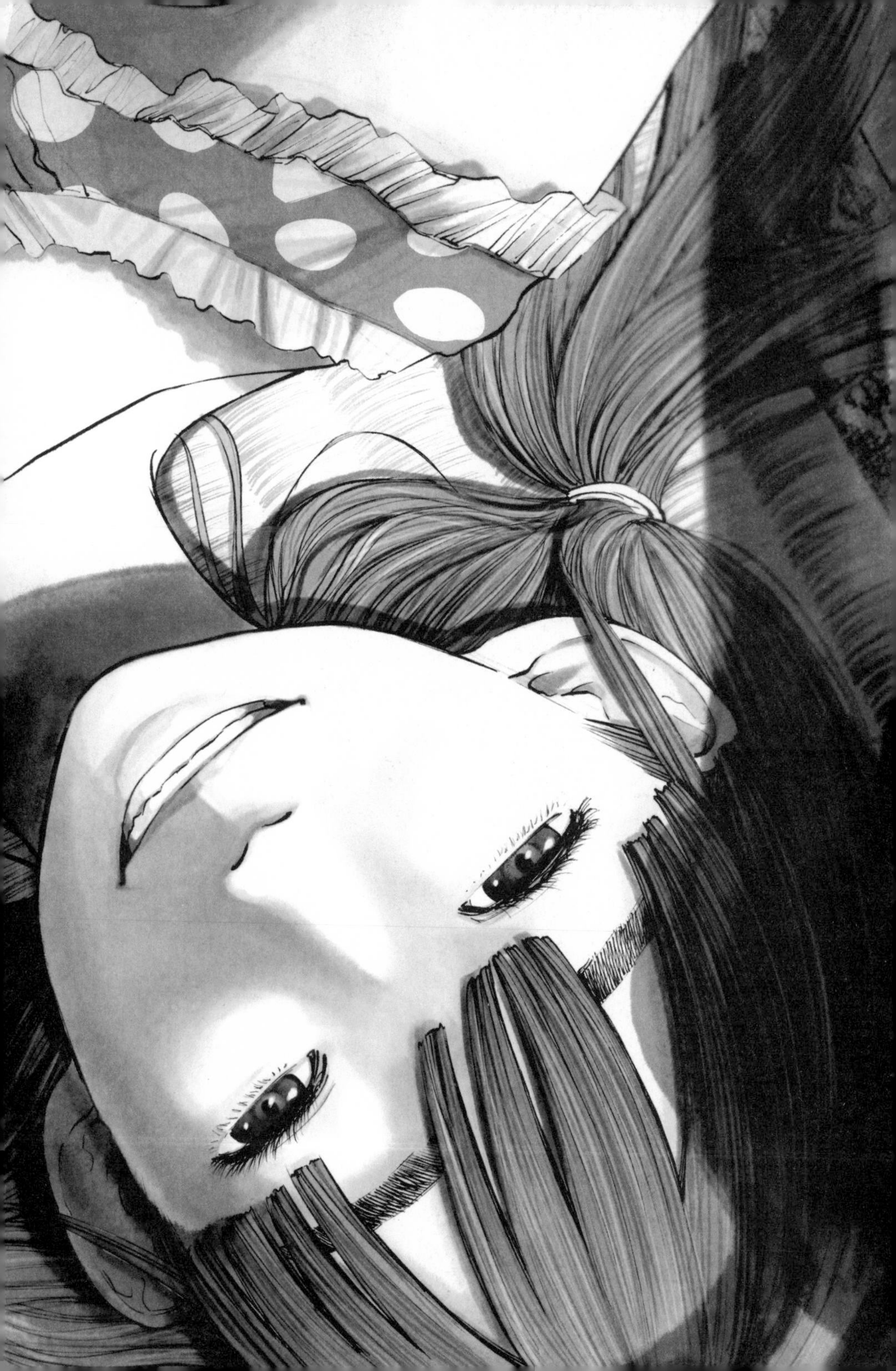

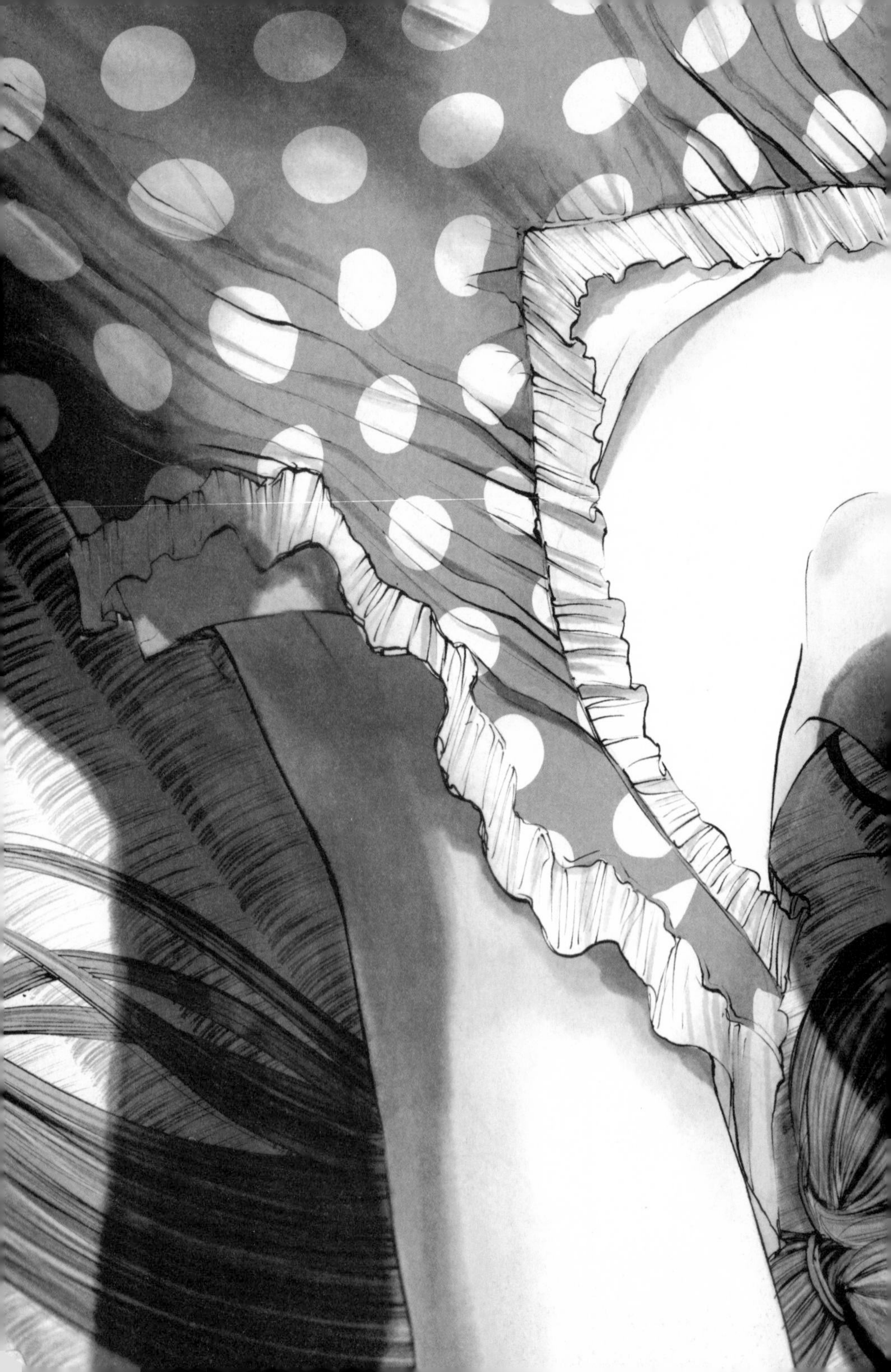

[เนื้อเรื่องที่ผ่านมาจนถึงเล่ม 10]

ทานากะไอโกะเพื่อนรุ่นเดียวกันกลับมาเรียนที่โรงเรียนขับรถอีกครั้งเธอใช้ชีวิตรันทดภายใต้การควบคุมจากแม่โอนาเดระปุนปุนไปหาแม่ของไอโกะเพื่อให้ได้รับอนุญาตให้อยู่ร่วมชายคาเดียวกันกับไอโกะ

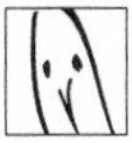

ตัวละครในเรื่อง

โอโนเดระ ปุนปุน
ทำงานพาร์ทไทม์ นิสัยไม่ค่อยสู้คนและมักหดหู่เป็นประจำ อายุ 20 ปี

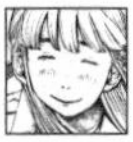

ทานากะ ไอโกะ
อดีตเพื่อนร่วมห้องของปุนปุน ทำงานที่โรงงานรับจ้างของร้านซักรีด

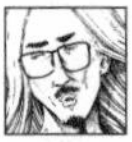

โฮชิคาวะ โทชิกิ
ลูกชายคนรองของโฮชิคาวะฮิโรชิกิและเป็นตัวแทนของศาสนาใหม่ที่ชื่อว่า "ศูนย์สุขภาพคุณคอสโม"
อวดอ้างว่าตัวเองรู้อนาคตได้

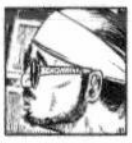

พี่ชายขนฟู Sweet Pretty Lonely (**วาดะ**)
เพื่อนสมัยเรียนมหาวิทยาลัยของโฮชิคาวะ โทชิกิ ครูโรงเรียนกวดวิชา ขนทั่วร่างหนาดก

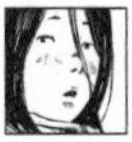

เซกิ มาสึมิ
อดีตเพื่อนร่วมห้องของปุนปุนทำอาชีพรวบรวมขยะรีไซเคิลขายมักไปอาศัยอยู่ในห้องแฟนประจำ

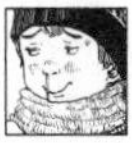

ชิมิซึ
อดีตเพื่อนร่วมห้องของปุนปุนตอนนี้เป็นนักศึกษามหาวิทยาลัยสามารถมองเห็น "เทพอุจจาระ" ได้

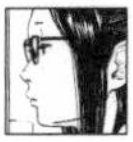

นันโจ ซาจิ
ครูโรงเรียนกวดวิชา เพื่อนสนิทของปุนปุน กำลังตั้งครรภ์ อายุ 25 ปี

[สารบัญ]

Chapter 111

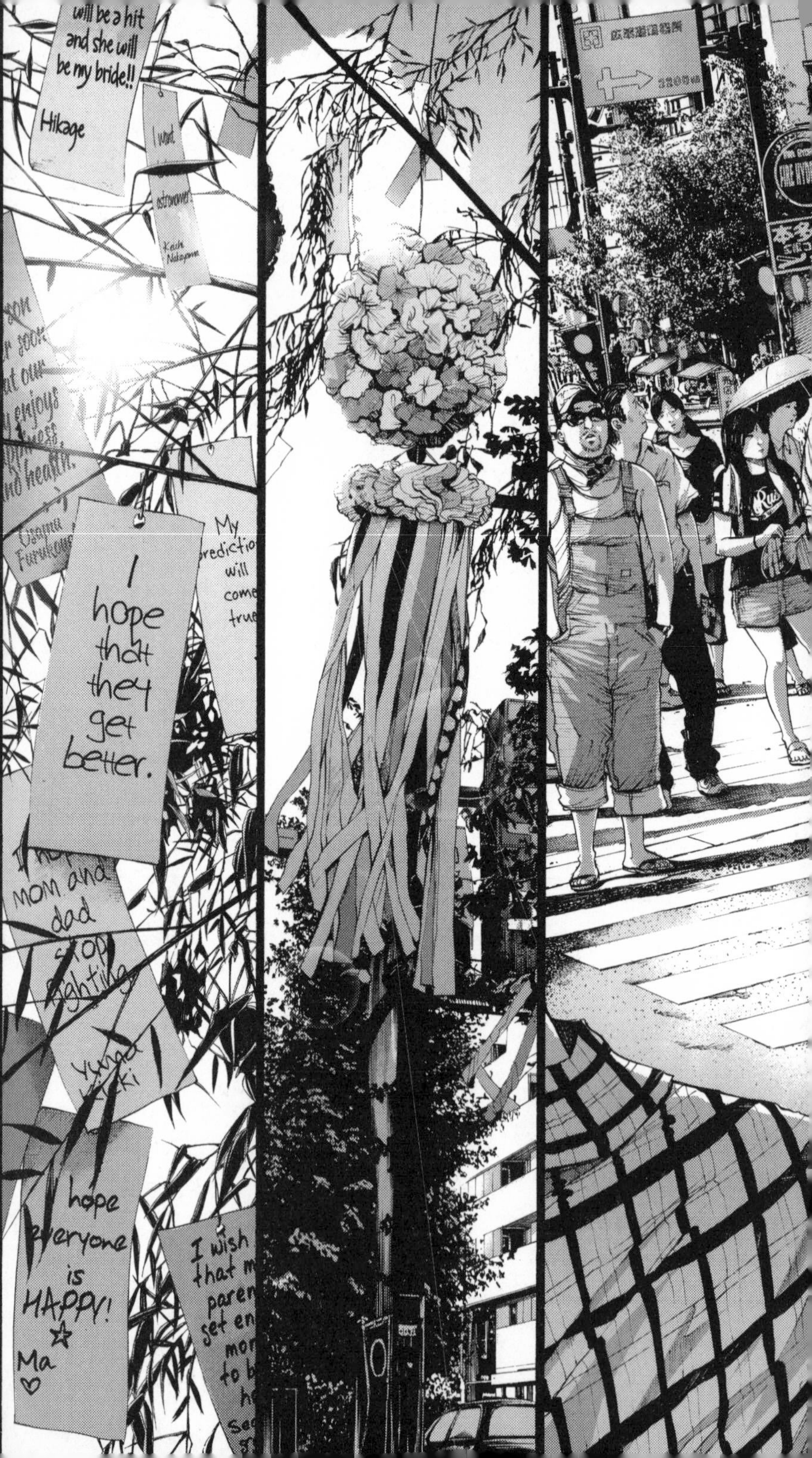
will be a hit
and she will
be my bride!!
Hikage
I hope that they get better.
My prediction will come true
hope
everyone
is
HAPPY!
☆

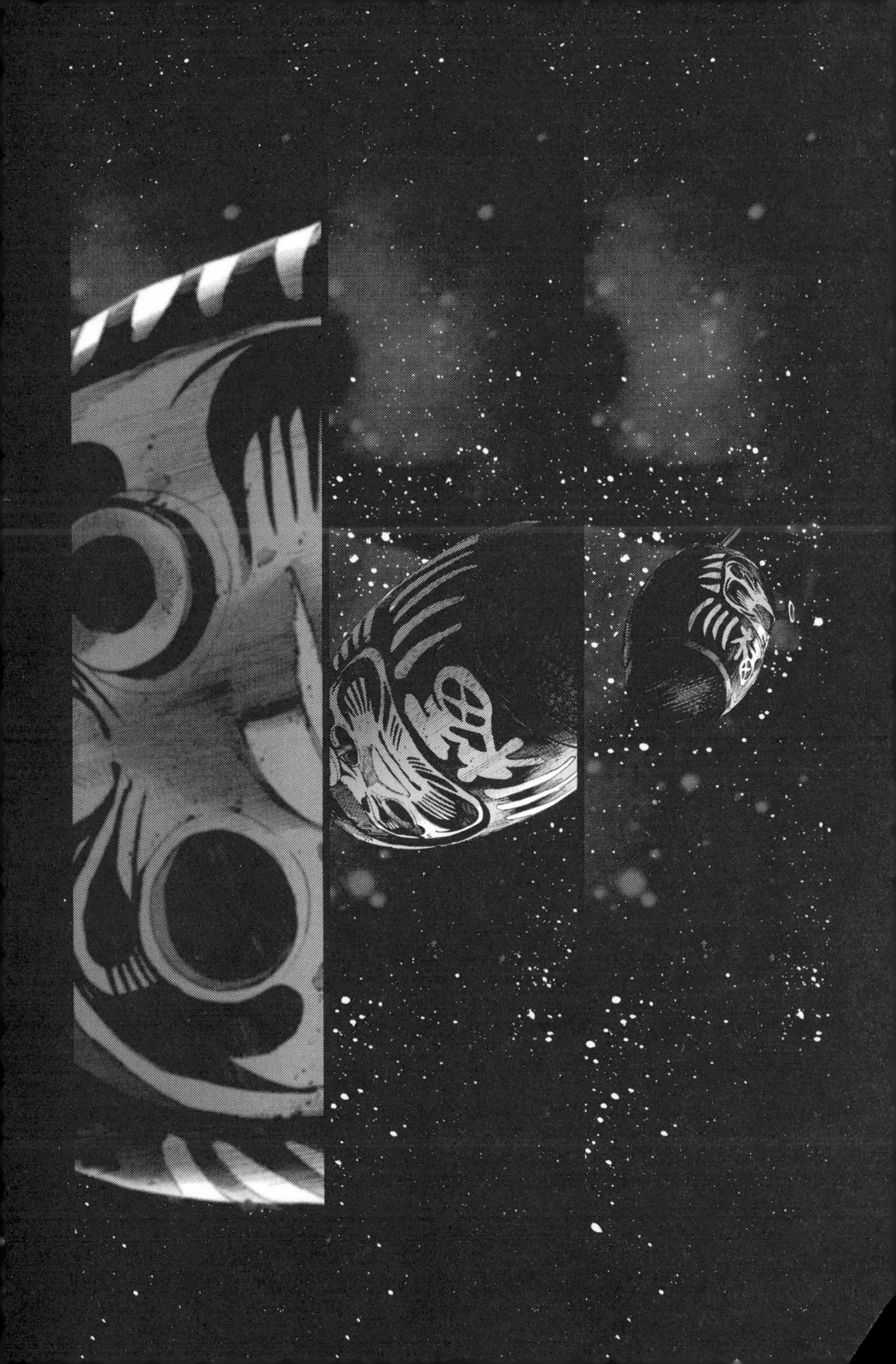

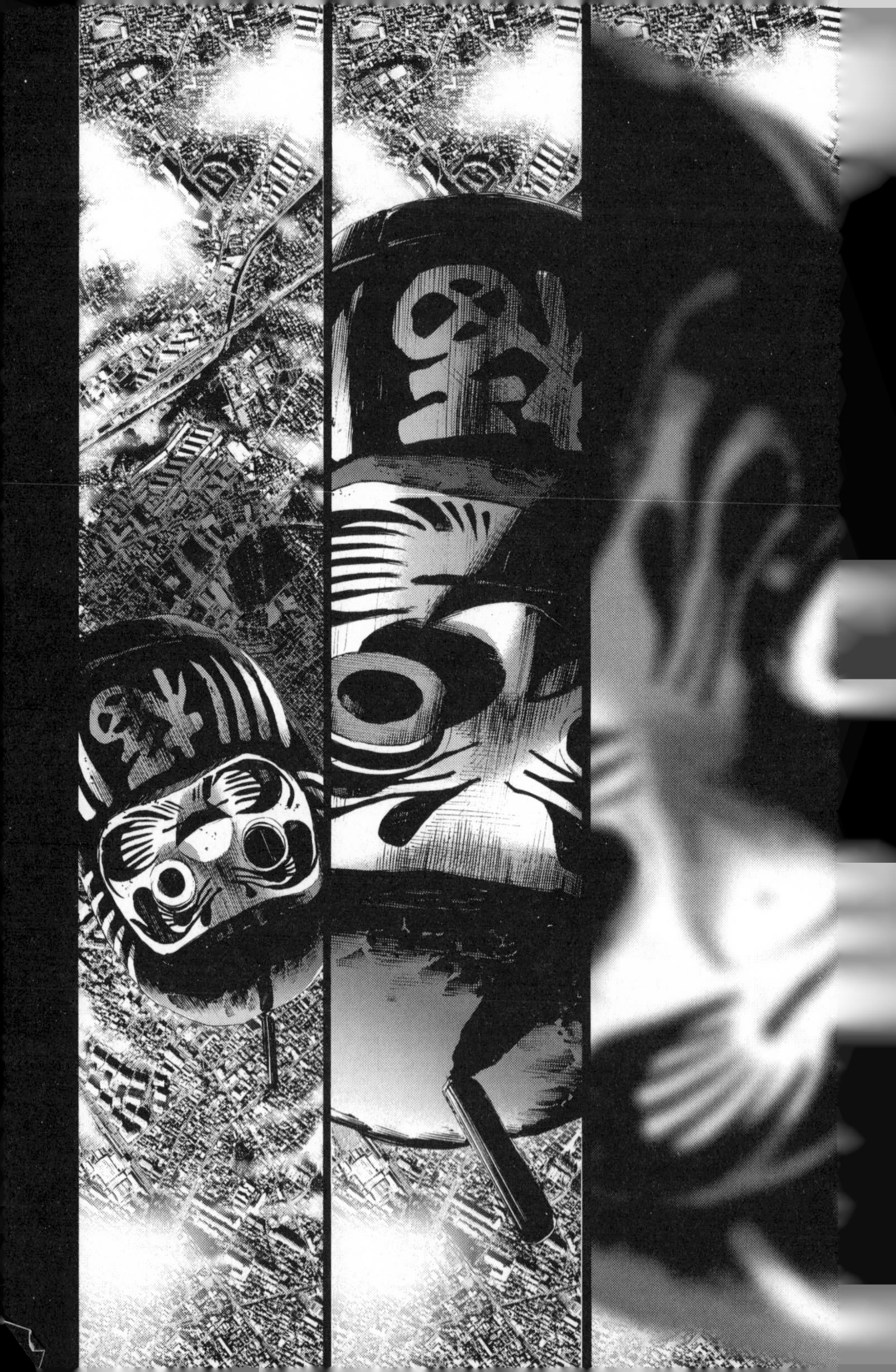

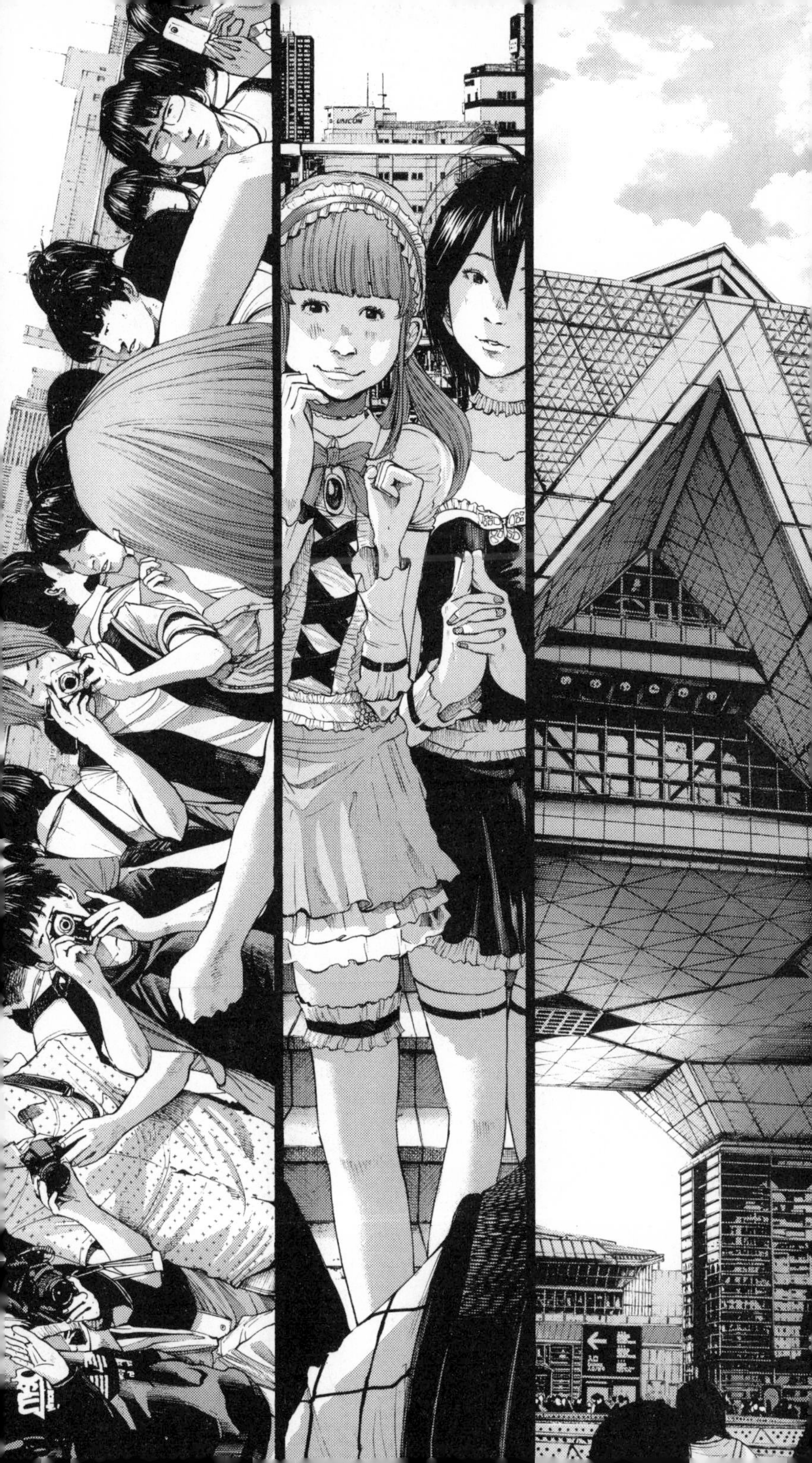

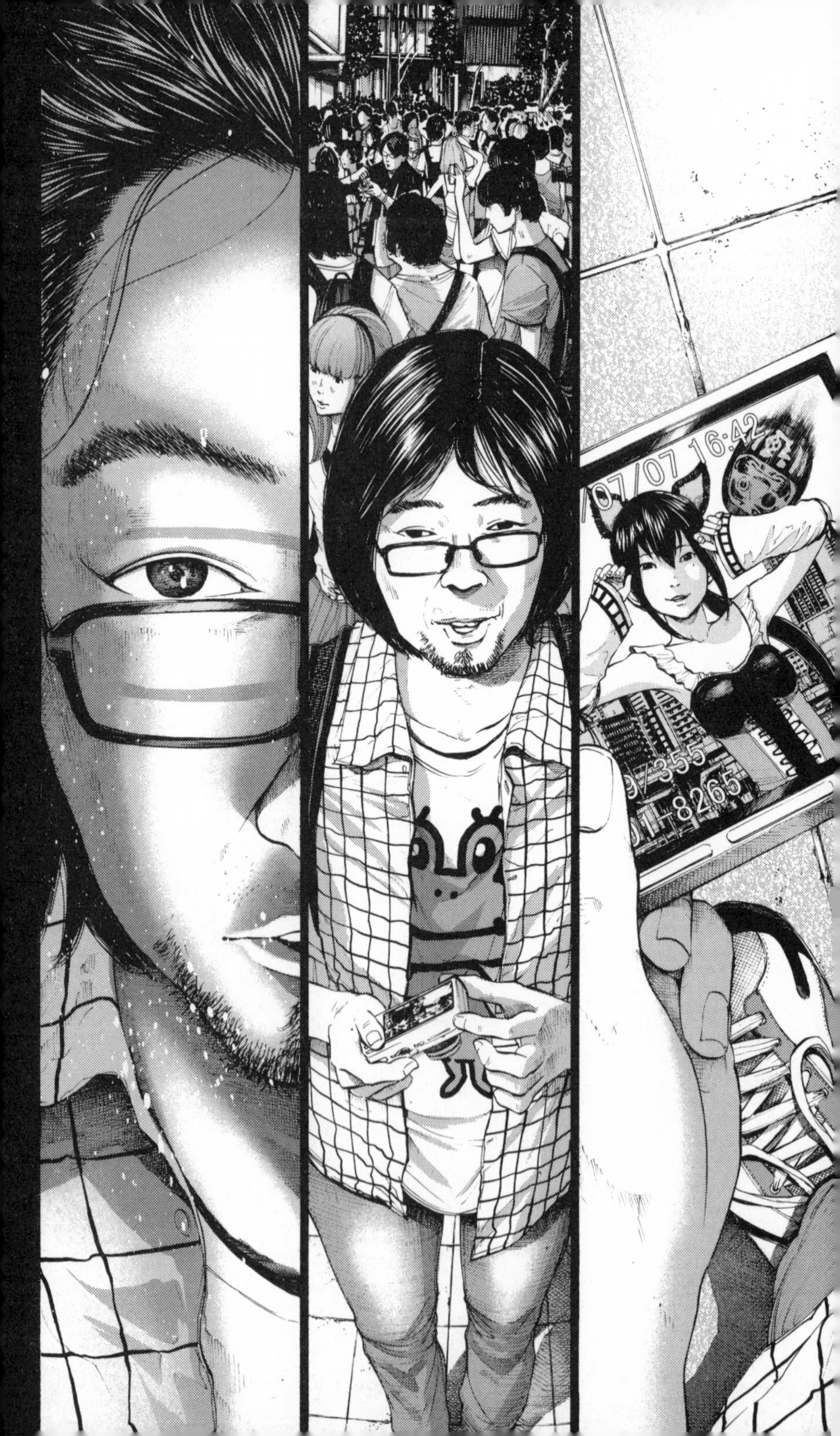

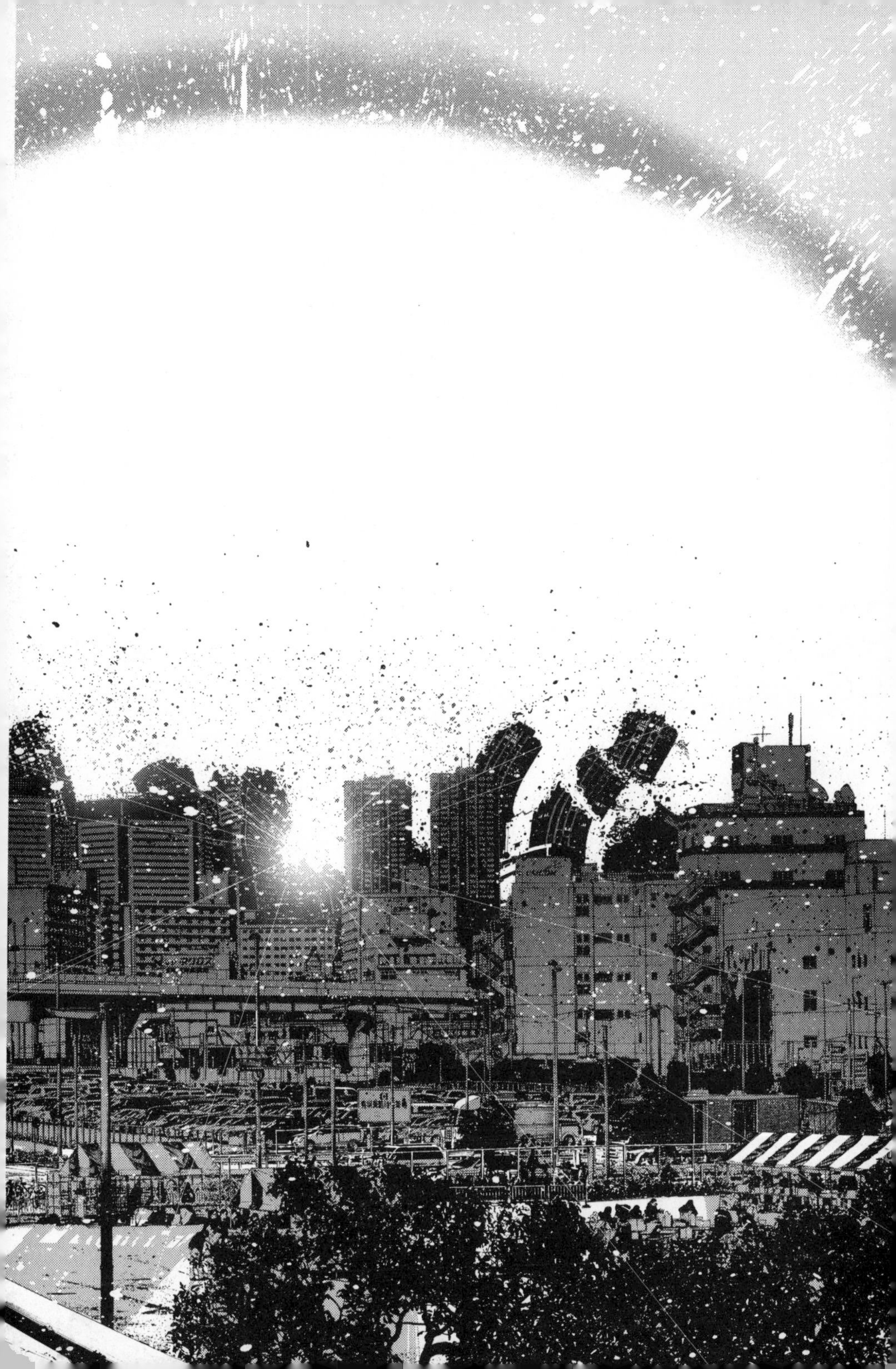

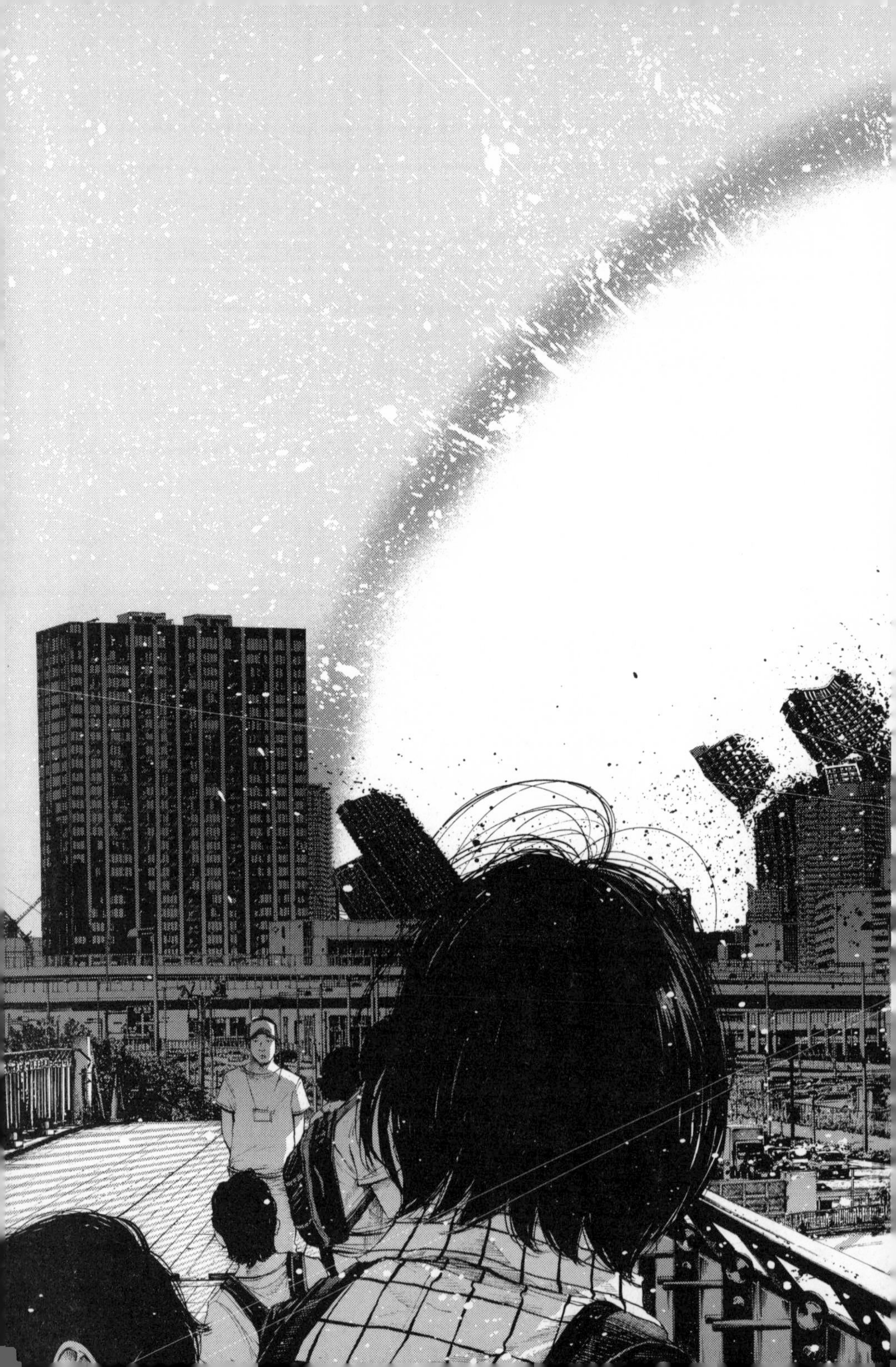

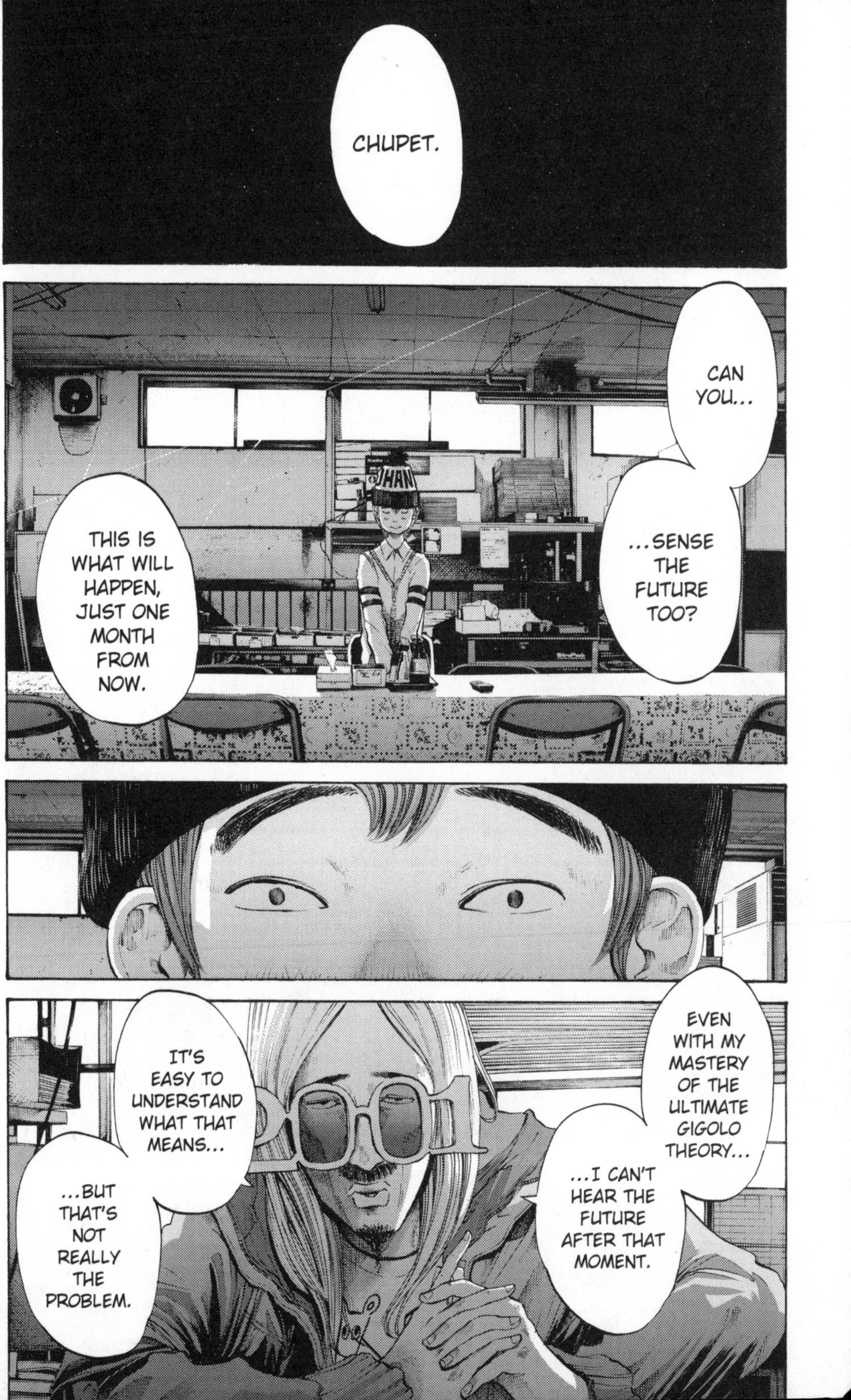
CHUPET.
CAN YOU...
...SENSE THE FUTURE TOO?
THIS IS WHAT WILL HAPPEN, JUST ONE MONTH FROM NOW.
EVEN WITH MY MASTERY OF THE ULTIMATE GIGOLO THEORY...
...I CAN'T HEAR THE FUTURE AFTER THAT MOMENT.
IT'S EASY TO UNDERSTAND WHAT THAT MEANS...
...BUT THAT'S NOT REALLY THE PROBLEM.

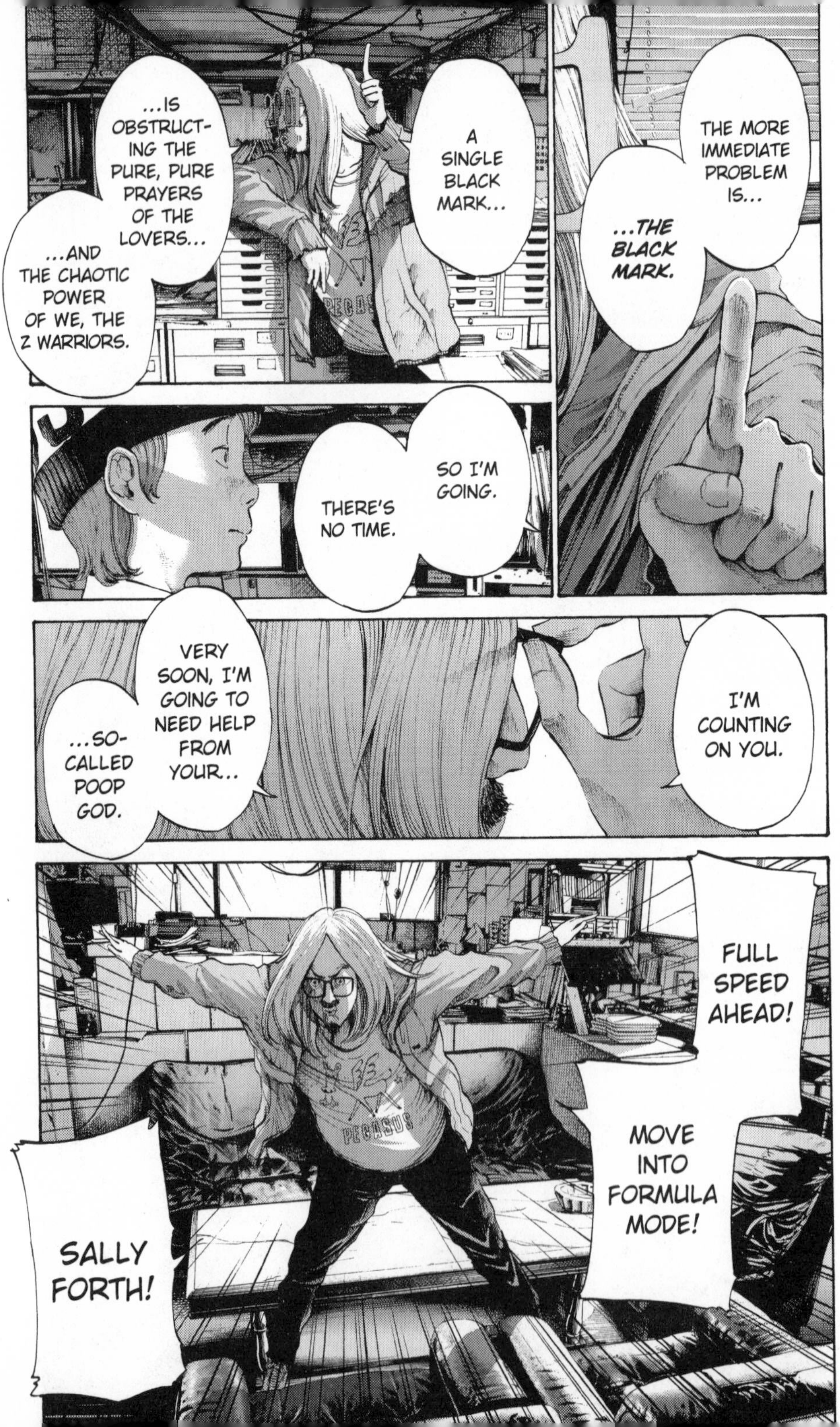
THE MORE IMMEDIATE PROBLEM IS...
...*THE BLACK MARK.*
A SINGLE BLACK MARK...
...IS OBSTRUCTING THE PURE, PURE PRAYERS OF THE LOVERS...
...AND THE CHAOTIC POWER OF WE, THE Z WARRIORS.
SO I'M GOING.
THERE'S NO TIME.
I'M COUNTING ON YOU.
VERY SOON, I'M GOING TO NEED HELP FROM YOUR...
...SO-CALLED POOP GOD.
FULL SPEED AHEAD!
MOVE INTO FORMULA MODE!
SALLY FORTH!

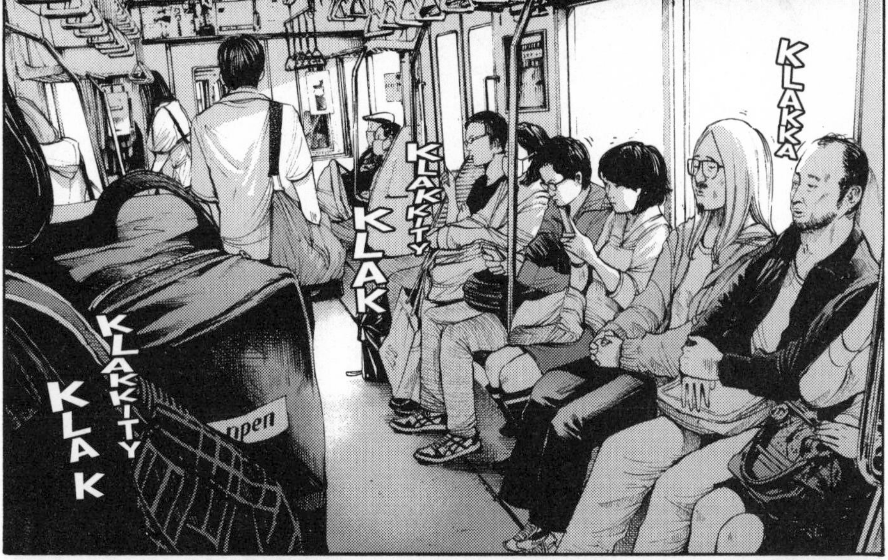
KLAKKA
KLAKKITY
KLAK
KLAKKITY
KLAK

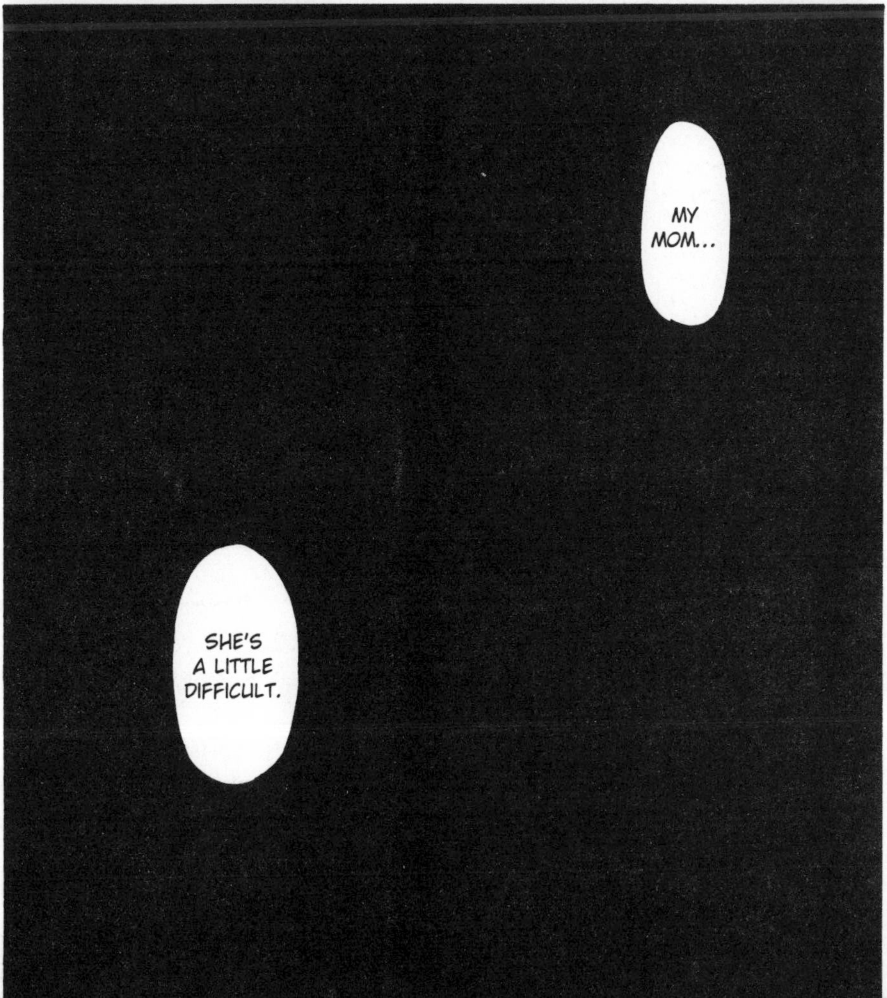
MY MOM...
SHE'S A LITTLE DIFFICULT.

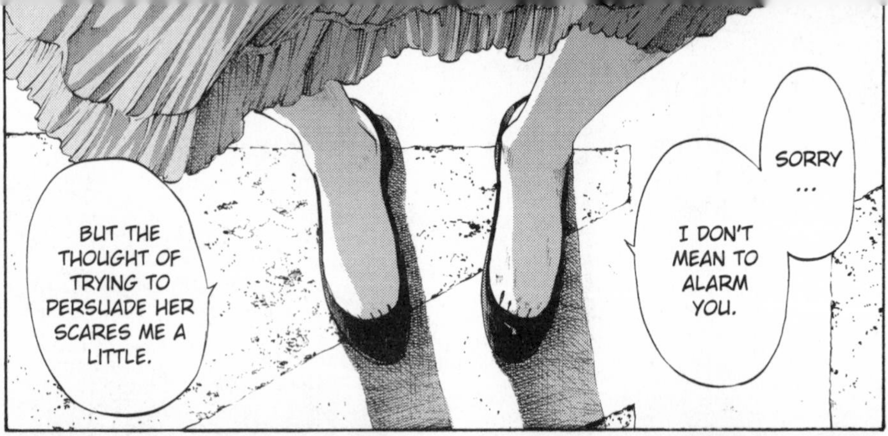
SORRY... I DON'T MEAN TO ALARM YOU.
BUT THE THOUGHT OF TRYING TO PERSUADE HER SCARES ME A LITTLE.

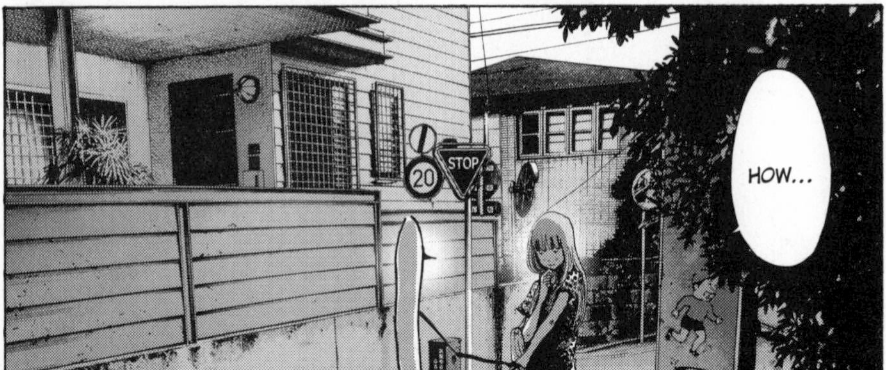
HOW...
STOP
20
...DO I LOOK?

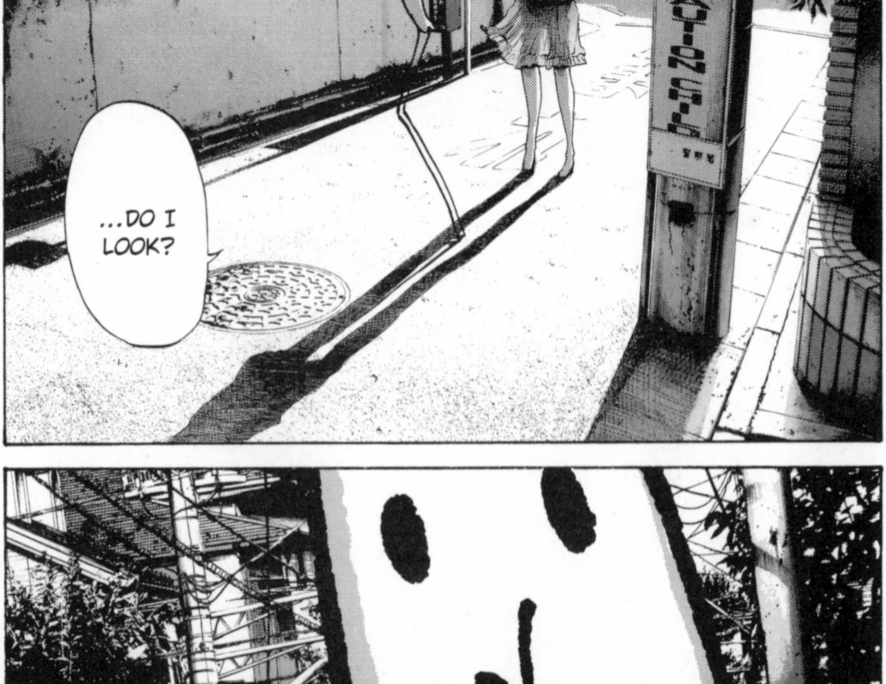

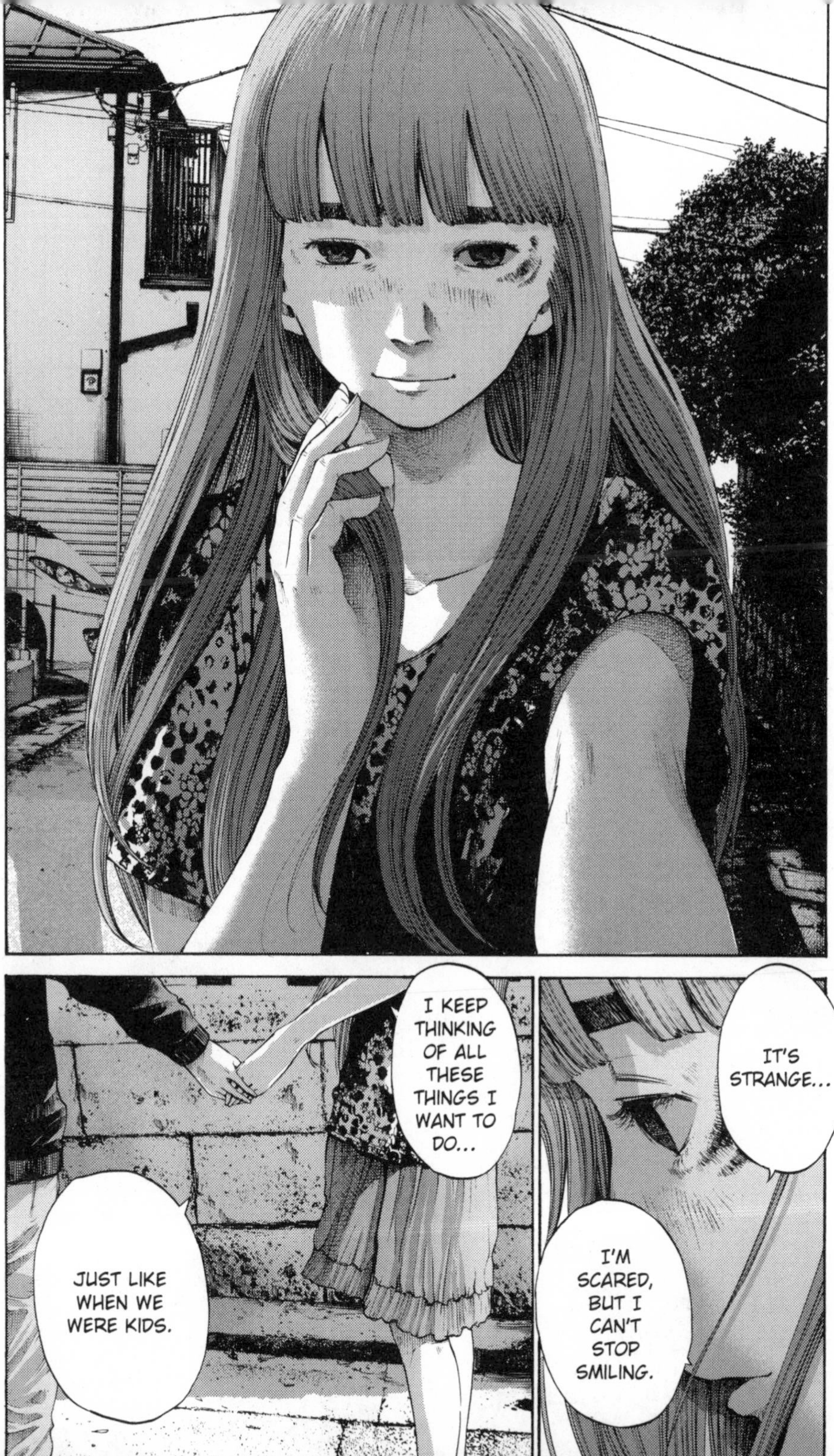
IT'S STRANGE…
I'M SCARED, BUT I CAN'T STOP SMILING.
I KEEP THINKING OF ALL THESE THINGS I WANT TO DO…
JUST LIKE WHEN WE WERE KIDS.

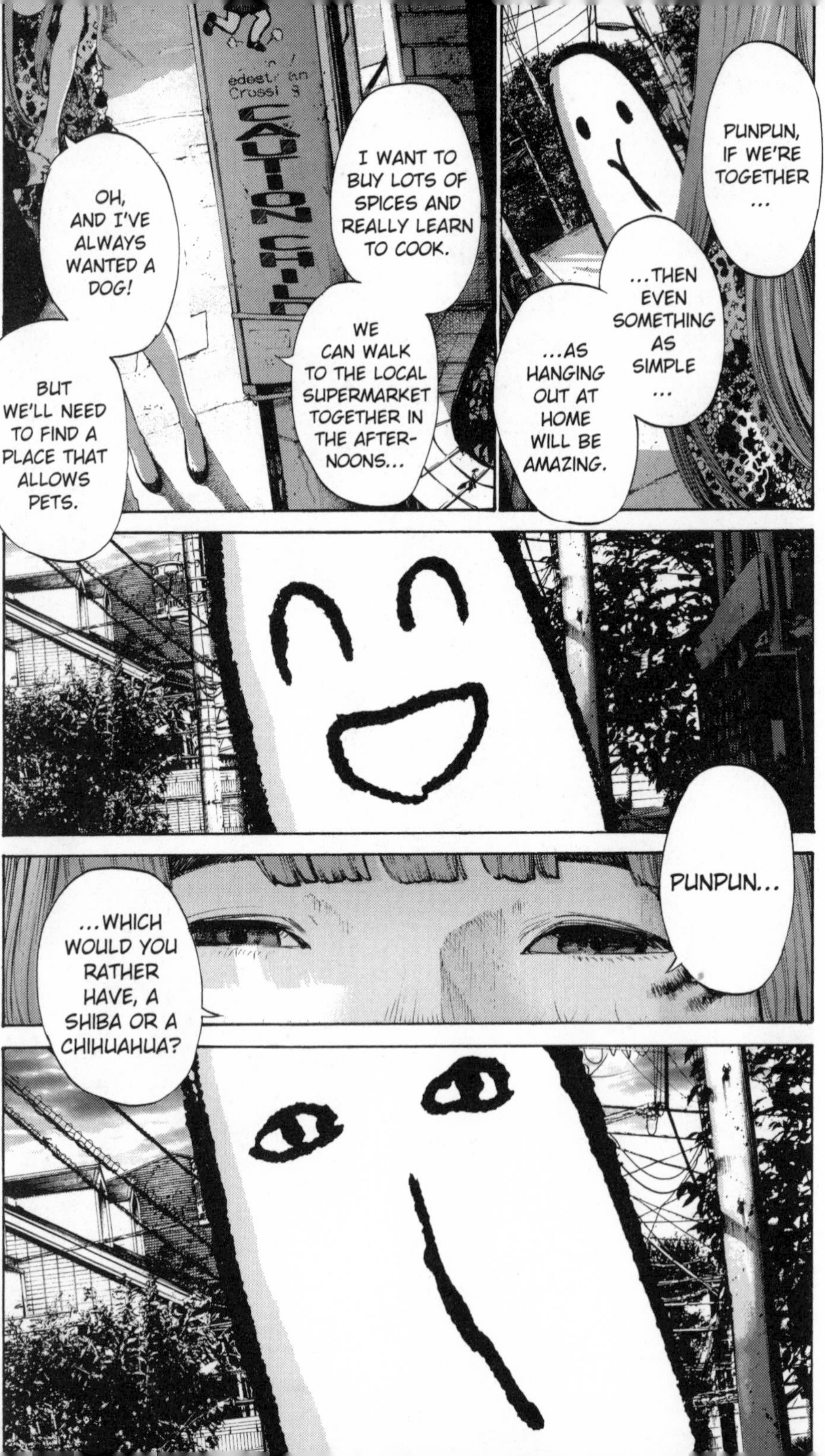
PUNPUN, IF WE'RE TOGETHER ...
...THEN EVEN SOMETHING AS SIMPLE ...
...AS HANGING OUT AT HOME WILL BE AMAZING.
I WANT TO BUY LOTS OF SPICES AND REALLY LEARN TO COOK.
WE CAN WALK TO THE LOCAL SUPERMARKET TOGETHER IN THE AFTER-NOONS...
OH, AND I'VE ALWAYS WANTED A DOG!
BUT WE'LL NEED TO FIND A PLACE THAT ALLOWS PETS.
PUNPUN...
...WHICH WOULD YOU RATHER HAVE, A SHIBA OR A CHIHUAHUA?

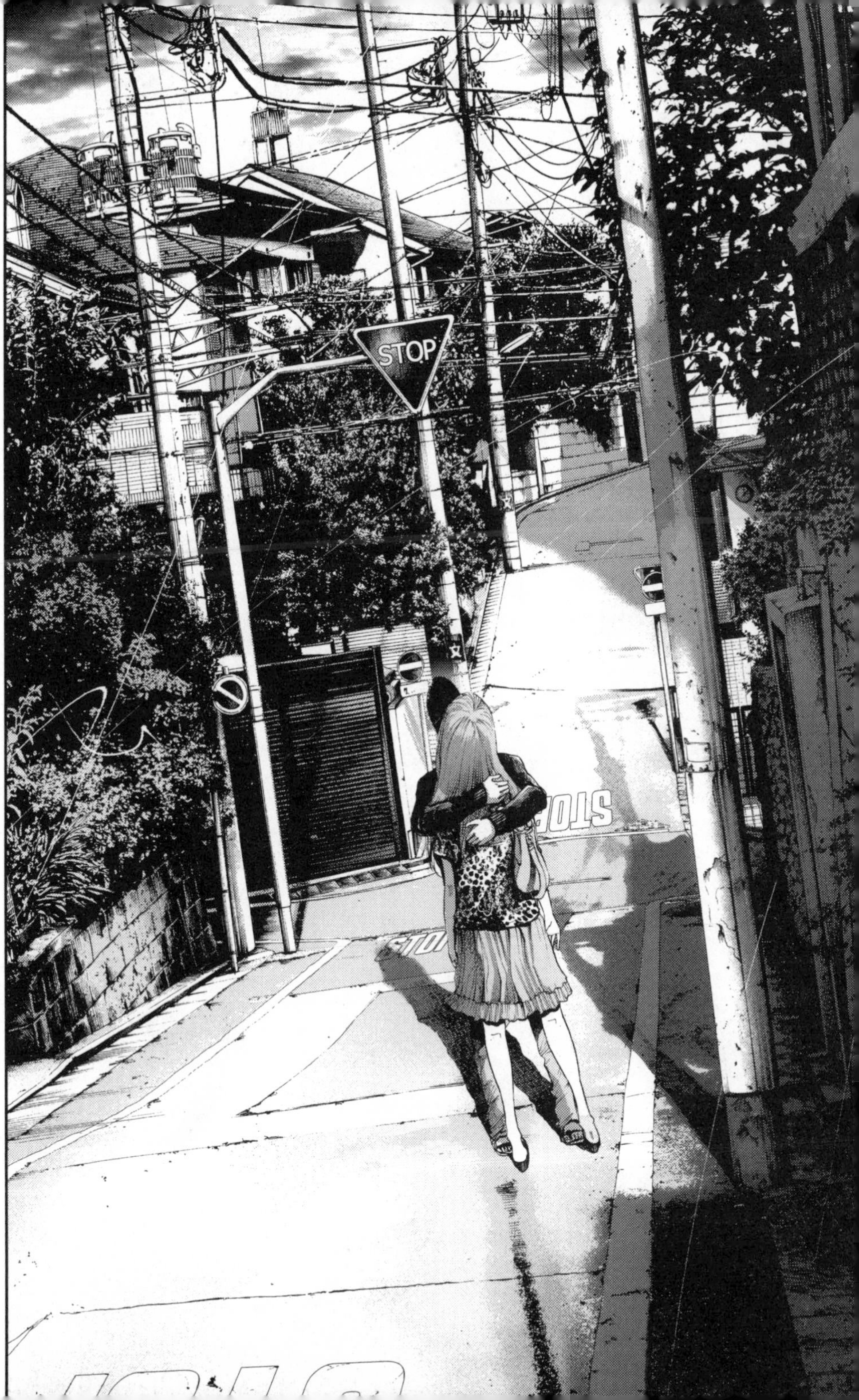
STOP

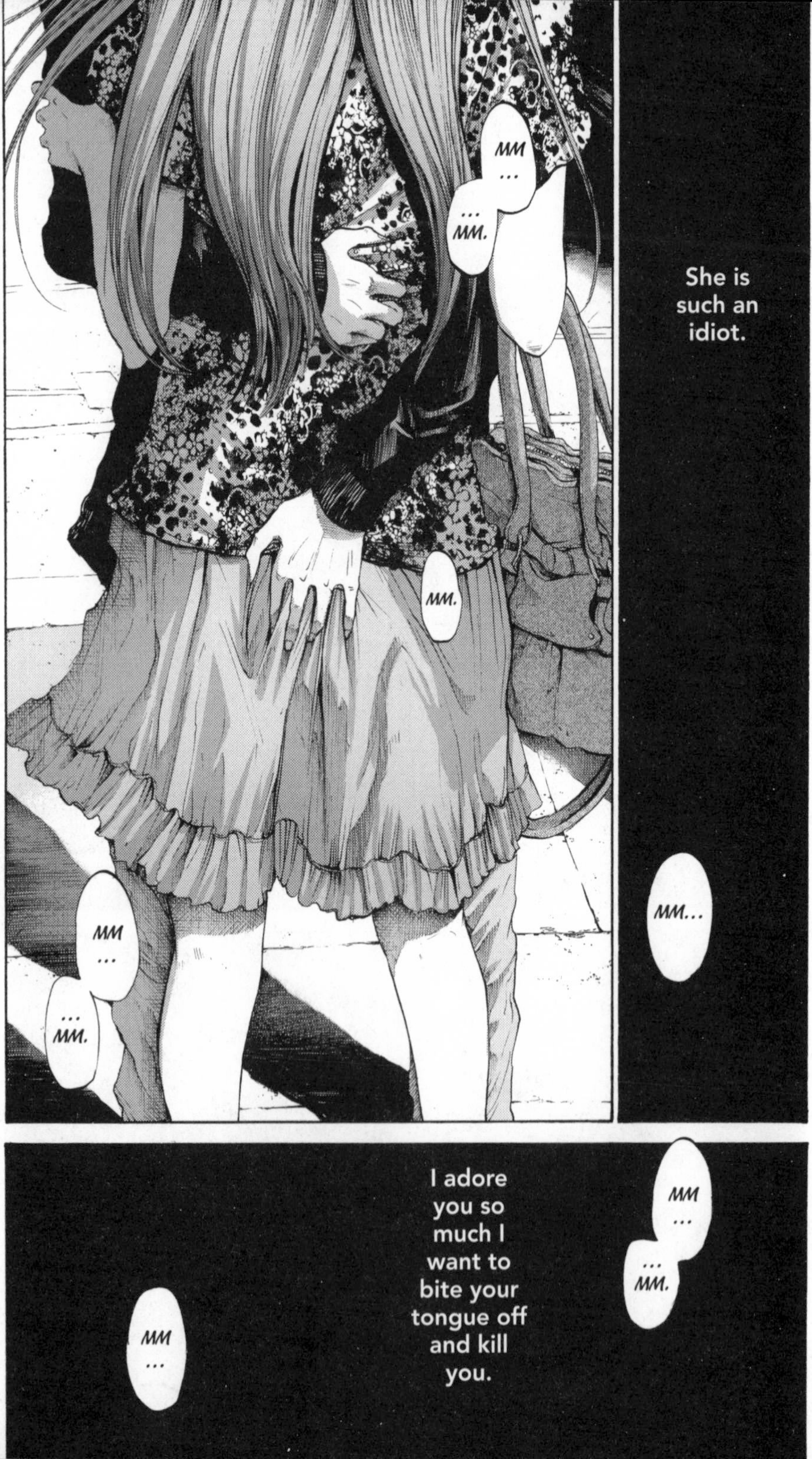
She is such an idiot.
MM...
MM ...
... MM.
MM.
MM ...
... MM.
MM ...
... MM.
I adore you so much I want to bite your tongue off and kill you.
MM ...

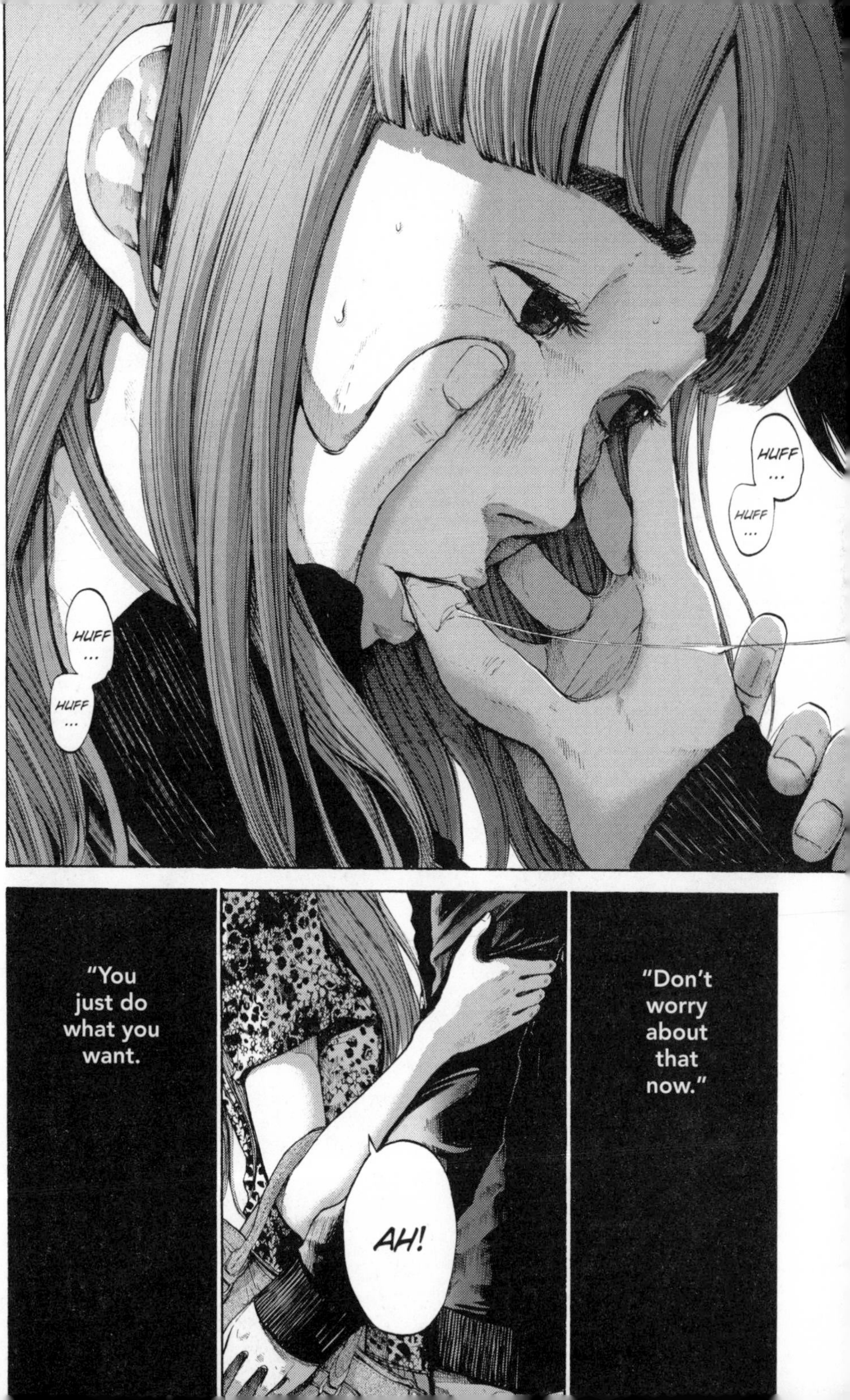
HUFF ...
HUFF ...
HUFF ...
HUFF ...
"Don't worry about that now."
AH!
"You just do what you want.

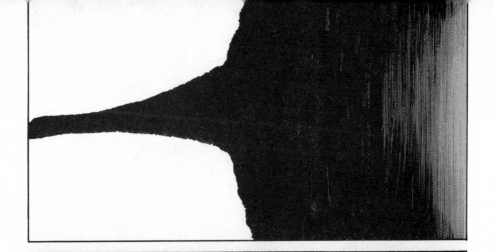

"No matter
what happens,
I'll protect you."

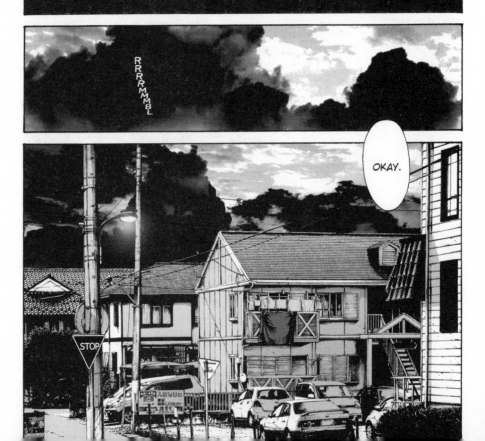

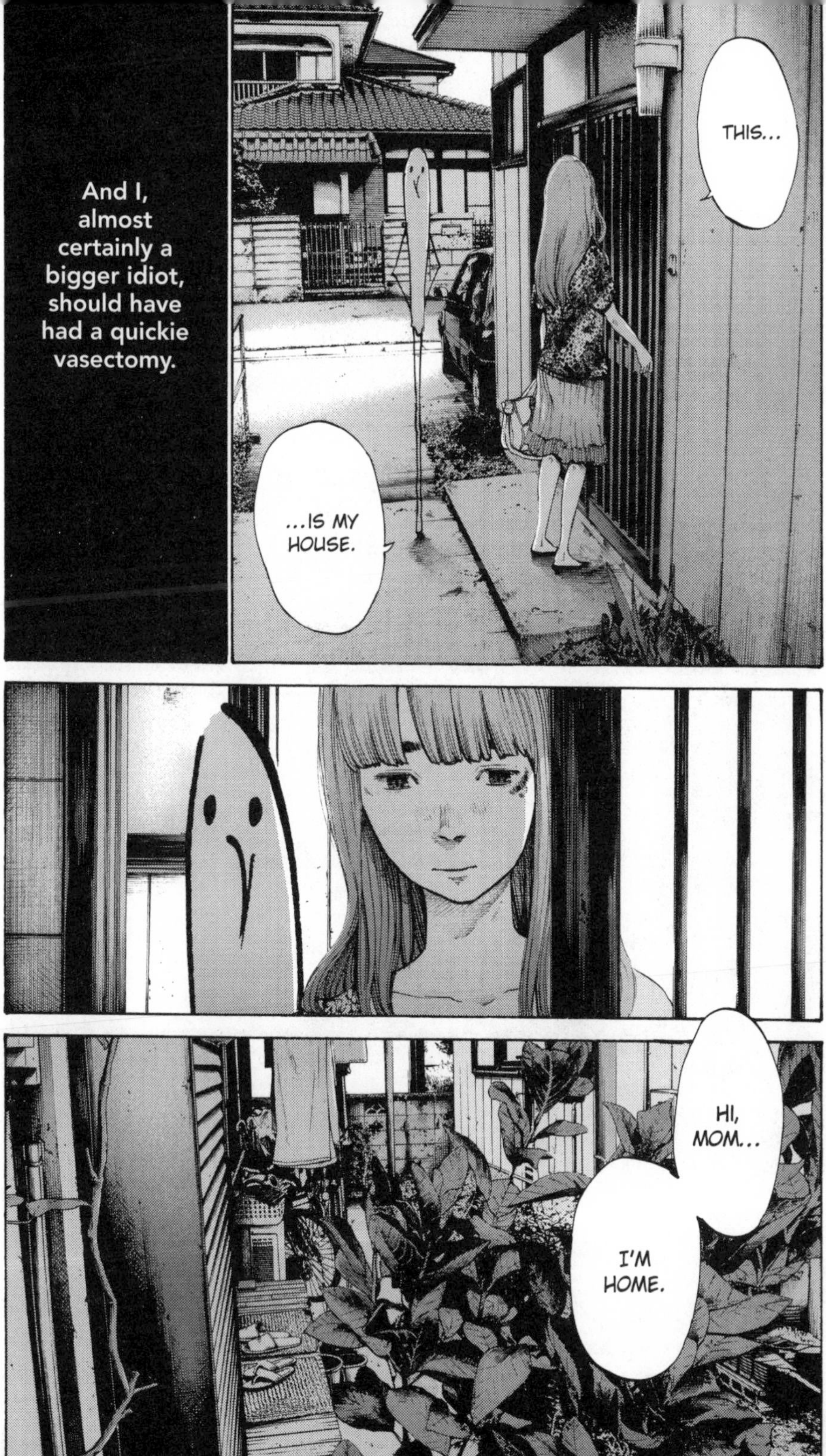
THIS...
...IS MY HOUSE.
And I, almost certainly a bigger idiot, should have had a quickie vasectomy.
HI, MOM...
I'M HOME.

Chapter 112.

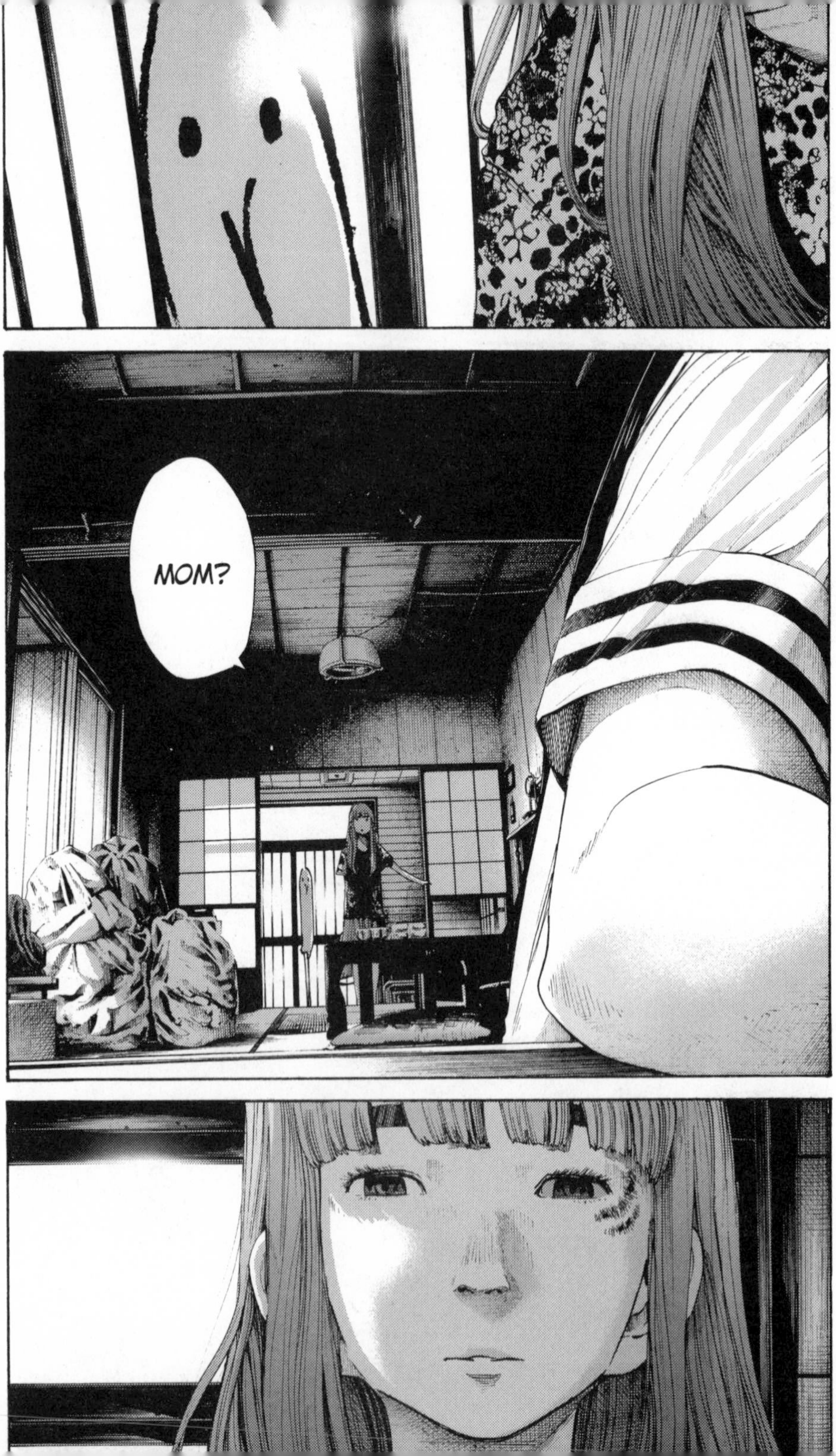
MOM?

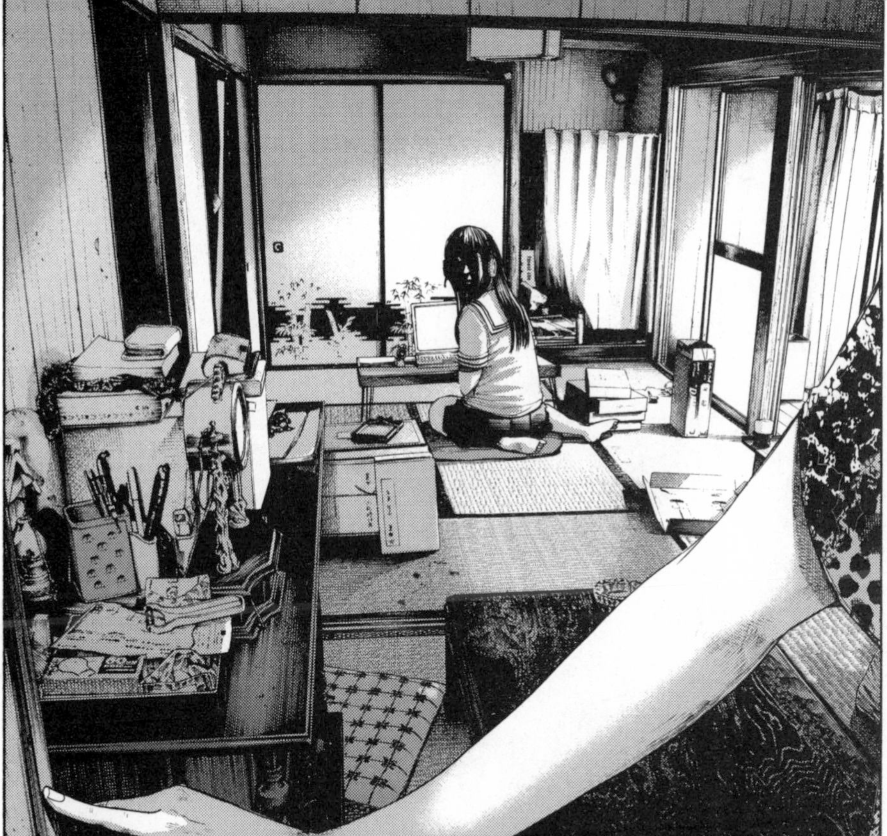
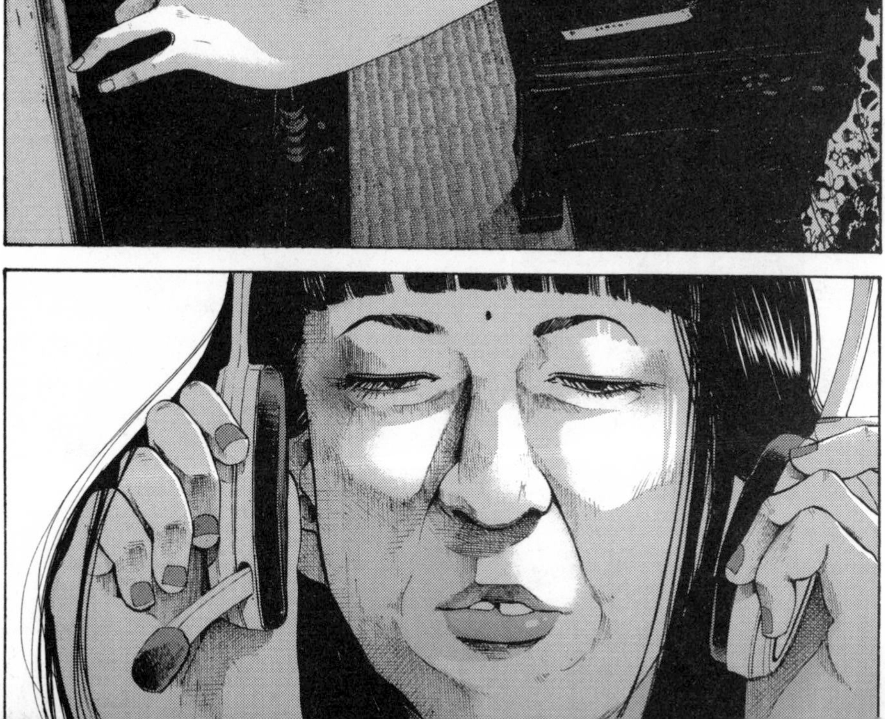

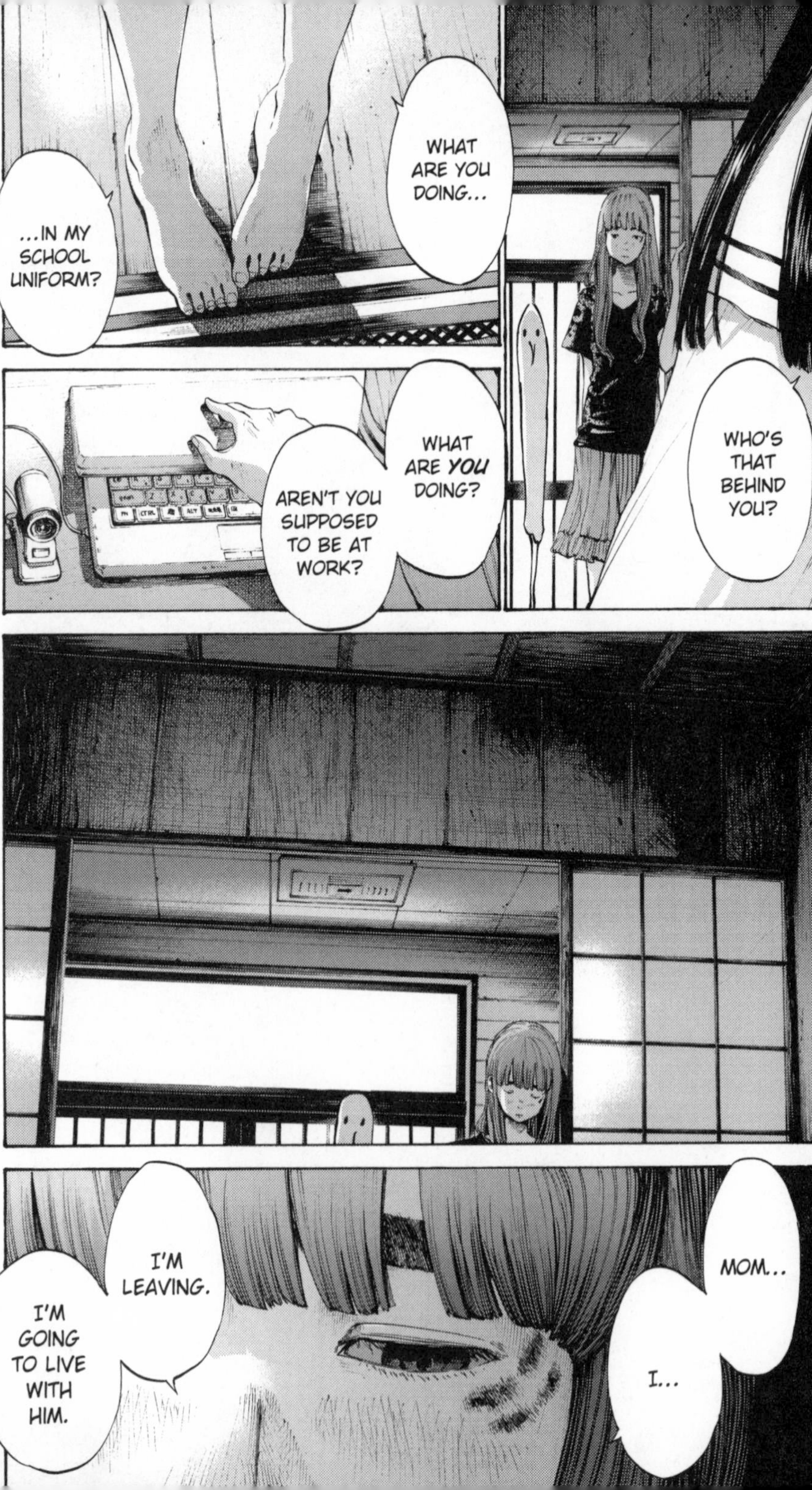
WHO'S THAT BEHIND YOU?
WHAT ARE YOU DOING...
...IN MY SCHOOL UNIFORM?
WHAT ARE *YOU* DOING?
AREN'T YOU SUPPOSED TO BE AT WORK?
MOM...
I...
I'M LEAVING.
I'M GOING TO LIVE WITH HIM.

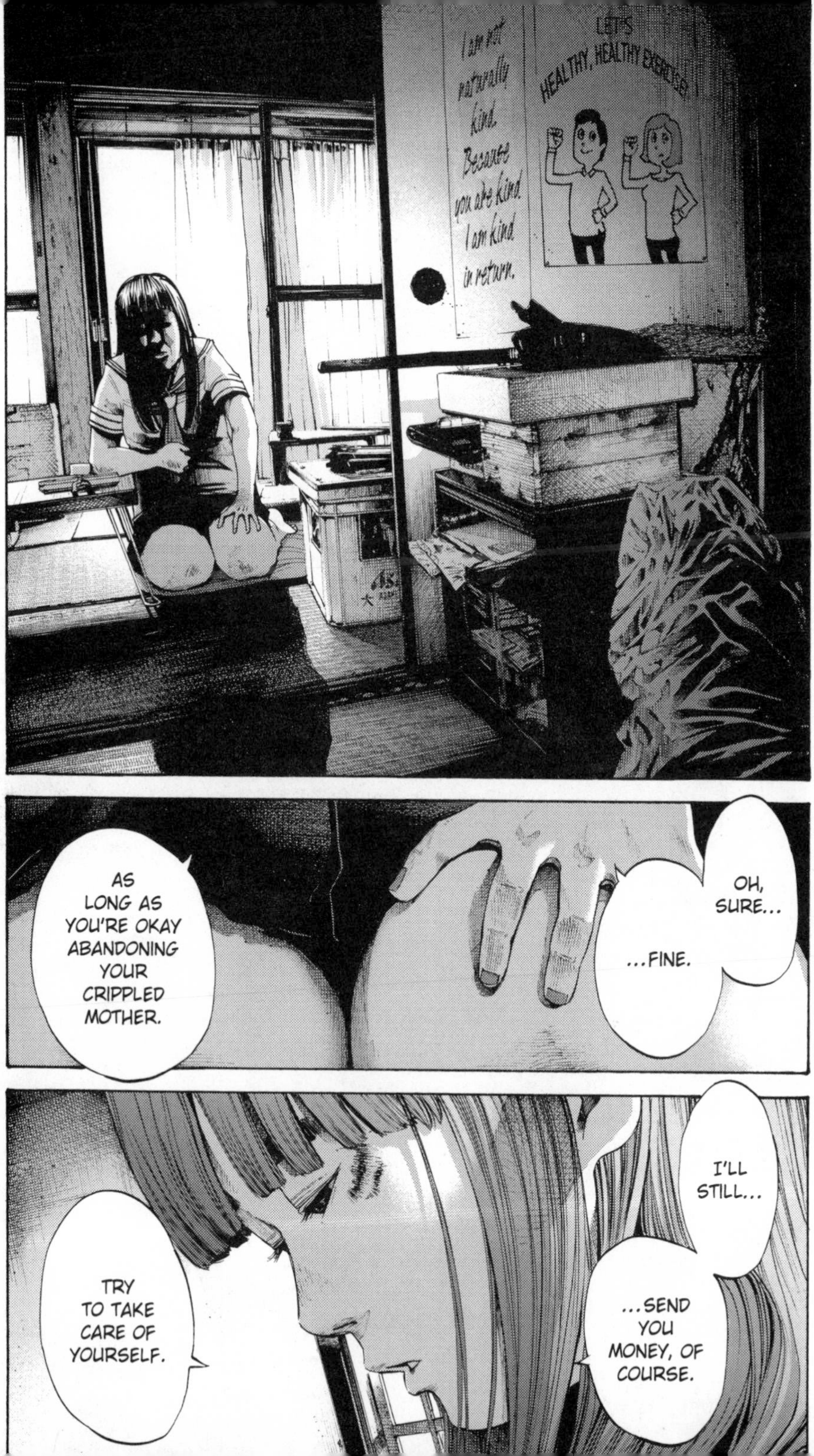
LET'S HEALTHY, HEALTHY EXERCISE!
I am not naturally kind. Because you are kind, I am kind in return.
OH, SURE...
...FINE.
AS LONG AS YOU'RE OKAY ABANDONING YOUR CRIPPLED MOTHER.
I'LL STILL...
...SEND YOU MONEY, OF COURSE.
TRY TO TAKE CARE OF YOURSELF.

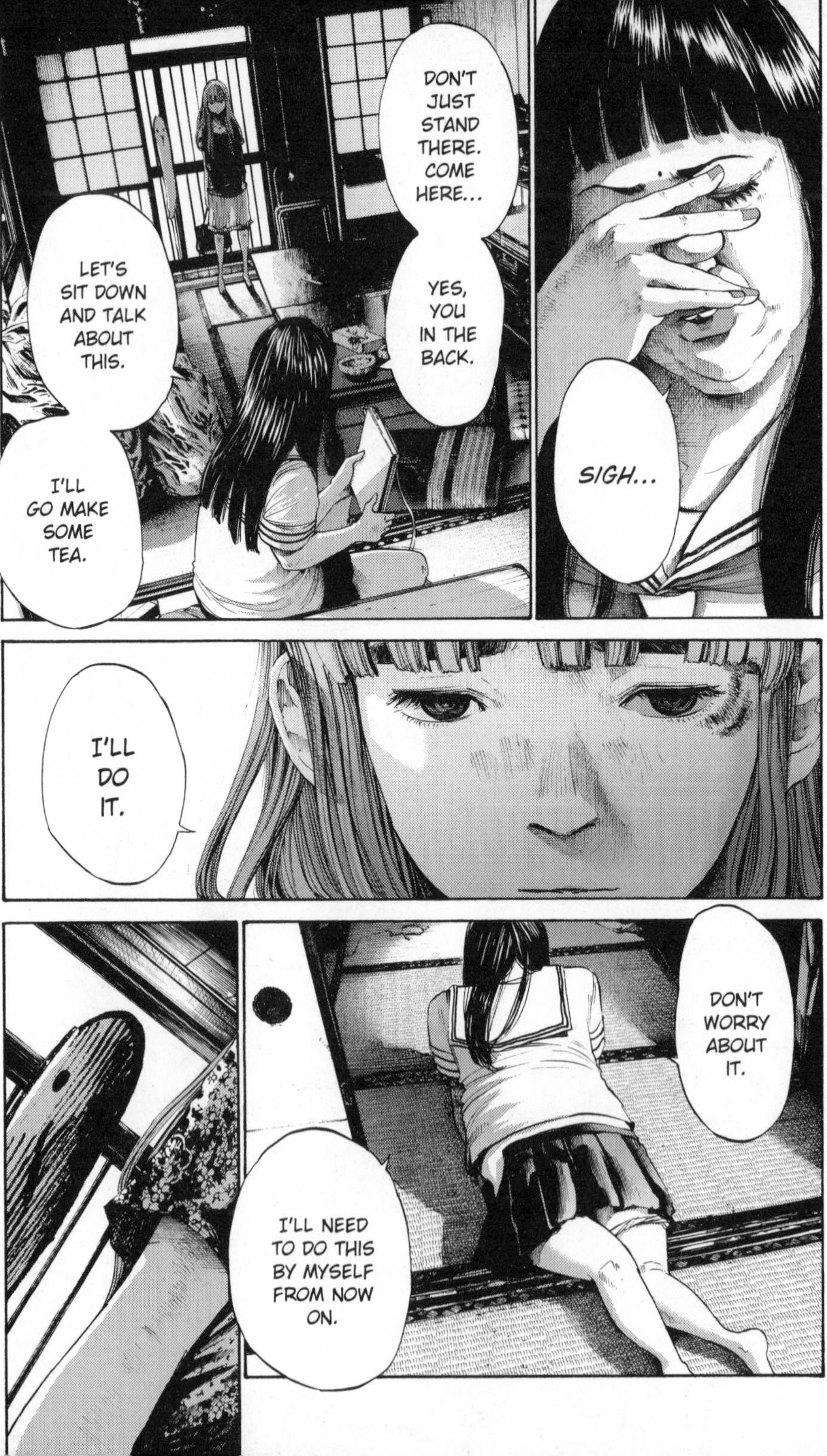
SIGH...
DON'T JUST STAND THERE. COME HERE...
YES, YOU IN THE BACK.
LET'S SIT DOWN AND TALK ABOUT THIS.
I'LL GO MAKE SOME TEA.
I'LL DO IT.
DON'T WORRY ABOUT IT.
I'LL NEED TO DO THIS BY MYSELF FROM NOW ON.

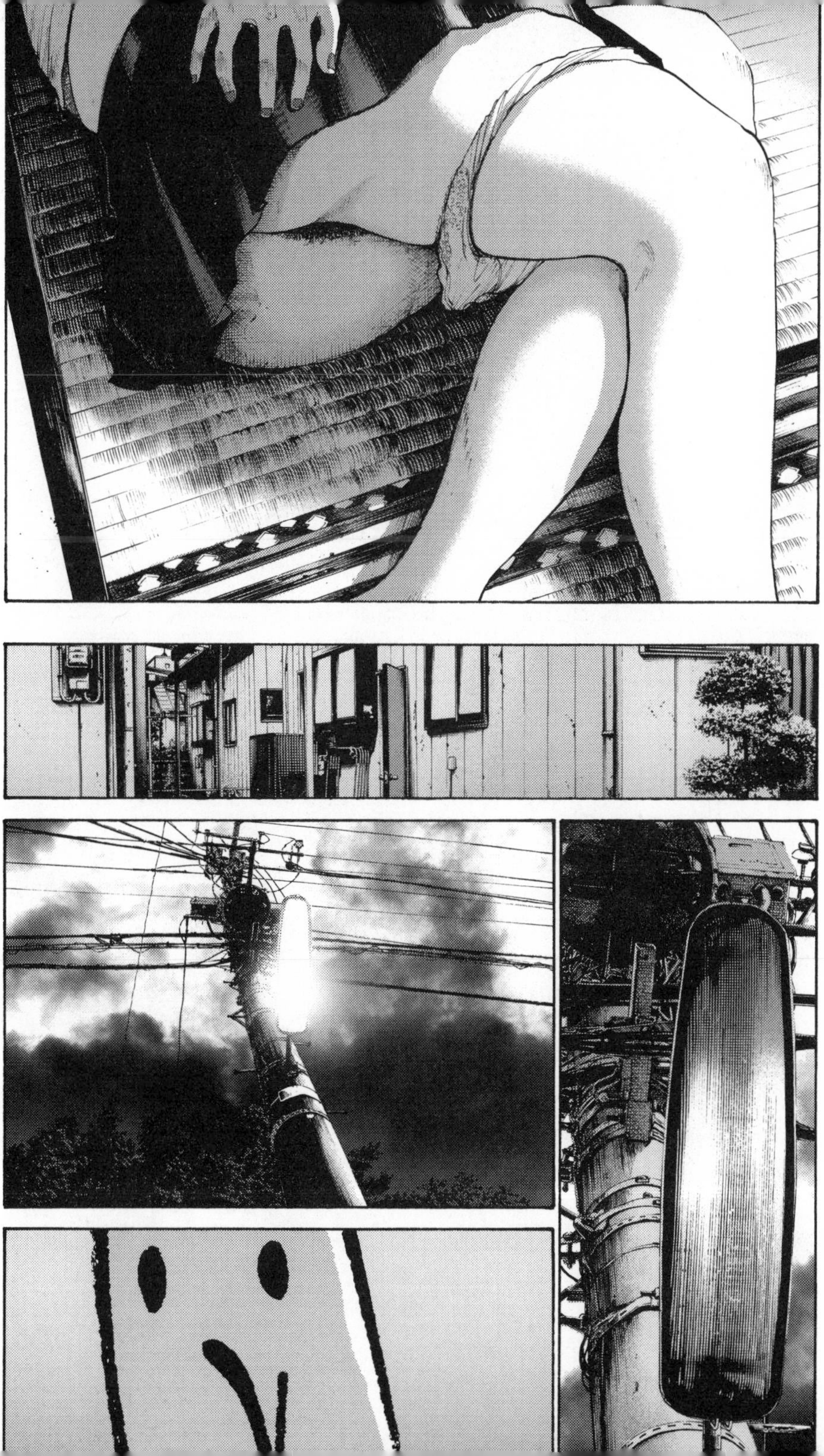

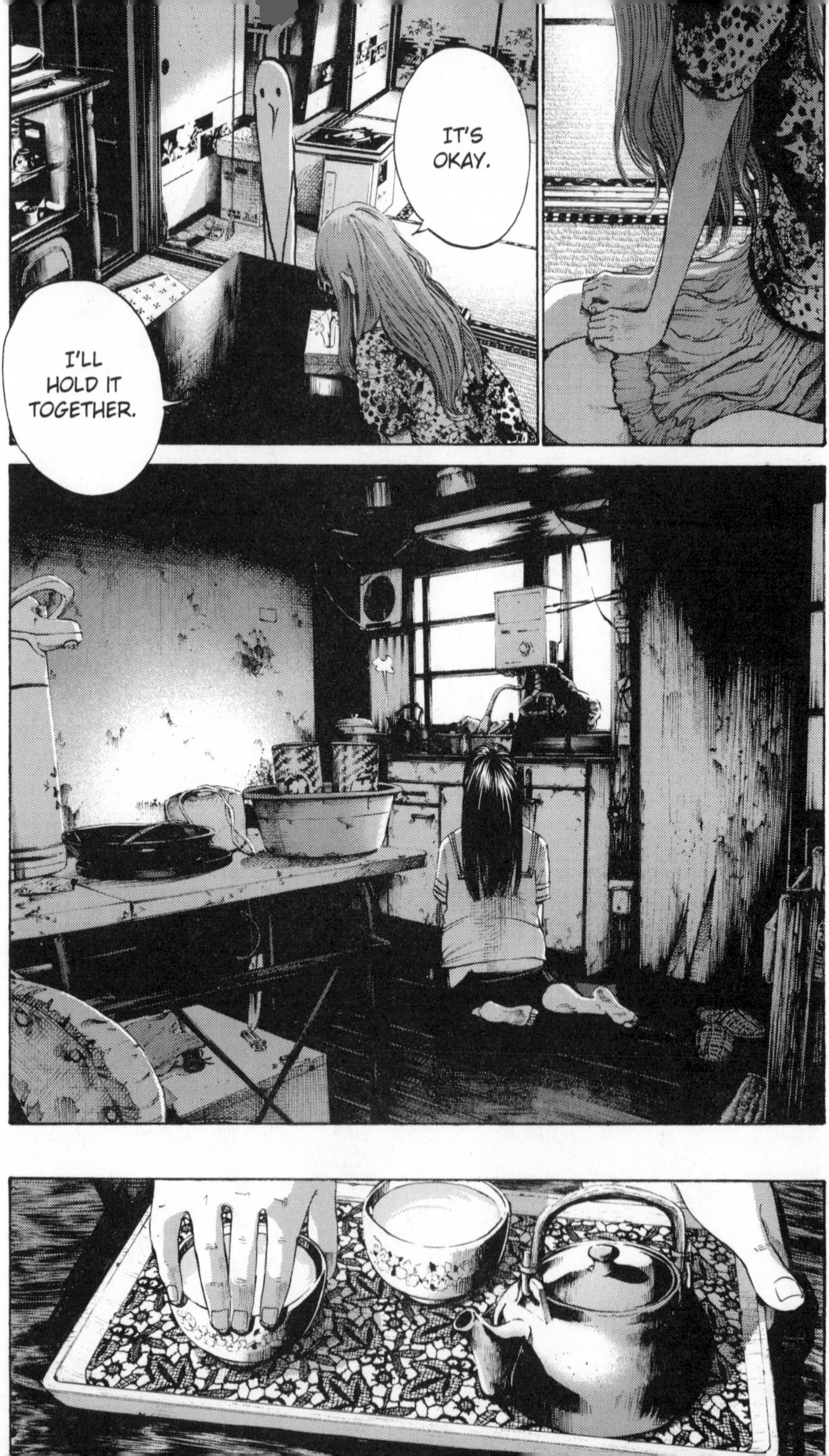
IT'S OKAY.
I'LL HOLD IT TOGETHER.

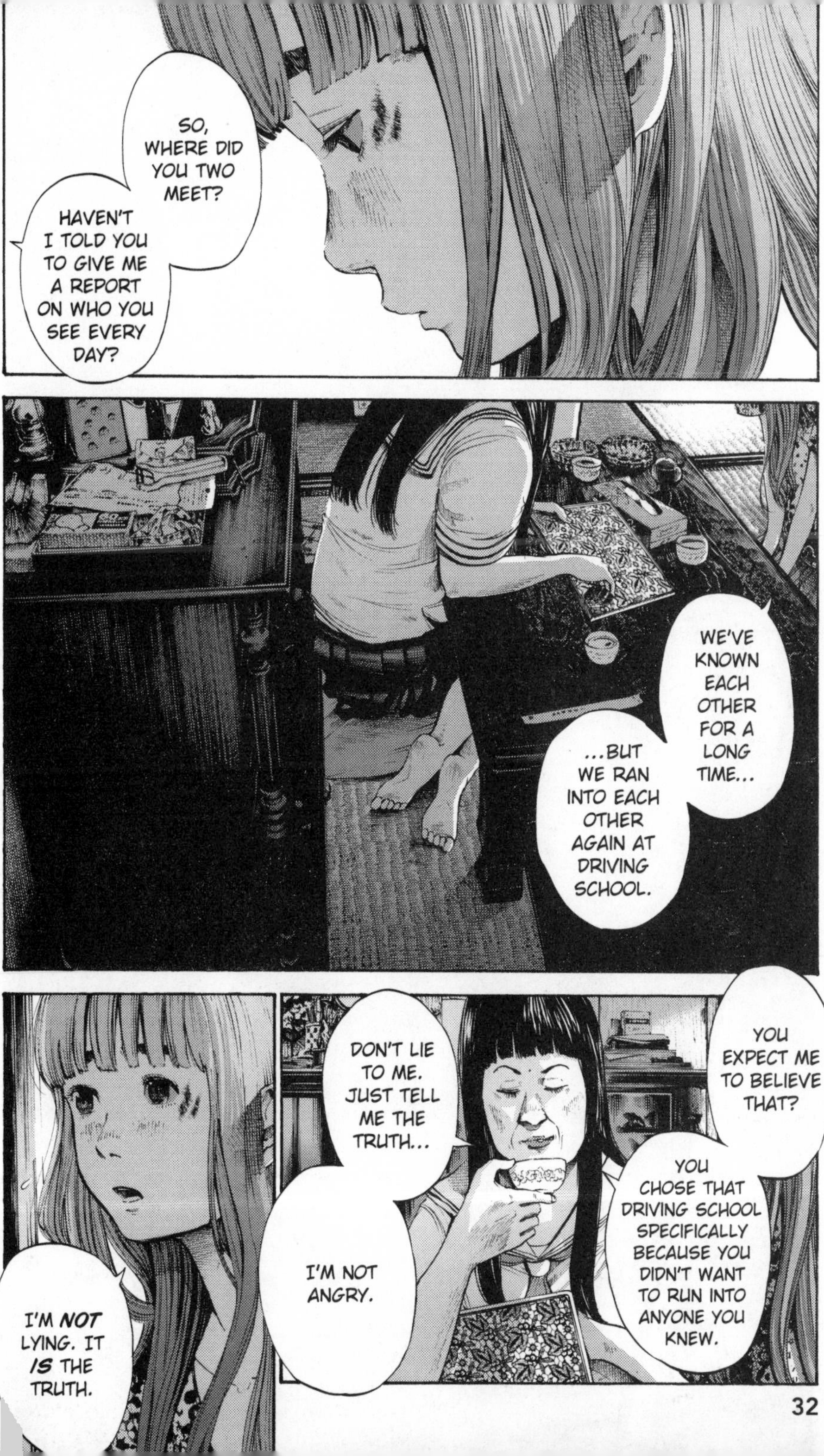
SO, WHERE DID YOU TWO MEET?
HAVEN'T I TOLD YOU TO GIVE ME A REPORT ON WHO YOU SEE EVERY DAY?
WE'VE KNOWN EACH OTHER FOR A LONG TIME...
...BUT WE RAN INTO EACH OTHER AGAIN AT DRIVING SCHOOL.
YOU EXPECT ME TO BELIEVE THAT?
DON'T LIE TO ME. JUST TELL ME THE TRUTH...
YOU CHOSE THAT DRIVING SCHOOL SPECIFICALLY BECAUSE YOU DIDN'T WANT TO RUN INTO ANYONE YOU KNEW.
I'M NOT ANGRY.
I'M ***NOT*** LYING. IT ***IS*** THE TRUTH.

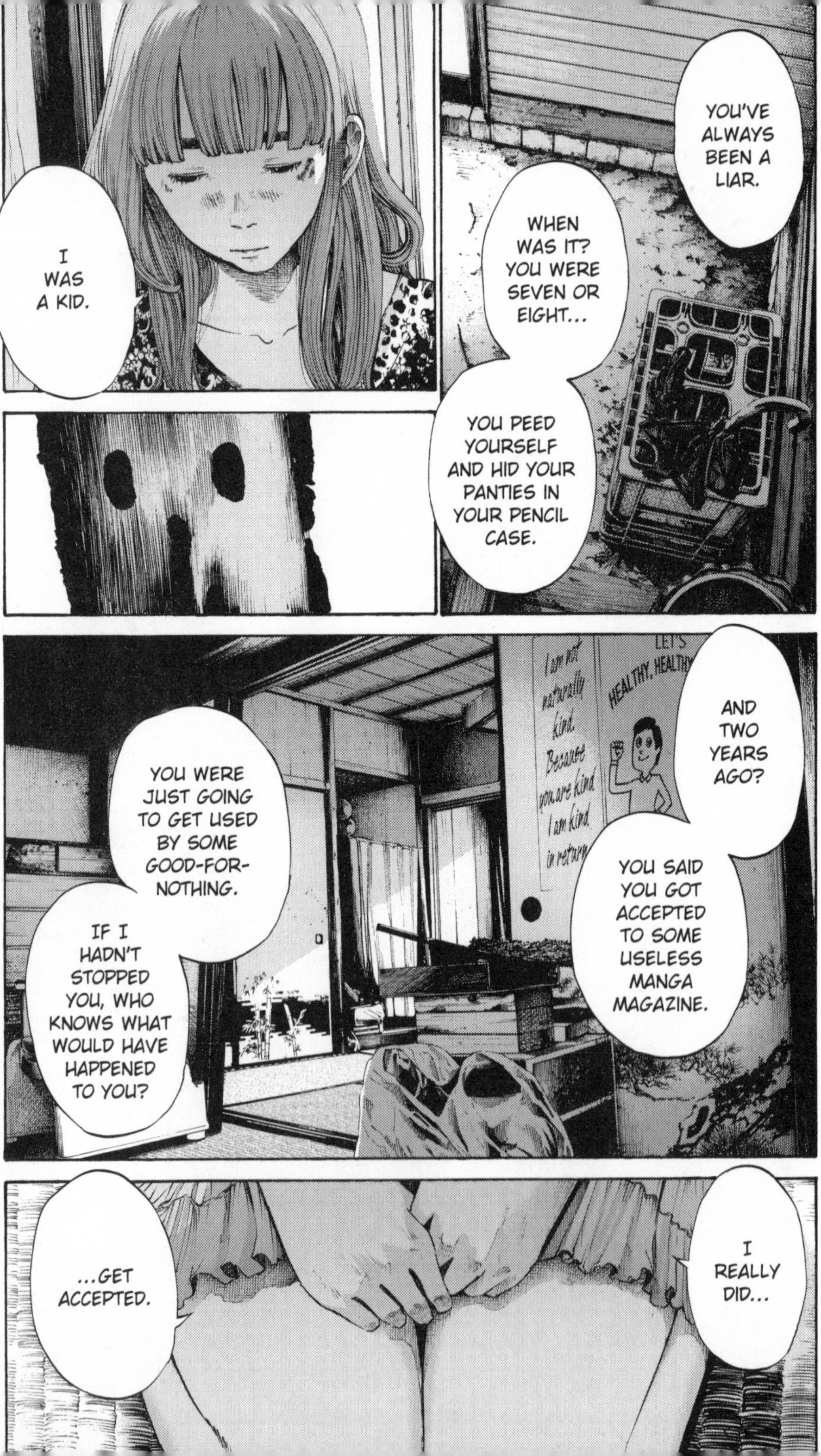
YOU'VE ALWAYS BEEN A LIAR.
WHEN WAS IT? YOU WERE SEVEN OR EIGHT...
YOU PEED YOURSELF AND HID YOUR PANTIES IN YOUR PENCIL CASE.
I WAS A KID.
LET'S
HEALTHY, HEALTHY
I am not naturally kind. Because you are kind I am kind in return
AND TWO YEARS AGO?
YOU SAID YOU GOT ACCEPTED TO SOME USELESS MANGA MAGAZINE.
YOU WERE JUST GOING TO GET USED BY SOME GOOD-FOR-NOTHING.
IF I HADN'T STOPPED YOU, WHO KNOWS WHAT WOULD HAVE HAPPENED TO YOU?
I REALLY DID...
...GET ACCEPTED.

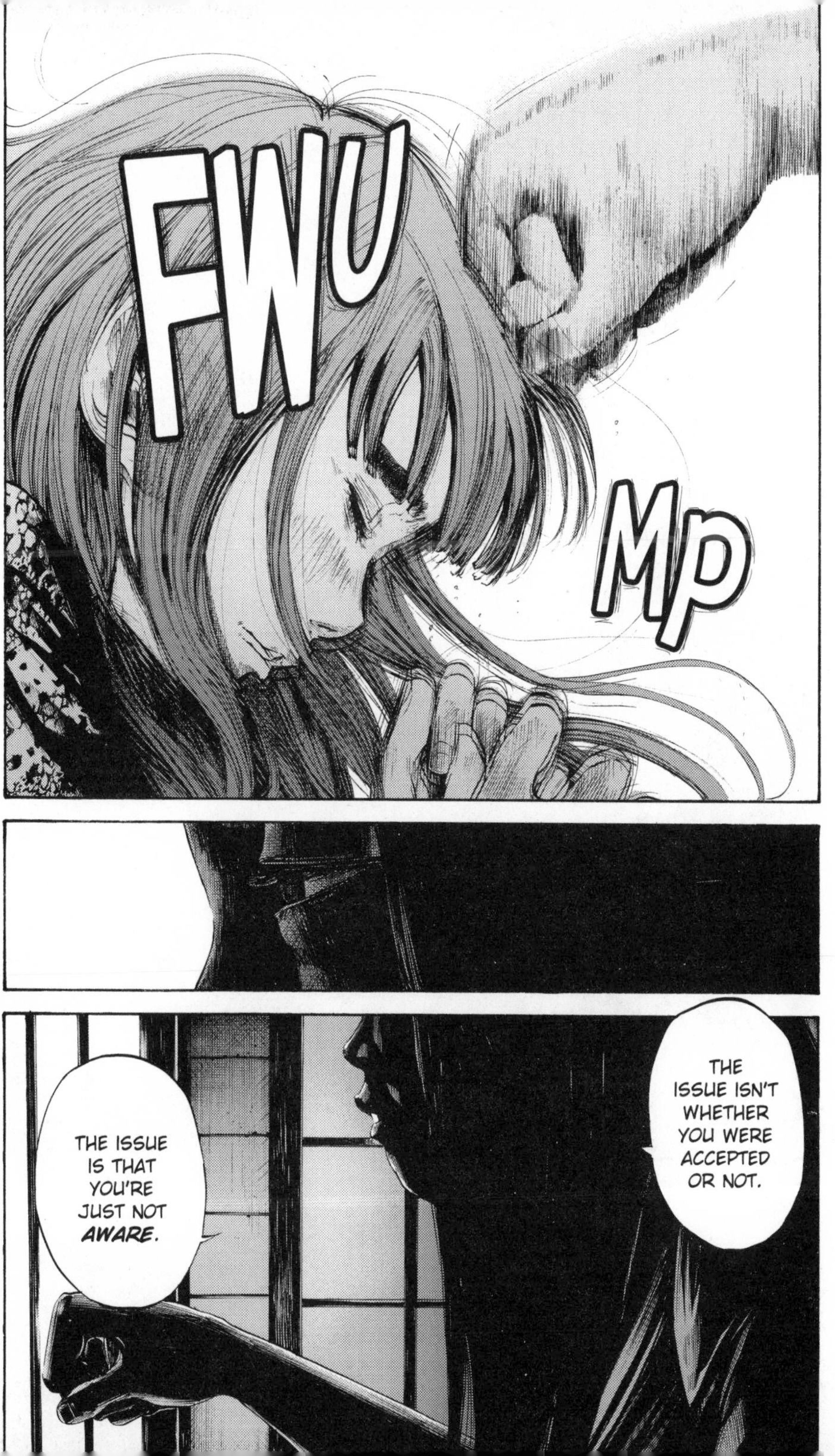
FWUMP
THE ISSUE ISN'T WHETHER YOU WERE ACCEPTED OR NOT.
THE ISSUE IS THAT YOU'RE JUST NOT *AWARE*.

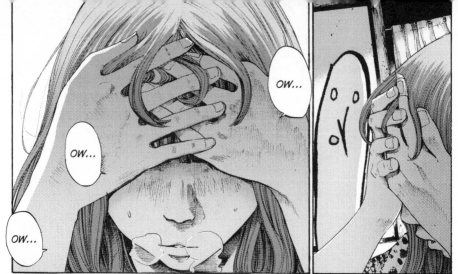

OW...

OW...

OW...

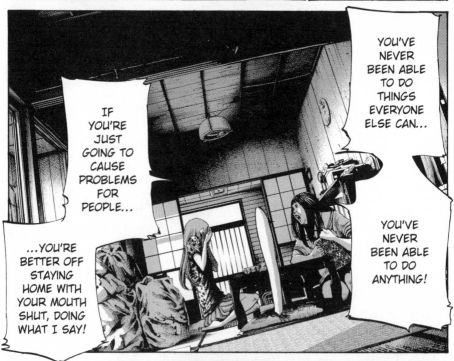

YOU'VE NEVER BEEN ABLE TO DO THINGS EVERYONE ELSE CAN...

IF YOU'RE JUST GOING TO CAUSE PROBLEMS FOR PEOPLE...

YOU'VE NEVER BEEN ABLE TO DO ANYTHING!

...YOU'RE BETTER OFF STAYING HOME WITH YOUR MOUTH SHUT, DOING WHAT I SAY!

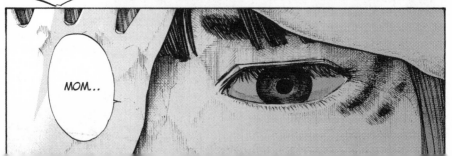

MOM...

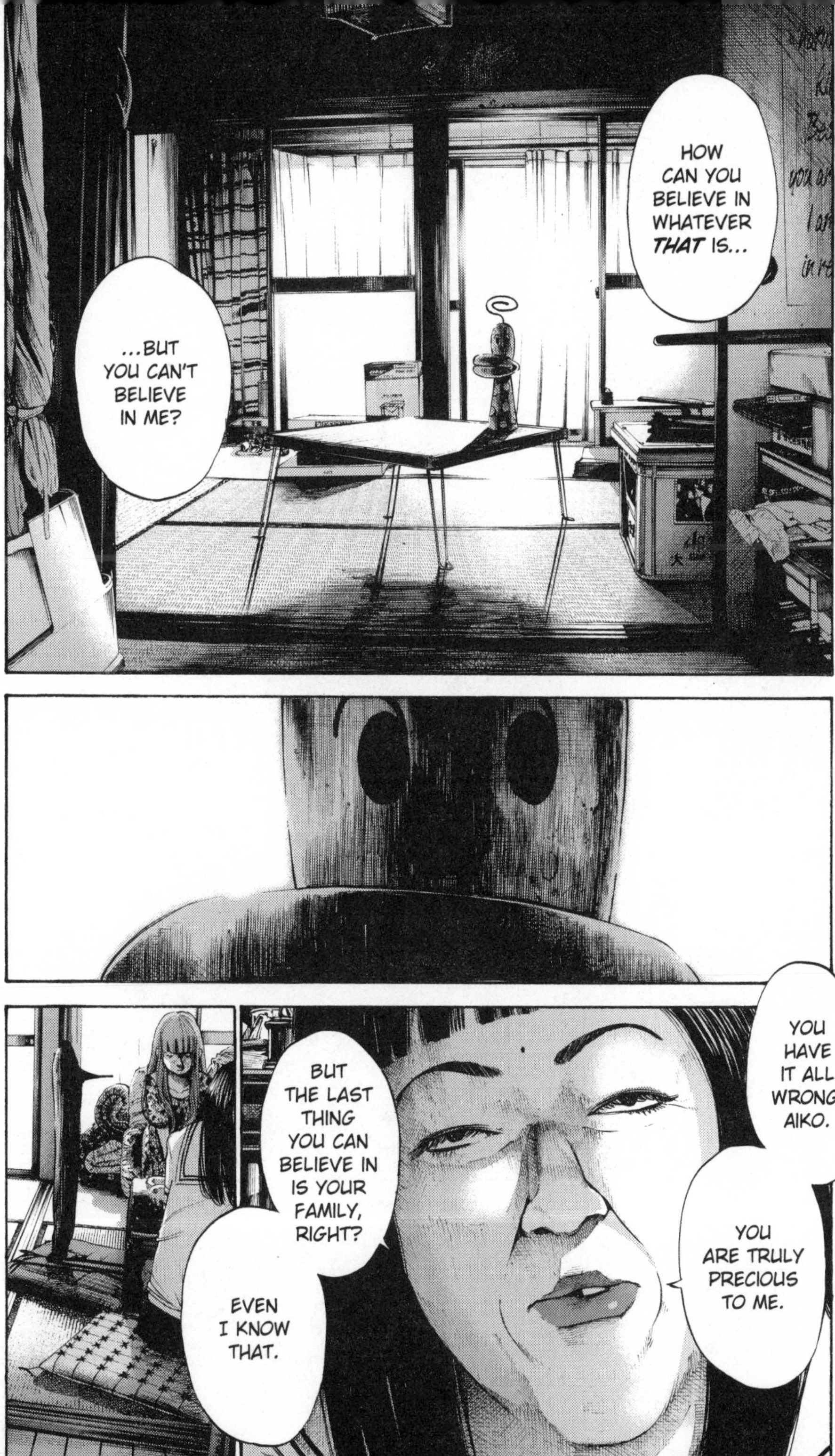
HOW CAN YOU BELIEVE IN WHATEVER *THAT* IS...
...BUT YOU CAN'T BELIEVE IN ME?
YOU HAVE IT ALL WRONG, AIKO.
YOU ARE TRULY PRECIOUS TO ME.
BUT THE LAST THING YOU CAN BELIEVE IN IS YOUR FAMILY, RIGHT?
EVEN I KNOW THAT.

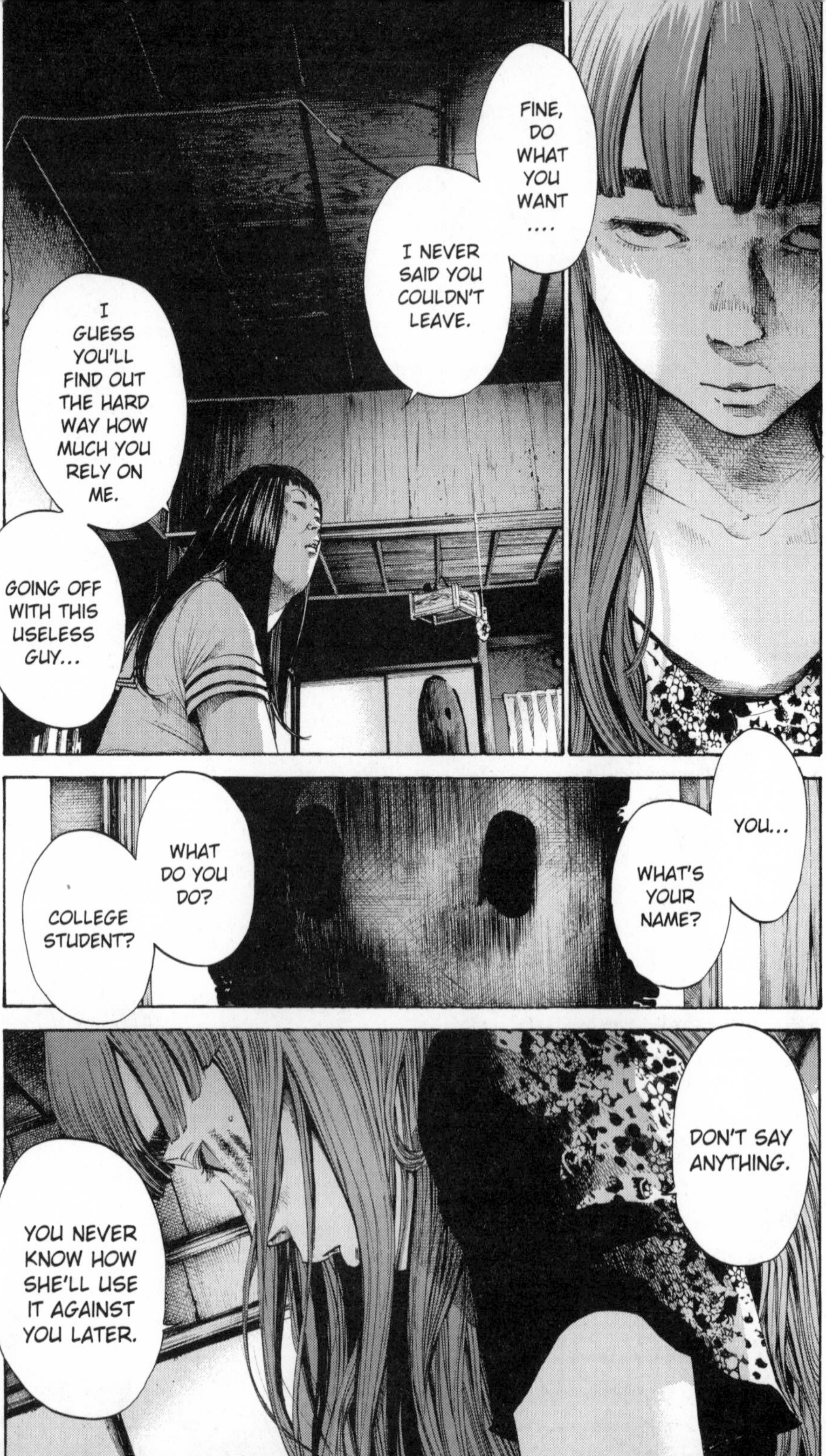
FINE, DO WHAT YOU WANT....
I NEVER SAID YOU COULDN'T LEAVE.
I GUESS YOU'LL FIND OUT THE HARD WAY HOW MUCH YOU RELY ON ME.
GOING OFF WITH THIS USELESS GUY...
YOU...
WHAT'S YOUR NAME?
WHAT DO YOU DO?
COLLEGE STUDENT?
DON'T SAY ANYTHING.
YOU NEVER KNOW HOW SHE'LL USE IT AGAINST YOU LATER.

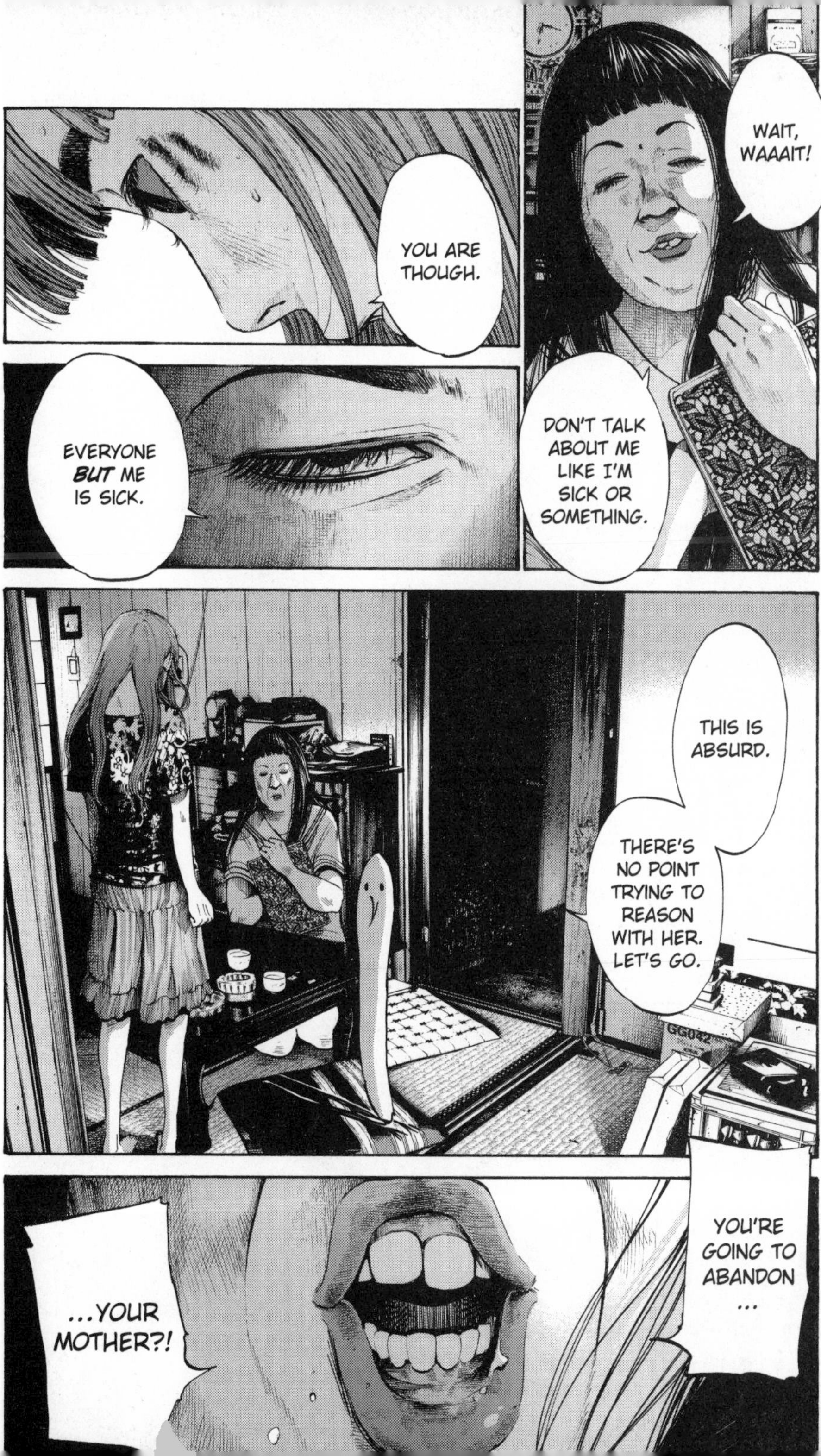
WAIT, WAAAIT!
DON'T TALK ABOUT ME LIKE I'M SICK OR SOMETHING.
YOU ARE THOUGH.
EVERYONE BUT ME IS SICK.
THIS IS ABSURD.
THERE'S NO POINT TRYING TO REASON WITH HER. LET'S GO.
YOU'RE GOING TO ABANDON ...
...YOUR MOTHER?!

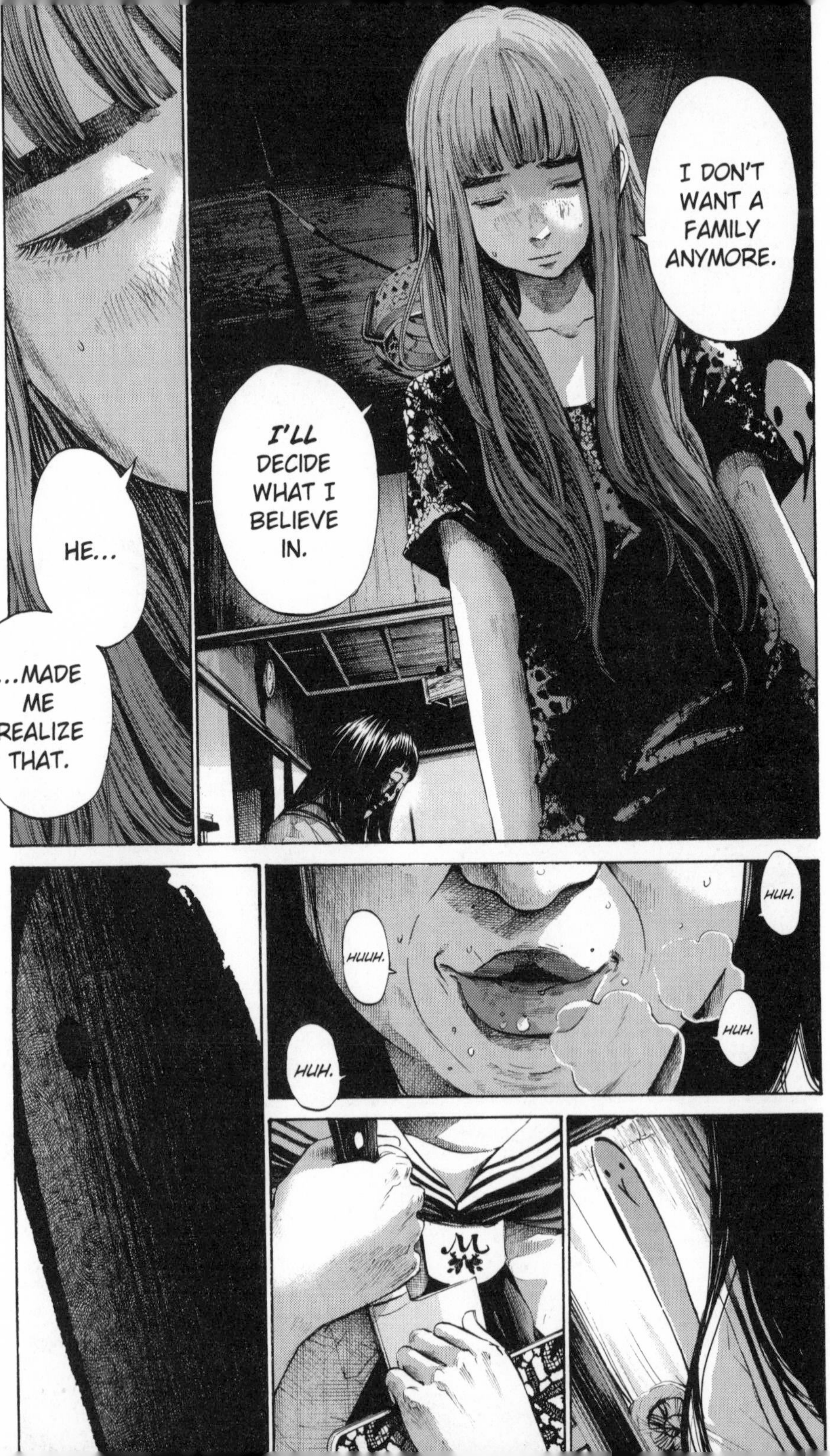
I DON'T WANT A FAMILY ANYMORE.
I'LL DECIDE WHAT I BELIEVE IN.
HE...
...MADE ME REALIZE THAT.
HUH.
HUUH.
HUH.
HUH.

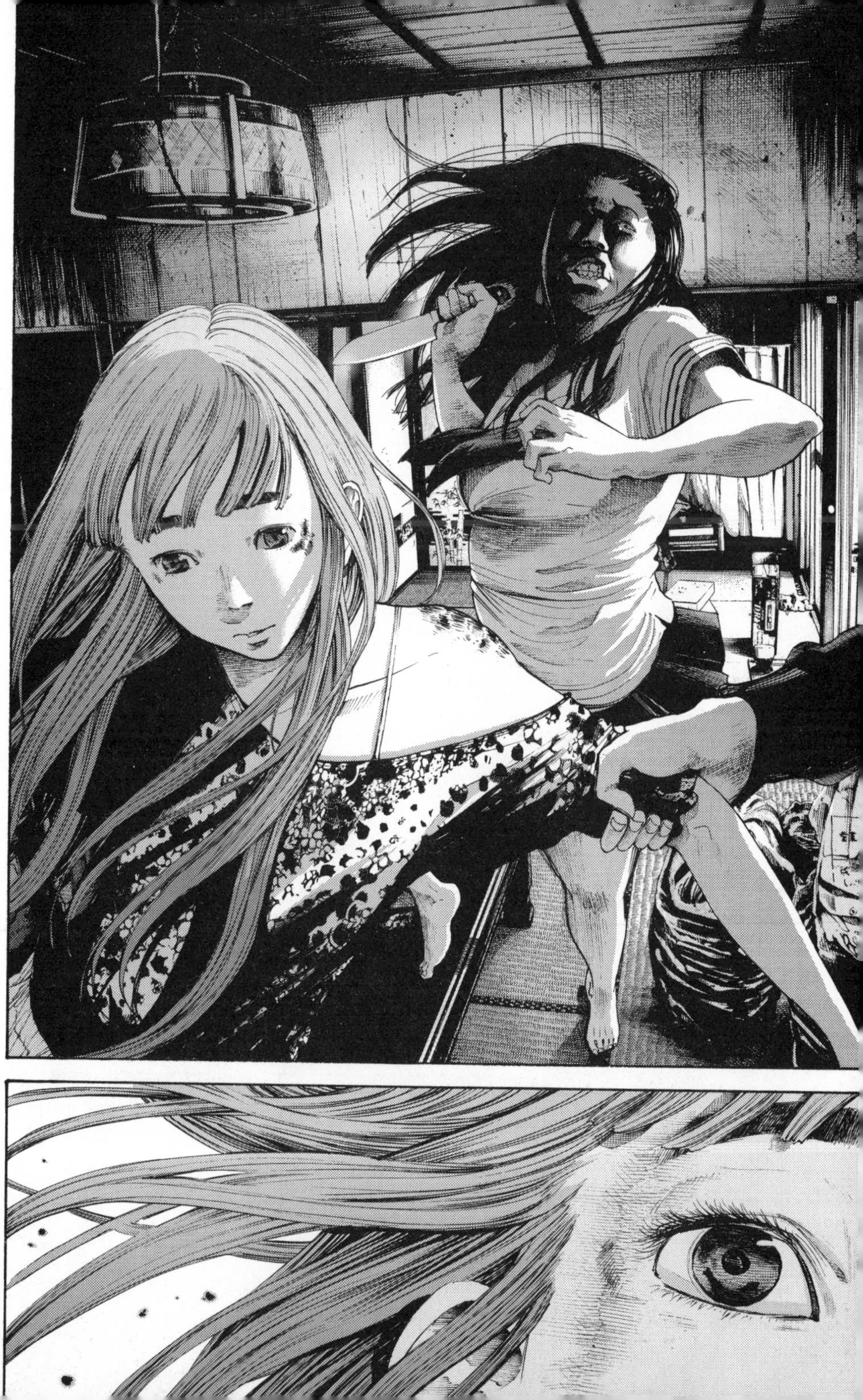

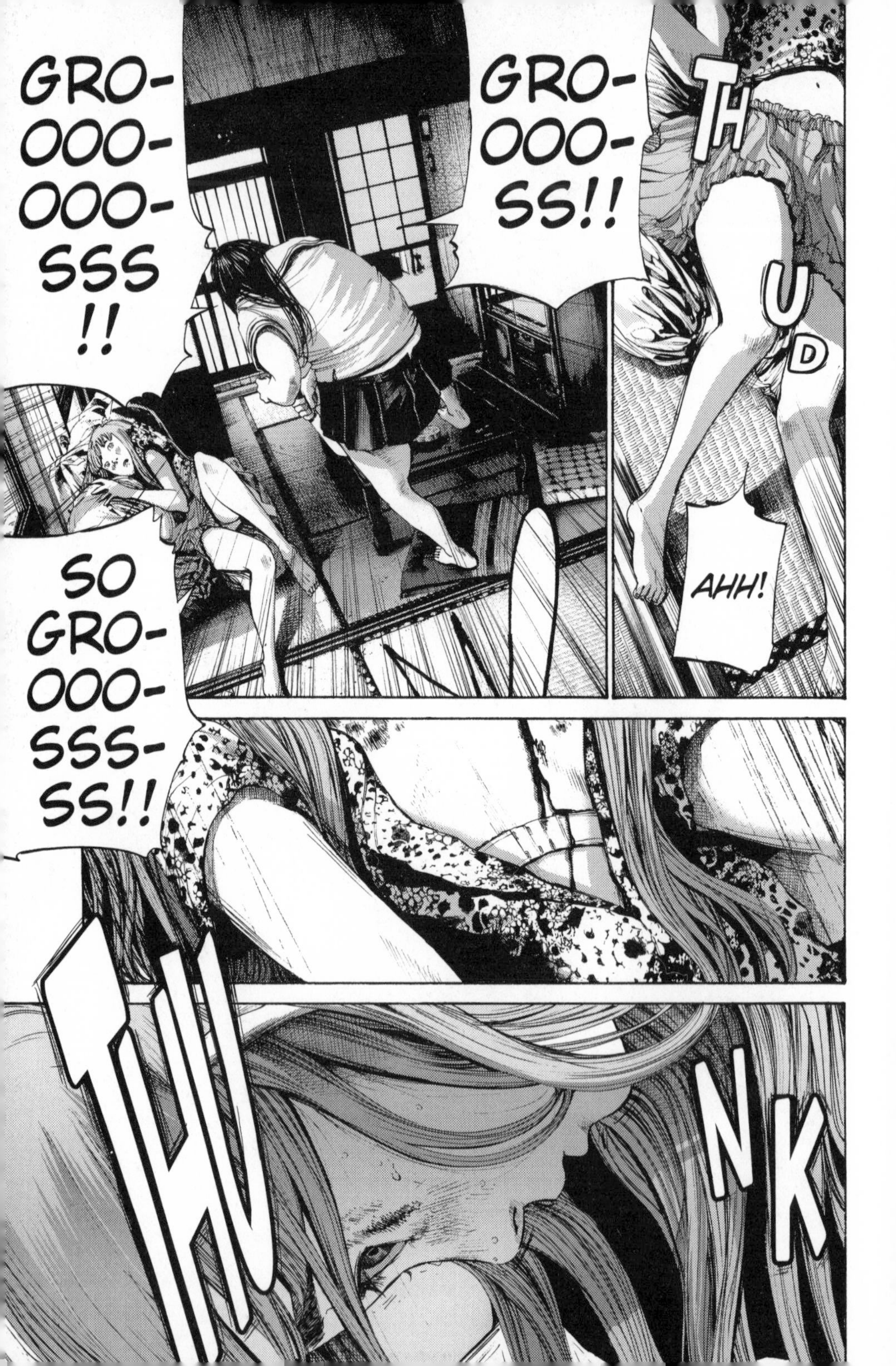
THUD
AHH!
GRO-OOO-SS!!
GRO-OOO-OOO-SSS!!
SO GRO-OOO-SSS-SS!!
THUNK

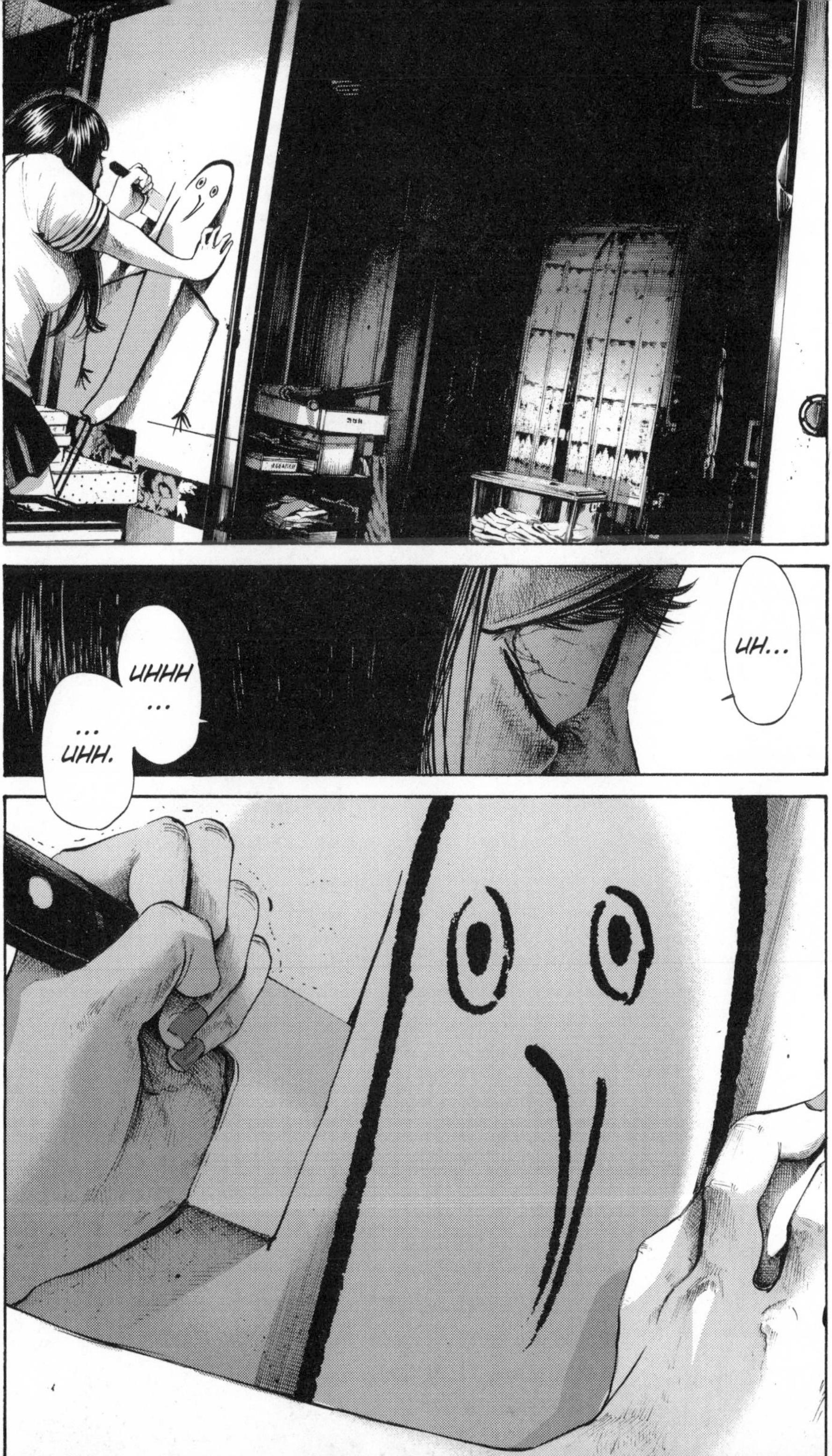
UH...
UHHH
...
...
UHH.

Chapter 113

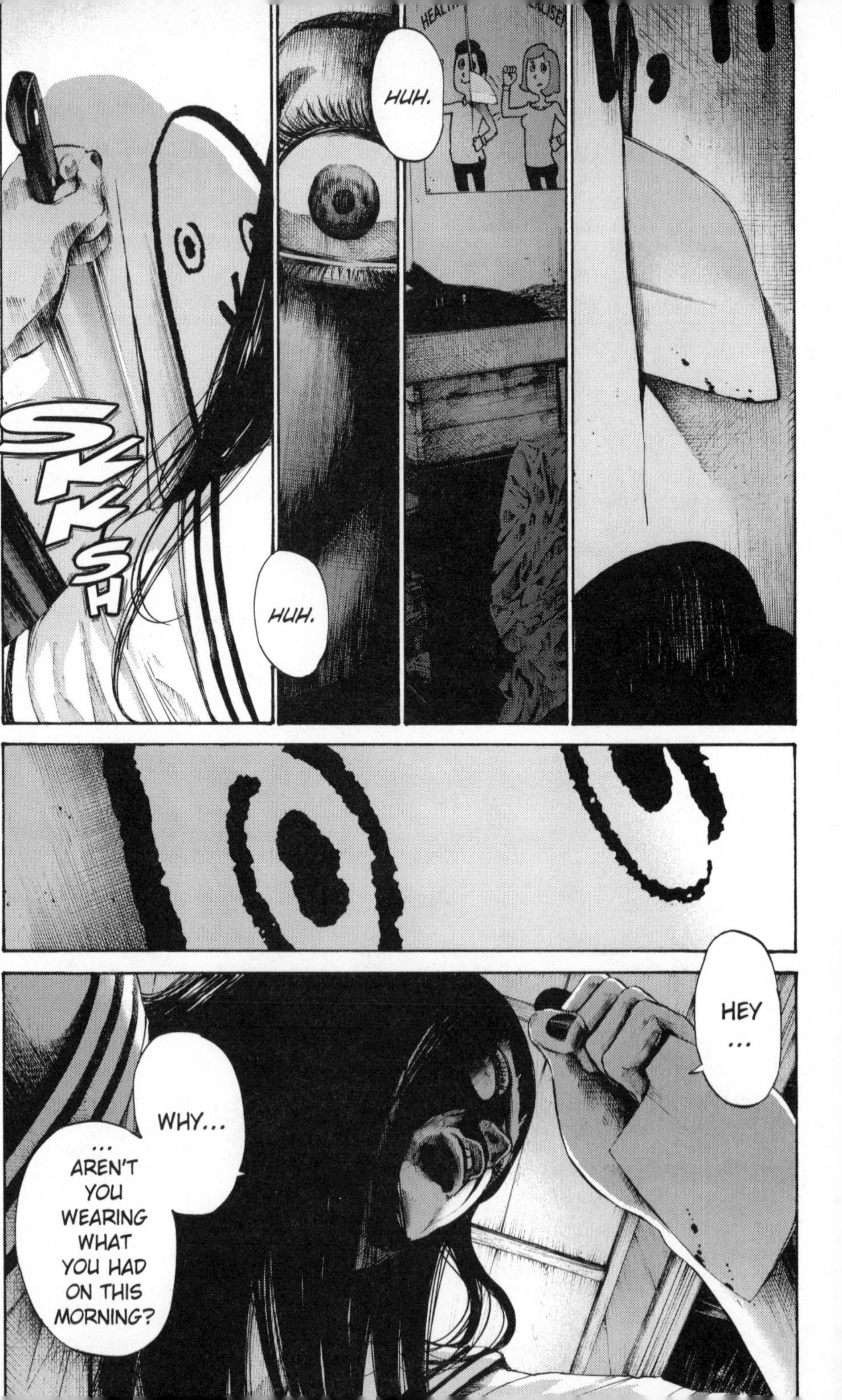
HUH.
HUH.
SKKSH
HEY ...
WHY...
... AREN'T YOU WEARING WHAT YOU HAD ON THIS MORNING?

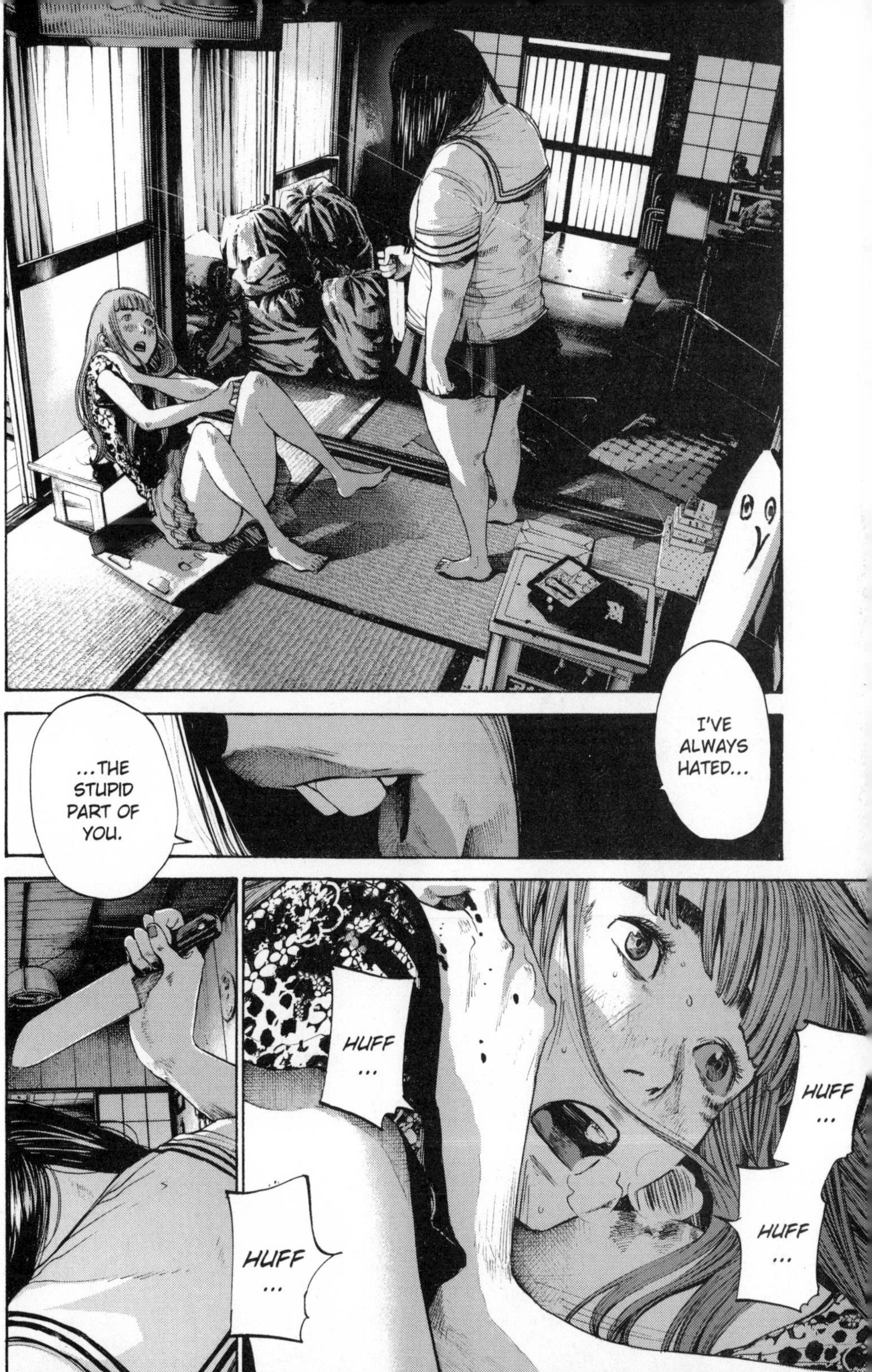
I'VE ALWAYS HATED...
...THE STUPID PART OF YOU.
HUFF ...
HUFF ...
HUFF ...
HUFF ...

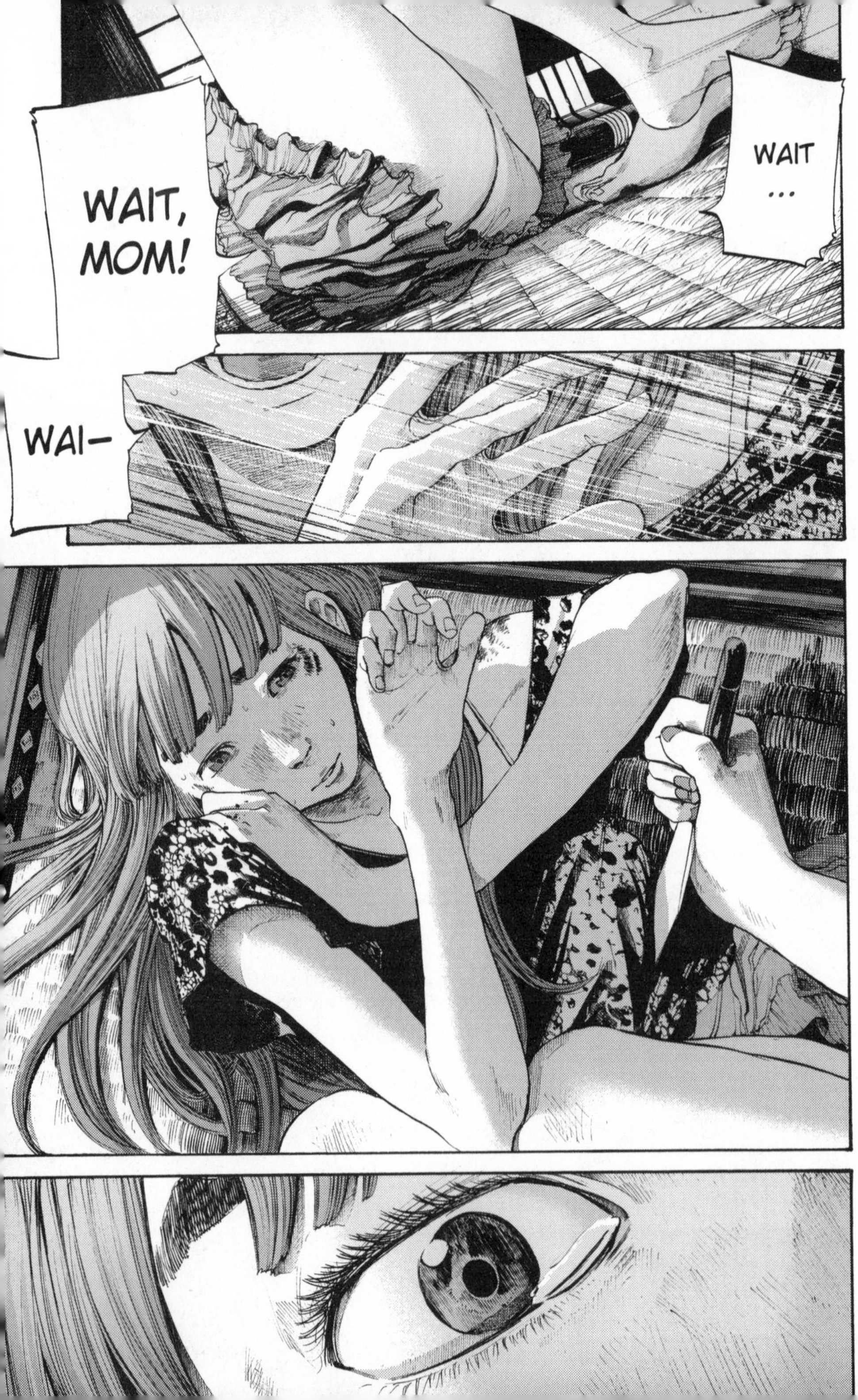
WAIT ...
WAIT, MOM!
WAI-

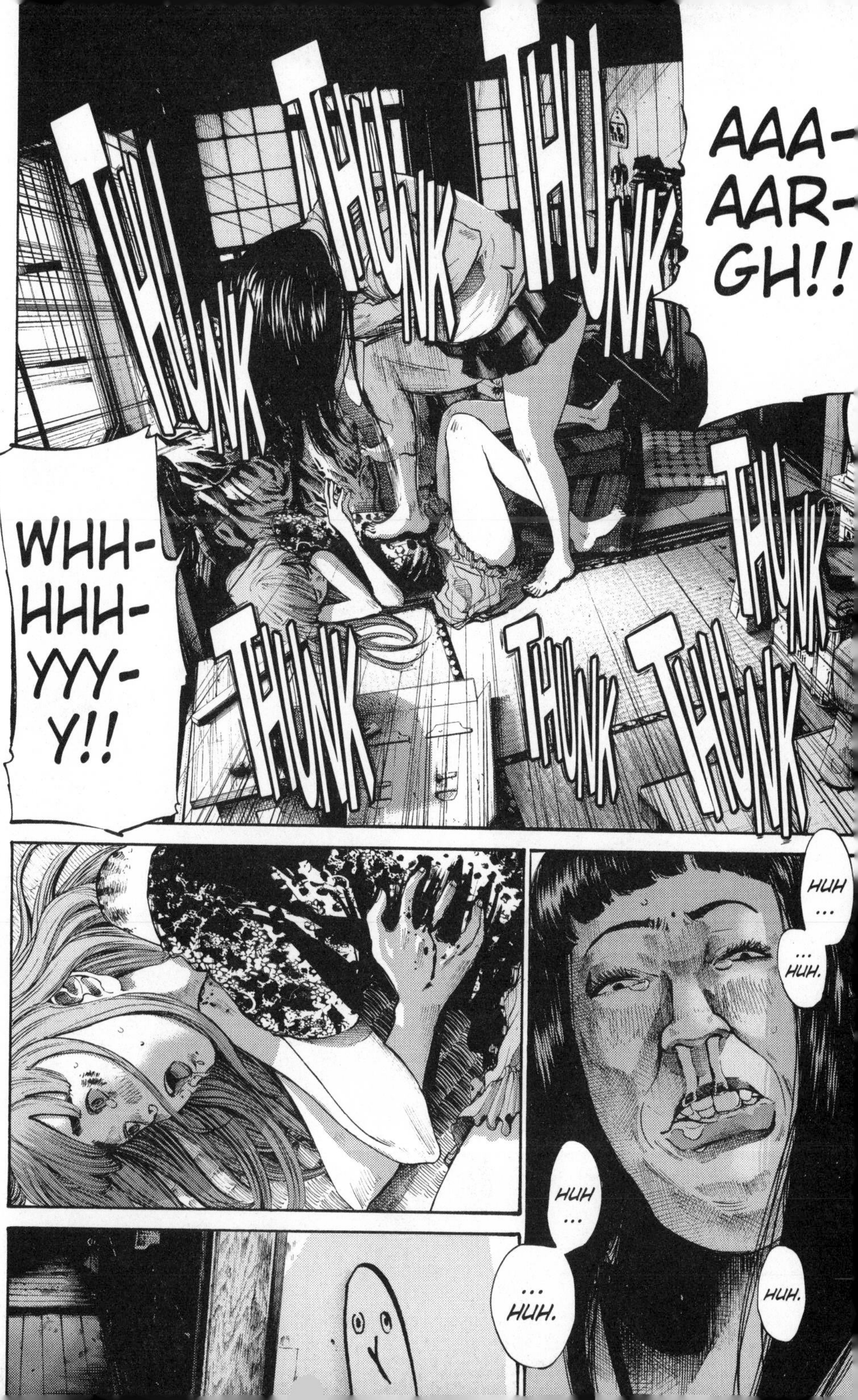
AAA-AAR-GH!!
THUNK
THUNK
THUNK
THUNK
THUNK
THUNK
THUNK
WHH-HHH-YYYY-Y!!
HUH...
...HUH.
HUH...
HUH.
...HUH.

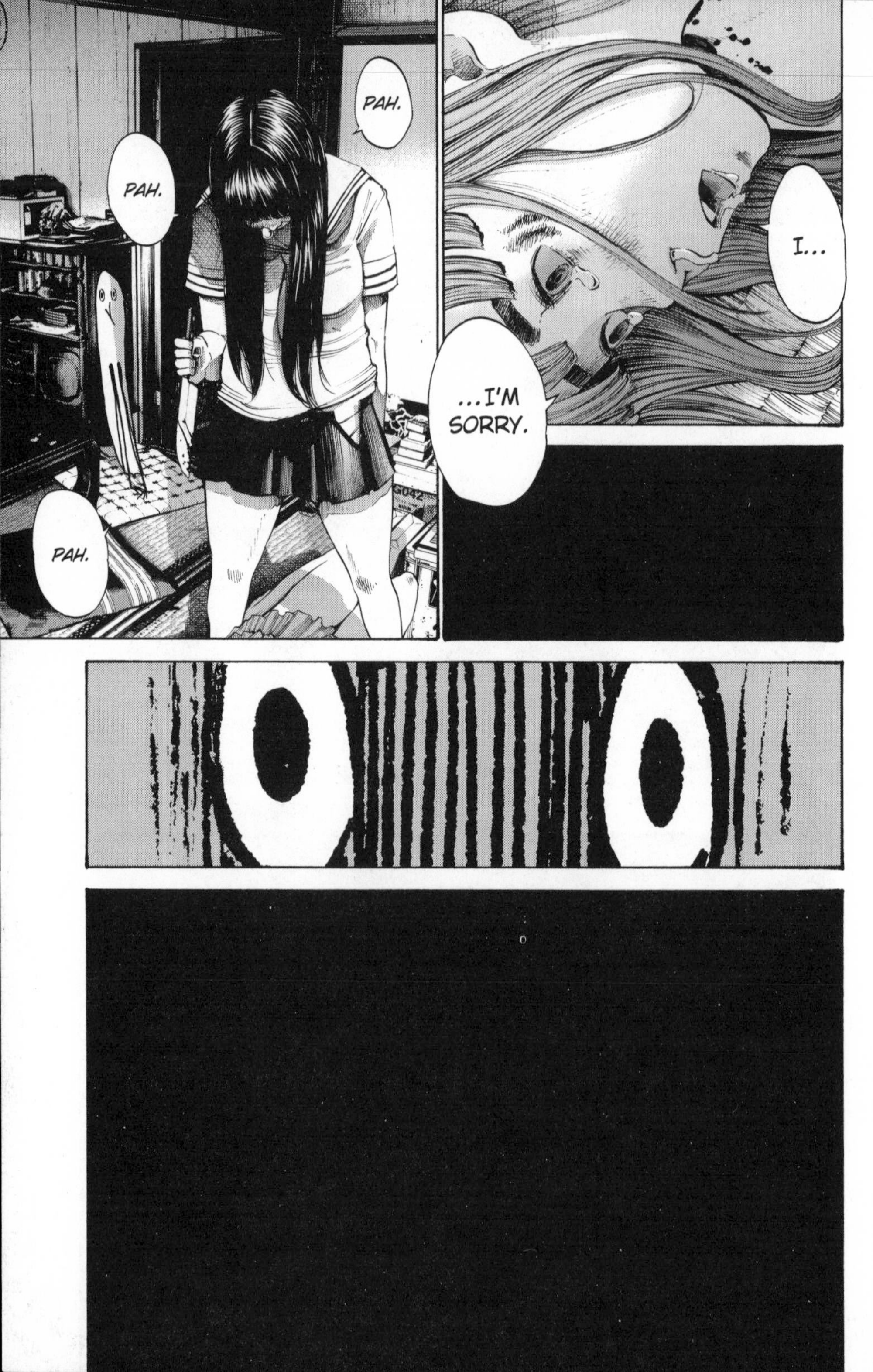
I...
...I'M SORRY.
PAH.
PAH.
PAH.

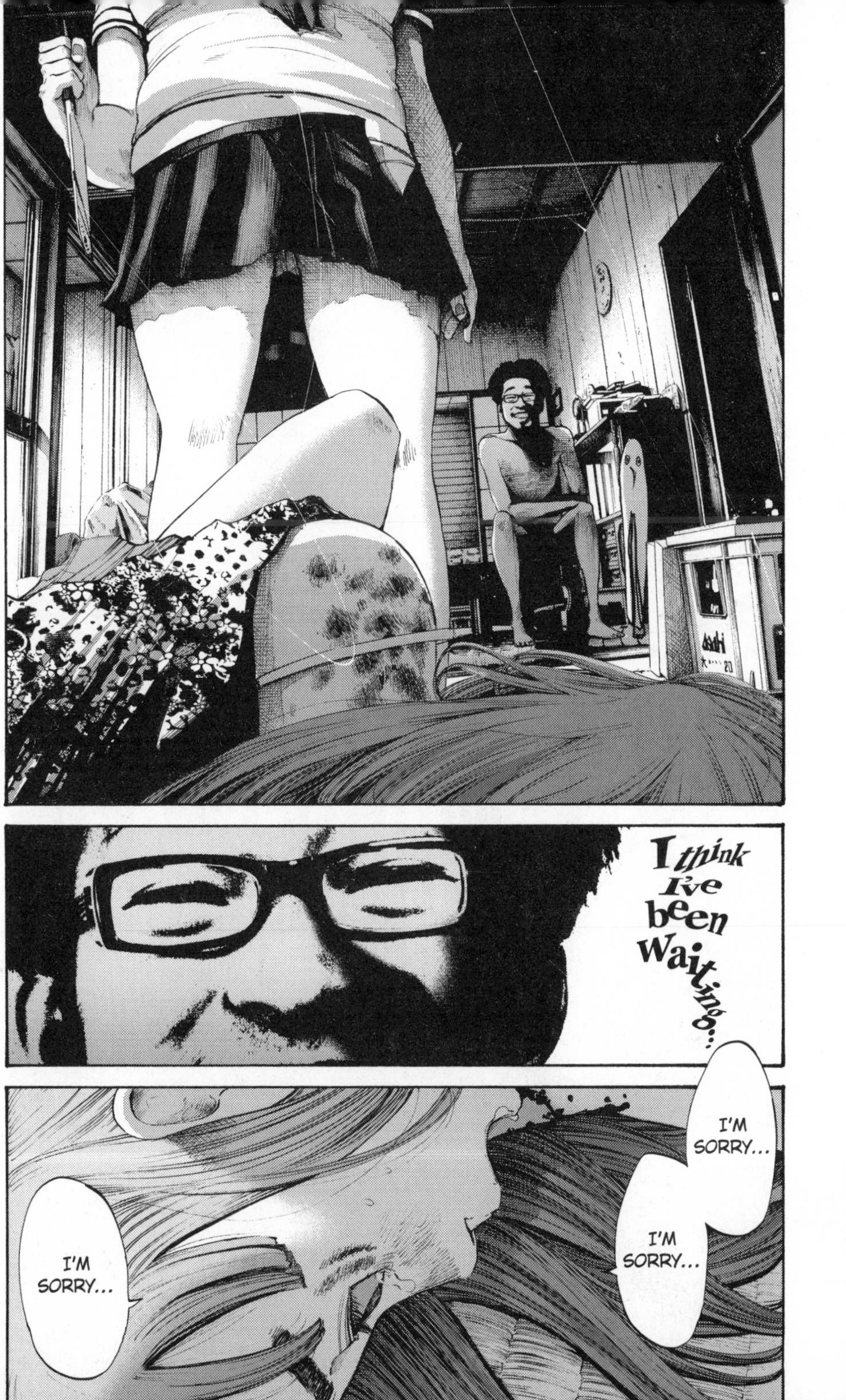
I think I've been waiting...
I'M SORRY...
I'M SORRY...
I'M SORRY...

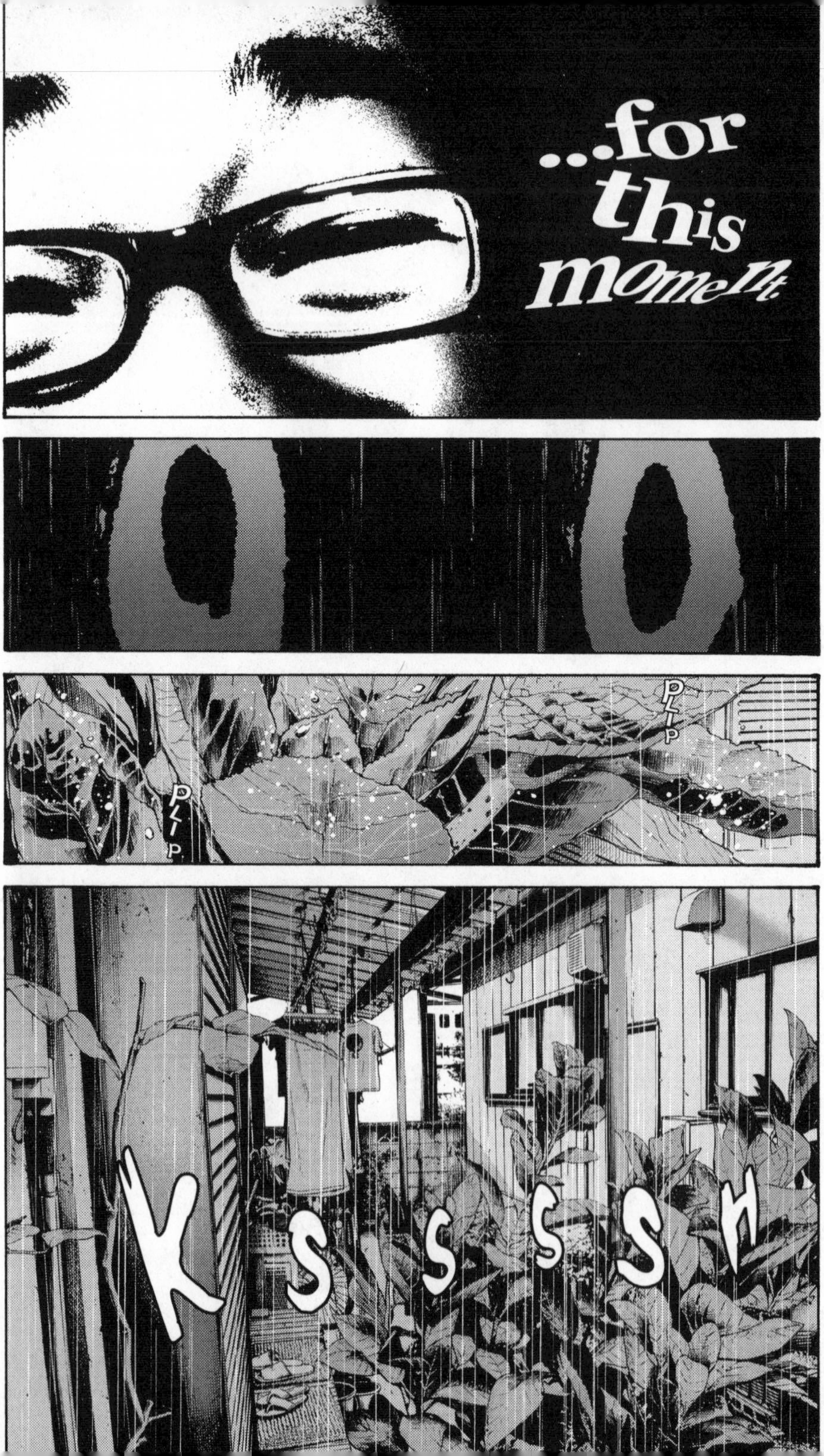
...for this moment.
PLIP PLIP
PLIP
KSSSSH

Good morning, PunPun.

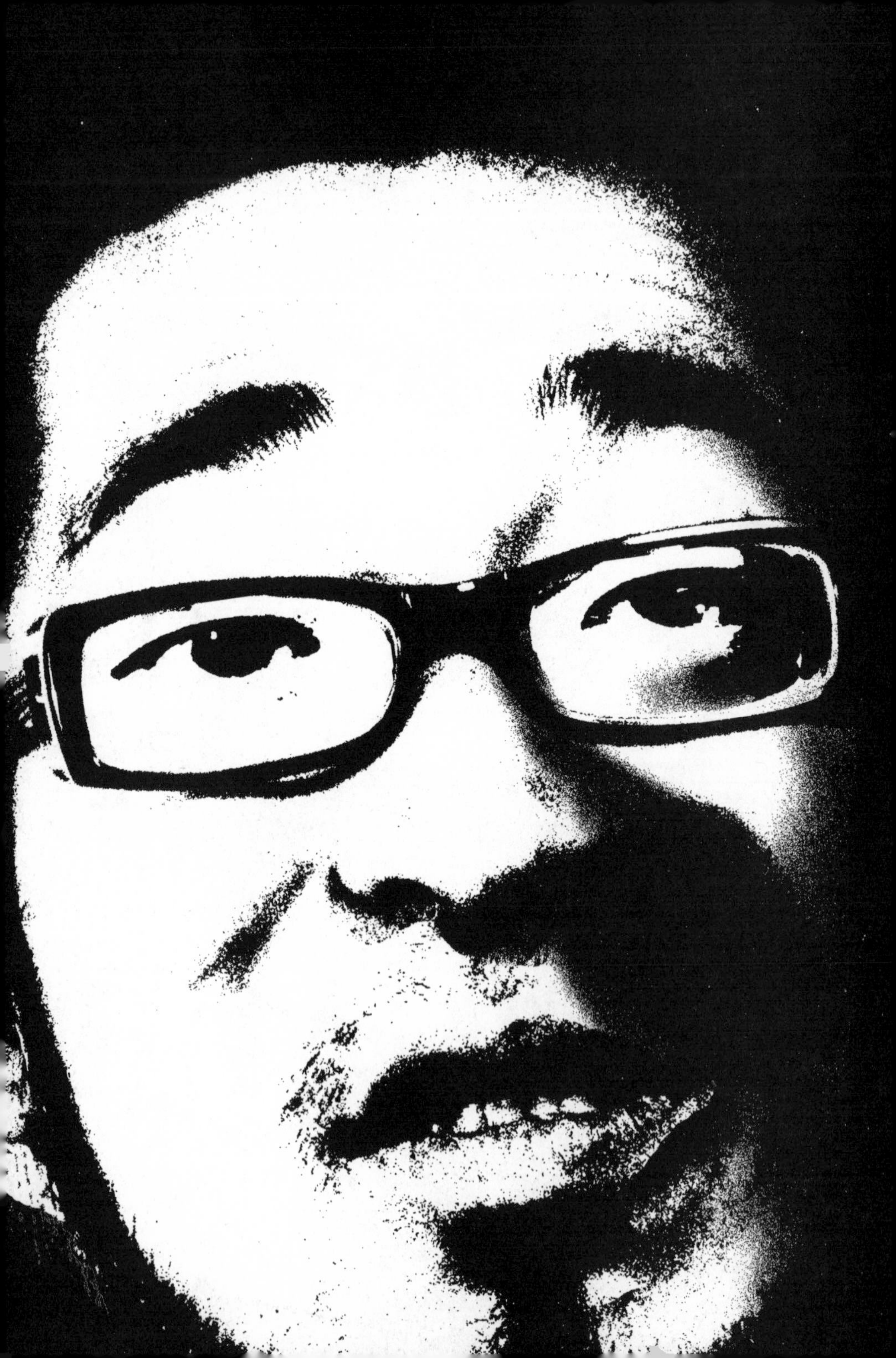

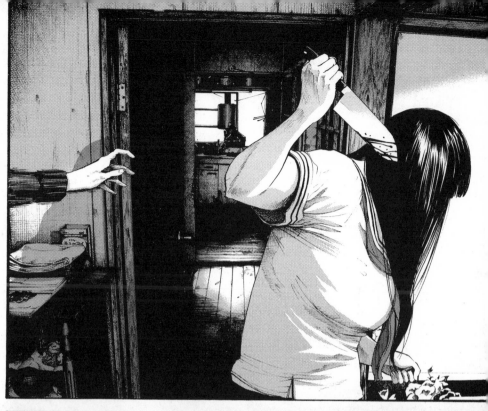
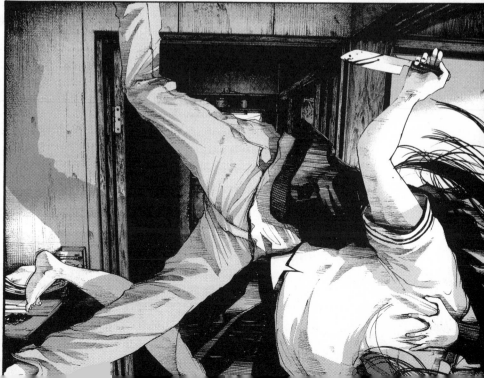

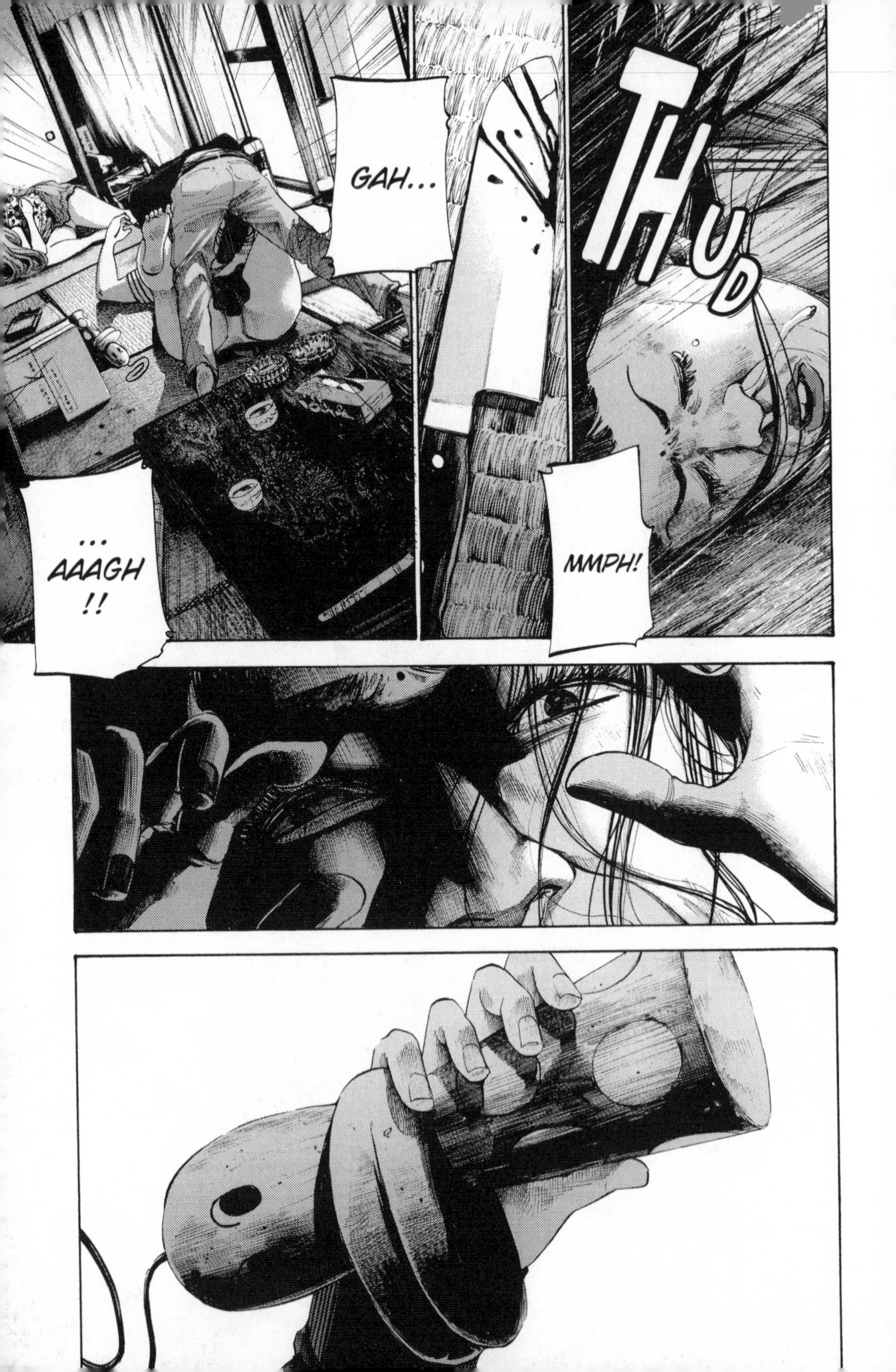
THUD
MMPH!
GAH...
... AAAGH !!

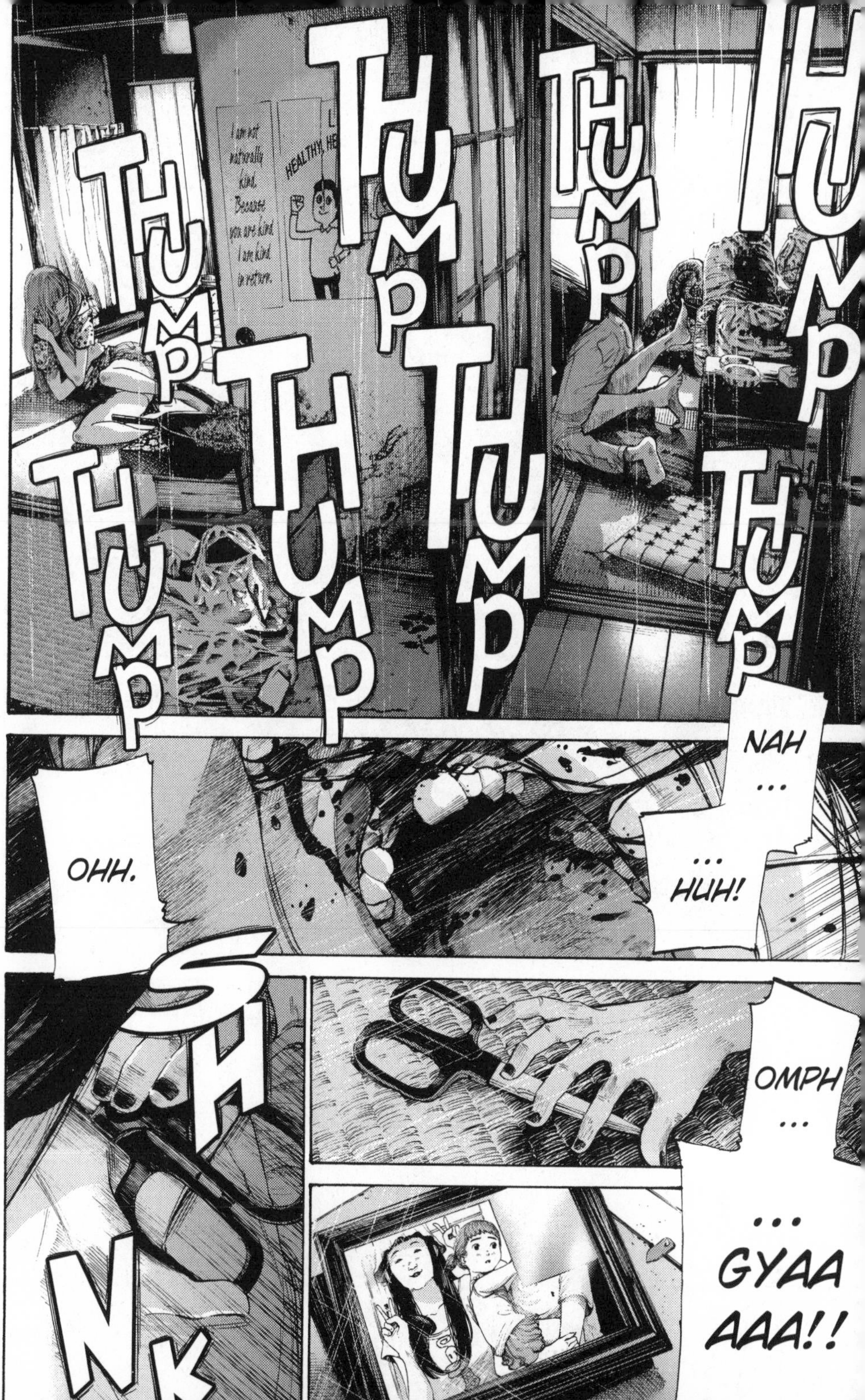
THUMP
THUMP
THUMP
THUMP
I am not naturally kind. Because you are kind, I am kind in return.
THUMP
THUMP
THUMP
THUMP
NAH ...
... HUH!
OHH.
OMPH ...
... GYAA AAA!!
SHNK

HUH ...
GUH ...
... GUH.
GUH.
GUH.

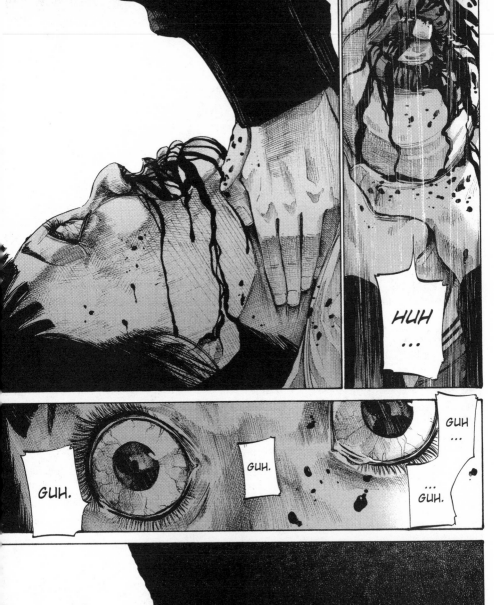

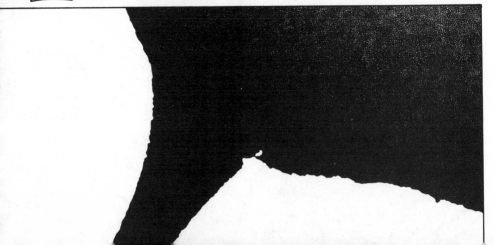

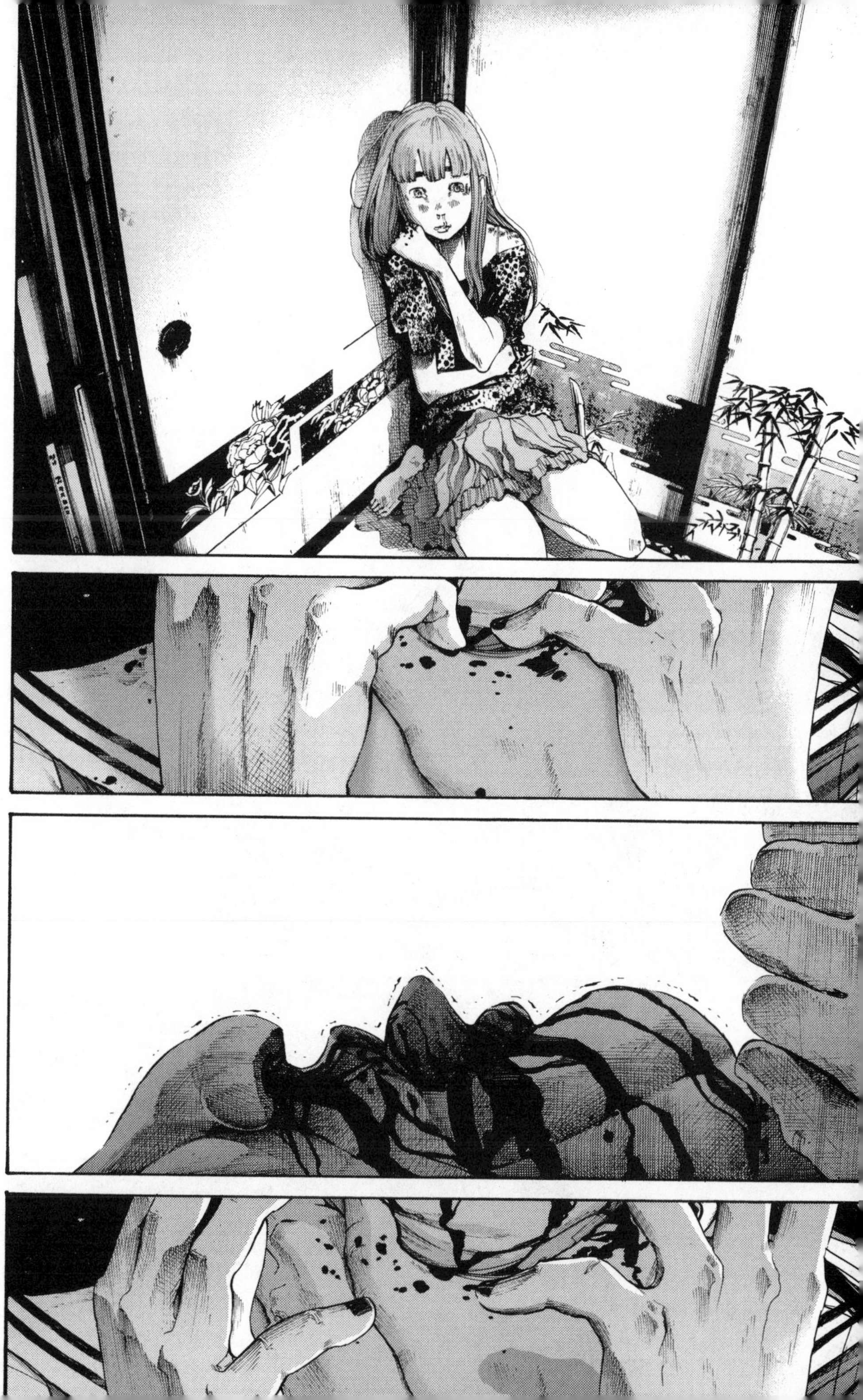

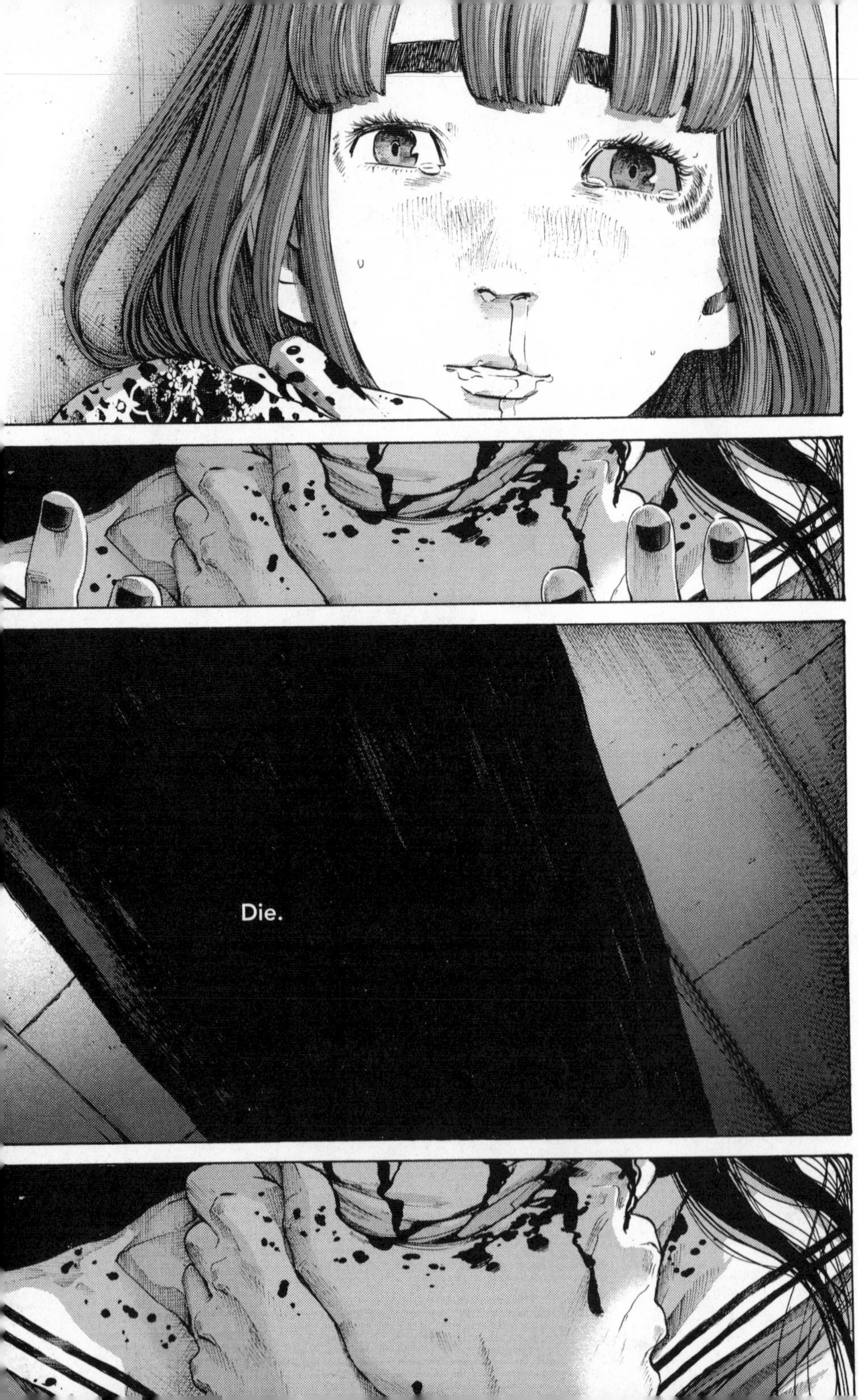
Die.

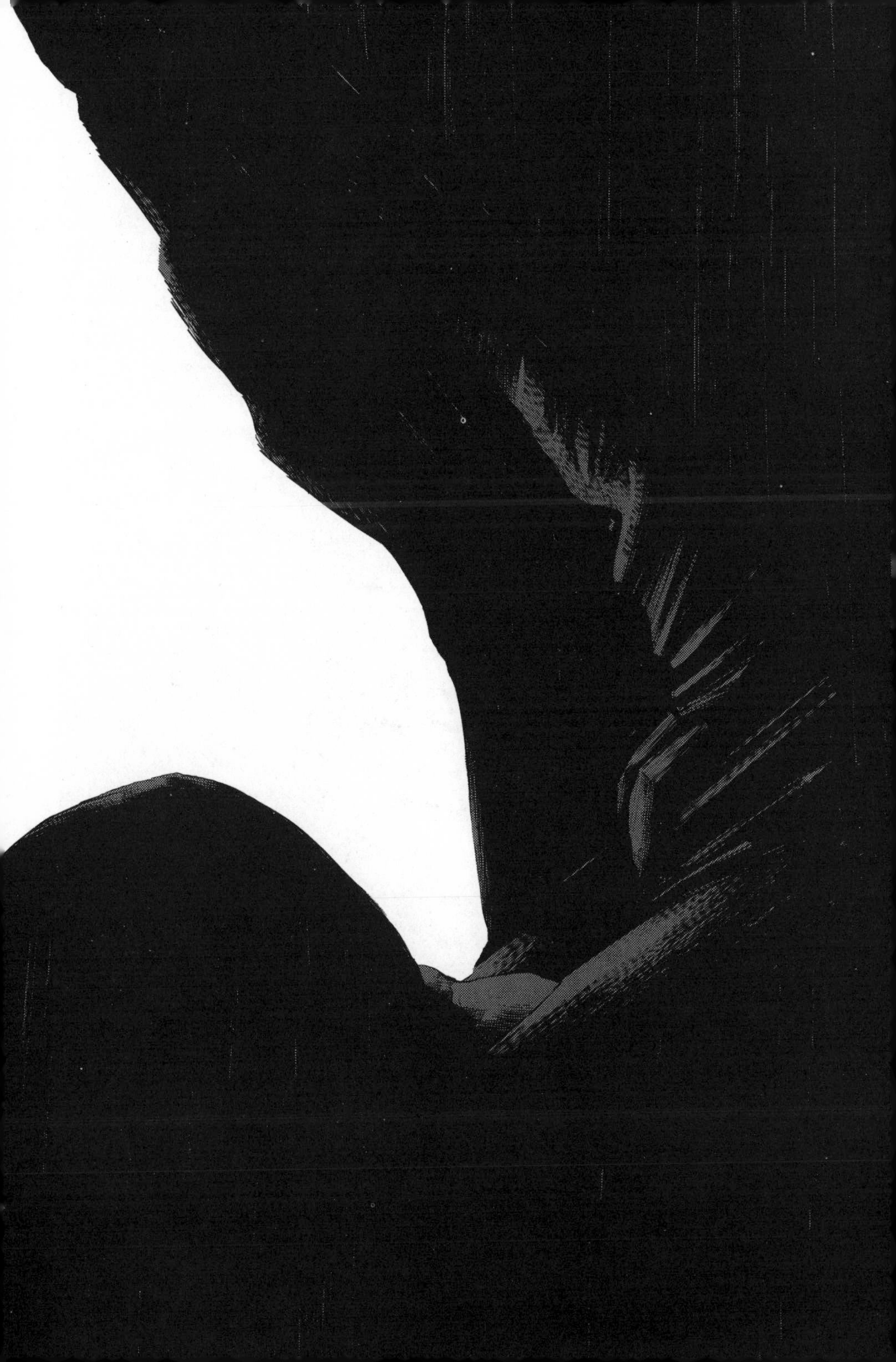

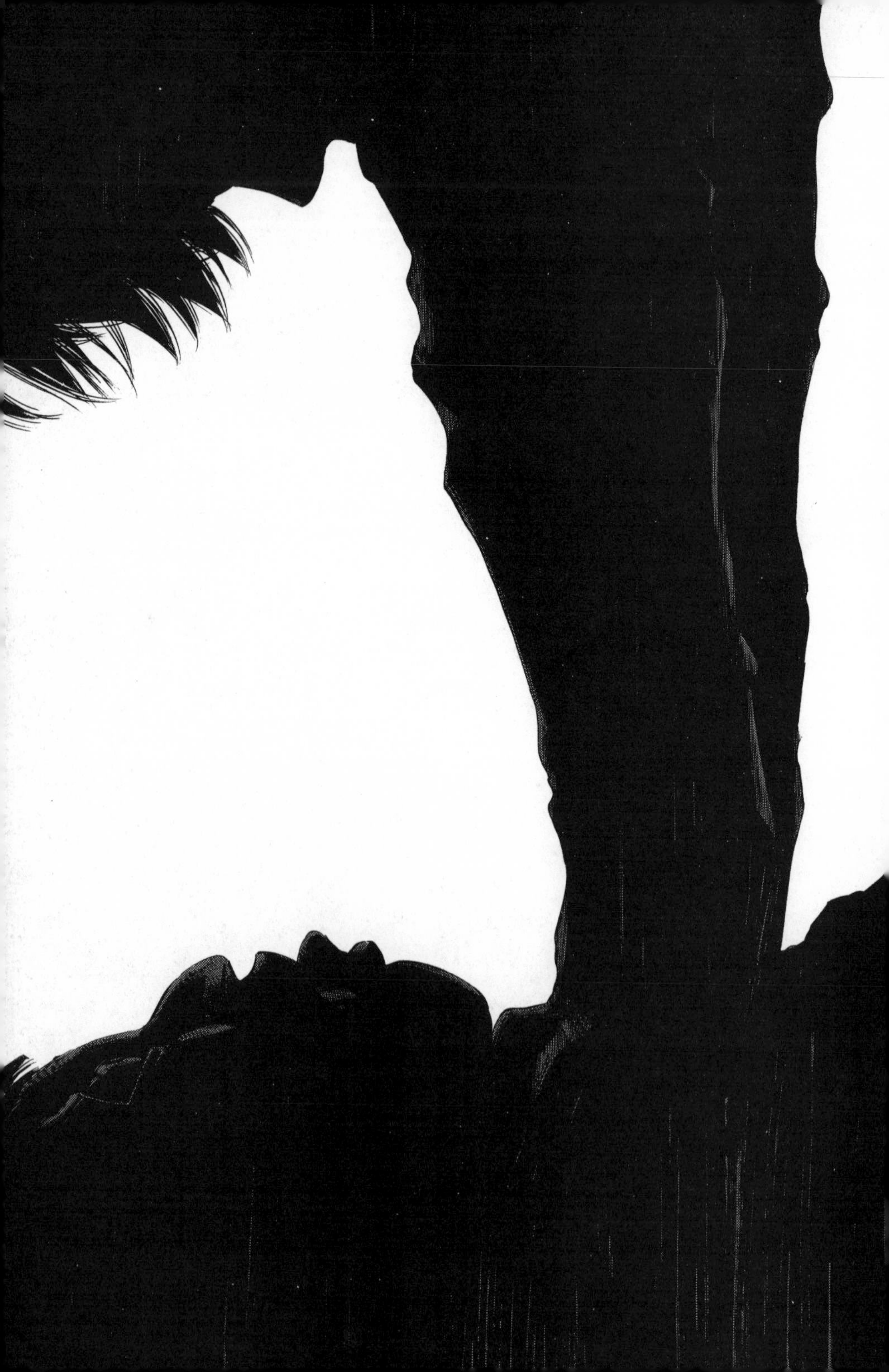

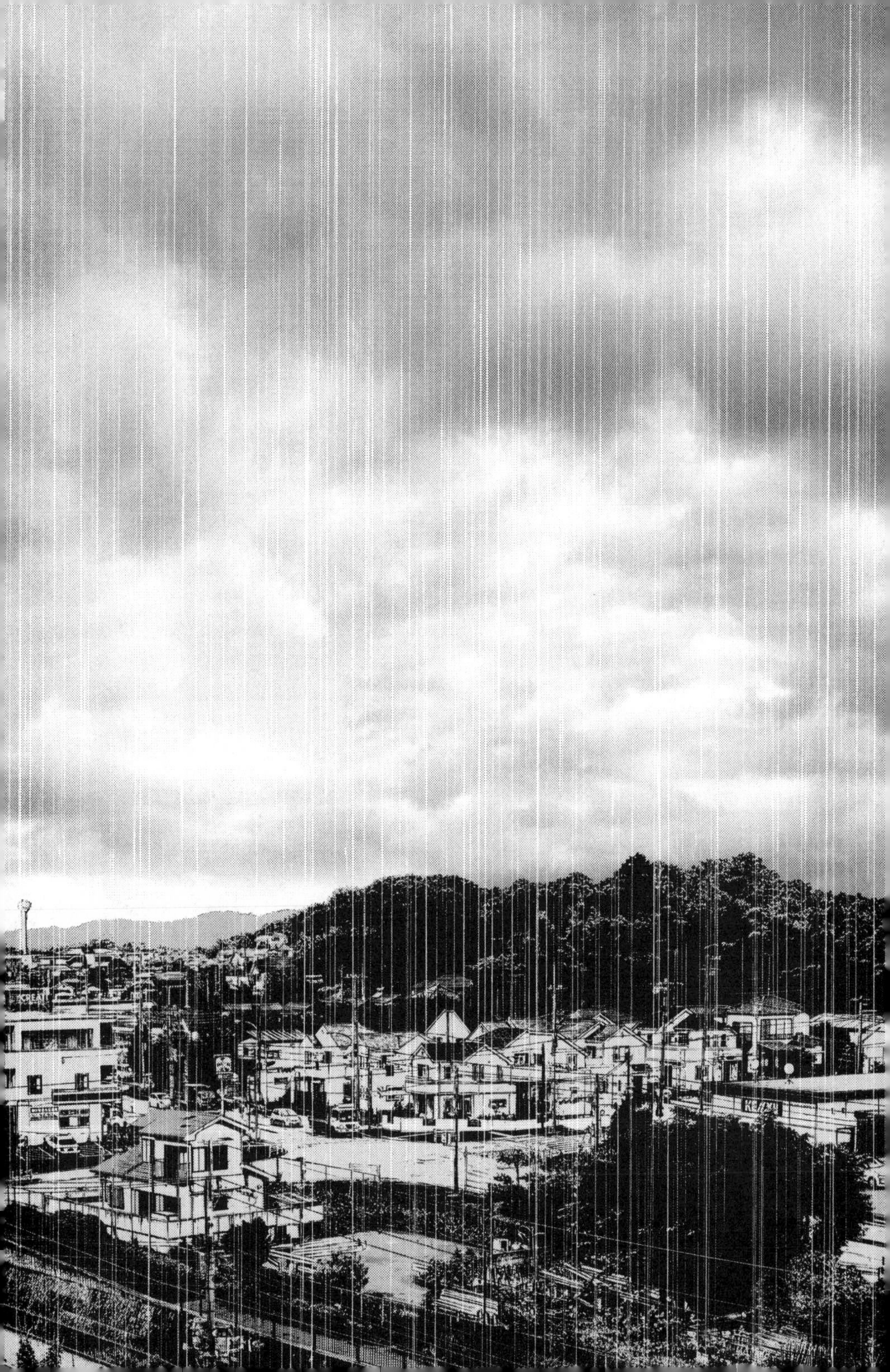

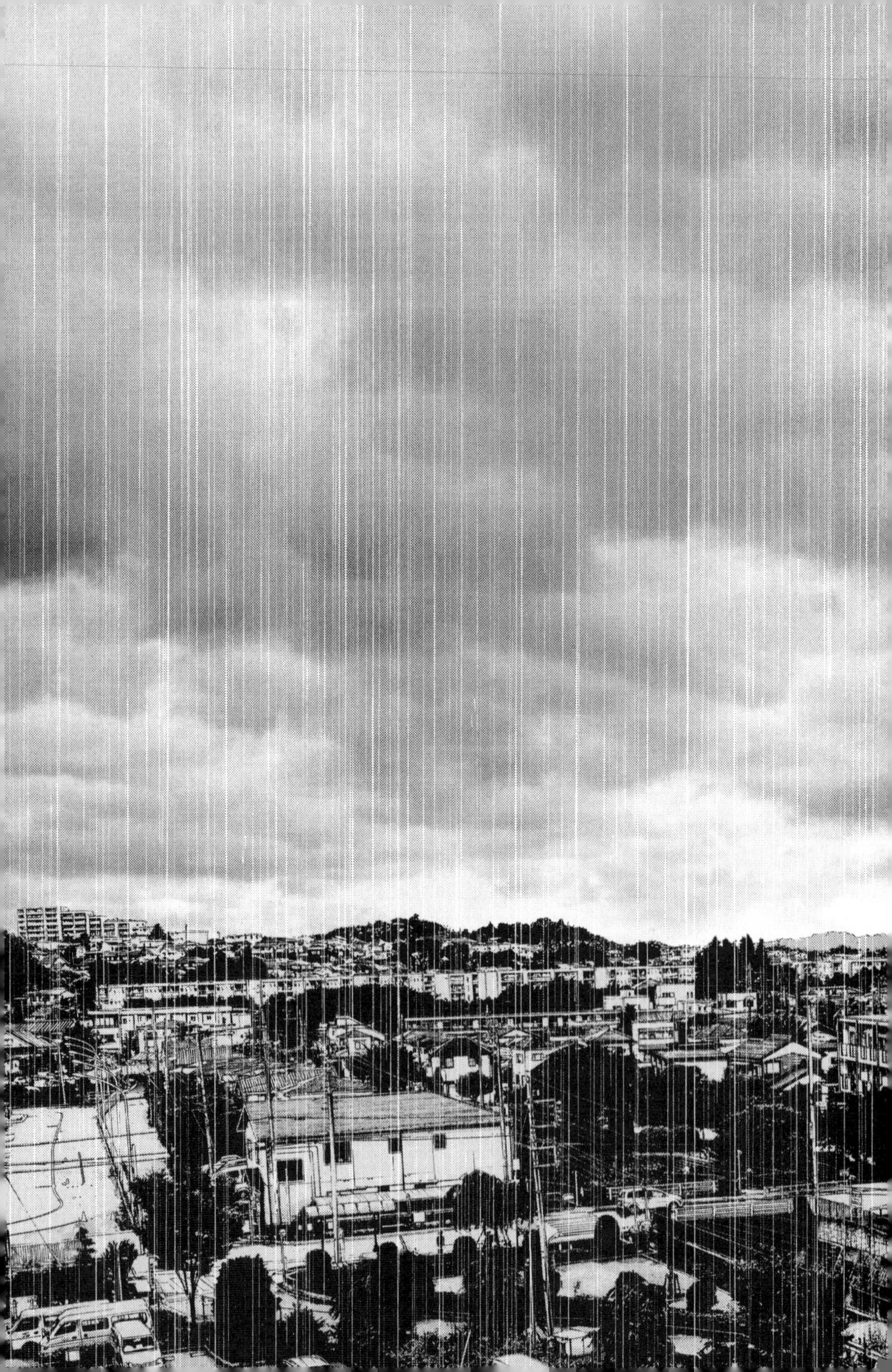

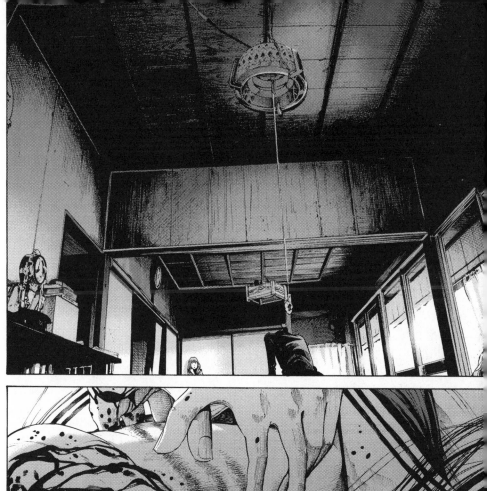
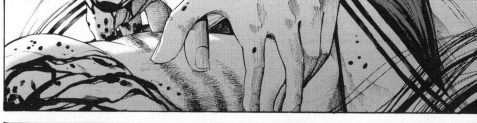
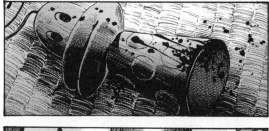
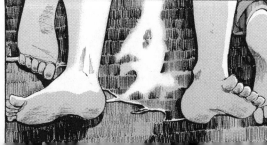
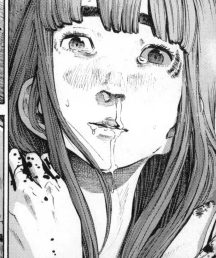

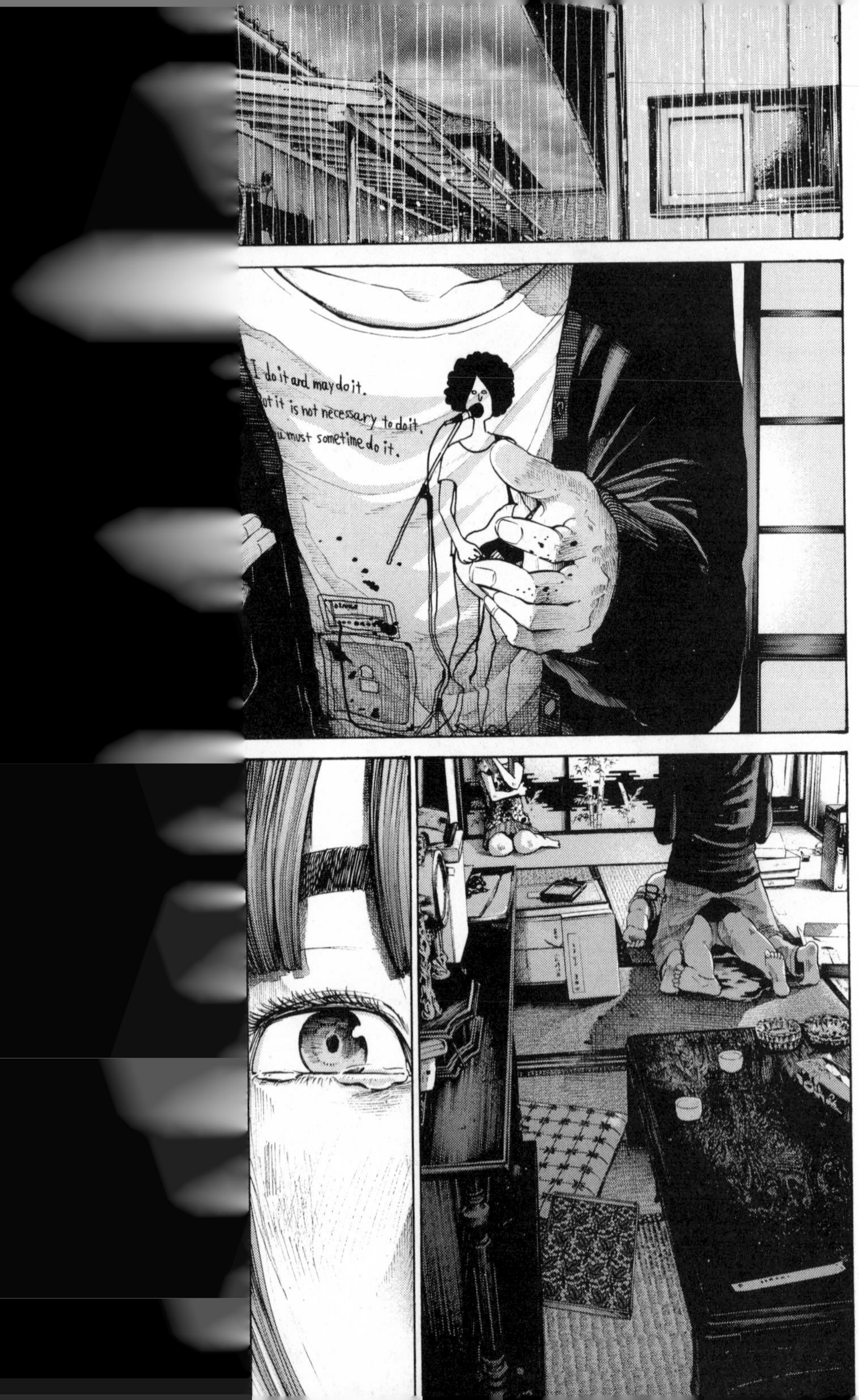

I do it and may do it.
ut it is not necessary to do it.
u must sometime do it.

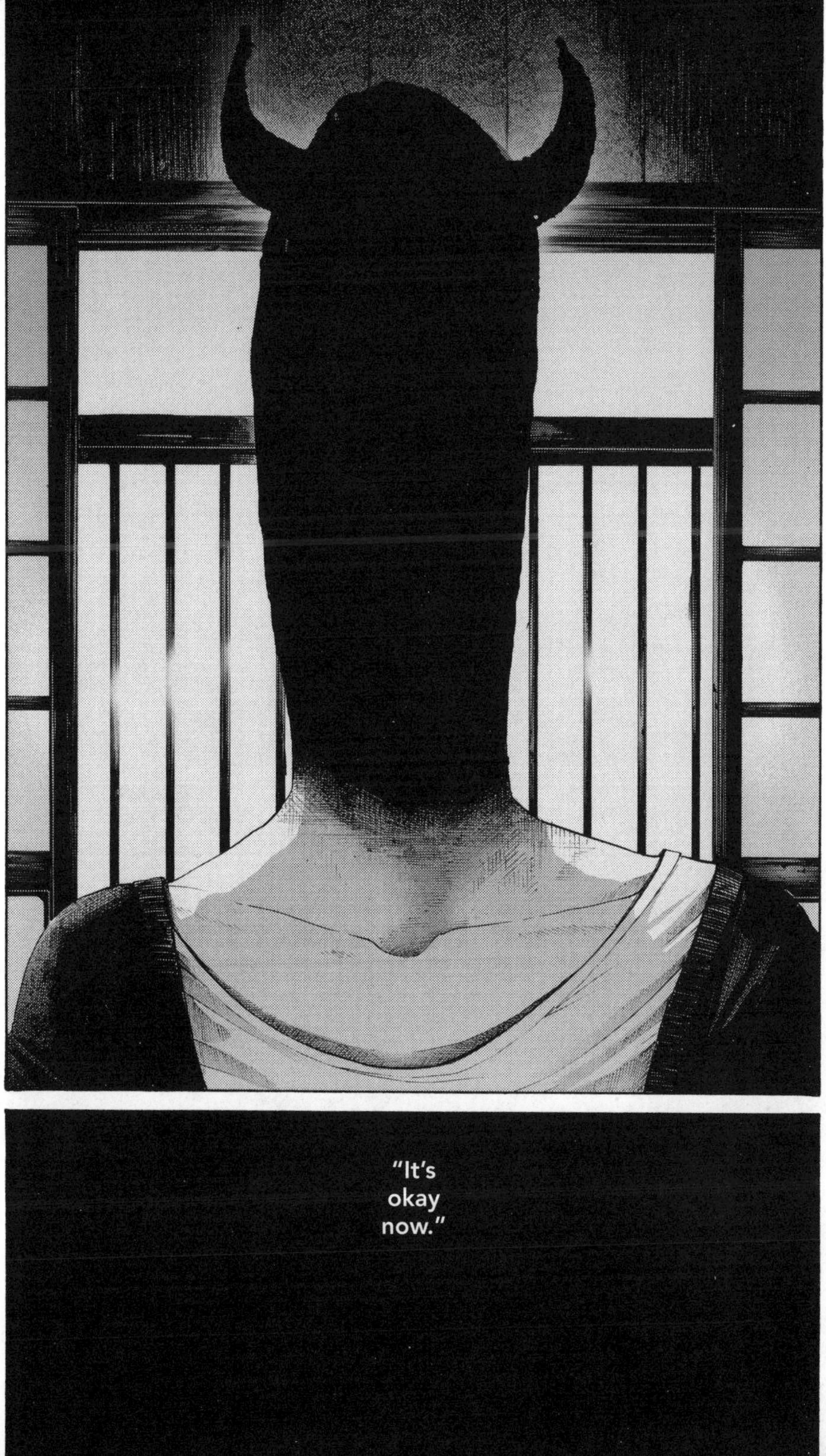

"It's
okay
now."

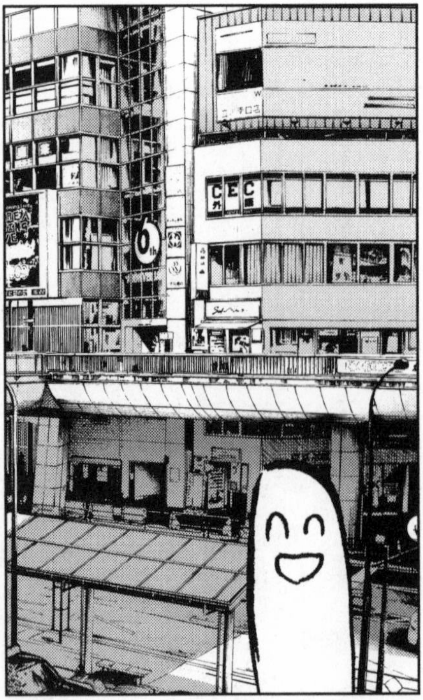
CEC

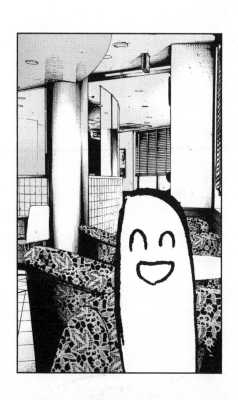

Chapter 114

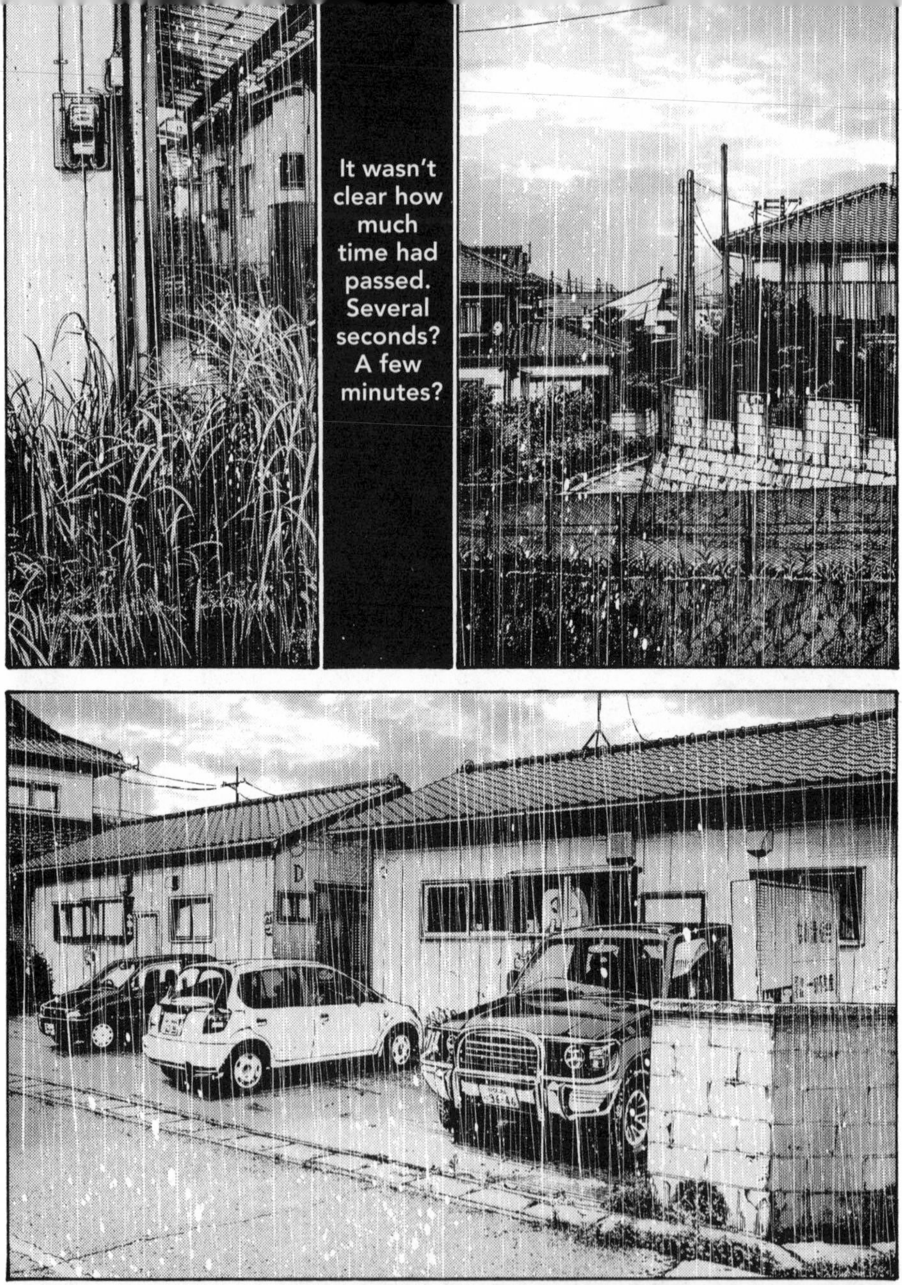
It wasn't clear how much time had passed. Several seconds? A few minutes?

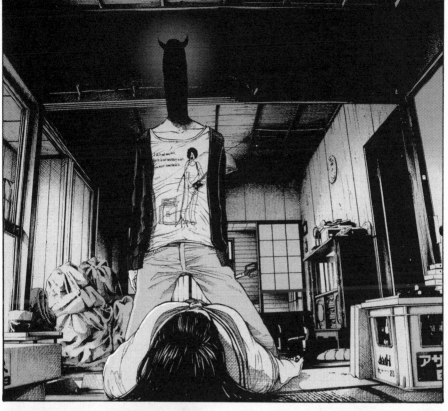

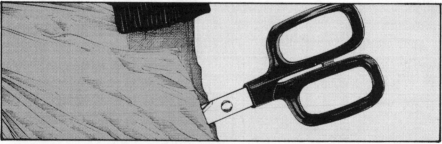

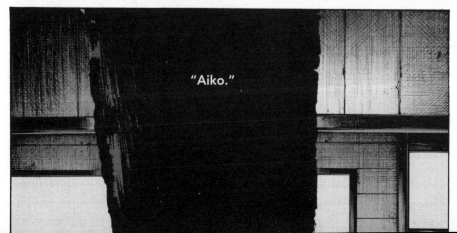

"Aiko."

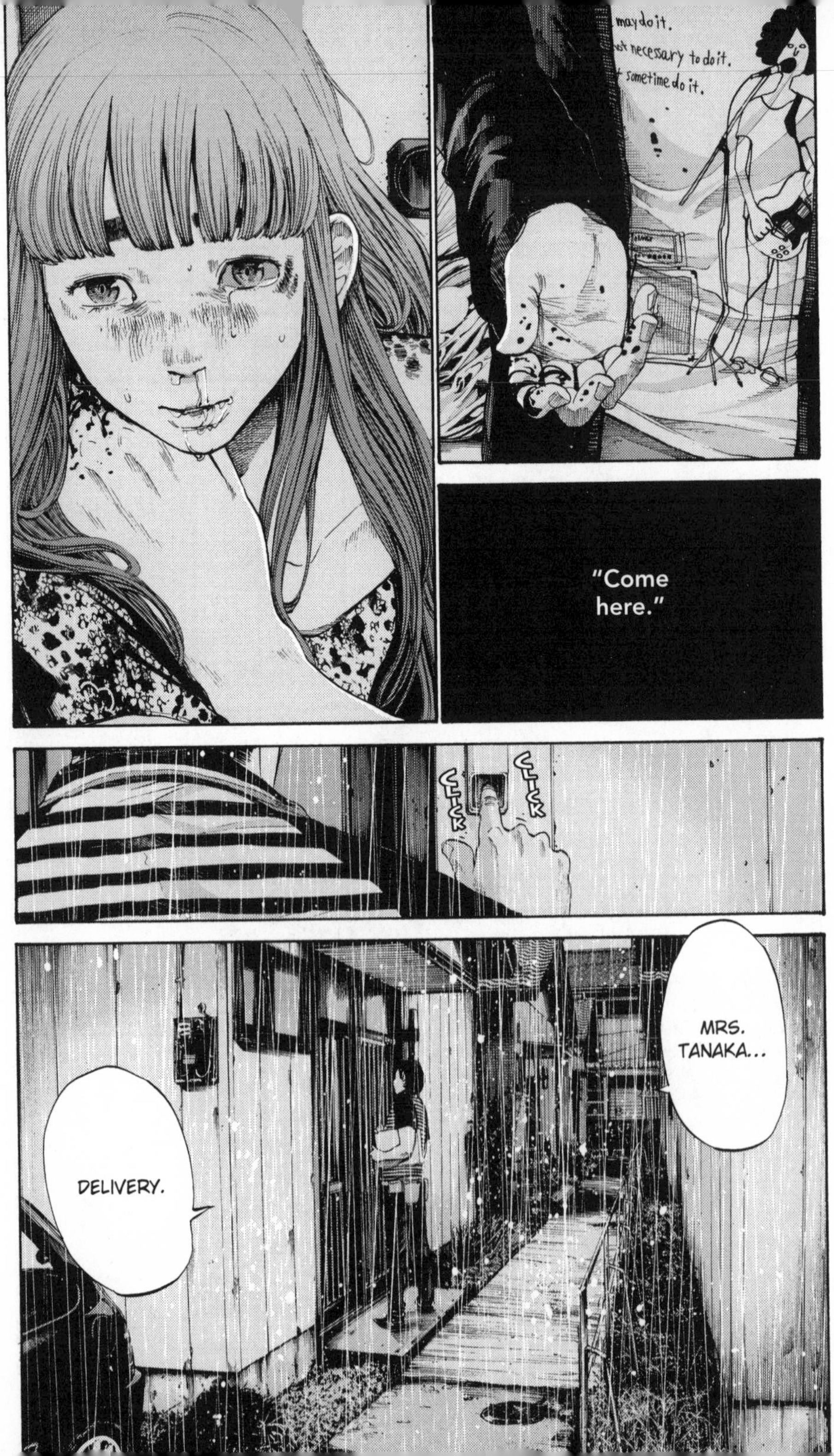
may do it.
necessary to do it.
sometime do it.
"Come here."
CLICK
CLICK
MRS. TANAKA...
DELIVERY.

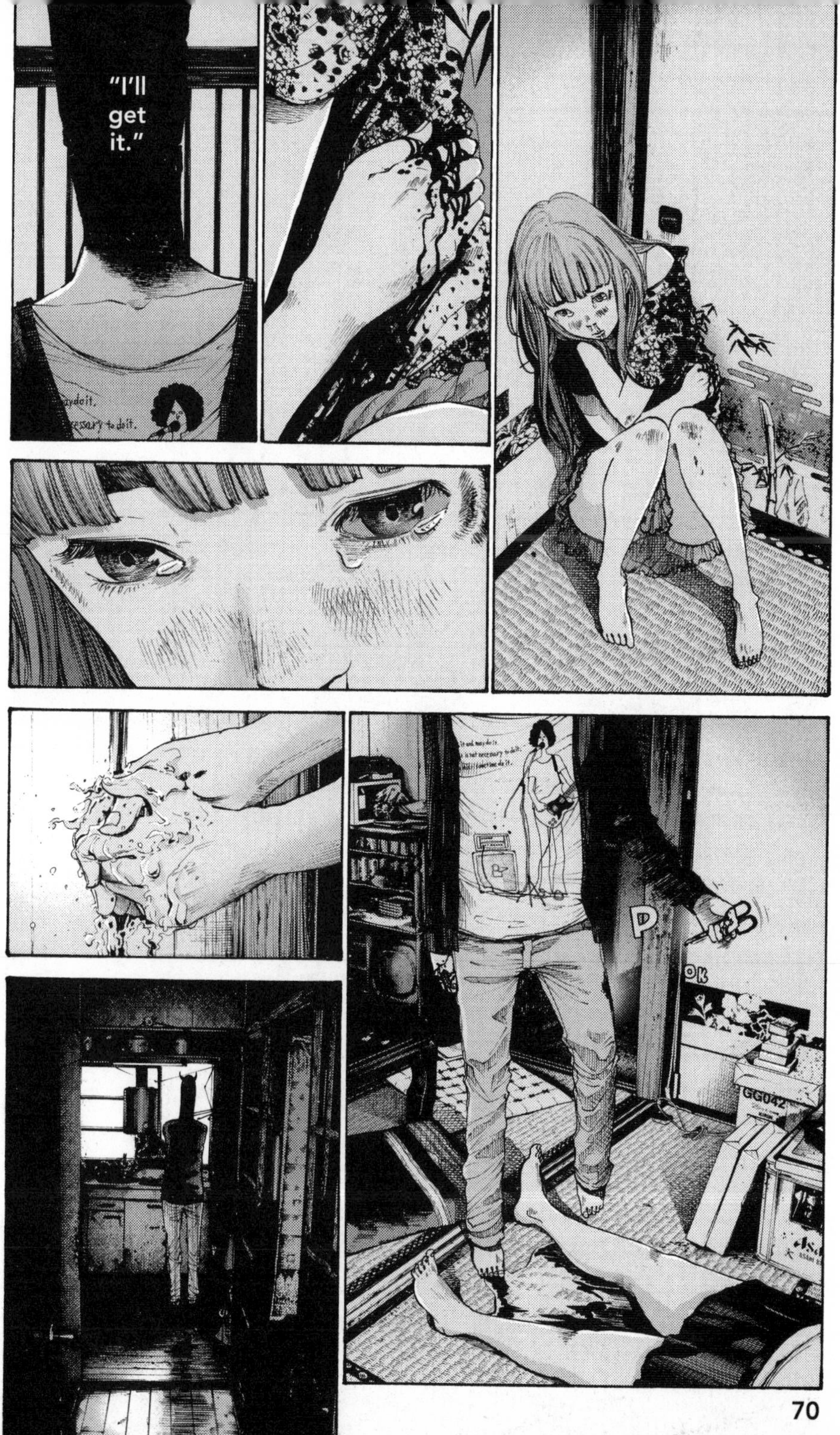
“I'll get it.”
P
GG042

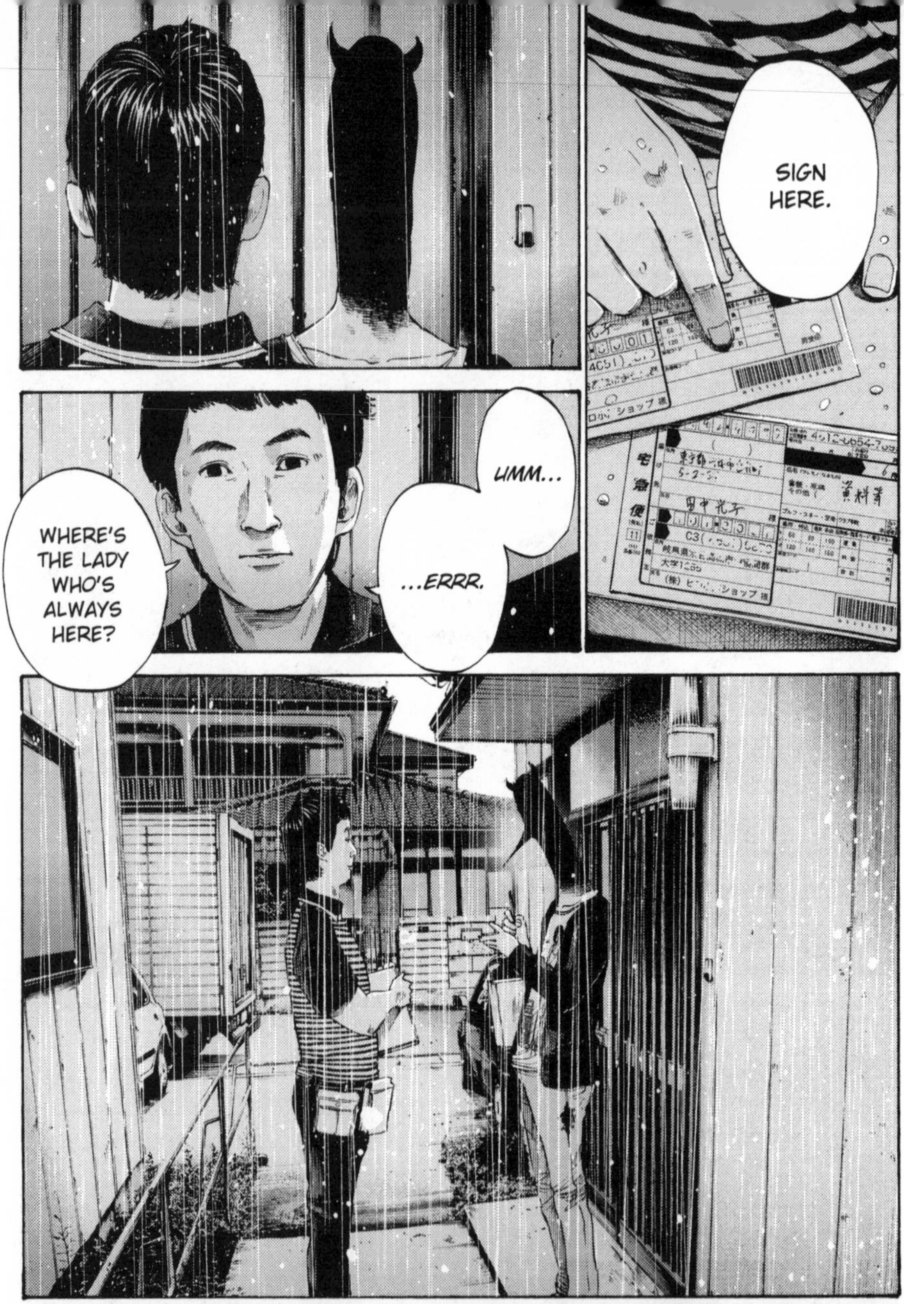
SIGN HERE.
UMM...
...ERRR.
WHERE'S THE LADY WHO'S ALWAYS HERE?

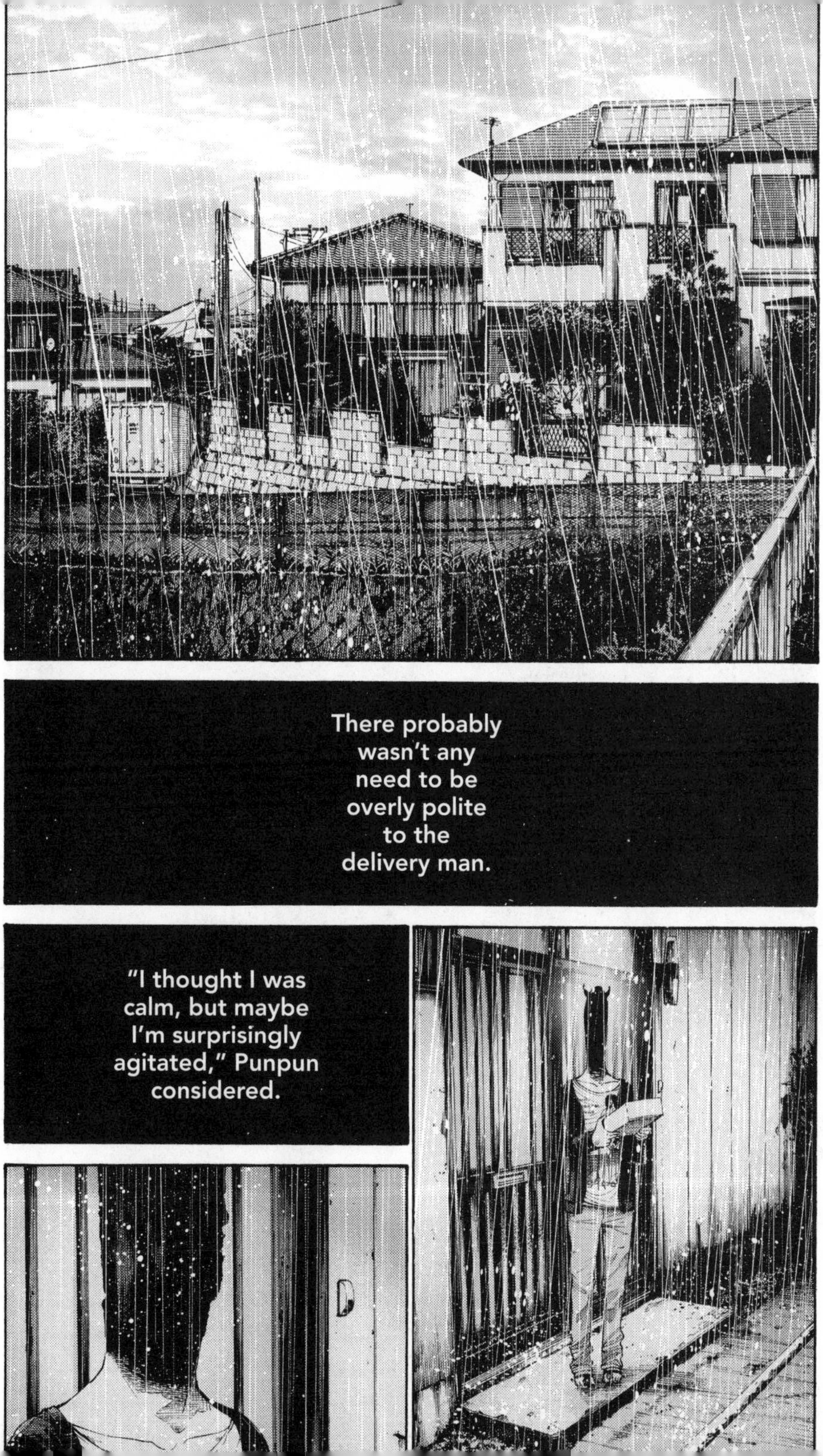
There probably wasn't any need to be overly polite to the delivery man.
"I thought I was calm, but maybe I'm surprisingly agitated," Punpun considered.

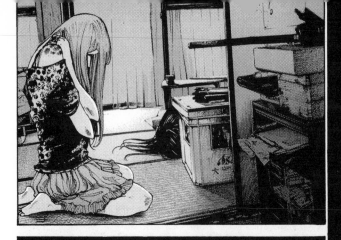

The dark gray sky, the worn-out building…

The scene reflected into his eyes seemed like just a backdrop.

Maybe if he went back into the room…

…a young, up-and-coming comedian would burst grinning out of the shadows as the instigator of an elaborate prank.

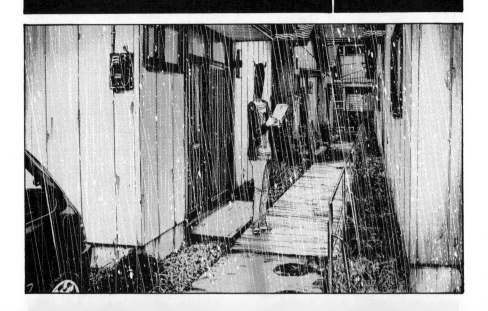

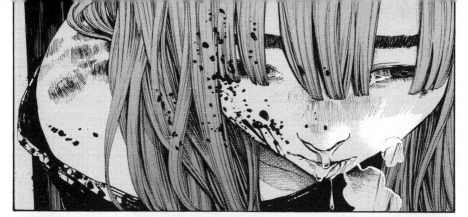

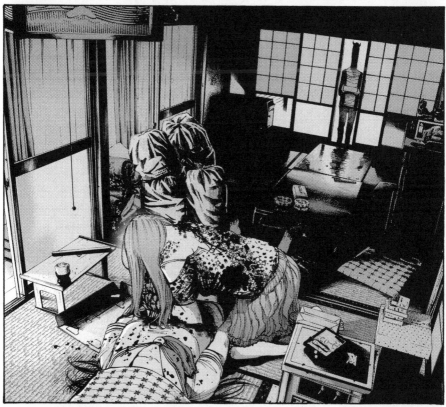

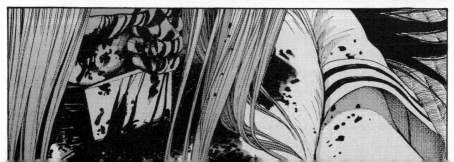

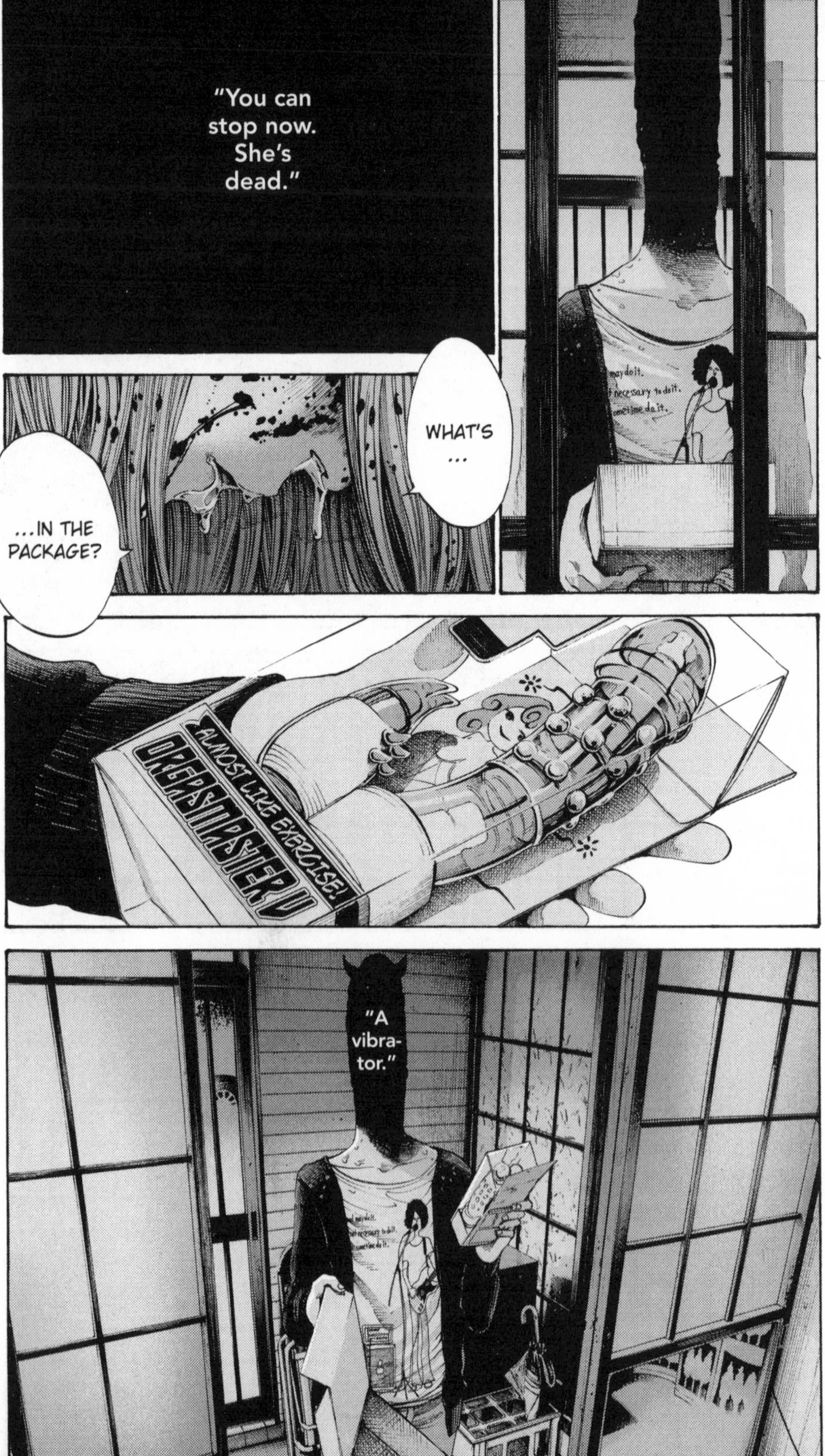
"You can stop now. She's dead."
WHAT'S ...
...IN THE PACKAGE?
ALMOST LIKE EXERCISE!
ORGASMASTER V
"A vibra-tor."

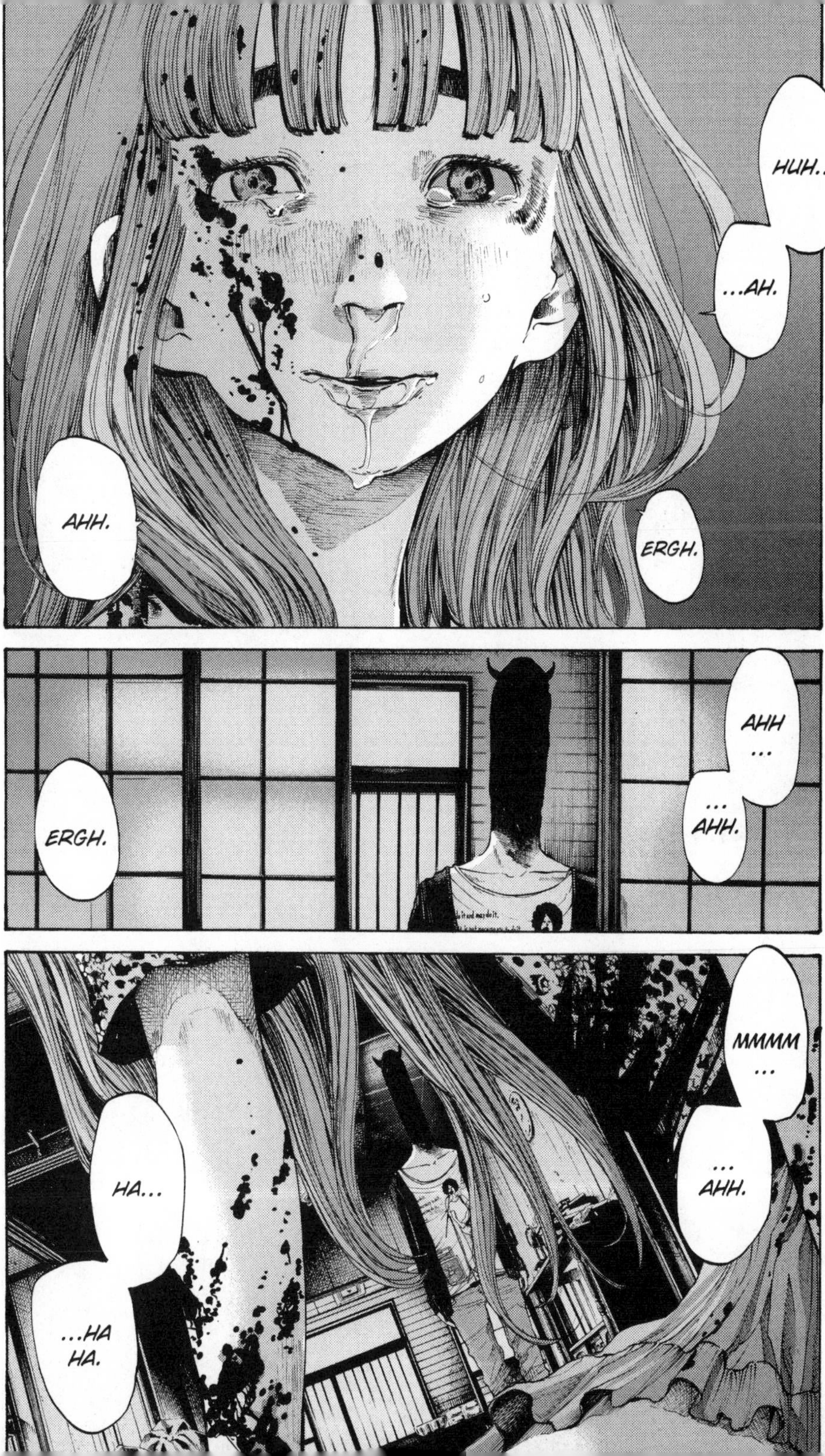
HUH...
...AH.
ERGH.
AHH.
AHH...
...AHH.
ERGH.
MMMM...
...AHH.
HA...
...HA HA.

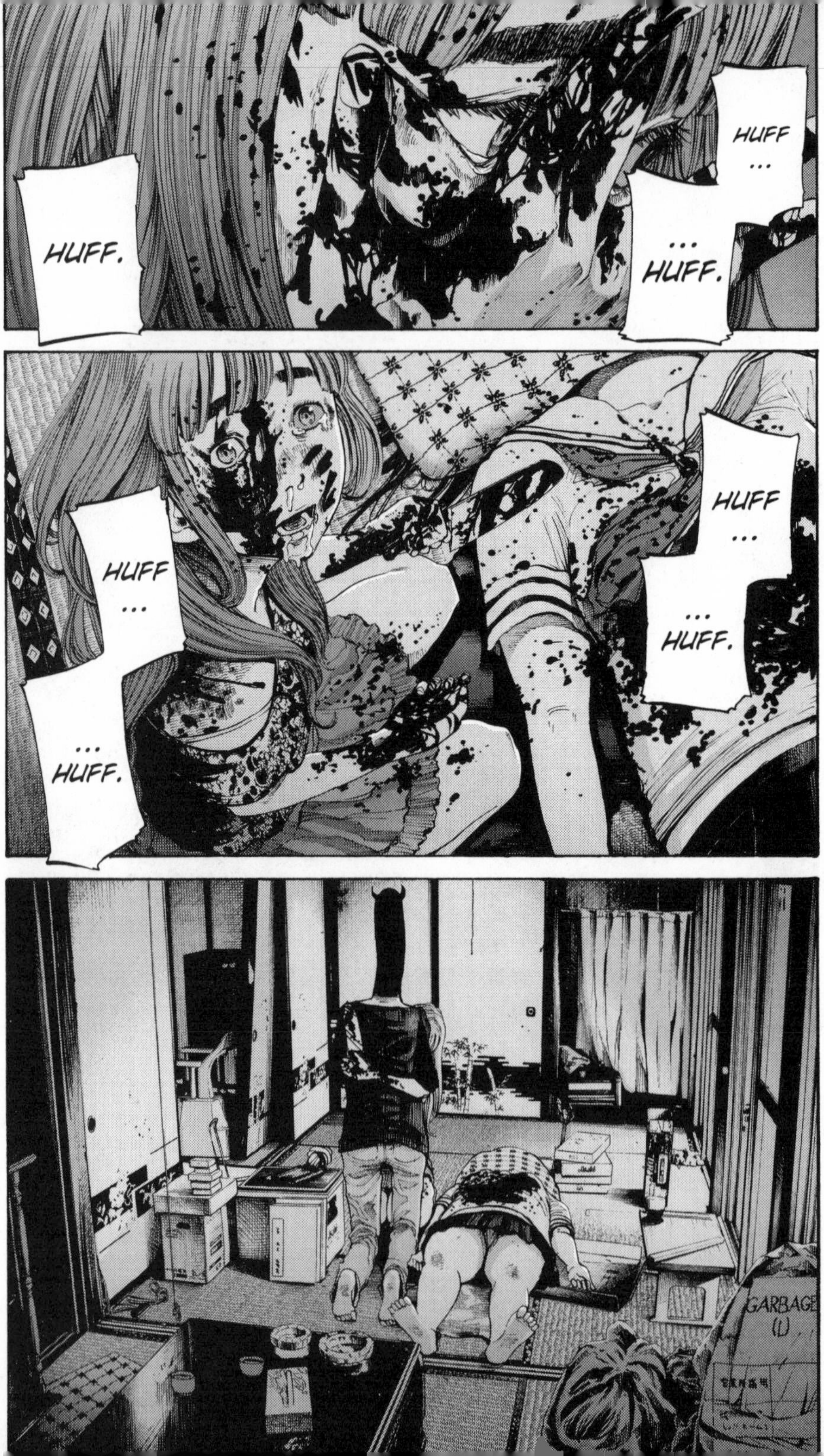
HUFF ...
... HUFF.
HUFF.
HUFF ...
... HUFF.
HUFF ...
... HUFF.
GARBAGE
(L)

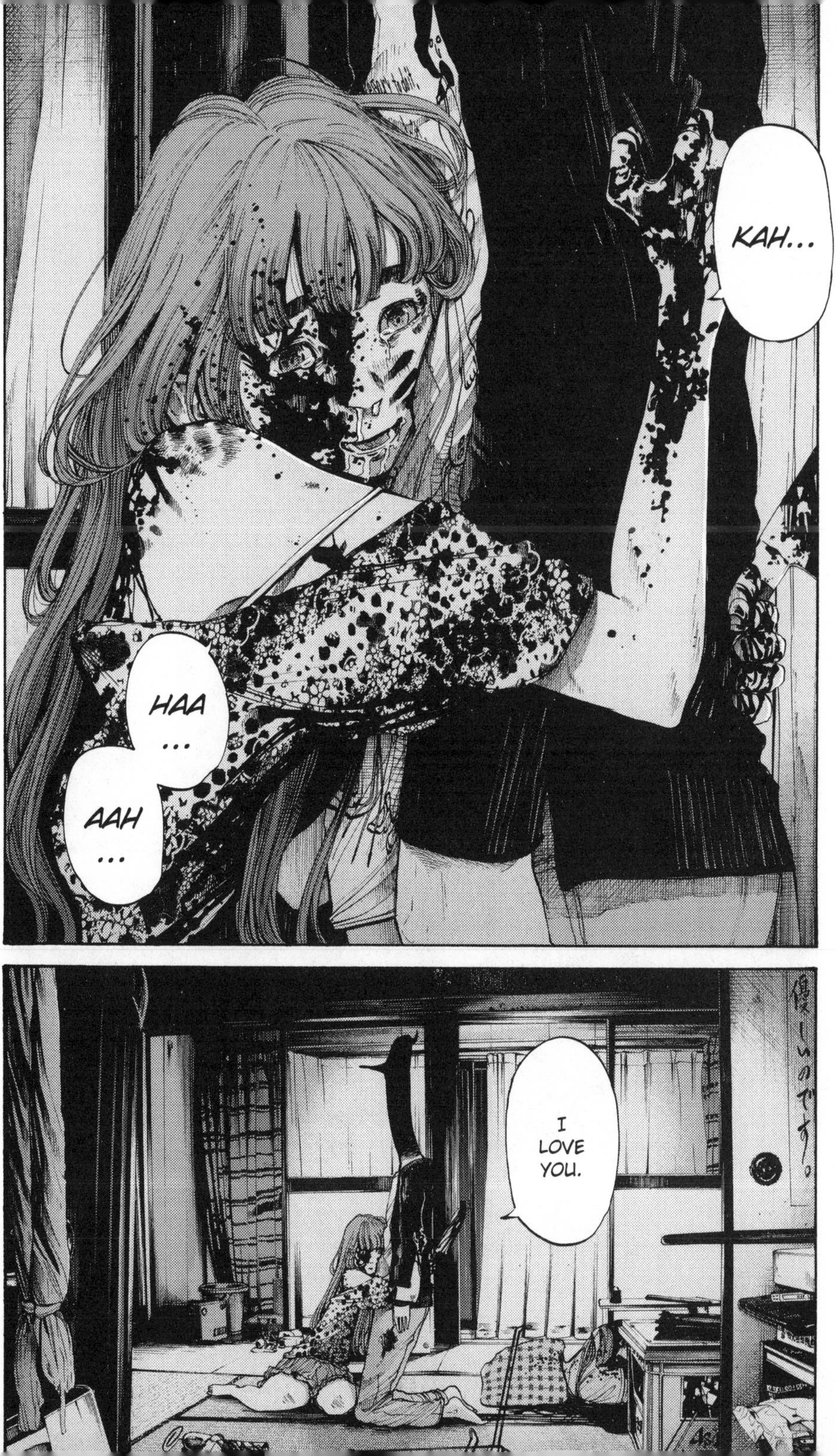
KAH...
HAA...
AAH...
優しいのです。
I LOVE YOU.

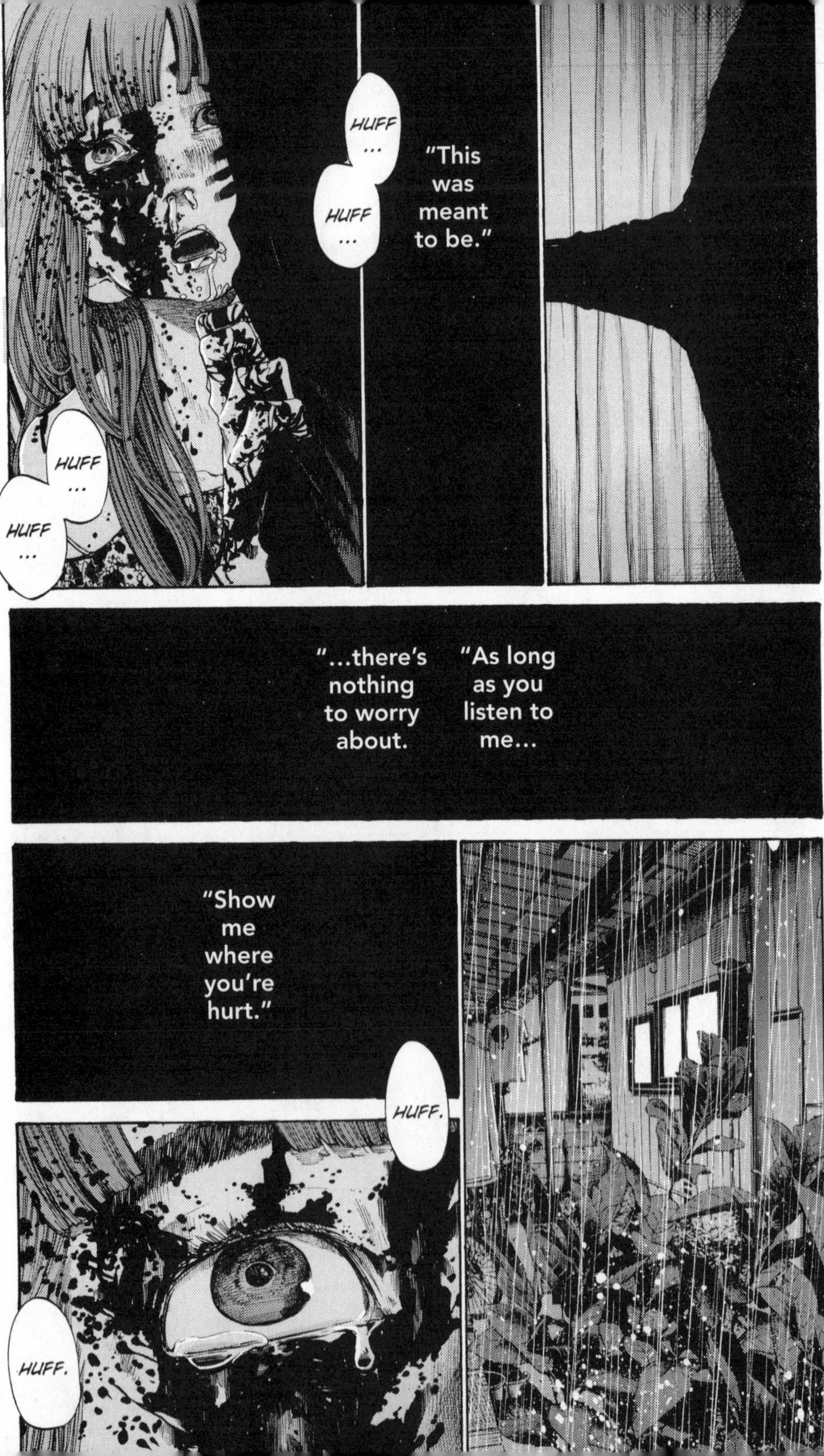
"This was meant to be."
HUFF...
HUFF...
HUFF...
HUFF...
"As long as you listen to me...
"...there's nothing to worry about.
"Show me where you're hurt."
HUFF.
HUFF.

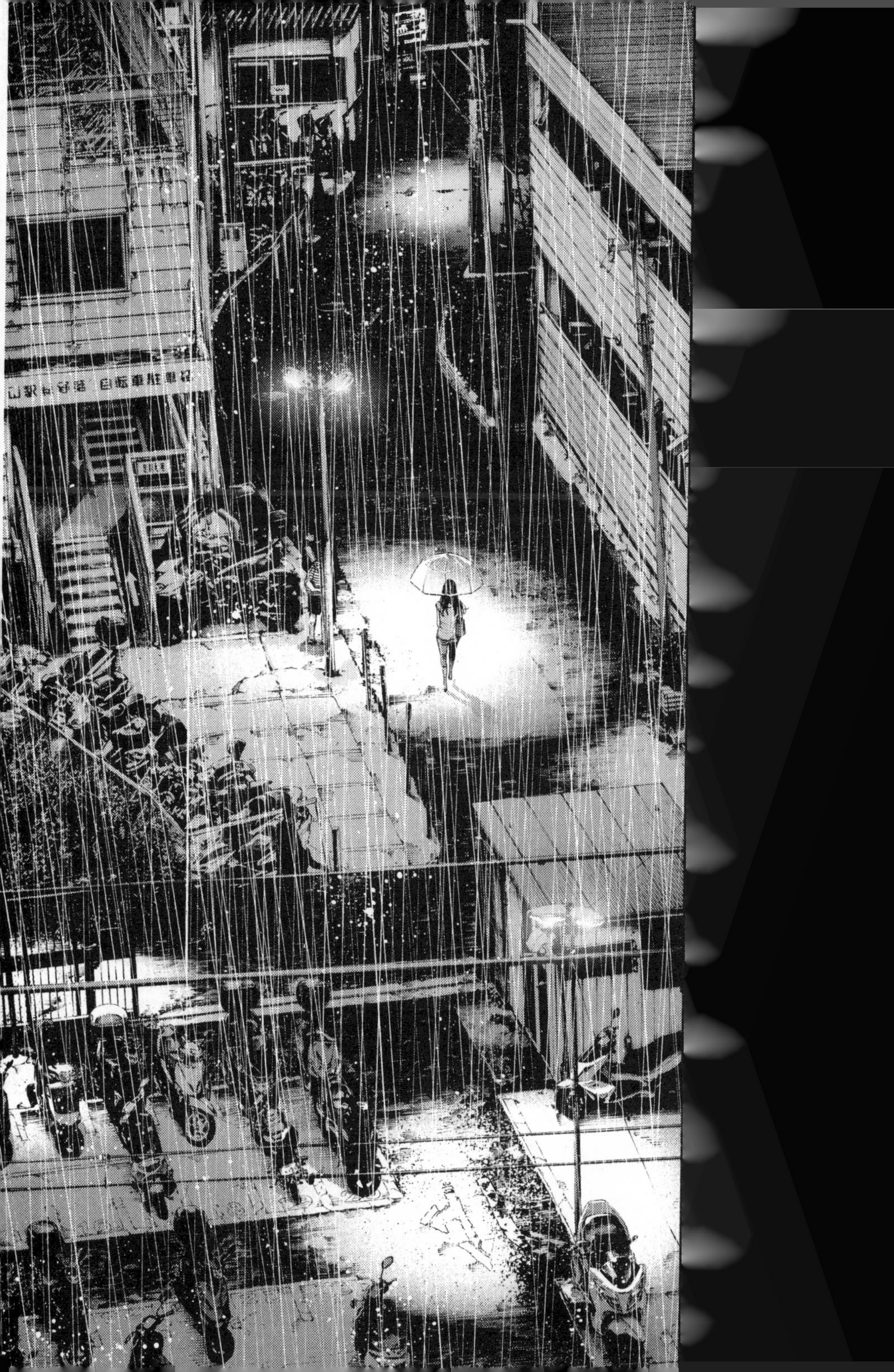

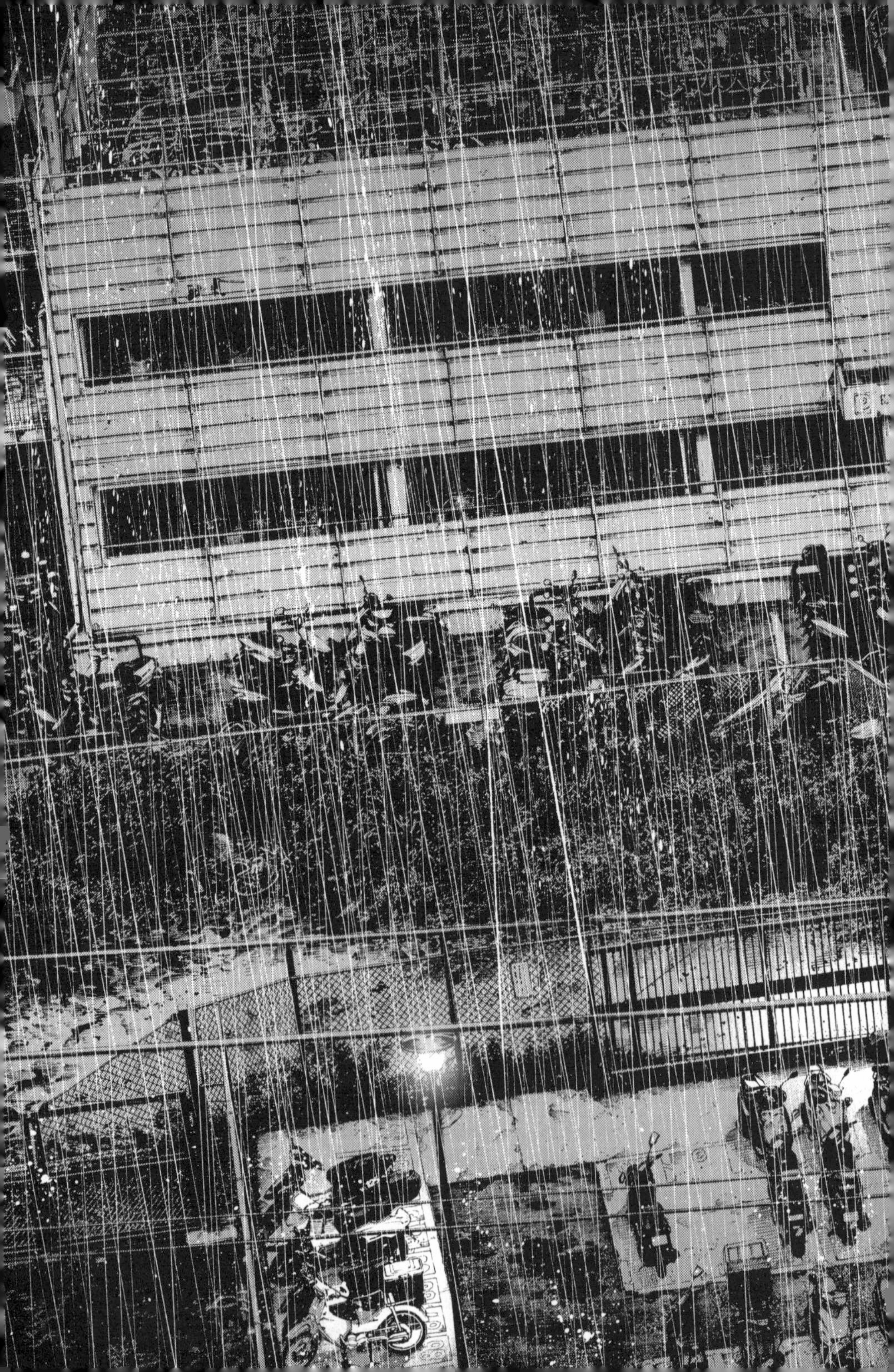

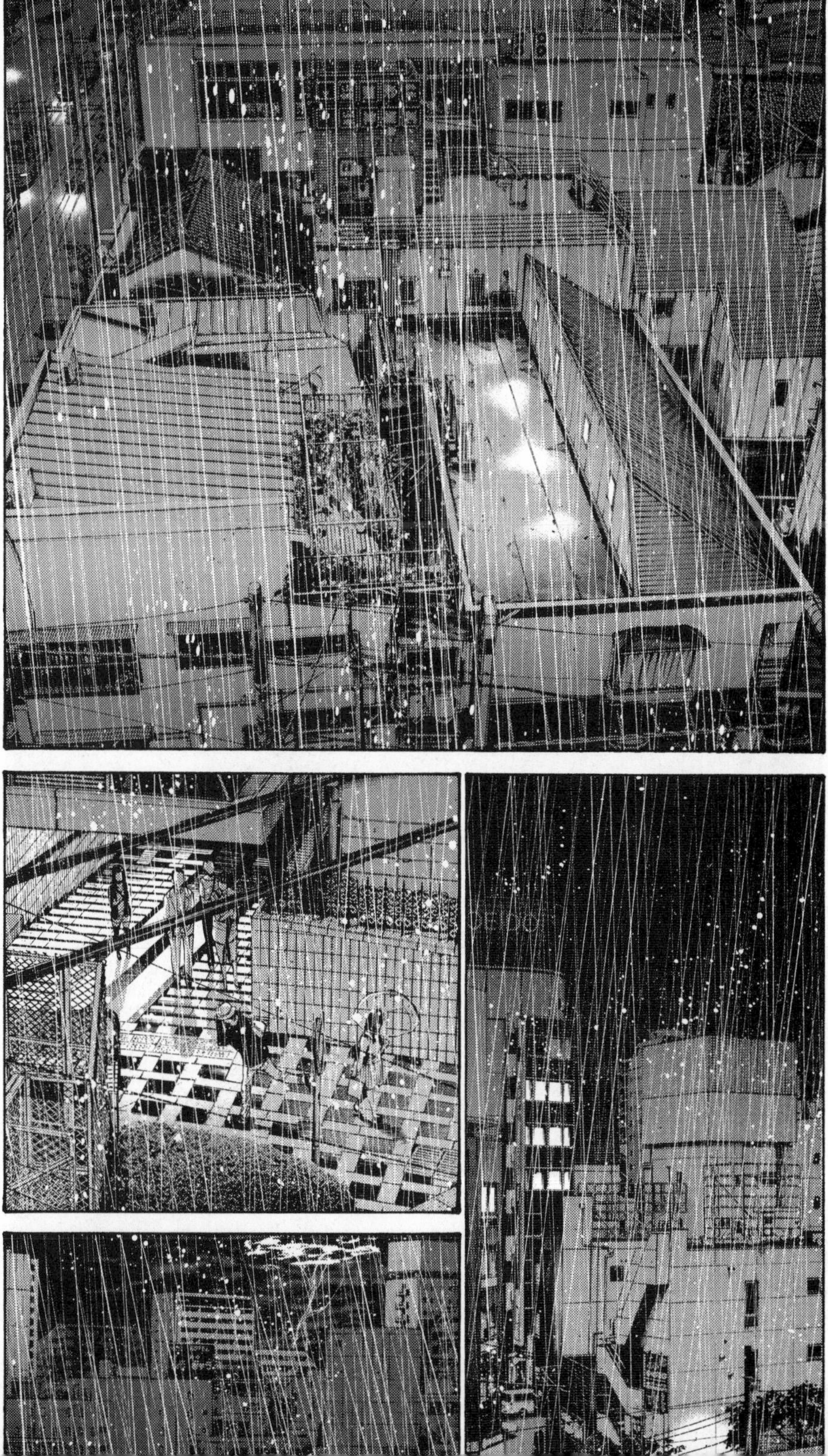

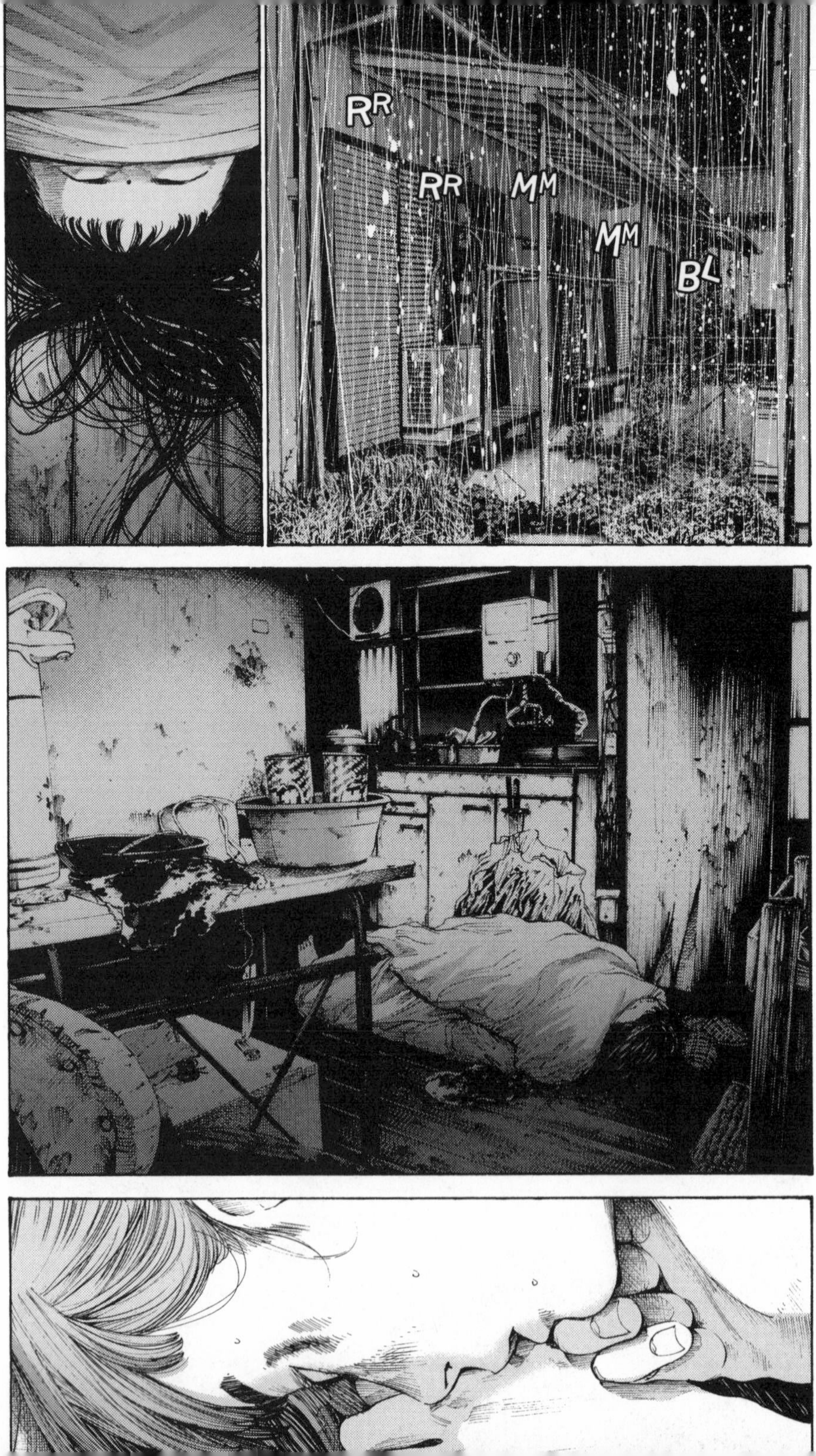
RR
RR
MM
MM
BL

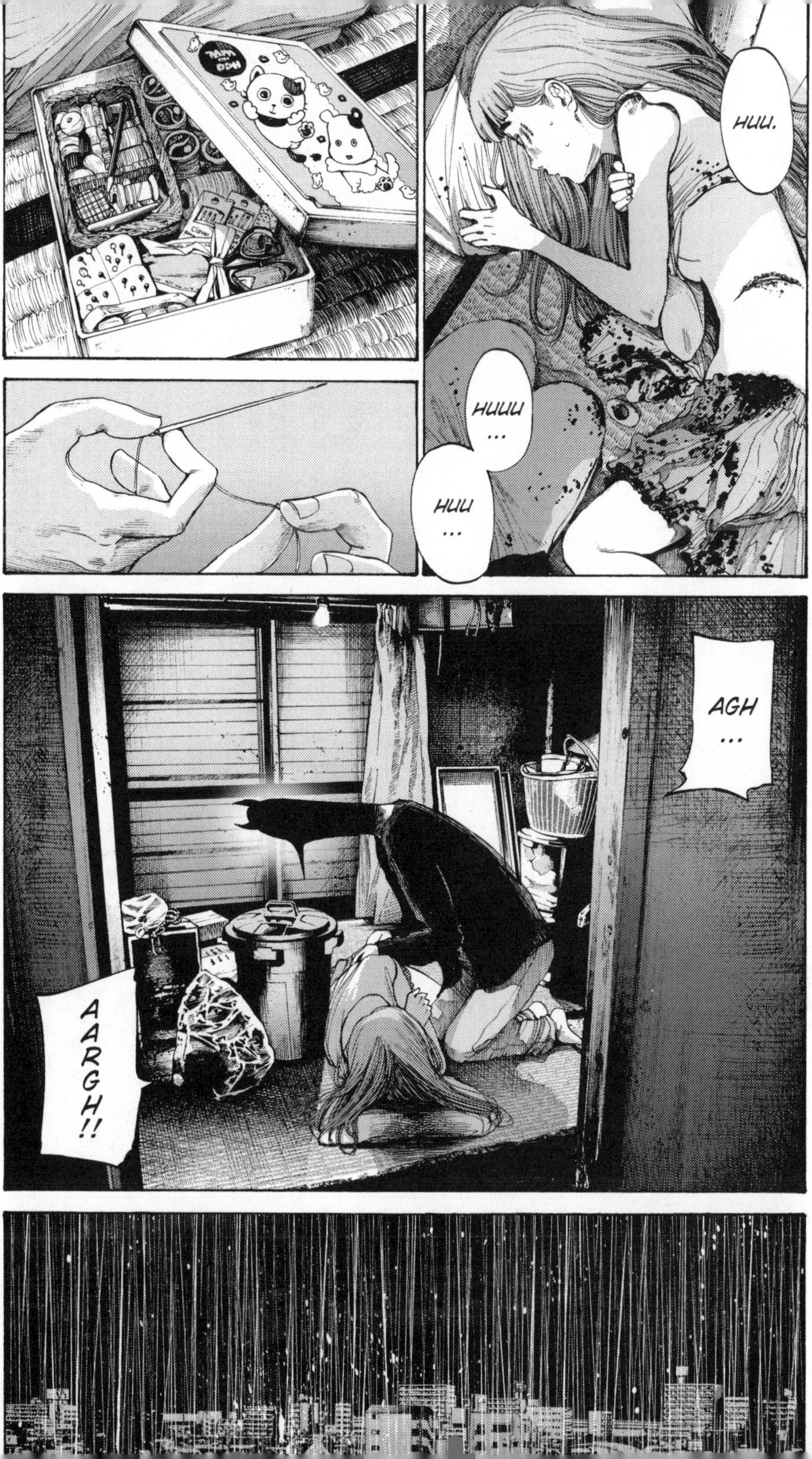
HUU.
HUUU ...
HUU ...
AGH ...
AARGH!!

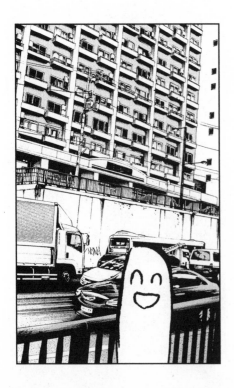

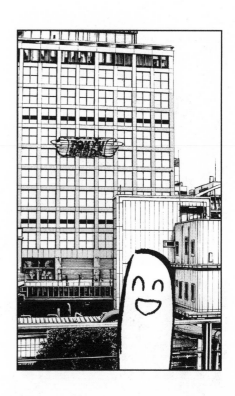

"WHY DON'T YOU FIND HAPPINESS...

"...WITH ME?"

"I...

"UNFORTUNATELY..

"...I CAN'T HELP..

"... YOU."

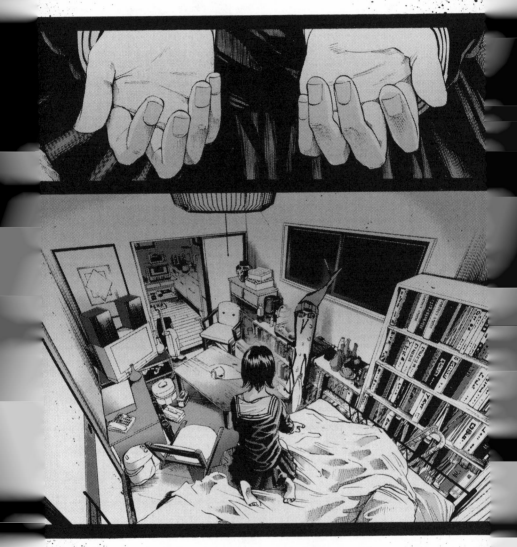

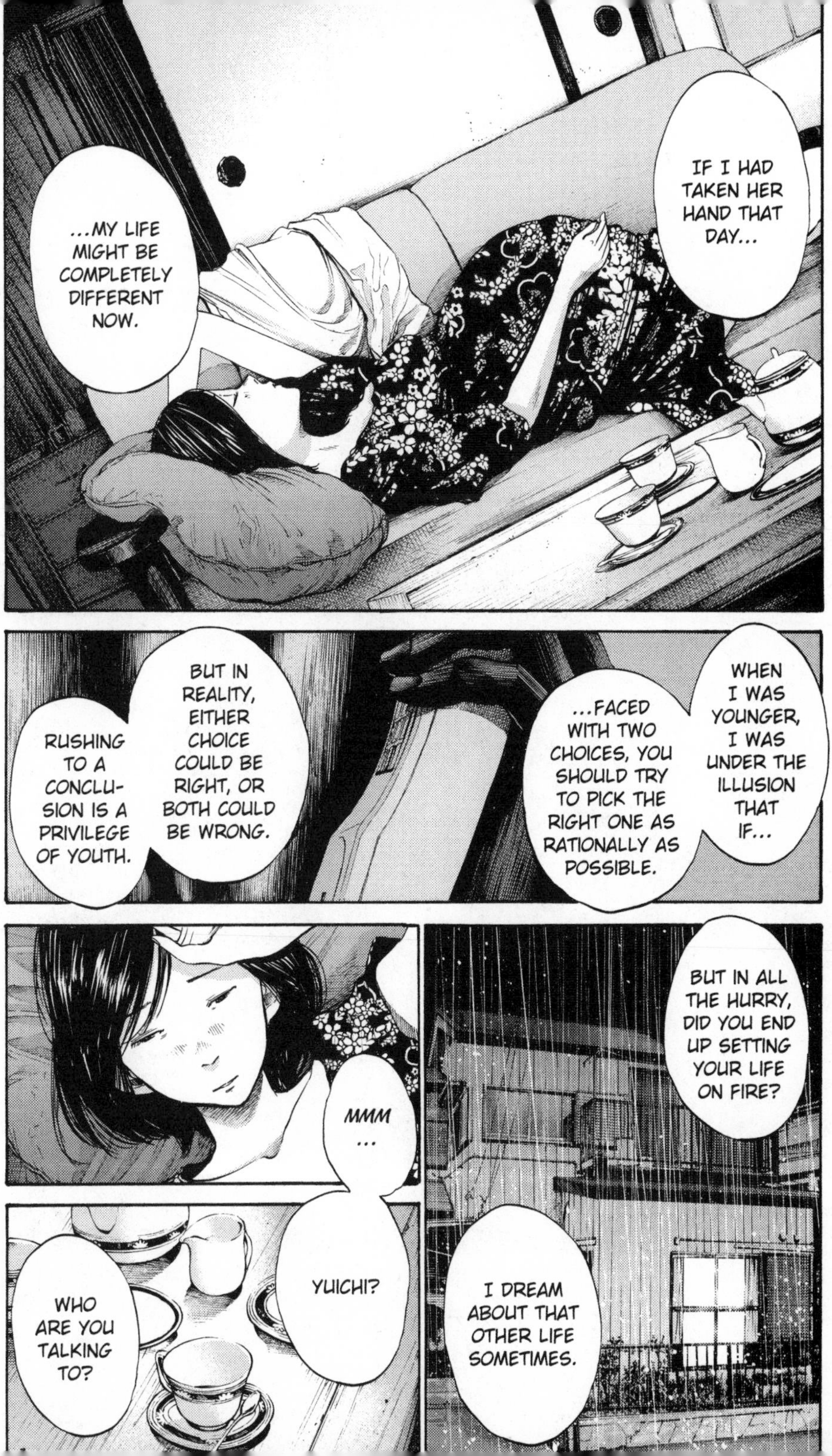
IF I HAD TAKEN HER HAND THAT DAY...
...MY LIFE MIGHT BE COMPLETELY DIFFERENT NOW.
WHEN I WAS YOUNGER, I WAS UNDER THE ILLUSION THAT IF...
...FACED WITH TWO CHOICES, YOU SHOULD TRY TO PICK THE RIGHT ONE AS RATIONALLY AS POSSIBLE.
BUT IN REALITY, EITHER CHOICE COULD BE RIGHT, OR BOTH COULD BE WRONG.
RUSHING TO A CONCLU-SION IS A PRIVILEGE OF YOUTH.
BUT IN ALL THE HURRY, DID YOU END UP SETTING YOUR LIFE ON FIRE?
I DREAM ABOUT THAT OTHER LIFE SOMETIMES.
MMM ...
YUICHI?
WHO ARE YOU TALKING TO?

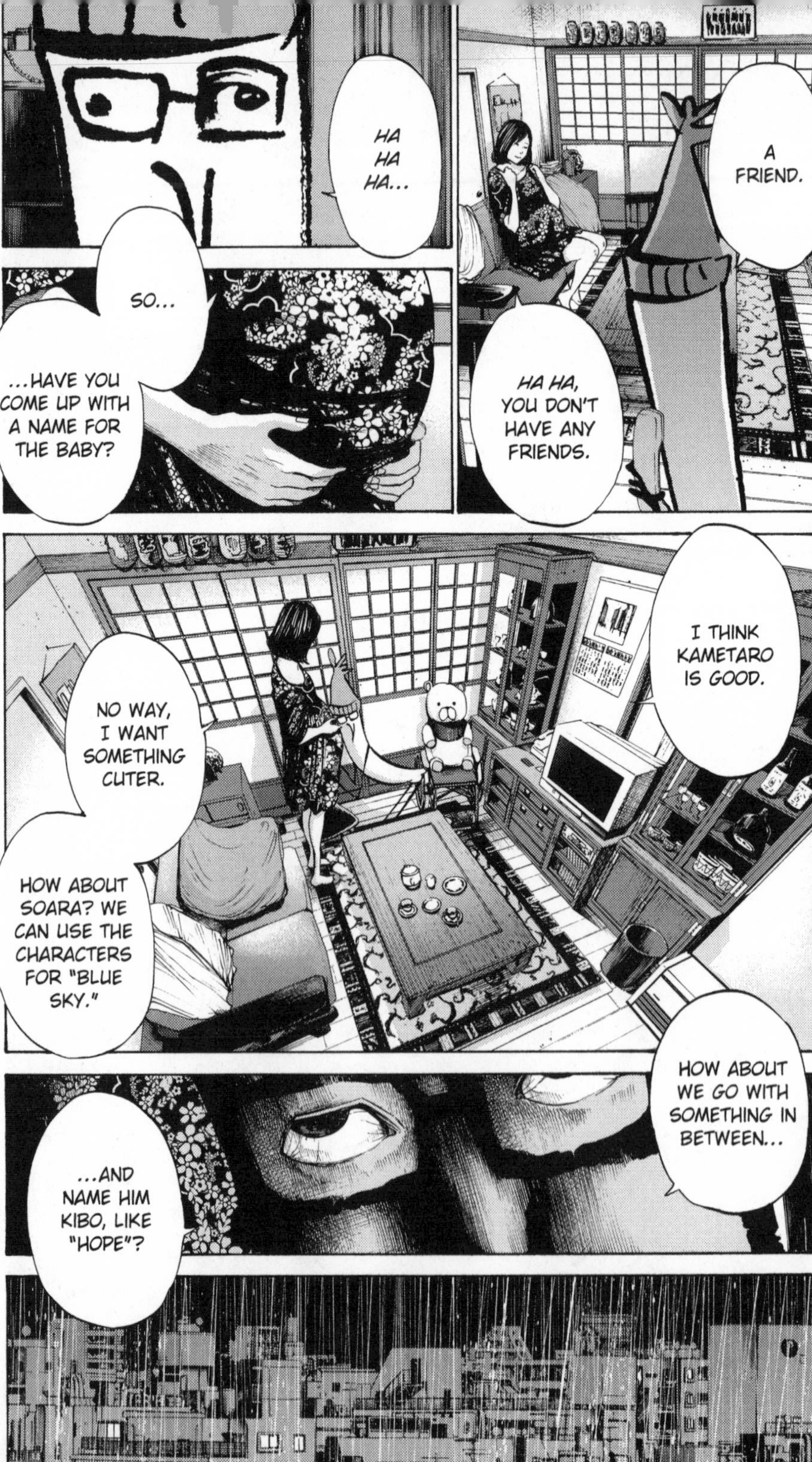
A FRIEND.
HA HA, YOU DON'T HAVE ANY FRIENDS.
HA HA HA...
SO...
...HAVE YOU COME UP WITH A NAME FOR THE BABY?
I THINK KAMETARO IS GOOD.
NO WAY, I WANT SOMETHING CUTER.
HOW ABOUT SOARA? WE CAN USE THE CHARACTERS FOR "BLUE SKY."
HOW ABOUT WE GO WITH SOMETHING IN BETWEEN...
...AND NAME HIM KIBO, LIKE "HOPE"?

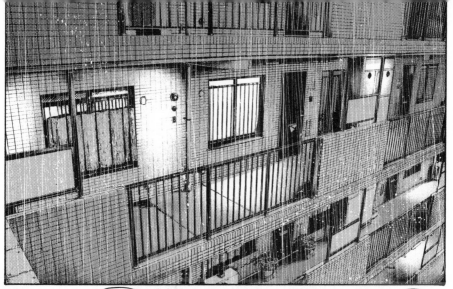

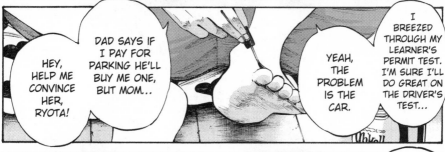

I BREEZED THROUGH MY LEARNER'S PERMIT TEST. I'M SURE I'LL DO GREAT ON THE DRIVER'S TEST...
YEAH, THE PROBLEM IS THE CAR.
DAD SAYS IF I PAY FOR PARKING HE'LL BUY ME ONE, BUT MOM...
HEY, HELP ME CONVINCE HER, RYOTA!
OH. WELL, I NEVER REALLY EXPECTED YOU TO. BESIDES, MY MOM SAYS SHE DOESN'T LIKE YOUR BLEACHED HAIR.
SHE *IS* REALLY STUBBORN. SHE'S SUPER UPTIGHT AND WON'T CHANGE HER MIND.
MICRO
SO I GUESS FOR THE TIME BEING, I'LL JUST HAVE TO BORROW HER SCOOTER...
OH YEAH, ABOUT TOMORROW—

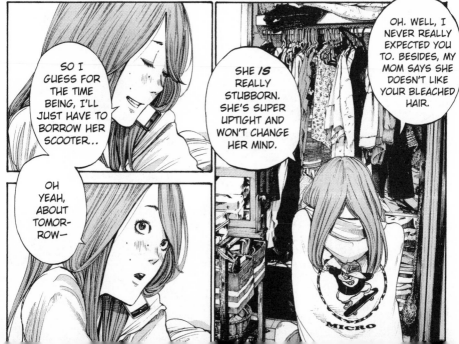

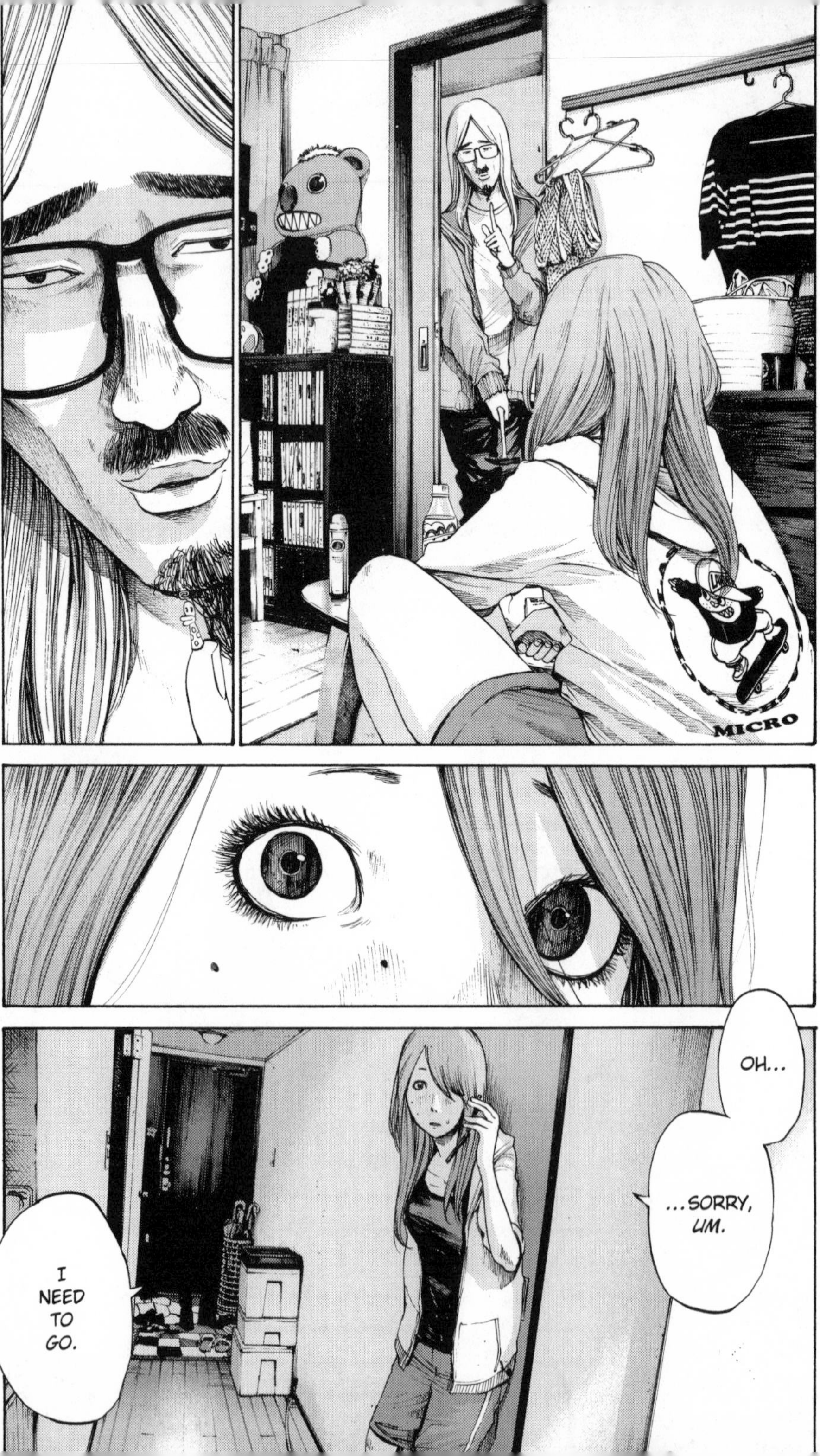
MICRO
OH...
...SORRY, UM.
I NEED TO GO.

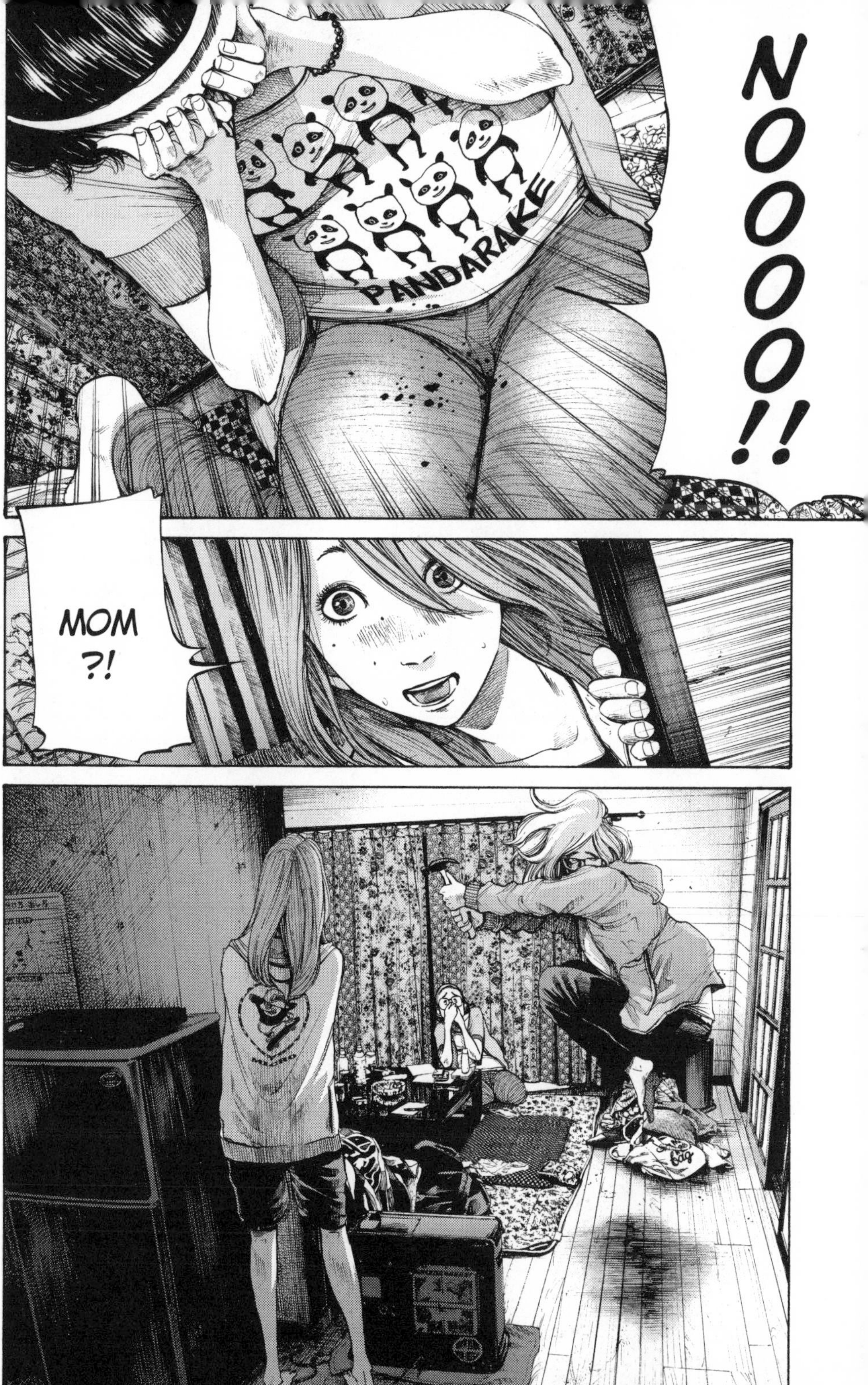
NOOOOO!!
PANDARAKE
MOM ?!

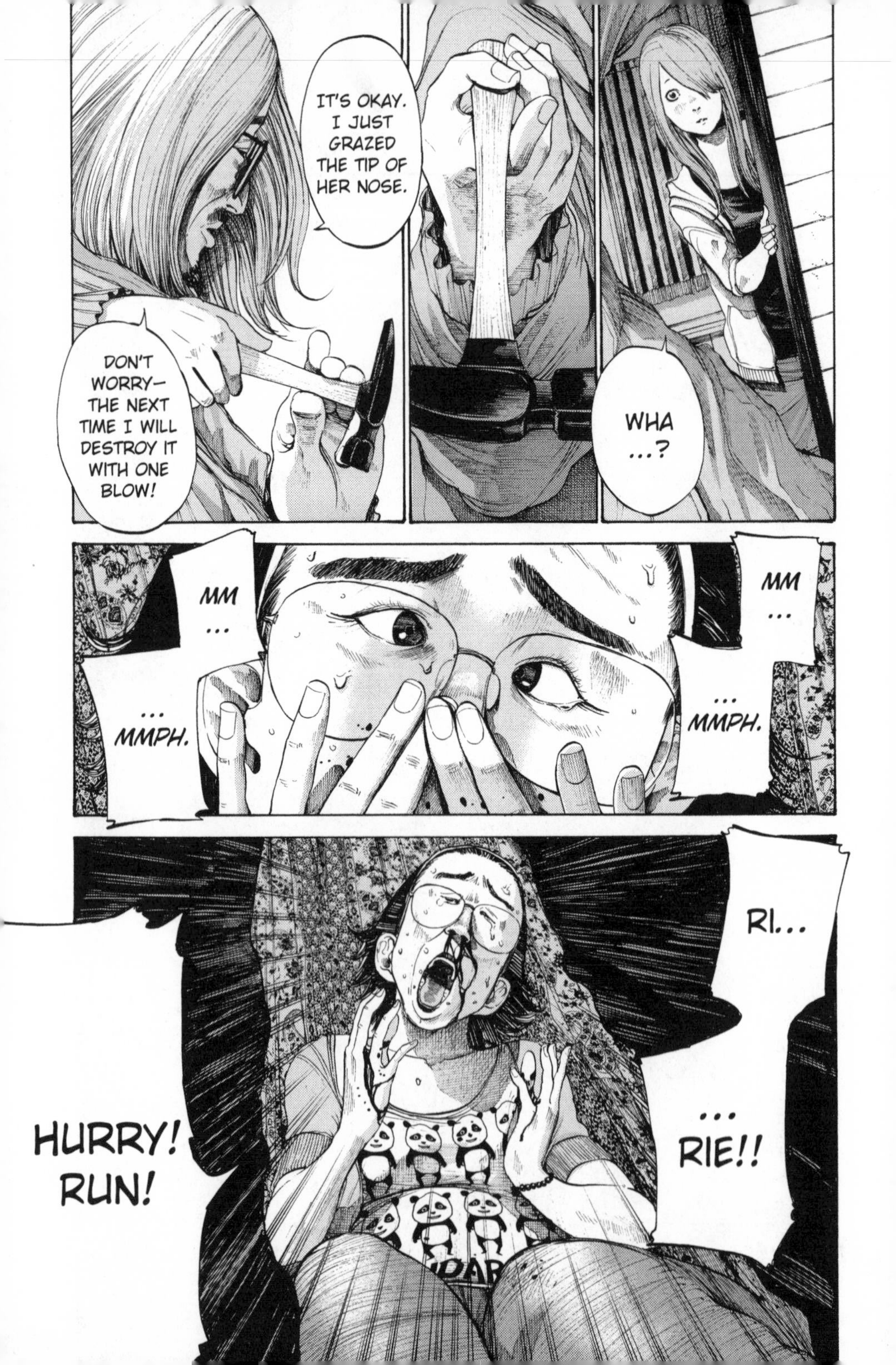
WHA ...?
IT'S OKAY. I JUST GRAZED THE TIP OF HER NOSE.
DON'T WORRY— THE NEXT TIME I WILL DESTROY IT WITH ONE BLOW!
MM ...
... MMPH.
MM ...
... MMPH.
RI...
... RIE!!
HURRY! RUN!

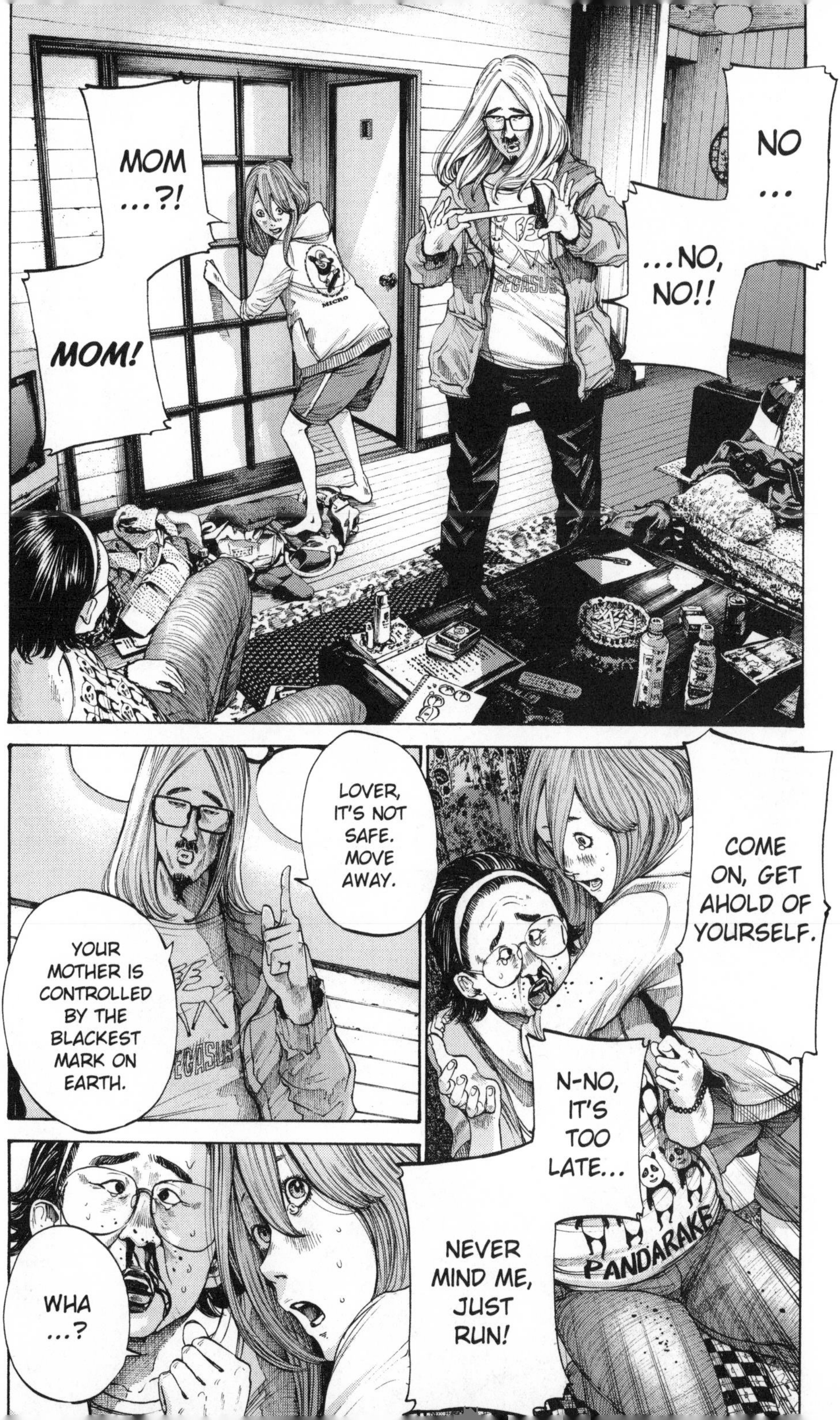
NO ...
MOM ...?!
...NO, NO!!
MOM!
COME ON, GET AHOLD OF YOURSELF.
N-NO, IT'S TOO LATE...
NEVER MIND ME, JUST RUN!
LOVER, IT'S NOT SAFE. MOVE AWAY.
YOUR MOTHER IS CONTROLLED BY THE BLACKEST MARK ON EARTH.
WHA ...?

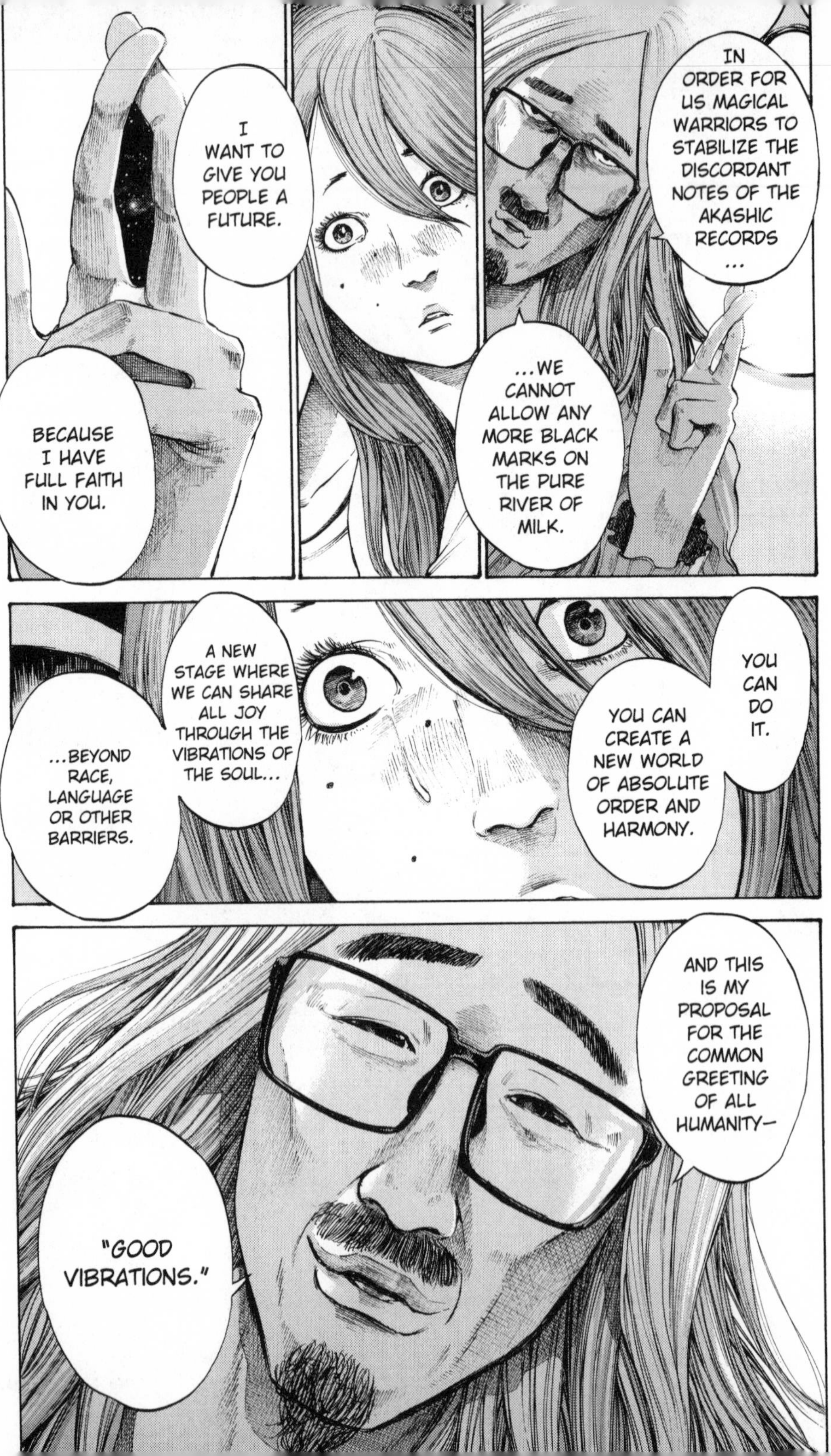
IN ORDER FOR US MAGICAL WARRIORS TO STABILIZE THE DISCORDANT NOTES OF THE AKASHIC RECORDS ...
...WE CANNOT ALLOW ANY MORE BLACK MARKS ON THE PURE RIVER OF MILK.
I WANT TO GIVE YOU PEOPLE A FUTURE.
BECAUSE I HAVE FULL FAITH IN YOU.
YOU CAN DO IT.
YOU CAN CREATE A NEW WORLD OF ABSOLUTE ORDER AND HARMONY.
A NEW STAGE WHERE WE CAN SHARE ALL JOY THROUGH THE VIBRATIONS OF THE SOUL...
...BEYOND RACE, LANGUAGE OR OTHER BARRIERS.
AND THIS IS MY PROPOSAL FOR THE COMMON GREETING OF ALL HUMANITY—
"GOOD VIBRATIONS."

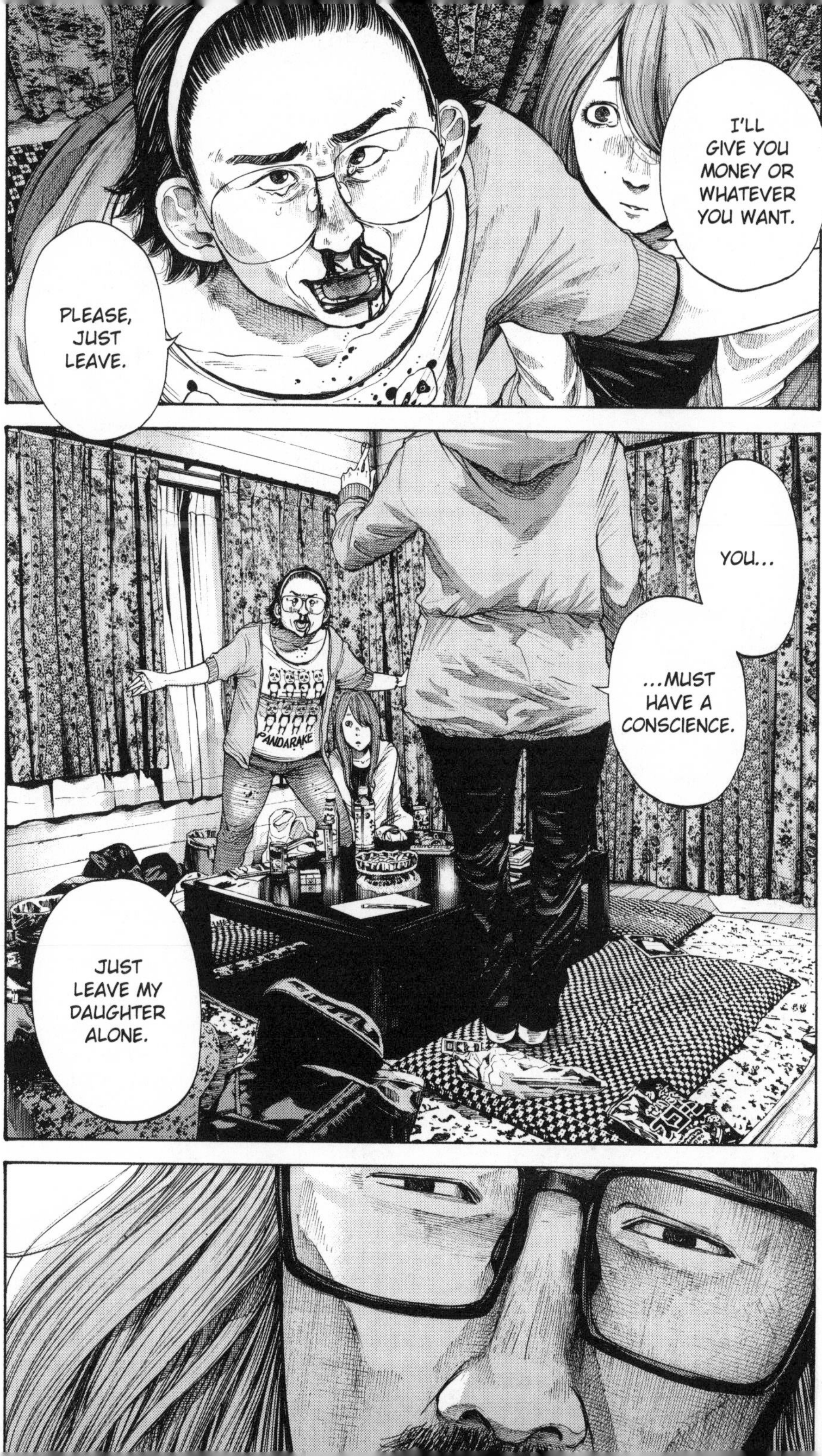
I'LL GIVE YOU MONEY OR WHATEVER YOU WANT.
PLEASE, JUST LEAVE.
YOU...
...MUST HAVE A CONSCIENCE.
JUST LEAVE MY DAUGHTER ALONE.
PANDARAKE

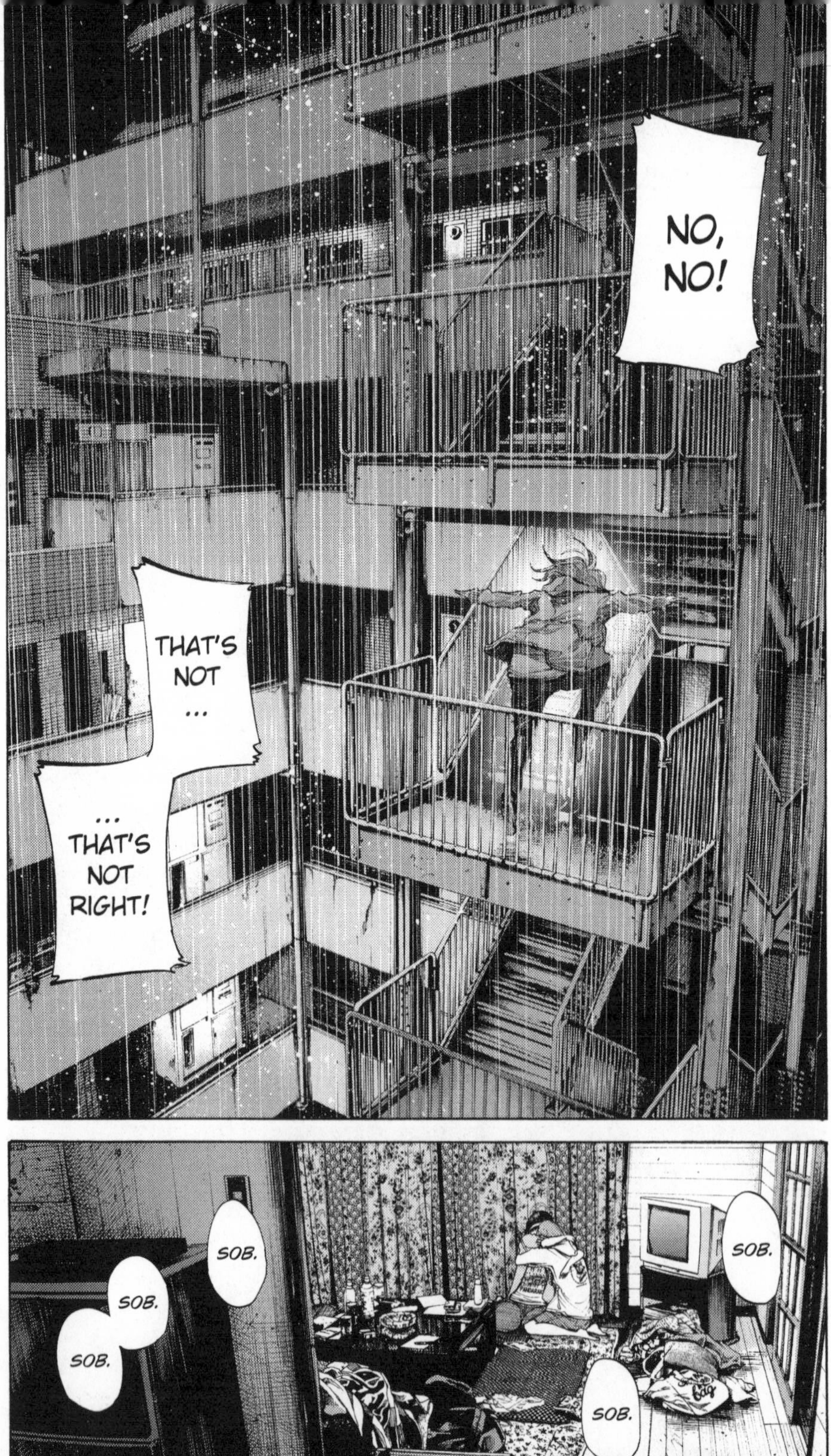
NO, NO!
THAT'S NOT ...
... THAT'S NOT RIGHT!
SOB.
SOB.
SOB.
SOB.
SOB.

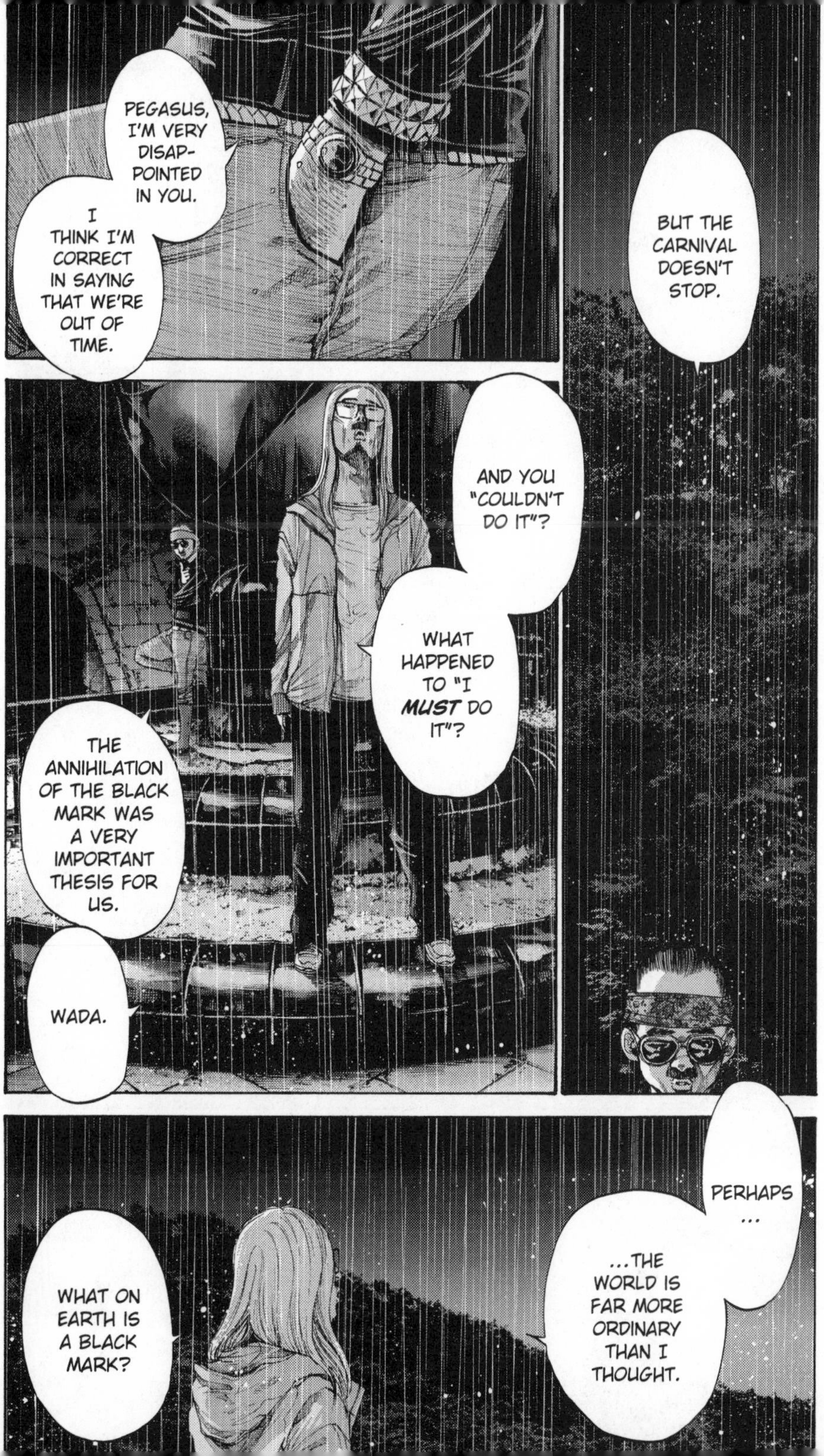

BUT THE CARNIVAL DOESN'T STOP.
PEGASUS, I'M VERY DISAP-POINTED IN YOU.
I THINK I'M CORRECT IN SAYING THAT WE'RE OUT OF TIME.
AND YOU "COULDN'T DO IT"?
WHAT HAPPENED TO "I *MUST* DO IT"?
THE ANNIHILATION OF THE BLACK MARK WAS A VERY IMPORTANT THESIS FOR US.
WADA.
PERHAPS...
...THE WORLD IS FAR MORE ORDINARY THAN I THOUGHT.
WHAT ON EARTH IS A BLACK MARK?

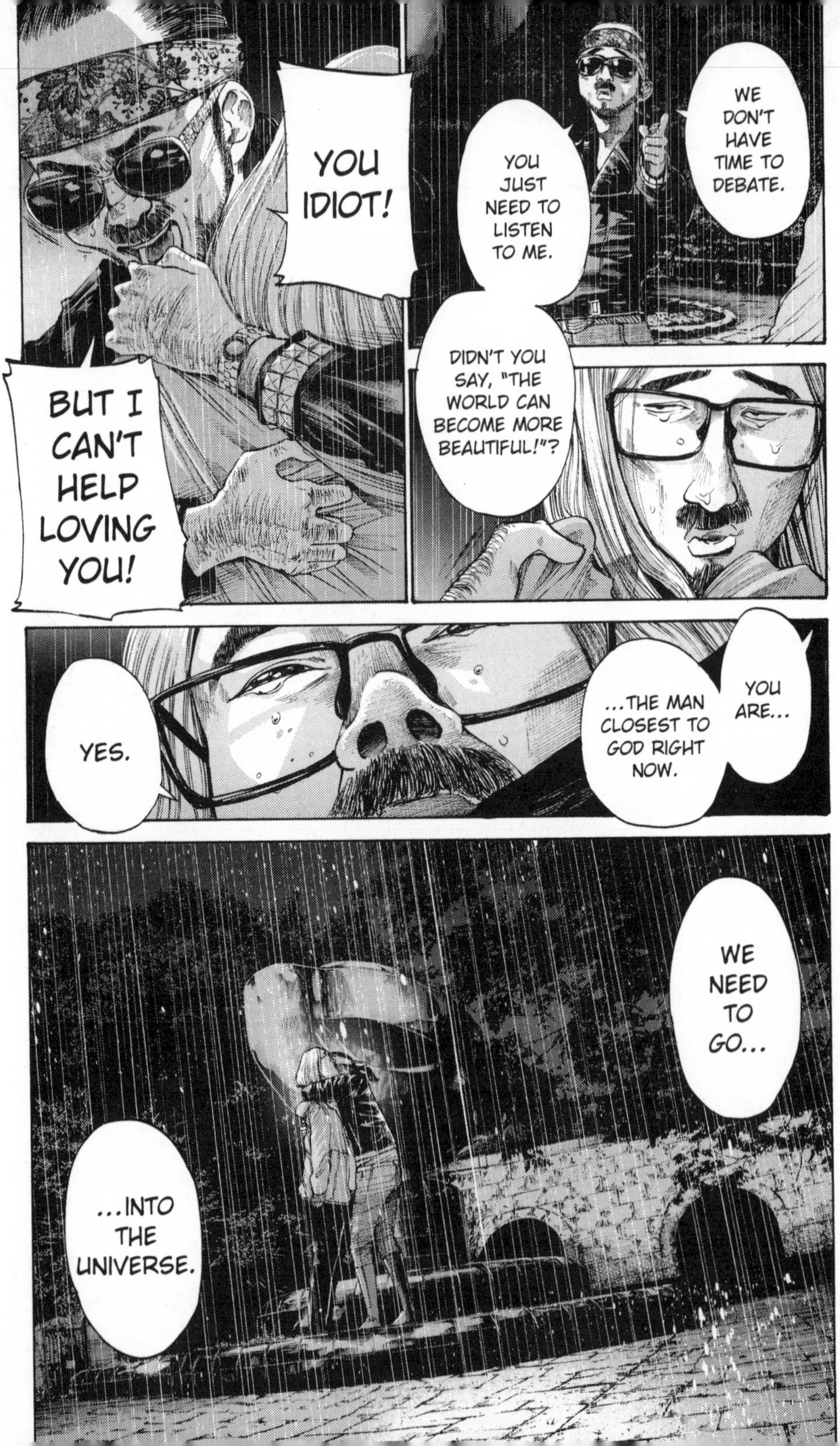
WE DON'T HAVE TIME TO DEBATE.
YOU JUST NEED TO LISTEN TO ME.
DIDN'T YOU SAY, "THE WORLD CAN BECOME MORE BEAUTIFUL!"?
YOU IDIOT!
BUT I CAN'T HELP LOVING YOU!
YOU ARE...
...THE MAN CLOSEST TO GOD RIGHT NOW.
YES.
WE NEED TO GO...
...INTO THE UNIVERSE.

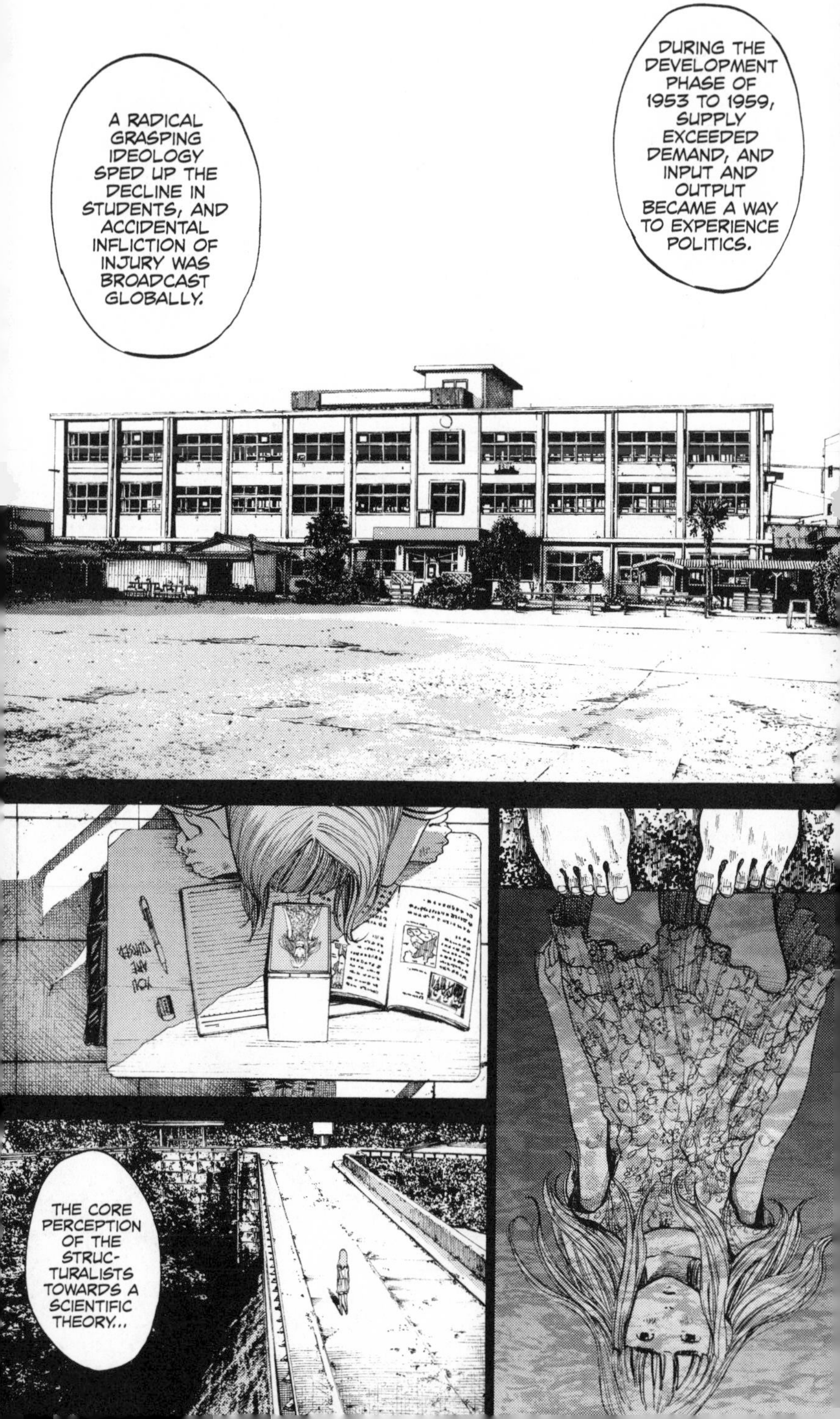
DURING THE DEVELOPMENT PHASE OF 1953 TO 1959, SUPPLY EXCEEDED DEMAND, AND INPUT AND OUTPUT BECAME A WAY TO EXPERIENCE POLITICS.
A RADICAL GRASPING IDEOLOGY SPED UP THE DECLINE IN STUDENTS, AND ACCIDENTAL INFLICTION OF INJURY WAS BROADCAST GLOBALLY.
THE CORE PERCEPTION OF THE STRUC-TURALISTS TOWARDS A SCIENTIFIC THEORY...

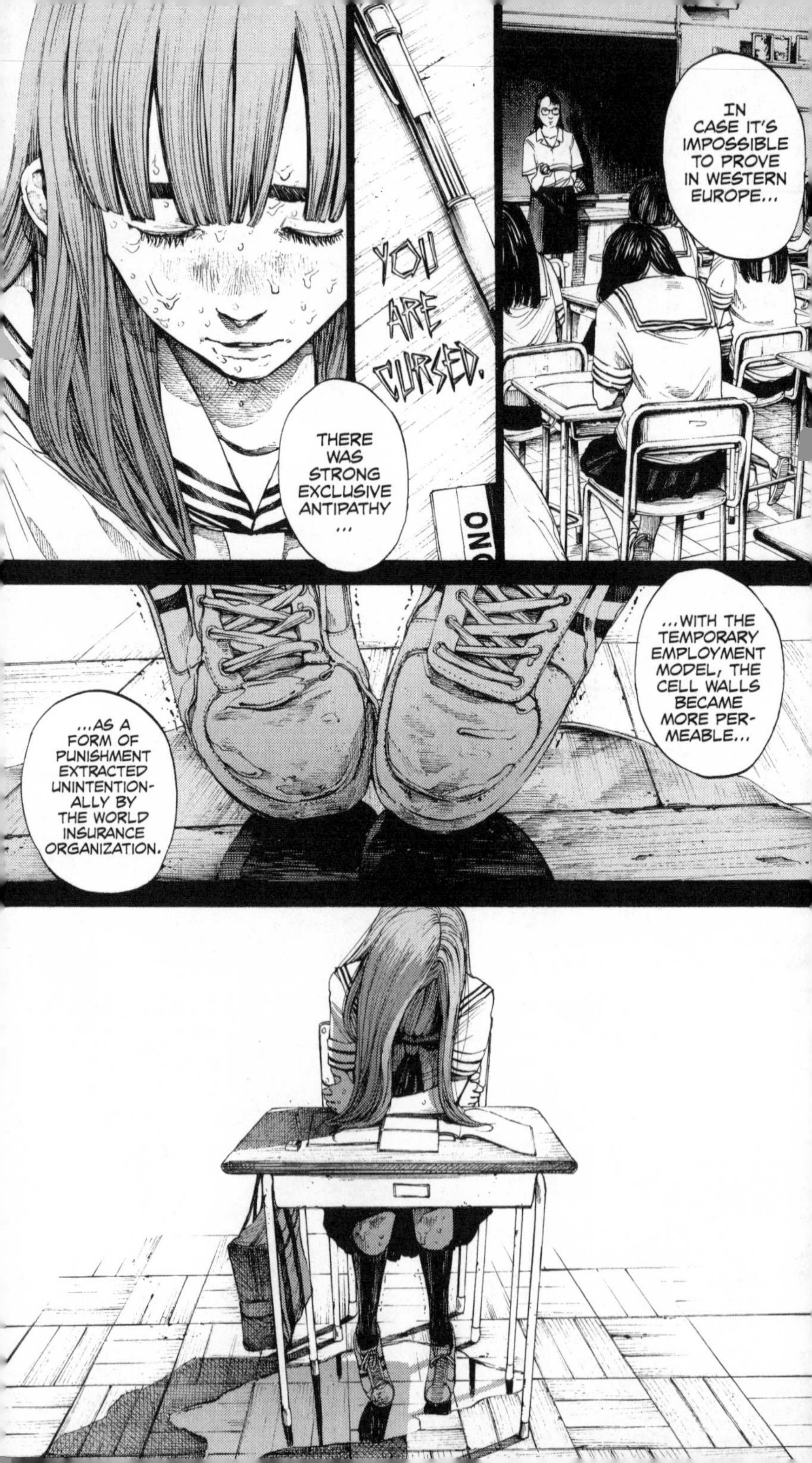
IN CASE IT'S IMPOSSIBLE TO PROVE IN WESTERN EUROPE...
YOU ARE CURSED.
ONO
THERE WAS STRONG EXCLUSIVE ANTIPATHY ...
...WITH THE TEMPORARY EMPLOYMENT MODEL, THE CELL WALLS BECAME MORE PER-MEABLE...
...AS A FORM OF PUNISHMENT EXTRACTED UNINTENTION-ALLY BY THE WORLD INSURANCE ORGANIZATION.

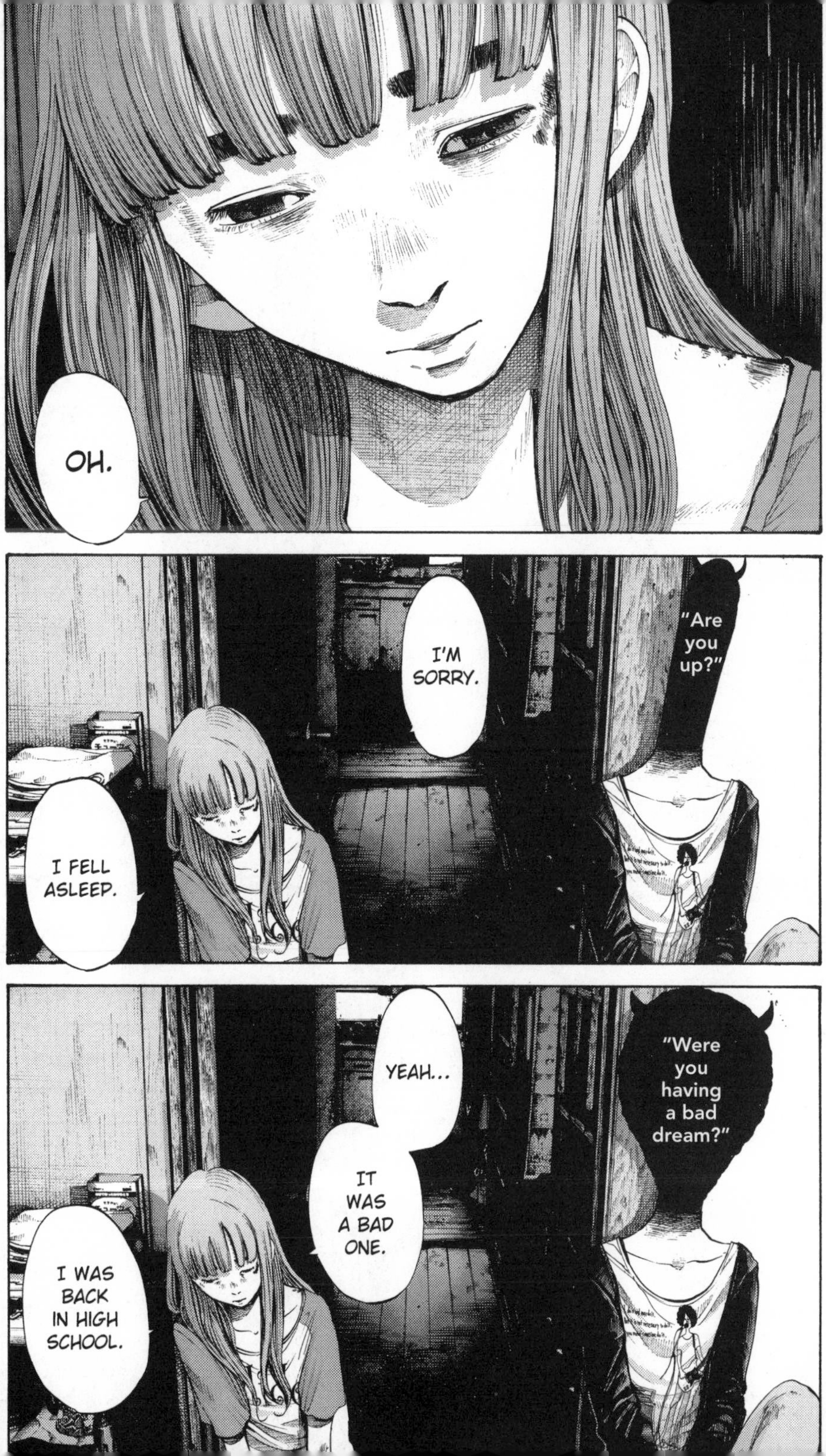
OH.
"Are you up?"
I'M SORRY.
I FELL ASLEEP.
"Were you having a bad dream?"
YEAH...
IT WAS A BAD ONE.
I WAS BACK IN HIGH SCHOOL.

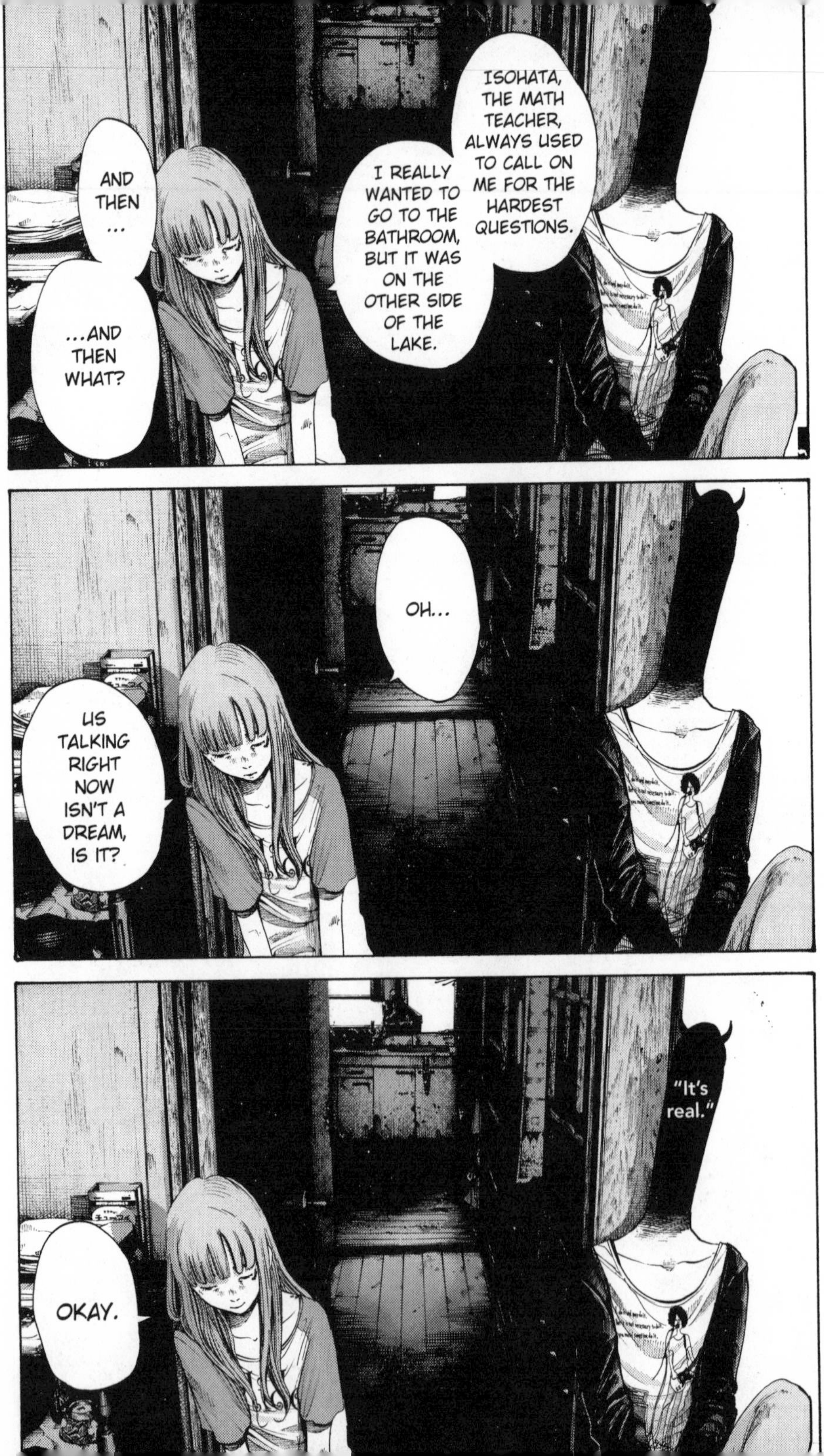
ISOHATA, THE MATH TEACHER, ALWAYS USED TO CALL ON ME FOR THE HARDEST QUESTIONS.
I REALLY WANTED TO GO TO THE BATHROOM, BUT IT WAS ON THE OTHER SIDE OF THE LAKE.
AND THEN ...
...AND THEN WHAT?
OH...
US TALKING RIGHT NOW ISN'T A DREAM, IS IT?
"It's real."
OKAY.

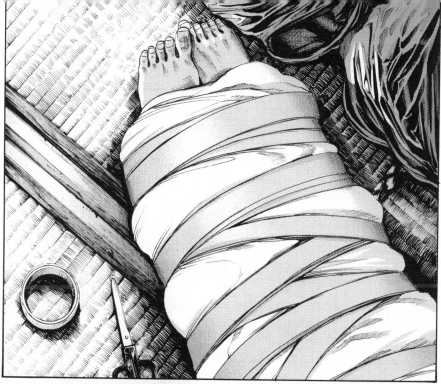

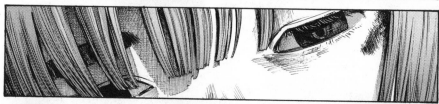

OKAY.

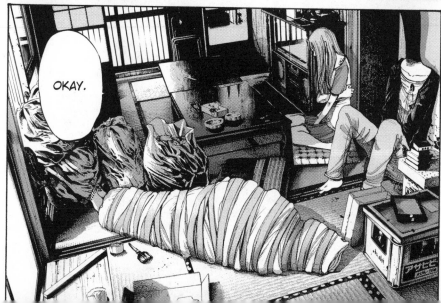

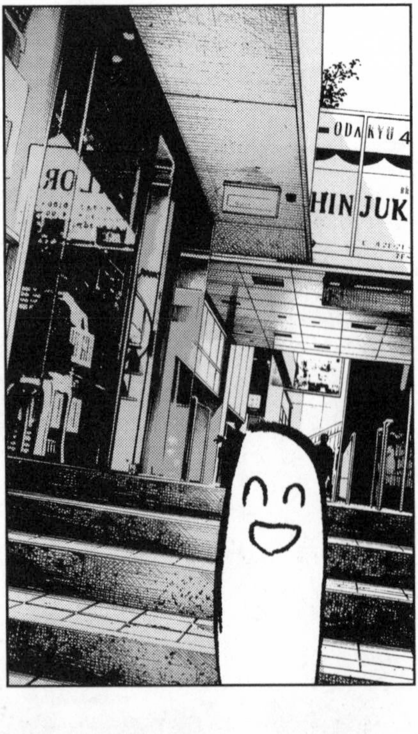
ODA KYU 4
HIN JUK

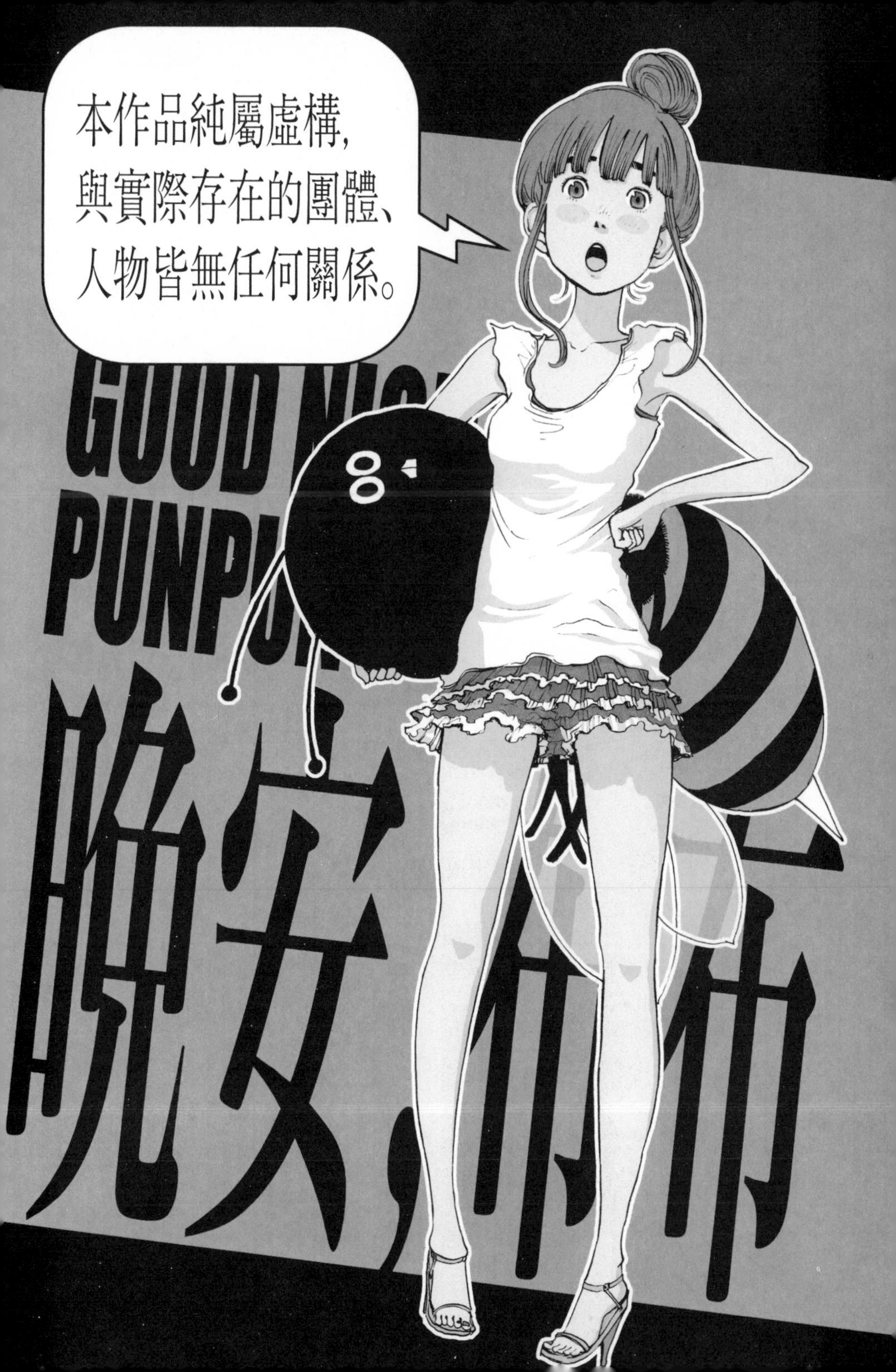
本作品純屬虛構,與實際存在的團體、人物皆無任何關係。
GOOD
晚安

Chapter 116

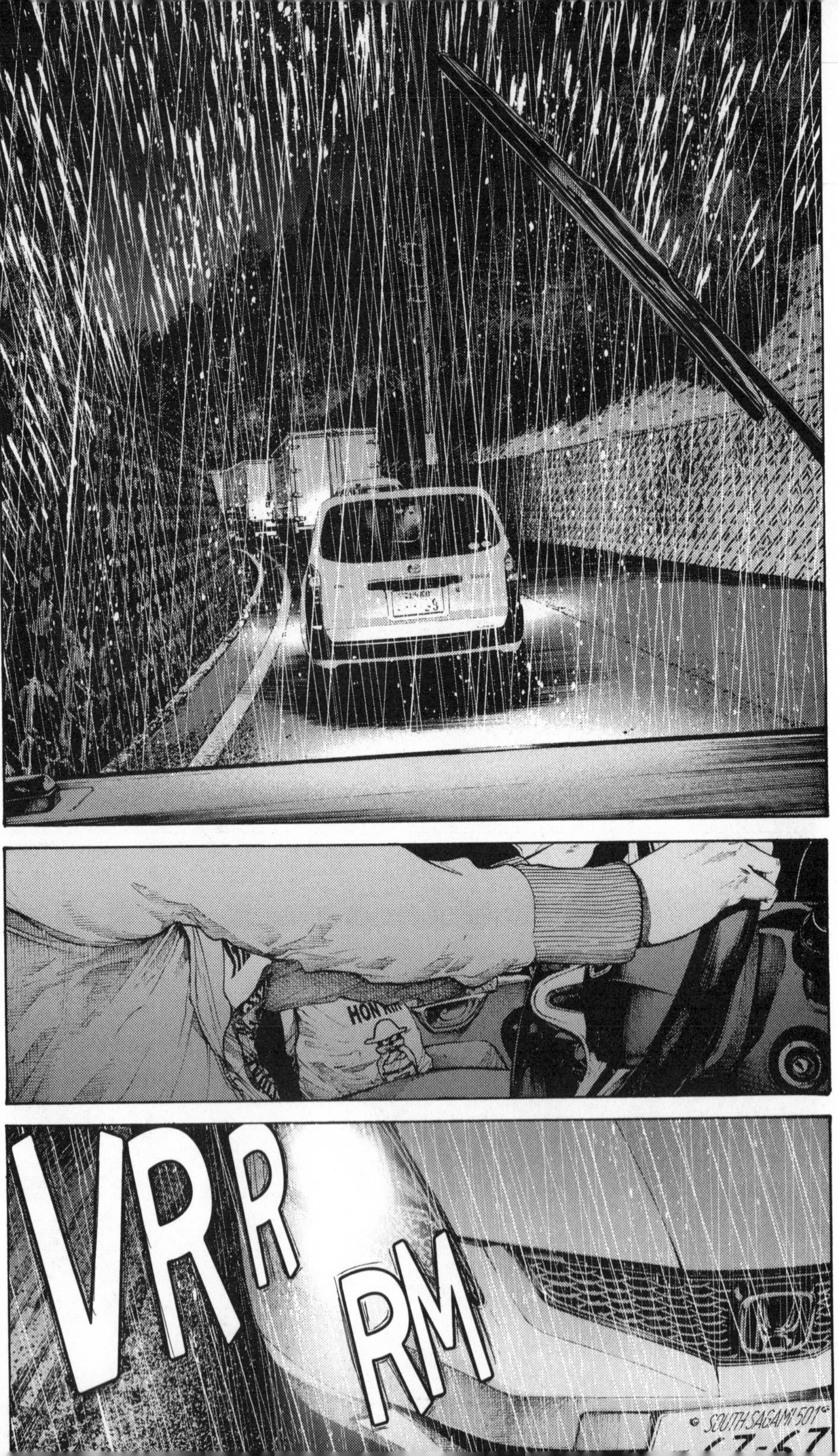
VRR
RM
SOUTH SAGAMI 501

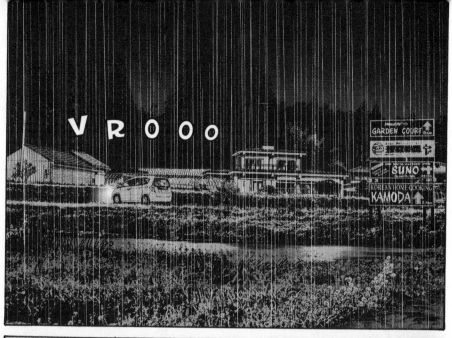

VROOO

GARDEN COURT
SUNO
KOREAN HOME COOKING
KAMODA

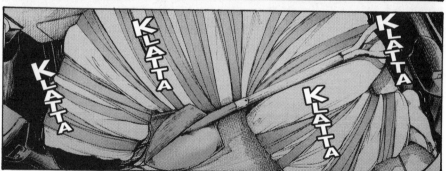

KLATTA KLATTA KLATTA KLATTA KLATTA

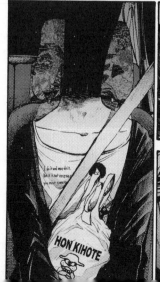

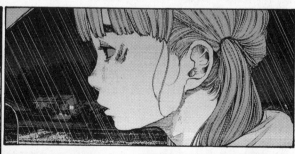

HON KIHOTE

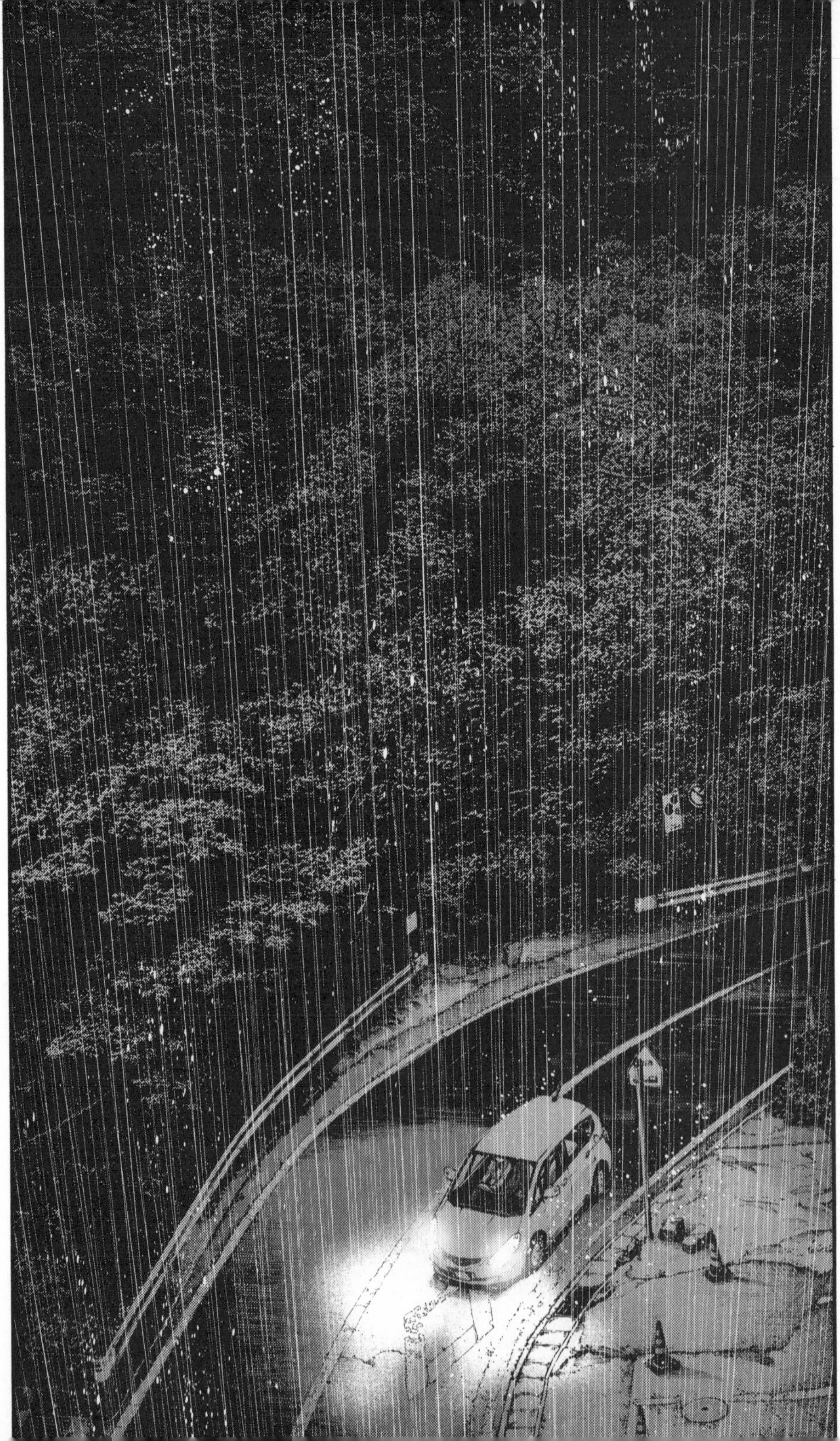

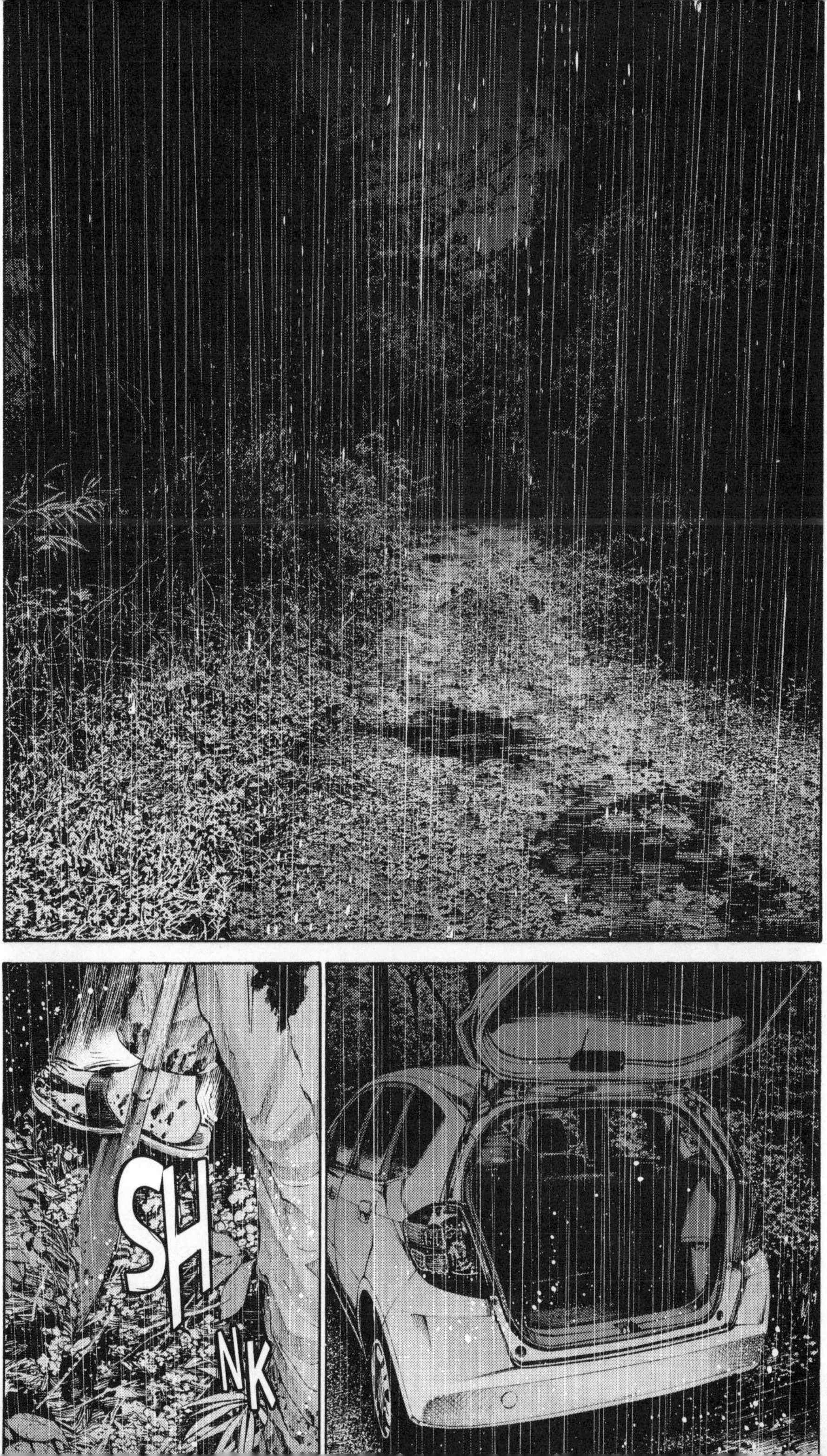
SHNK

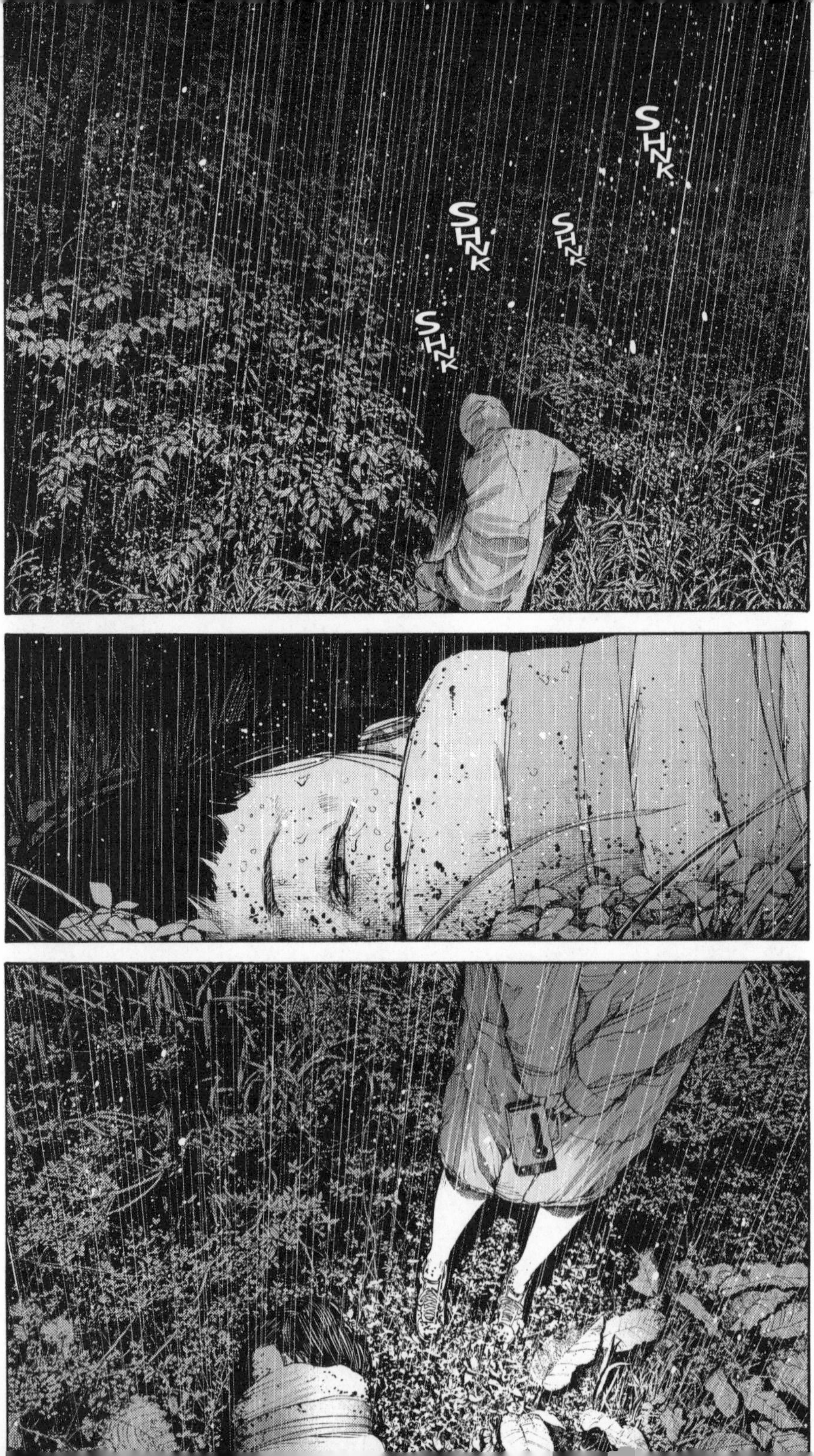
SHNK
SHNK
SHNK
SHNK

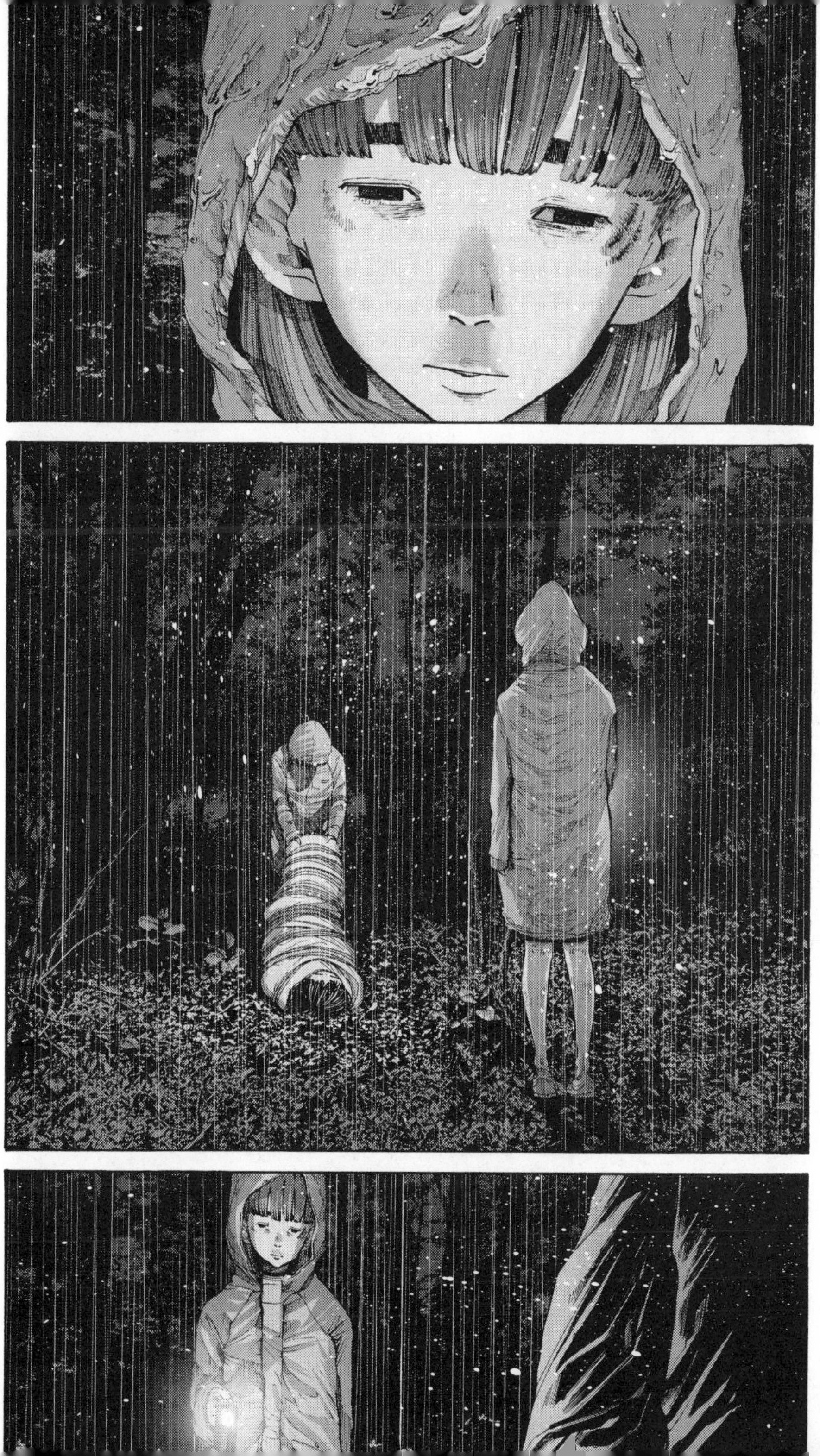

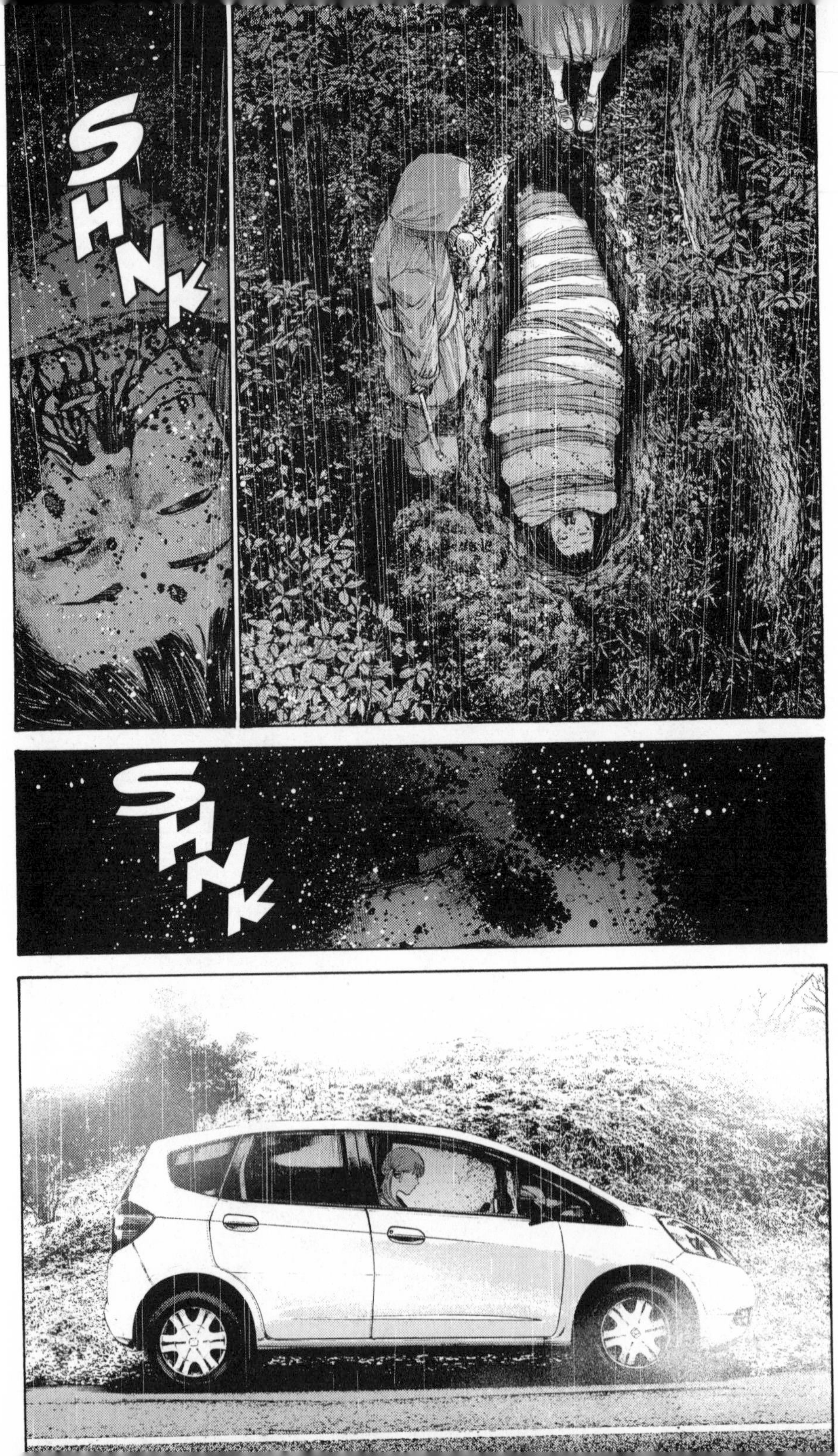
SHNK
SHNK

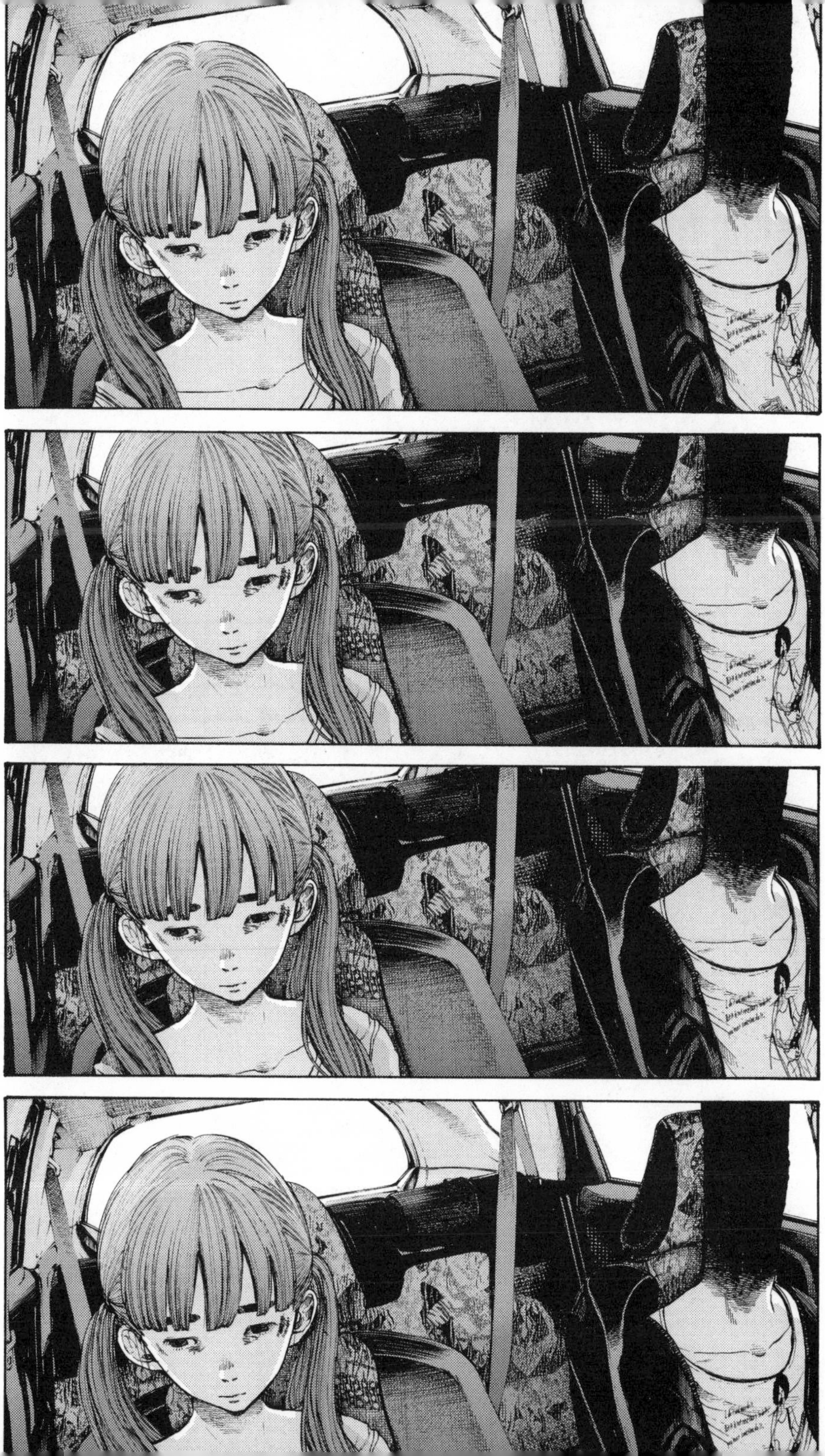

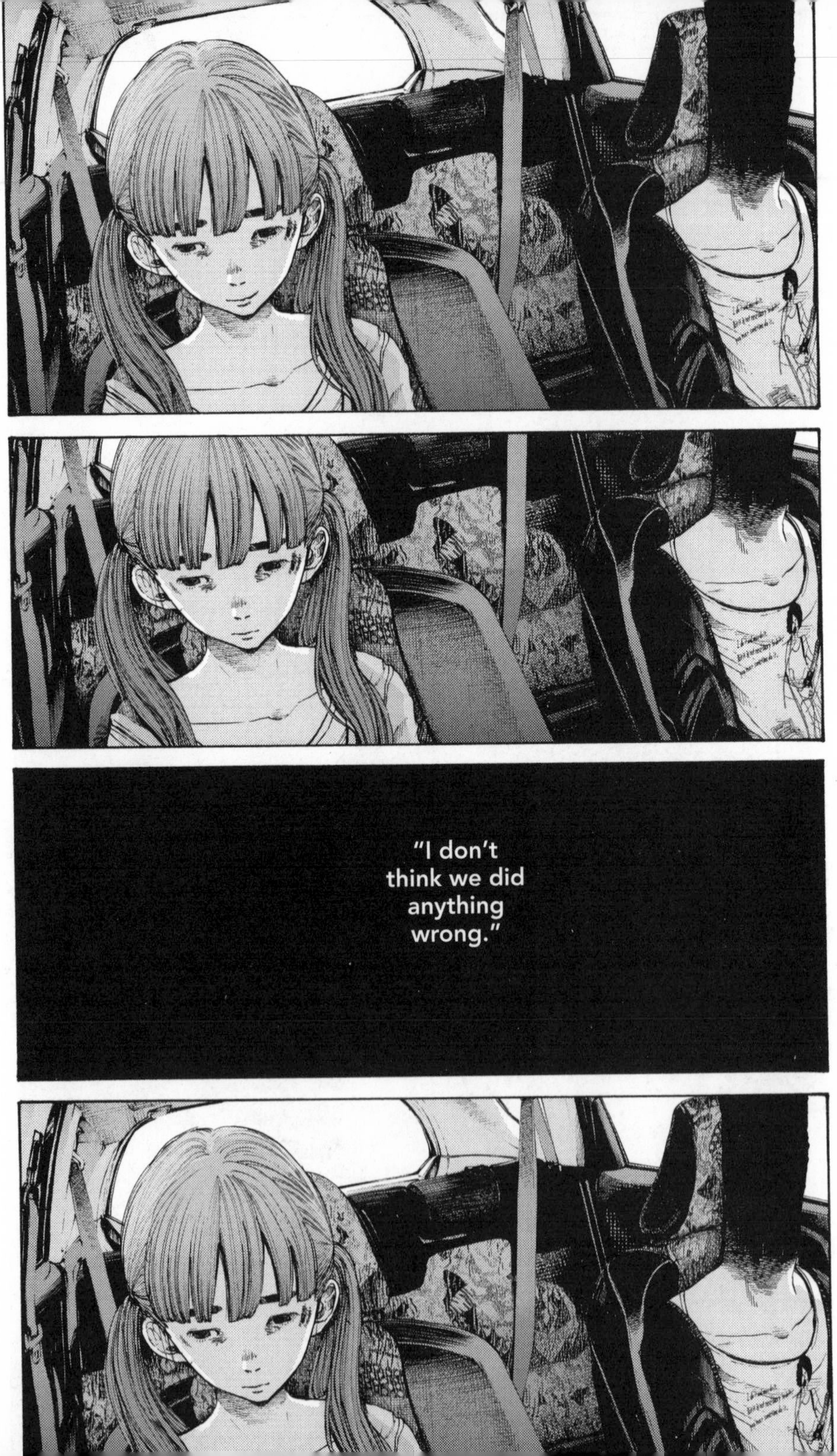
"I don't think we did anything wrong."

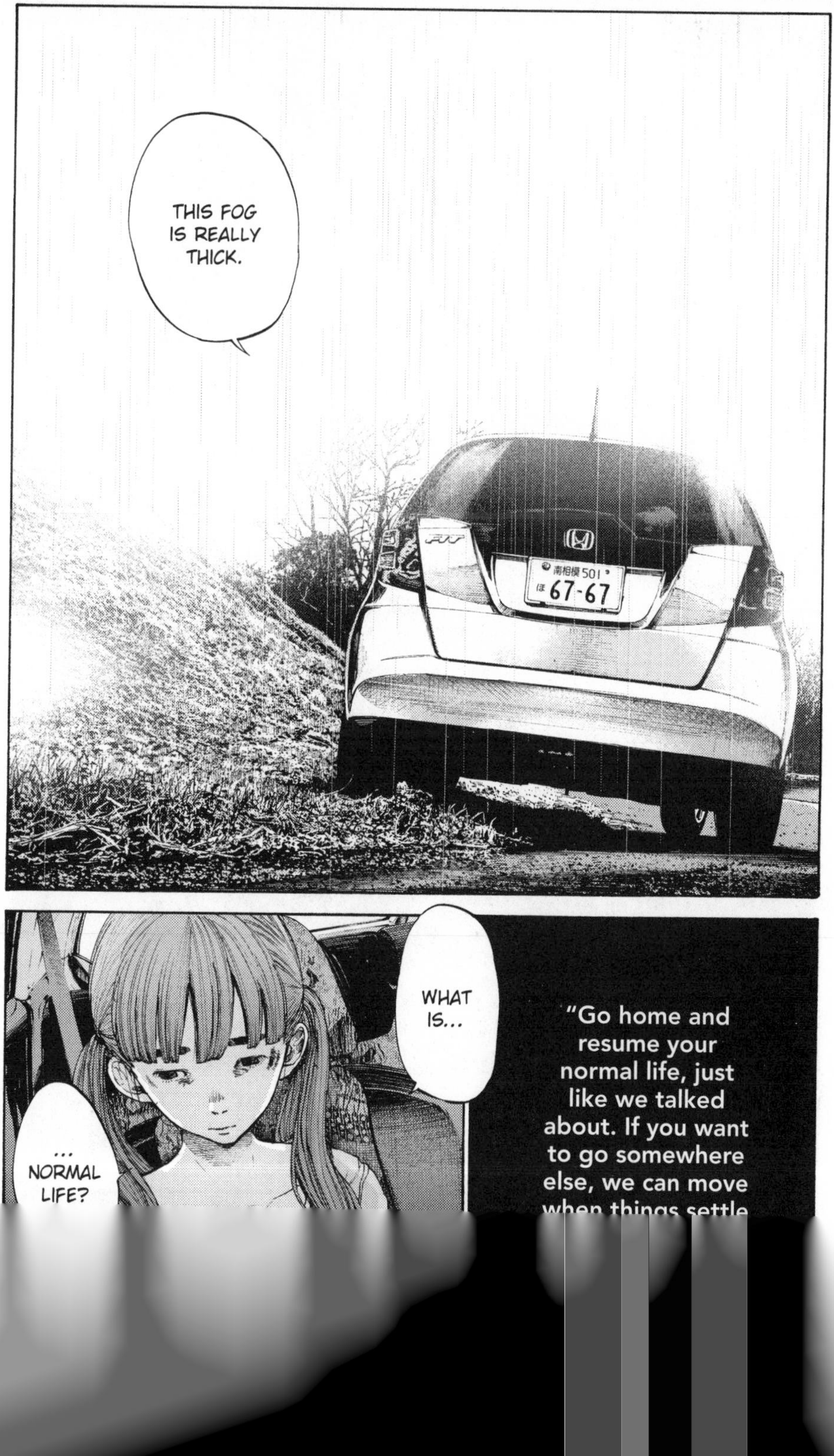
THIS FOG IS REALLY THICK.
"Go home and resume your normal life, just like we talked about. If you want to go somewhere else, we can move when things settle
WHAT IS...
...NORMAL LIFE?

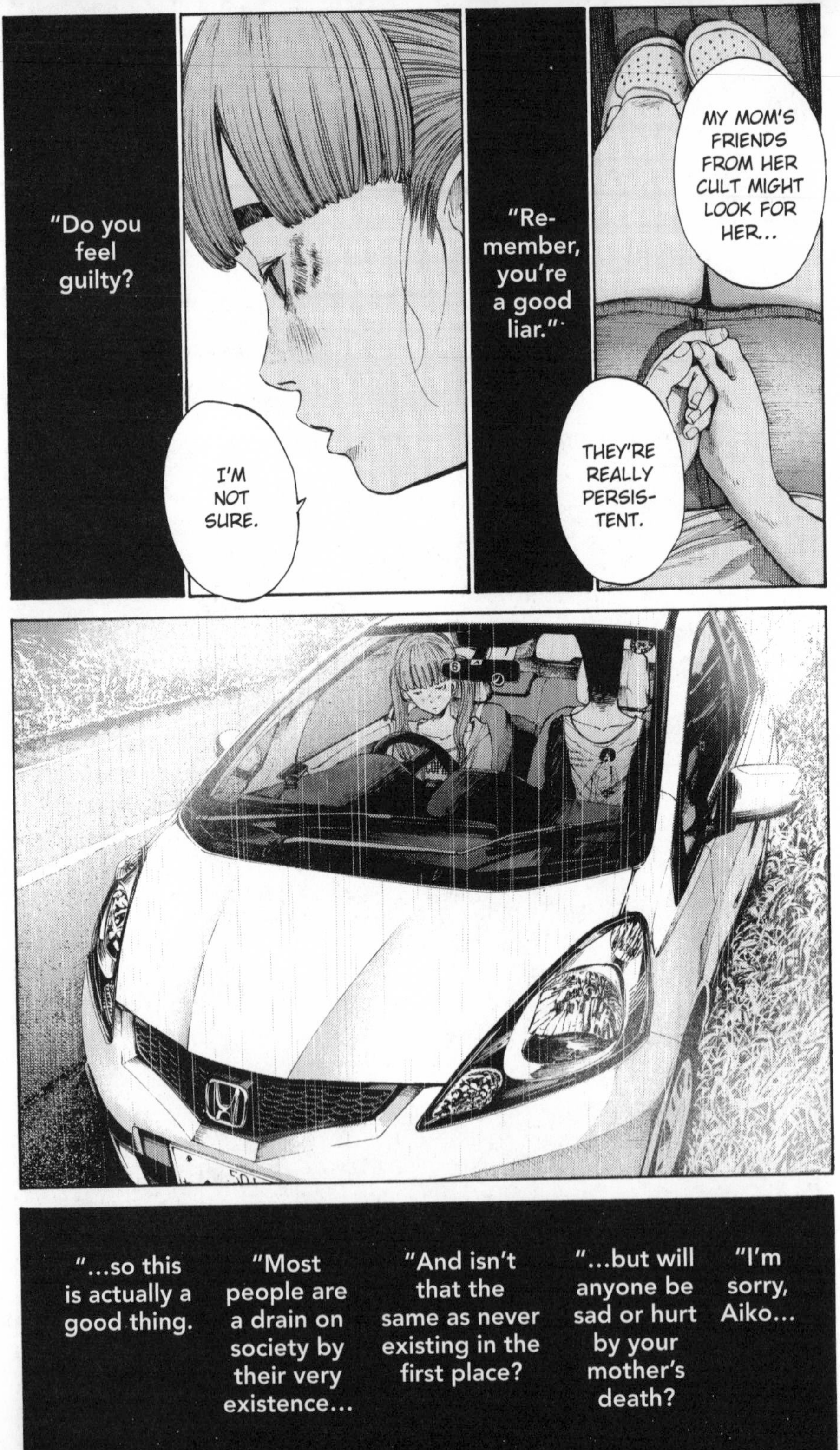
MY MOM'S FRIENDS FROM HER CULT MIGHT LOOK FOR HER...
THEY'RE REALLY PERSISTENT.
"Re-member, you're a good liar."
I'M NOT SURE.
"Do you feel guilty?
"I'm sorry, Aiko...
"...but will anyone be sad or hurt by your mother's death?
"And isn't that the same as never existing in the first place?
"Most people are a drain on society by their very existence...
"...so this is actually a good thing.

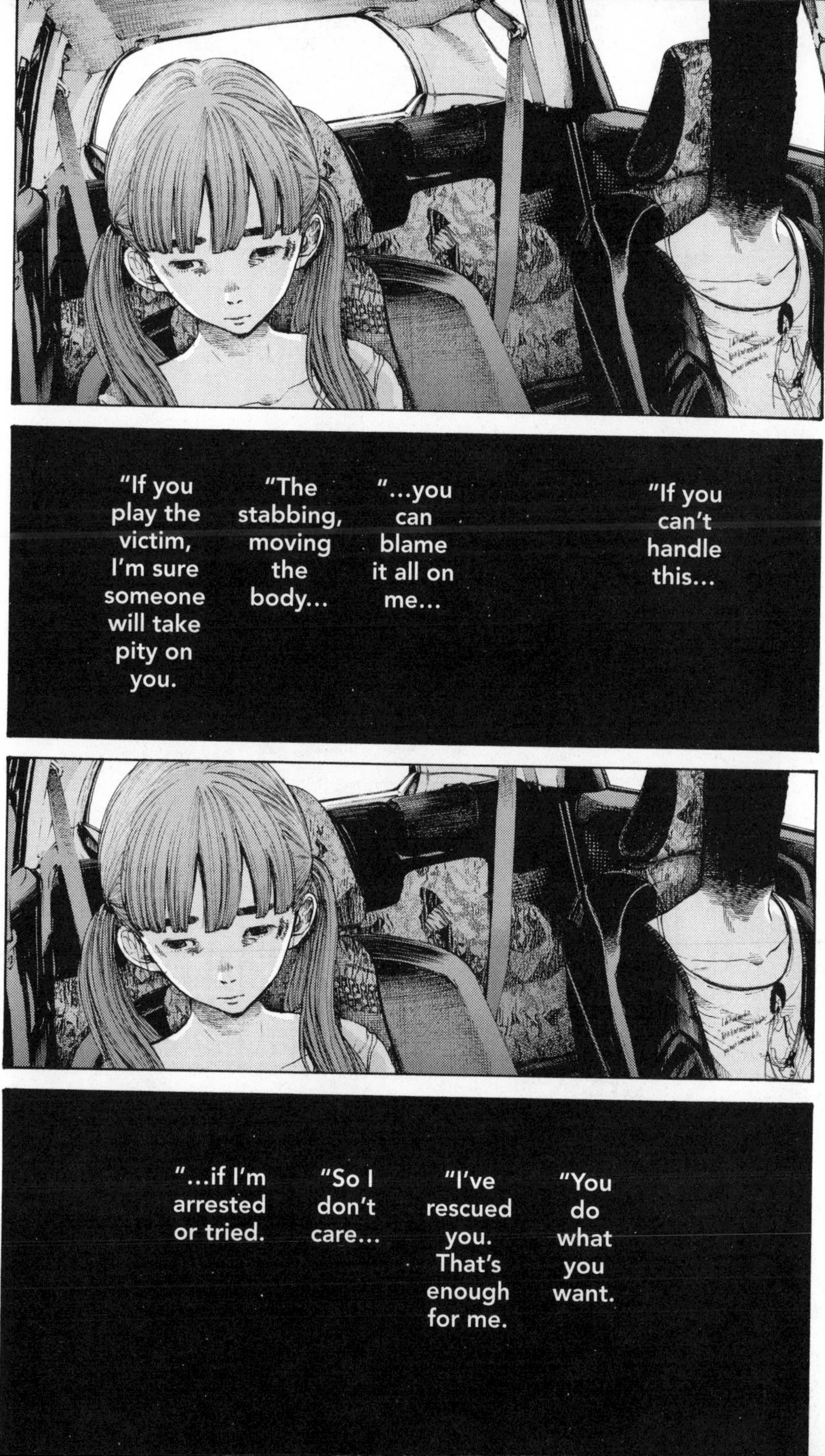
"If you can't handle this...
"...you can blame it all on me...
"The stabbing, moving the body...
"If you play the victim, I'm sure someone will take pity on you.
"You do what you want.
"I've rescued you. That's enough for me.
"So I don't care...
"...if I'm arrested or tried.

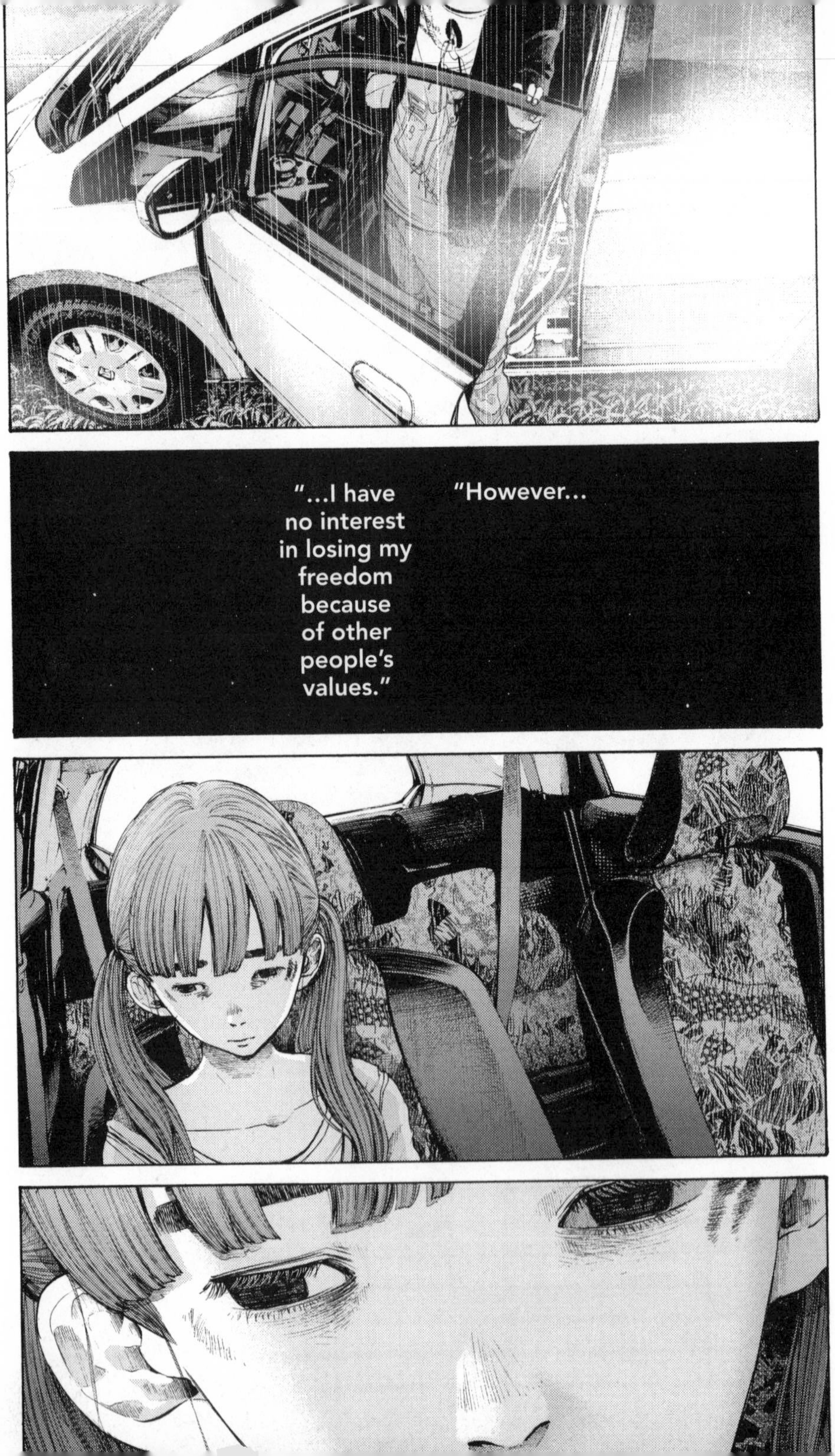
"However...
"...I have no interest in losing my freedom because of other people's values."

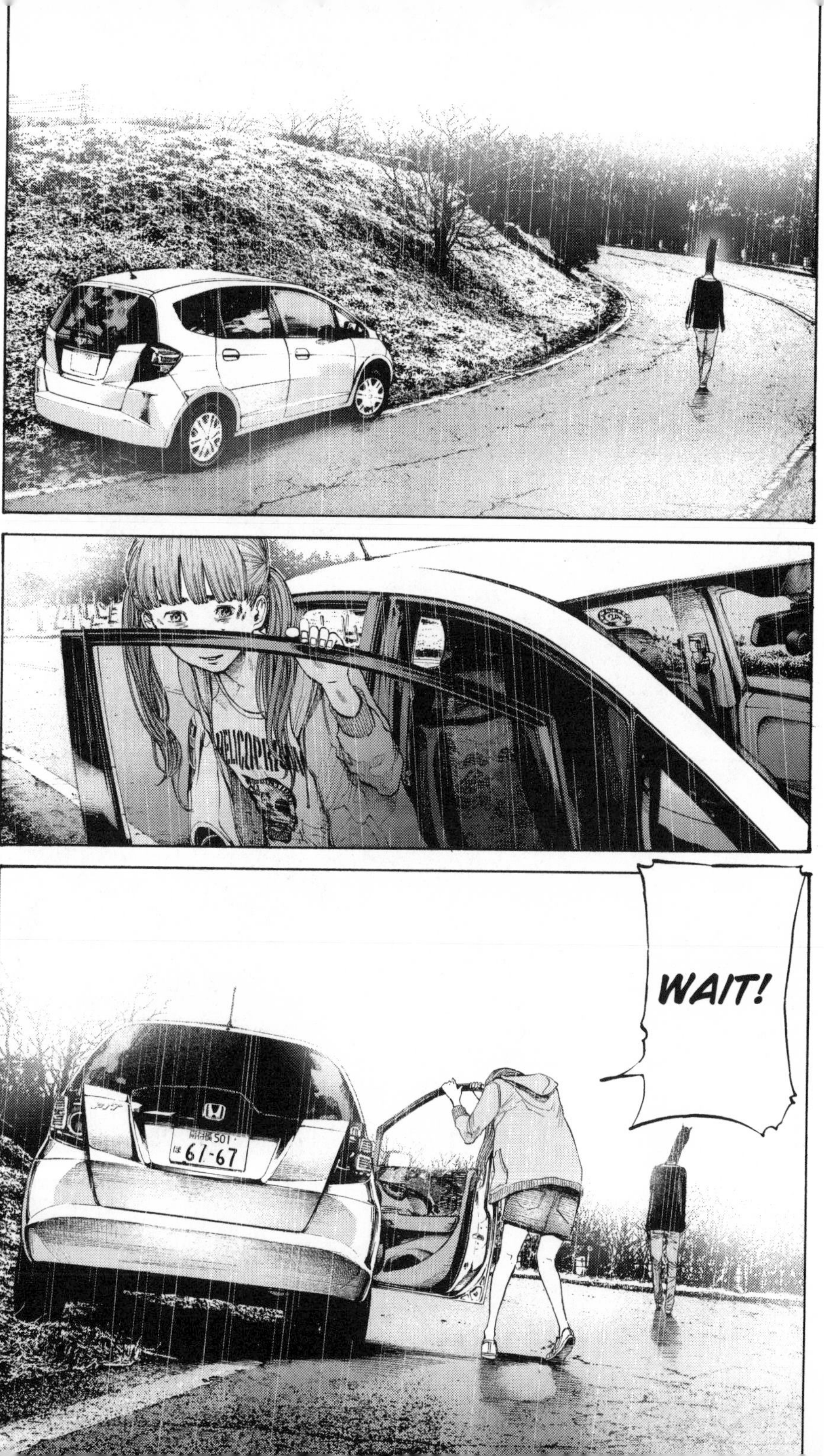
WAIT!

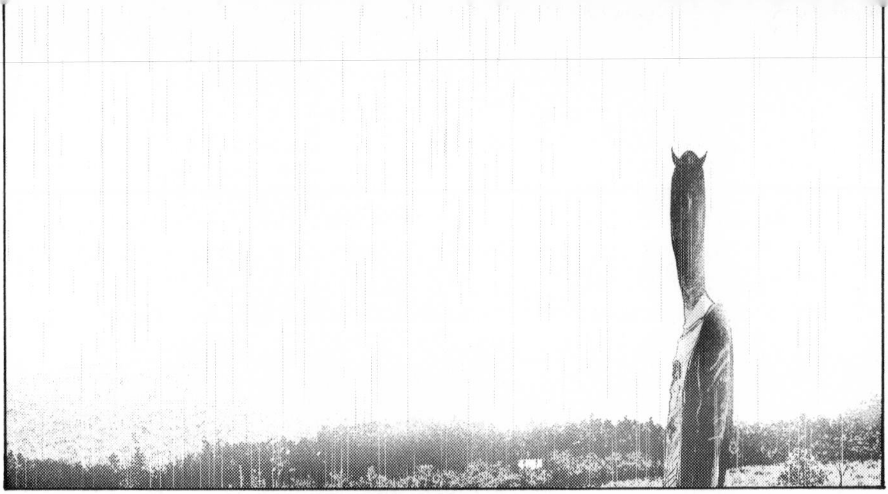
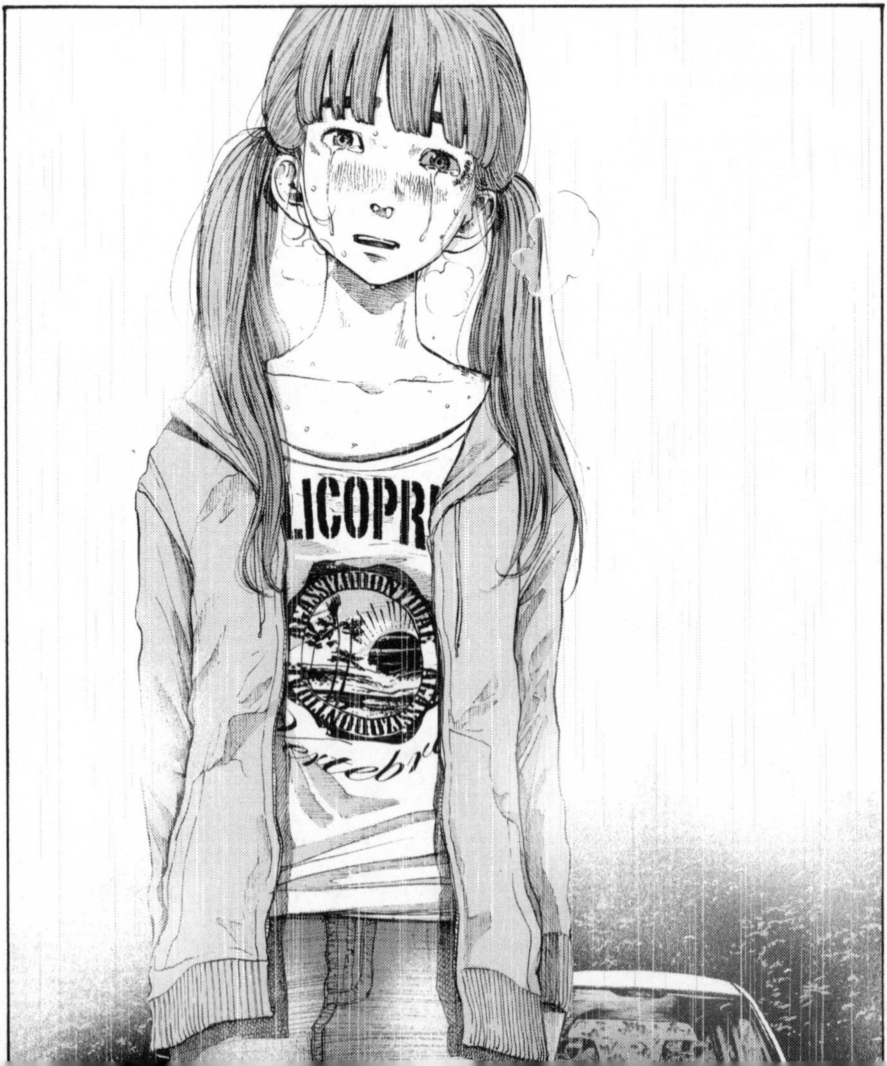

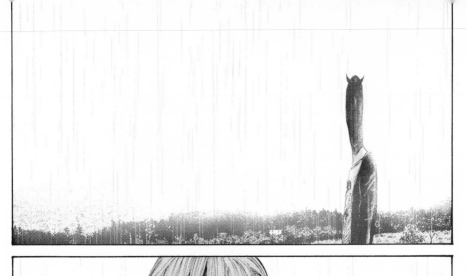

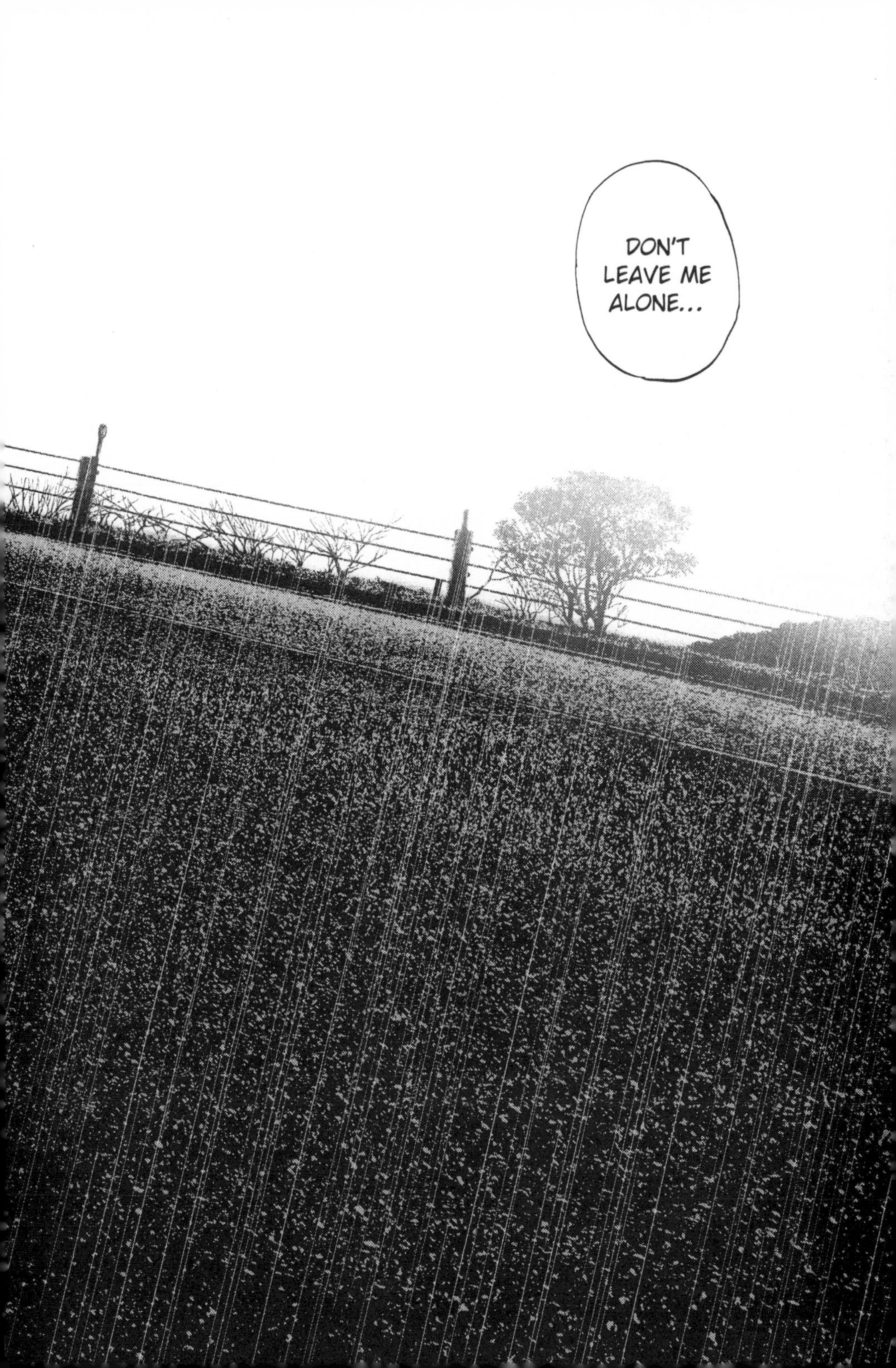
DON'T LEAVE ME ALONE...

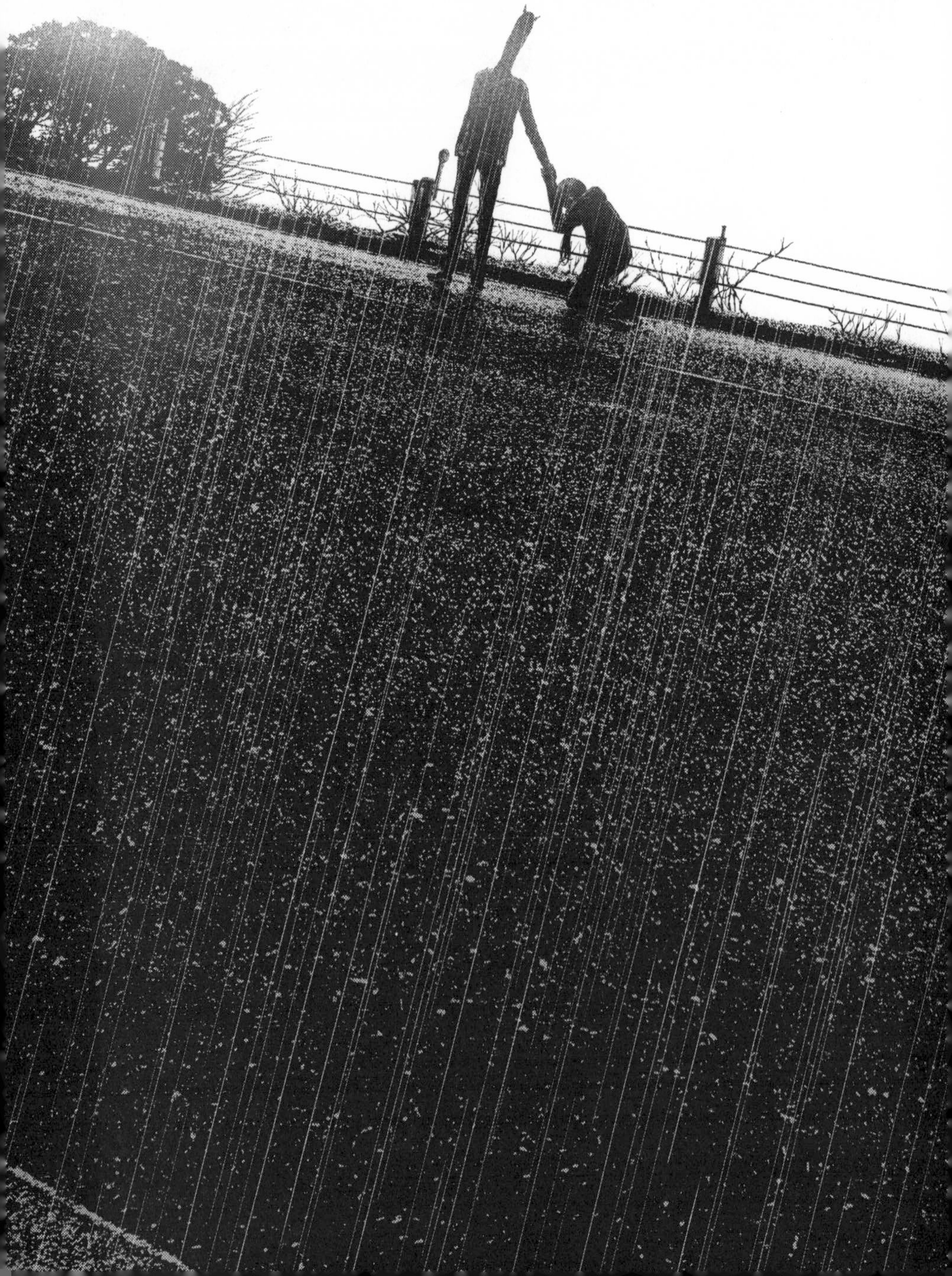

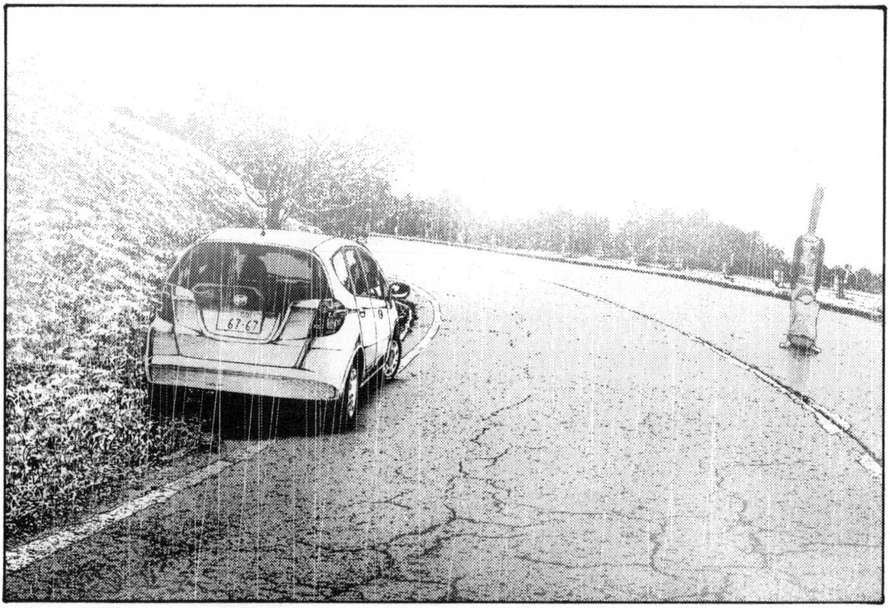

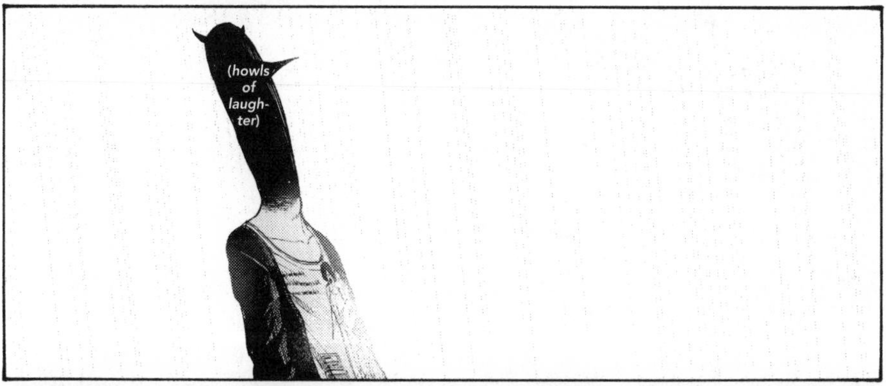
(howls of laugh-ter)

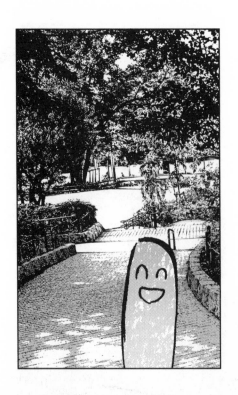

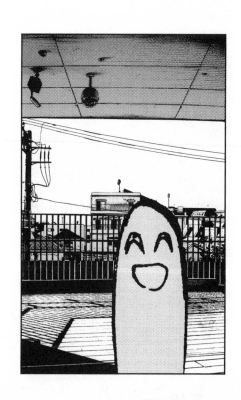

Chapter 117

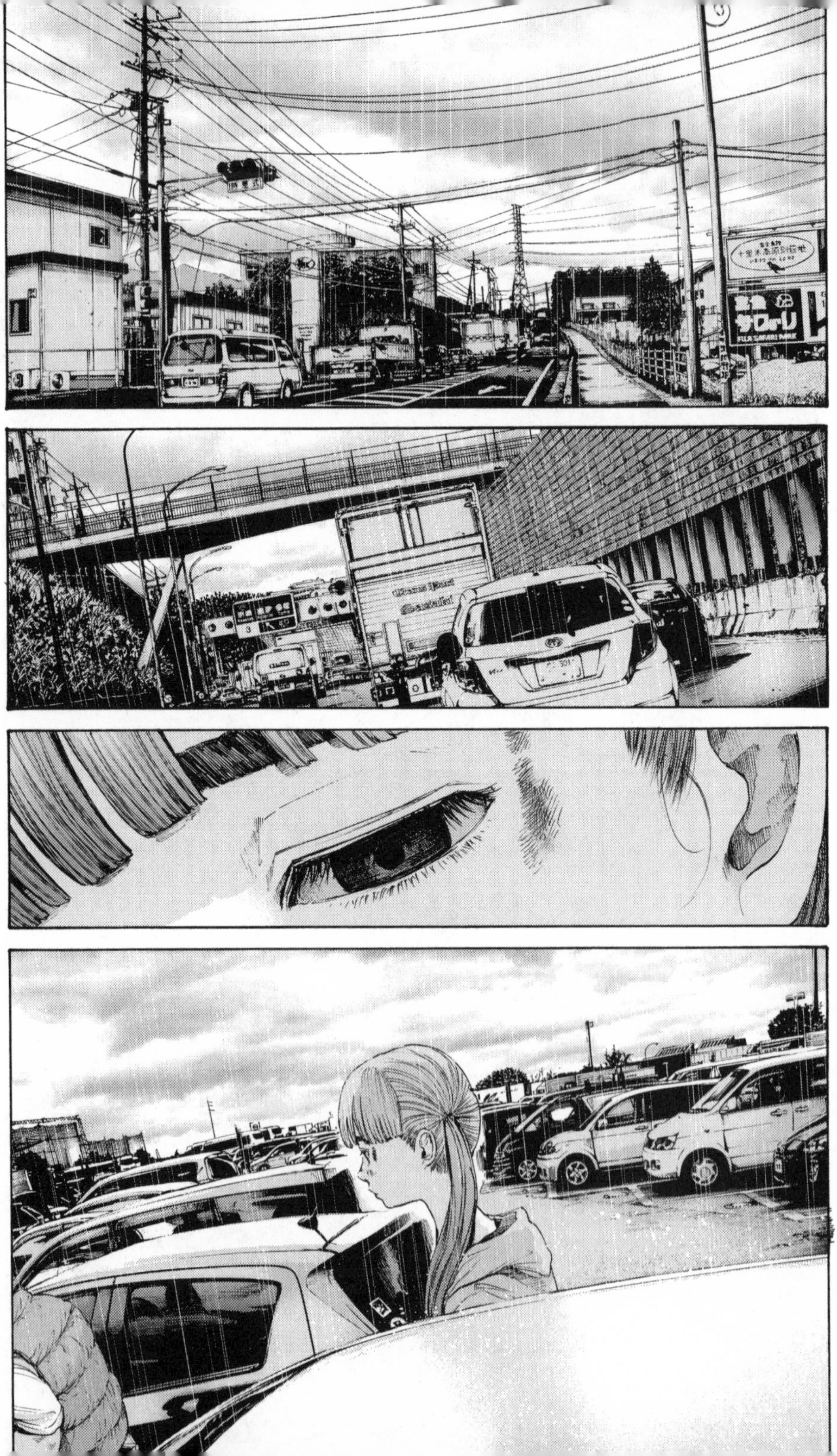

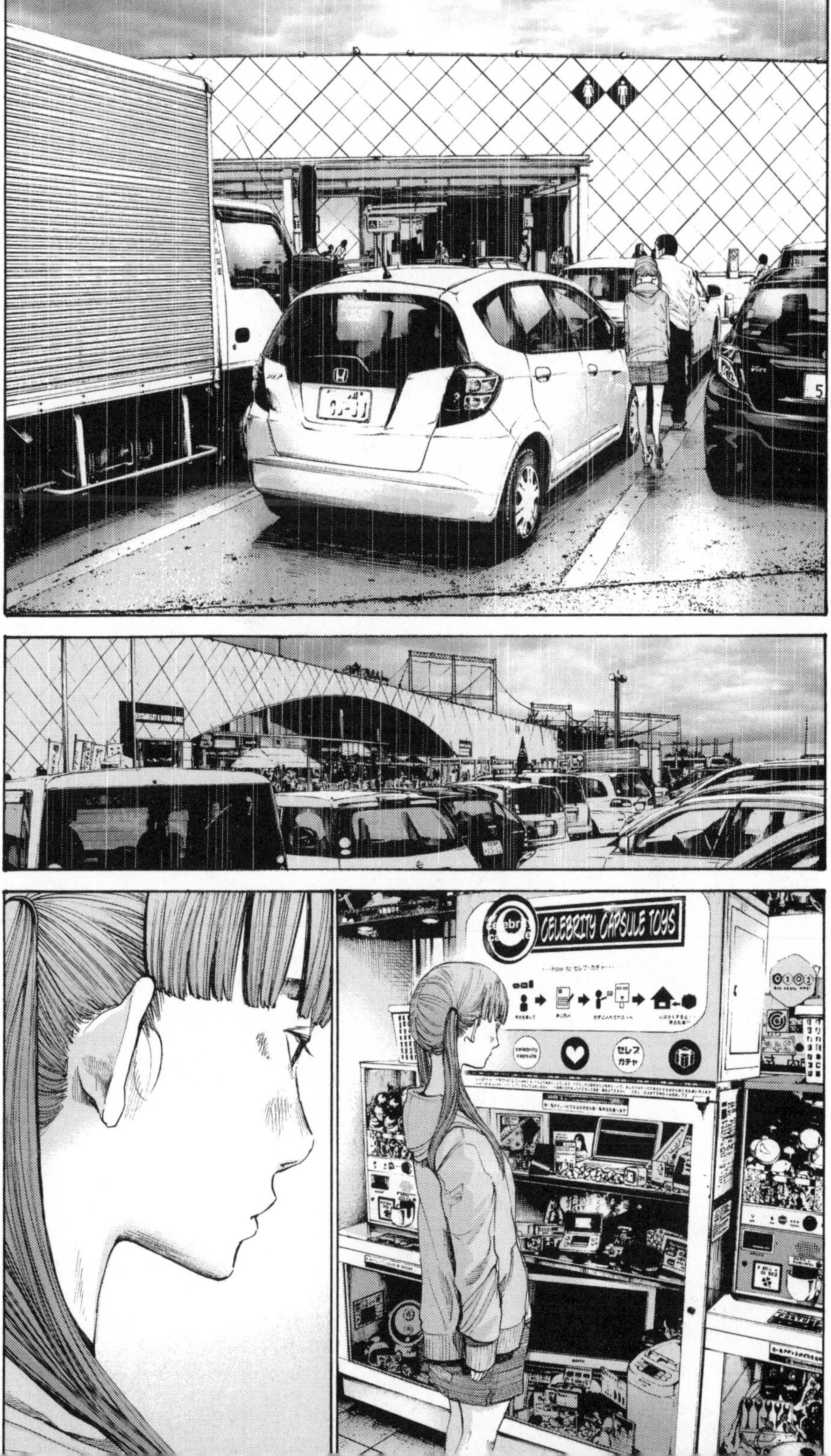
CELEBRITY CAPSULE TOYS
celebrity capsule
How to セレフ・ガチャ
celebrity capsule
セレフ ガチャ

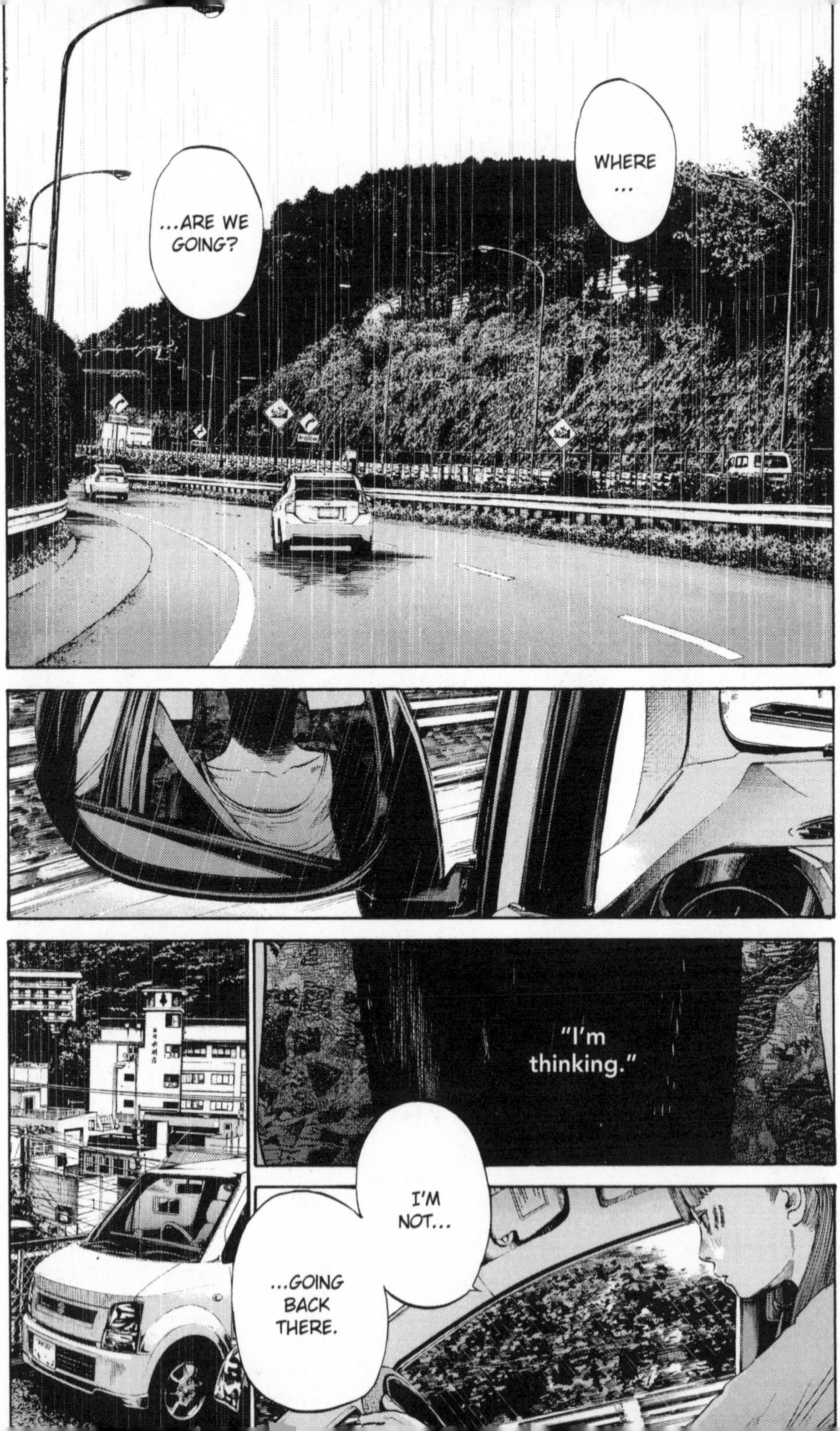
WHERE ...
...ARE WE GOING?
"I'm thinking."
I'M NOT...
...GOING BACK THERE.

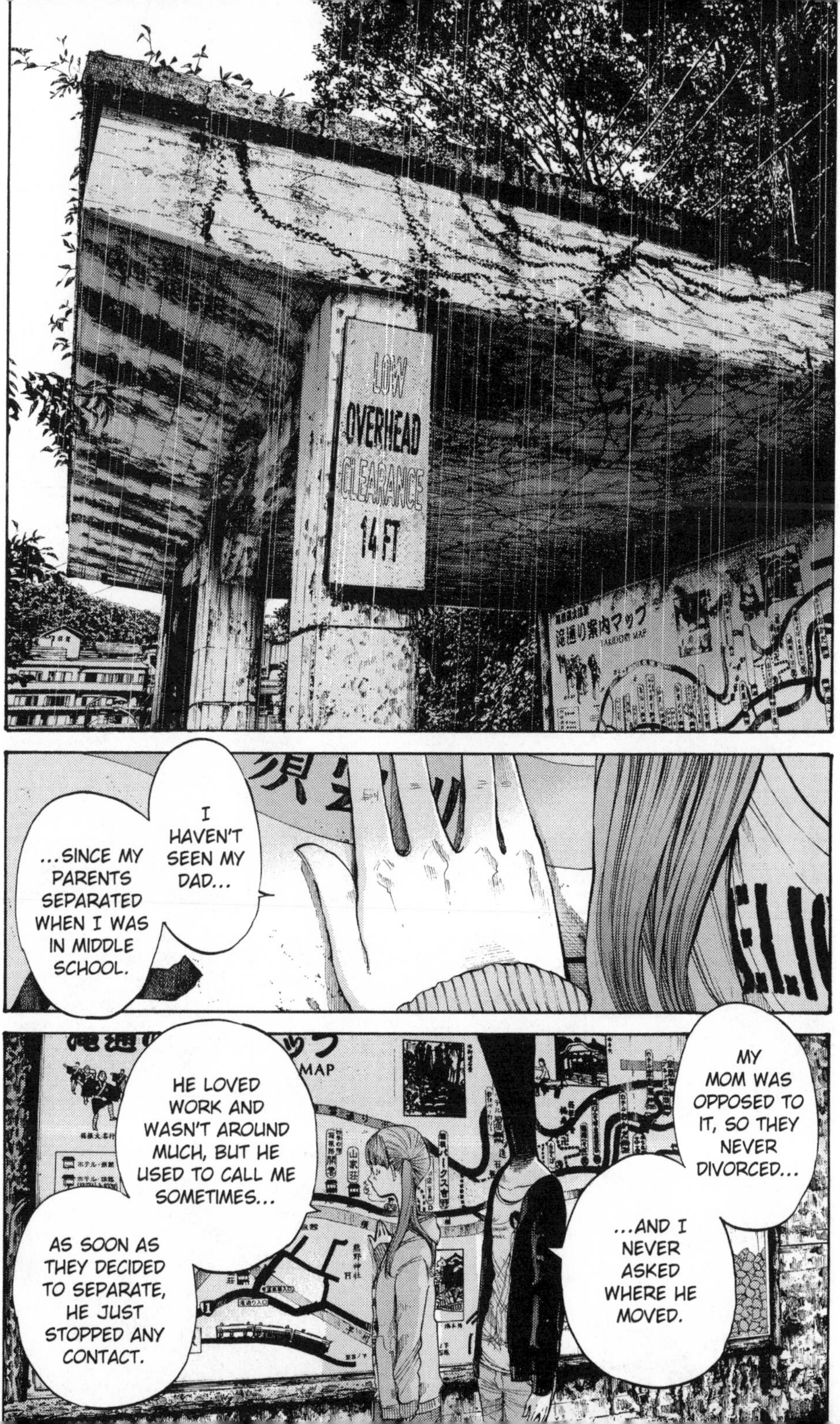
LOW
OVERHEAD
CLEARANCE
14 FT
I HAVEN'T SEEN MY DAD...
...SINCE MY PARENTS SEPARATED WHEN I WAS IN MIDDLE SCHOOL.
MAP
MY MOM WAS OPPOSED TO IT, SO THEY NEVER DIVORCED...
...AND I NEVER ASKED WHERE HE MOVED.
HE LOVED WORK AND WASN'T AROUND MUCH, BUT HE USED TO CALL ME SOMETIMES...
AS SOON AS THEY DECIDED TO SEPARATE, HE JUST STOPPED ANY CONTACT.

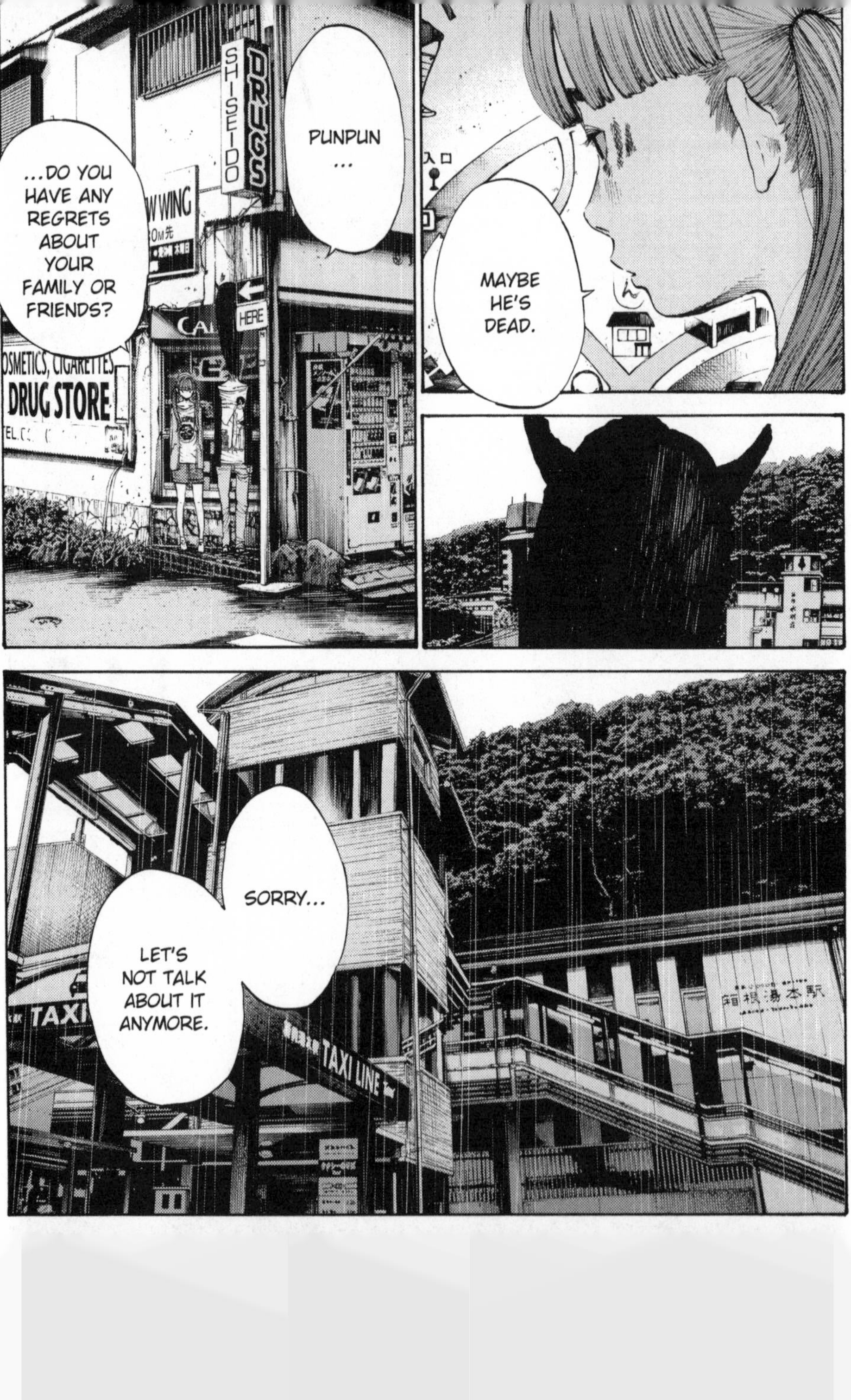
MAYBE HE'S DEAD.
PUNPUN ...
SHISEIDO
DRUGS
DRUG STORE
HERE
...DO YOU HAVE ANY REGRETS ABOUT YOUR FAMILY OR FRIENDS?
箱根湯本駅
SORRY...
LET'S NOT TALK ABOUT IT ANYMORE.
TAXI LINE
TAXI

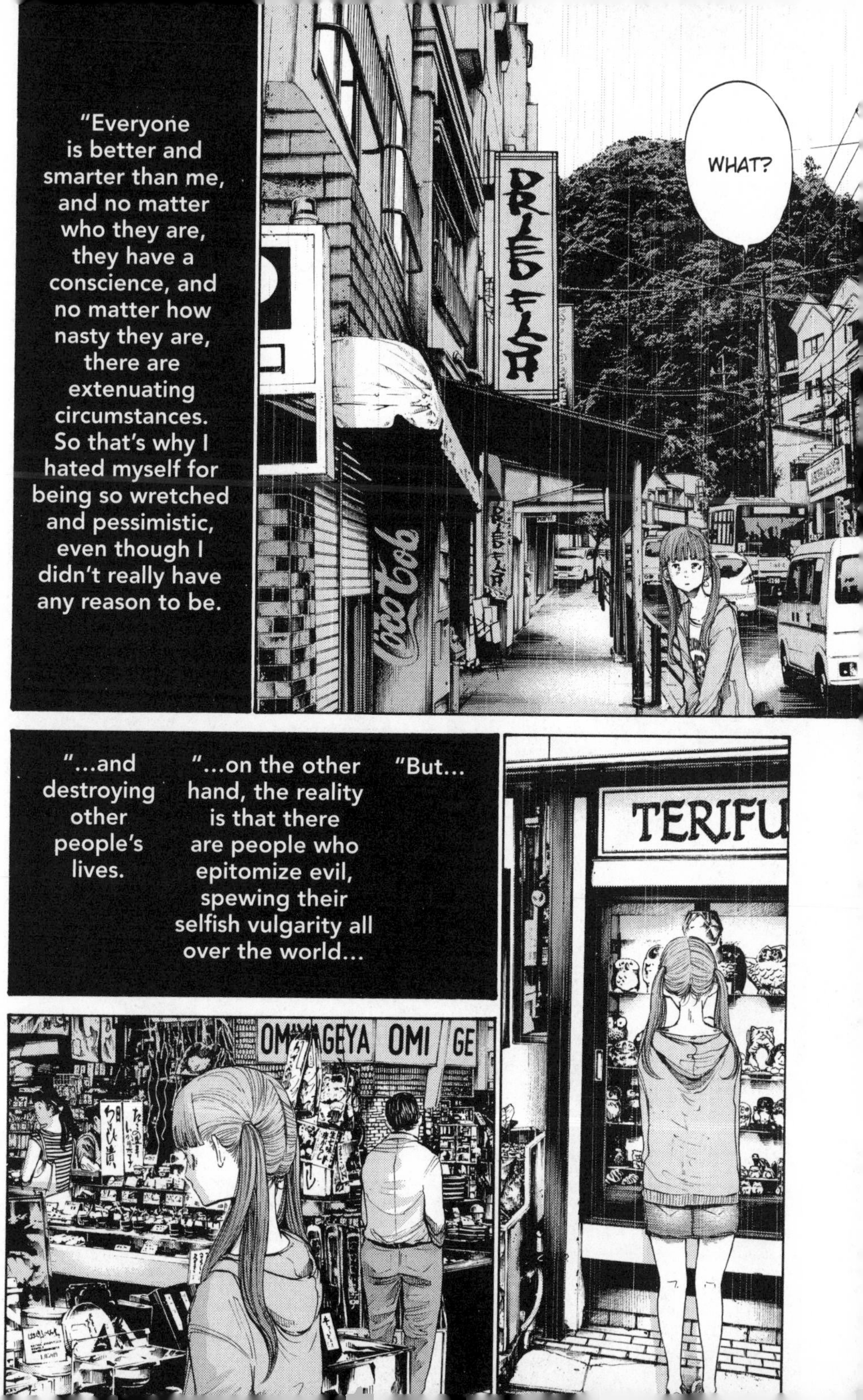
DRIED FISH
WHAT?
"Everyone is better and smarter than me, and no matter who they are, they have a conscience, and no matter how nasty they are, there are extenuating circumstances. So that's why I hated myself for being so wretched and pessimistic, even though I didn't really have any reason to be.
TERIFU
"But...
"...on the other hand, the reality is that there are people who epitomize evil, spewing their selfish vulgarity all over the world...
"...and destroying other people's lives.
OMIYAGEYA OMI GE

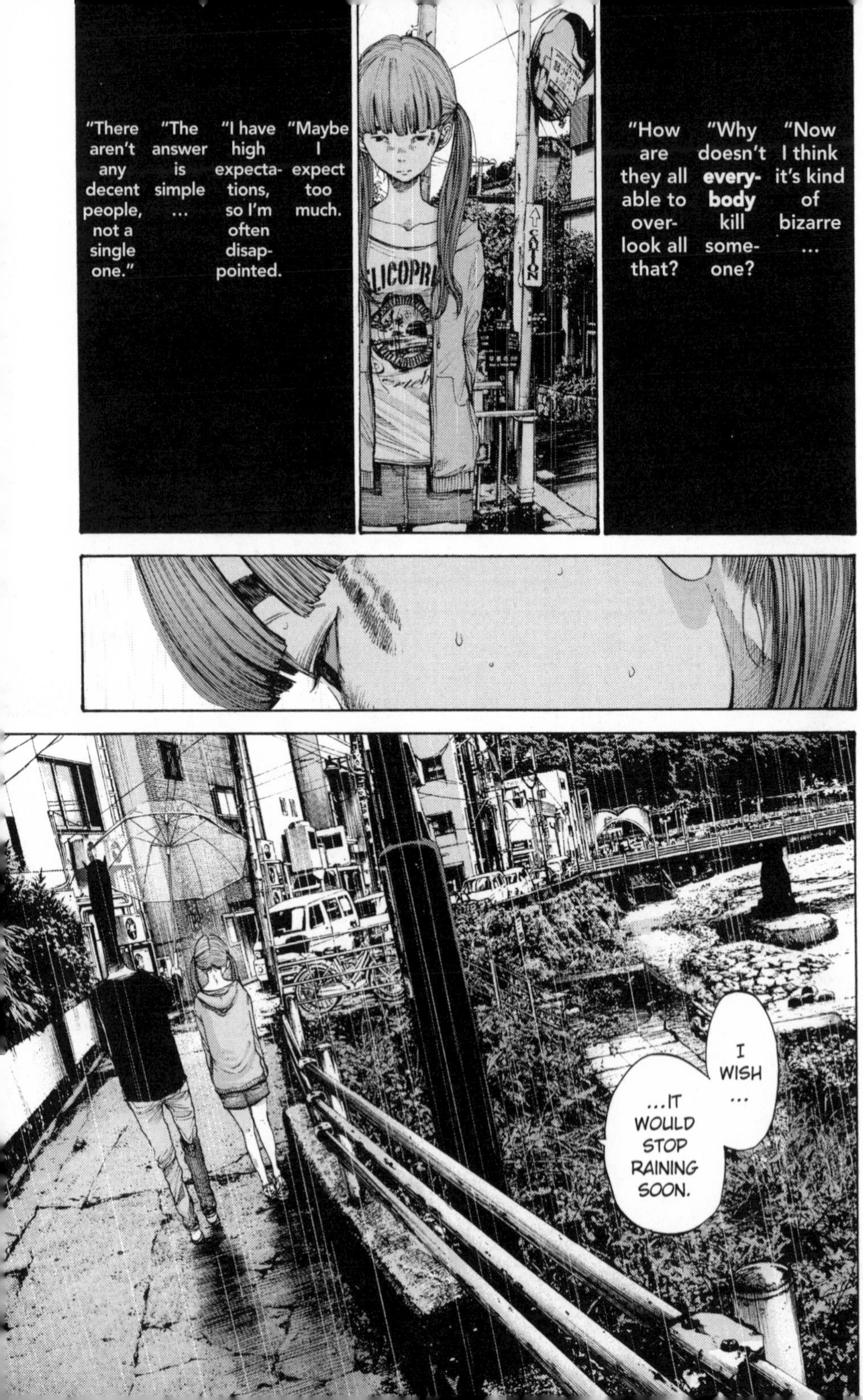
"Now I think it's kind of bizarre…
"Why doesn't **everybody** kill someone?
"How are they all able to overlook all that?
"Maybe I expect too much.
"I have high expectations, so I'm often disappointed.
"The answer is simple…
"There aren't any decent people, not a single one."
I WISH…
…IT WOULD STOP RAINING SOON.

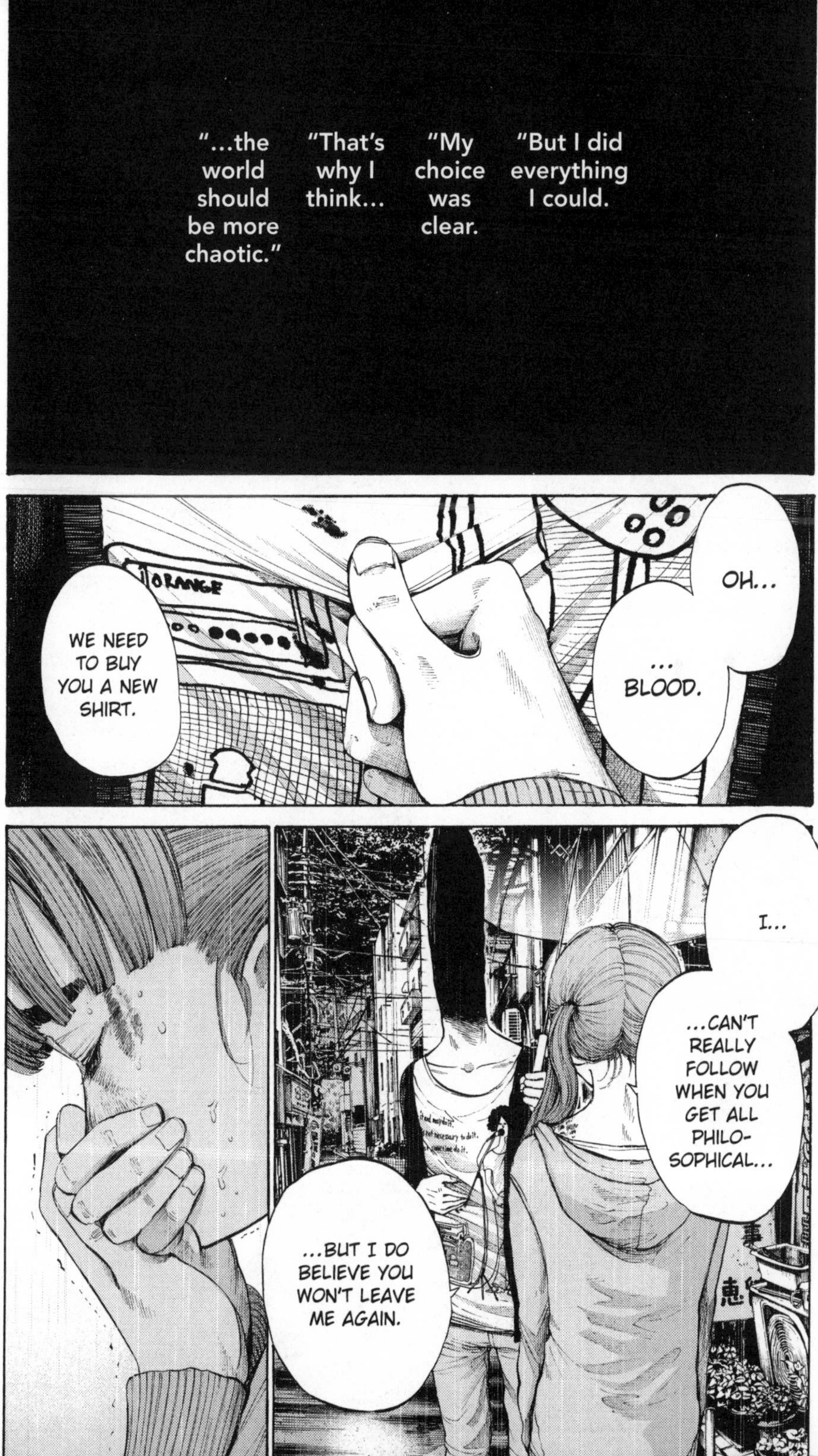
"But I did everything I could.
"My choice was clear.
"That's why I think...
"...the world should be more chaotic."
OH...
...BLOOD.
ORANGE
WE NEED TO BUY YOU A NEW SHIRT.
I...
...CAN'T REALLY FOLLOW WHEN YOU GET ALL PHILO-SOPHICAL...
...BUT I DO BELIEVE YOU WON'T LEAVE ME AGAIN.

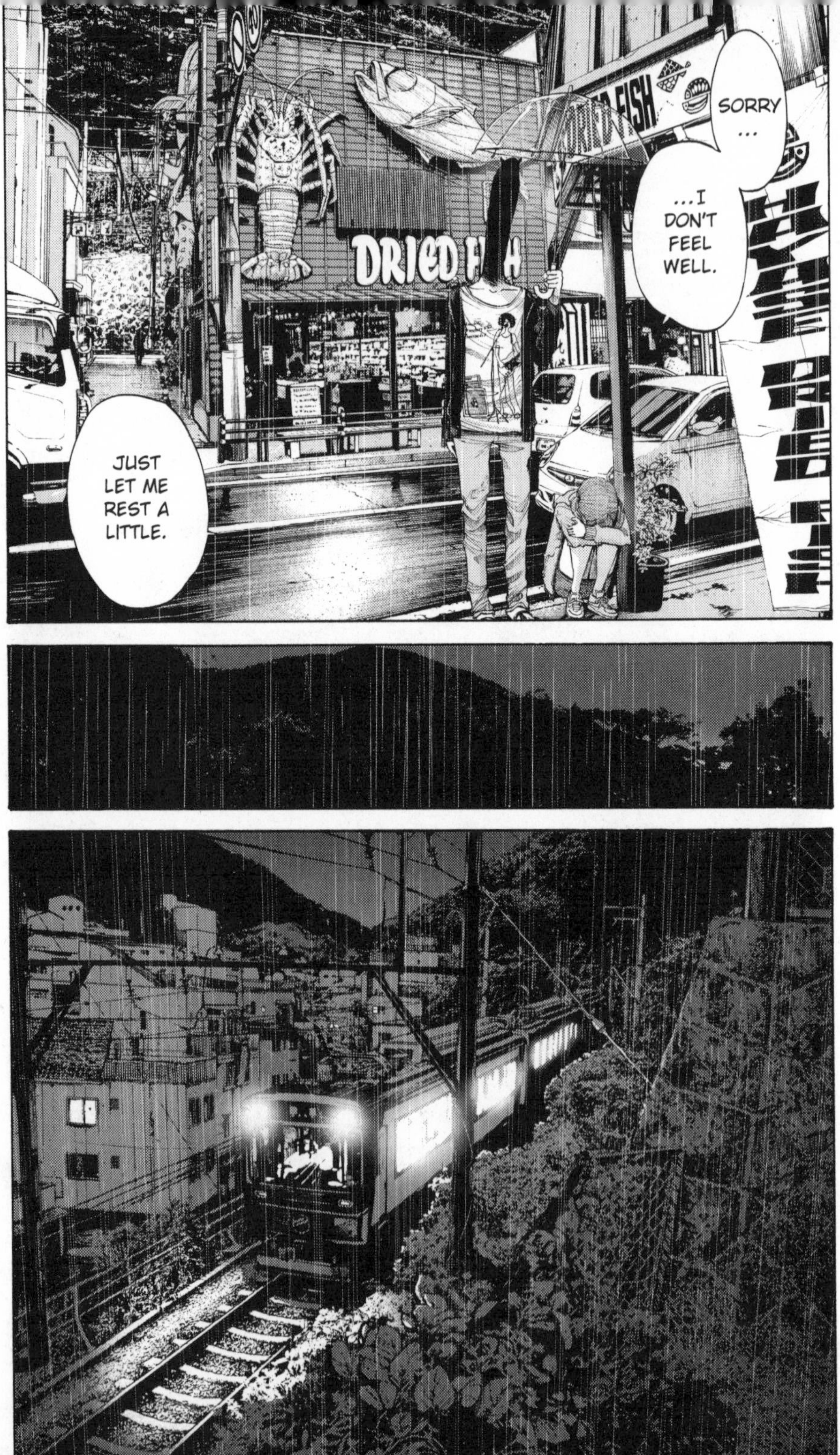
SORRY ...
...I DON'T FEEL WELL.
DRIED FISH
JUST LET ME REST A LITTLE.

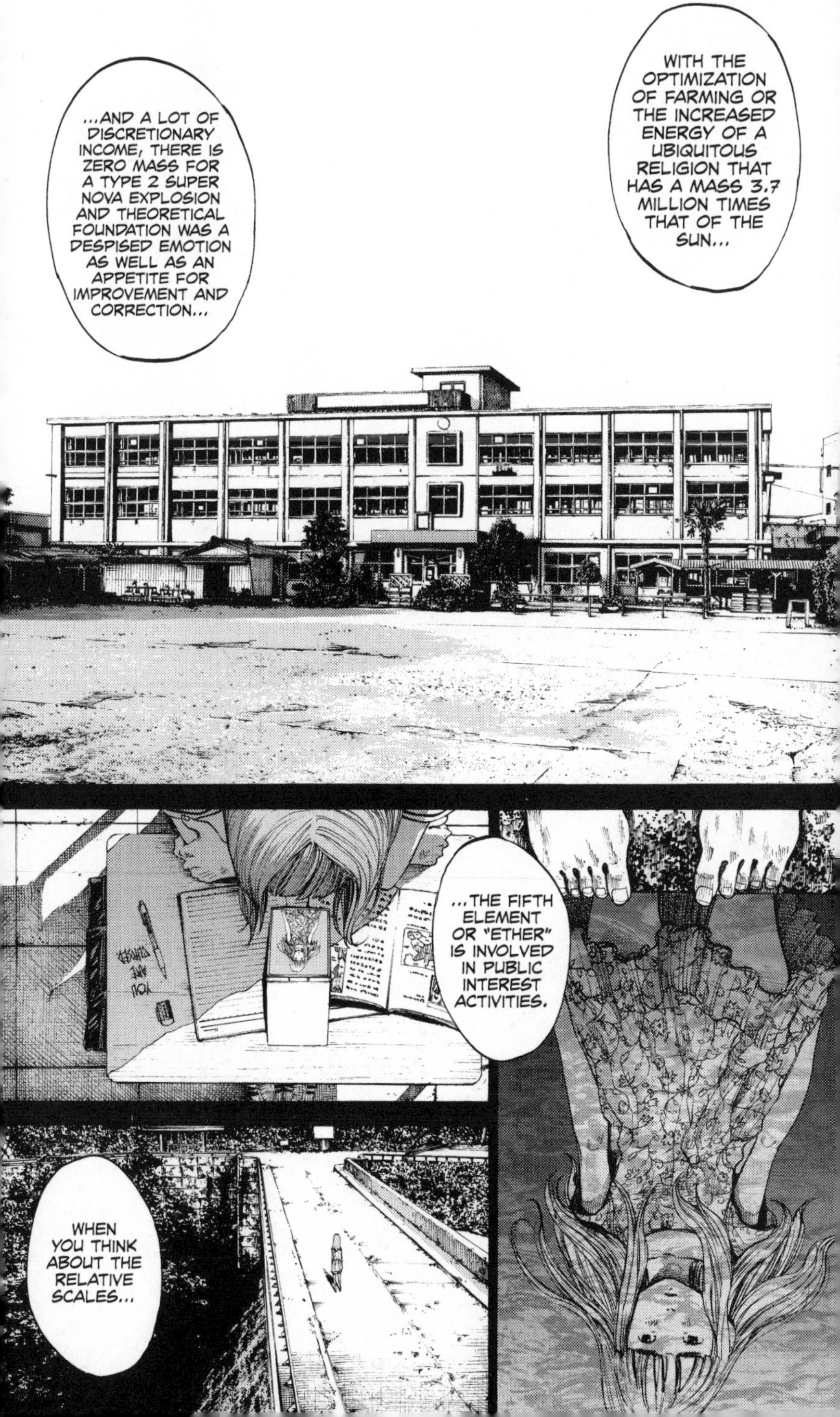
WITH THE OPTIMIZATION OF FARMING OR THE INCREASED ENERGY OF A UBIQUITOUS RELIGION THAT HAS A MASS 3.7 MILLION TIMES THAT OF THE SUN...
...AND A LOT OF DISCRETIONARY INCOME, THERE IS ZERO MASS FOR A TYPE 2 SUPER NOVA EXPLOSION AND THEORETICAL FOUNDATION WAS A DESPISED EMOTION AS WELL AS AN APPETITE FOR IMPROVEMENT AND CORRECTION...
...THE FIFTH ELEMENT OR "ETHER" IS INVOLVED IN PUBLIC INTEREST ACTIVITIES.
WHEN YOU THINK ABOUT THE RELATIVE SCALES...

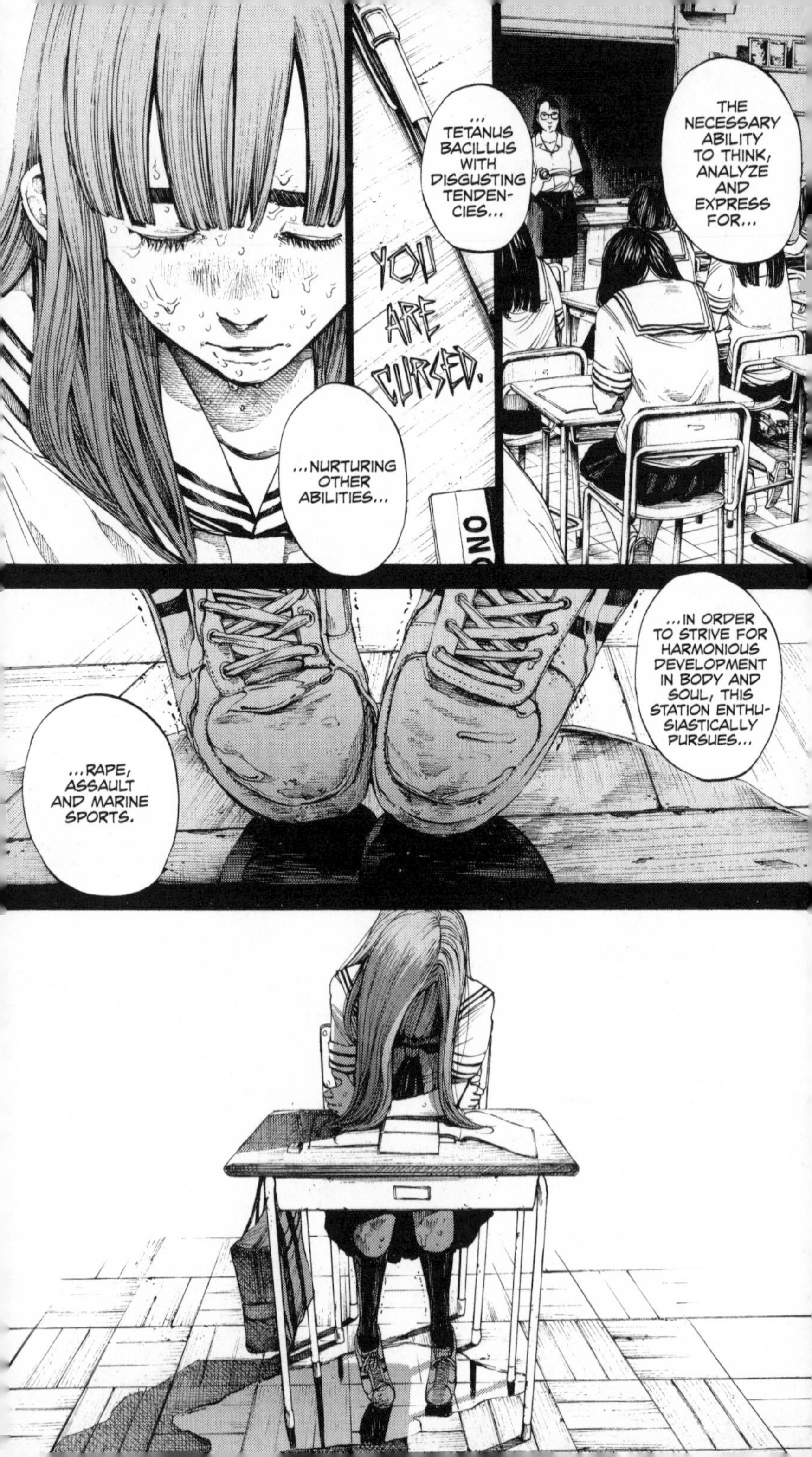
THE NECESSARY ABILITY TO THINK, ANALYZE AND EXPRESS FOR...
...TETANUS BACILLUS WITH DISGUSTING TENDENCIES...
YOU ARE CURSED.
...NURTURING OTHER ABILITIES...
ONO
...IN ORDER TO STRIVE FOR HARMONIOUS DEVELOPMENT IN BODY AND SOUL, THIS STATION ENTHUSIASTICALLY PURSUES...
...RAPE, ASSAULT AND MARINE SPORTS.

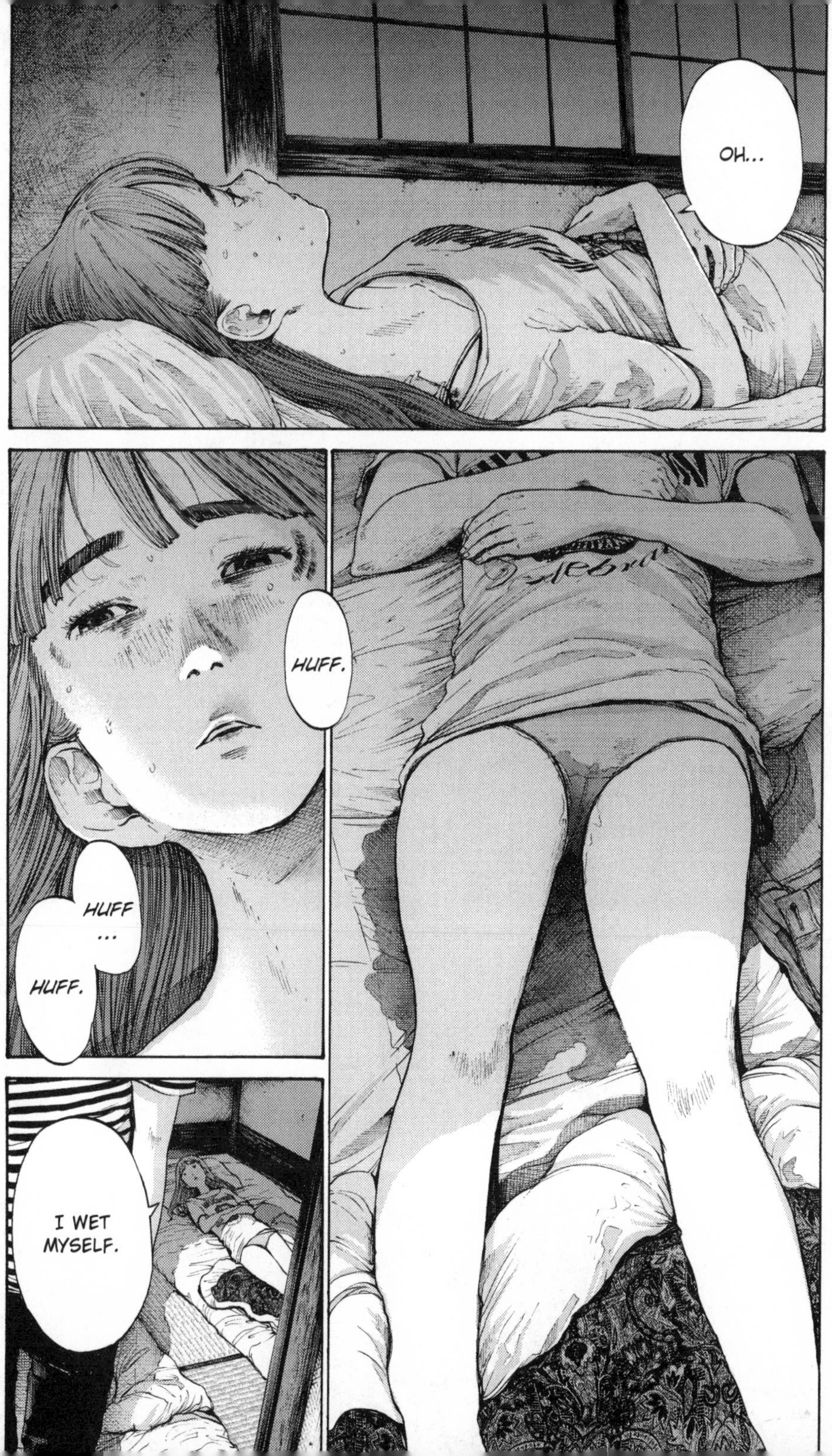
OH...
HUFF.
HUFF ... HUFF.
I WET MYSELF.

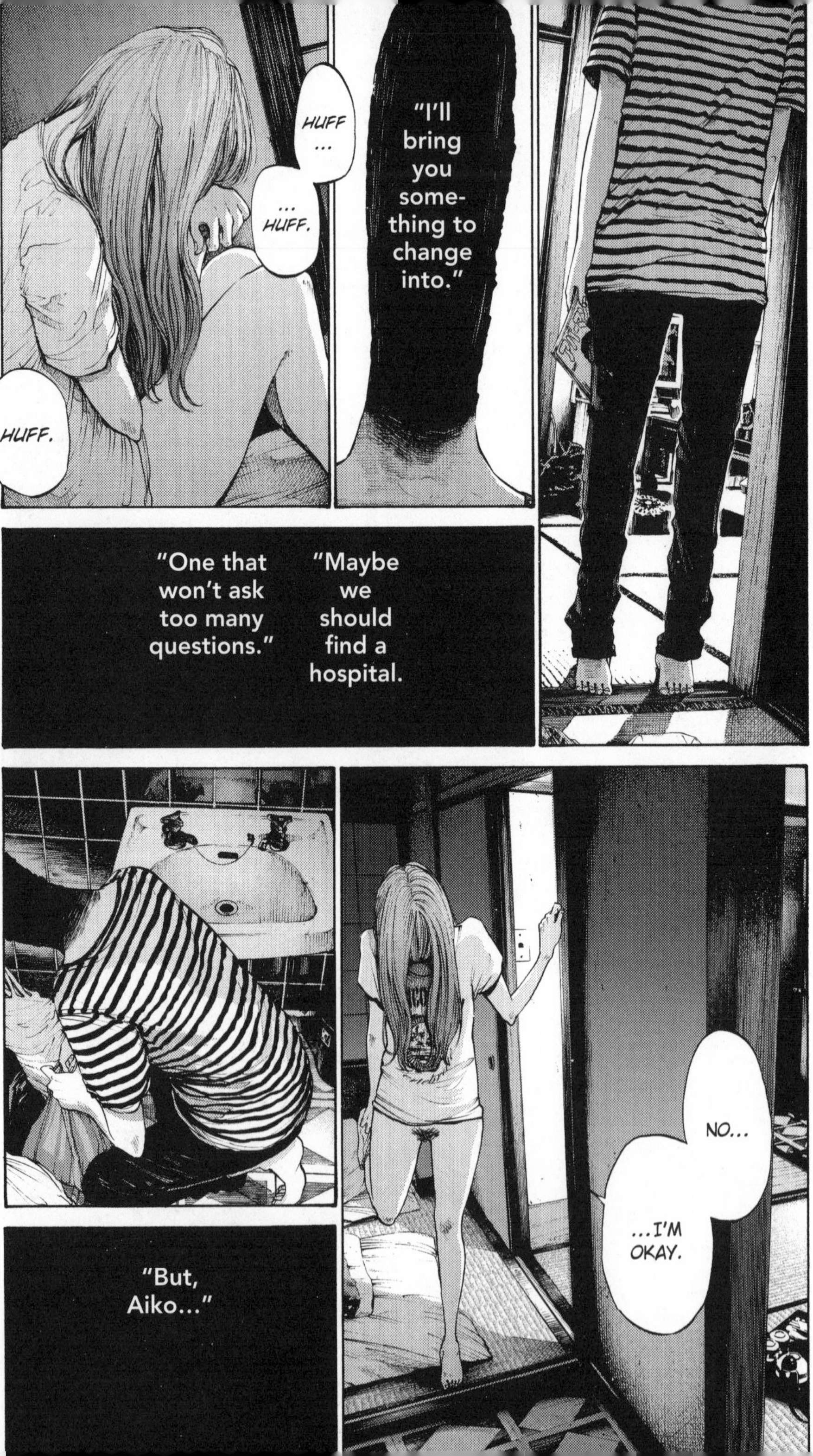
"I'll bring you some-thing to change into."
HUFF...
...HUFF.
HUFF.
"Maybe we should find a hospital.
"One that won't ask too many questions."
NO...
...I'M OKAY.
"But, Aiko..."

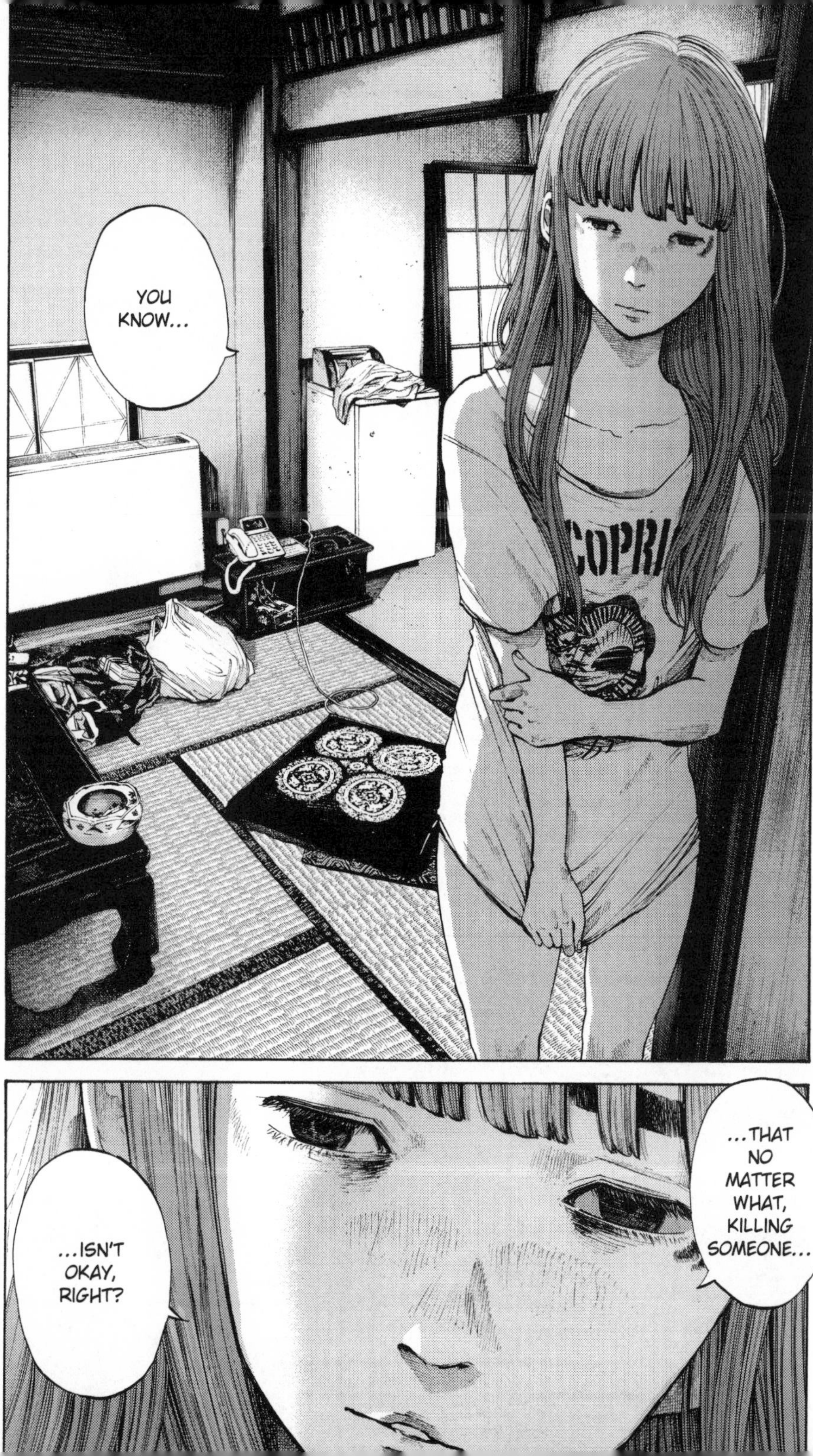
YOU KNOW...
COPRI
...THAT NO MATTER WHAT, KILLING SOMEONE...
...ISN'T OKAY, RIGHT?

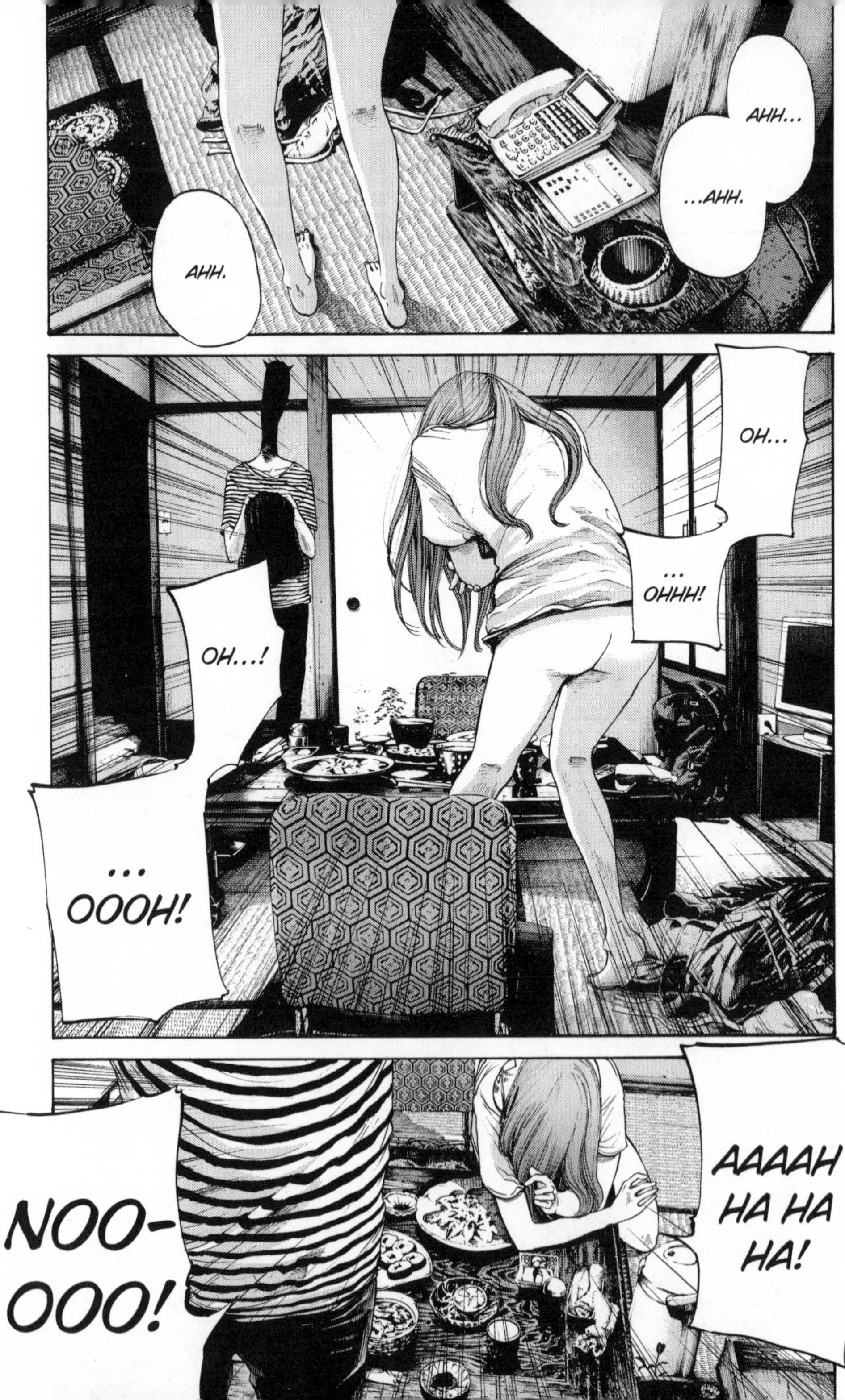
AHH...
...AHH.
AHH.
OH...
... OHHH!
OH...!
... OOOH!
AAAAH HA HA HA!
NOO-OOO!

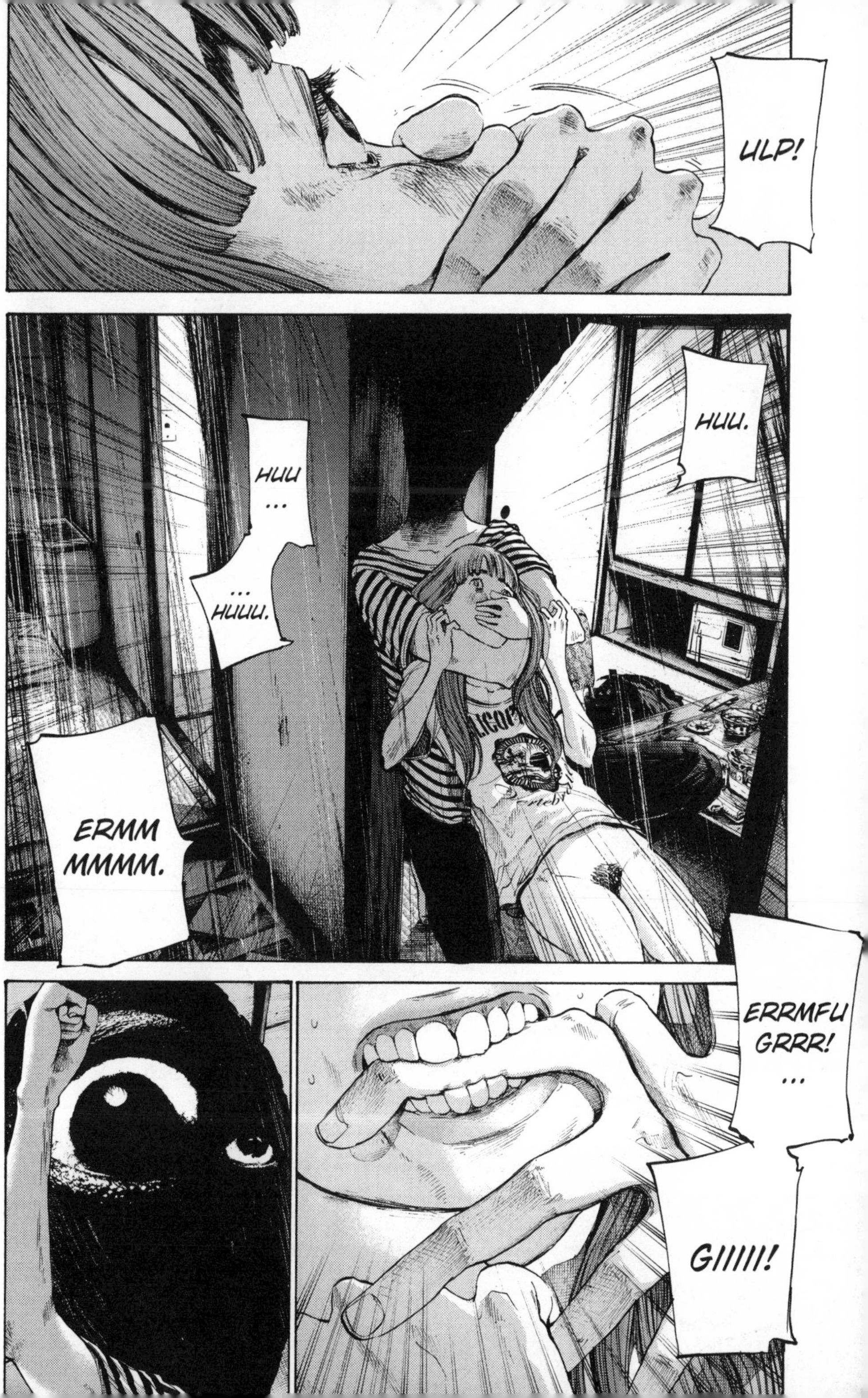
ULP!
HUU.
HUU ...
... HUUU.
ERMM MMMM.
ERRMFU GRRR! ...
GIIIII!

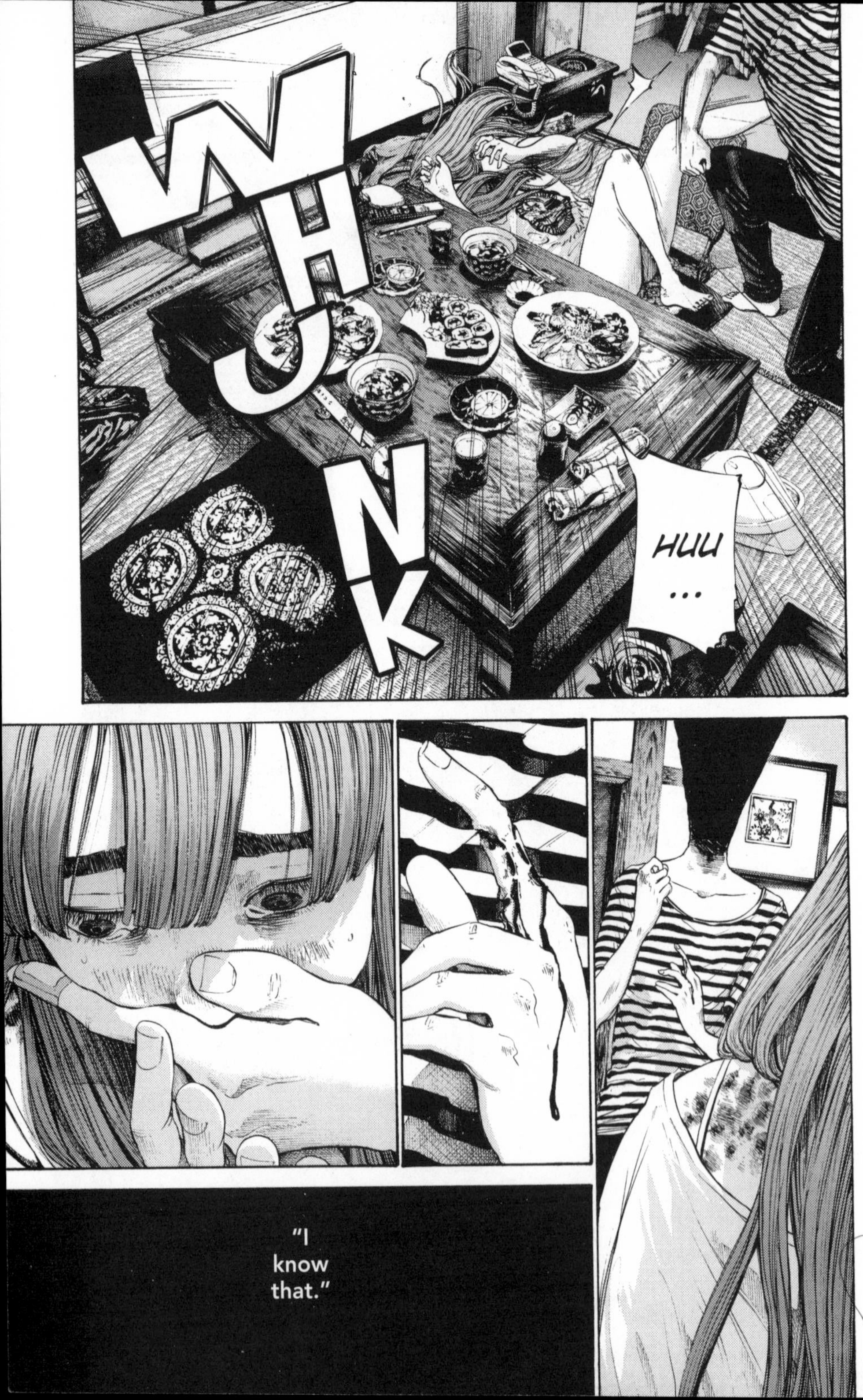
WHUNK
HUU...
"I know that."

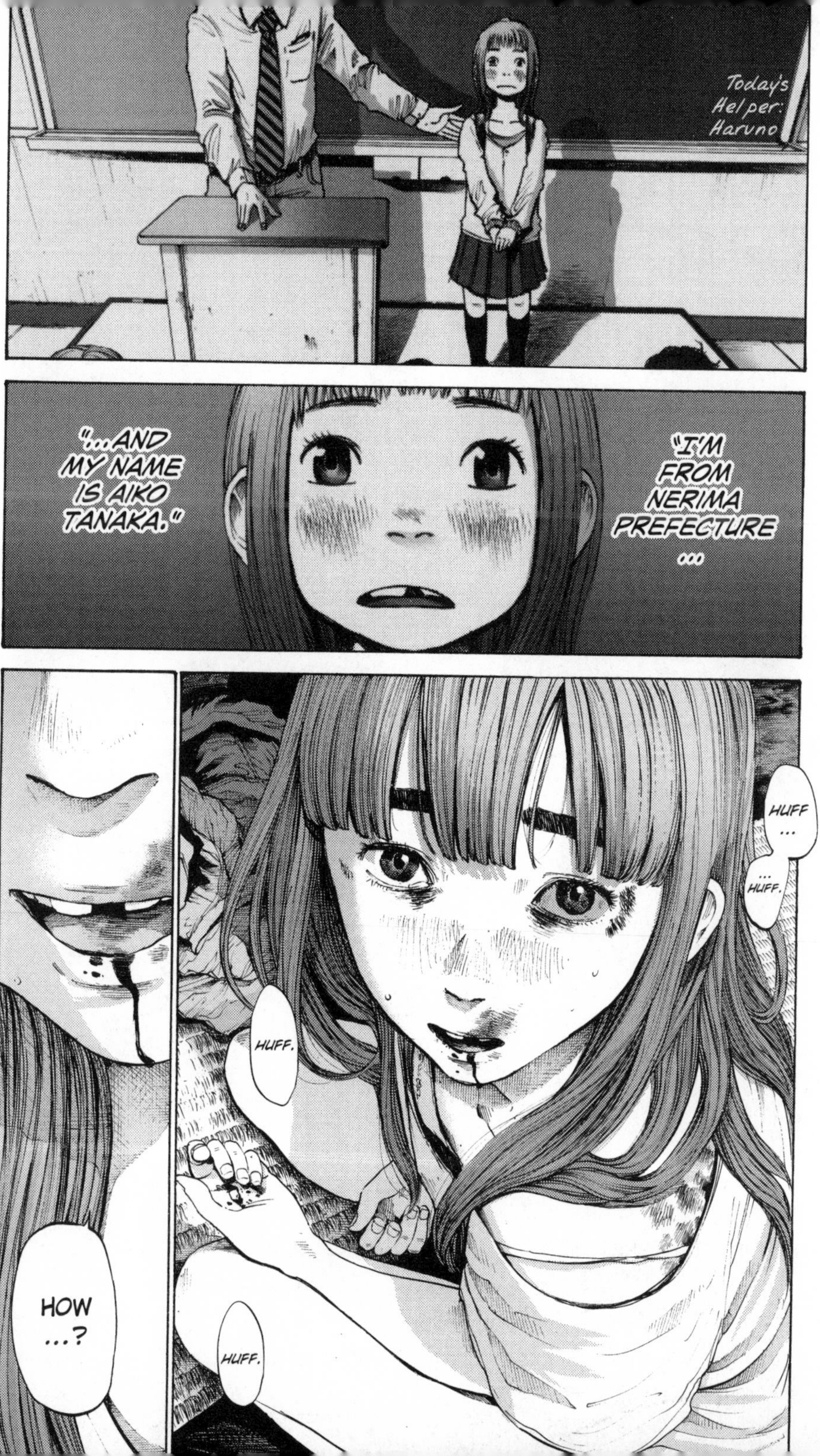
Today's Helper: Haruno
"I'M FROM NERIMA PREFECTURE ...
"...AND MY NAME IS AIKO TANAKA."
HUFF ...
... HUFF.
HUFF.
HUFF.
HOW ...?

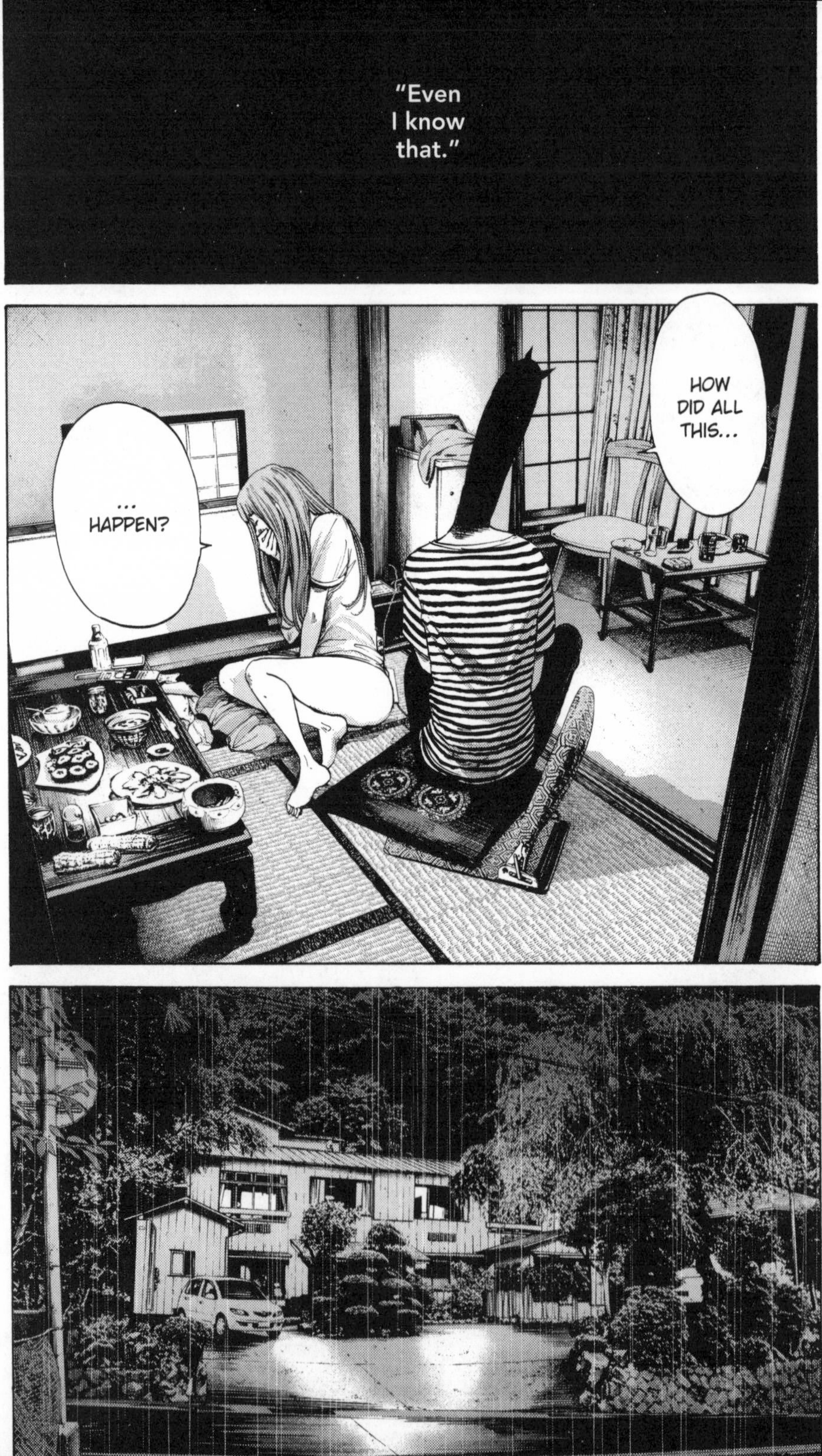
"Even I know that."
HOW DID ALL THIS...
... HAPPEN?

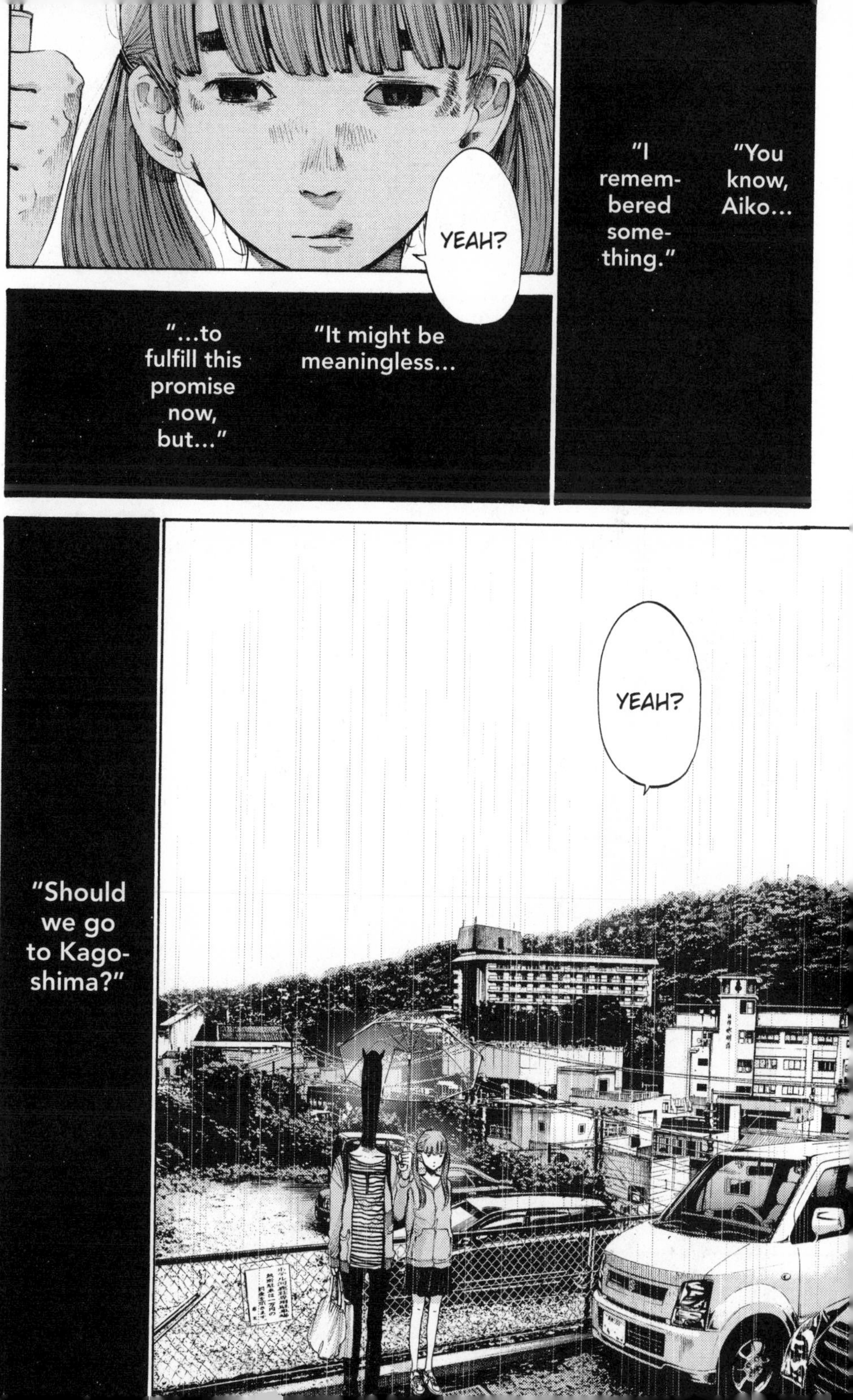
"You know, Aiko...
"I remembered something."
YEAH?
"It might be meaningless...
"...to fulfill this promise now, but..."
YEAH?
"Should we go to Kagoshima?"

Chapter 118

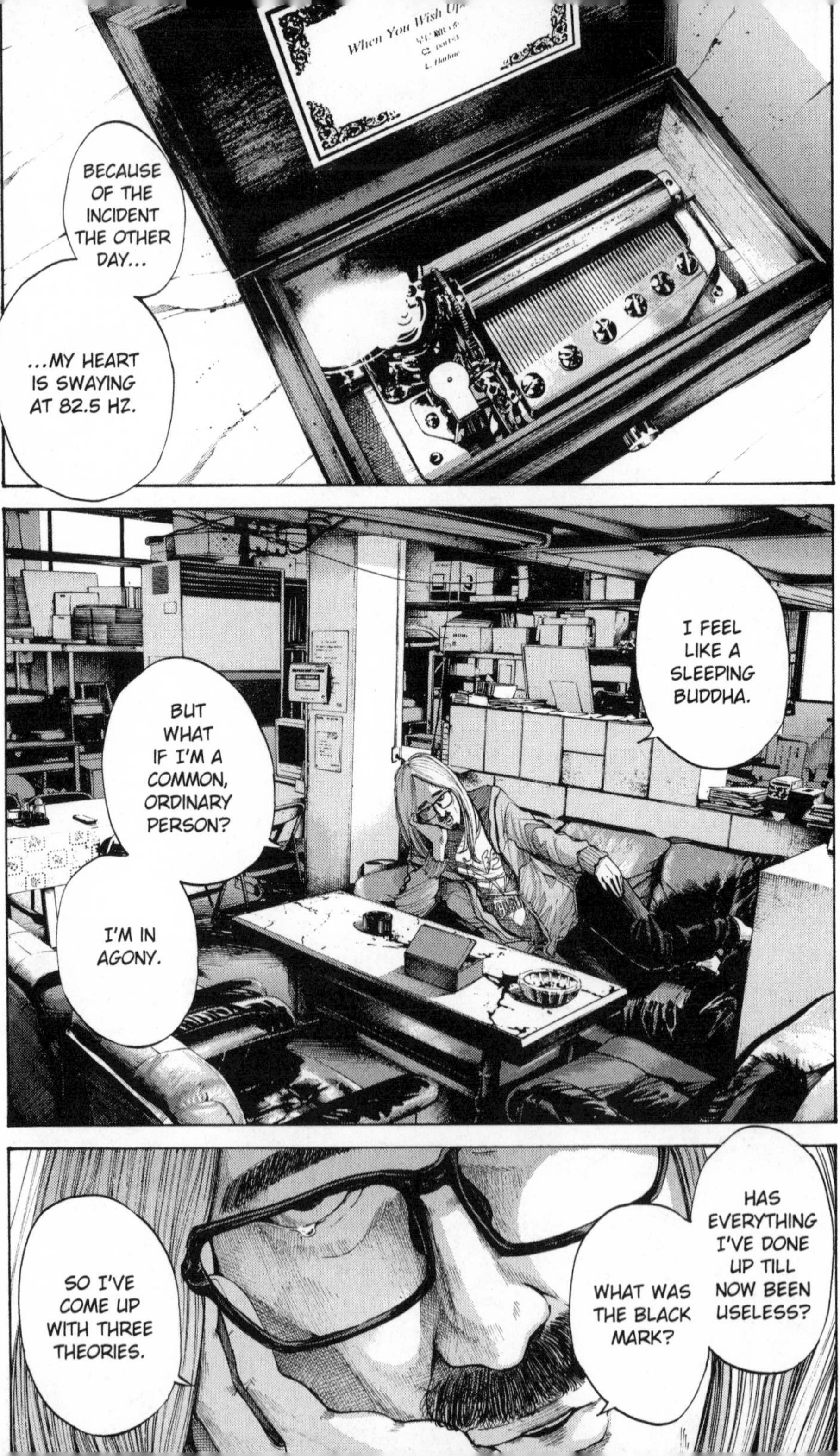

BECAUSE OF THE INCIDENT THE OTHER DAY...
...MY HEART IS SWAYING AT 82.5 HZ.
I FEEL LIKE A SLEEPING BUDDHA.
BUT WHAT IF I'M A COMMON, ORDINARY PERSON?
I'M IN AGONY.
HAS EVERYTHING I'VE DONE UP TILL NOW BEEN USELESS?
WHAT WAS THE BLACK MARK?
SO I'VE COME UP WITH THREE THEORIES.

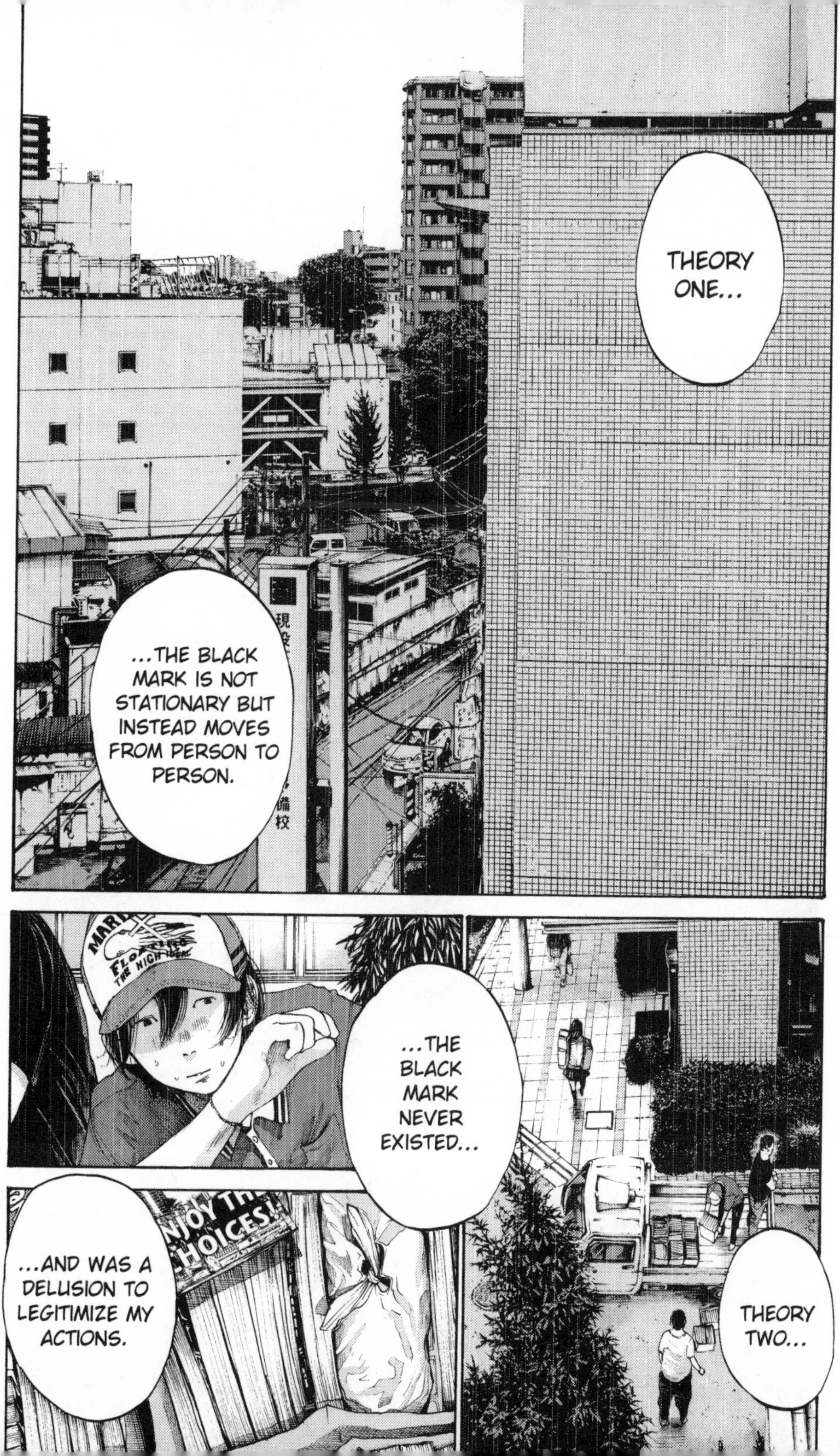
THEORY ONE...
...THE BLACK MARK IS NOT STATIONARY BUT INSTEAD MOVES FROM PERSON TO PERSON.
THEORY TWO...
...THE BLACK MARK NEVER EXISTED...
...AND WAS A DELUSION TO LEGITIMIZE MY ACTIONS.

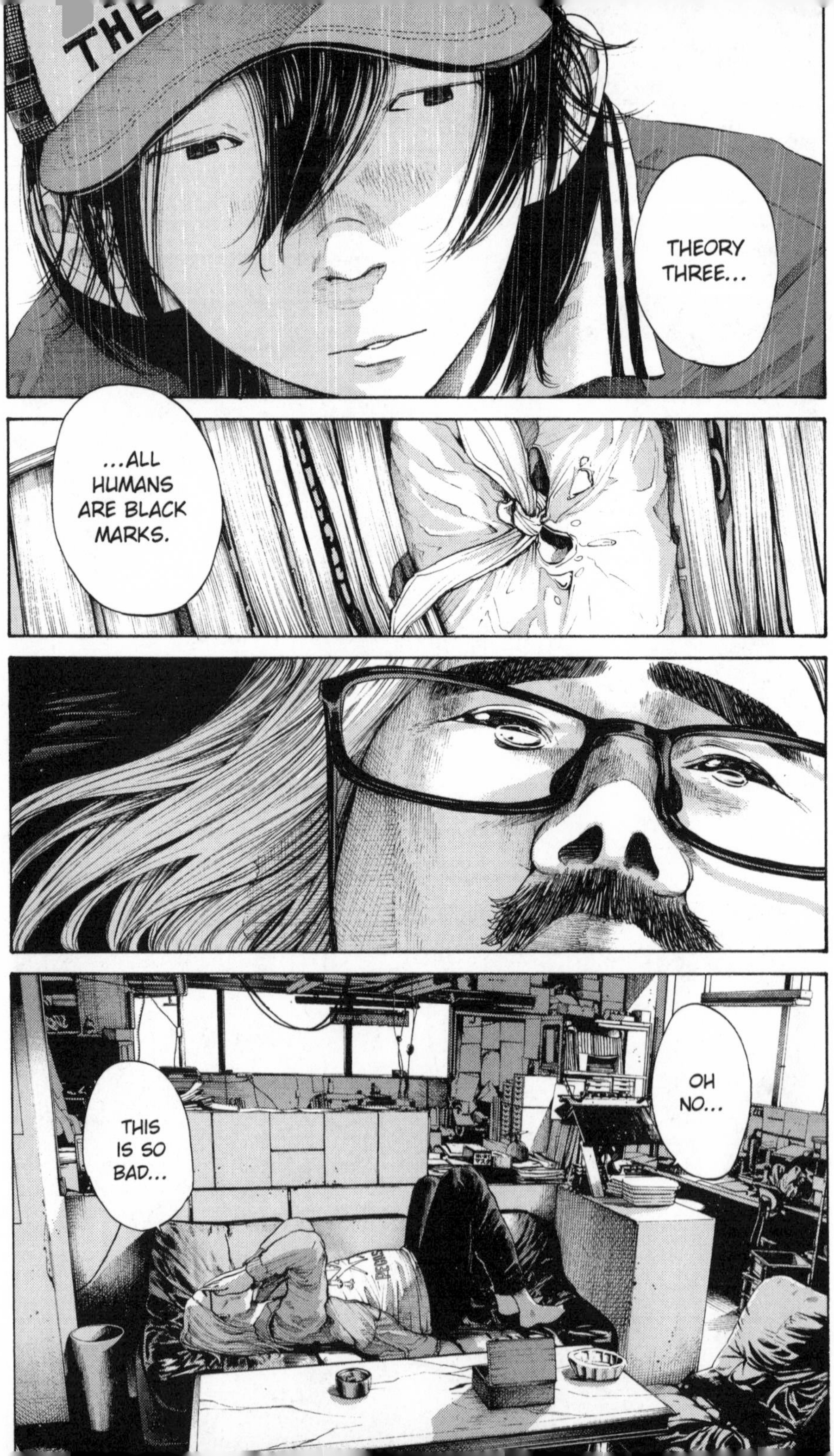
THEORY THREE...
...ALL HUMANS ARE BLACK MARKS.
OH NO...
THIS IS SO BAD...

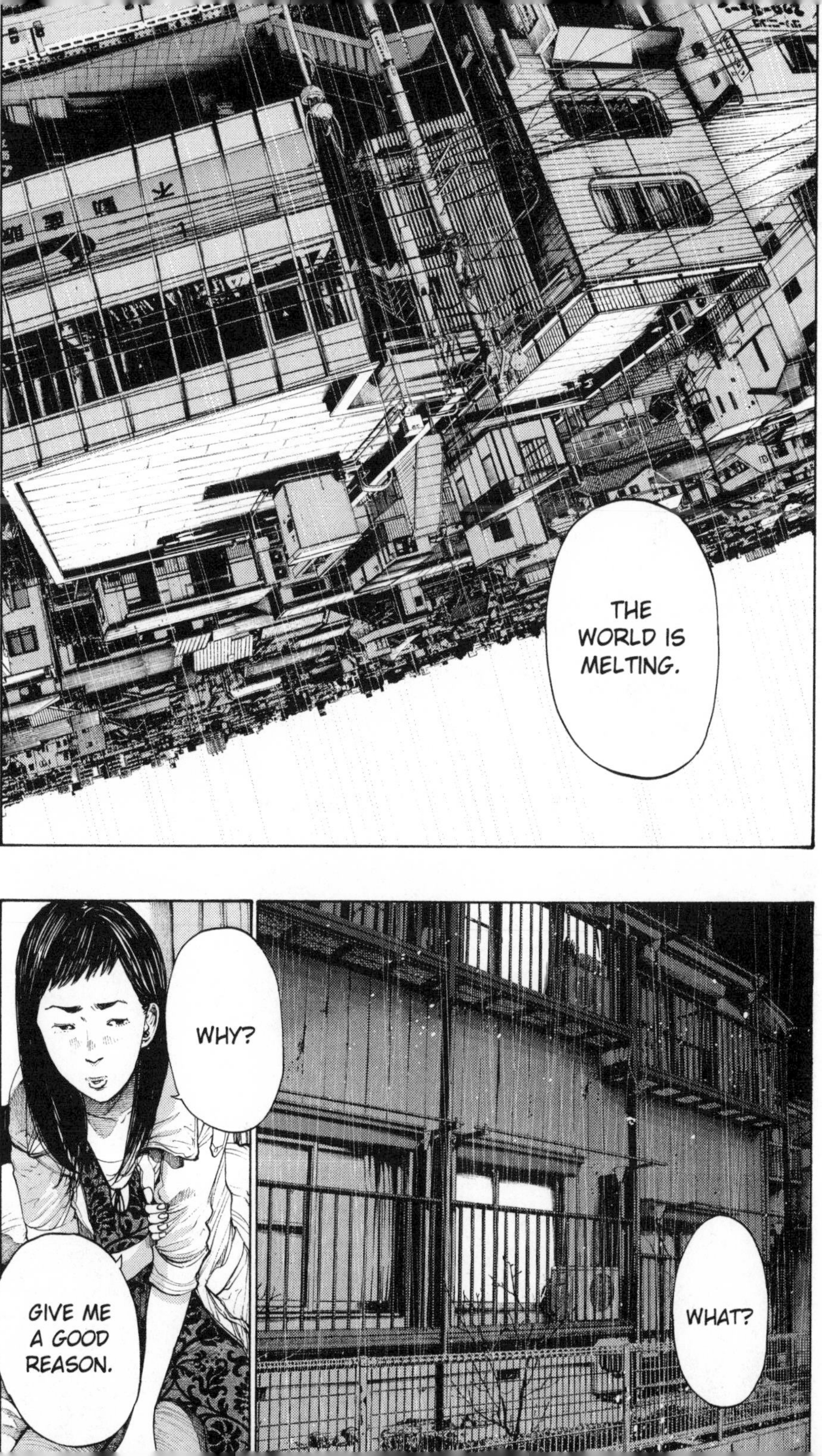
THE WORLD IS MELTING.
WHAT?
WHY?
GIVE ME A GOOD REASON.

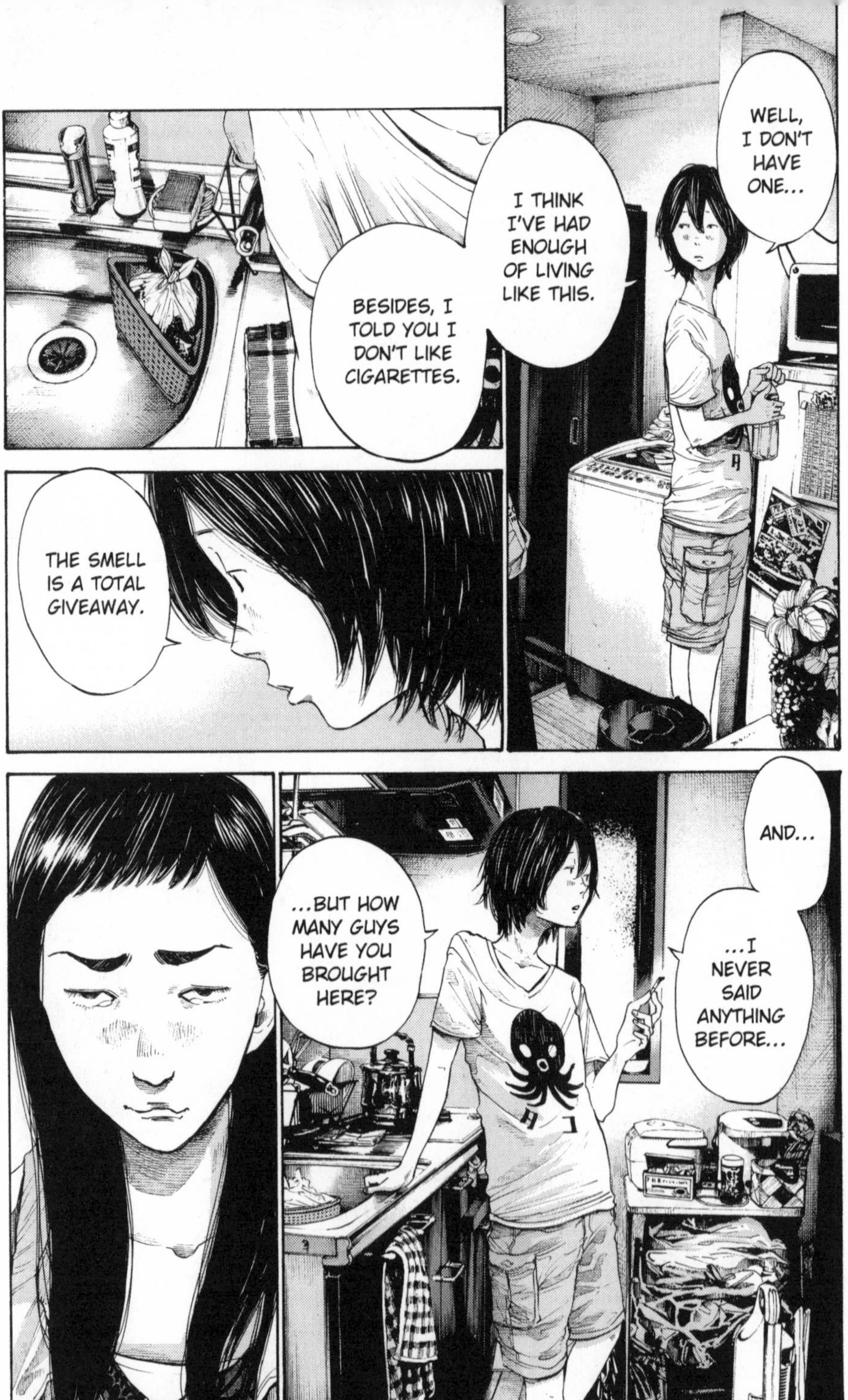
WELL, I DON'T HAVE ONE...
I THINK I'VE HAD ENOUGH OF LIVING LIKE THIS.
BESIDES, I TOLD YOU I DON'T LIKE CIGARETTES.
THE SMELL IS A TOTAL GIVEAWAY.
AND...
...I NEVER SAID ANYTHING BEFORE...
...BUT HOW MANY GUYS HAVE YOU BROUGHT HERE?

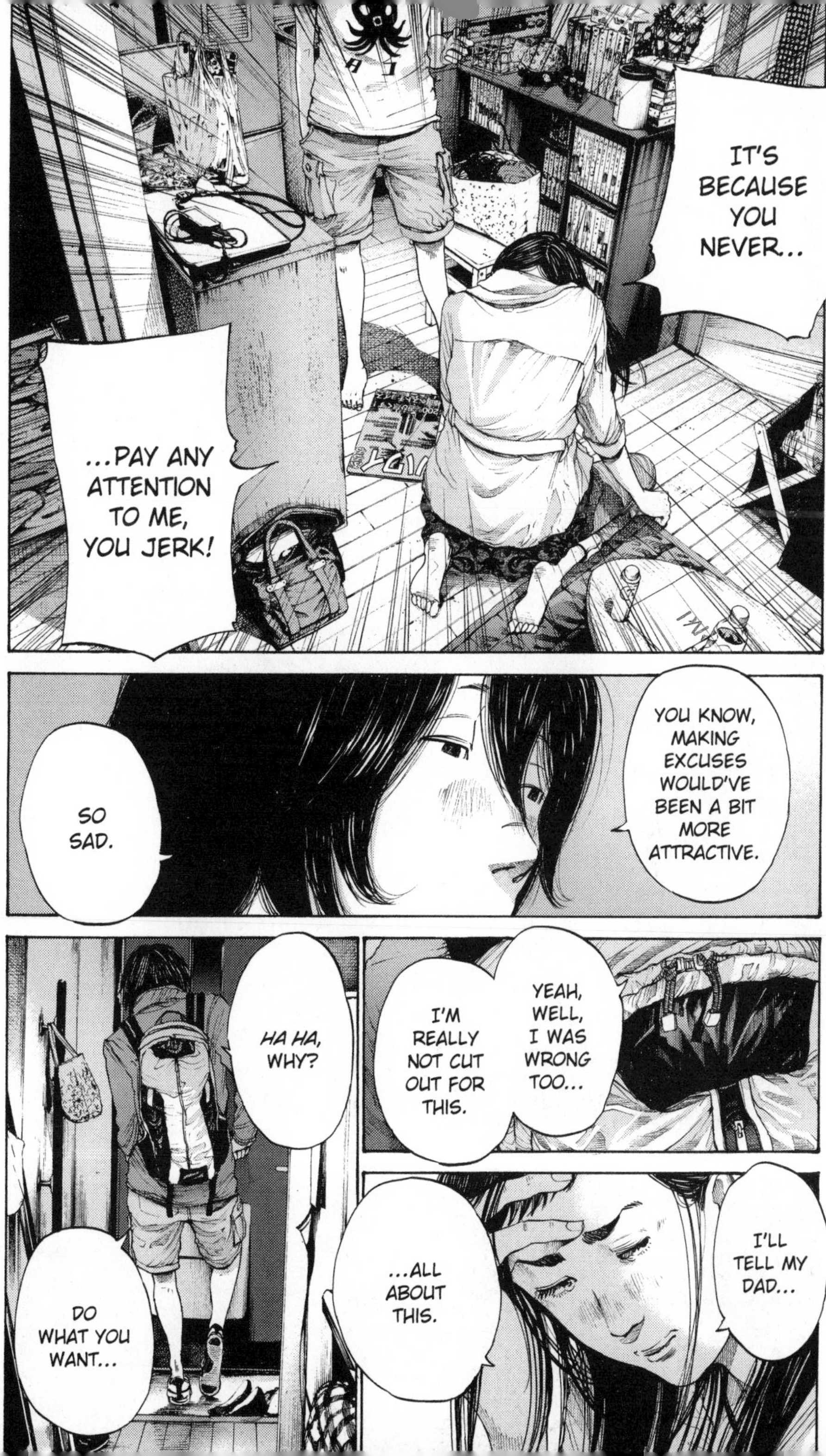
IT'S BECAUSE YOU NEVER...
...PAY ANY ATTENTION TO ME, YOU JERK!
YOU KNOW, MAKING EXCUSES WOULD'VE BEEN A BIT MORE ATTRACTIVE.
SO SAD.
YEAH, WELL, I WAS WRONG TOO...
I'M REALLY NOT CUT OUT FOR THIS.
I'LL TELL MY DAD...
...ALL ABOUT THIS.
HA HA, WHY?
DO WHAT YOU WANT...

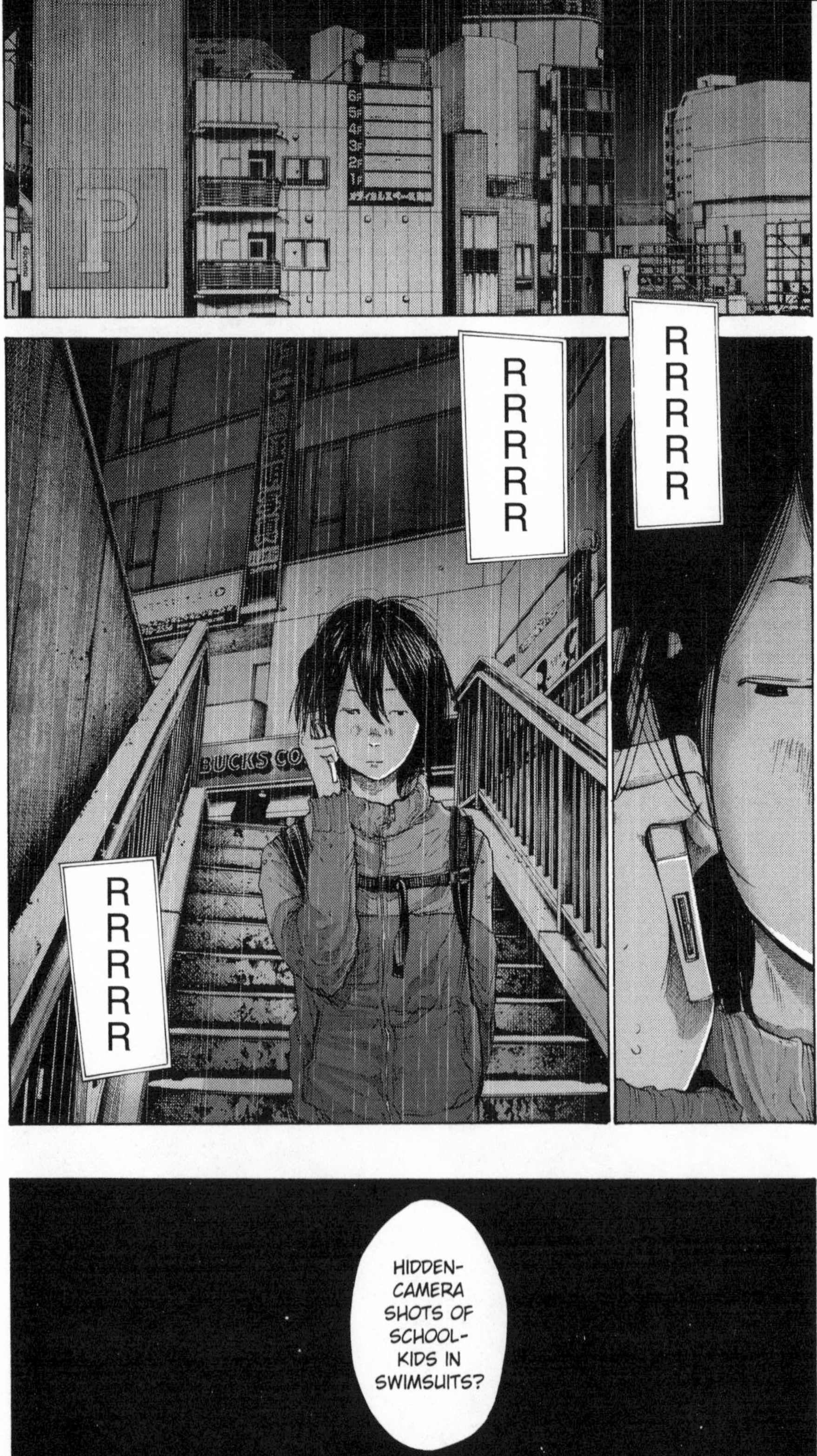
RRRRR
RRRRR
RRRRR
HIDDEN-CAMERA SHOTS OF SCHOOL-KIDS IN SWIMSUITS?

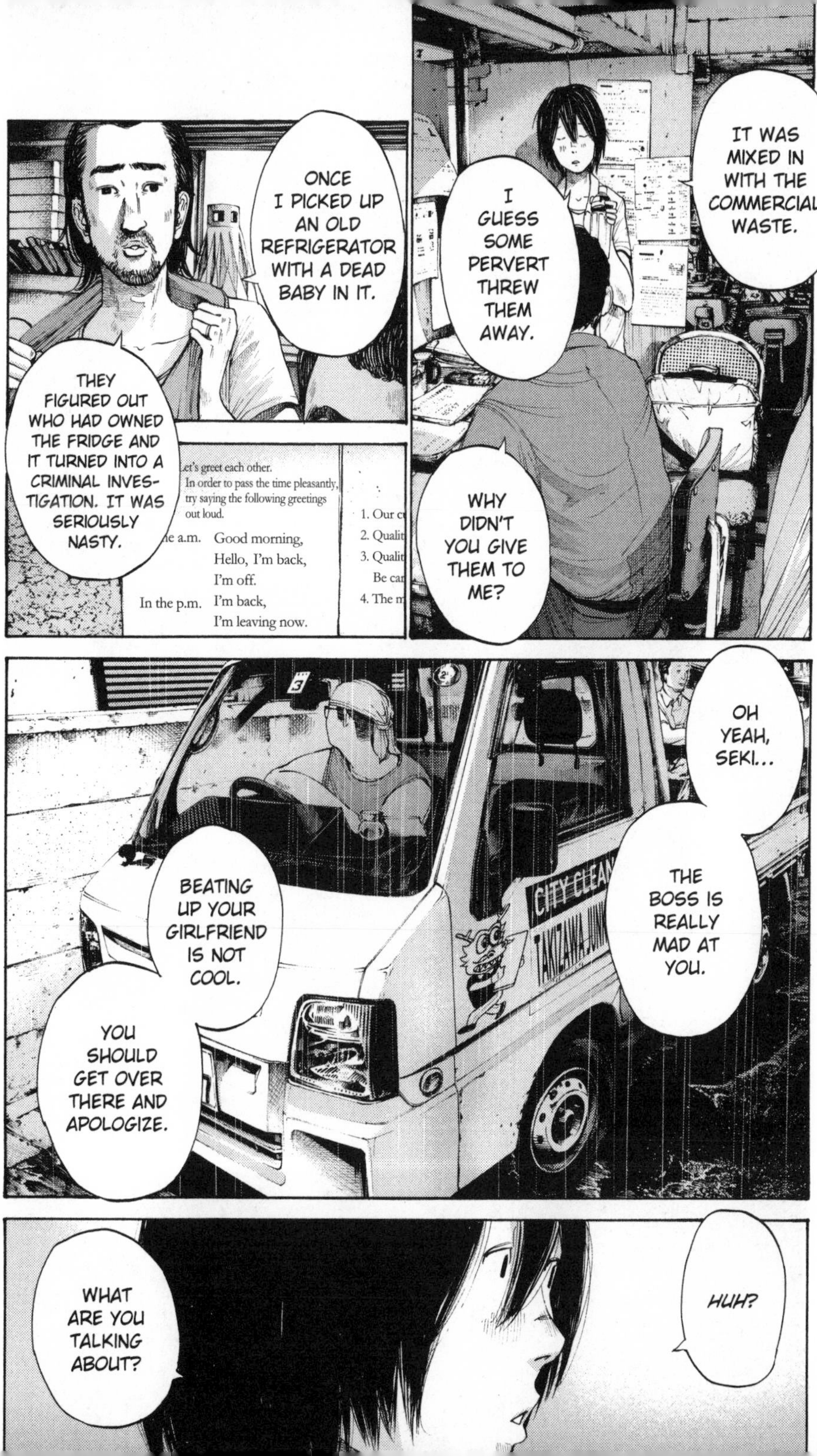
IT WAS MIXED IN WITH THE COMMERCIAL WASTE.
I GUESS SOME PERVERT THREW THEM AWAY.
WHY DIDN'T YOU GIVE THEM TO ME?
ONCE I PICKED UP AN OLD REFRIGERATOR WITH A DEAD BABY IN IT.
THEY FIGURED OUT WHO HAD OWNED THE FRIDGE AND IT TURNED INTO A CRIMINAL INVESTIGATION. IT WAS SERIOUSLY NASTY.
In order to pass the time pleasantly, try saying the following greetings out loud.
Good morning, Hello, I'm back, I'm off.
In the p.m. I'm back, I'm leaving now.
OH YEAH, SEKI...
THE BOSS IS REALLY MAD AT YOU.
BEATING UP YOUR GIRLFRIEND IS NOT COOL.
YOU SHOULD GET OVER THERE AND APOLOGIZE.
HUH?
WHAT ARE YOU TALKING ABOUT?

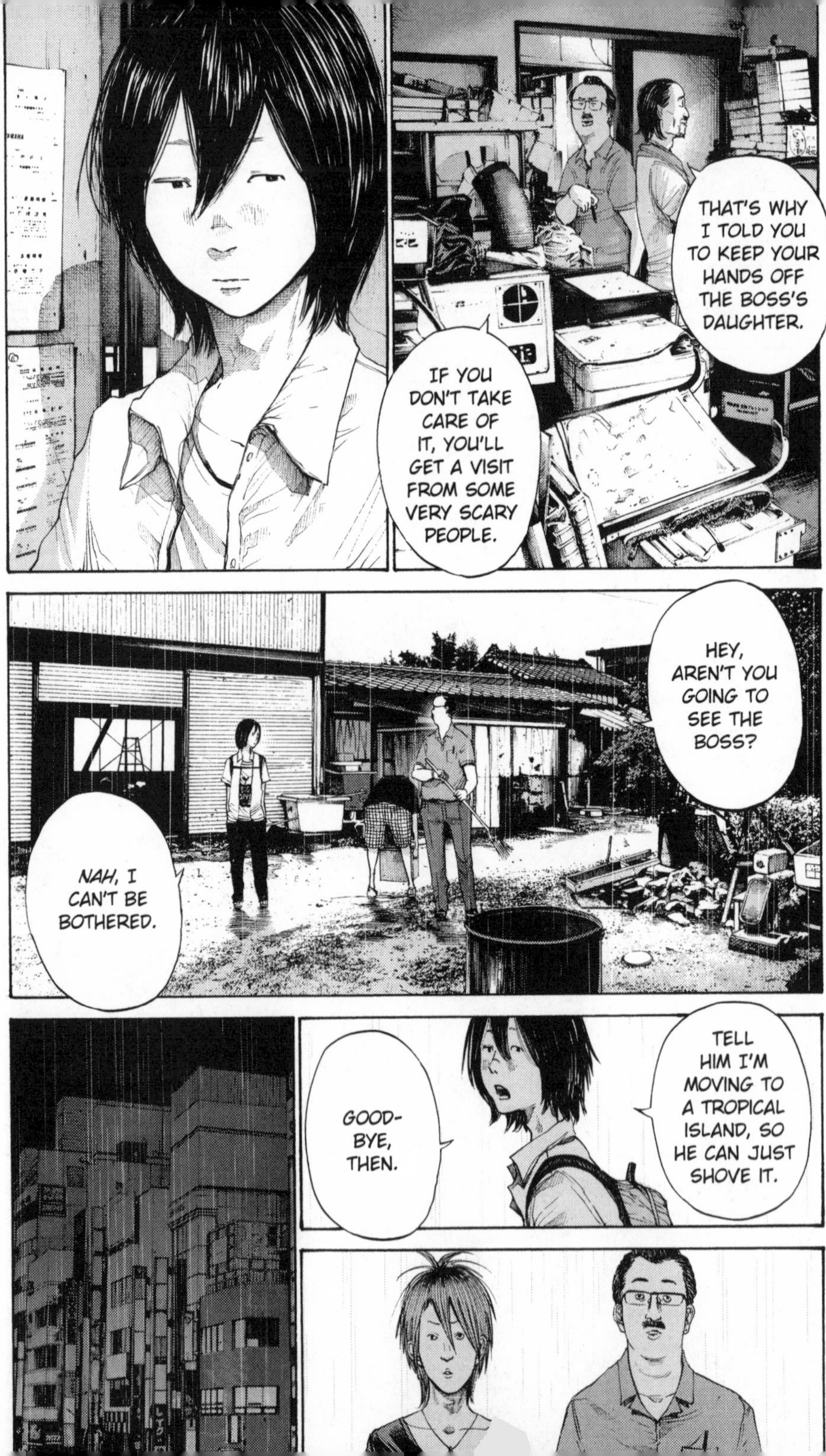
THAT'S WHY I TOLD YOU TO KEEP YOUR HANDS OFF THE BOSS'S DAUGHTER.
IF YOU DON'T TAKE CARE OF IT, YOU'LL GET A VISIT FROM SOME VERY SCARY PEOPLE.
HEY, AREN'T YOU GOING TO SEE THE BOSS?
NAH, I CAN'T BE BOTHERED.
TELL HIM I'M MOVING TO A TROPICAL ISLAND, SO HE CAN JUST SHOVE IT.
GOOD-BYE, THEN.

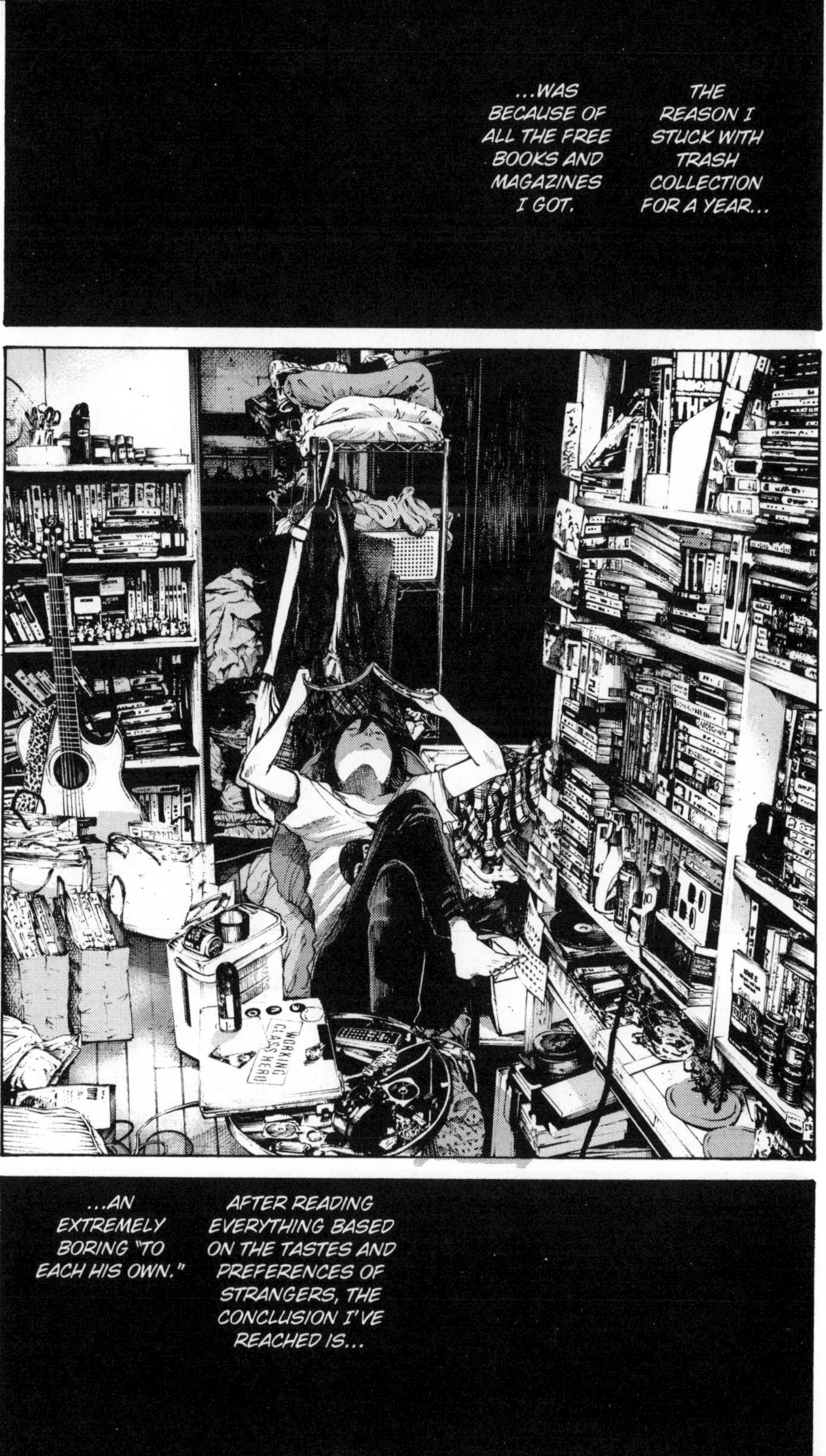
THE REASON I STUCK WITH TRASH COLLECTION FOR A YEAR...
...WAS BECAUSE OF ALL THE FREE BOOKS AND MAGAZINES I GOT.
WORKING CLASS HERO
AFTER READING EVERYTHING BASED ON THE TASTES AND PREFERENCES OF STRANGERS, THE CONCLUSION I'VE REACHED IS...
...AN EXTREMELY BORING "TO EACH HIS OWN."

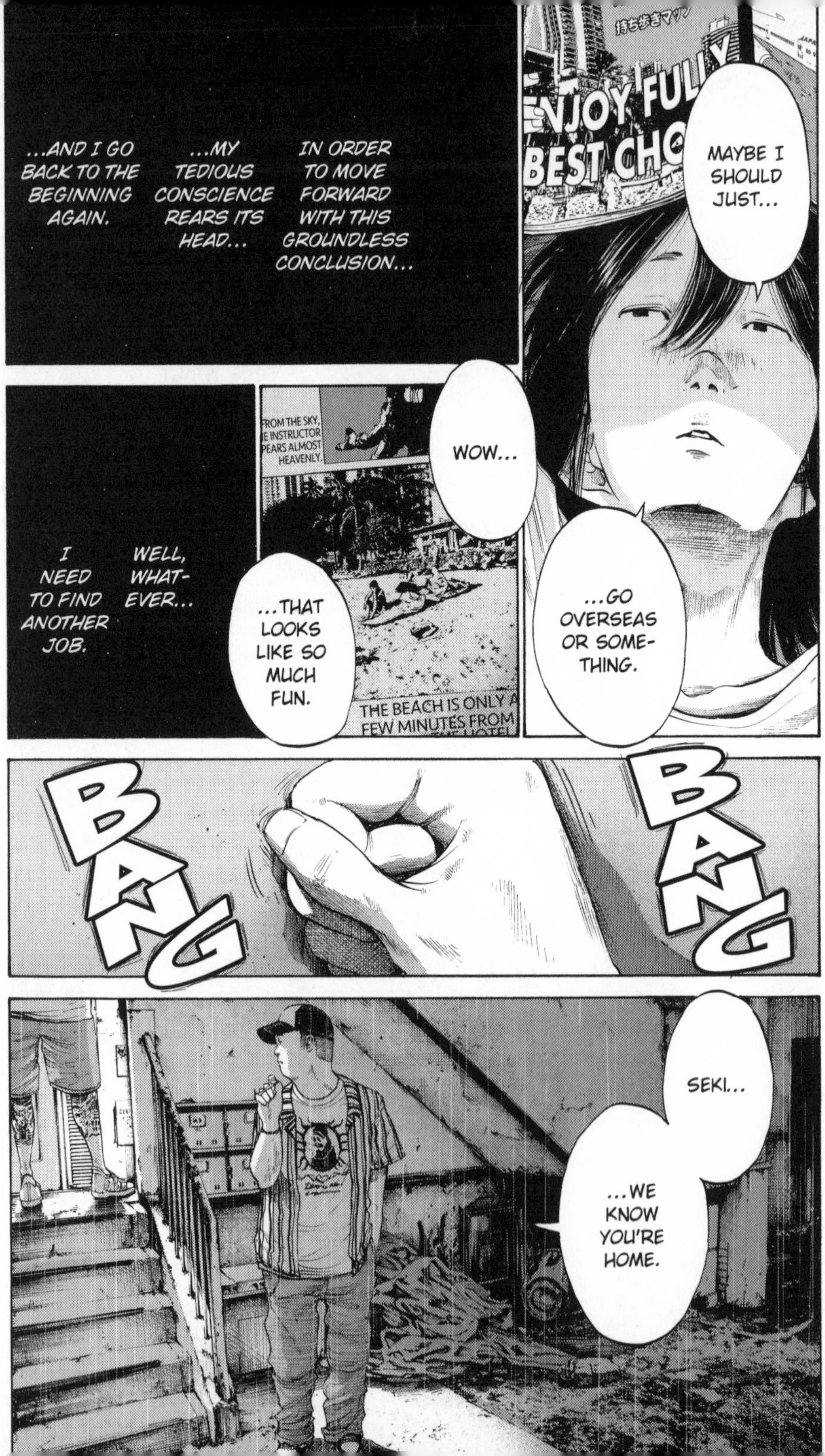
持ち歩きマップ
MAYBE I SHOULD JUST...
...GO OVERSEAS OR SOME-THING.
IN ORDER TO MOVE FORWARD WITH THIS GROUNDLESS CONCLUSION...
...MY TEDIOUS CONSCIENCE REARS ITS HEAD...
...AND I GO BACK TO THE BEGINNING AGAIN.
FROM THE SKY,
HEAVENLY.
WOW...
...THAT LOOKS LIKE SO MUCH FUN.
THE BEACH IS ONLY A
WELL, WHAT-EVER...
I NEED TO FIND ANOTHER JOB.
BANG
BANG
SEKI...
...WE KNOW YOU'RE HOME.

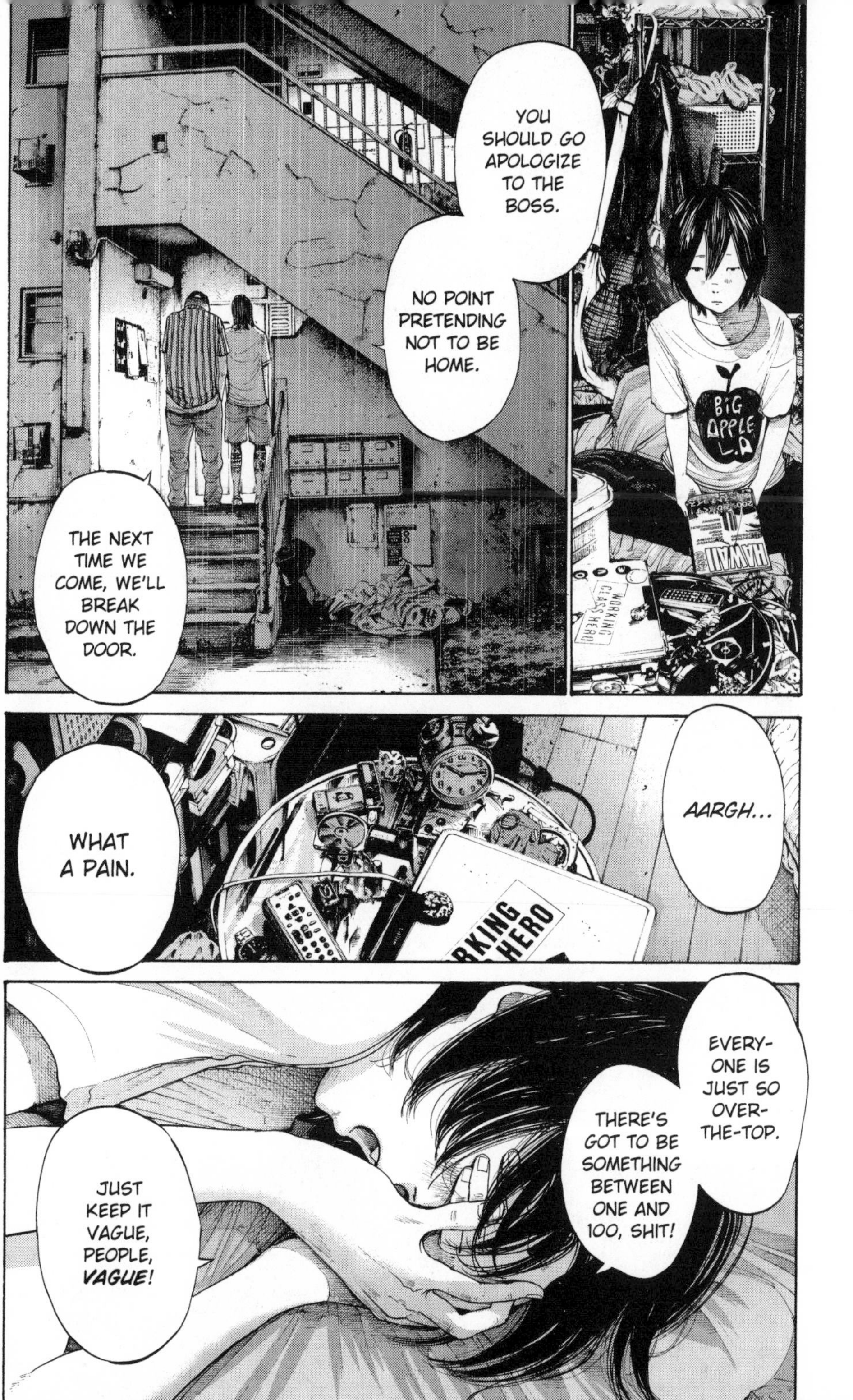
BIG APPLE L.A
HAWAII
WORKING CLASS HERO
YOU SHOULD GO APOLOGIZE TO THE BOSS.
NO POINT PRETENDING NOT TO BE HOME.
THE NEXT TIME WE COME, WE'LL BREAK DOWN THE DOOR.
AARGH...
WHAT A PAIN.
WORKING HERO
EVERY-ONE IS JUST SO OVER-THE-TOP.
THERE'S GOT TO BE SOMETHING BETWEEN ONE AND 100, SHIT!
JUST KEEP IT VAGUE, PEOPLE, *VAGUE*!

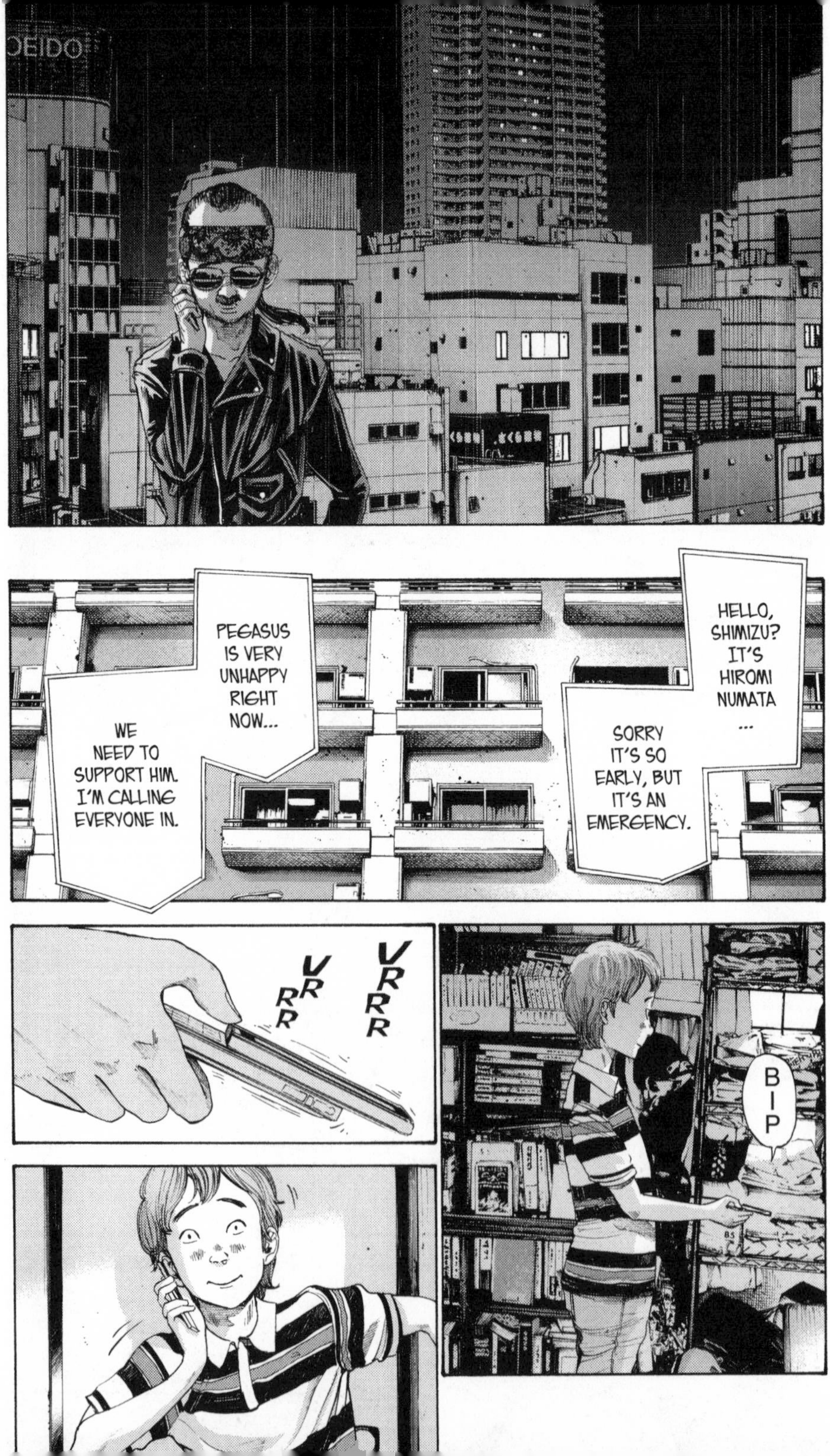
HELLO, SHIMIZU? IT'S HIROMI NUMATA ...
SORRY IT'S SO EARLY, BUT IT'S AN EMERGENCY.
PEGASUS IS VERY UNHAPPY RIGHT NOW...
WE NEED TO SUPPORT HIM. I'M CALLING EVERYONE IN.
BIP
VRRR
VRRR

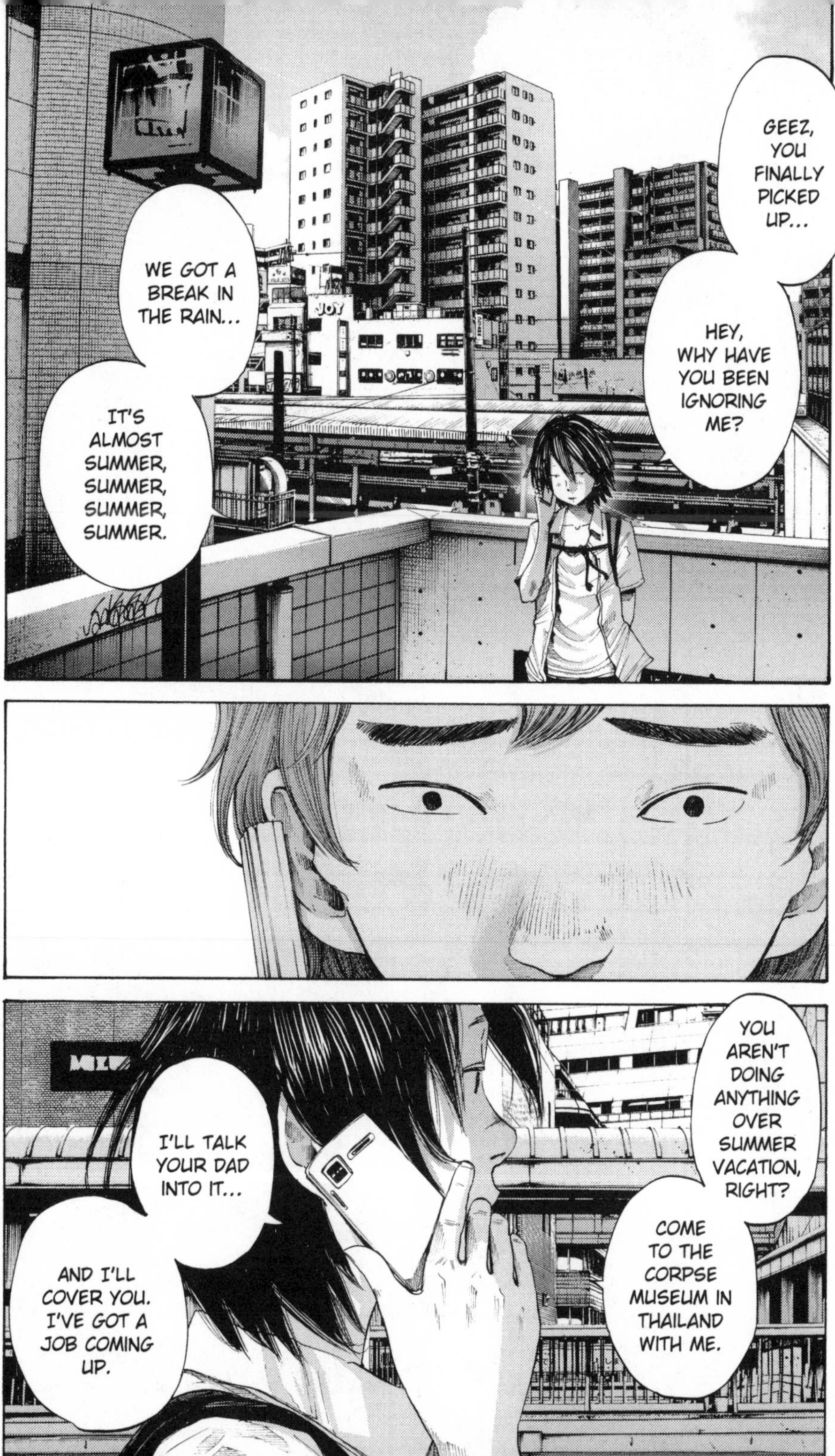
GEEZ, YOU FINALLY PICKED UP...
HEY, WHY HAVE YOU BEEN IGNORING ME?
WE GOT A BREAK IN THE RAIN...
IT'S ALMOST SUMMER, SUMMER, SUMMER, SUMMER.
JOY
YOU AREN'T DOING ANYTHING OVER SUMMER VACATION, RIGHT?
COME TO THE CORPSE MUSEUM IN THAILAND WITH ME.
I'LL TALK YOUR DAD INTO IT...
AND I'LL COVER YOU. I'VE GOT A JOB COMING UP.

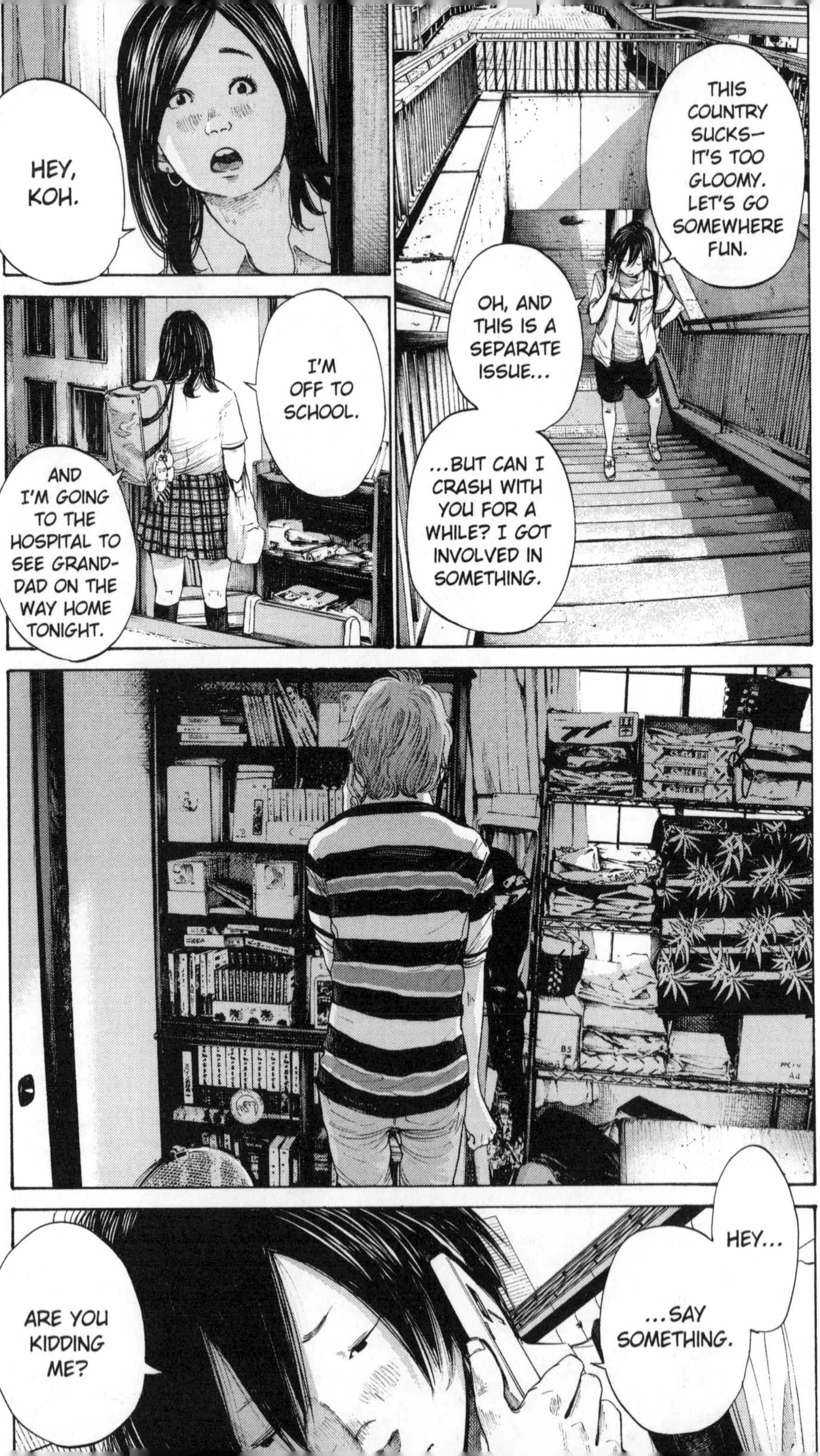

THIS COUNTRY SUCKS— IT'S TOO GLOOMY. LET'S GO SOMEWHERE FUN.
OH, AND THIS IS A SEPARATE ISSUE...
...BUT CAN I CRASH WITH YOU FOR A WHILE? I GOT INVOLVED IN SOMETHING.
HEY, KOH.
I'M OFF TO SCHOOL.
AND I'M GOING TO THE HOSPITAL TO SEE GRAND-DAD ON THE WAY HOME TONIGHT.
HEY...
...SAY SOMETHING.
ARE YOU KIDDING ME?

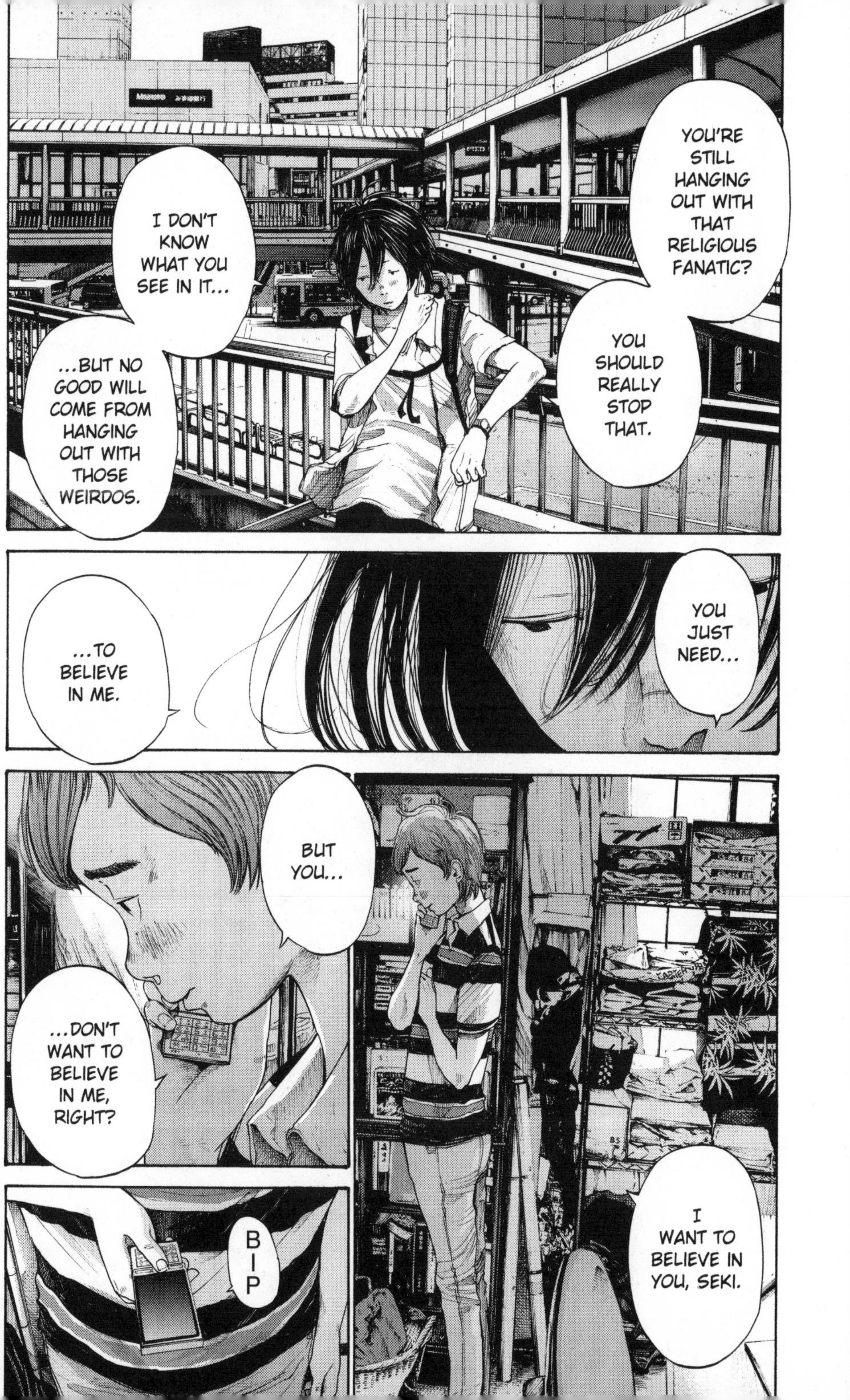
YOU'RE STILL HANGING OUT WITH THAT RELIGIOUS FANATIC?
YOU SHOULD REALLY STOP THAT.
I DON'T KNOW WHAT YOU SEE IN IT...
...BUT NO GOOD WILL COME FROM HANGING OUT WITH THOSE WEIRDOS.
YOU JUST NEED...
...TO BELIEVE IN ME.
BUT YOU...
...DON'T WANT TO BELIEVE IN ME, RIGHT?
I WANT TO BELIEVE IN YOU, SEKI.
BIP

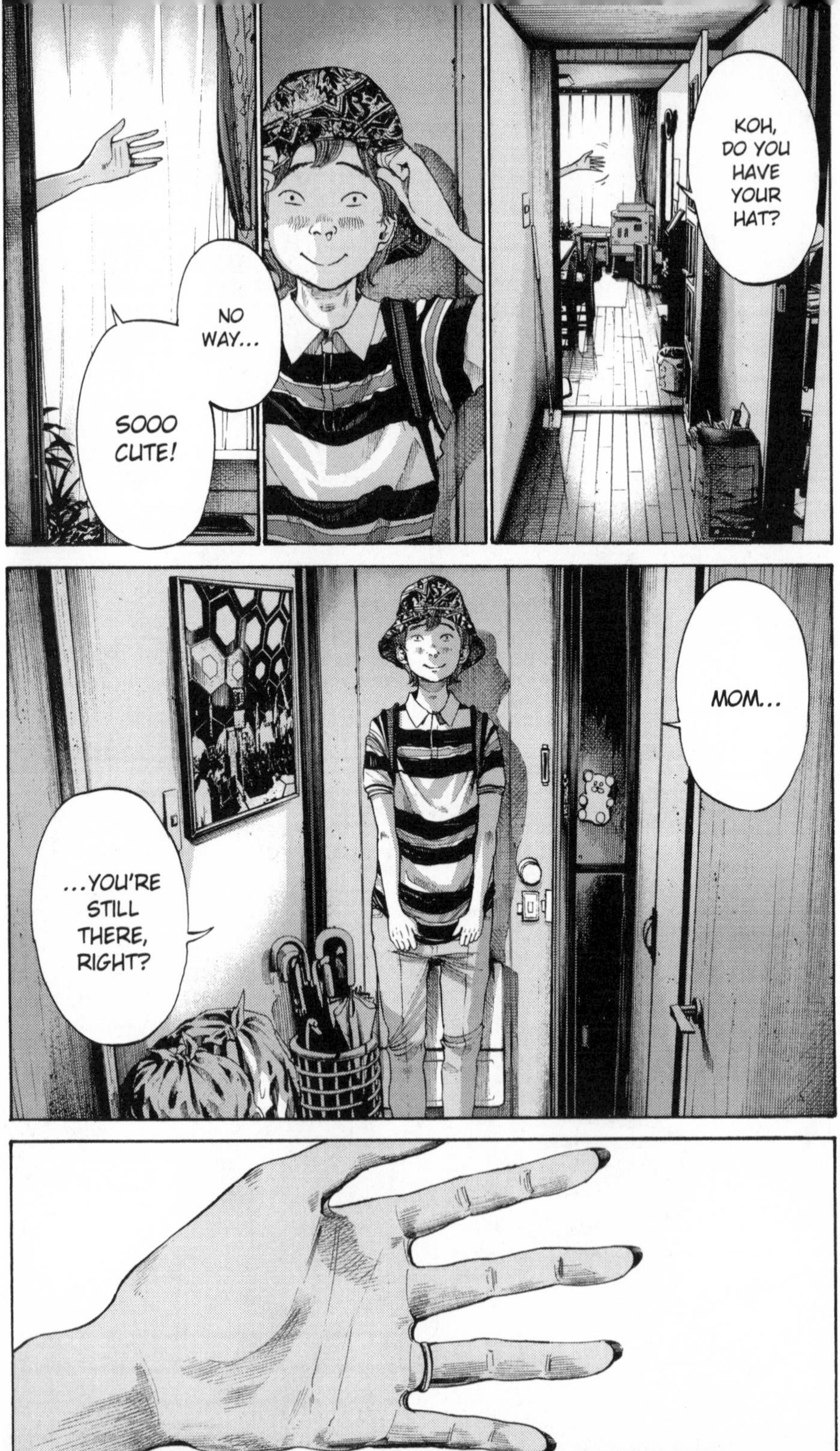
KOH, DO YOU HAVE YOUR HAT?
NO WAY...
SOOO CUTE!
MOM...
...YOU'RE STILL THERE, RIGHT?

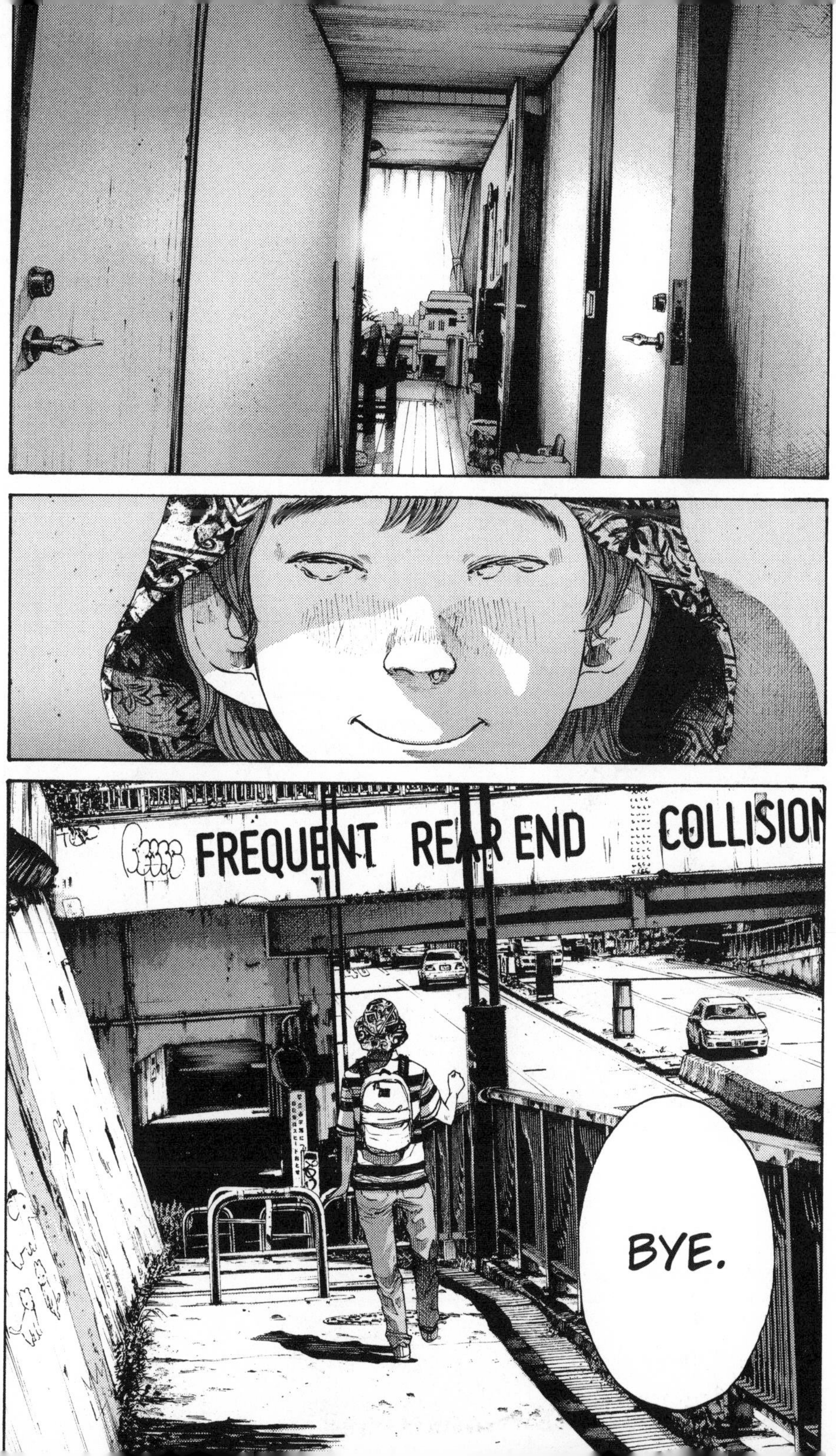
FREQUENT REAR END COLLISION
BYE.

Chapter 119

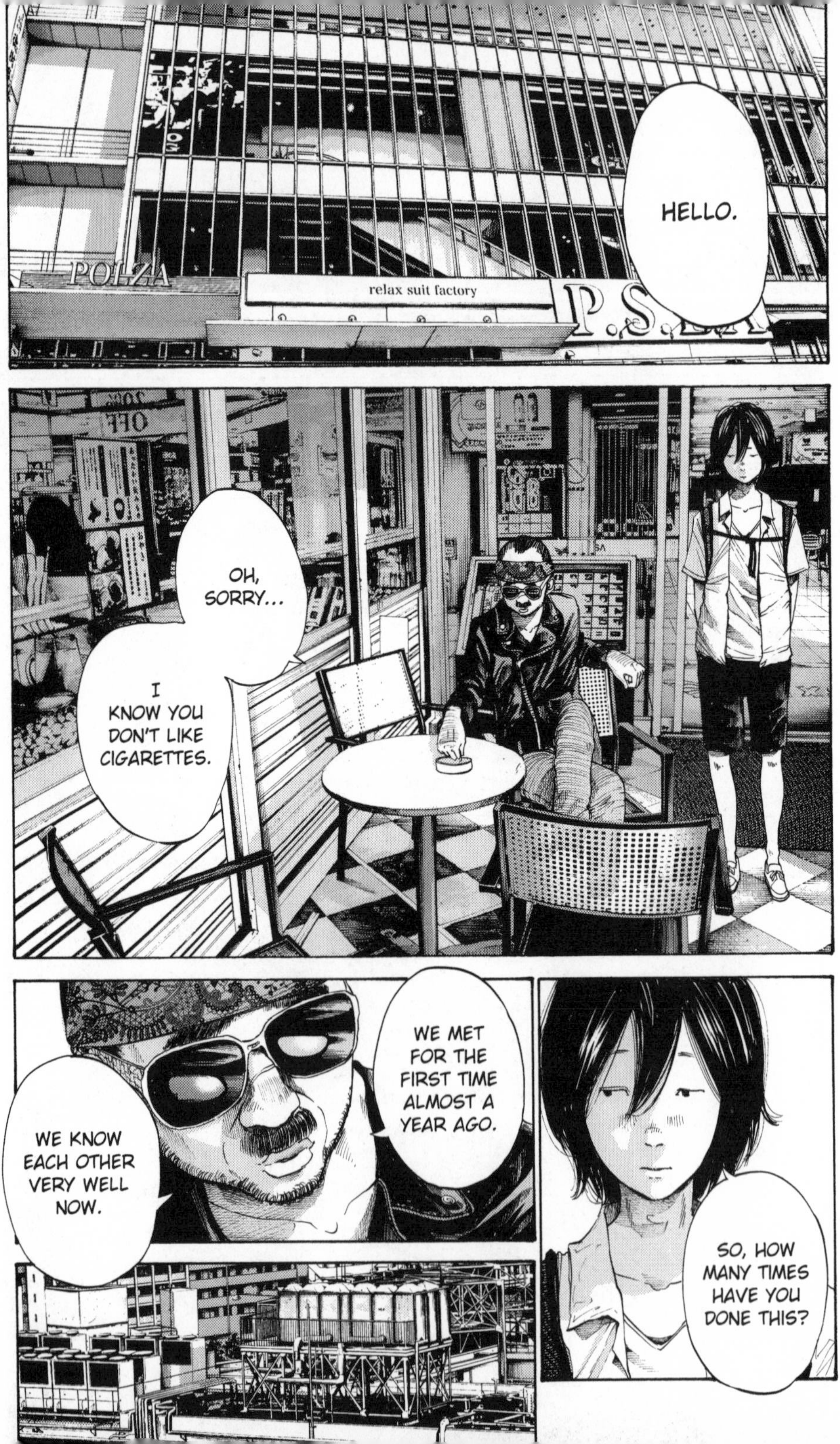
POLZA
relax suit factory
HELLO.
OH, SORRY...
I KNOW YOU DON'T LIKE CIGARETTES.
SO, HOW MANY TIMES HAVE YOU DONE THIS?
WE MET FOR THE FIRST TIME ALMOST A YEAR AGO.
WE KNOW EACH OTHER VERY WELL NOW.

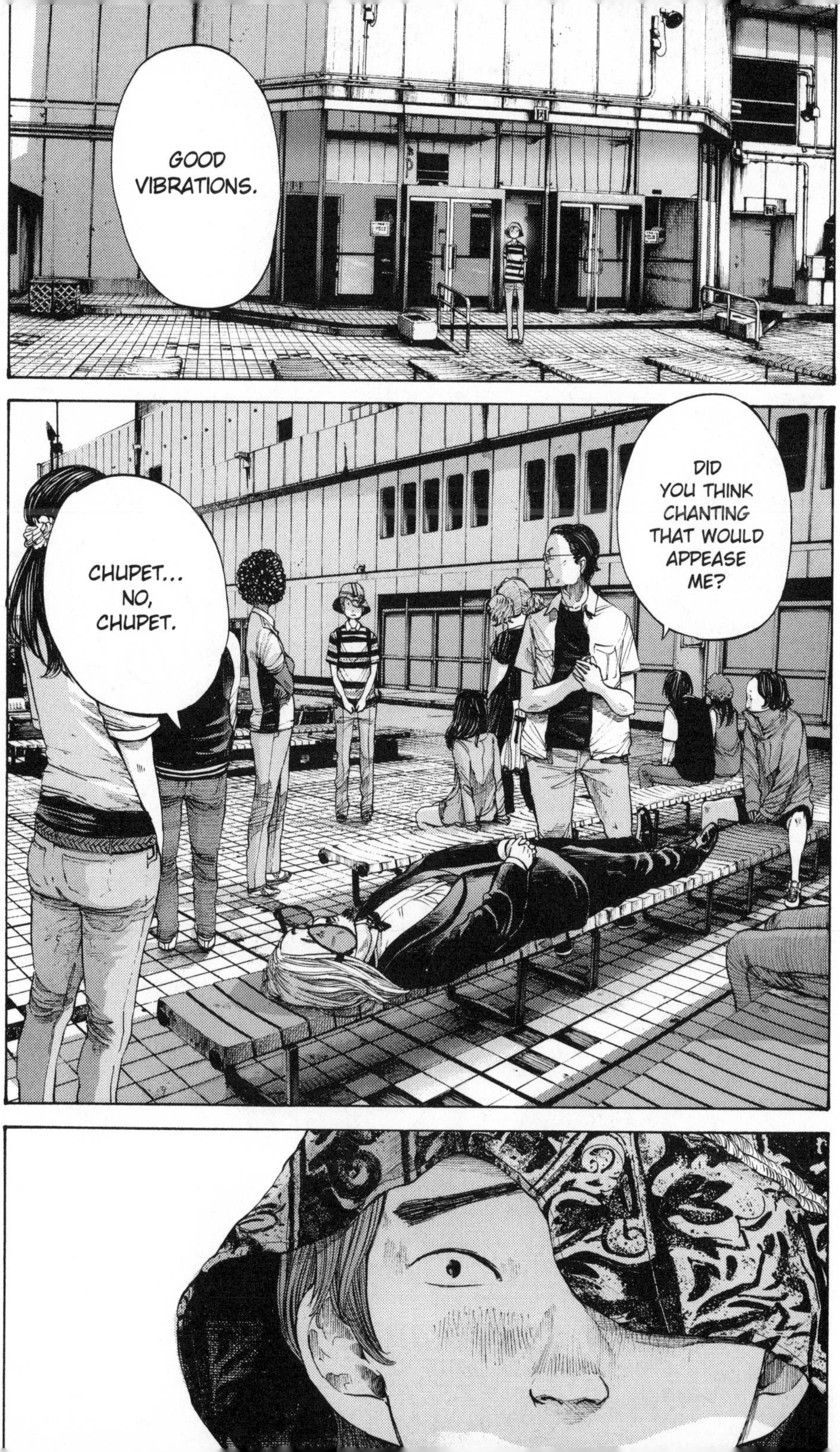
GOOD VIBRATIONS.
DID YOU THINK CHANTING THAT WOULD APPEASE ME?
CHUPET… NO, CHUPET.

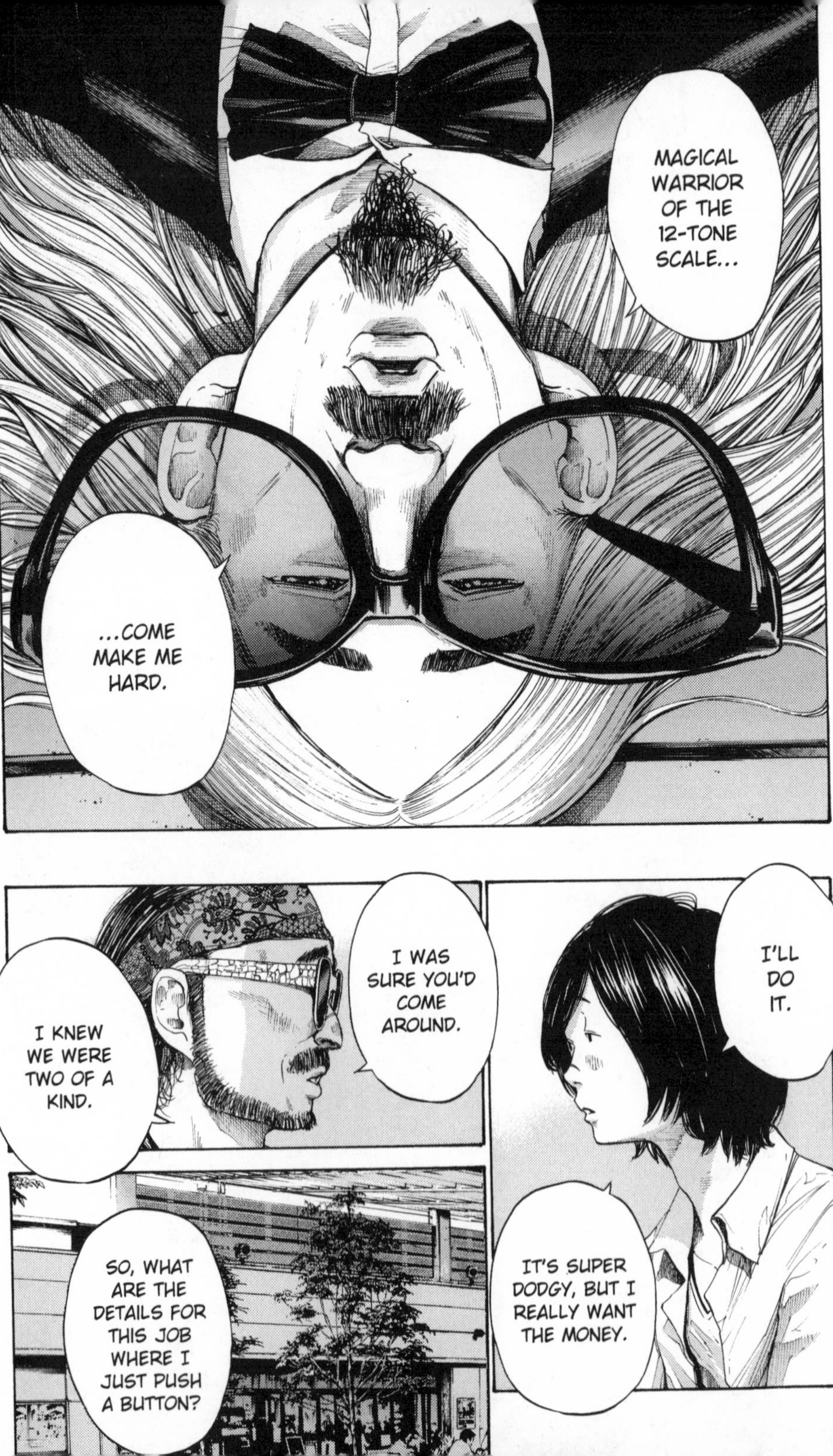
MAGICAL WARRIOR OF THE 12-TONE SCALE...
...COME MAKE ME HARD.
I'LL DO IT.
IT'S SUPER DODGY, BUT I REALLY WANT THE MONEY.
I WAS SURE YOU'D COME AROUND.
I KNEW WE WERE TWO OF A KIND.
SO, WHAT ARE THE DETAILS FOR THIS JOB WHERE I JUST PUSH A BUTTON?

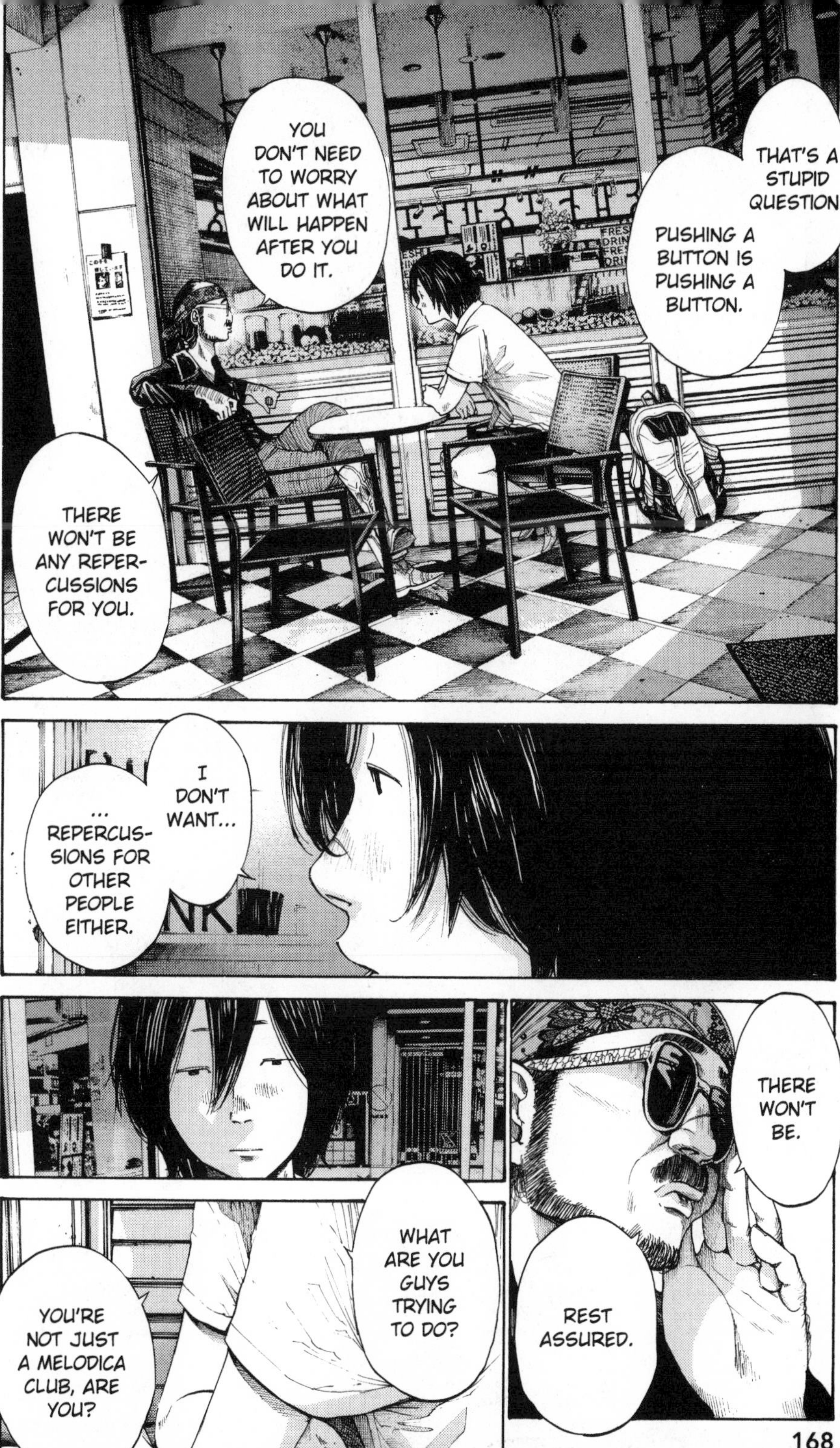
THAT'S A STUPID QUESTION.
PUSHING A BUTTON IS PUSHING A BUTTON.
YOU DON'T NEED TO WORRY ABOUT WHAT WILL HAPPEN AFTER YOU DO IT.
THERE WON'T BE ANY REPERCUSSIONS FOR YOU.
I DON'T WANT...
...REPERCUSSIONS FOR OTHER PEOPLE EITHER.
THERE WON'T BE.
REST ASSURED.
WHAT ARE YOU GUYS TRYING TO DO?
YOU'RE NOT JUST A MELODICA CLUB, ARE YOU?

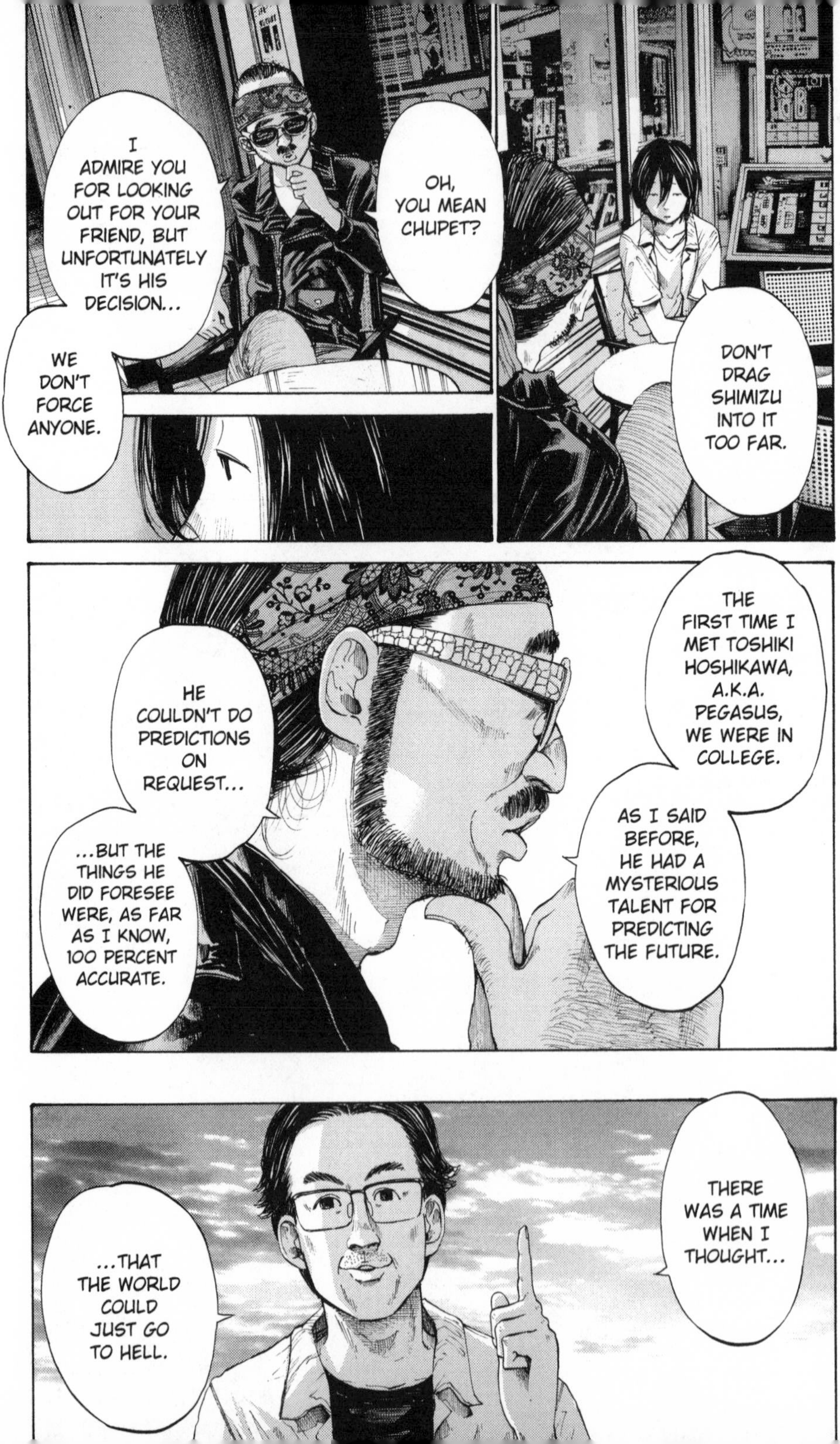
DON'T DRAG SHIMIZU INTO IT TOO FAR.
OH, YOU MEAN CHUPET?
I ADMIRE YOU FOR LOOKING OUT FOR YOUR FRIEND, BUT UNFORTUNATELY IT'S HIS DECISION...
WE DON'T FORCE ANYONE.
THE FIRST TIME I MET TOSHIKI HOSHIKAWA, A.K.A. PEGASUS, WE WERE IN COLLEGE.
AS I SAID BEFORE, HE HAD A MYSTERIOUS TALENT FOR PREDICTING THE FUTURE.
HE COULDN'T DO PREDICTIONS ON REQUEST...
...BUT THE THINGS HE DID FORESEE WERE, AS FAR AS I KNOW, 100 PERCENT ACCURATE.
THERE WAS A TIME WHEN I THOUGHT...
...THAT THE WORLD COULD JUST GO TO HELL.

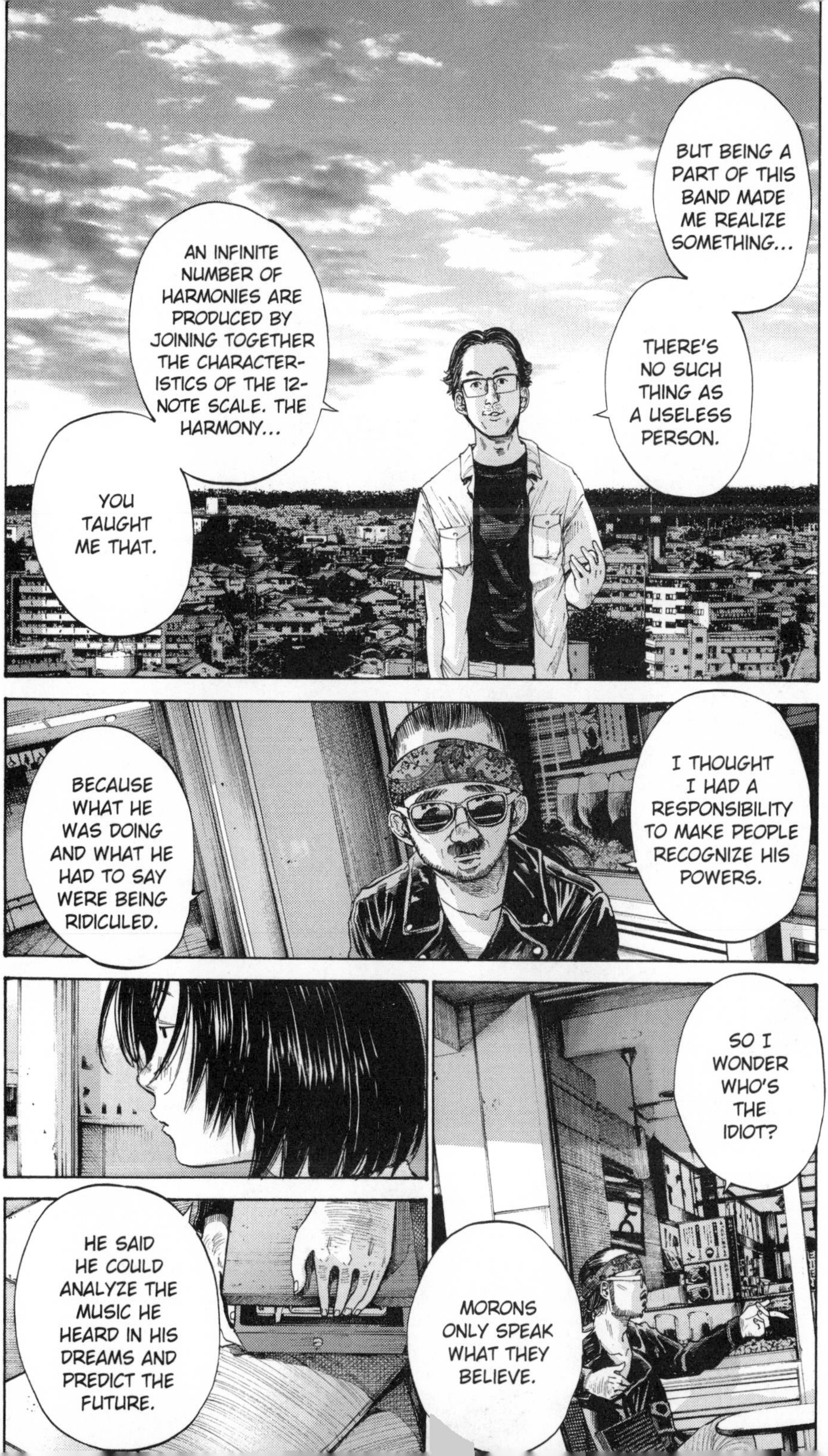
BUT BEING A PART OF THIS BAND MADE ME REALIZE SOMETHING…
THERE'S NO SUCH THING AS A USELESS PERSON.
AN INFINITE NUMBER OF HARMONIES ARE PRODUCED BY JOINING TOGETHER THE CHARACTER-ISTICS OF THE 12-NOTE SCALE. THE HARMONY…
YOU TAUGHT ME THAT.
I THOUGHT I HAD A RESPONSIBILITY TO MAKE PEOPLE RECOGNIZE HIS POWERS.
BECAUSE WHAT HE WAS DOING AND WHAT HE HAD TO SAY WERE BEING RIDICULED.
SO I WONDER WHO'S THE IDIOT?
MORONS ONLY SPEAK WHAT THEY BELIEVE.
HE SAID HE COULD ANALYZE THE MUSIC HE HEARD IN HIS DREAMS AND PREDICT THE FUTURE.

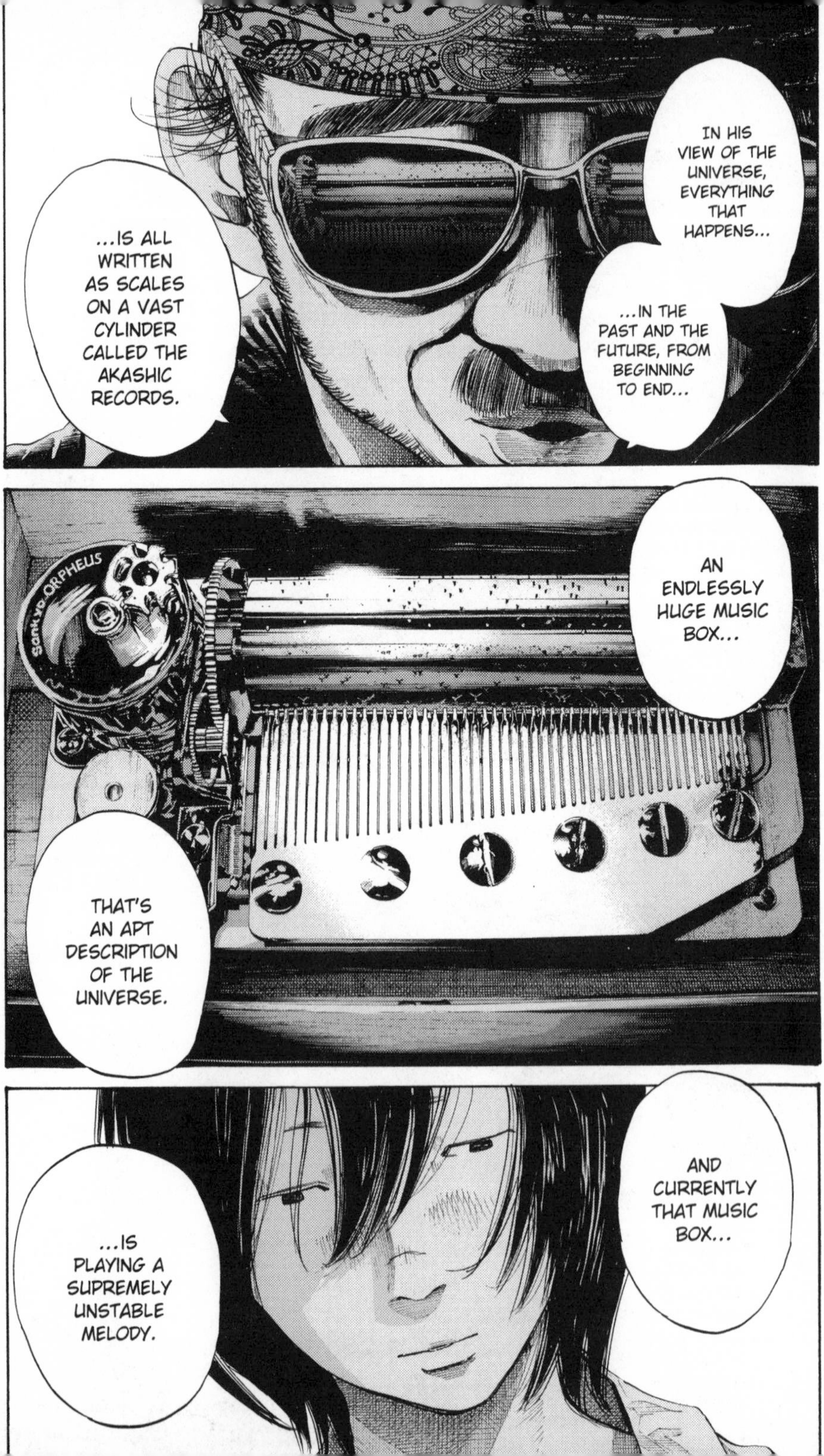
IN HIS VIEW OF THE UNIVERSE, EVERYTHING THAT HAPPENS...
...IN THE PAST AND THE FUTURE, FROM BEGINNING TO END...
...IS ALL WRITTEN AS SCALES ON A VAST CYLINDER CALLED THE AKASHIC RECORDS.
AN ENDLESSLY HUGE MUSIC BOX...
Sankyo ORPHEUS
THAT'S AN APT DESCRIPTION OF THE UNIVERSE.
AND CURRENTLY THAT MUSIC BOX...
...IS PLAYING A SUPREMELY UNSTABLE MELODY.

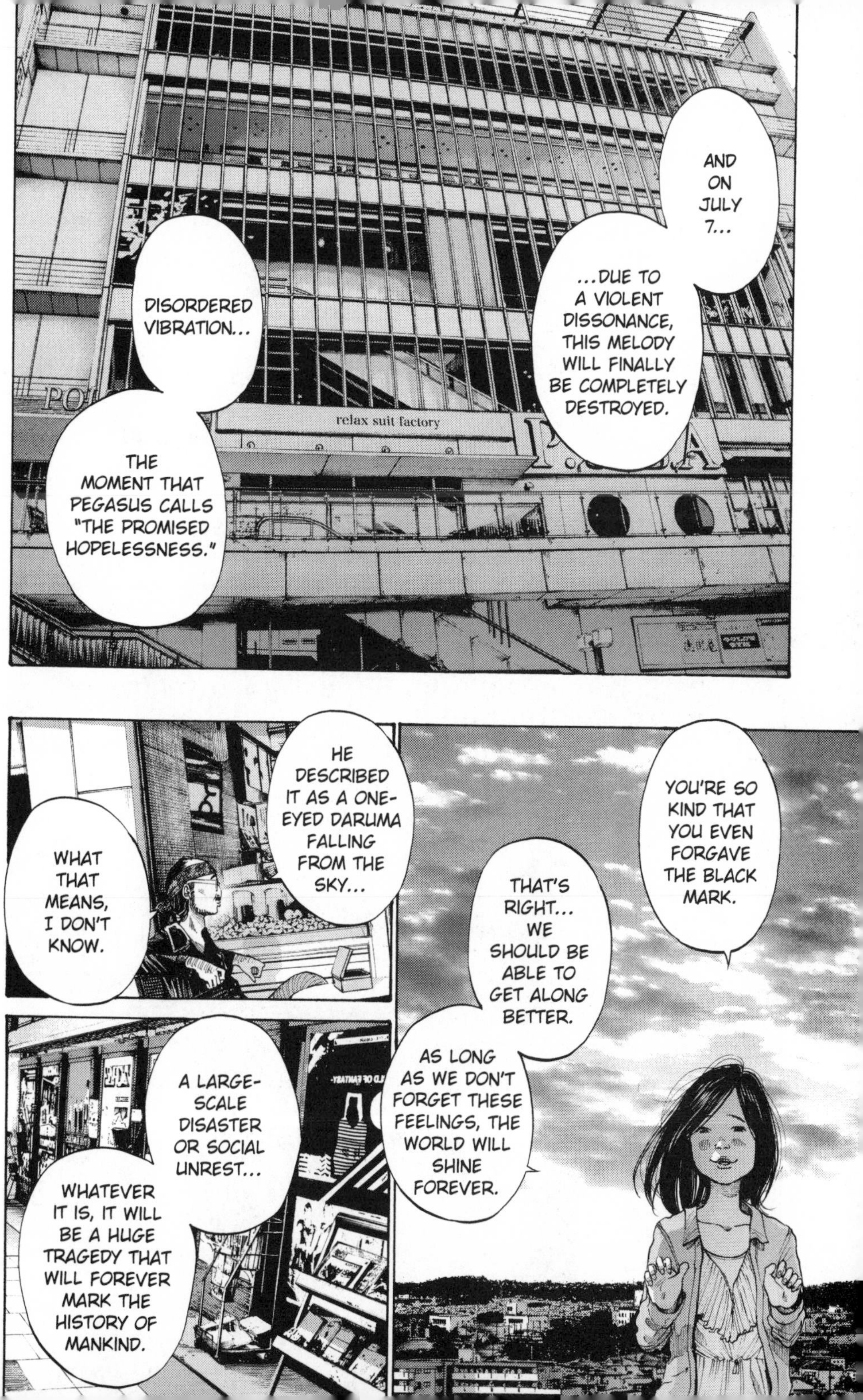
AND ON JULY 7...
...DUE TO A VIOLENT DISSONANCE, THIS MELODY WILL FINALLY BE COMPLETELY DESTROYED.
relax suit factory
DISORDERED VIBRATION...
THE MOMENT THAT PEGASUS CALLS "THE PROMISED HOPELESSNESS."
YOU'RE SO KIND THAT YOU EVEN FORGAVE THE BLACK MARK.
THAT'S RIGHT... WE SHOULD BE ABLE TO GET ALONG BETTER.
AS LONG AS WE DON'T FORGET THESE FEELINGS, THE WORLD WILL SHINE FOREVER.
HE DESCRIBED IT AS A ONE-EYED DARUMA FALLING FROM THE SKY...
WHAT THAT MEANS, I DON'T KNOW.
A LARGE-SCALE DISASTER OR SOCIAL UNREST...
WHATEVER IT IS, IT WILL BE A HUGE TRAGEDY THAT WILL FOREVER MARK THE HISTORY OF MANKIND.

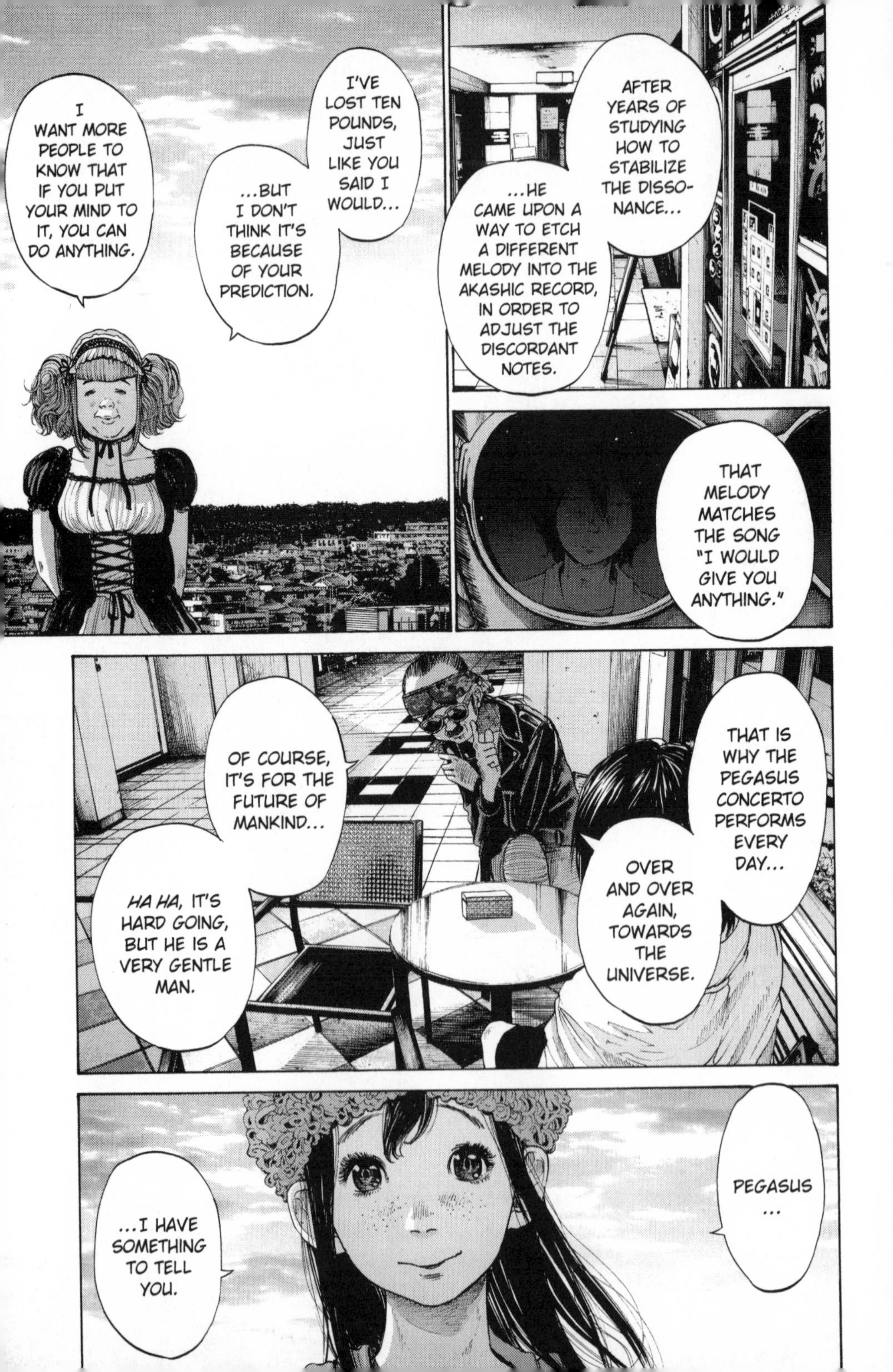
AFTER YEARS OF STUDYING HOW TO STABILIZE THE DISSO- NANCE...
...HE CAME UPON A WAY TO ETCH A DIFFERENT MELODY INTO THE AKASHIC RECORD, IN ORDER TO ADJUST THE DISCORDANT NOTES.
THAT MELODY MATCHES THE SONG "I WOULD GIVE YOU ANYTHING."
I'VE LOST TEN POUNDS, JUST LIKE YOU SAID I WOULD...
...BUT I DON'T THINK IT'S BECAUSE OF YOUR PREDICTION.
I WANT MORE PEOPLE TO KNOW THAT IF YOU PUT YOUR MIND TO IT, YOU CAN DO ANYTHING.
THAT IS WHY THE PEGASUS CONCERTO PERFORMS EVERY DAY...
OVER AND OVER AGAIN, TOWARDS THE UNIVERSE.
OF COURSE, IT'S FOR THE FUTURE OF MANKIND...
HA HA, IT'S HARD GOING, BUT HE IS A VERY GENTLE MAN.
PEGASUS ...
...I HAVE SOMETHING TO TELL YOU.

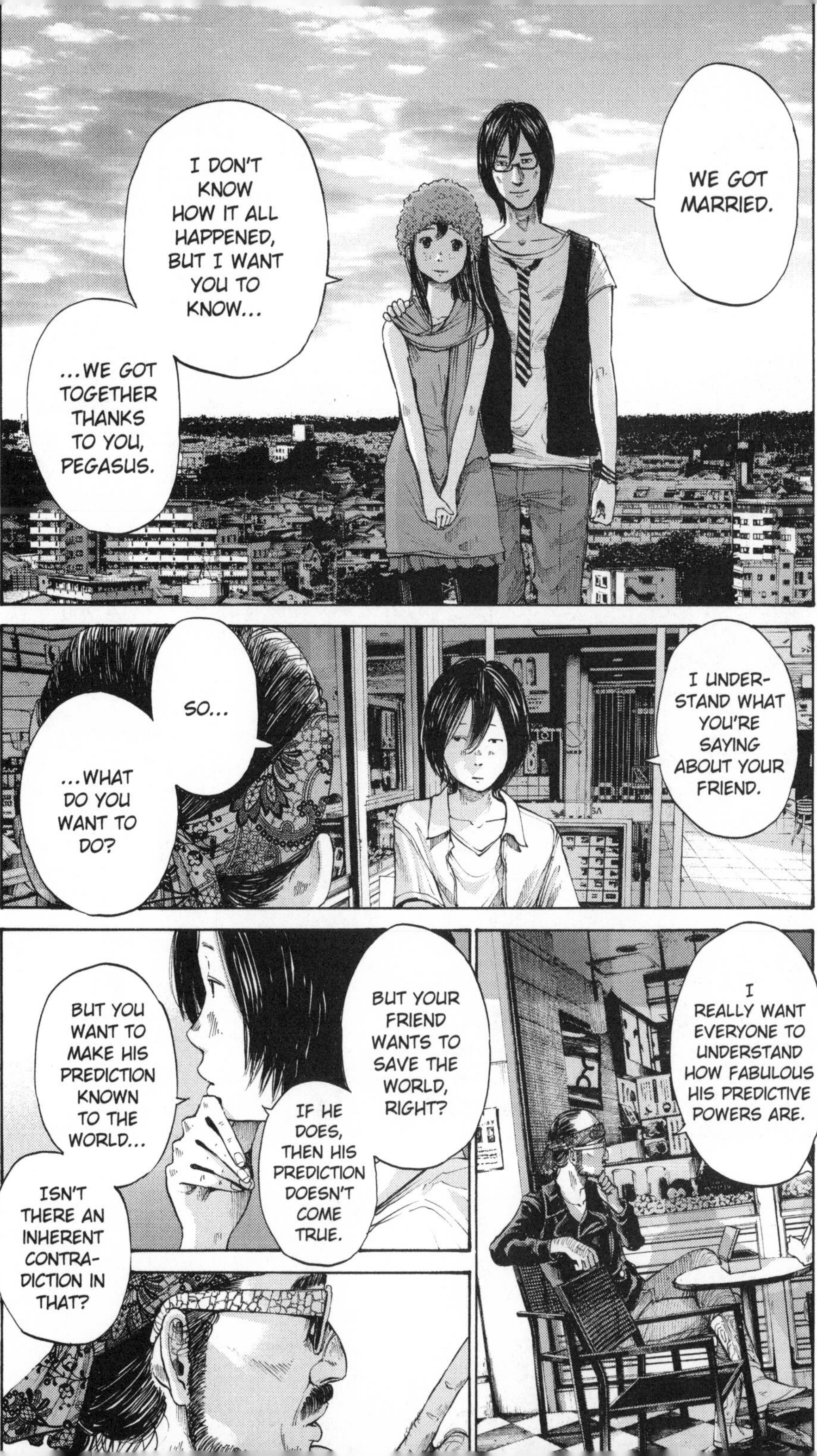
WE GOT MARRIED.
I DON'T KNOW HOW IT ALL HAPPENED, BUT I WANT YOU TO KNOW...
...WE GOT TOGETHER THANKS TO YOU, PEGASUS.
I UNDERSTAND WHAT YOU'RE SAYING ABOUT YOUR FRIEND.
SO...
...WHAT DO YOU WANT TO DO?
I REALLY WANT EVERYONE TO UNDERSTAND HOW FABULOUS HIS PREDICTIVE POWERS ARE.
BUT YOUR FRIEND WANTS TO SAVE THE WORLD, RIGHT?
IF HE DOES, THEN HIS PREDICTION DOESN'T COME TRUE.
BUT YOU WANT TO MAKE HIS PREDICTION KNOWN TO THE WORLD...
ISN'T THERE AN INHERENT CONTRADICTION IN THAT?

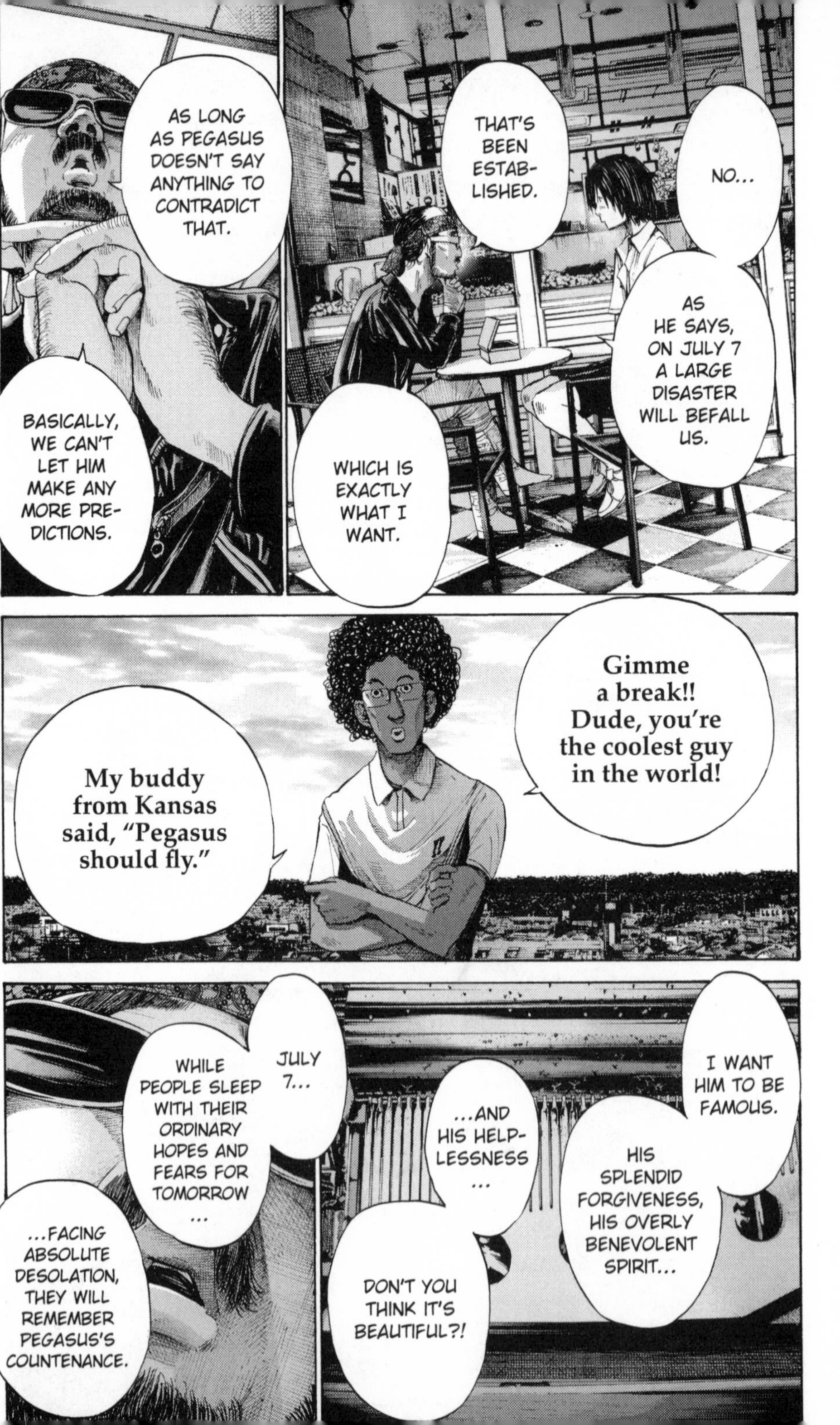
NO...
AS HE SAYS, ON JULY 7 A LARGE DISASTER WILL BEFALL US.
THAT'S BEEN ESTAB-LISHED.
WHICH IS EXACTLY WHAT I WANT.
AS LONG AS PEGASUS DOESN'T SAY ANYTHING TO CONTRADICT THAT.
BASICALLY, WE CAN'T LET HIM MAKE ANY MORE PRE-DICTIONS.
Gimme a break!! Dude, you're the coolest guy in the world!
My buddy from Kansas said, "Pegasus should fly."
I WANT HIM TO BE FAMOUS.
HIS SPLENDID FORGIVENESS, HIS OVERLY BENEVOLENT SPIRIT...
...AND HIS HELP-LESSNESS...
DON'T YOU THINK IT'S BEAUTIFUL?!
JULY 7...
WHILE PEOPLE SLEEP WITH THEIR ORDINARY HOPES AND FEARS FOR TOMORROW...
...FACING ABSOLUTE DESOLATION, THEY WILL REMEMBER PEGASUS'S COUNTENANCE.

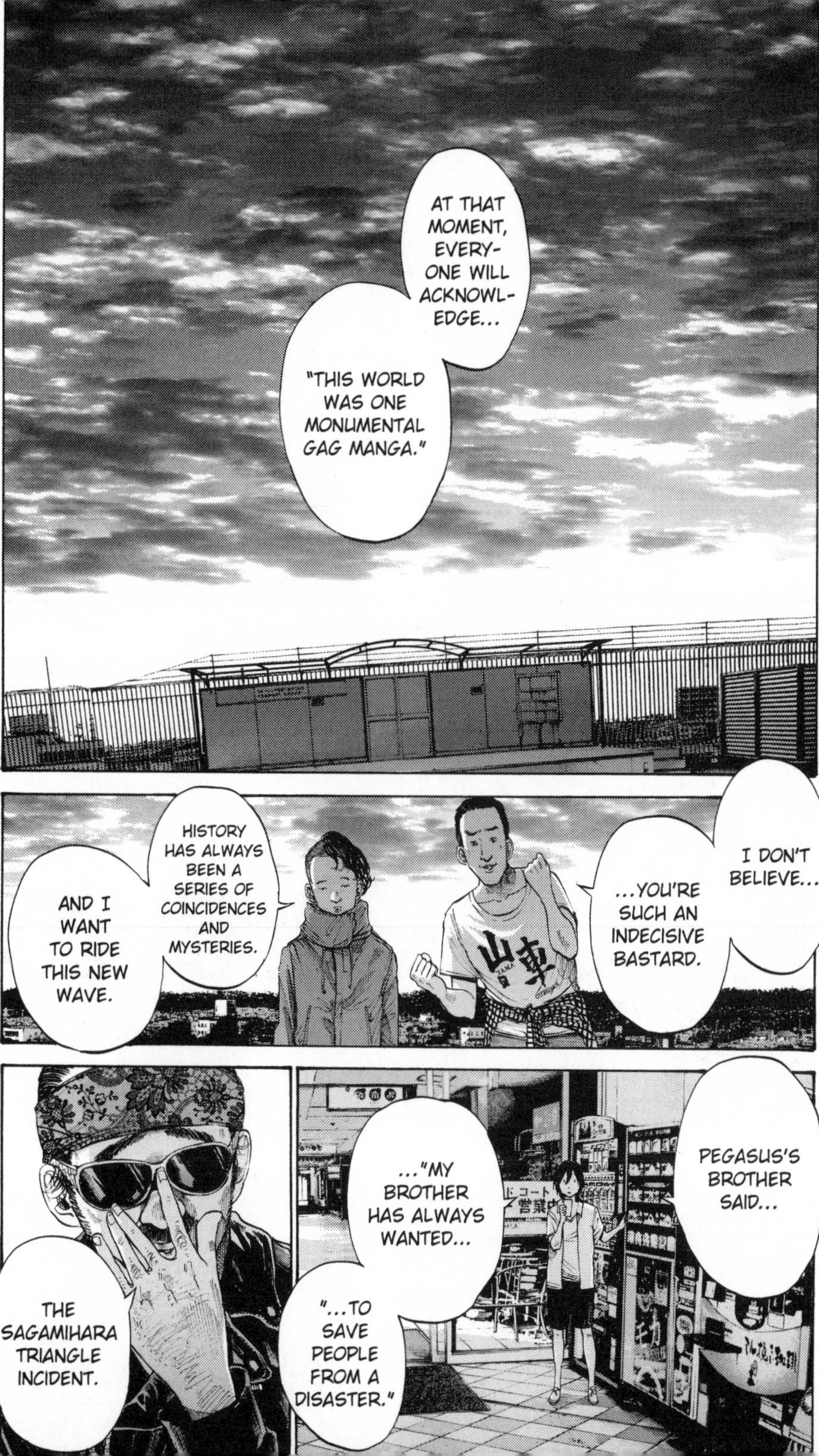
AT THAT MOMENT, EVERYONE WILL ACKNOWLEDGE...
"THIS WORLD WAS ONE MONUMENTAL GAG MANGA."
I DON'T BELIEVE...
...YOU'RE SUCH AN INDECISIVE BASTARD.
HISTORY HAS ALWAYS BEEN A SERIES OF COINCIDENCES AND MYSTERIES.
AND I WANT TO RIDE THIS NEW WAVE.
PEGASUS'S BROTHER SAID...
..."MY BROTHER HAS ALWAYS WANTED...
"...TO SAVE PEOPLE FROM A DISASTER."
THE SAGAMIHARA TRIANGLE INCIDENT.

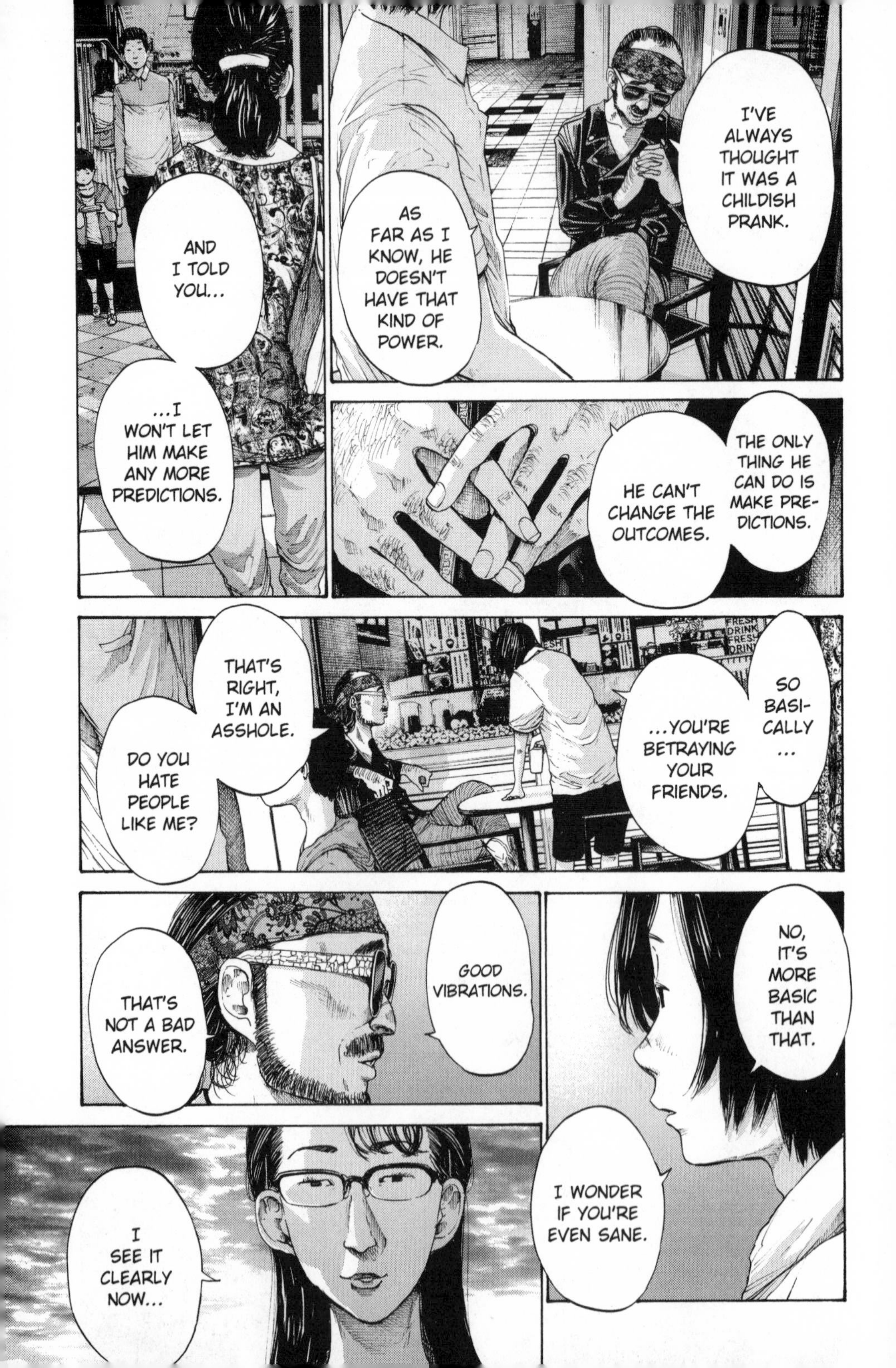
I'VE ALWAYS THOUGHT IT WAS A CHILDISH PRANK.
AS FAR AS I KNOW, HE DOESN'T HAVE THAT KIND OF POWER.
THE ONLY THING HE CAN DO IS MAKE PRE-DICTIONS.
HE CAN'T CHANGE THE OUTCOMES.
AND I TOLD YOU...
...I WON'T LET HIM MAKE ANY MORE PREDICTIONS.
SO BASI-CALLY...
...YOU'RE BETRAYING YOUR FRIENDS.
THAT'S RIGHT, I'M AN ASSHOLE.
DO YOU HATE PEOPLE LIKE ME?
NO, IT'S MORE BASIC THAN THAT.
I WONDER IF YOU'RE EVEN SANE.
GOOD VIBRATIONS.
THAT'S NOT A BAD ANSWER.
I SEE IT CLEARLY NOW...

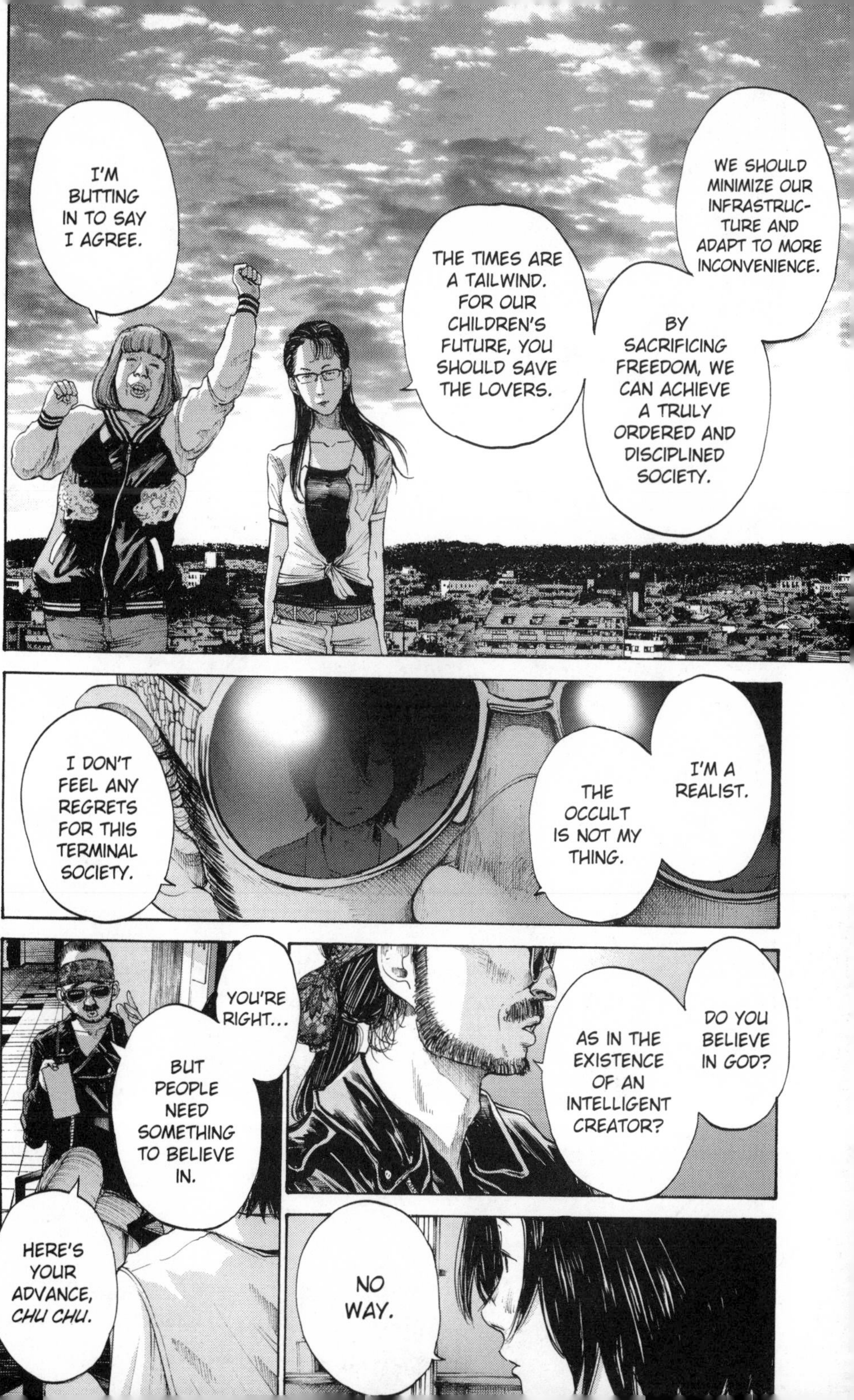
WE SHOULD MINIMIZE OUR INFRASTRUC-TURE AND ADAPT TO MORE INCONVENIENCE.
BY SACRIFICING FREEDOM, WE CAN ACHIEVE A TRULY ORDERED AND DISCIPLINED SOCIETY.
THE TIMES ARE A TAILWIND. FOR OUR CHILDREN'S FUTURE, YOU SHOULD SAVE THE LOVERS.
I'M BUTTING IN TO SAY I AGREE.
I'M A REALIST.
THE OCCULT IS NOT MY THING.
I DON'T FEEL ANY REGRETS FOR THIS TERMINAL SOCIETY.
DO YOU BELIEVE IN GOD?
AS IN THE EXISTENCE OF AN INTELLIGENT CREATOR?
YOU'RE RIGHT...
BUT PEOPLE NEED SOMETHING TO BELIEVE IN.
NO WAY.
HERE'S YOUR ADVANCE, *CHU CHU*.

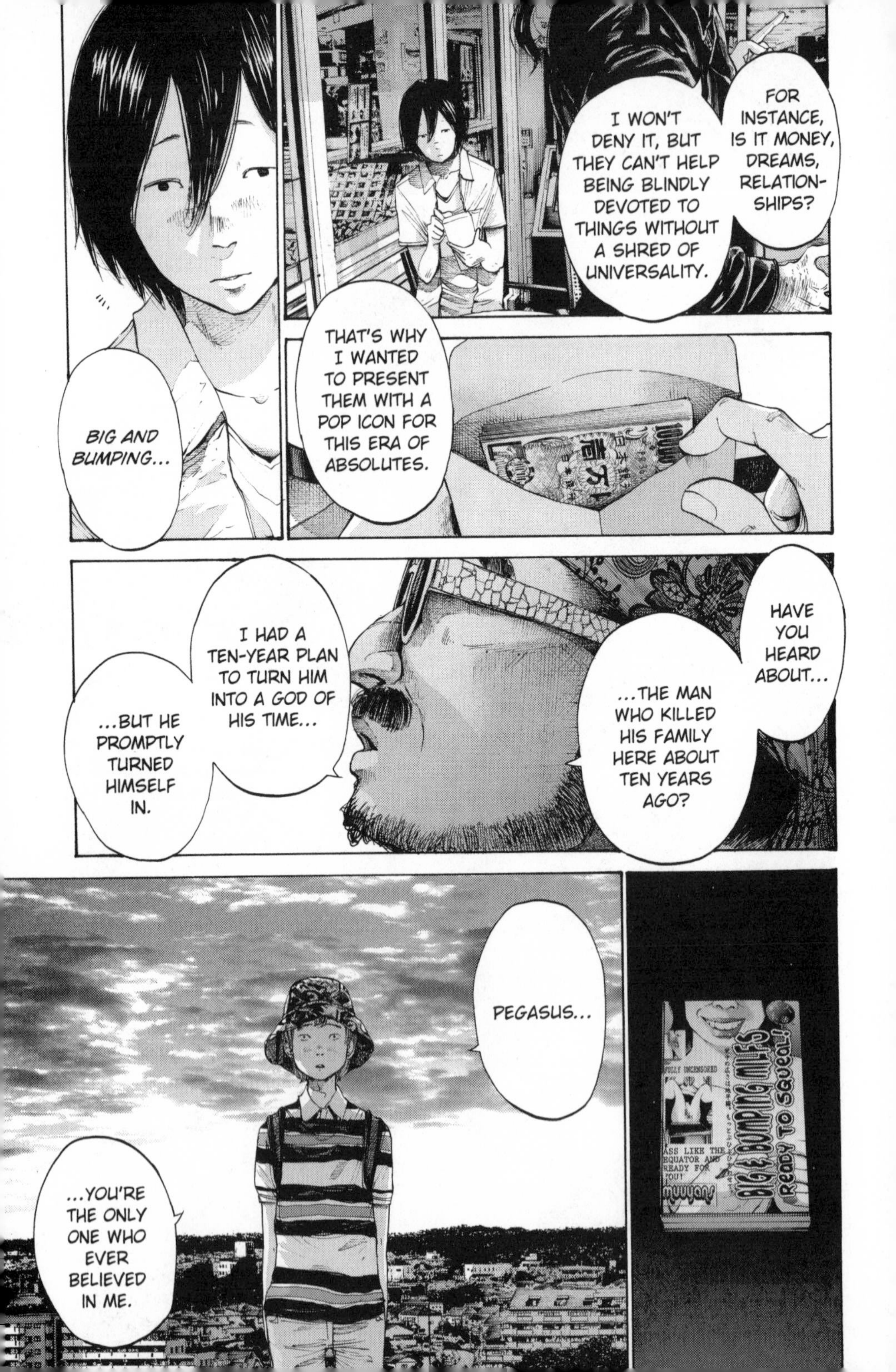
FOR INSTANCE, IS IT MONEY, DREAMS, RELATION-SHIPS?
I WON'T DENY IT, BUT THEY CAN'T HELP BEING BLINDLY DEVOTED TO THINGS WITHOUT A SHRED OF UNIVERSALITY.
THAT'S WHY I WANTED TO PRESENT THEM WITH A POP ICON FOR THIS ERA OF ABSOLUTES.
BIG AND BUMPING...
HAVE YOU HEARD ABOUT...
...THE MAN WHO KILLED HIS FAMILY HERE ABOUT TEN YEARS AGO?
I HAD A TEN-YEAR PLAN TO TURN HIM INTO A GOD OF HIS TIME...
...BUT HE PROMPTLY TURNED HIMSELF IN.
BIG & BUMPING MILFS
READY TO SQUEAL!
FULLY UNCENSORED
ASS LIKE THE EQUATOR AND READY FOR YOU!
PEGASUS...
...YOU'RE THE ONLY ONE WHO EVER BELIEVED IN ME.

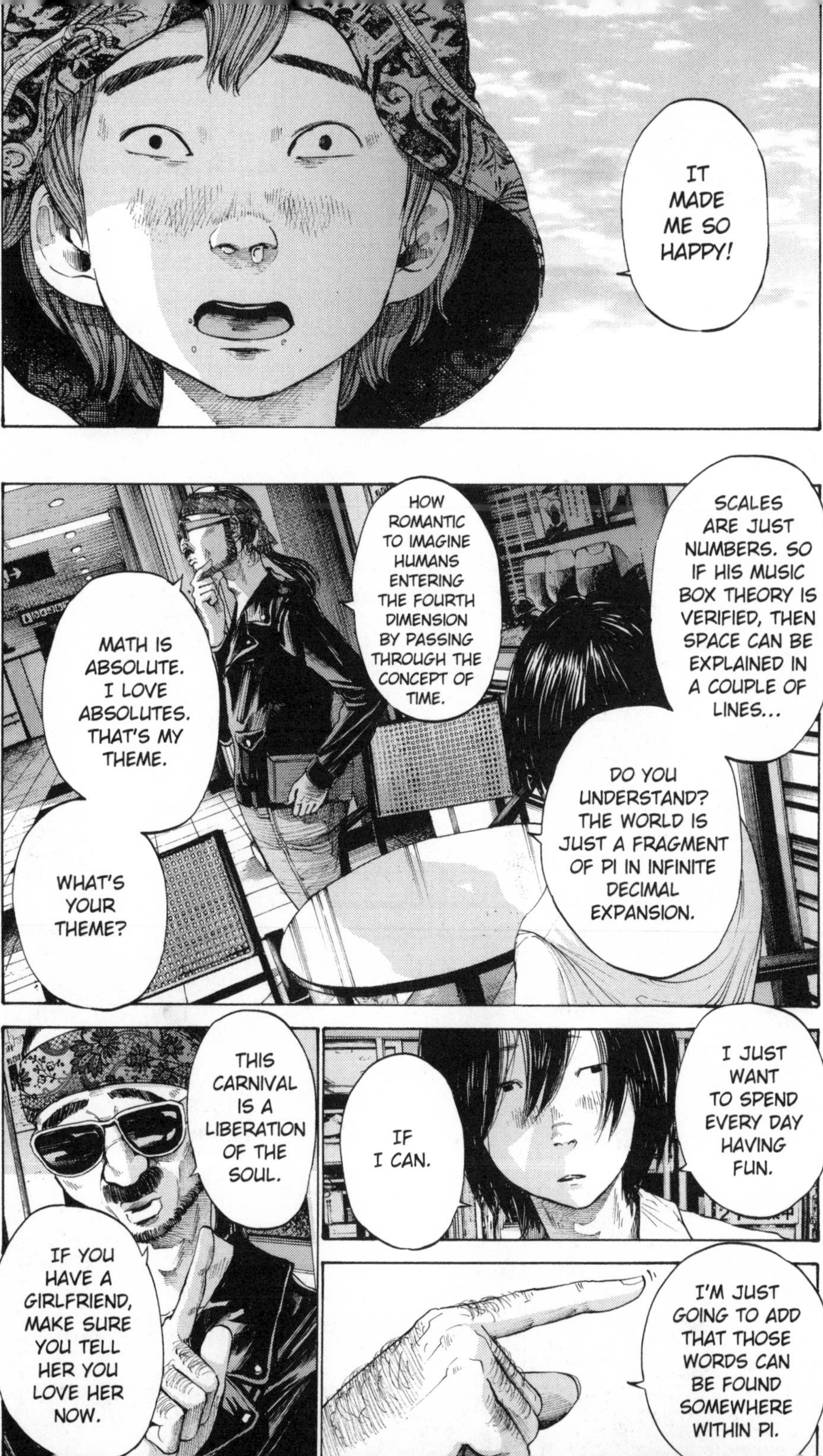
IT MADE ME SO HAPPY!
SCALES ARE JUST NUMBERS. SO IF HIS MUSIC BOX THEORY IS VERIFIED, THEN SPACE CAN BE EXPLAINED IN A COUPLE OF LINES...
HOW ROMANTIC TO IMAGINE HUMANS ENTERING THE FOURTH DIMENSION BY PASSING THROUGH THE CONCEPT OF TIME.
DO YOU UNDERSTAND? THE WORLD IS JUST A FRAGMENT OF PI IN INFINITE DECIMAL EXPANSION.
MATH IS ABSOLUTE. I LOVE ABSOLUTES. THAT'S MY THEME.
WHAT'S YOUR THEME?
I JUST WANT TO SPEND EVERY DAY HAVING FUN.
IF I CAN.
I'M JUST GOING TO ADD THAT THOSE WORDS CAN BE FOUND SOMEWHERE WITHIN PI.
THIS CARNIVAL IS A LIBERATION OF THE SOUL.
IF YOU HAVE A GIRLFRIEND, MAKE SURE YOU TELL HER YOU LOVE HER NOW.

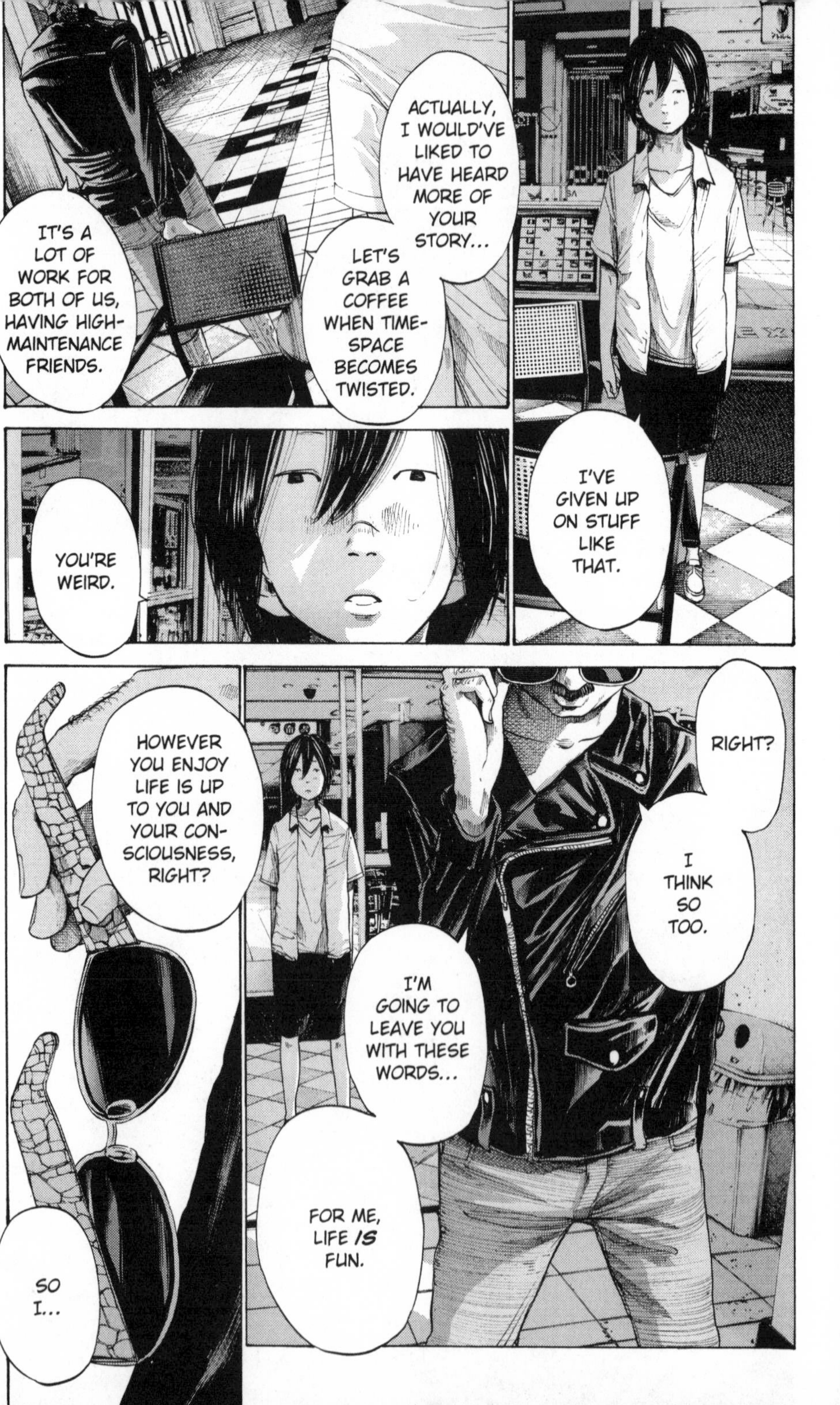
I'VE GIVEN UP ON STUFF LIKE THAT.
ACTUALLY, I WOULD'VE LIKED TO HAVE HEARD MORE OF YOUR STORY...
LET'S GRAB A COFFEE WHEN TIME-SPACE BECOMES TWISTED.
IT'S A LOT OF WORK FOR BOTH OF US, HAVING HIGH-MAINTENANCE FRIENDS.
YOU'RE WEIRD.
RIGHT?
I THINK SO TOO.
I'M GOING TO LEAVE YOU WITH THESE WORDS...
FOR ME, LIFE *IS* FUN.
HOWEVER YOU ENJOY LIFE IS UP TO YOU AND YOUR CONSCIOUSNESS, RIGHT?
SO I...

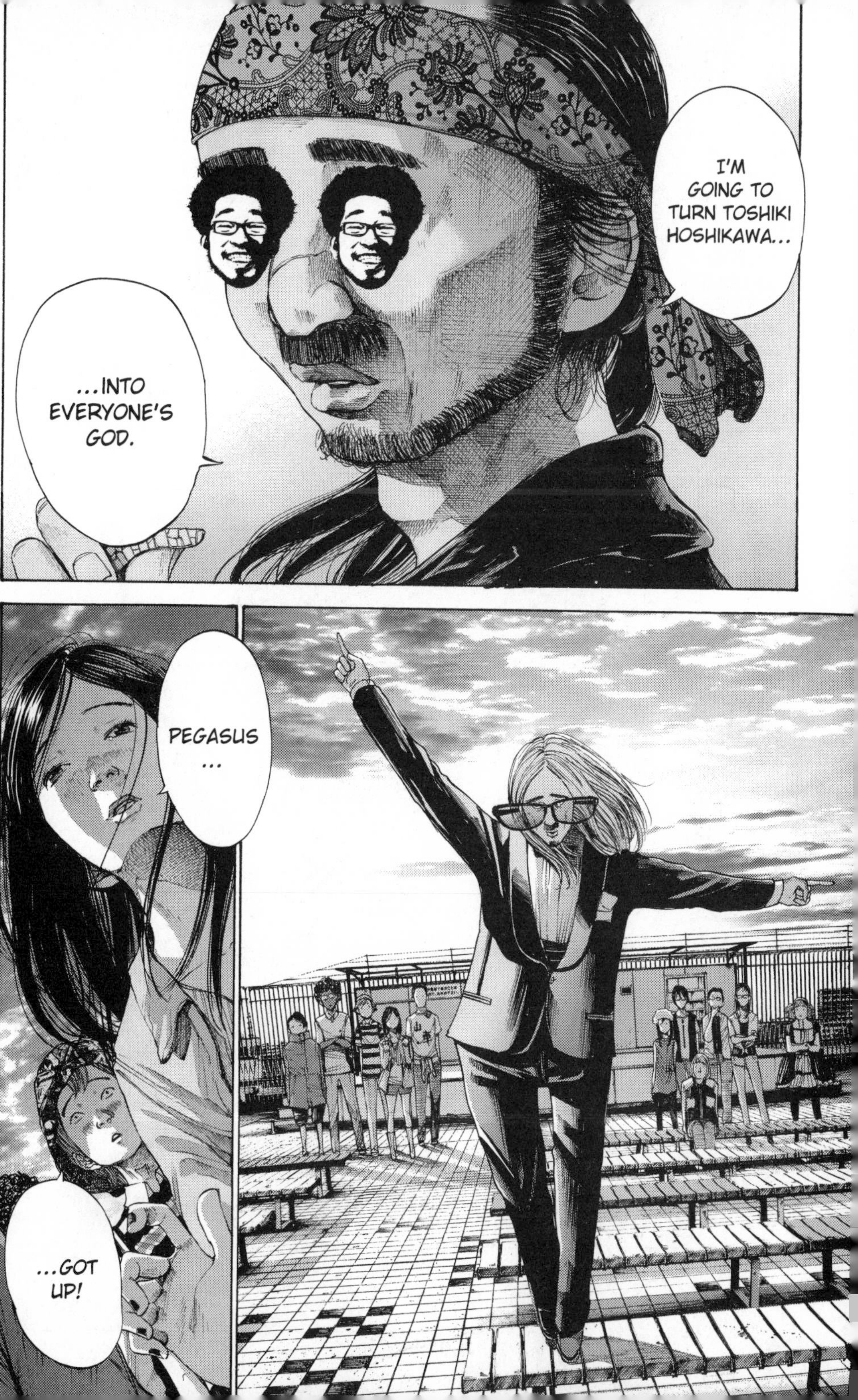
I'M GOING TO TURN TOSHIKI HOSHIKAWA...
...INTO EVERYONE'S GOD.
PEGASUS ...
...GOT UP!

Chapter 120

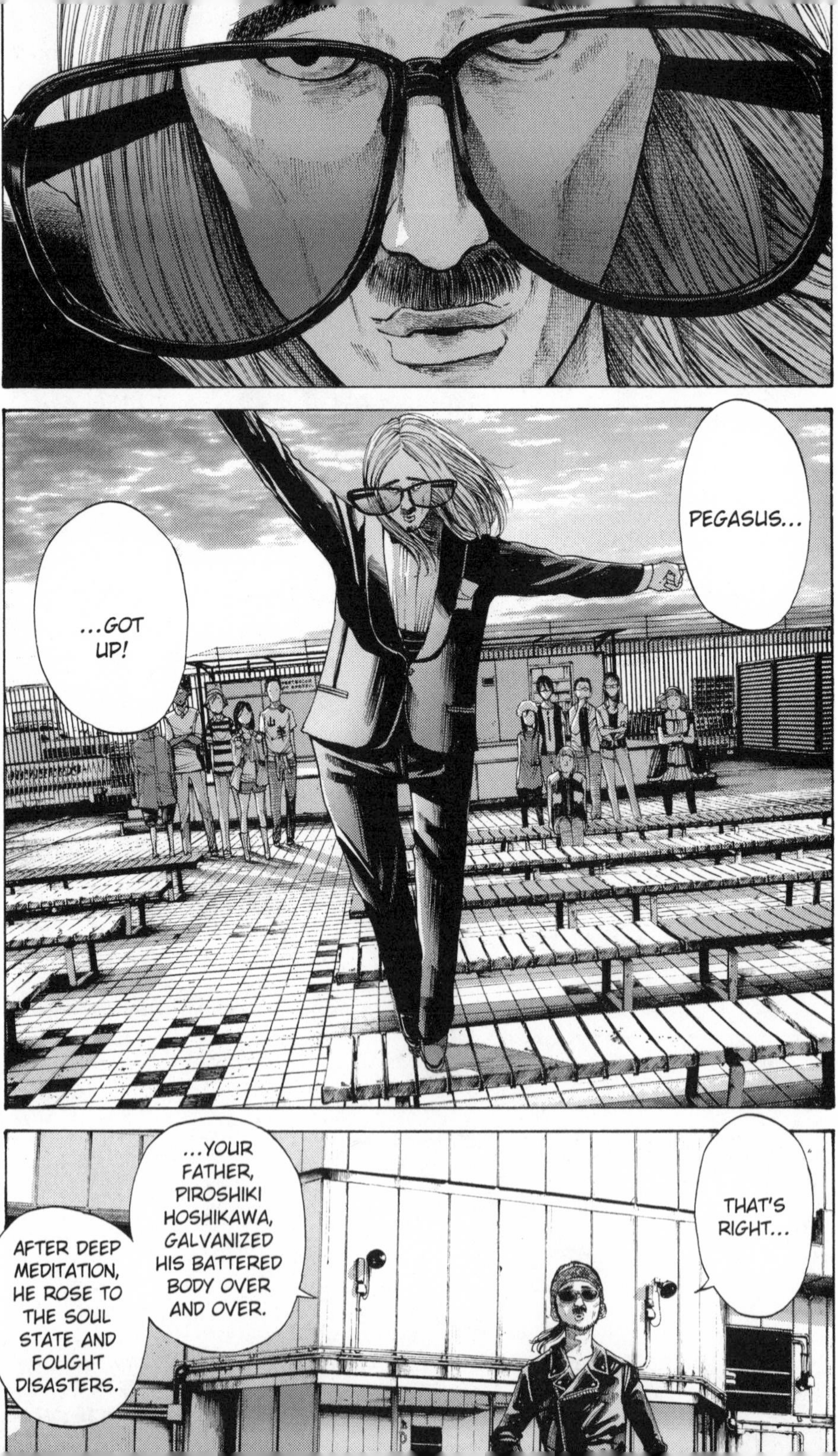
PEGASUS...
...GOT UP!
THAT'S RIGHT...
...YOUR FATHER, PIROSHIKI HOSHIKAWA, GALVANIZED HIS BATTERED BODY OVER AND OVER.
AFTER DEEP MEDITATION, HE ROSE TO THE SOUL STATE AND FOUGHT DISASTERS.

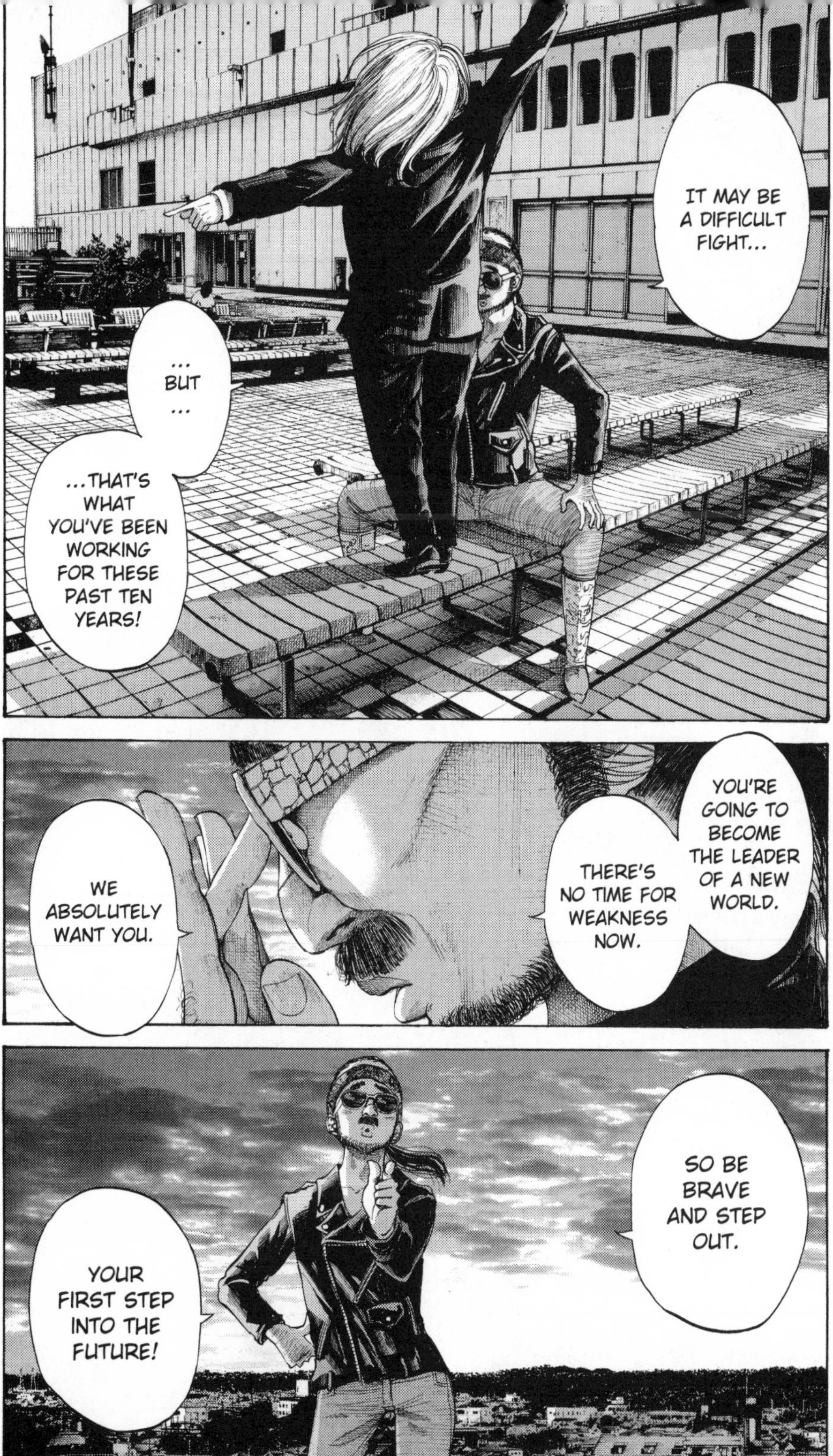
IT MAY BE A DIFFICULT FIGHT...
... BUT ...
...THAT'S WHAT YOU'VE BEEN WORKING FOR THESE PAST TEN YEARS!
YOU'RE GOING TO BECOME THE LEADER OF A NEW WORLD.
THERE'S NO TIME FOR WEAKNESS NOW.
WE ABSOLUTELY WANT YOU.
SO BE BRAVE AND STEP OUT.
YOUR FIRST STEP INTO THE FUTURE!

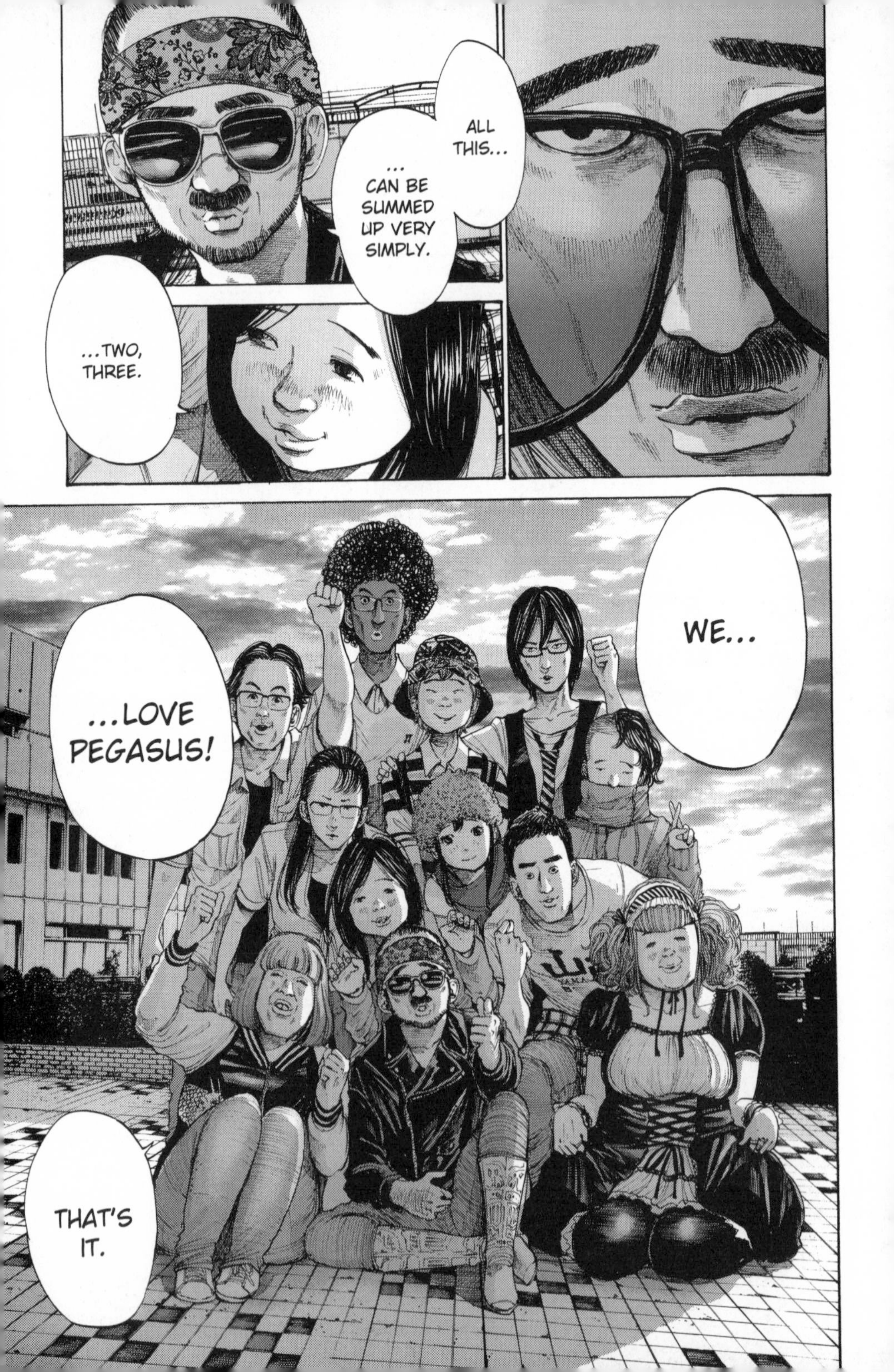
ALL THIS...
...CAN BE SUMMED UP VERY SIMPLY.
...TWO, THREE.
WE...
...LOVE PEGASUS!
THAT'S IT.

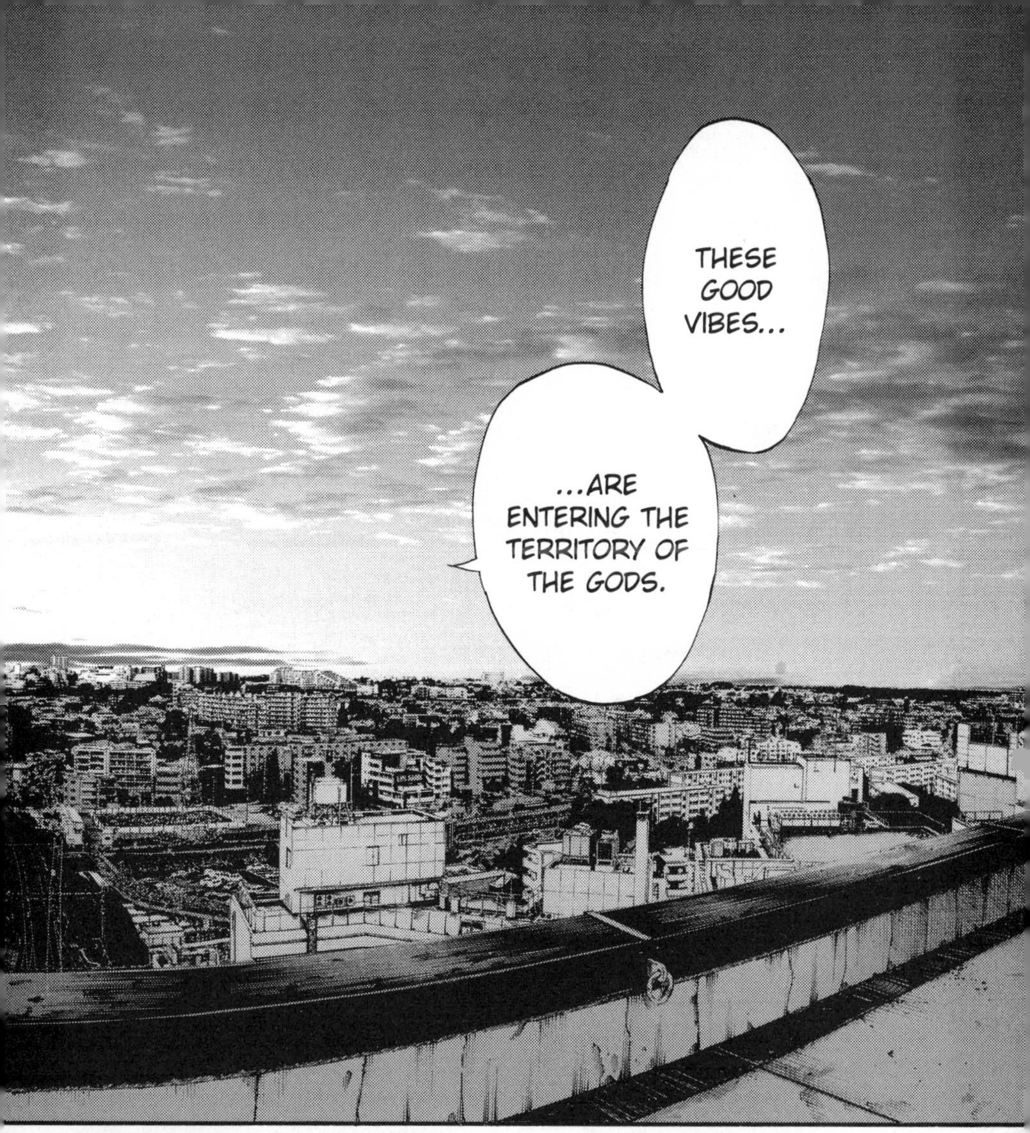
THESE GOOD VIBES...
...ARE ENTERING THE TERRITORY OF THE GODS.

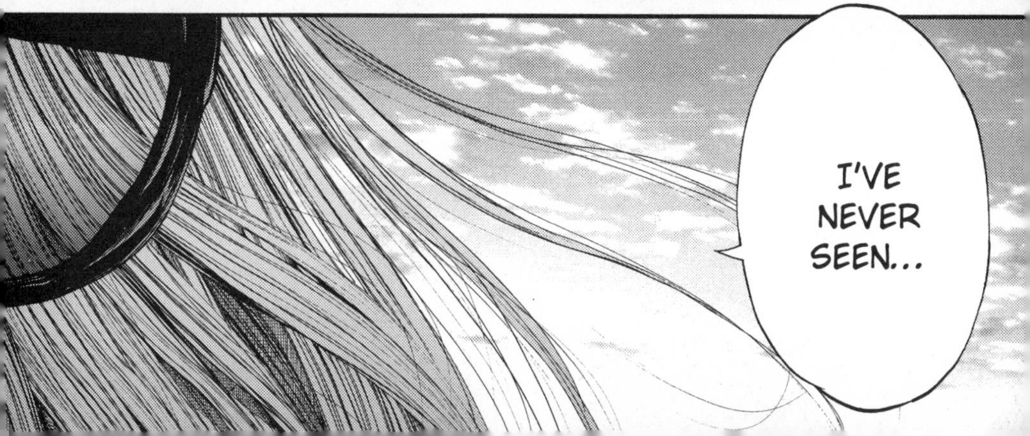
I'VE NEVER SEEN...

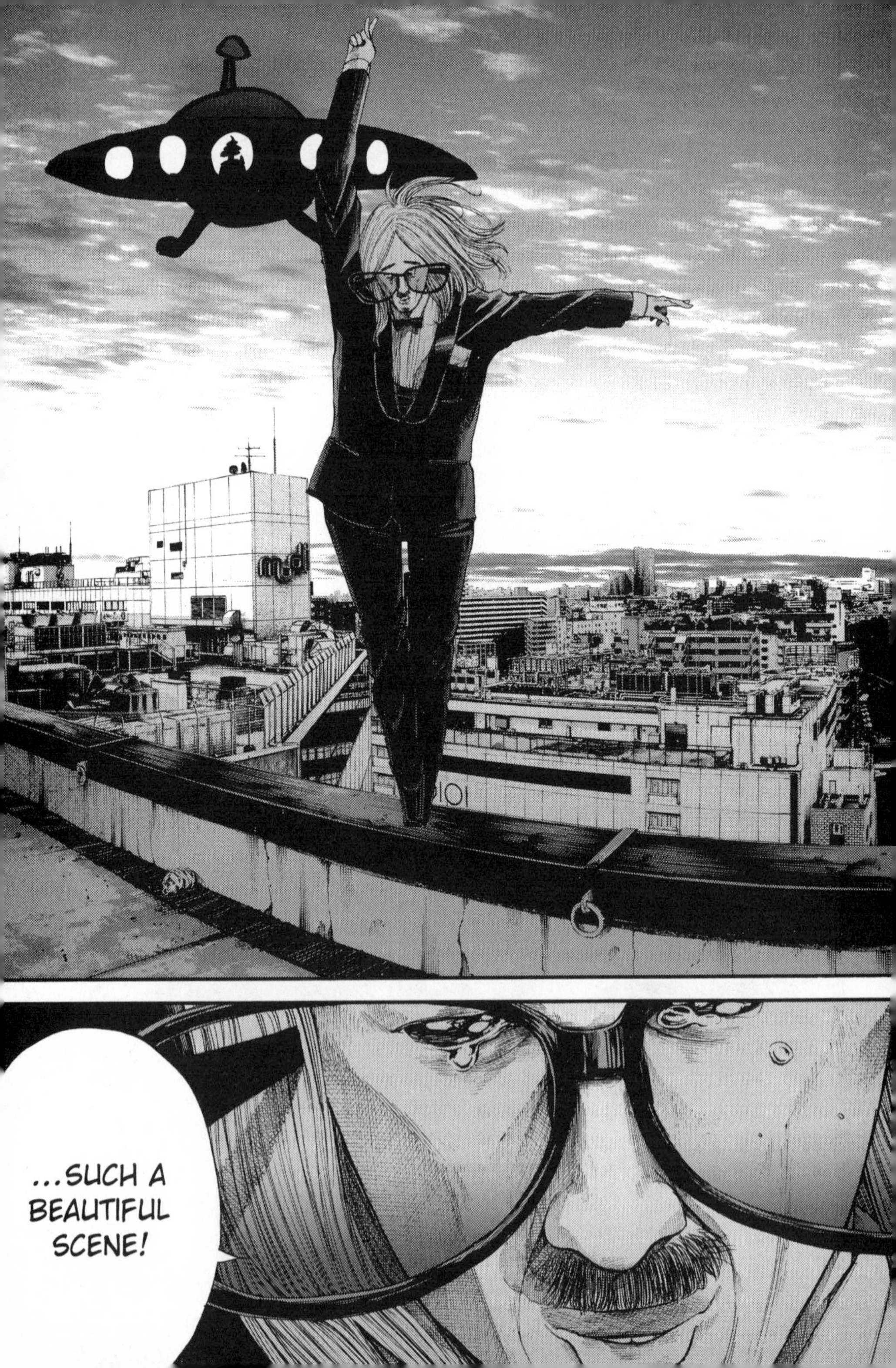
...SUCH A BEAUTIFUL SCENE!

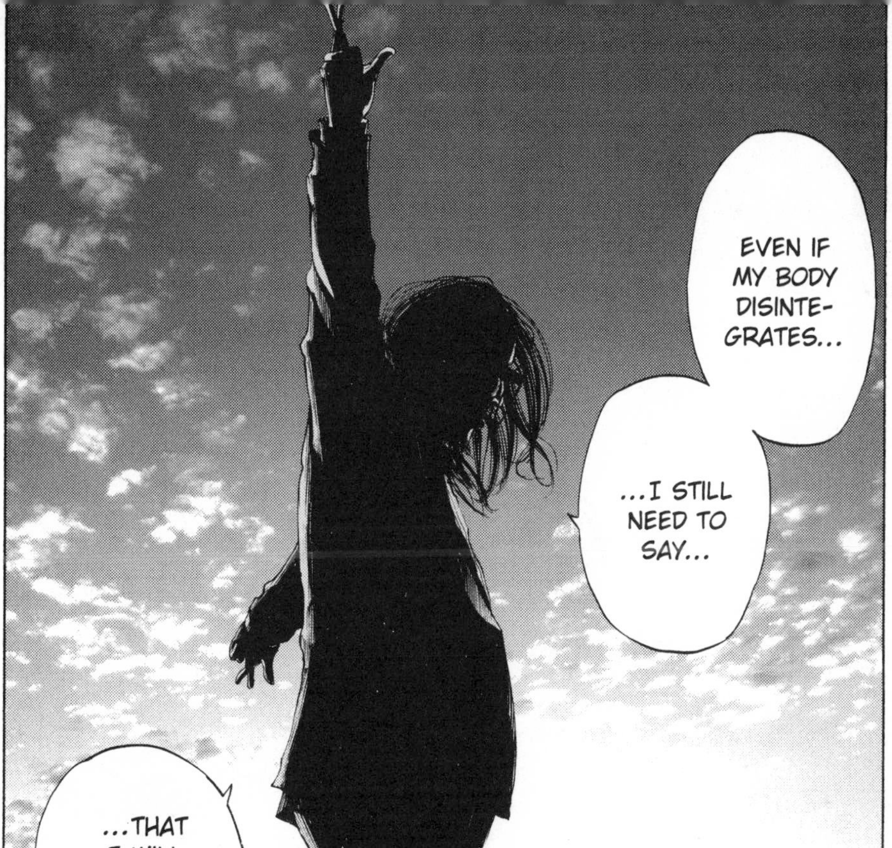
EVEN IF MY BODY DISINTE- GRATES...
...I STILL NEED TO SAY...
...THAT I WILL PROTECT THIS BEAUTIFUL WORLD!
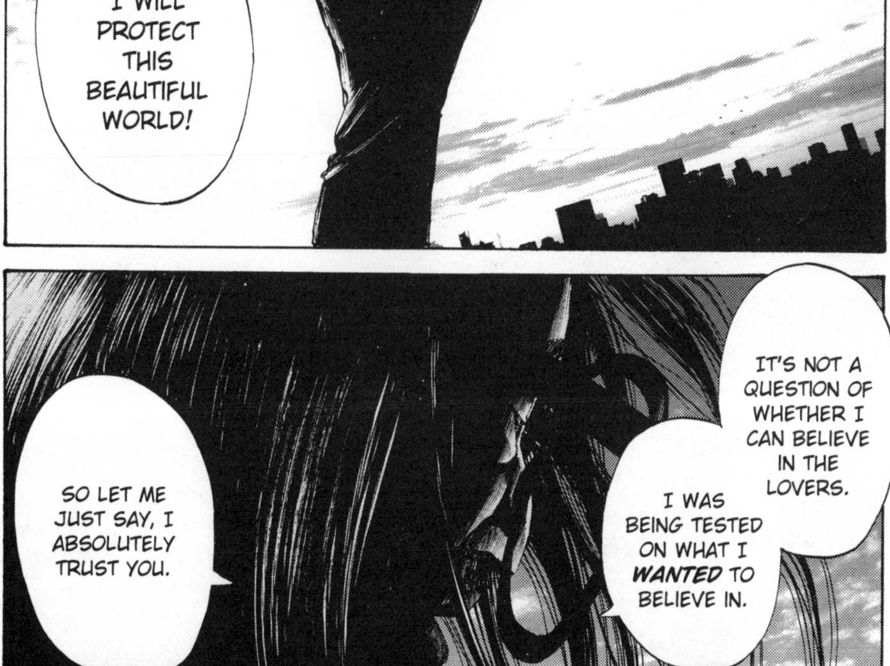
IT'S NOT A QUESTION OF WHETHER I CAN BELIEVE IN THE LOVERS.
I WAS BEING TESTED ON WHAT I *WANTED* TO BELIEVE IN.
SO LET ME JUST SAY, I ABSOLUTELY TRUST YOU.

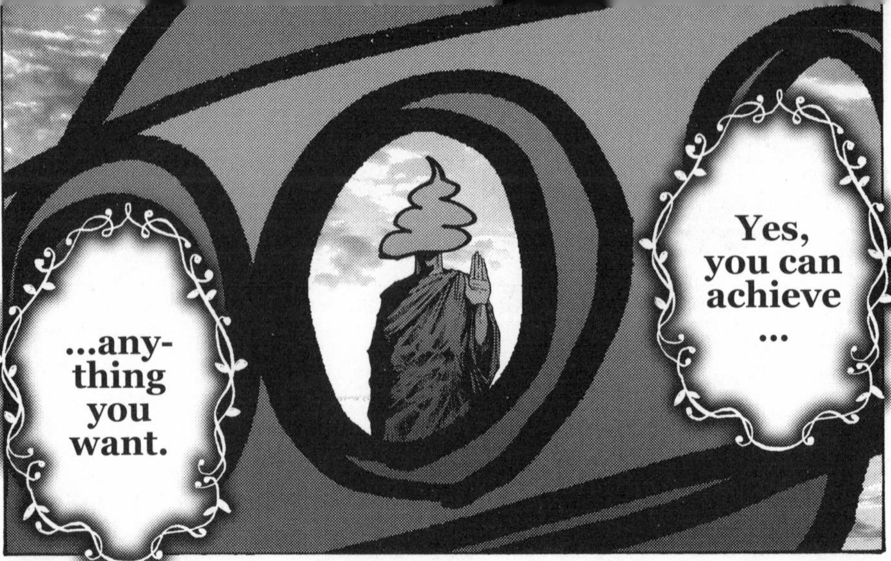
Yes, you can achieve ...
...any-thing you want.

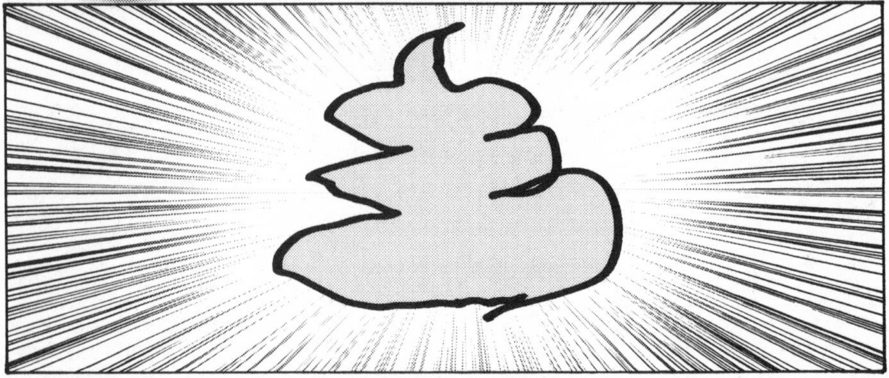

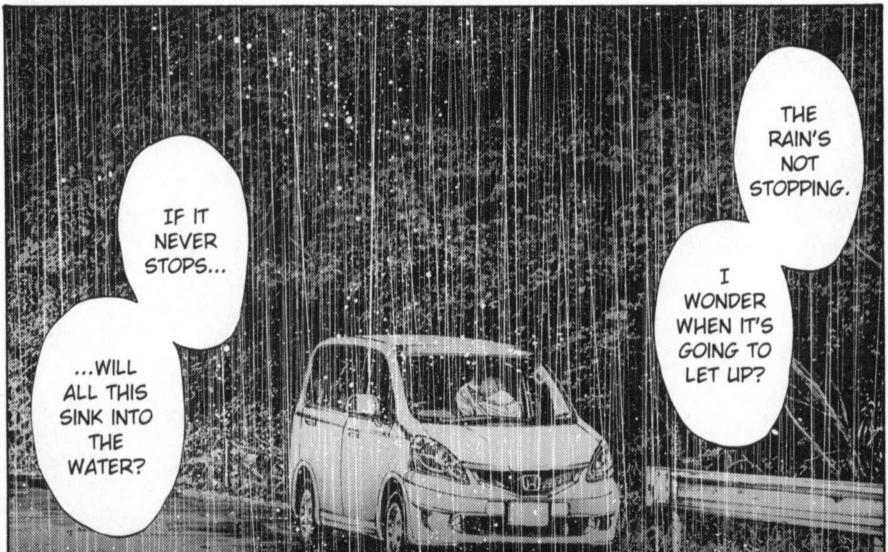
THE RAIN'S NOT STOPPING.
I WONDER WHEN IT'S GOING TO LET UP?
IF IT NEVER STOPS...
...WILL ALL THIS SINK INTO THE WATER?

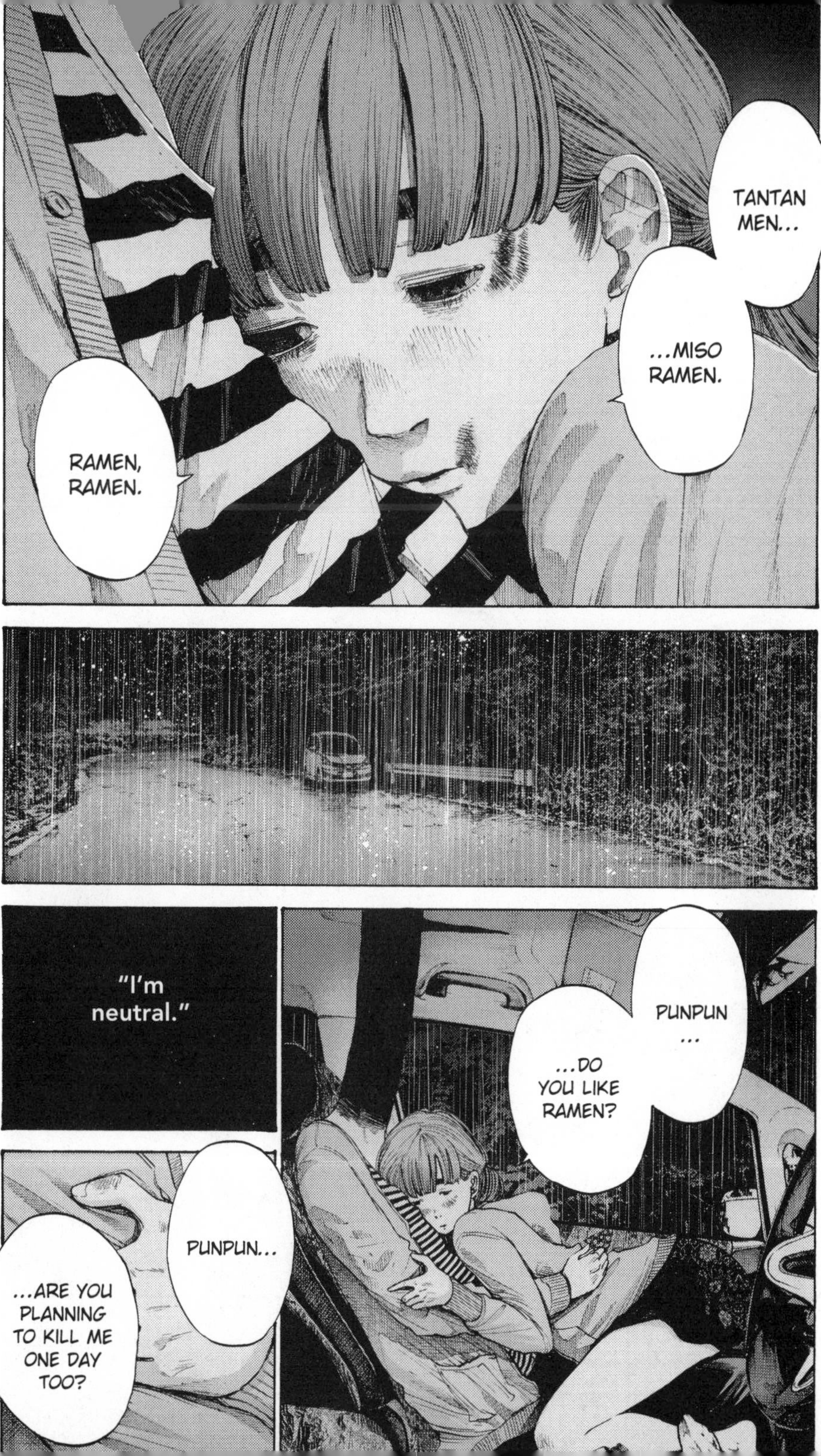
TANTAN MEN...
...MISO RAMEN.
RAMEN, RAMEN.
PUNPUN ...
...DO YOU LIKE RAMEN?
"I'm neutral."
PUNPUN...
...ARE YOU PLANNING TO KILL ME ONE DAY TOO?

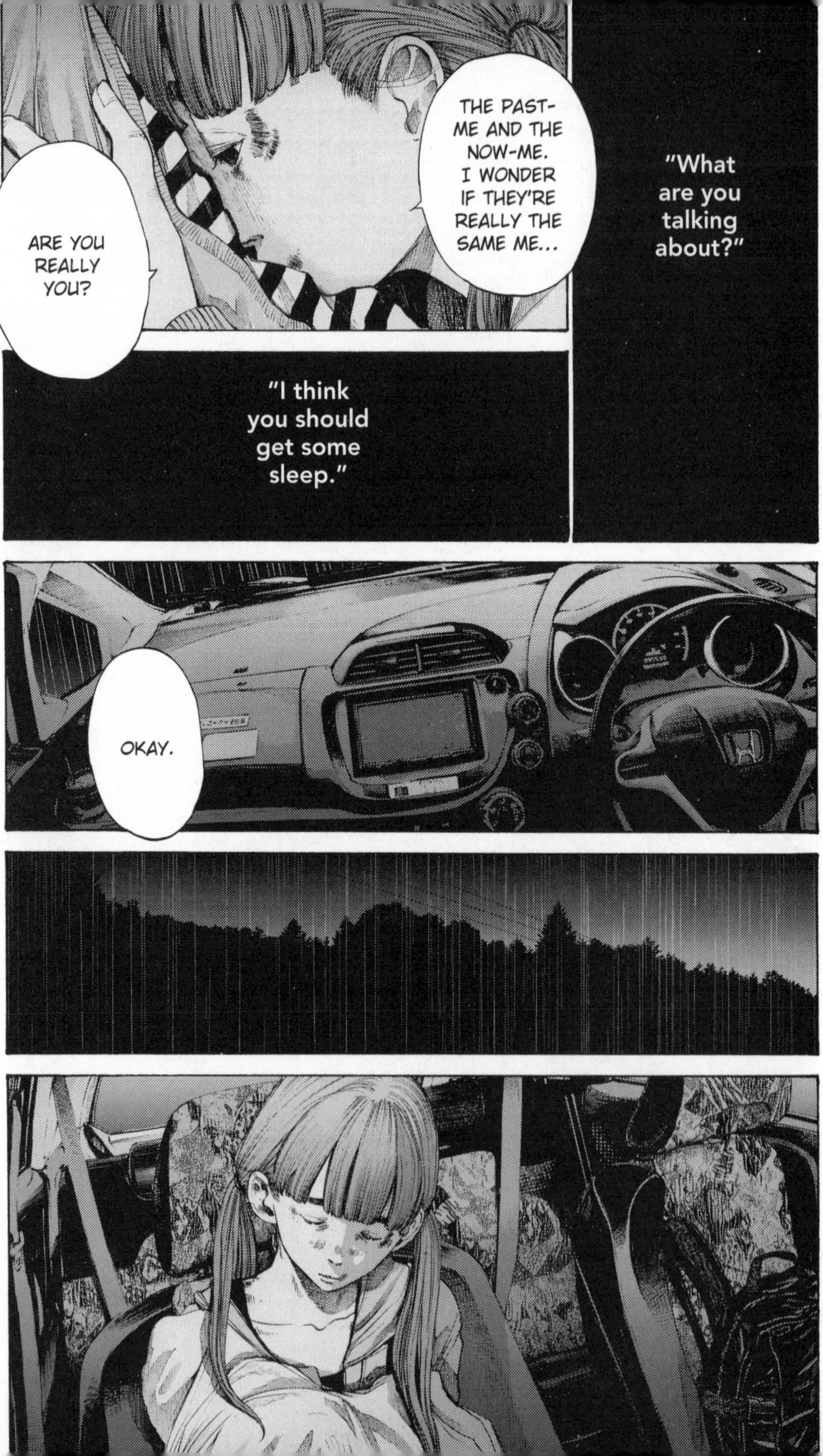
"What are you talking about?"
THE PAST-ME AND THE NOW-ME. I WONDER IF THEY'RE REALLY THE SAME ME...
ARE YOU REALLY YOU?
"I think you should get some sleep."
OKAY.

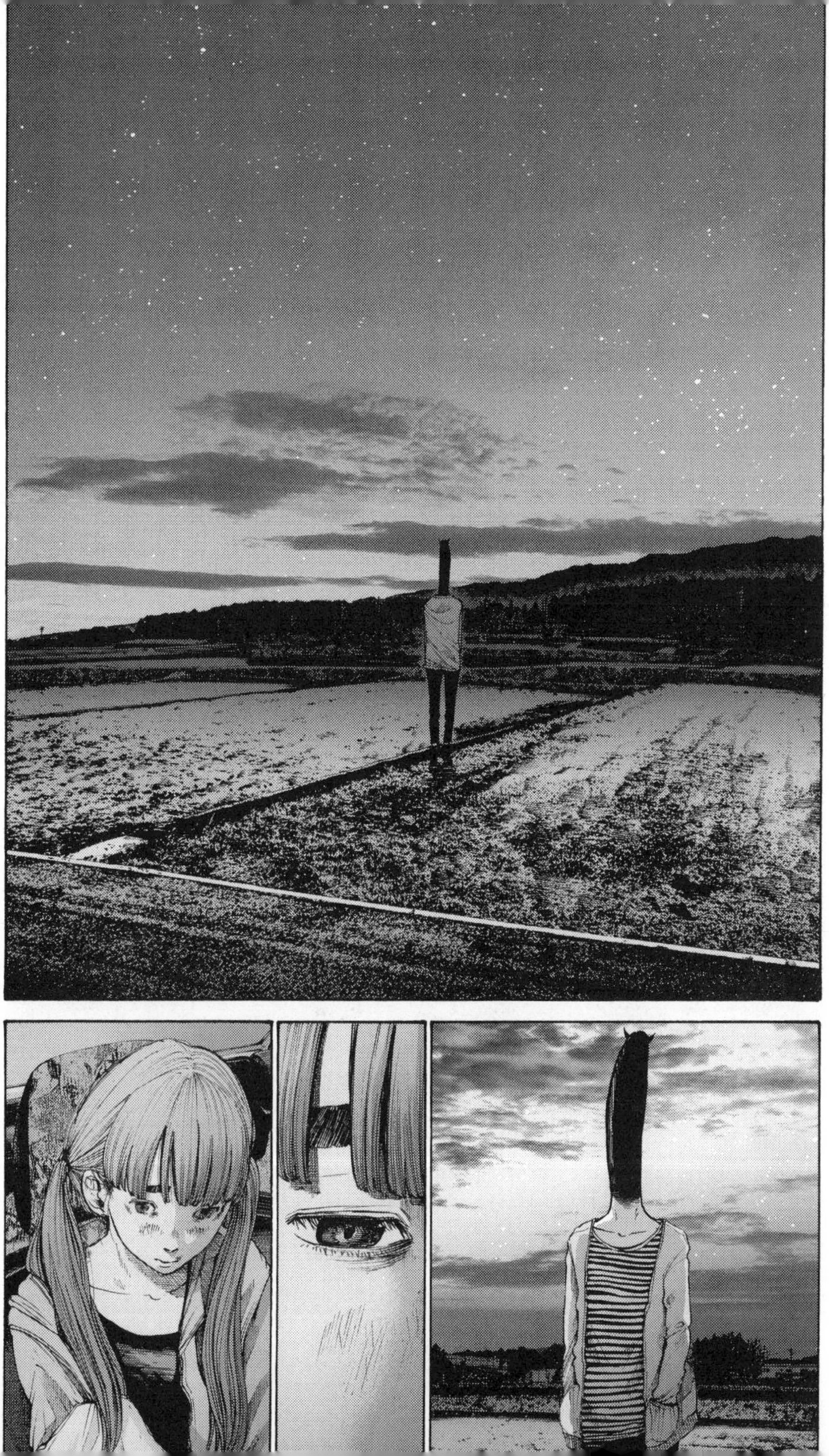

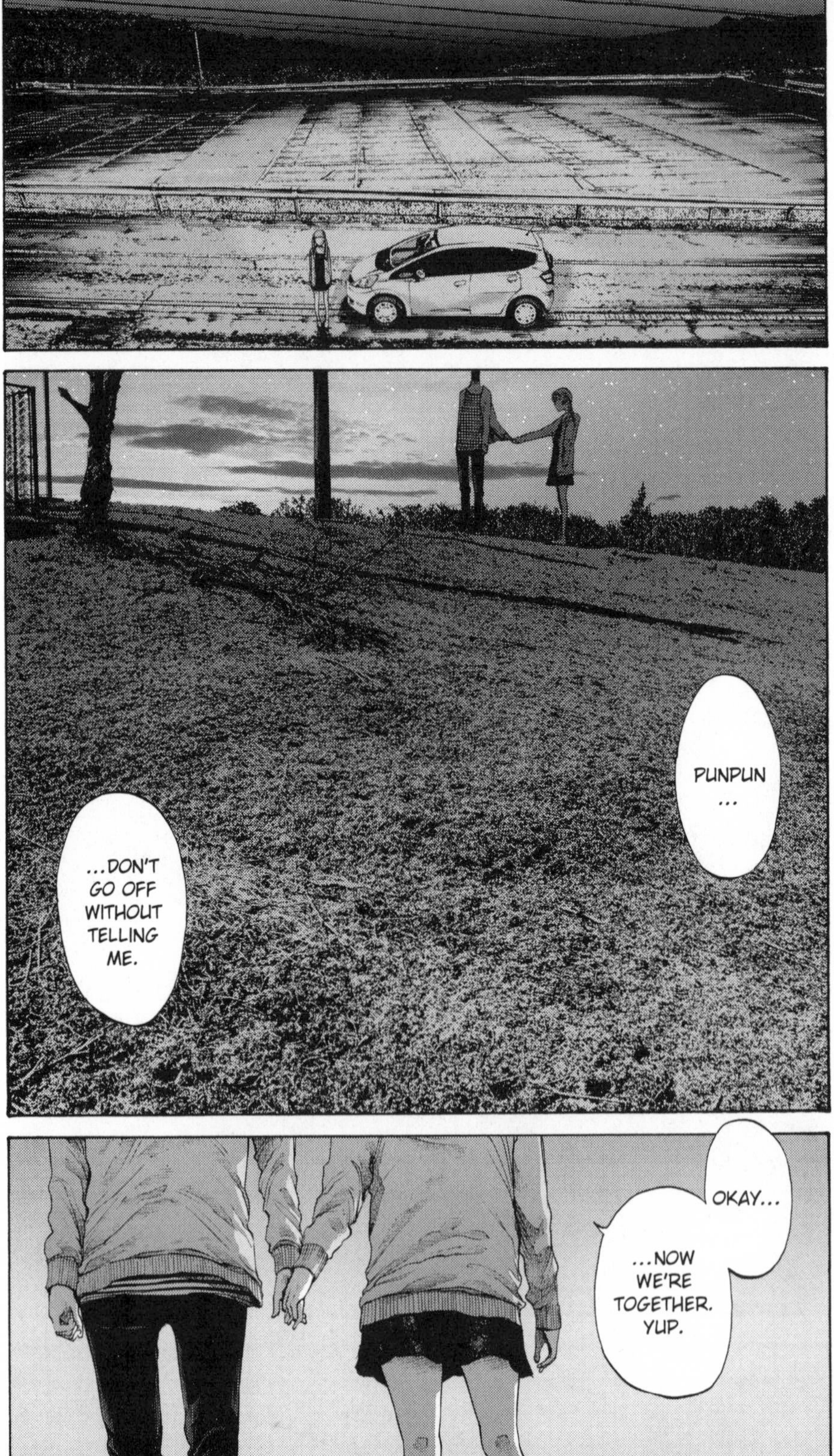
PUNPUN ...
...DON'T GO OFF WITHOUT TELLING ME.
OKAY...
...NOW WE'RE TOGETHER. YUP.

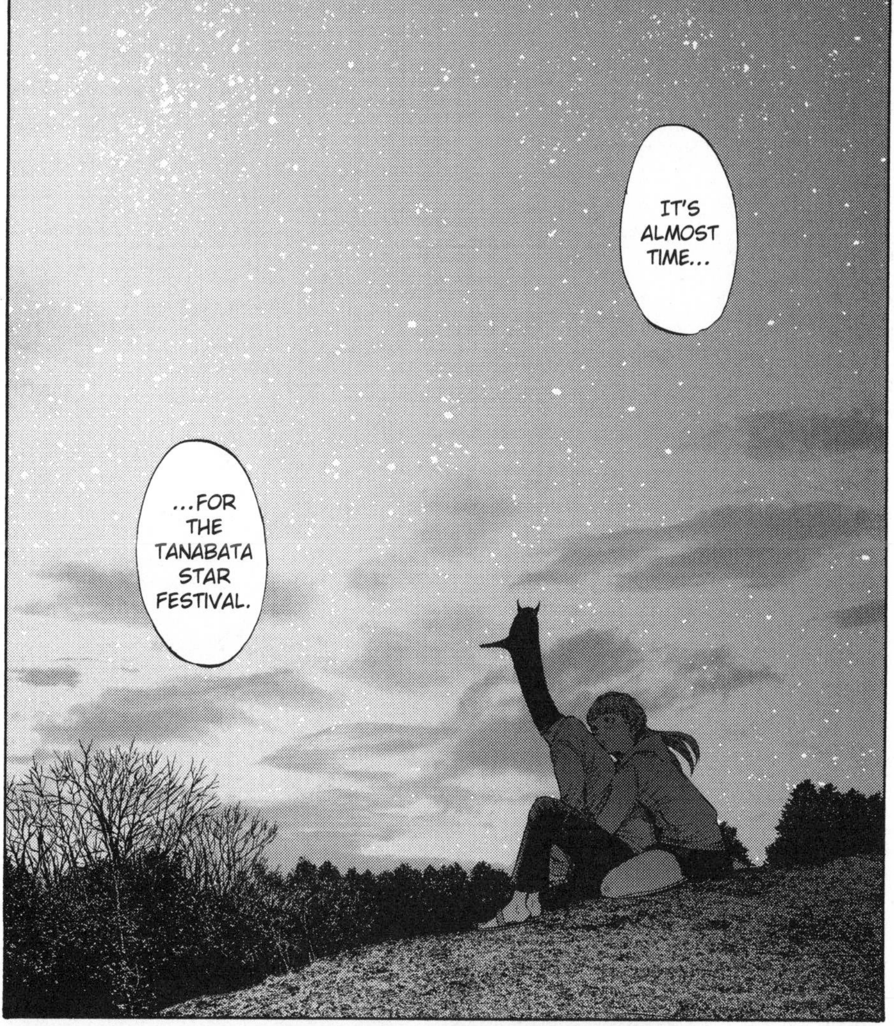
IT'S ALMOST TIME...
...FOR THE TANABATA STAR FESTIVAL.
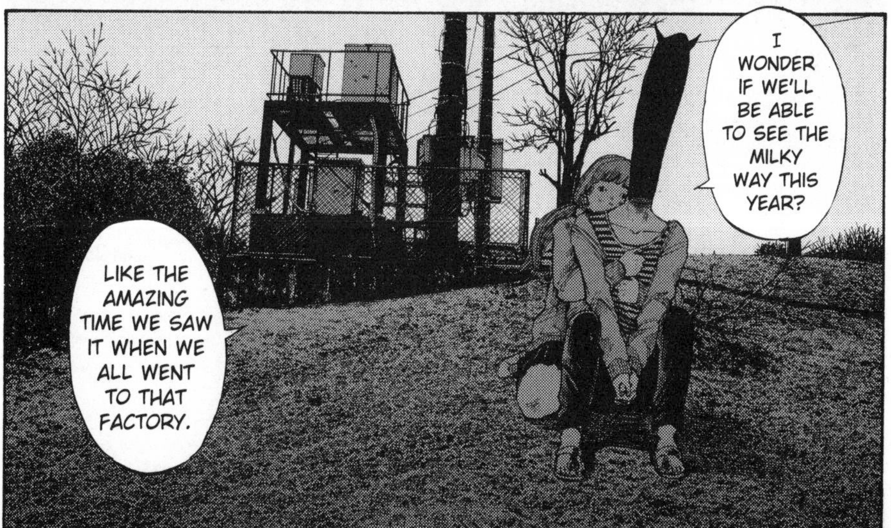
I WONDER IF WE'LL BE ABLE TO SEE THE MILKY WAY THIS YEAR?
LIKE THE AMAZING TIME WE SAW IT WHEN WE ALL WENT TO THAT FACTORY.

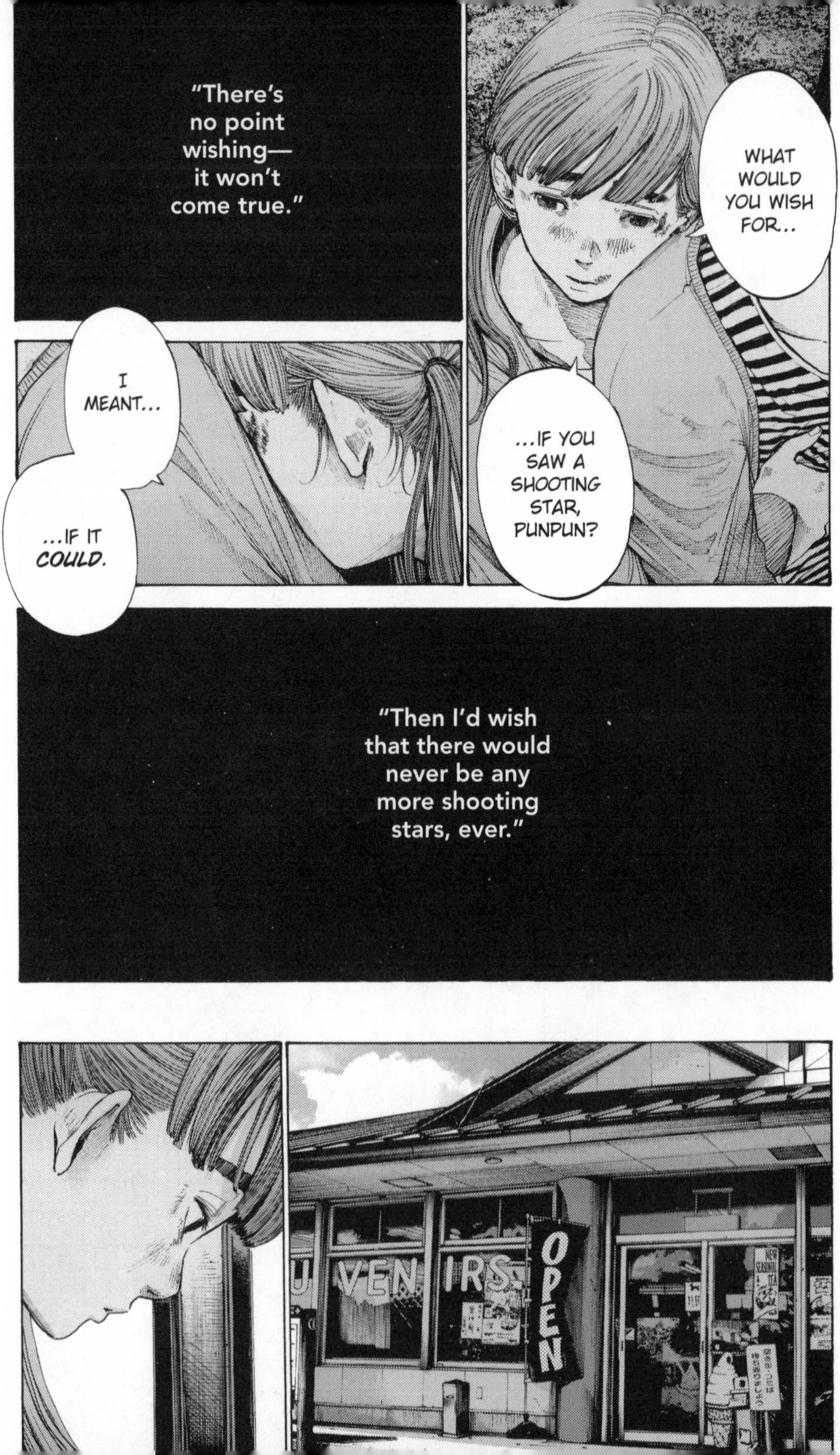
WHAT WOULD YOU WISH FOR..
...IF YOU SAW A SHOOTING STAR, PUNPUN?
"There's no point wishing— it won't come true."
I MEANT...
...IF IT *COULD.*
"Then I'd wish that there would never be any more shooting stars, ever."
OPEN
NEW SEASONAL TEA

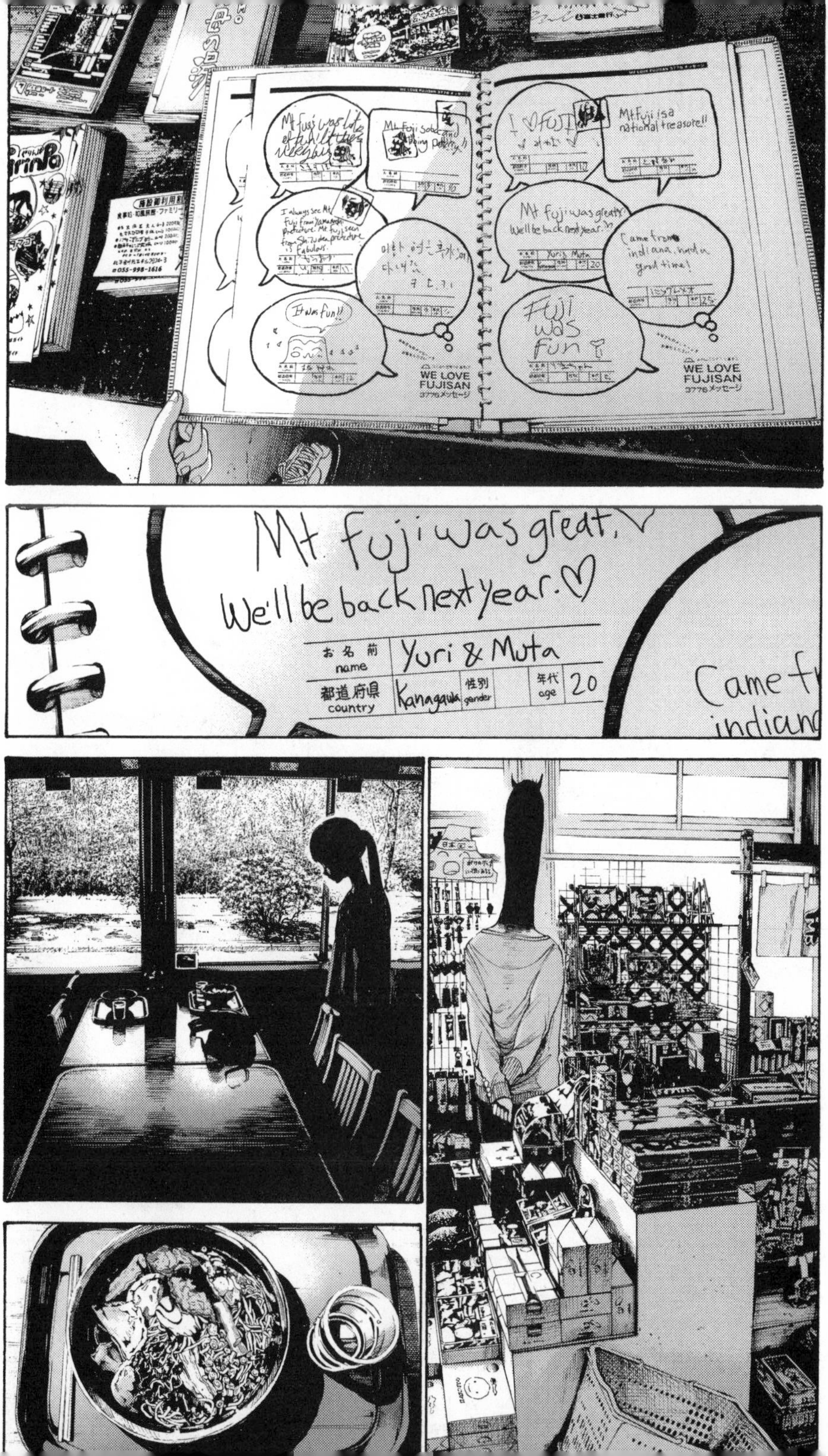

I ♡ FUJI
Mt Fuji is a national treasure!!
Mt fuji was great. We'll be back next year.
Came from indiana. had a good time!
Fuji was fun
It was fun!!
WE LOVE FUJISAN
3776メッセージ
WE LOVE FUJISAN
3776メッセージ
Mt. fuji was great.♡
We'll be back next year.♡
お名前 name
Yuri & Muta
都道府県 country
Kanagawa
性別 gender
年代 age
20

SPLLSH PSSH PSSH
YO!
HUFF.
HUFF.
SLURP ...
... SLURP.
SLURP.
SLURP.
SLURP ...
... SLURP.

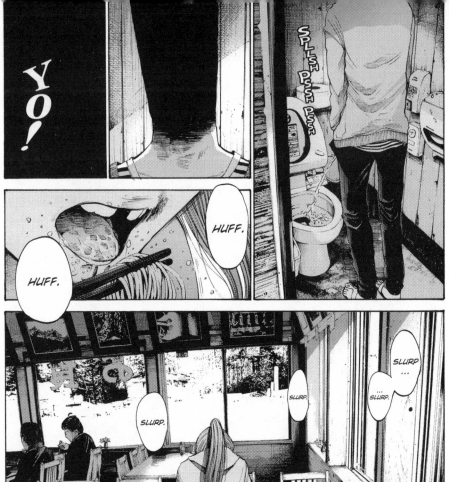

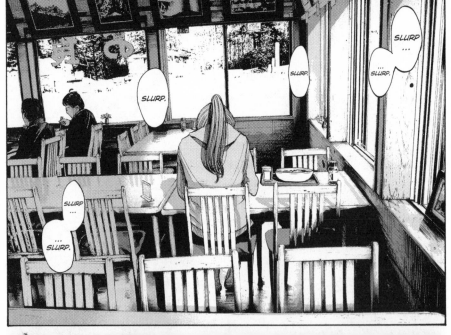

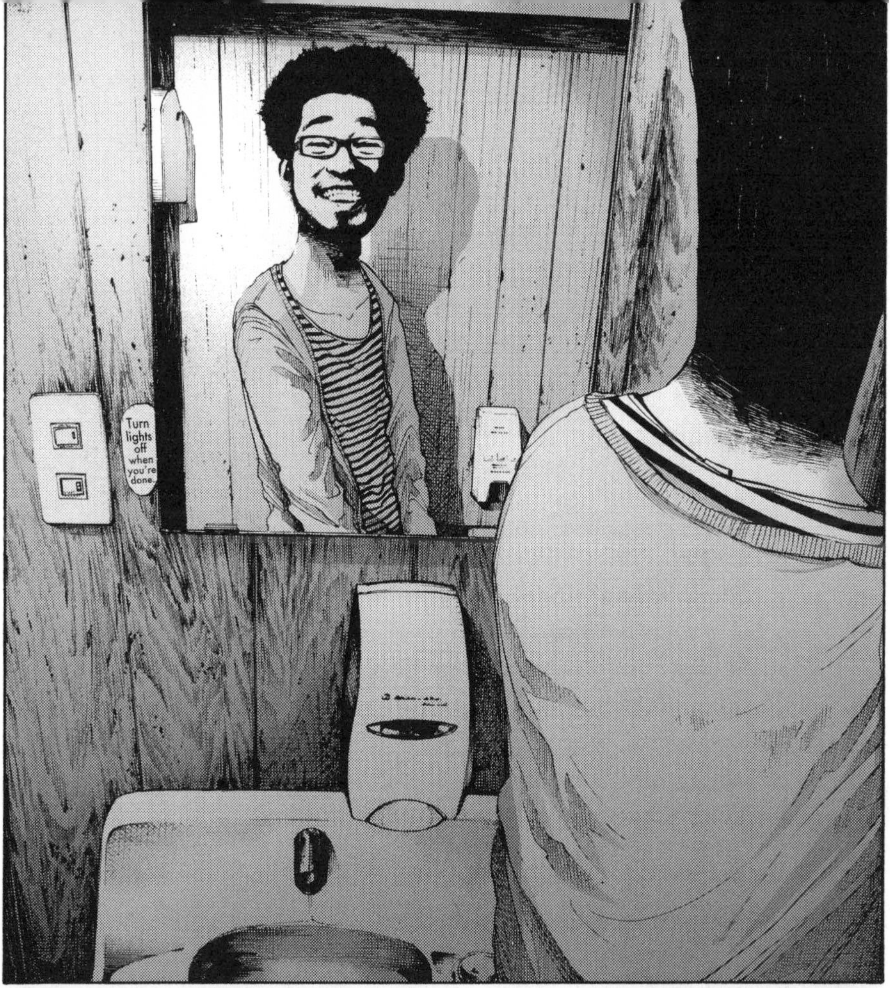
Turn lights off when you're done.
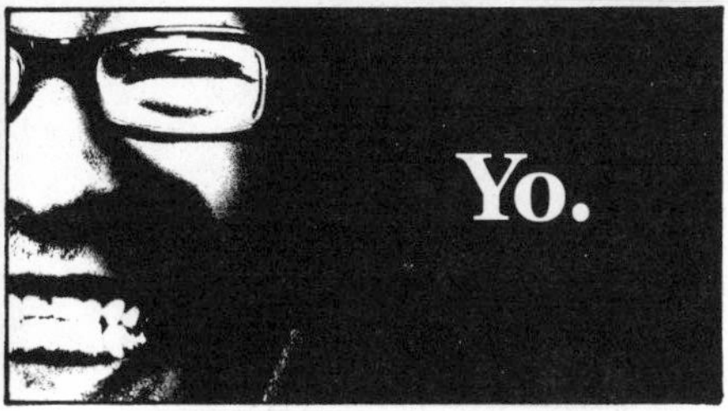
Yo.
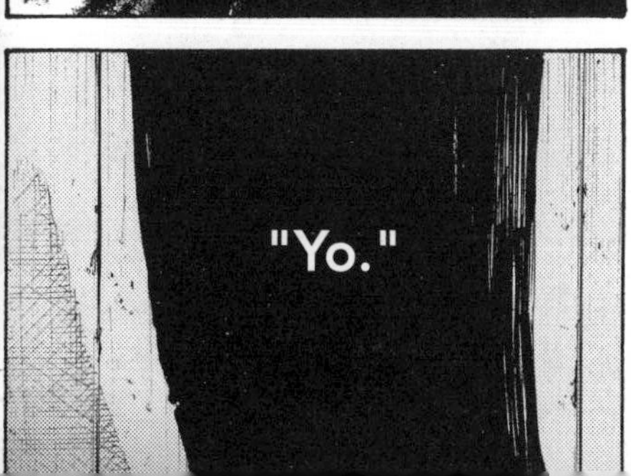
"Yo."
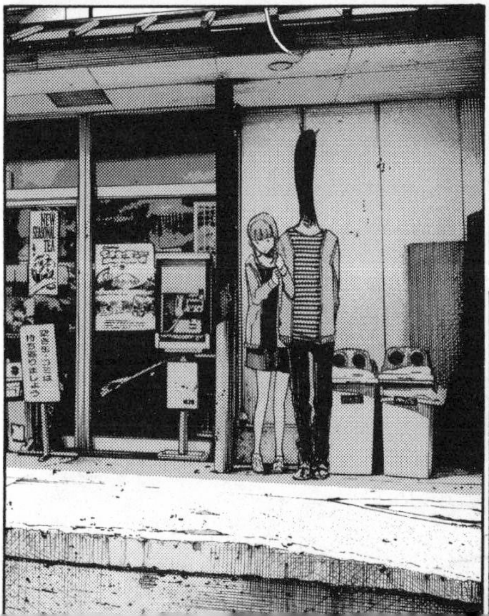

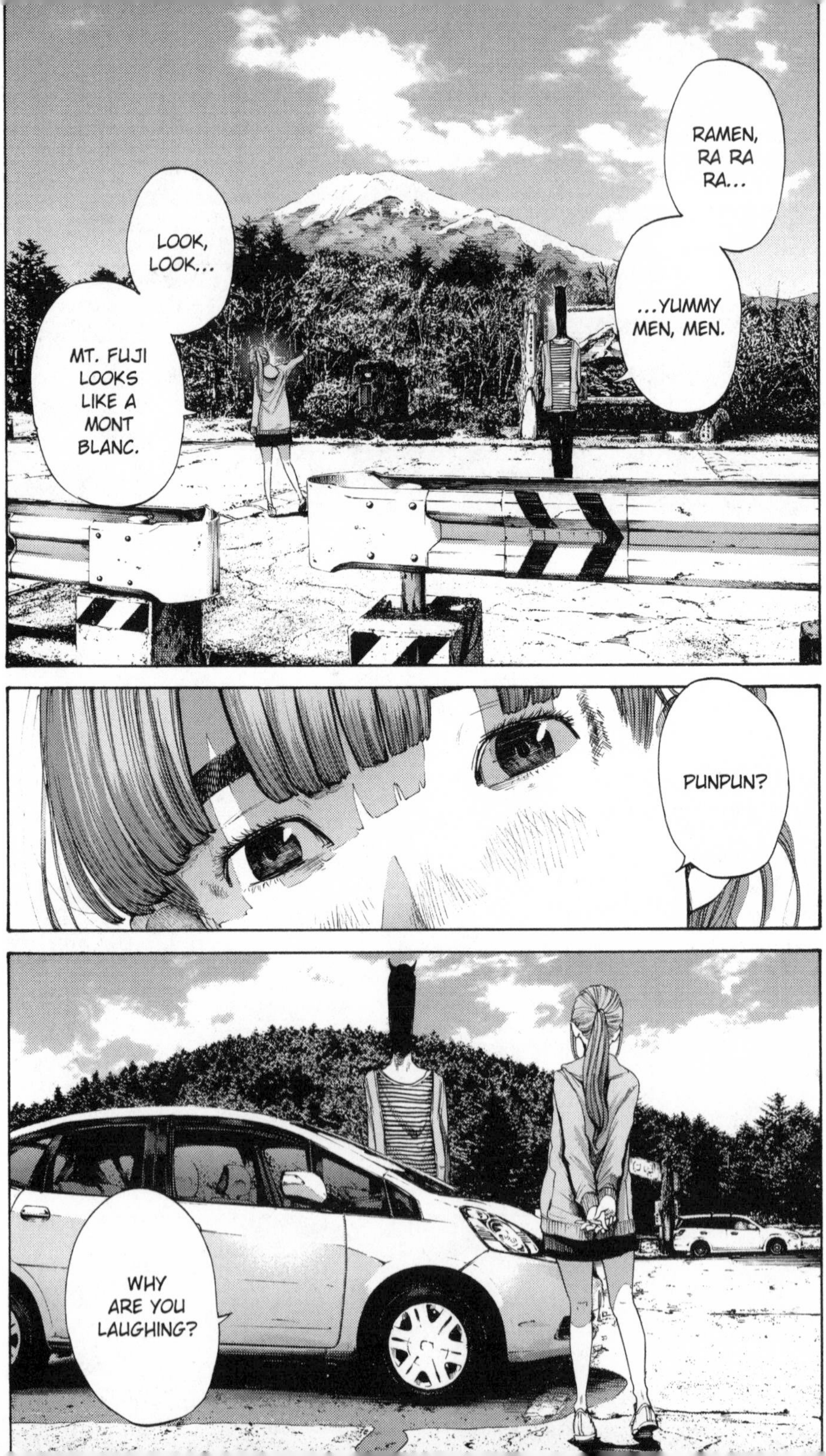
RAMEN, RA RA RA...
...YUMMY MEN, MEN.
LOOK, LOOK...
MT. FUJI LOOKS LIKE A MONT BLANC.
PUNPUN?
WHY ARE YOU LAUGHING?

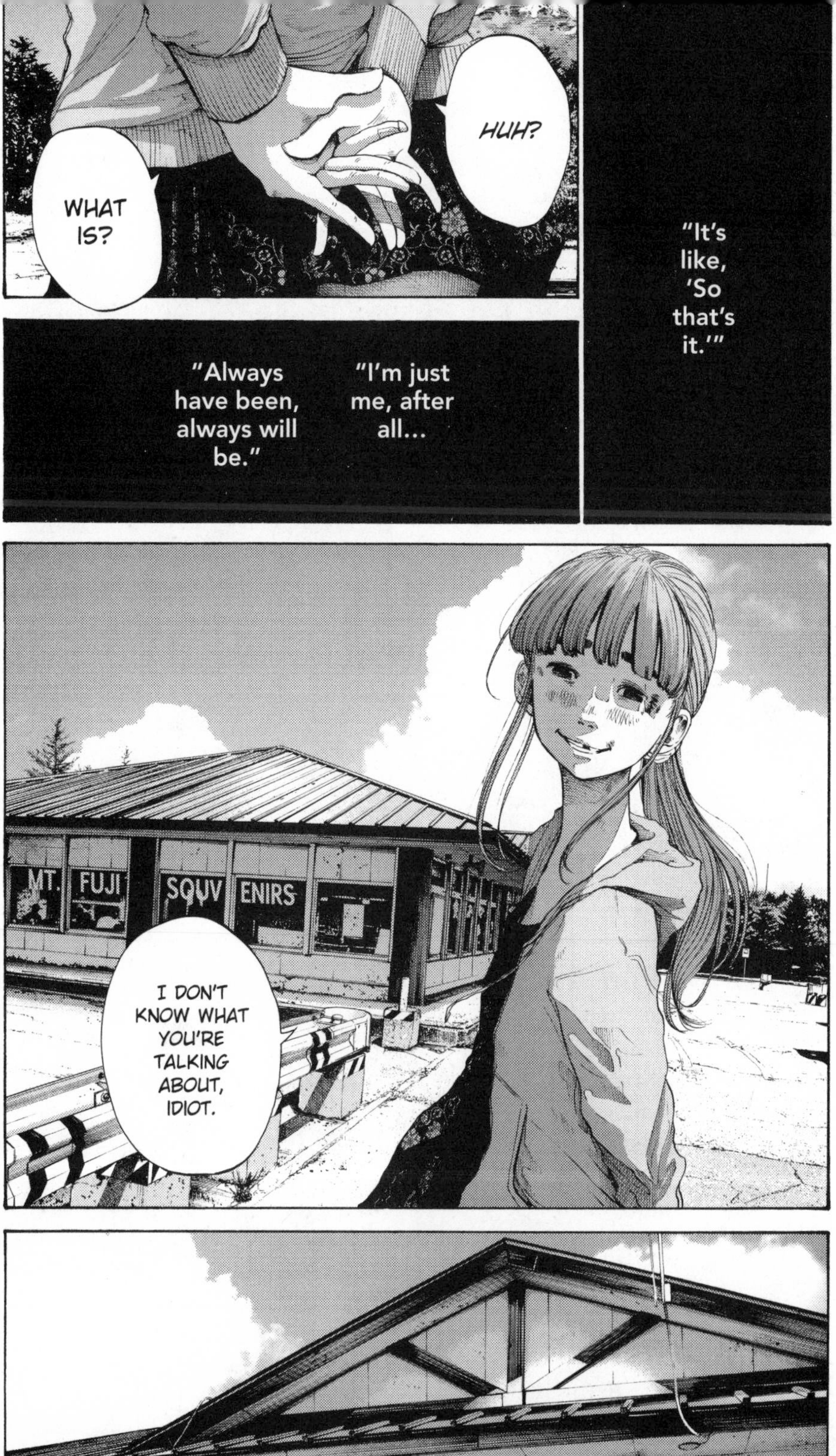
"It's like, 'So that's it.'"
HUH?
WHAT IS?
"I'm just me, after all...
"Always have been, always will be."
MT. FUJI SOUV ENIRS
I DON'T KNOW WHAT YOU'RE TALKING ABOUT, IDIOT.

Chapter 121.

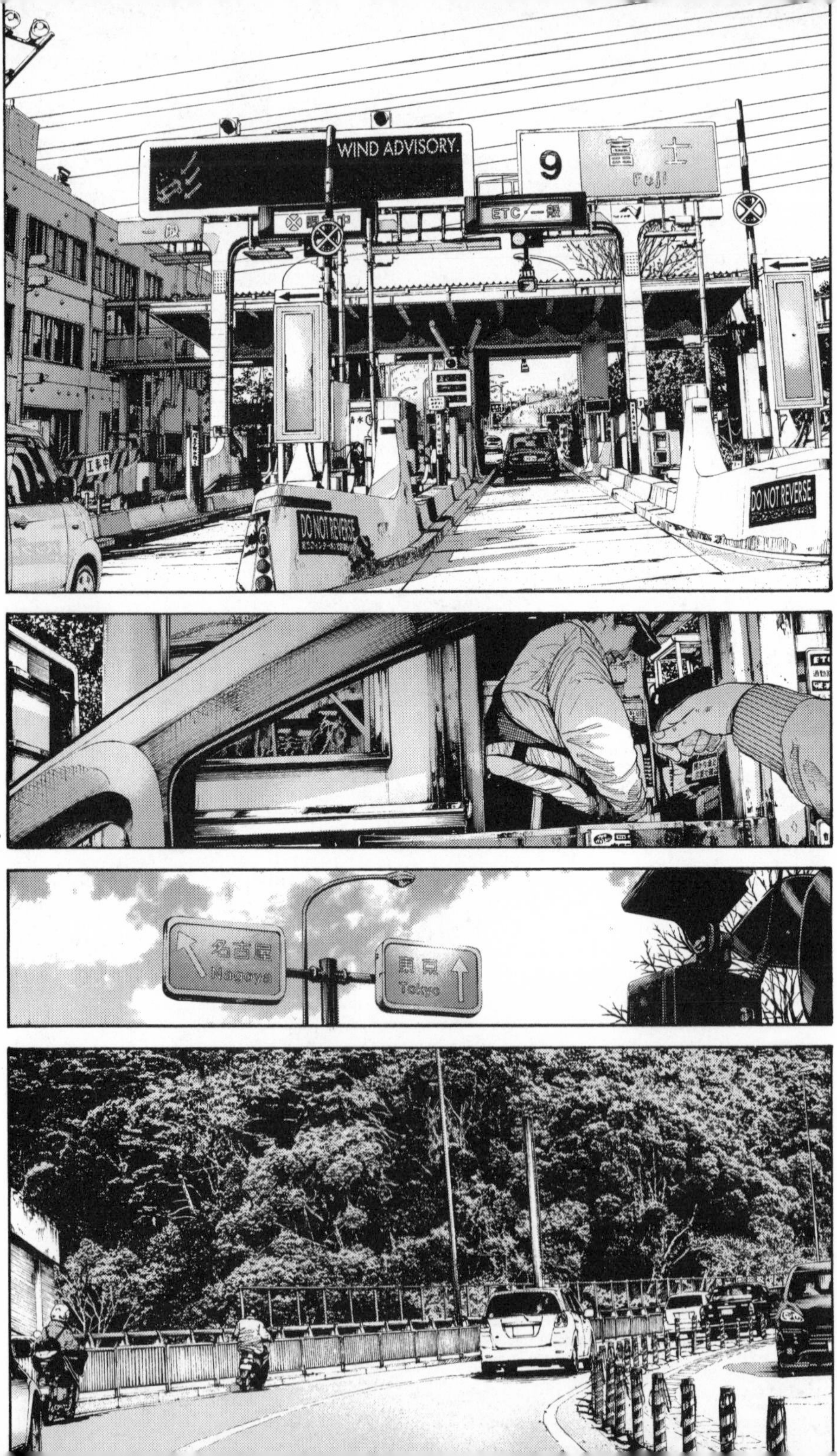
WIND ADVISORY.
9
富士
Fuji
ETC 一般
DO NOT REVERSE.
DO NOT REVERSE.
名古屋
Nagoya
東京
Tokyo

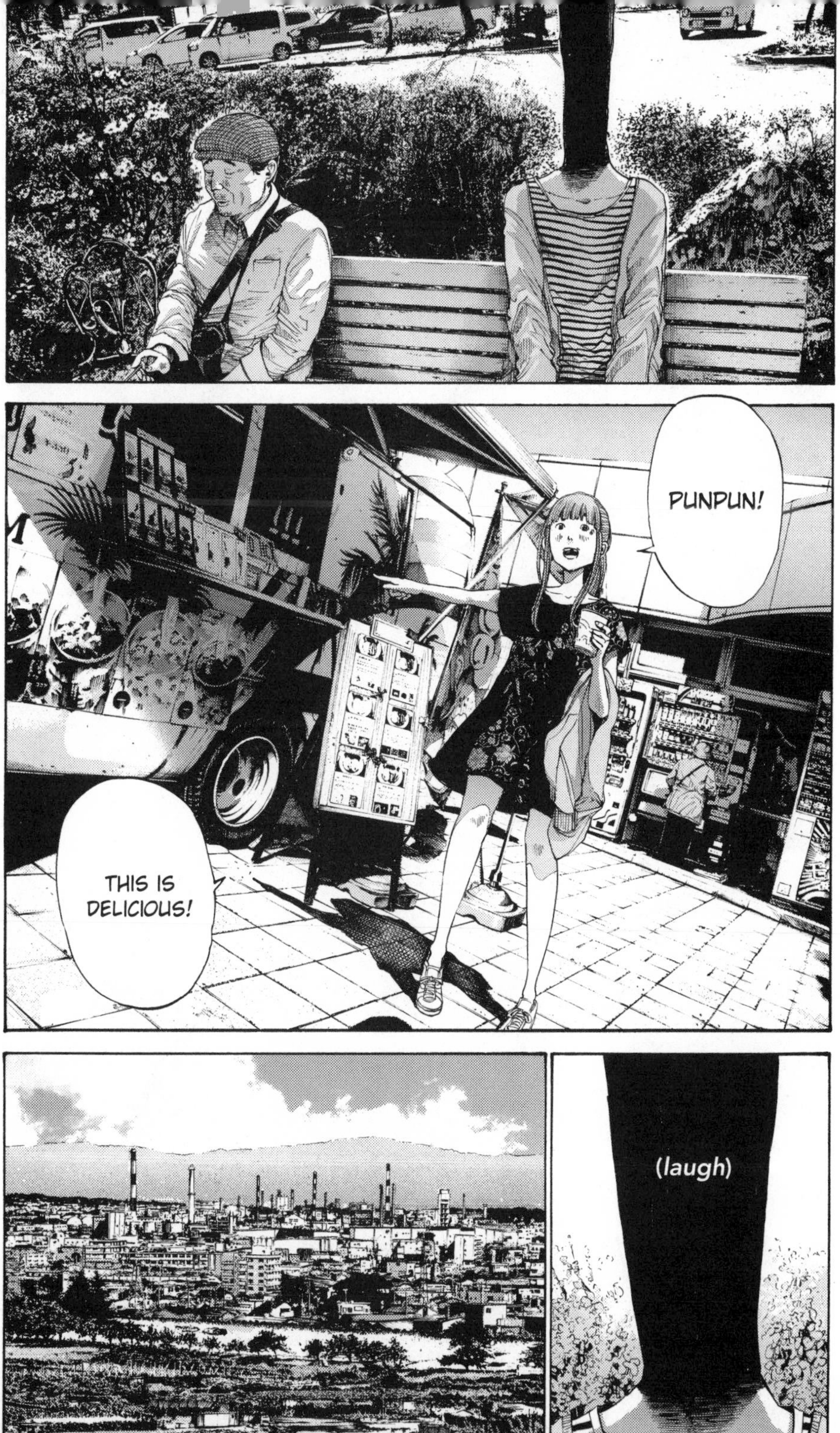
PUNPUN!
THIS IS DELICIOUS!
(laugh)

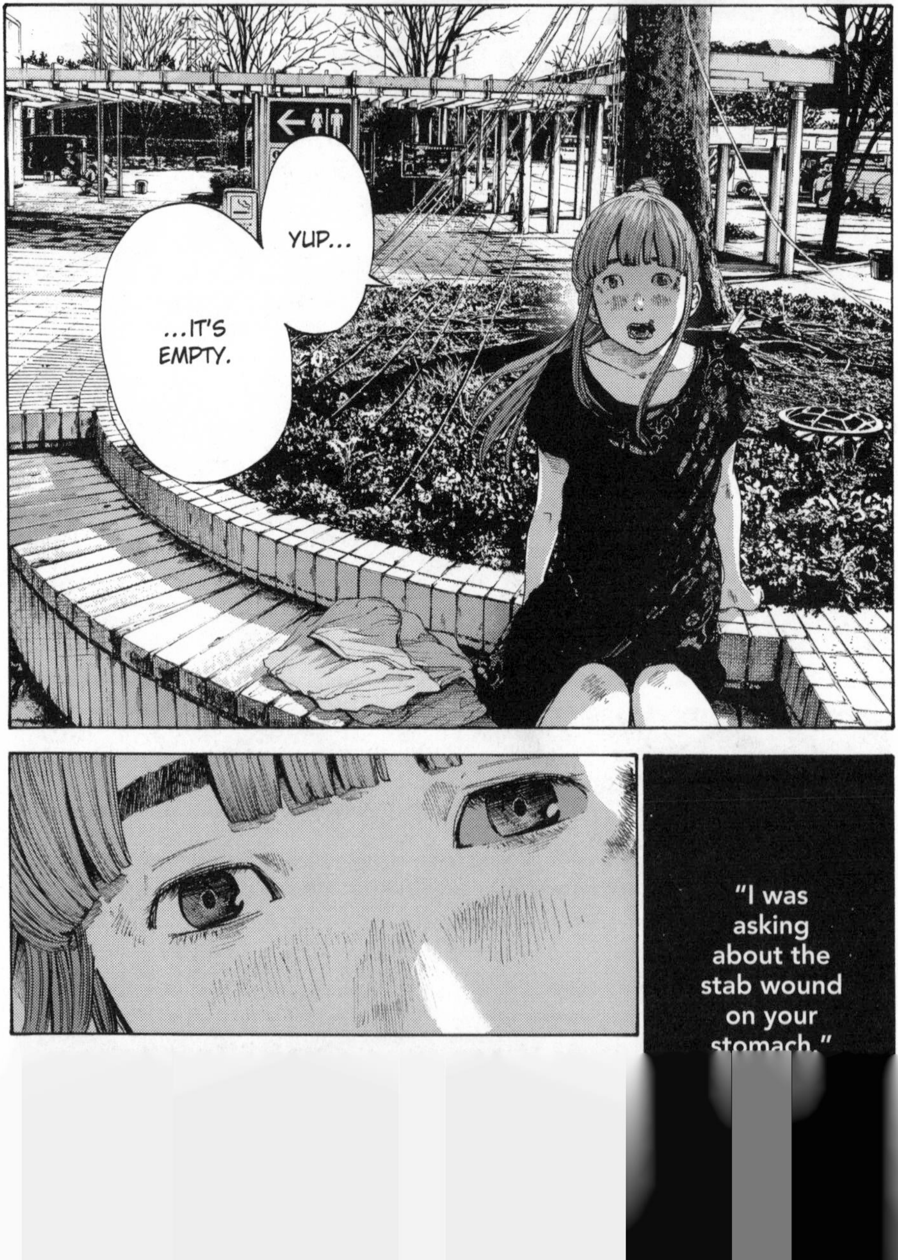
YUP...
...IT'S EMPTY.
"I was asking about the stab wound on your stomach."

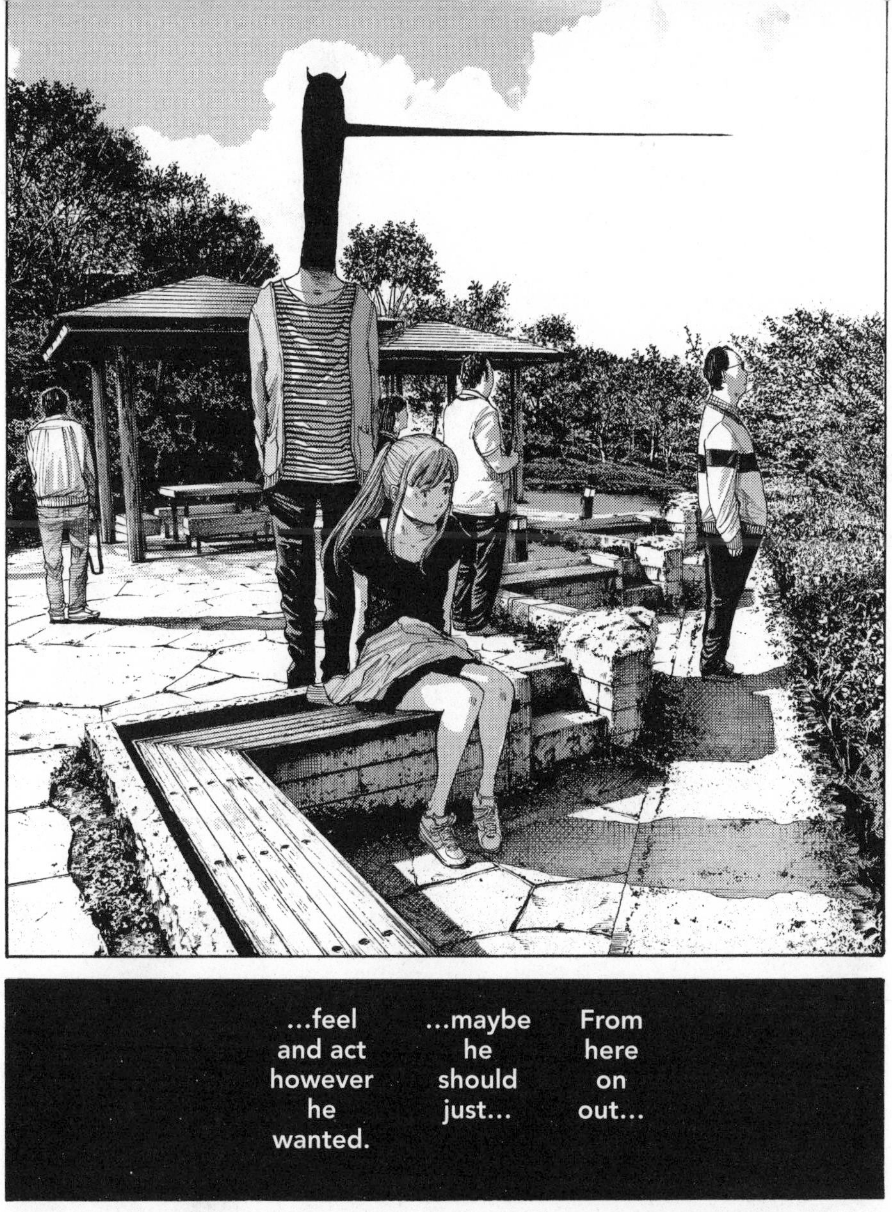

From here on out...

...maybe he should just...

...feel and act however he wanted.

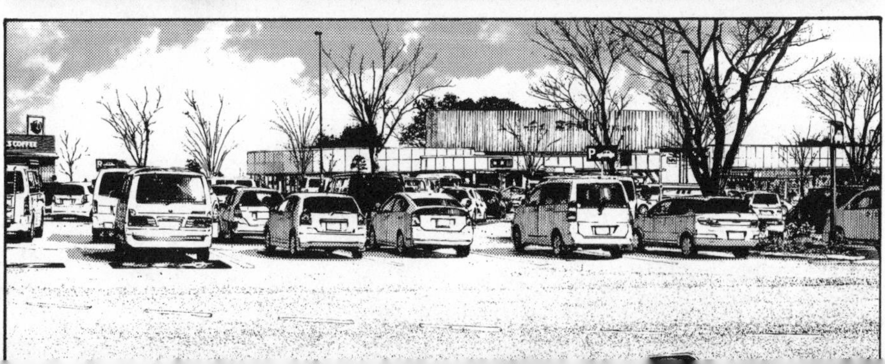

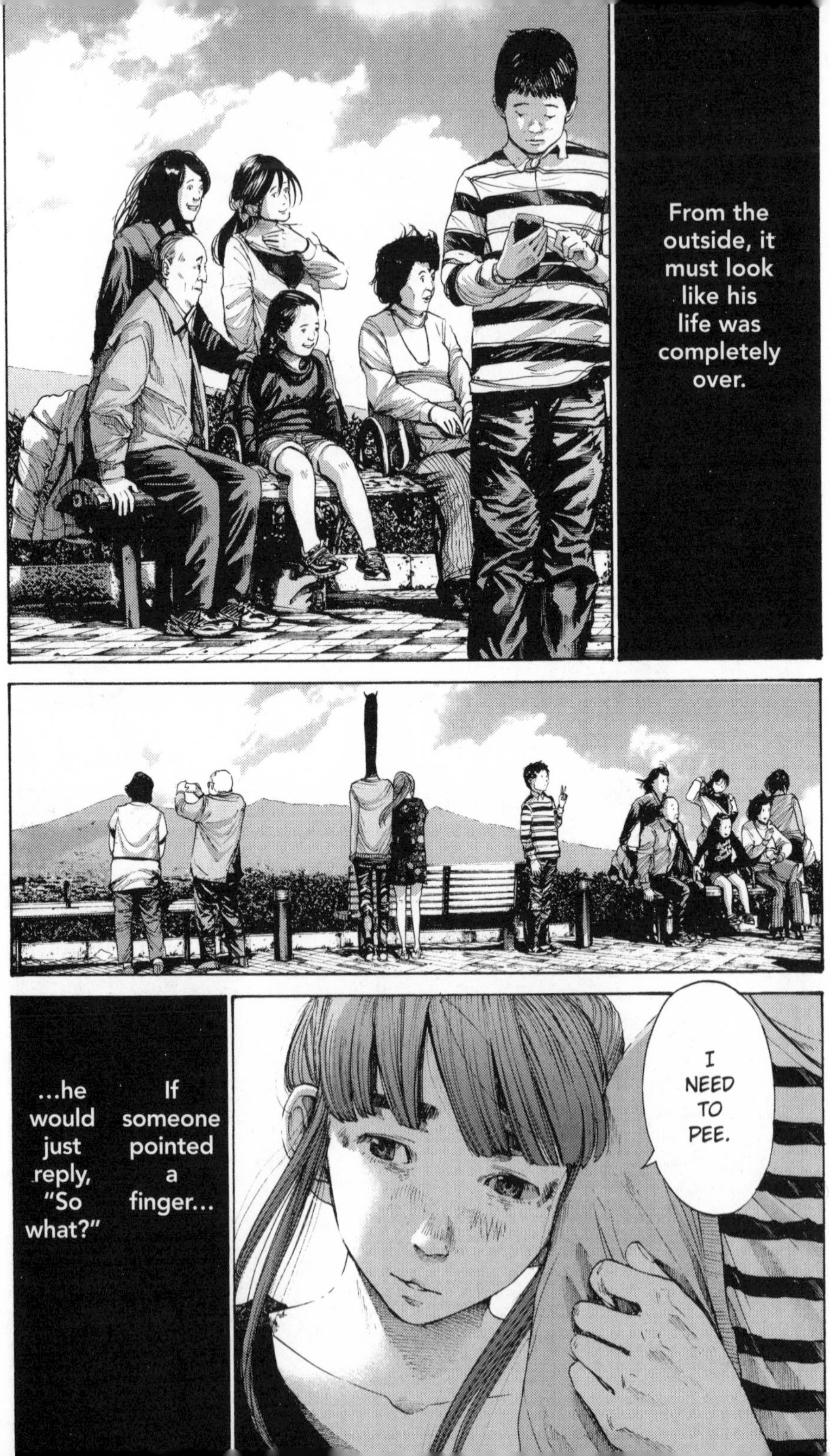
From the outside, it must look like his life was completely over.
I NEED TO PEE.
If someone pointed a finger...
...he would just reply, "So what?"

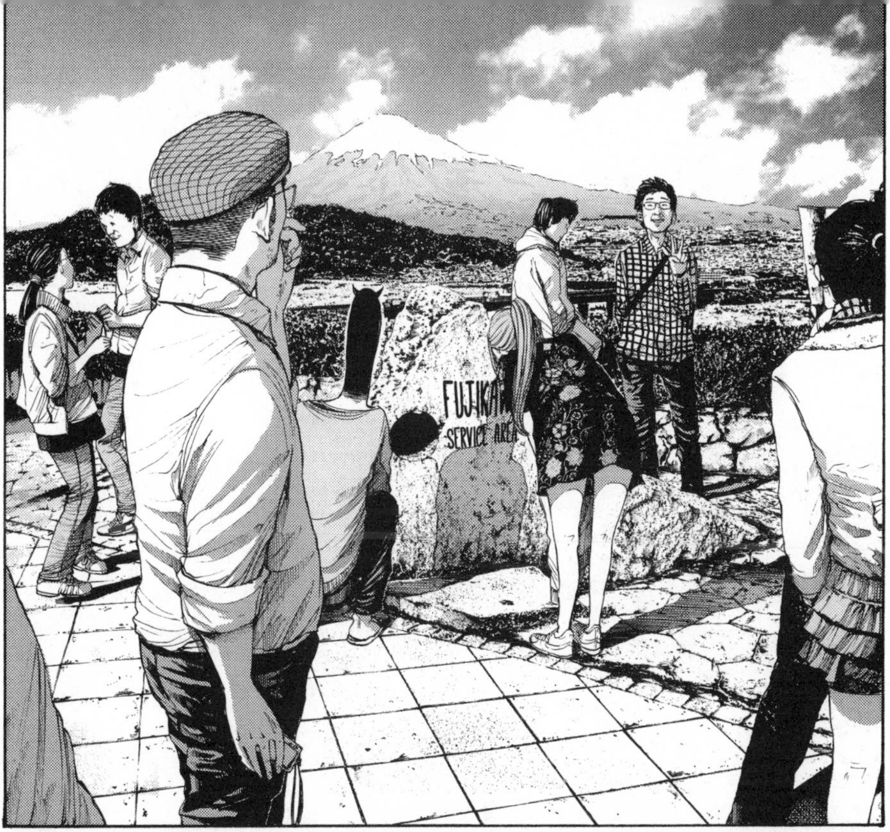
SERVICE AREA

Beyond this ending wasn't hell or despair...

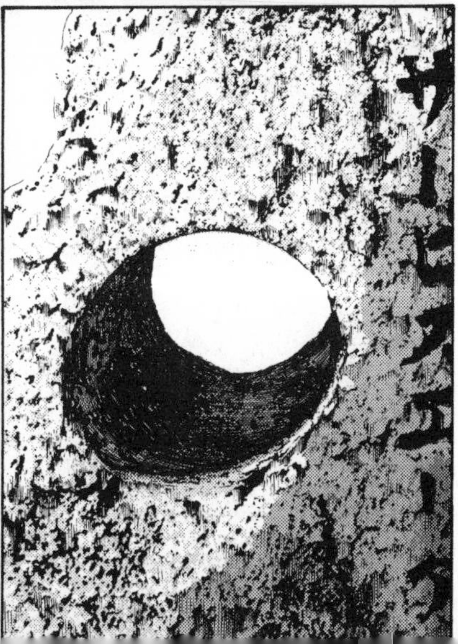

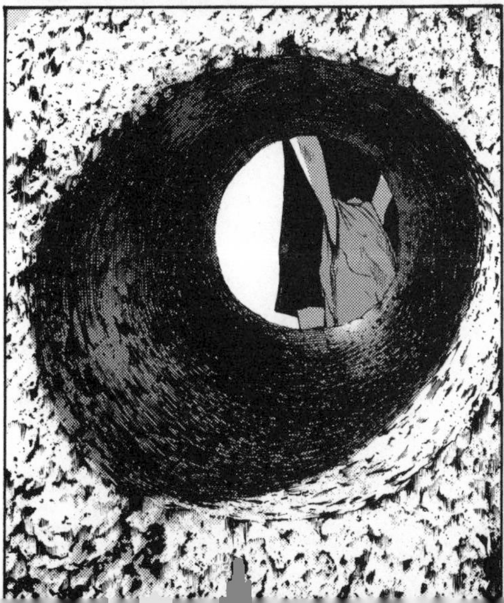

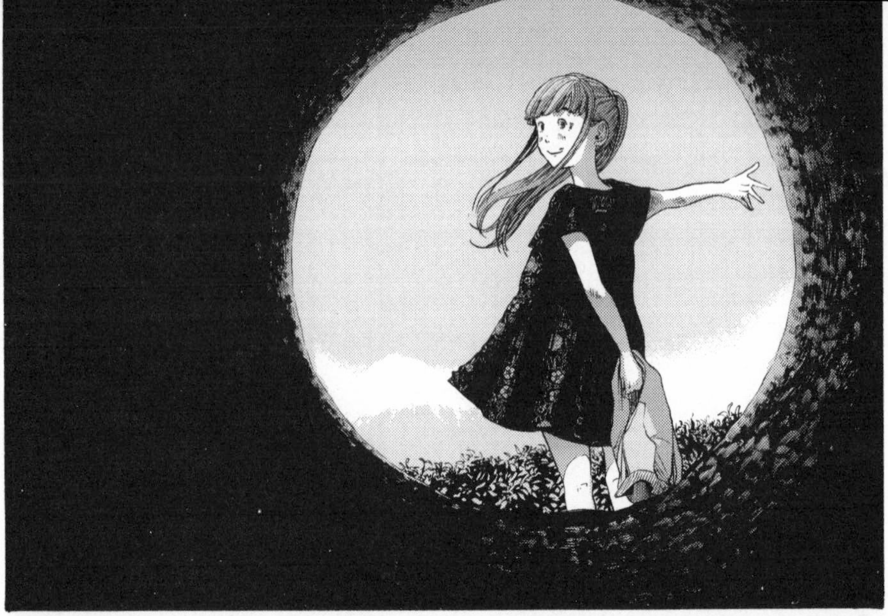

...even if the sound and fury was a momentary fuss about nothing.

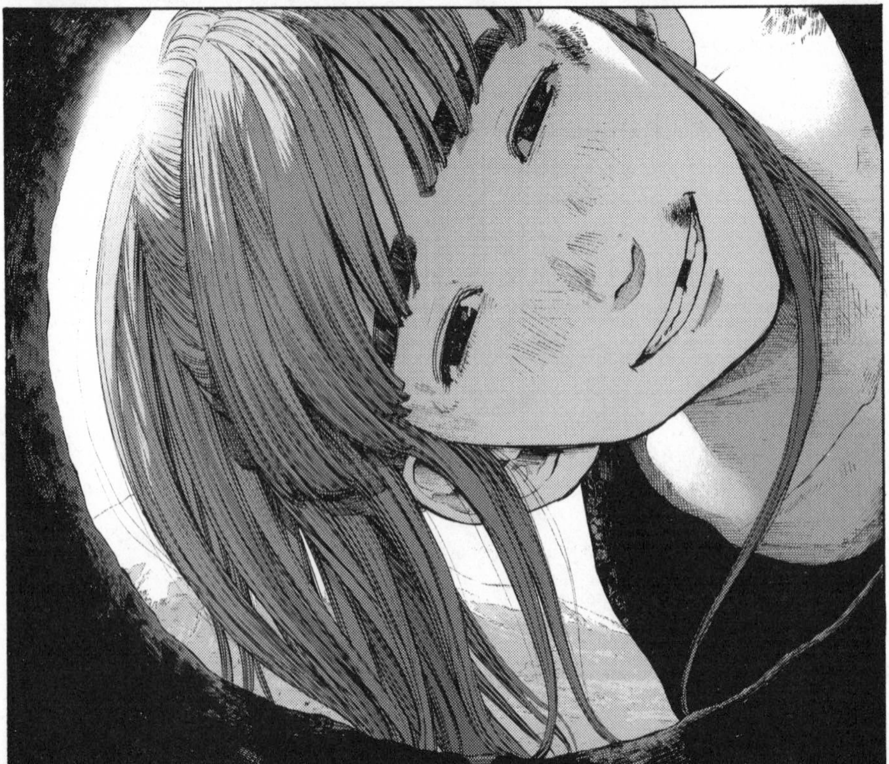

GOODNIGHT PUNPUN

Part Eleven

INIO ASANO

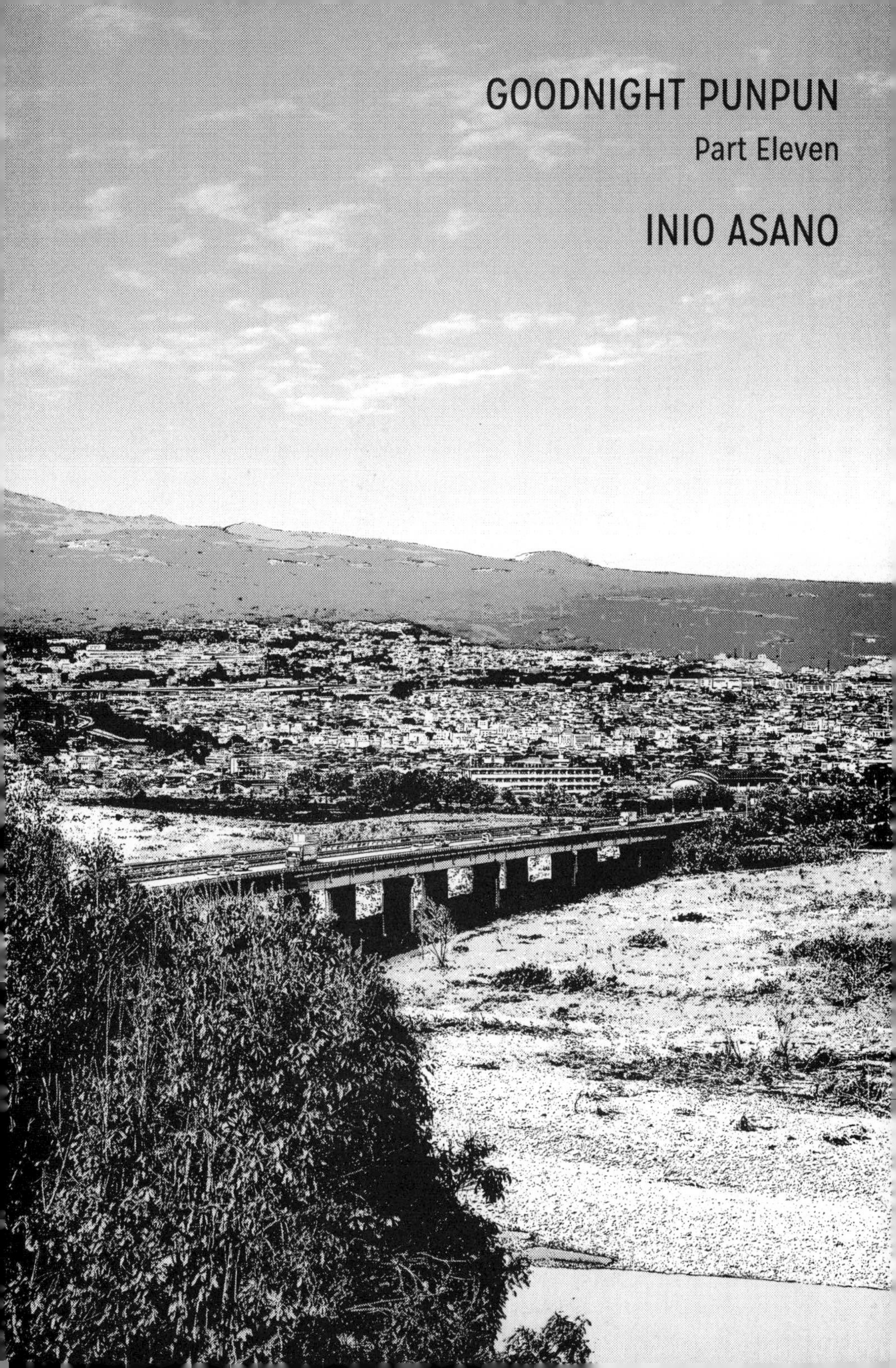

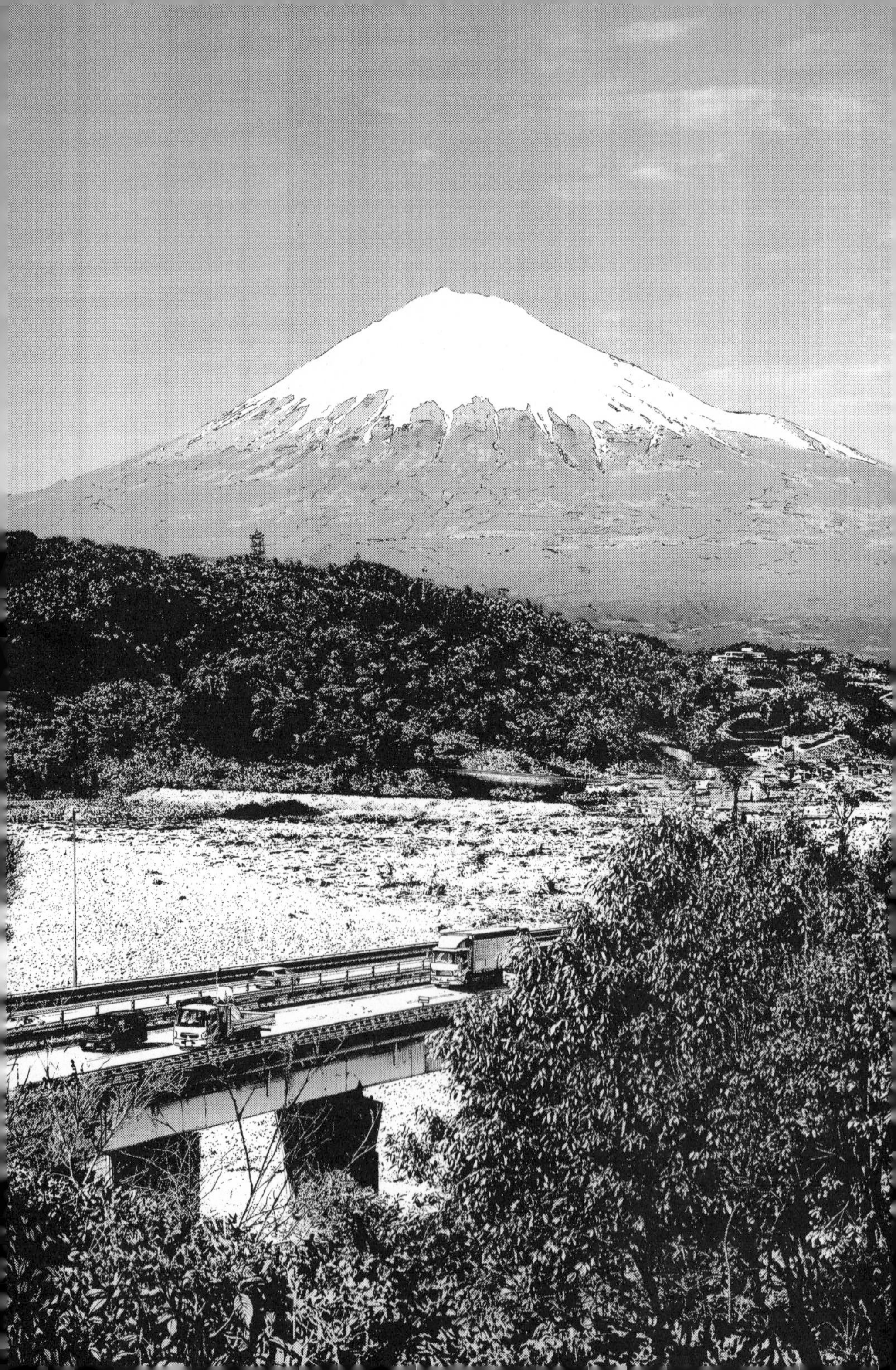

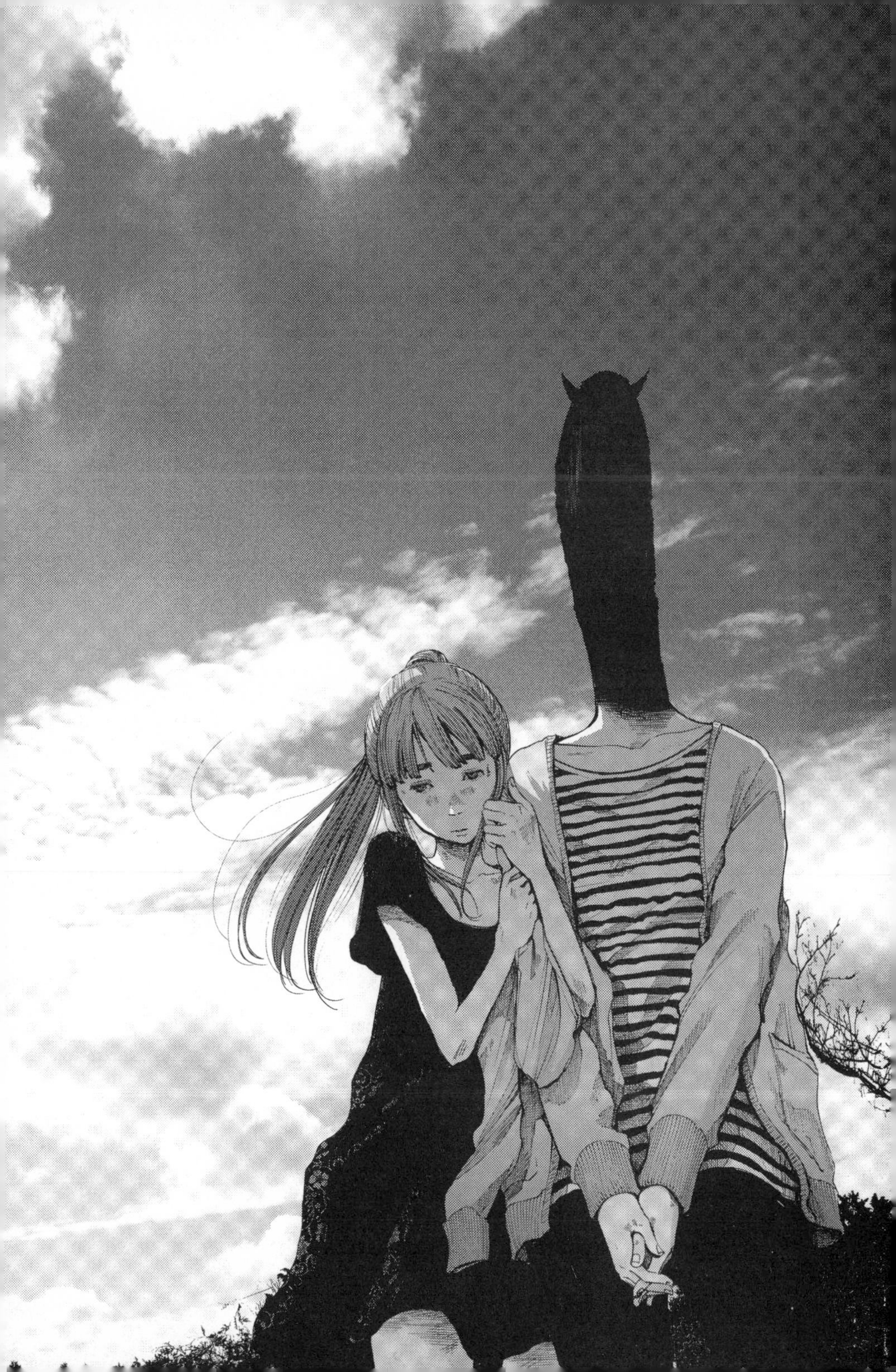

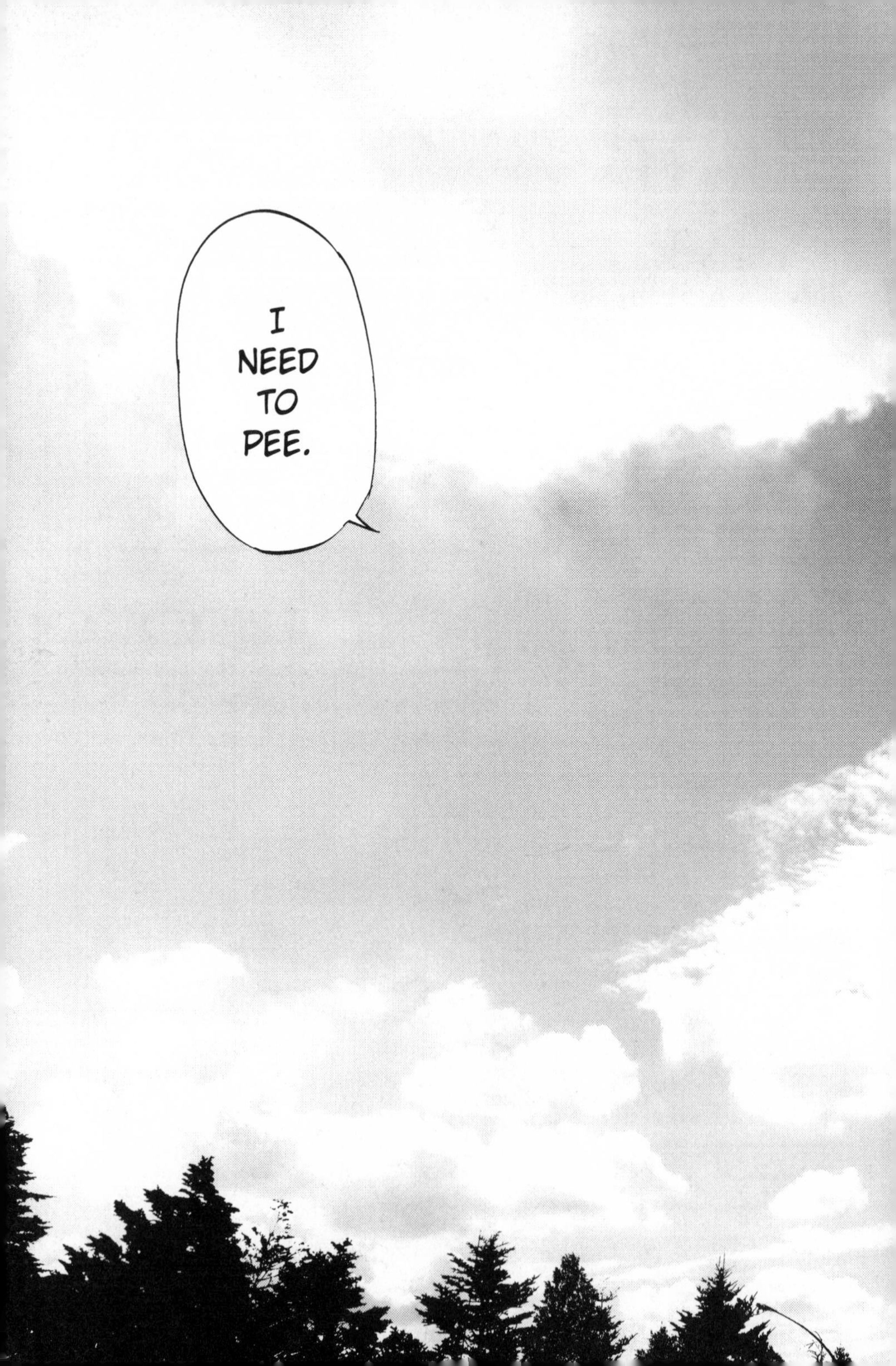
I NEED TO PEE.

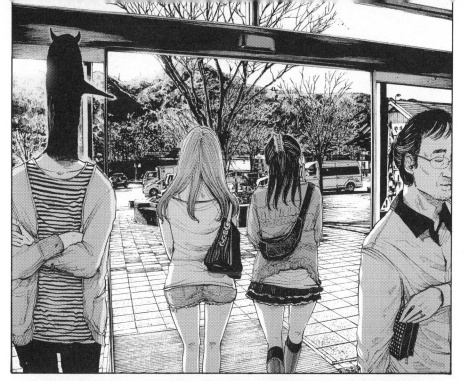

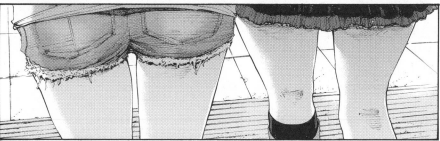

"You
were
gone
a long
time."

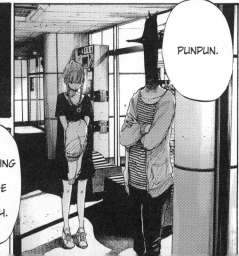

PUNPUN.

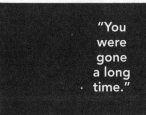

I WAS
REWRAPPING
THE
BANDAGE
ON MY
STOMACH.

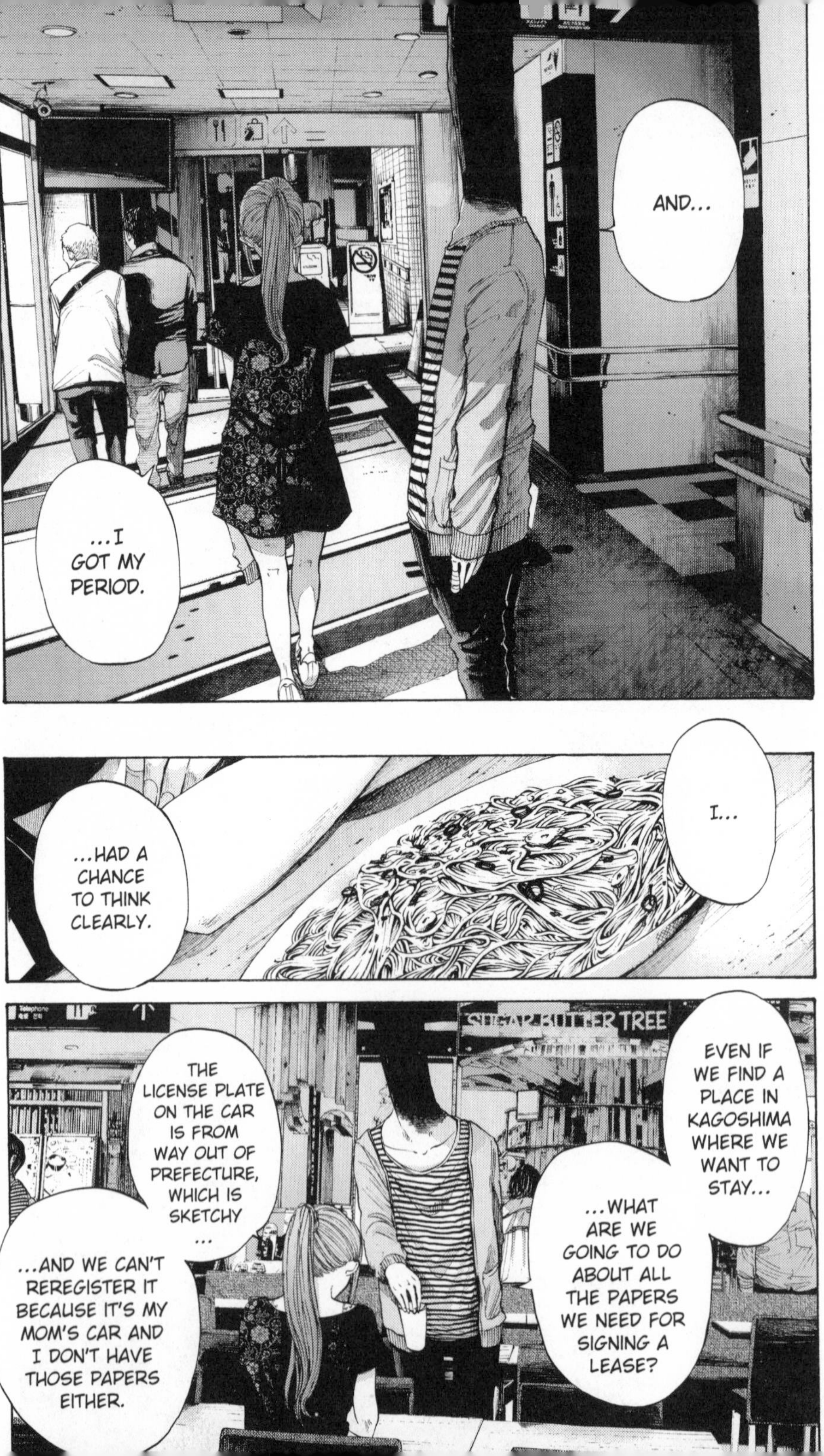
AND...
...I GOT MY PERIOD.
I...
...HAD A CHANCE TO THINK CLEARLY.
SUGAR BUTTER TREE
EVEN IF WE FIND A PLACE IN KAGOSHIMA WHERE WE WANT TO STAY...
...WHAT ARE WE GOING TO DO ABOUT ALL THE PAPERS WE NEED FOR SIGNING A LEASE?
THE LICENSE PLATE ON THE CAR IS FROM WAY OUT OF PREFECTURE, WHICH IS SKETCHY...
...AND WE CAN'T REREGISTER IT BECAUSE IT'S MY MOM'S CAR AND I DON'T HAVE THOSE PAPERS EITHER.

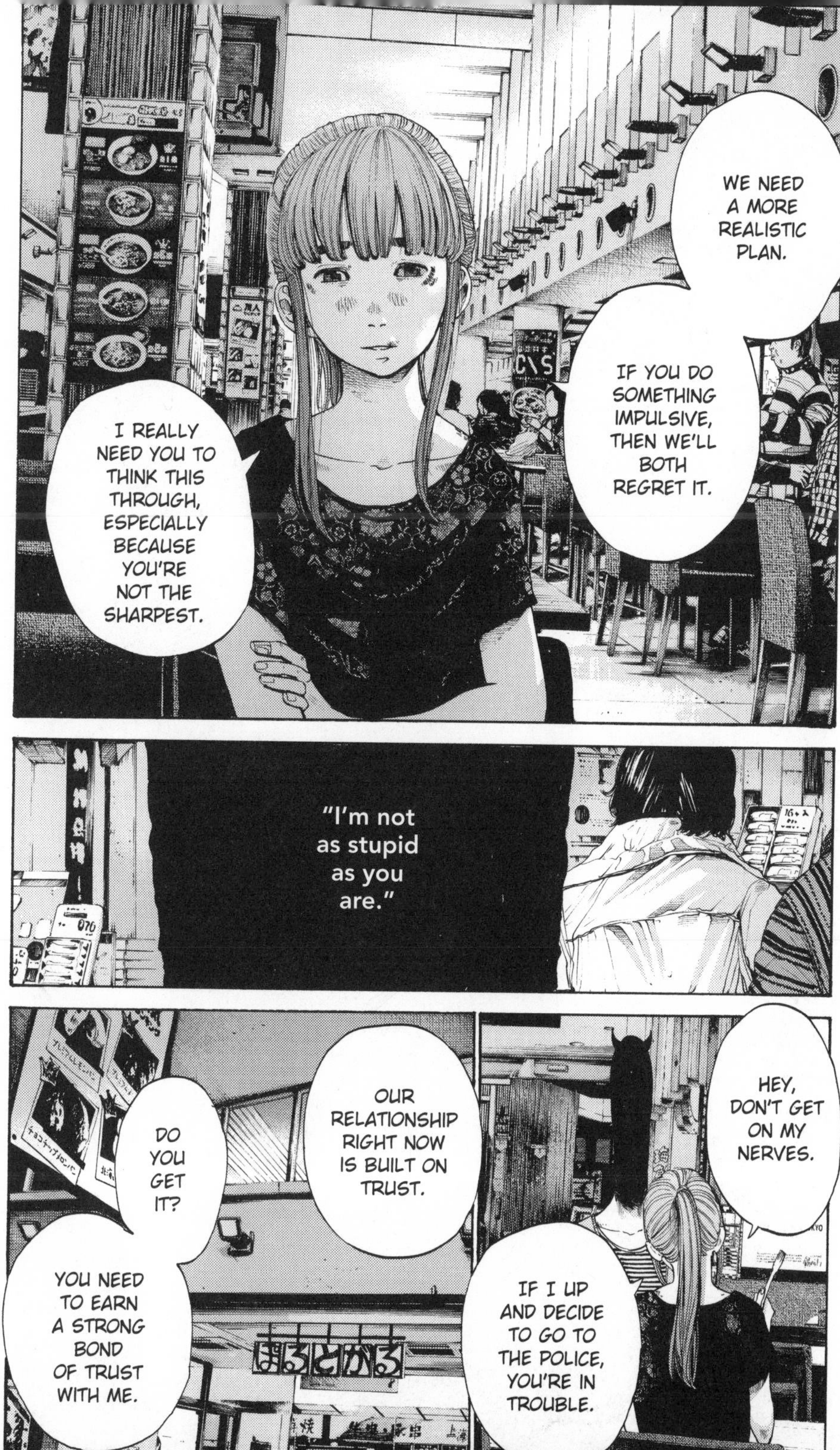
WE NEED A MORE REALISTIC PLAN.
IF YOU DO SOMETHING IMPULSIVE, THEN WE'LL BOTH REGRET IT.
I REALLY NEED YOU TO THINK THIS THROUGH, ESPECIALLY BECAUSE YOU'RE NOT THE SHARPEST.
"I'm not as stupid as you are."
HEY, DON'T GET ON MY NERVES.
IF I UP AND DECIDE TO GO TO THE POLICE, YOU'RE IN TROUBLE.
OUR RELATIONSHIP RIGHT NOW IS BUILT ON TRUST.
DO YOU GET IT?
YOU NEED TO EARN A STRONG BOND OF TRUST WITH ME.

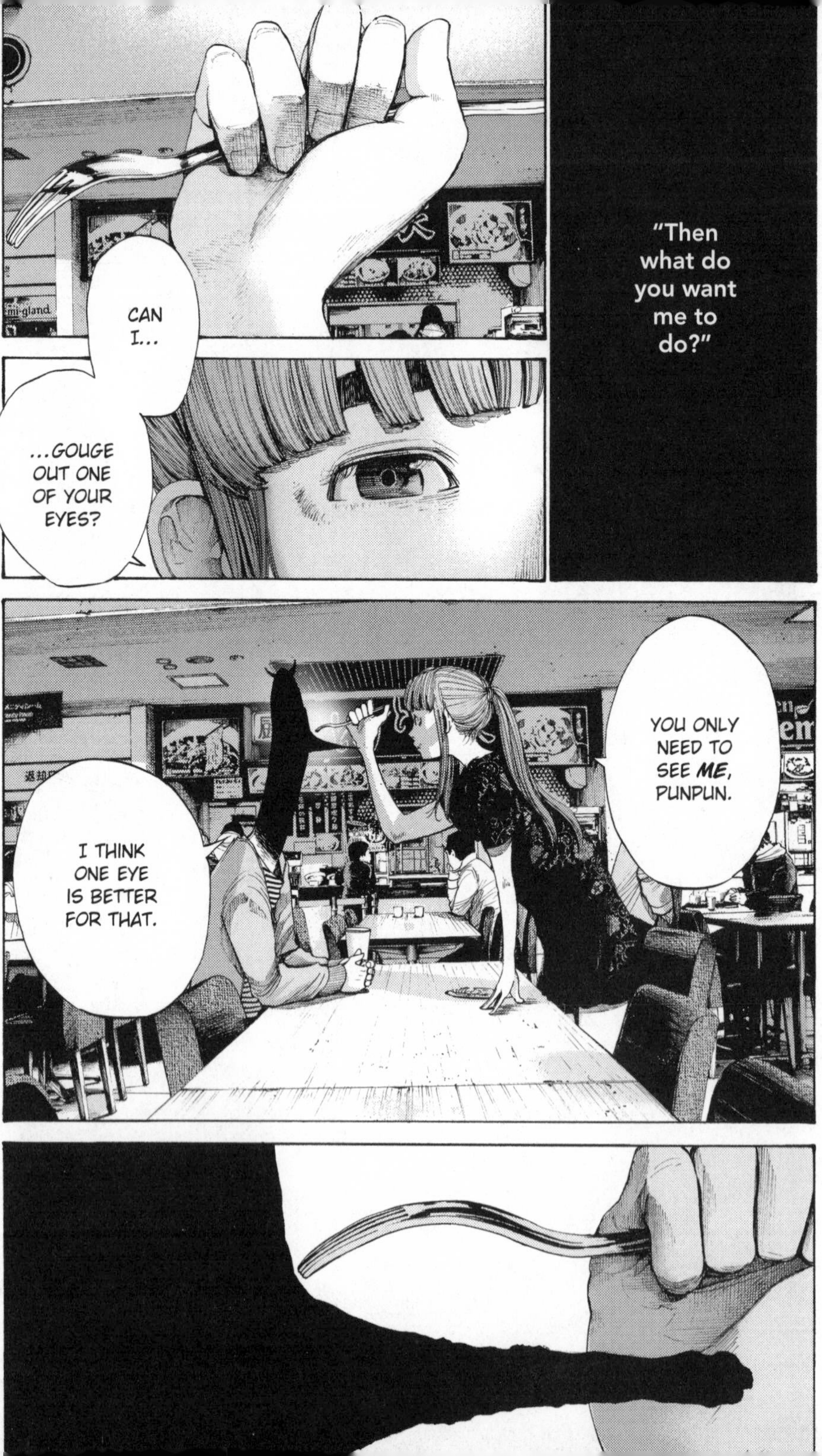
"Then what do you want me to do?"
CAN I...
...GOUGE OUT ONE OF YOUR EYES?
YOU ONLY NEED TO SEE *ME*, PUNPUN.
I THINK ONE EYE IS BETTER FOR THAT.

"You're
right."

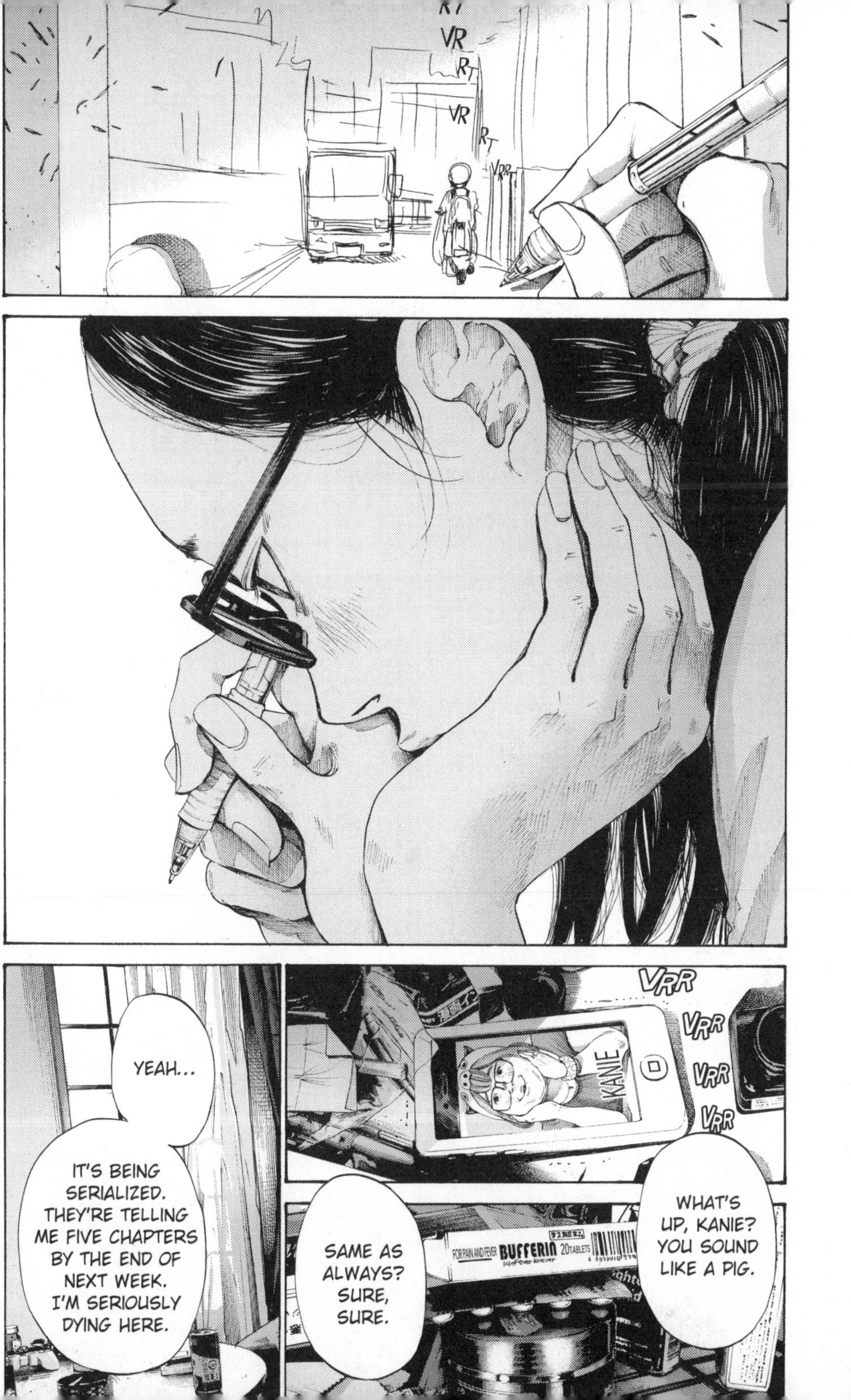
VR
RT
VR
RT
VRR
VRR
VRR
VRR
VRR
KANIE
WHAT'S UP, KANIE? YOU SOUND LIKE A PIG.
SAME AS ALWAYS? SURE, SURE.
FOR PAIN AND FEVER BUFFERIN 20 TABLETS
YEAH...
IT'S BEING SERIALIZED. THEY'RE TELLING ME FIVE CHAPTERS BY THE END OF NEXT WEEK. I'M SERIOUSLY DYING HERE.

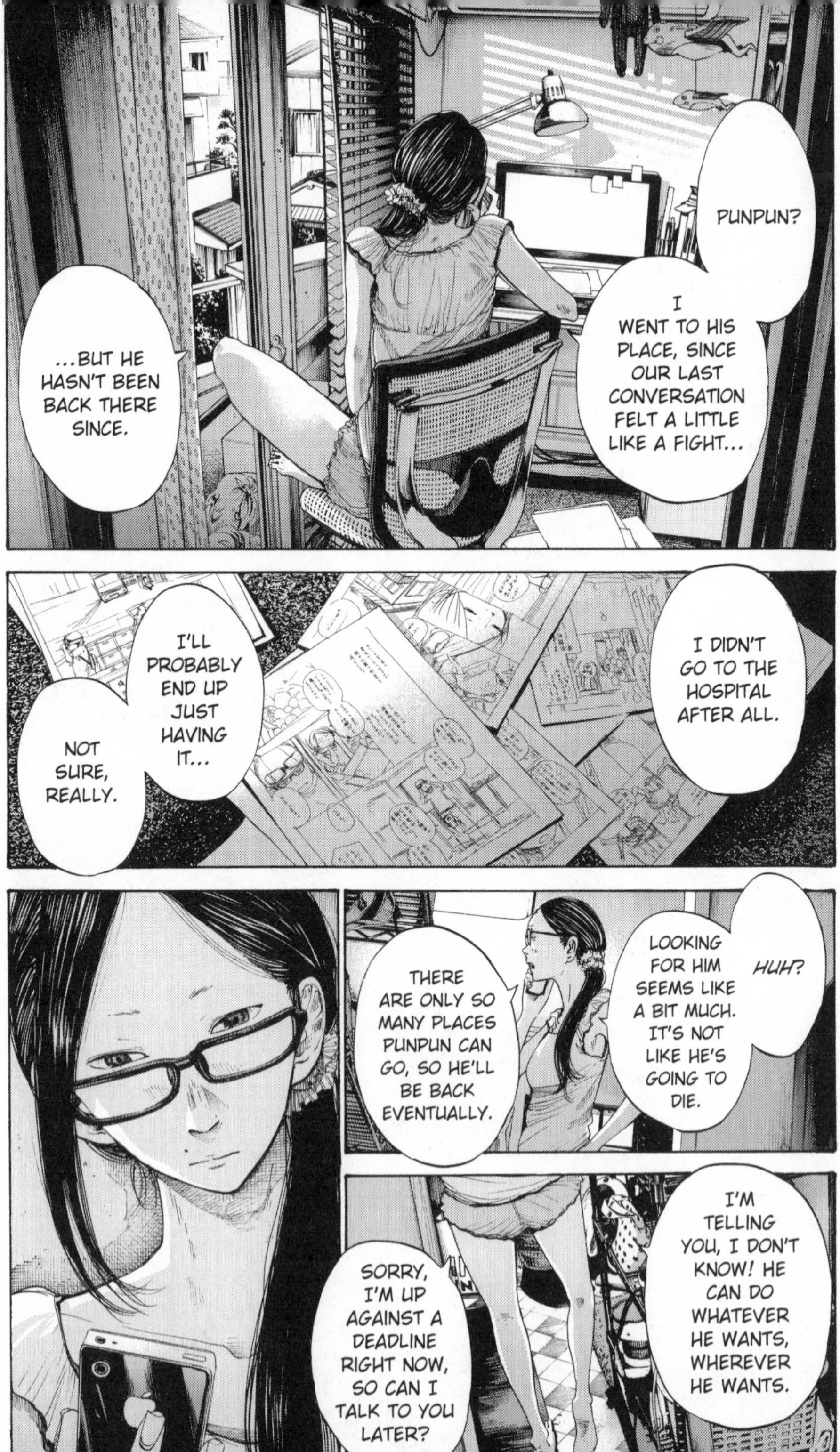
PUNPUN?
I WENT TO HIS PLACE, SINCE OUR LAST CONVERSATION FELT A LITTLE LIKE A FIGHT...
...BUT HE HASN'T BEEN BACK THERE SINCE.
I DIDN'T GO TO THE HOSPITAL AFTER ALL.
I'LL PROBABLY END UP JUST HAVING IT...
NOT SURE, REALLY.
HUH?
LOOKING FOR HIM SEEMS LIKE A BIT MUCH. IT'S NOT LIKE HE'S GOING TO DIE.
THERE ARE ONLY SO MANY PLACES PUNPUN CAN GO, SO HE'LL BE BACK EVENTUALLY.
I'M TELLING YOU, I DON'T KNOW! HE CAN DO WHATEVER HE WANTS, WHEREVER HE WANTS.
SORRY, I'M UP AGAINST A DEADLINE RIGHT NOW, SO CAN I TALK TO YOU LATER?

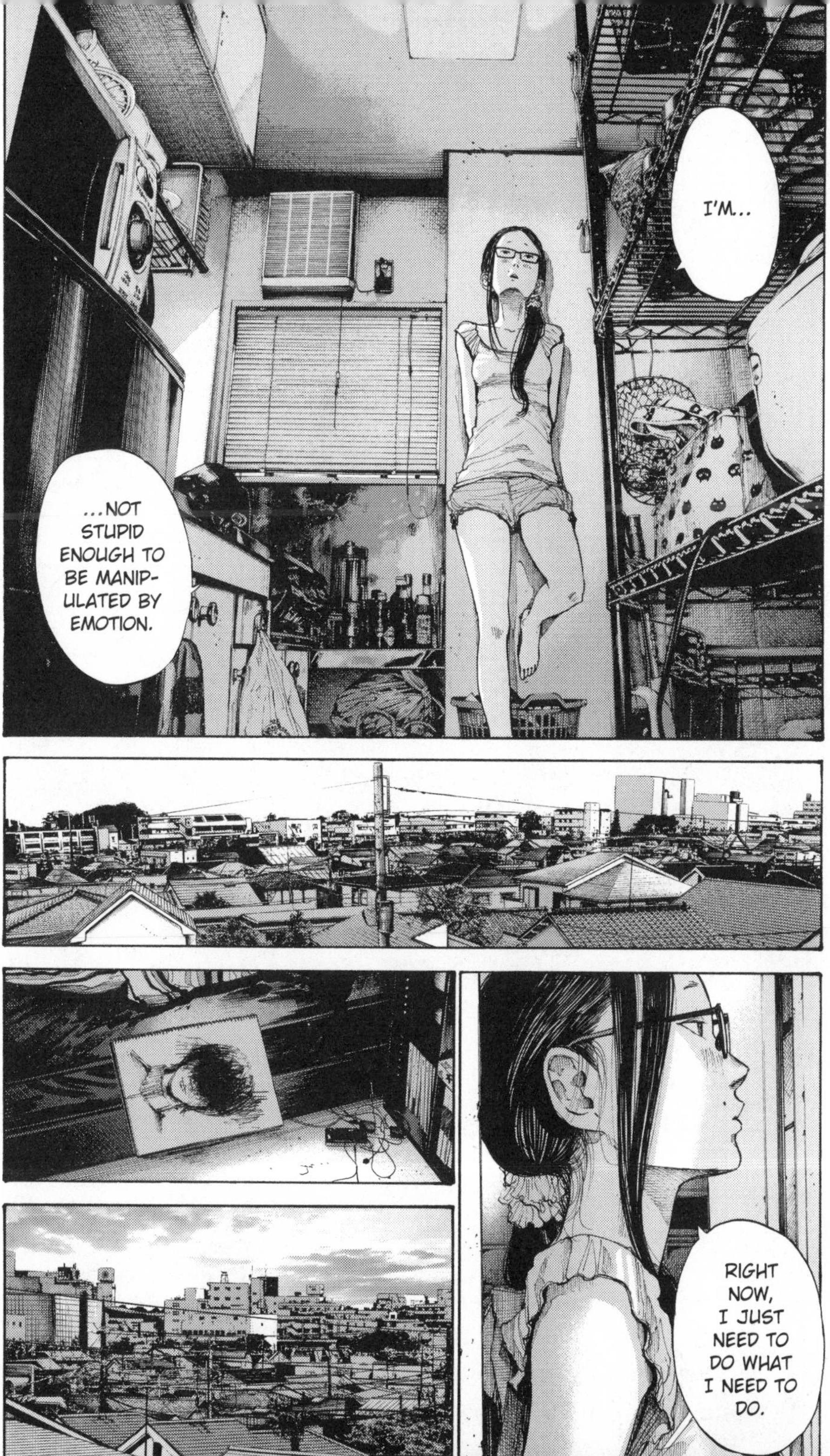
I'M...
...NOT STUPID ENOUGH TO BE MANIP-ULATED BY EMOTION.
RIGHT NOW, I JUST NEED TO DO WHAT I NEED TO DO.

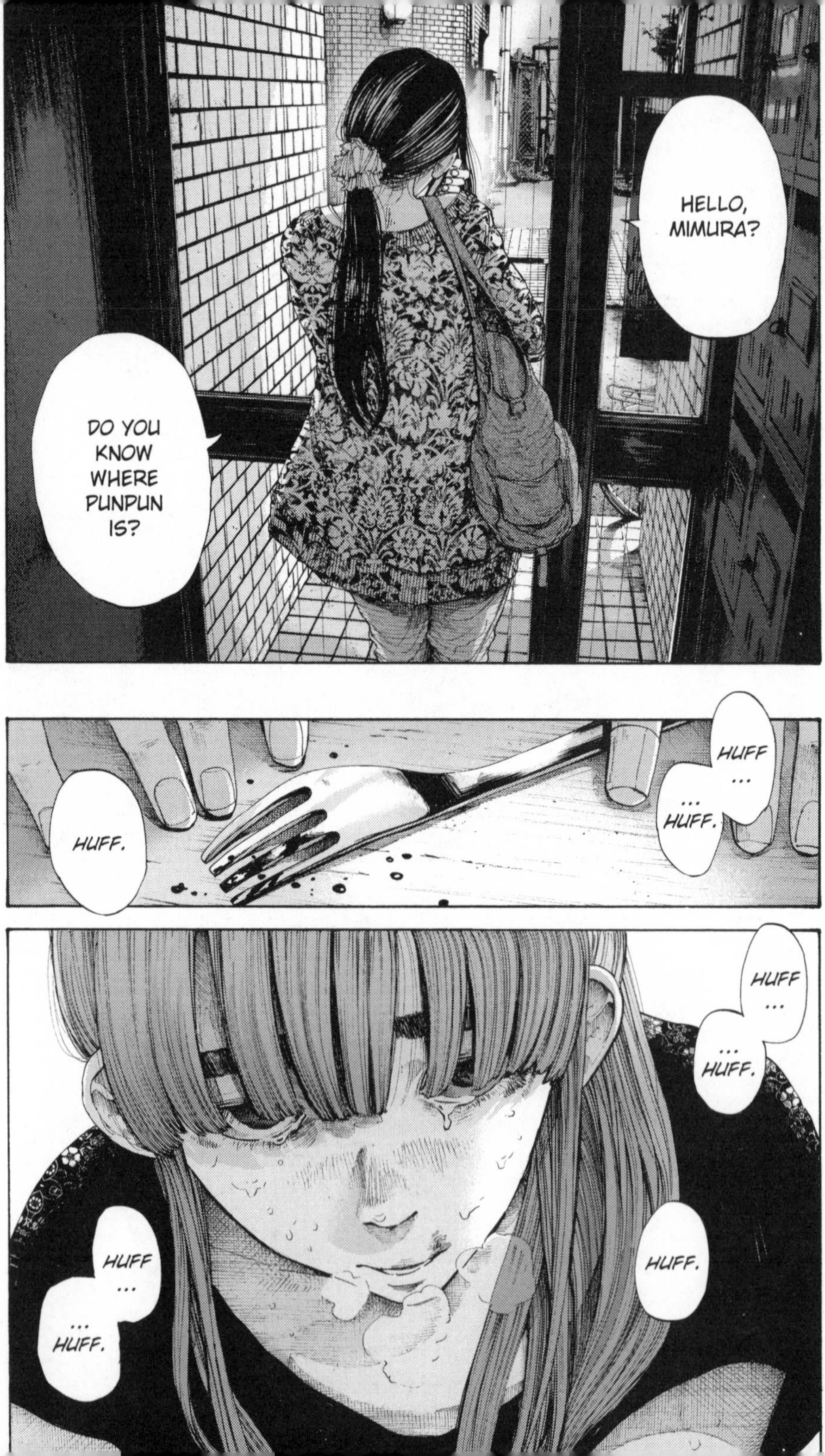
HELLO, MIMURA?
DO YOU KNOW WHERE PUNPUN IS?
HUFF ...
... HUFF.
HUFF.
HUFF ...
... HUFF.
HUFF.
HUFF ...
... HUFF.

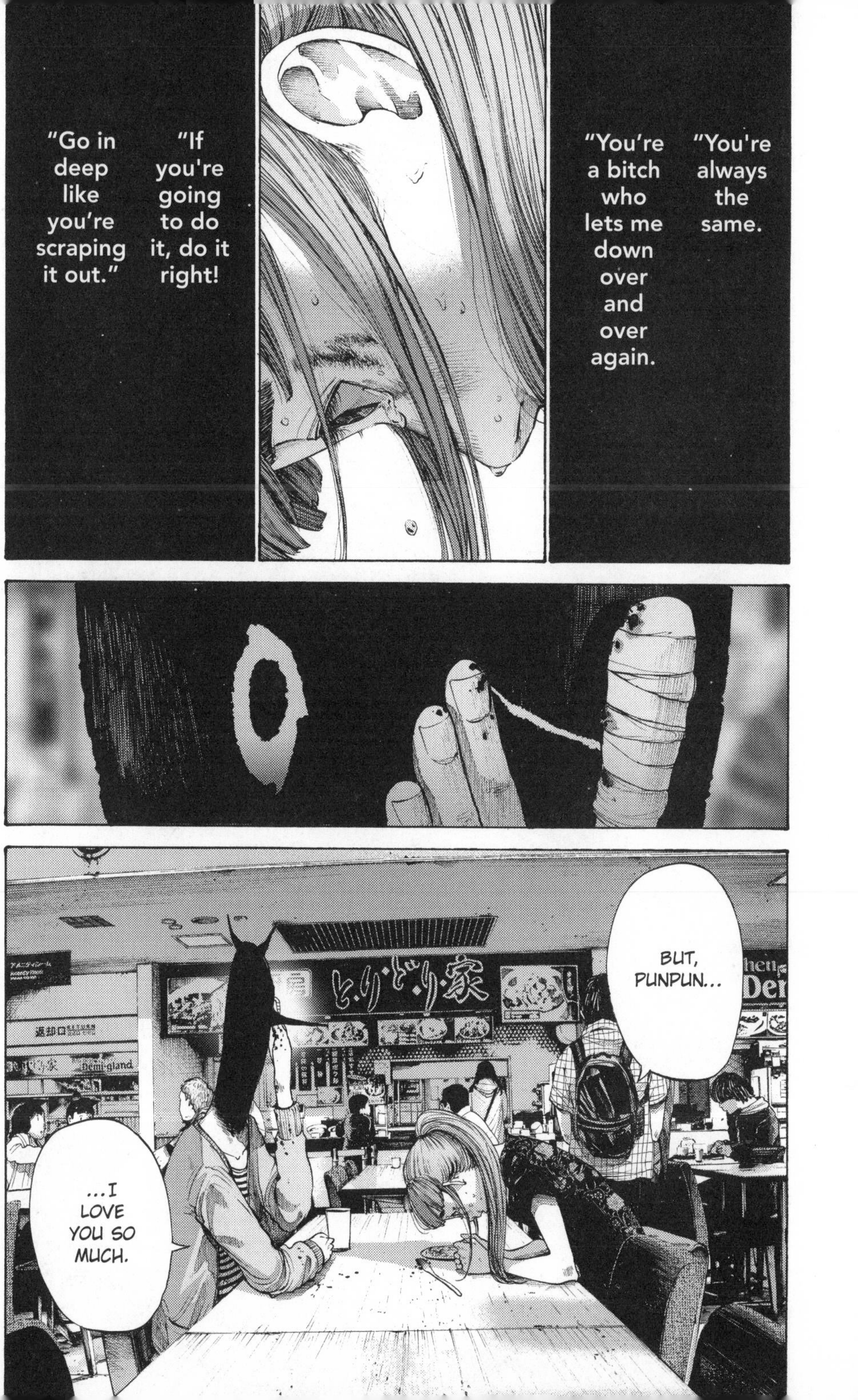
"You're always the same.
"You're a bitch who lets me down over and over again.
"If you're going to do it, do it right!
"Go in deep like you're scraping it out."
BUT, PUNPUN...
...I LOVE YOU SO MUCH.
とり・どり・家
返却口
Demi-gland

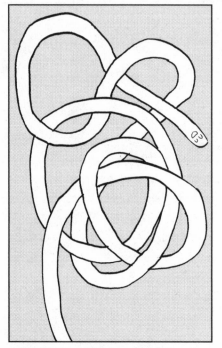

GOODNIGHT PUNPUN   INIO ASANO
Part Eleven

BACKGROUND ASSISTANTS: Satsuki Sato
Hiro Kashiwaba
Ran Atsumori
CG ASSISTANT: Hisashi Saito
COOPERATION: Kumatsuto
Yu Uehara

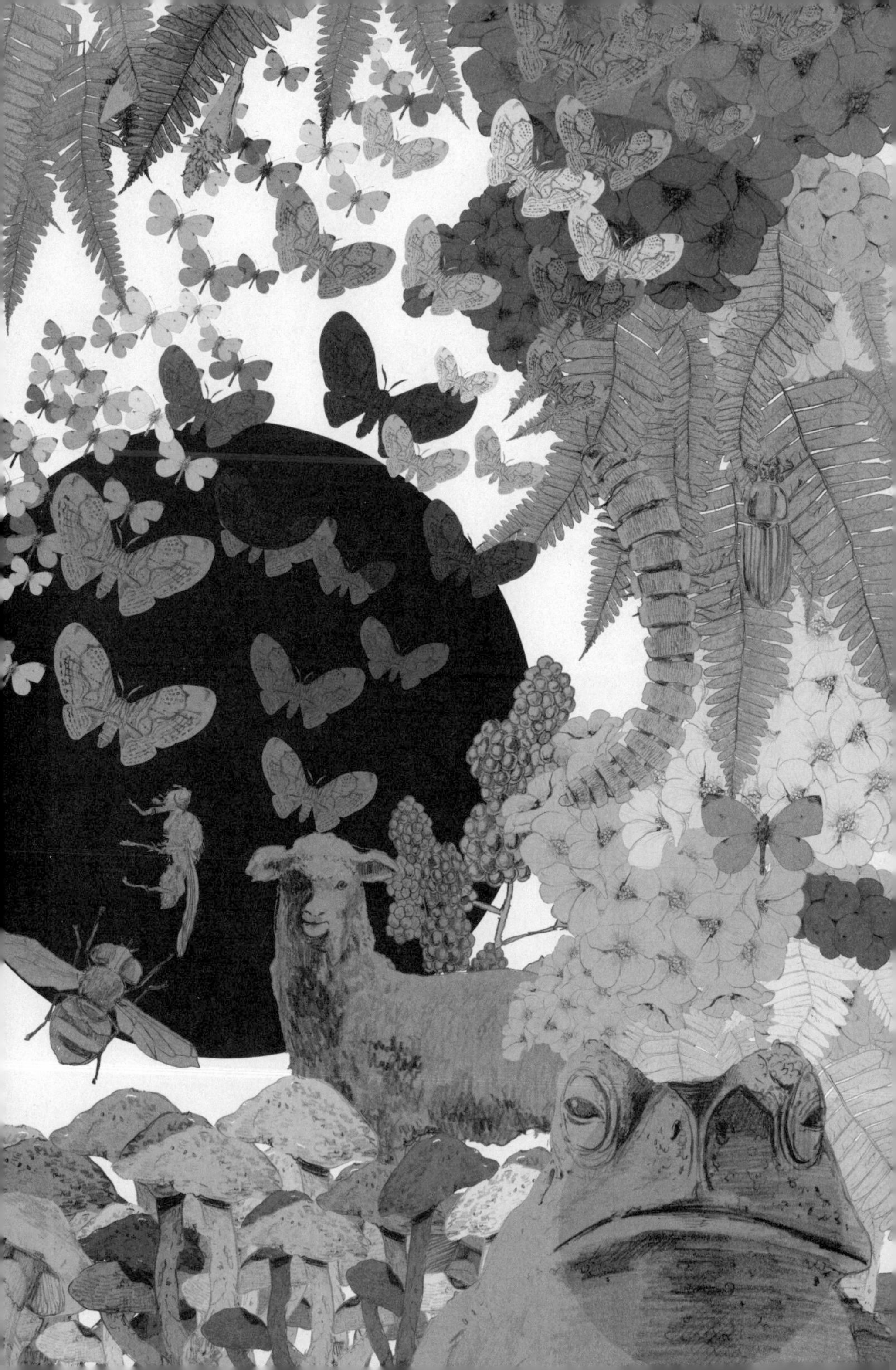

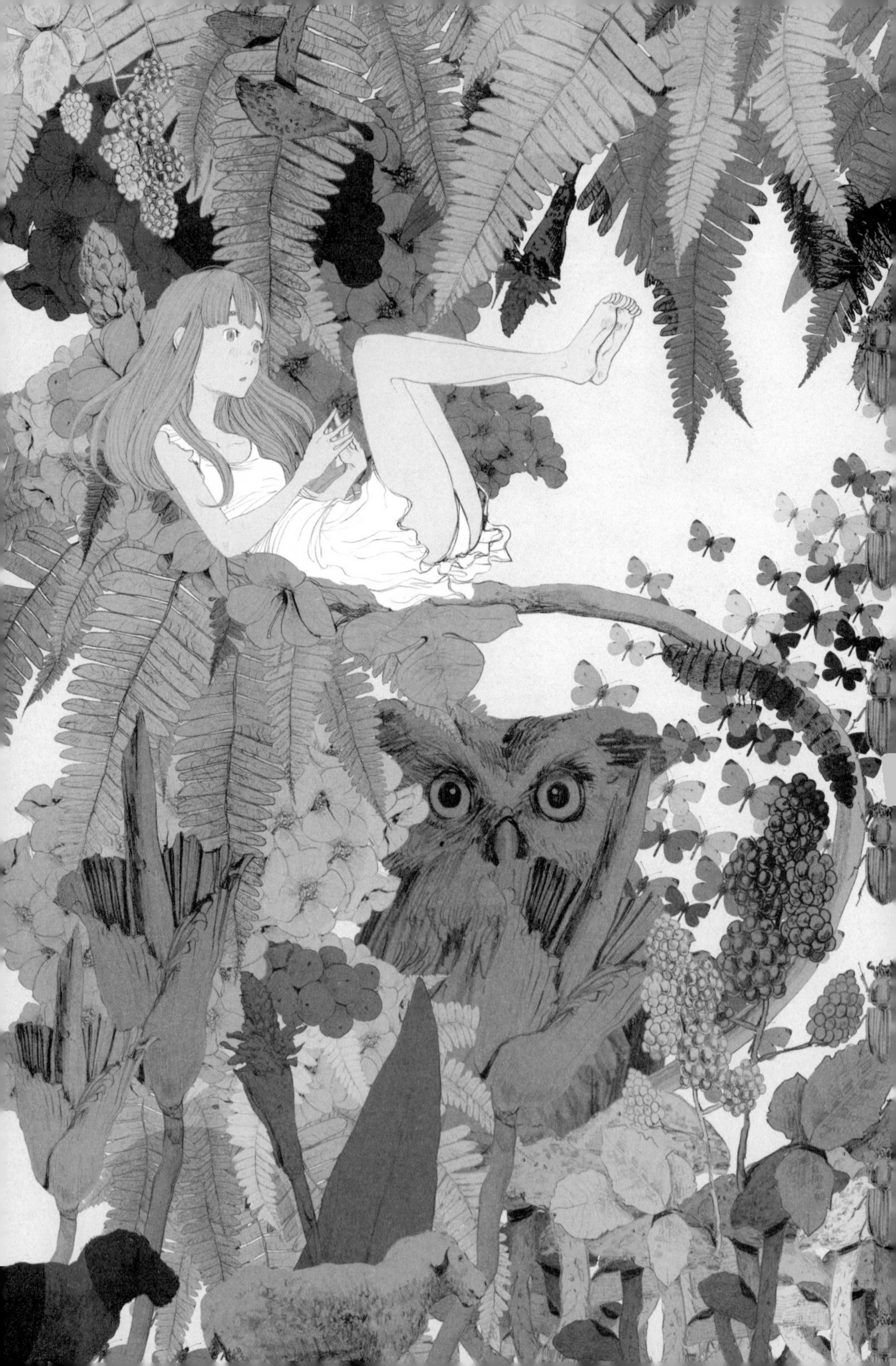

GOODNIGHT

PUNPUN

Part Twelve

OOD IGHT PUNPUN

VOLUME 1–11 SYNOPSIS

STORY THUS FAR..

Pegasus, the youngest person to ever receive Superpower Certification, dreamed of the end of the world at the age of eight. One day, he met Wada, a physicist with an IQ of 300, and set off on a journey to learn the true meaning of his dream. After beating back continuous attacks from brainwashed super beings and liberated evils in a harmonic interdimensional battle, Pegasus learned of the existence of a disaster born of mass unconsciousness. As his group of colleagues grew, so too did his enlightenment. He was a descendant of the enlightened one and was fated to confront the disaster with the Majestic Twelve, a band of hidden warriors.

In spite of the chase, the disaster escaped to the 25th dimension, and Pegasus fell into an enigma. But with support from the Majestic Twelve, he returned safely. Then Wada said to Pegasus...

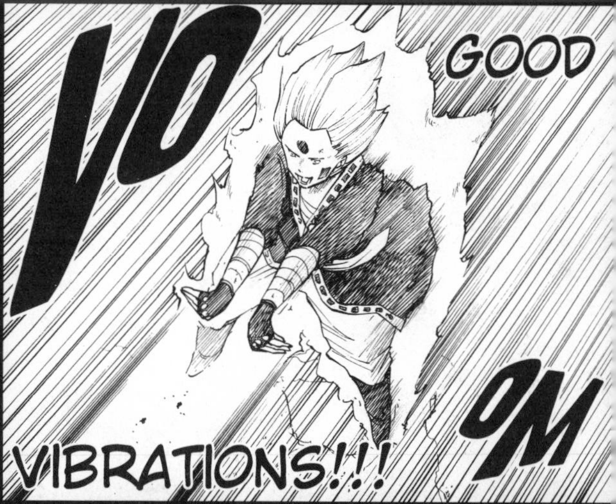
VO
GOOD
OM
VIBRATIONS!!!

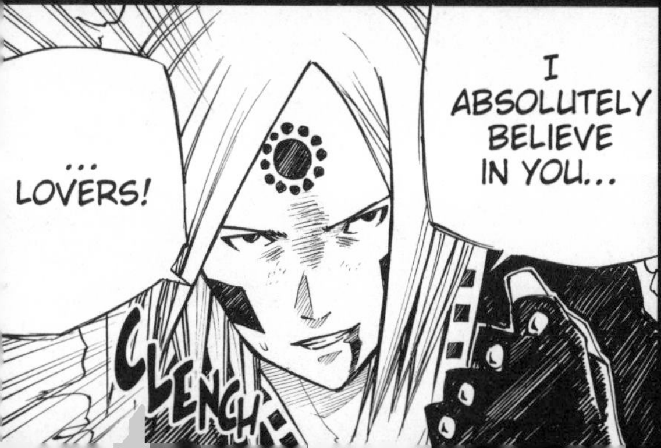
I ABSOLUTELY BELIEVE IN YOU...
... LOVERS!
CLENCH

"The only way to win is by using the forbidden treasure, Redkiss, even though the wielder always loses his life. You and the Majestic Twelve will become Super Spirits and go down with the disaster in its zero magnetic zone." The battle for Harmony, the last dimension, begins. The existence of mankind is at stake.

CAST OF CHARACTERS

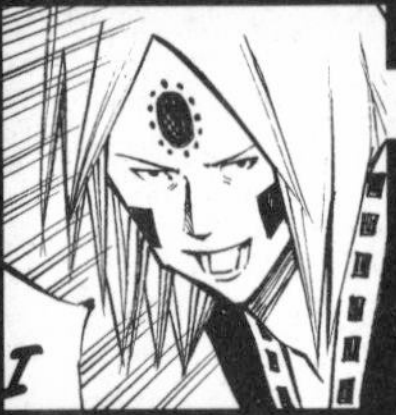
I

PEGASUS

Thirteenth Sorcery Unit. An enlightened one who leads the Majestic Twelve.

Powers: Prescience, Thought JACK

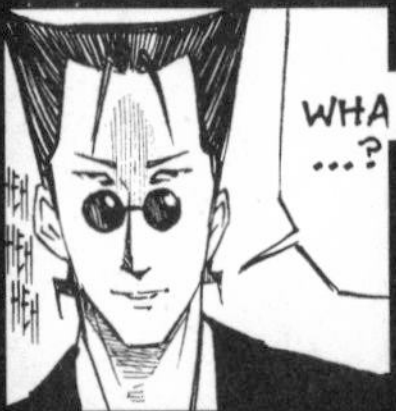
WHA ...?
HEH HEH HEH

WADA (BIG BRO MOFUMOFU SWEET PRETTY LONELY HEART)

Genius physicist. Former head of the Shinei Knights of the eastern lands.

Powers: Super brainy

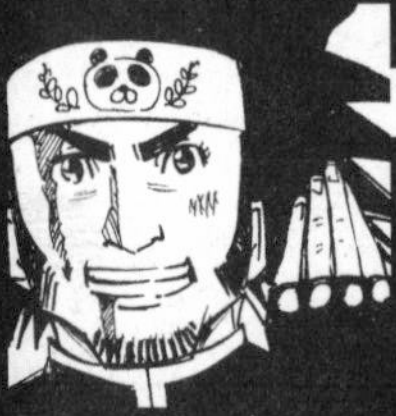

PAOPAO CHANNEL

A wanted ex-big-time burglar. Made a living as a hacker after retiring.

Powers: Gouen (Mongolian Death Arm)

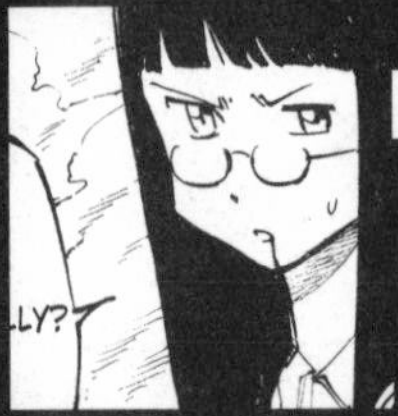
LLY?

ECO BAG

An international investigator chasing Paopao Channel.

Powers: Telekinesis

WHITE PIG

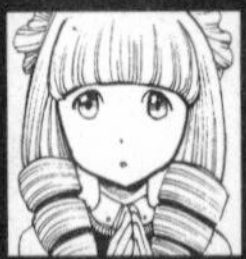

A princess who was imprisoned for ten years by Lord Heinrich Altair.

Powers: Boundary of pure blood

CONTRARY TO...

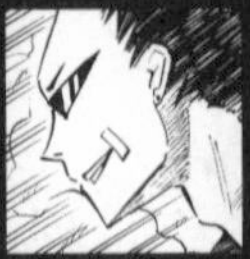

A world-traveling messenger. Second of the three Jet Brothers.

Powers: Sound movement

CHUPET

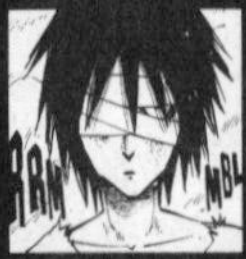

An orphan who lived in a bottomless village. His hidden powers are the strongest of the group.

Powers: Weather control, recalling flying objects

IT'S AWKWARD WHEN YOU ONLY HAVE ONE BATTERY LEFT

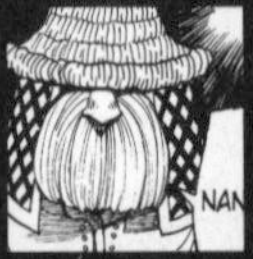
NAN

A martial arts genius who fought in the great war a thousand year ago. He was left apparently dead but has been resurrected.

Powers: Qigong, mantis boxing, 88 form Tai Chi Chuan

WEEKLY BIG COMIC SPIRITS

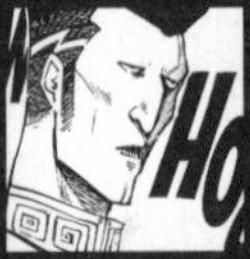
HO

Captain of the armored ship *New Nessie*. Came from the continent as an observer.

Powers: A grave wind (*mokele mbembe*)

PRINCESS PUSSY

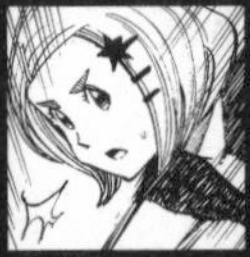

A failed ninja who escaped from the Tsuchinoko Kingdom after civil war broke out.

Powers: Opening locks

INFINITE ★ LOVE

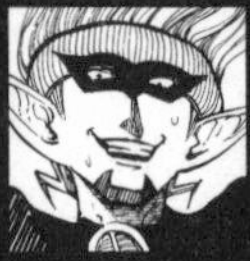

Worked as a clown in a traveling magic show but is really the scion of the Mothman Foundation.

Powers: Shape-shifting, information acquisition

BUTT HAMBURGER

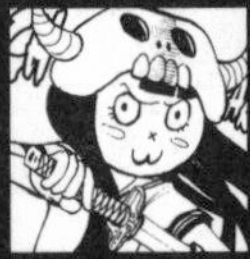

A high school student who lost her memory after being possessed by an evil sword. She is on a journey to find her family.

Powers: Evil Sword Nozuchi

GUARDIAN ANGEL GIBOBOGIGI

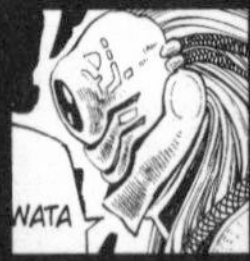
WATA

A wandering swordswoman. She was severely wounded in a battle with the Black Mark, and 90 percent of her body is now mechanical.

Powers: Cosmic Beam Level 3

BLACK MARK

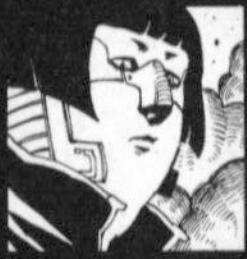

A mysterious woman who obstructs Pegasus and his group. She was a regular citizen who became deranged by the overwhelming pressure of mass unconsciousness.

THE DISASTER

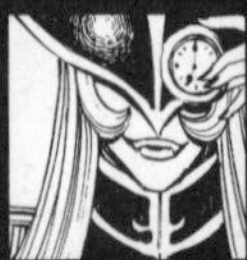

An evil presence that was vanquished in the last great war. Currently plotting from the 25th dimension to return mankind to nothingness.

CONTENTS

Chapter 122

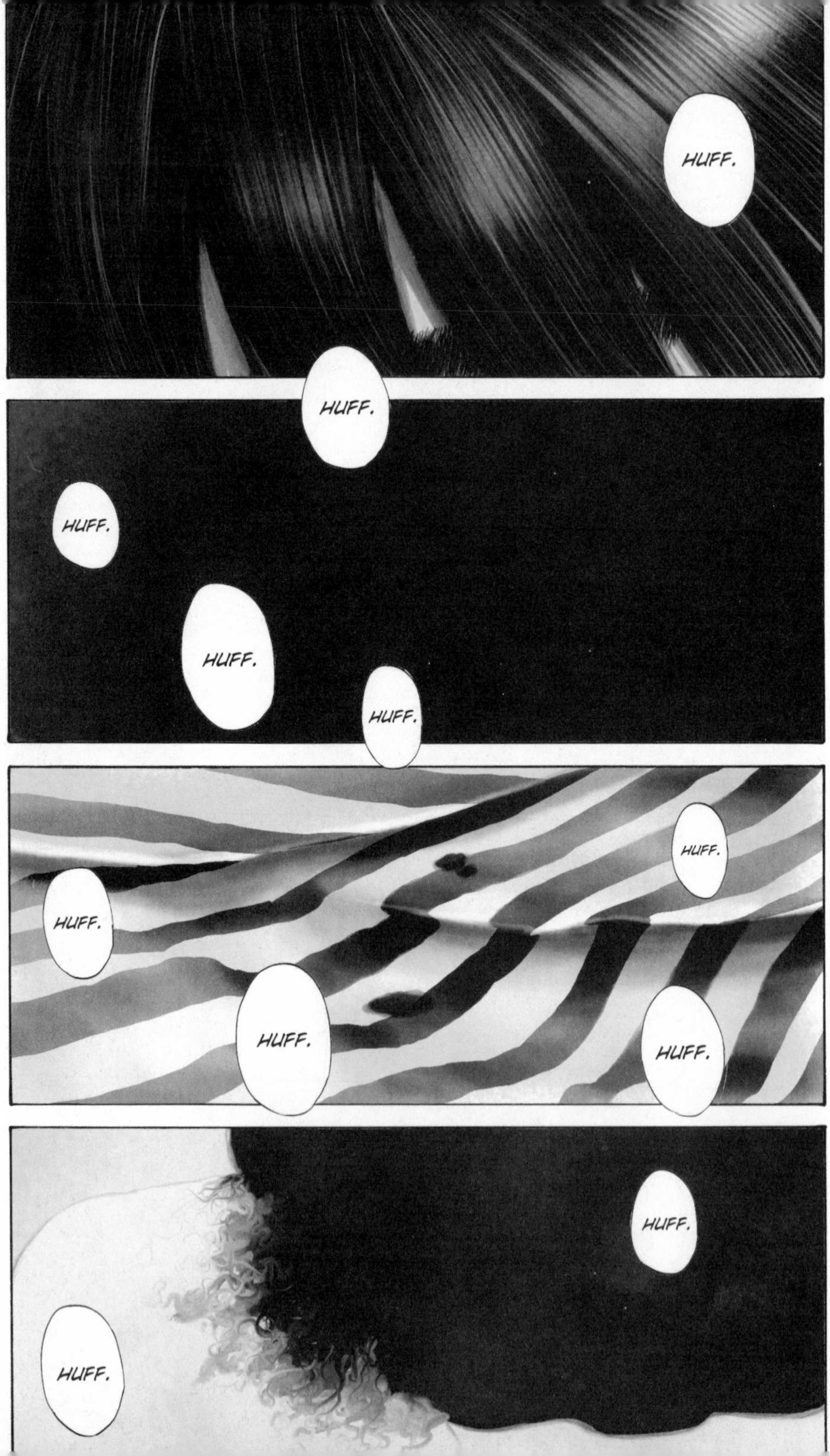
HUFF.
HUFF.
HUFF.
HUFF.
HUFF.
HUFF.
HUFF.
HUFF.
HUFF.
HUFF.
HUFF.

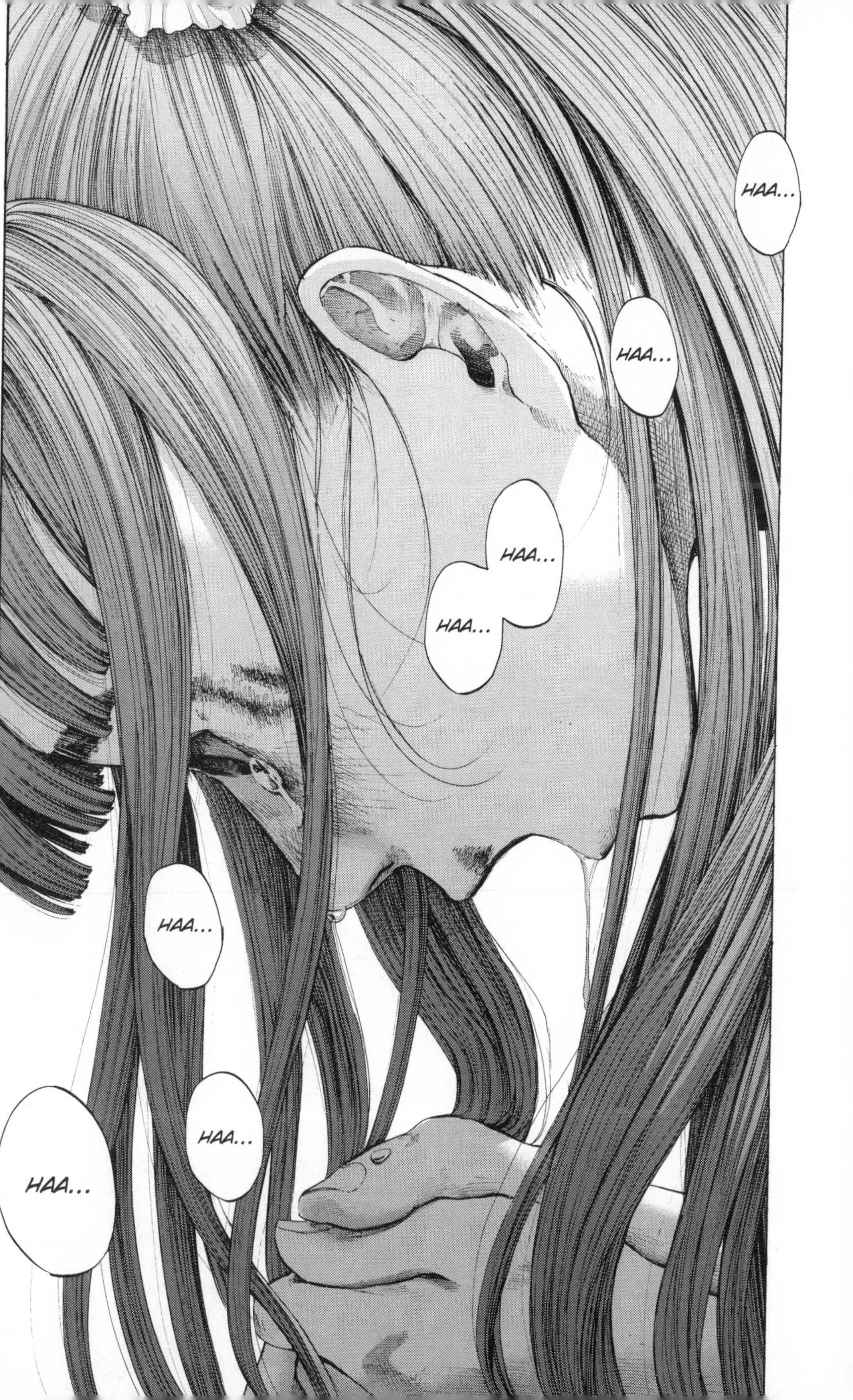
HAA...
HAA...
HAA...
HAA...
HAA...
HAA...
HAA...

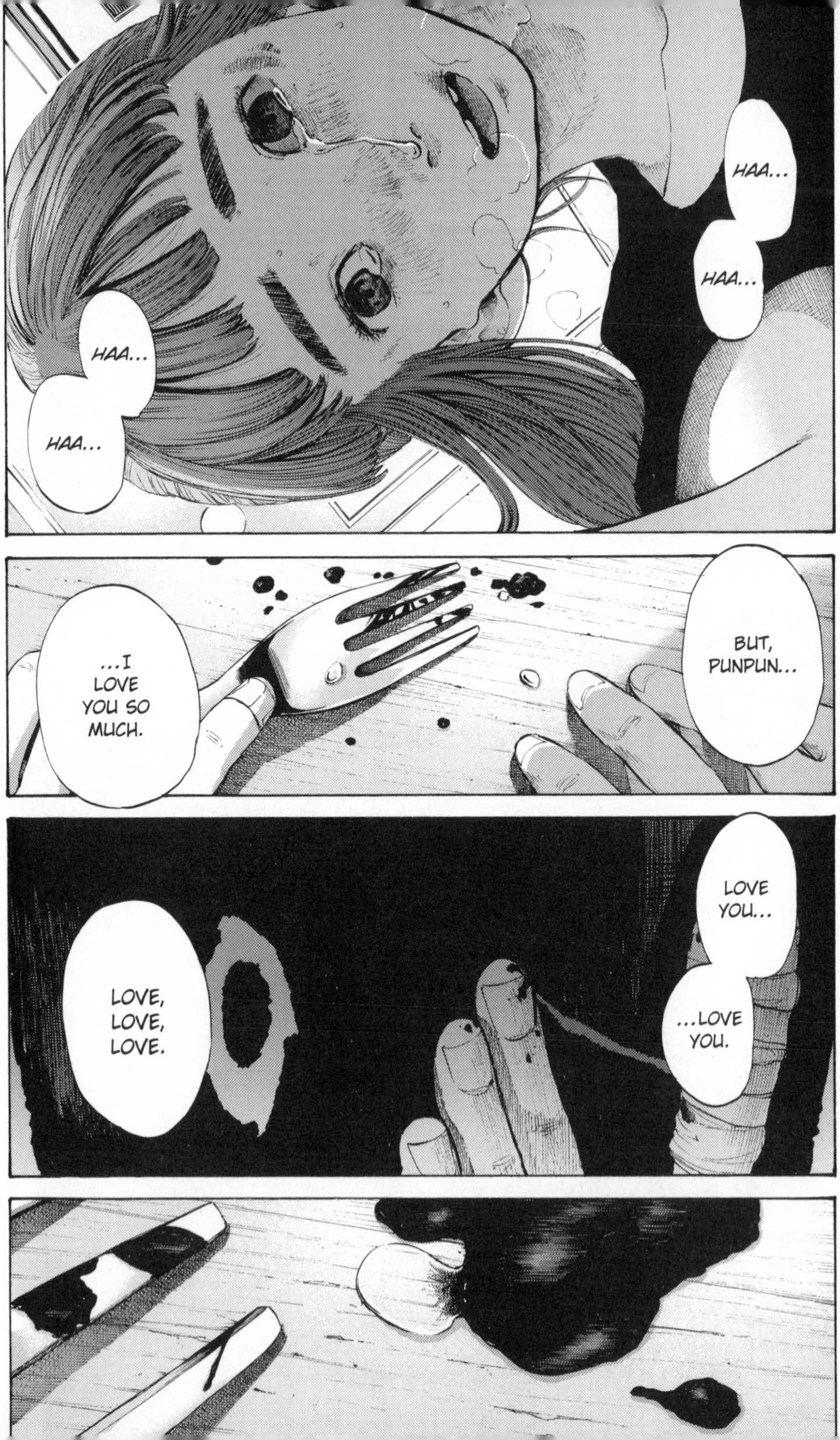
HAA...
HAA...
HAA...
HAA...
BUT, PUNPUN...
...I LOVE YOU SO MUCH.
LOVE YOU...
...LOVE YOU.
LOVE, LOVE, LOVE.

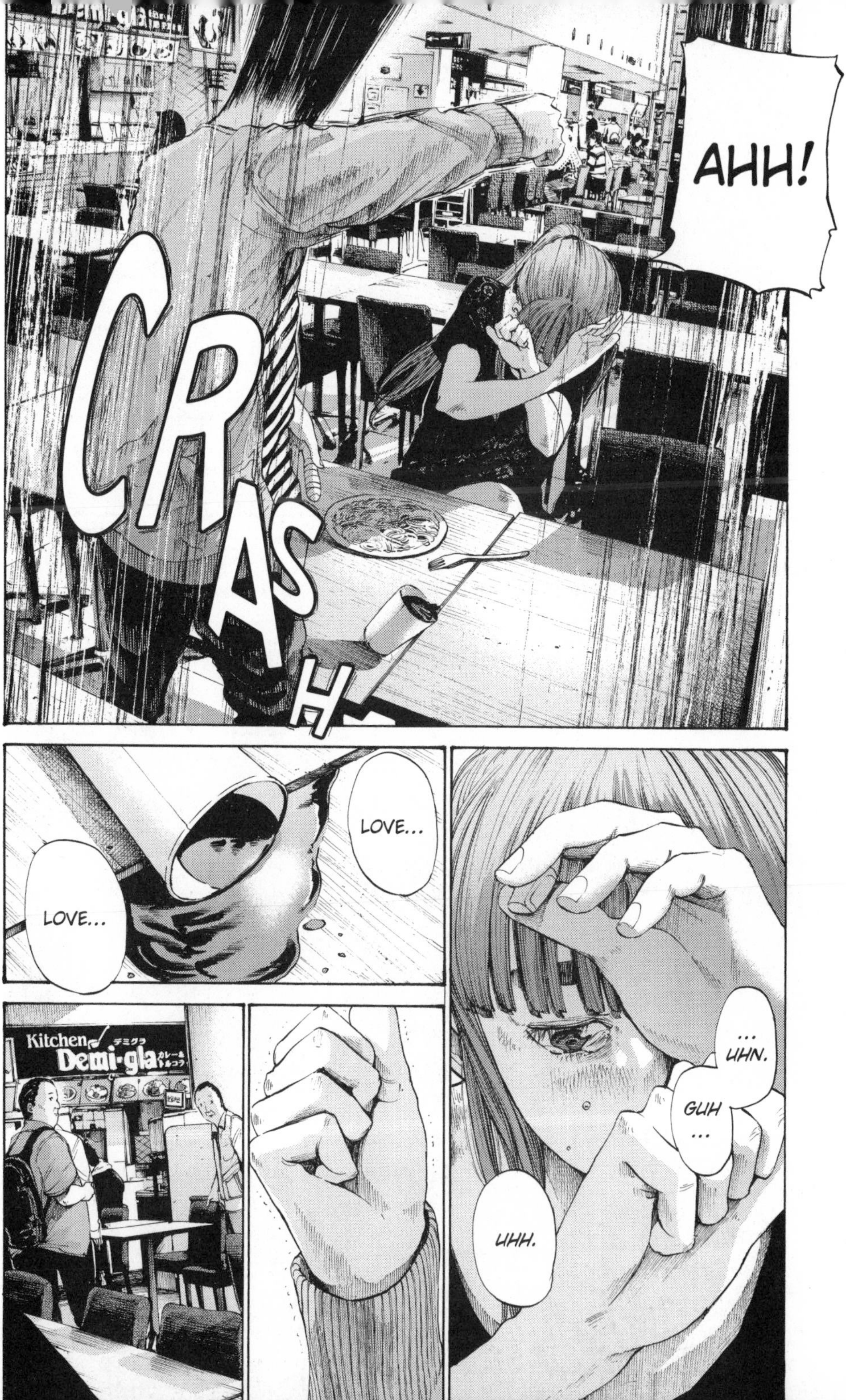
AHH!
CRASH
...UHN.
GUH...
UHH.
LOVE...
LOVE...
Kitchen
デミグラ
Demi-gla

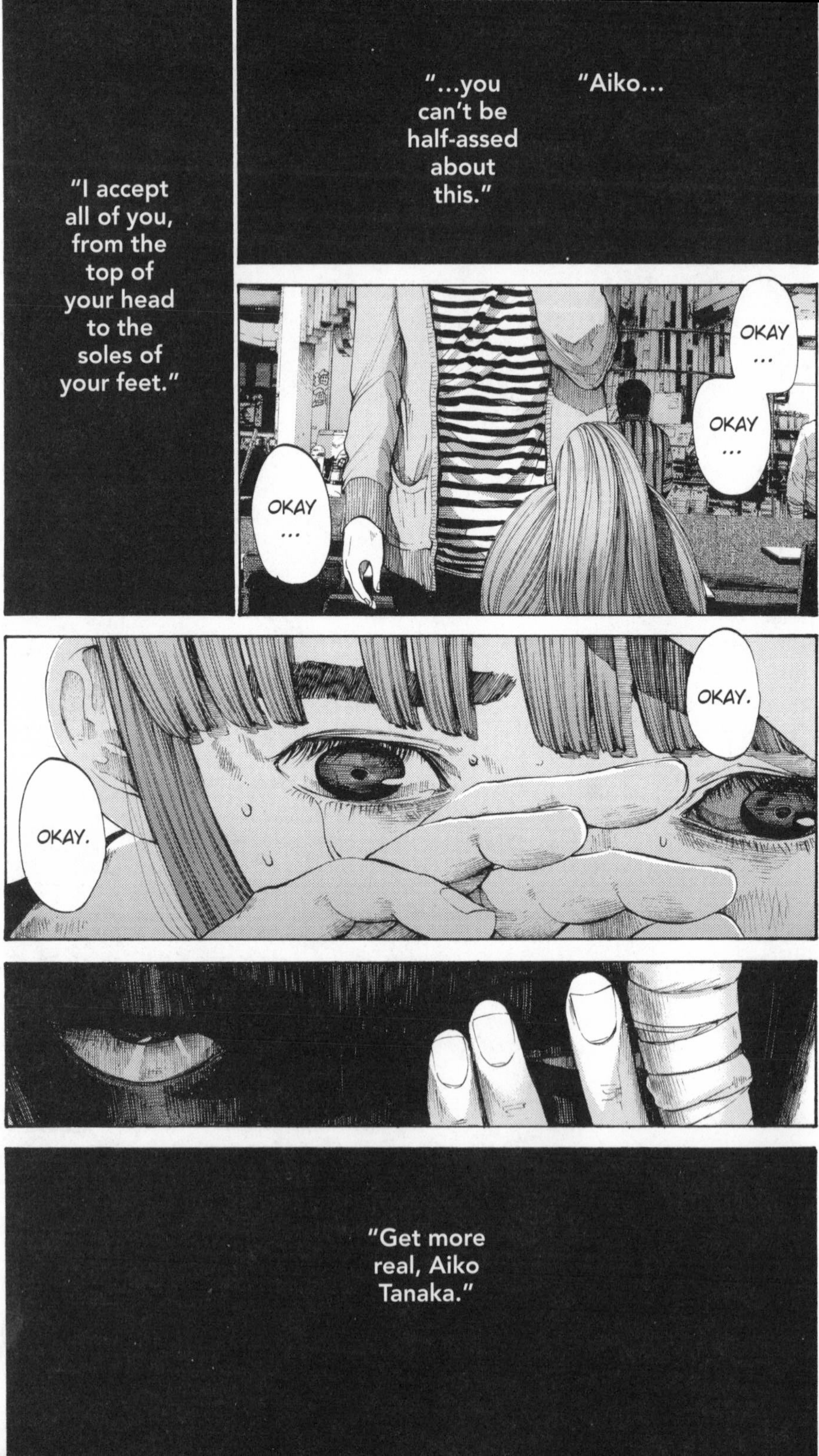
"Aiko...
"...you can't be half-assed about this."
OKAY ...
OKAY ...
OKAY ...
"I accept all of you, from the top of your head to the soles of your feet."
OKAY.
OKAY.
"Get more real, Aiko Tanaka."

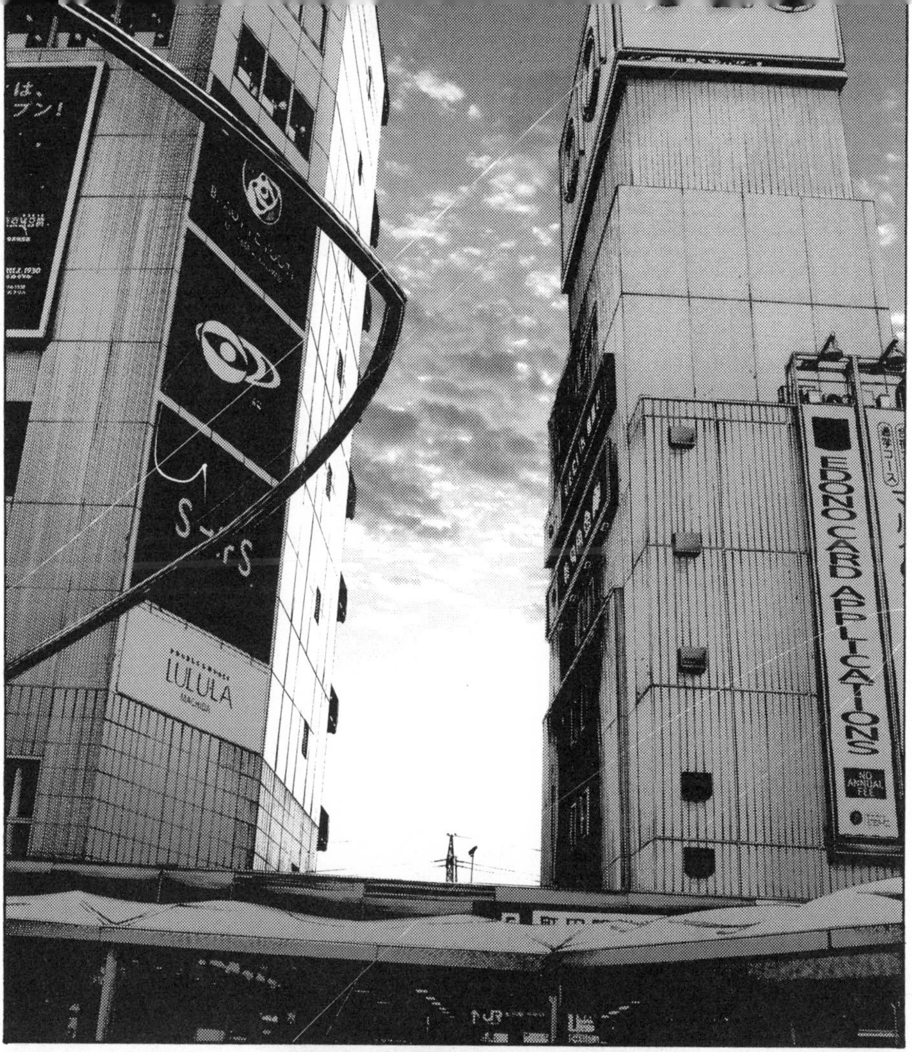
LULULA
EDONO CARD APPLICATIONS
NO ANNUAL FEE

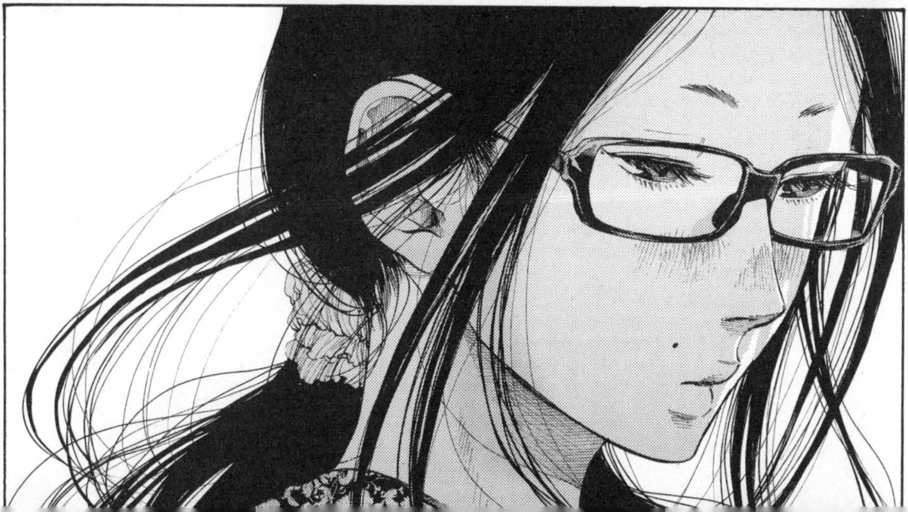

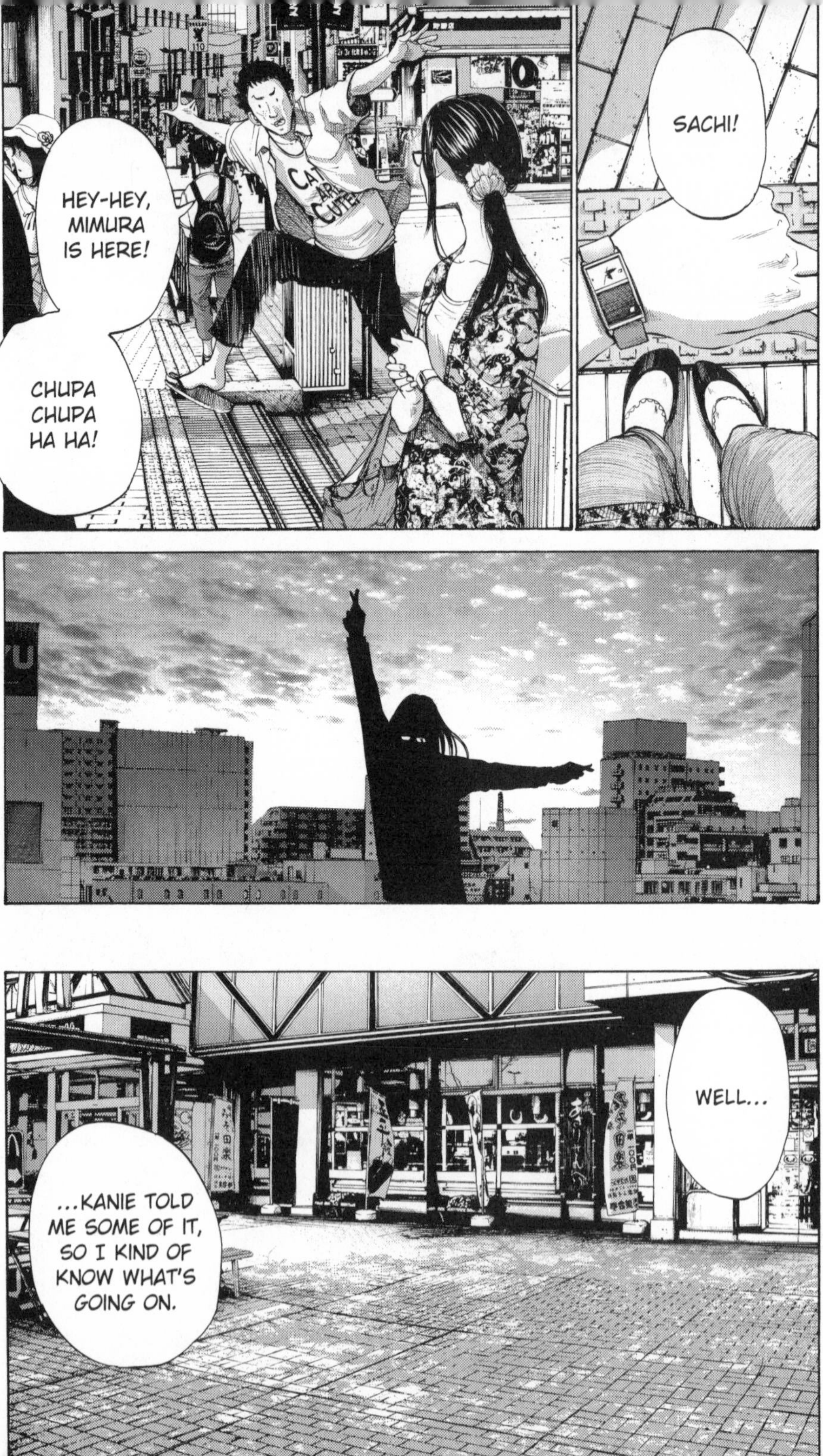
SACHI!
HEY-HEY, MIMURA IS HERE!
CHUPA CHUPA HA HA!
WELL...
...KANIE TOLD ME SOME OF IT, SO I KIND OF KNOW WHAT'S GOING ON.

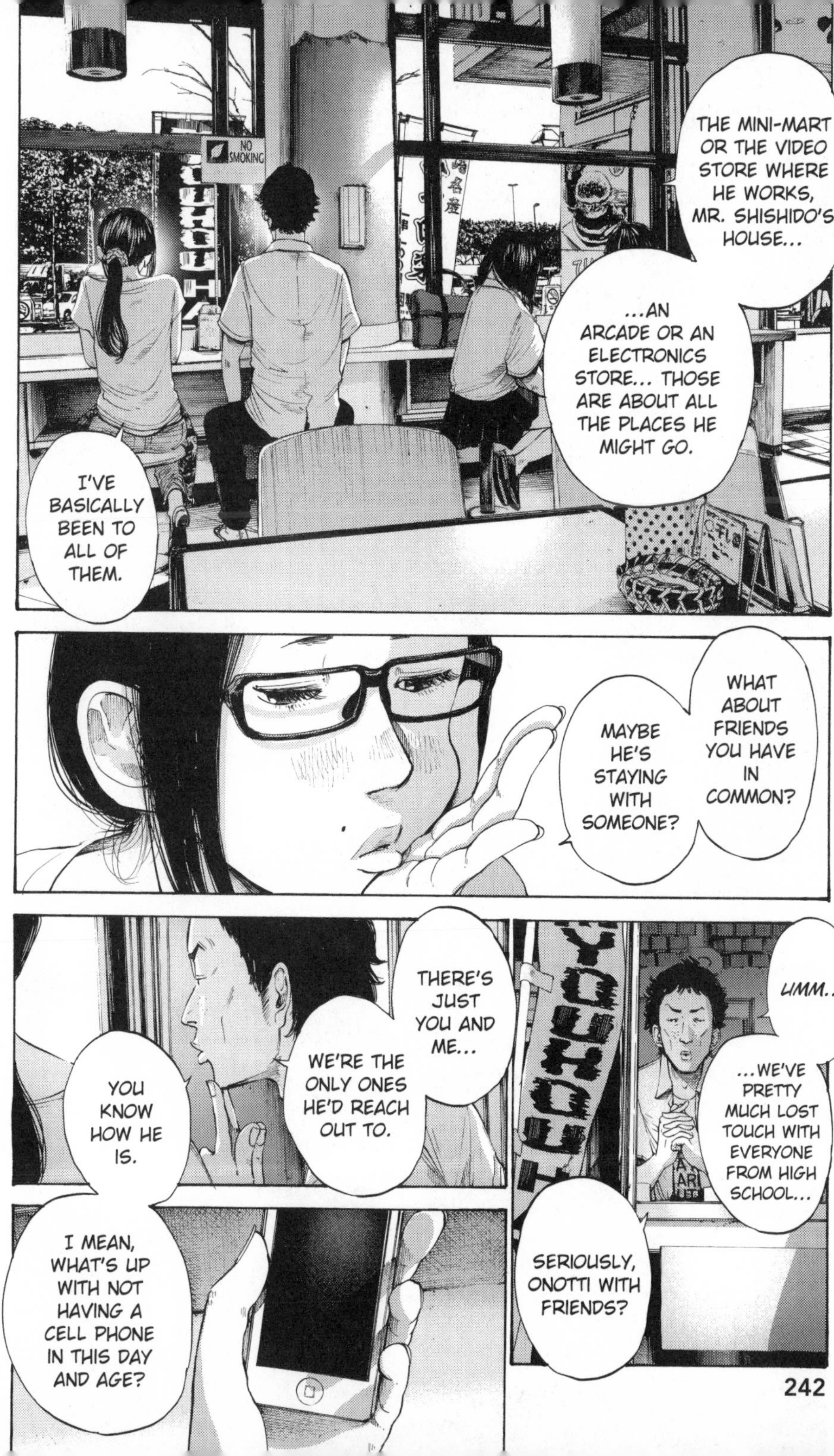
NO SMOKING
THE MINI-MART OR THE VIDEO STORE WHERE HE WORKS, MR. SHISHIDO'S HOUSE...
...AN ARCADE OR AN ELECTRONICS STORE... THOSE ARE ABOUT ALL THE PLACES HE MIGHT GO.
I'VE BASICALLY BEEN TO ALL OF THEM.
WHAT ABOUT FRIENDS YOU HAVE IN COMMON?
MAYBE HE'S STAYING WITH SOMEONE?
UMM...
...WE'VE PRETTY MUCH LOST TOUCH WITH EVERYONE FROM HIGH SCHOOL...
SERIOUSLY, ONOTTI WITH FRIENDS?
THERE'S JUST YOU AND ME...
WE'RE THE ONLY ONES HE'D REACH OUT TO.
YOU KNOW HOW HE IS.
I MEAN, WHAT'S UP WITH NOT HAVING A CELL PHONE IN THIS DAY AND AGE?

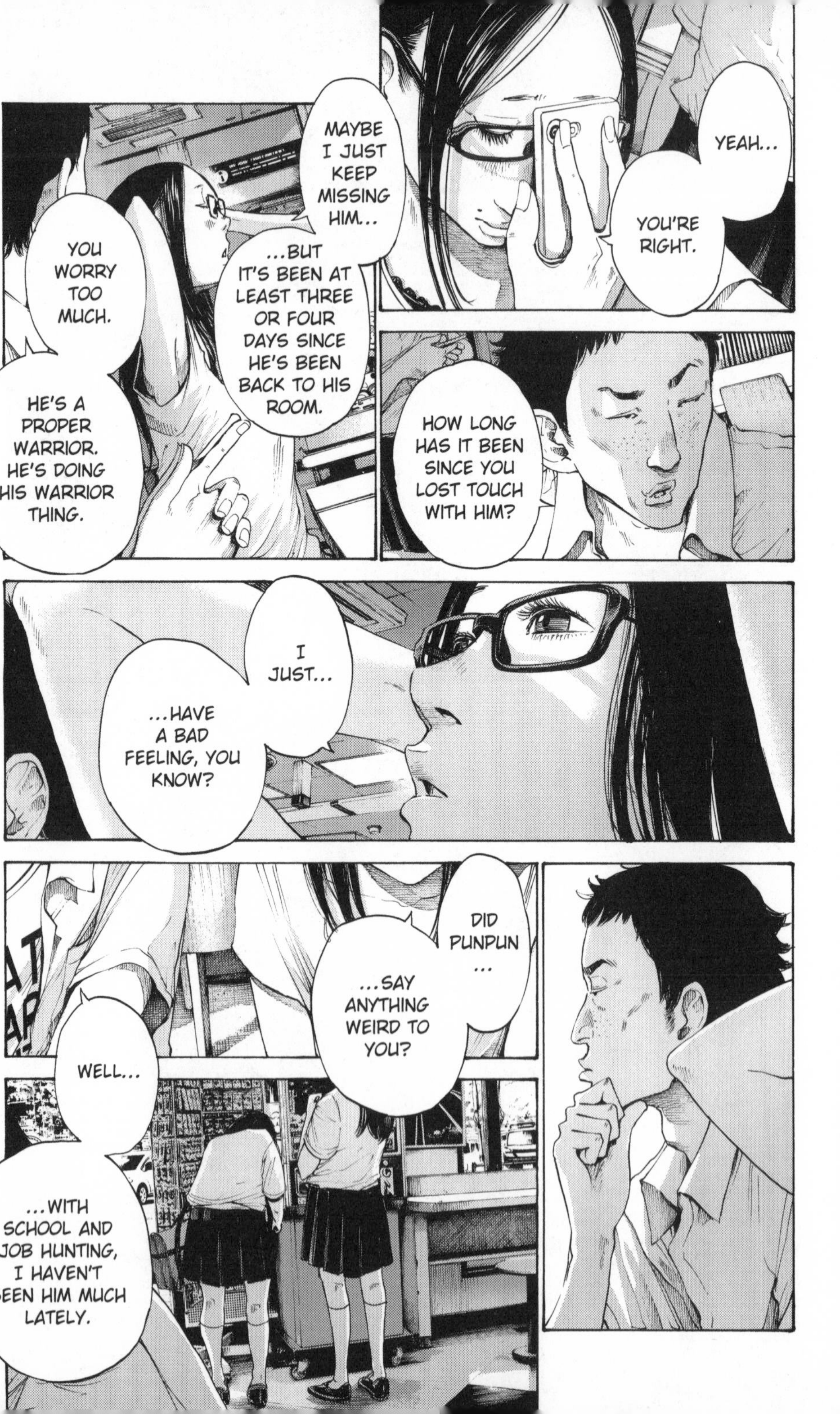
YEAH...
YOU'RE RIGHT.
HOW LONG HAS IT BEEN SINCE YOU LOST TOUCH WITH HIM?
MAYBE I JUST KEEP MISSING HIM...
...BUT IT'S BEEN AT LEAST THREE OR FOUR DAYS SINCE HE'S BEEN BACK TO HIS ROOM.
YOU WORRY TOO MUCH.
HE'S A PROPER WARRIOR. HE'S DOING HIS WARRIOR THING.
I JUST...
...HAVE A BAD FEELING, YOU KNOW?
DID PUNPUN...
...SAY ANYTHING WEIRD TO YOU?
WELL...
...WITH SCHOOL AND JOB HUNTING, I HAVEN'T SEEN HIM MUCH LATELY.

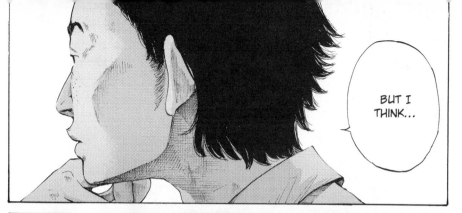

BUT I THINK...

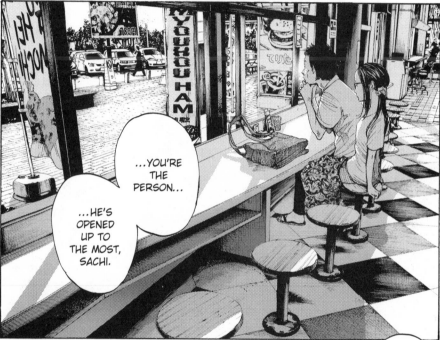

...YOU'RE THE PERSON...

...HE'S OPENED UP TO THE MOST, SACHI.

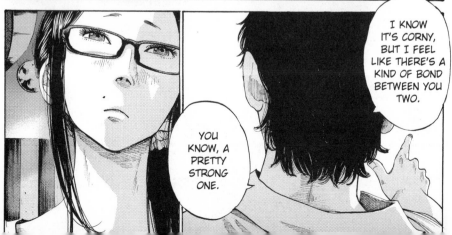

I KNOW IT'S CORNY, BUT I FEEL LIKE THERE'S A KIND OF BOND BETWEEN YOU TWO.

YOU KNOW, A PRETTY STRONG ONE.

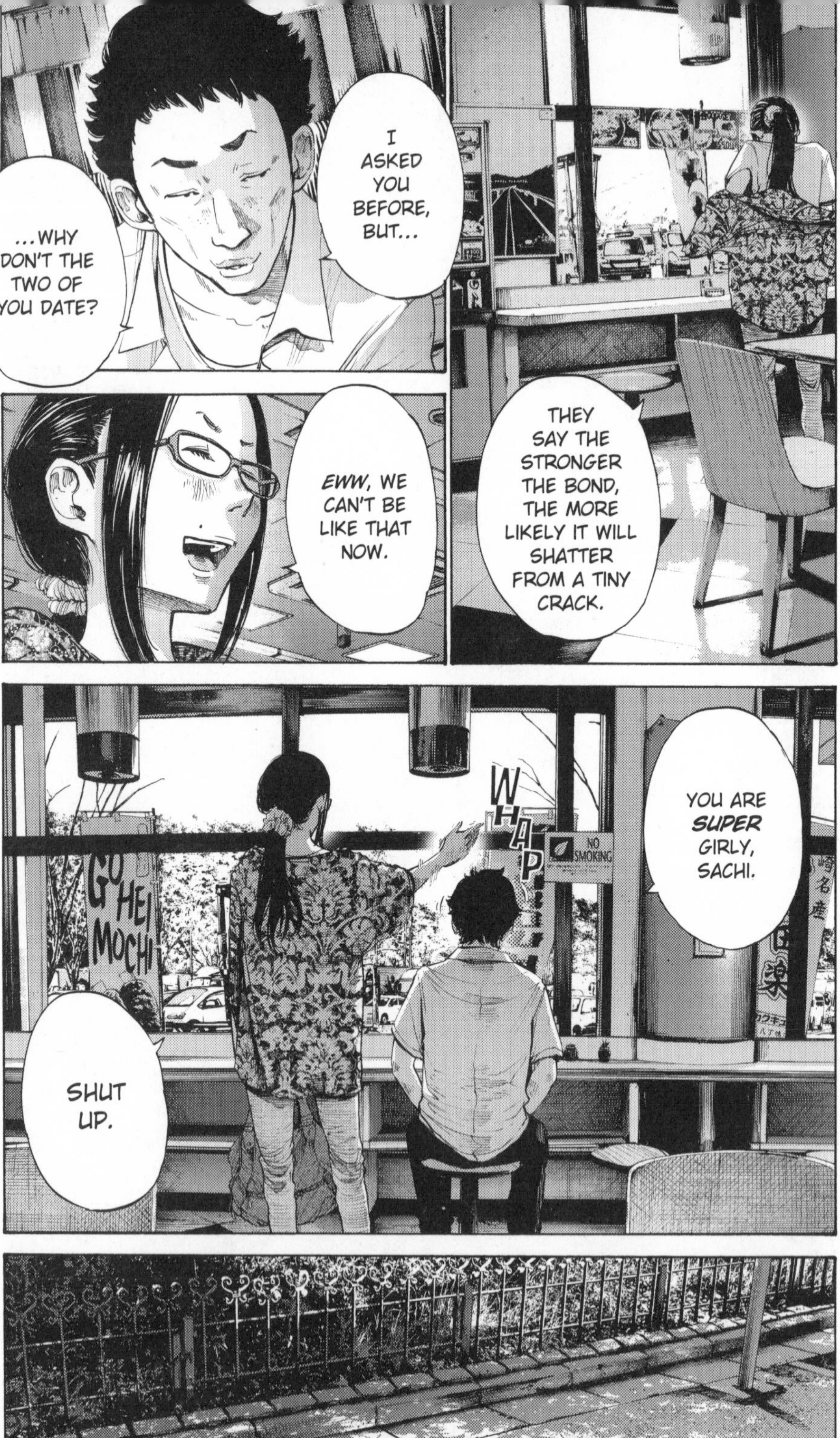
THEY SAY THE STRONGER THE BOND, THE MORE LIKELY IT WILL SHATTER FROM A TINY CRACK.
I ASKED YOU BEFORE, BUT...
...WHY DON'T THE TWO OF YOU DATE?
EWW, WE CAN'T BE LIKE THAT NOW.
YOU ARE ***SUPER*** GIRLY, SACHI.
NO SMOKING
WHAP
GOHEI MOCHI
SHUT UP.

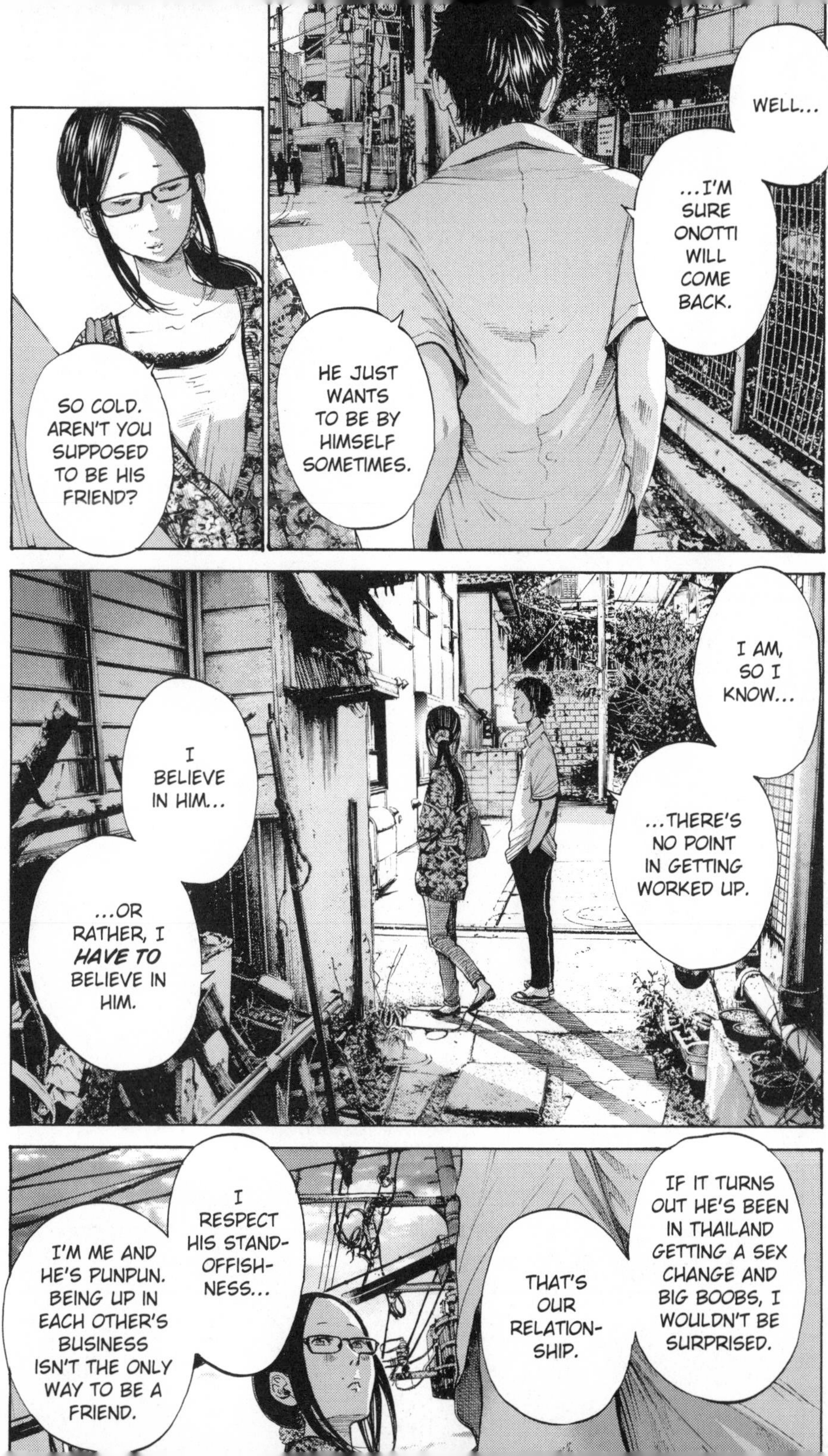
WELL...
...I'M SURE ONOTTI WILL COME BACK.
HE JUST WANTS TO BE BY HIMSELF SOMETIMES.
SO COLD. AREN'T YOU SUPPOSED TO BE HIS FRIEND?
I AM, SO I KNOW...
...THERE'S NO POINT IN GETTING WORKED UP.
I BELIEVE IN HIM...
...OR RATHER, I *HAVE TO* BELIEVE IN HIM.
IF IT TURNS OUT HE'S BEEN IN THAILAND GETTING A SEX CHANGE AND BIG BOOBS, I WOULDN'T BE SURPRISED.
THAT'S OUR RELATION-SHIP.
I RESPECT HIS STAND-OFFISH-NESS...
I'M ME AND HE'S PUNPUN. BEING UP IN EACH OTHER'S BUSINESS ISN'T THE ONLY WAY TO BE A FRIEND.

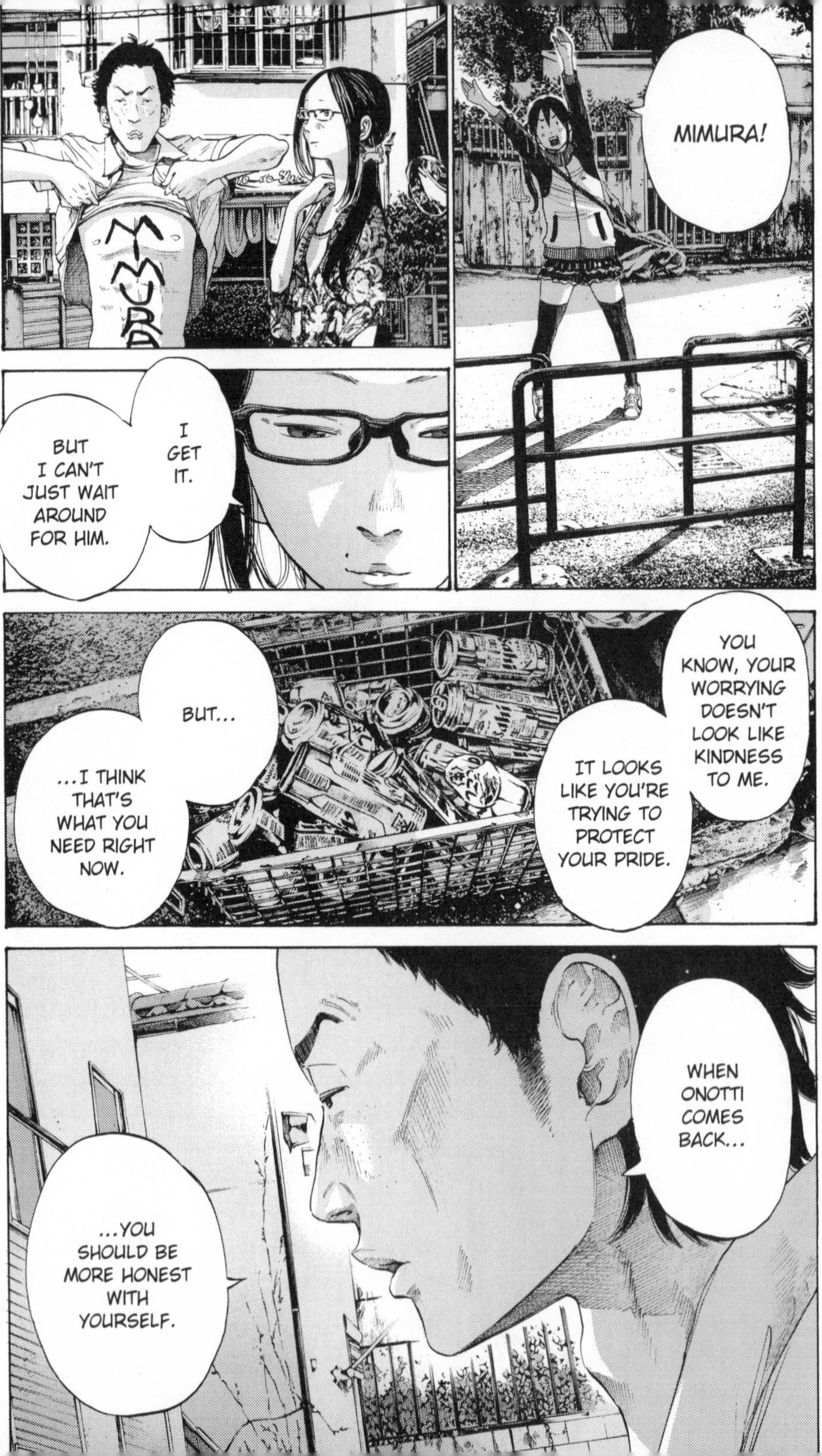
MIMURA!
MIMURA
I GET IT.
BUT I CAN'T JUST WAIT AROUND FOR HIM.
YOU KNOW, YOUR WORRYING DOESN'T LOOK LIKE KINDNESS TO ME.
IT LOOKS LIKE YOU'RE TRYING TO PROTECT YOUR PRIDE.
BUT...
...I THINK THAT'S WHAT YOU NEED RIGHT NOW.
WHEN ONOTTI COMES BACK...
...YOU SHOULD BE MORE HONEST WITH YOURSELF.

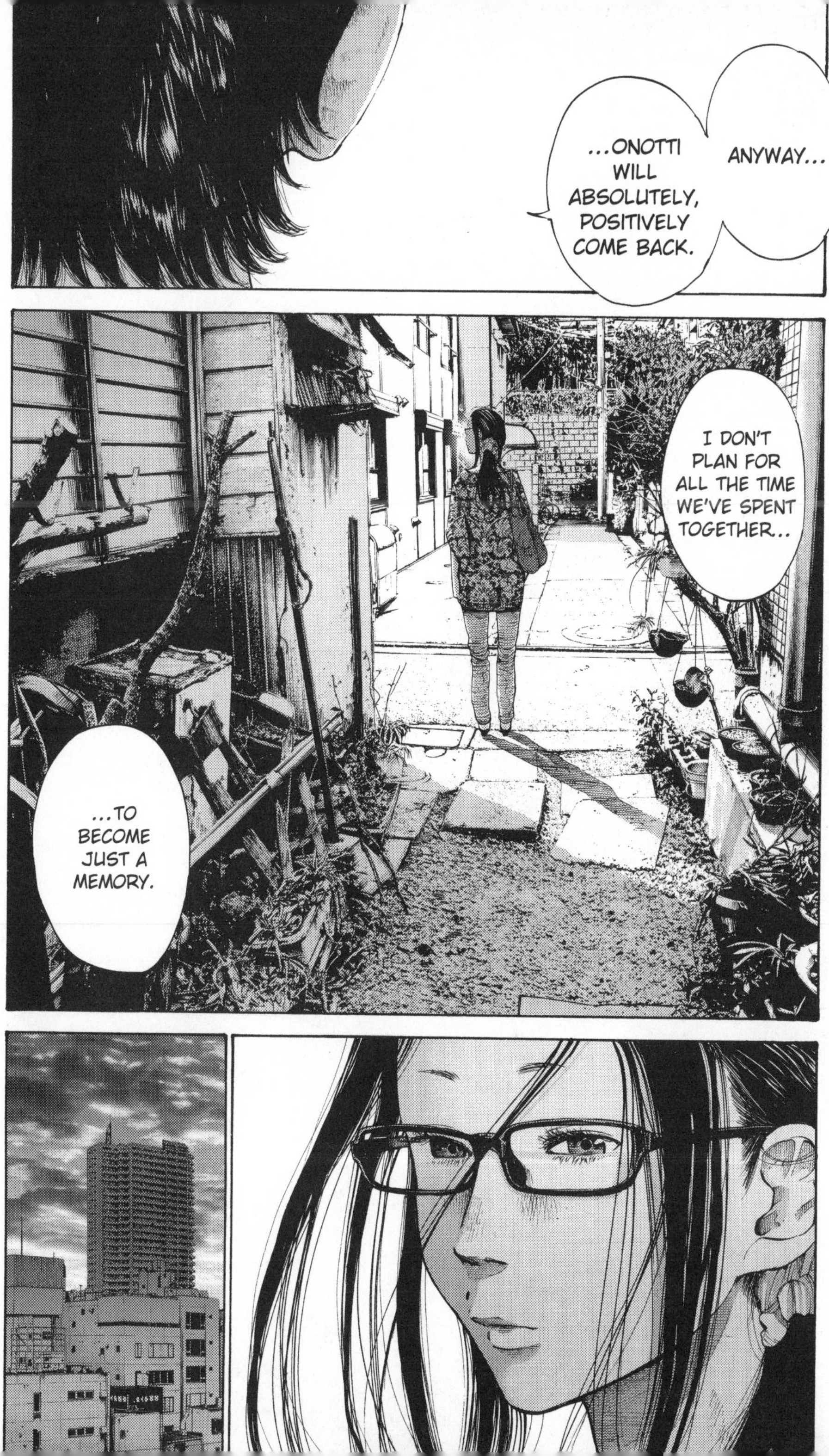
ANYWAY...
...ONOTTI WILL ABSOLUTELY, POSITIVELY COME BACK.
I DON'T PLAN FOR ALL THE TIME WE'VE SPENT TOGETHER...
...TO BECOME JUST A MEMORY.

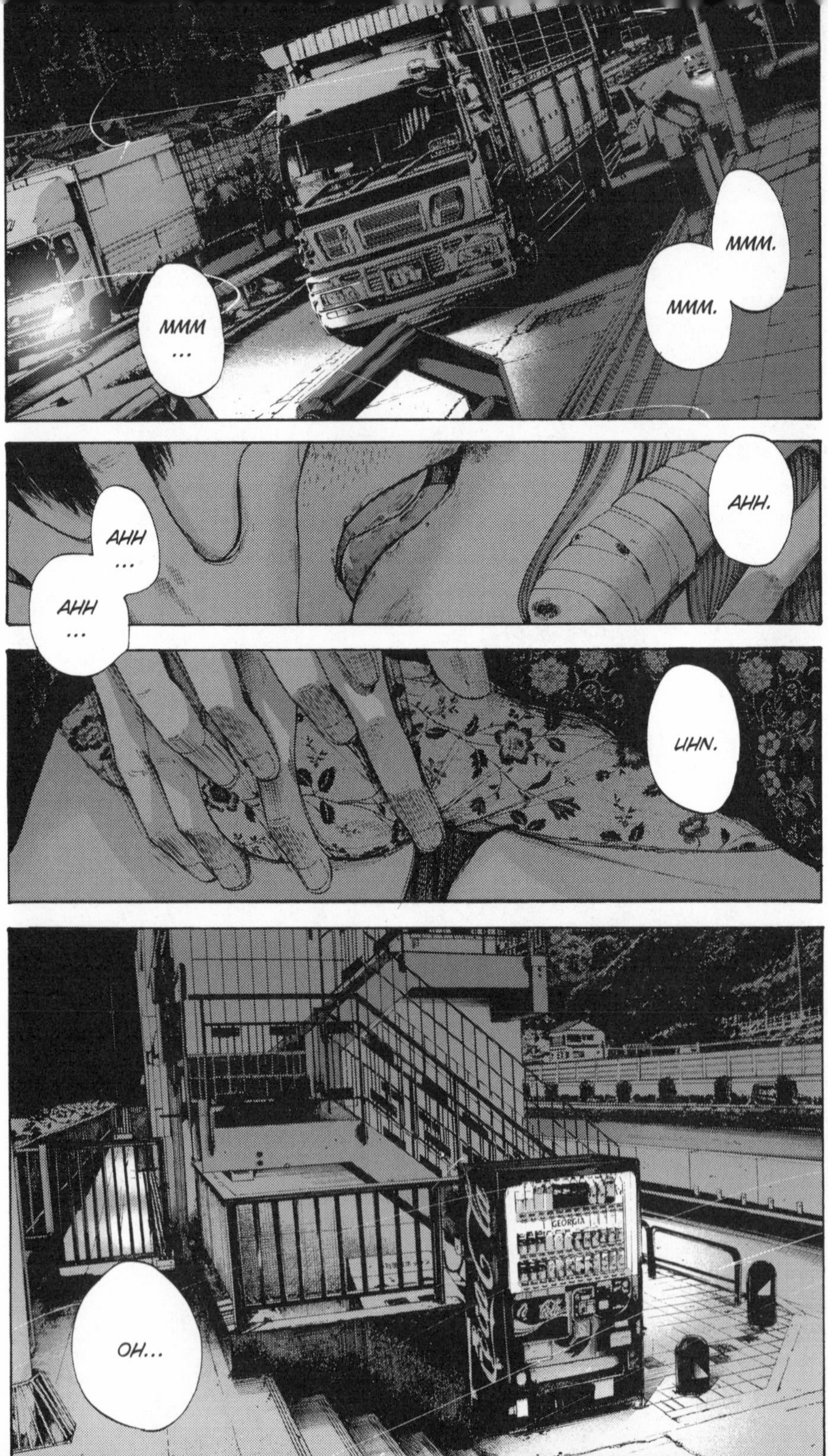
MMM.
MMM.
MMM ...
AHH.
AHH ...
AHH ...
UHN.
GEORGIA
OH...

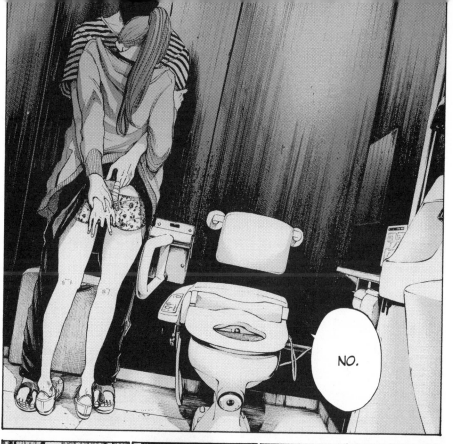

NO.

HUFF.

HUFF.

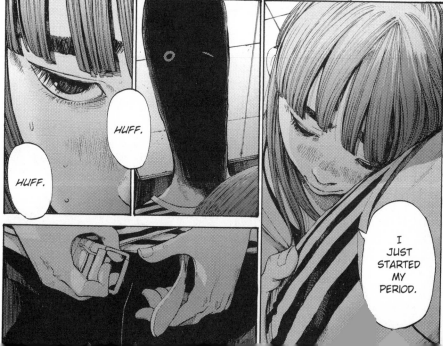

I JUST STARTED MY PERIOD.

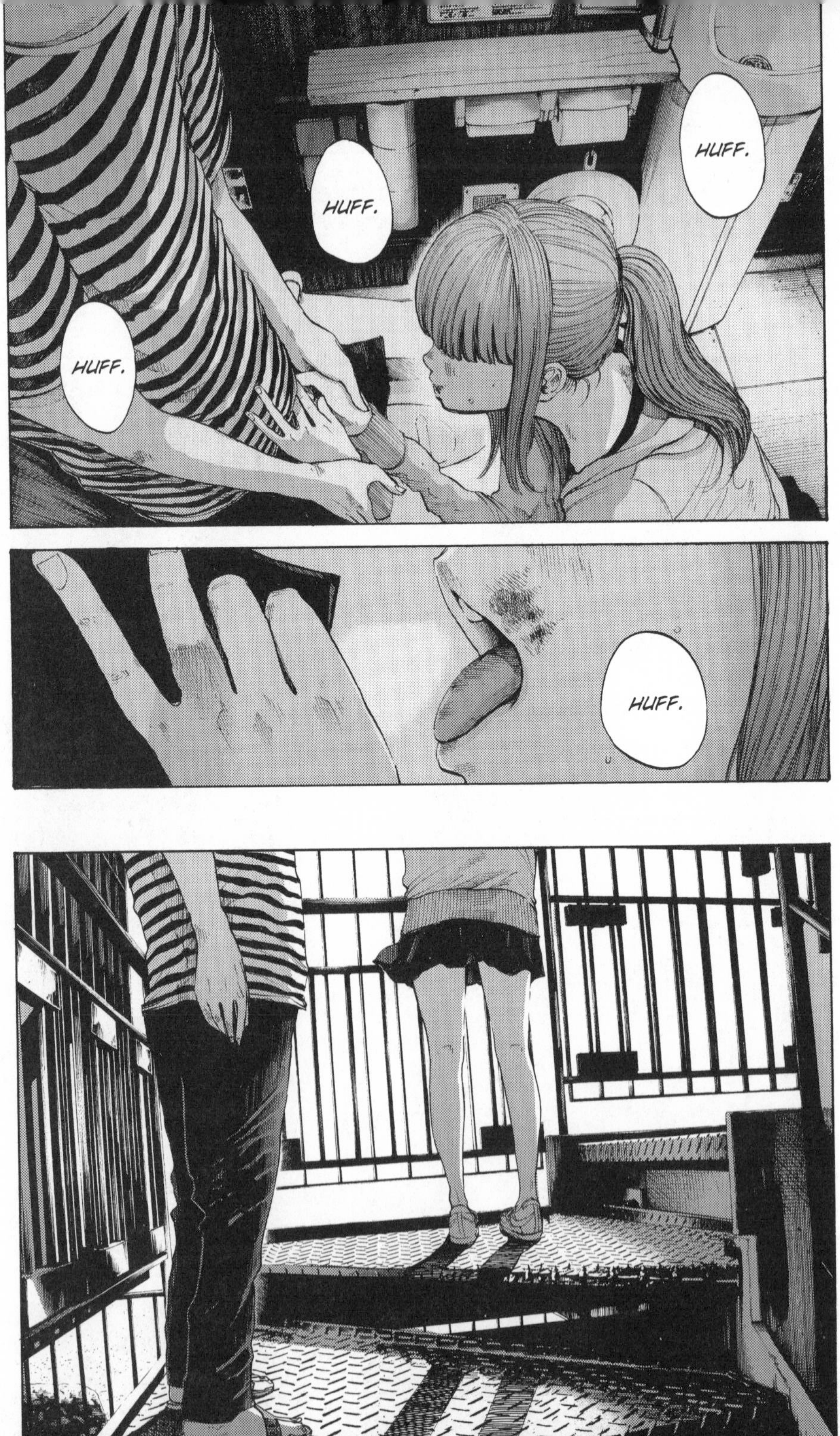
HUFF.
HUFF.
HUFF.
HUFF.

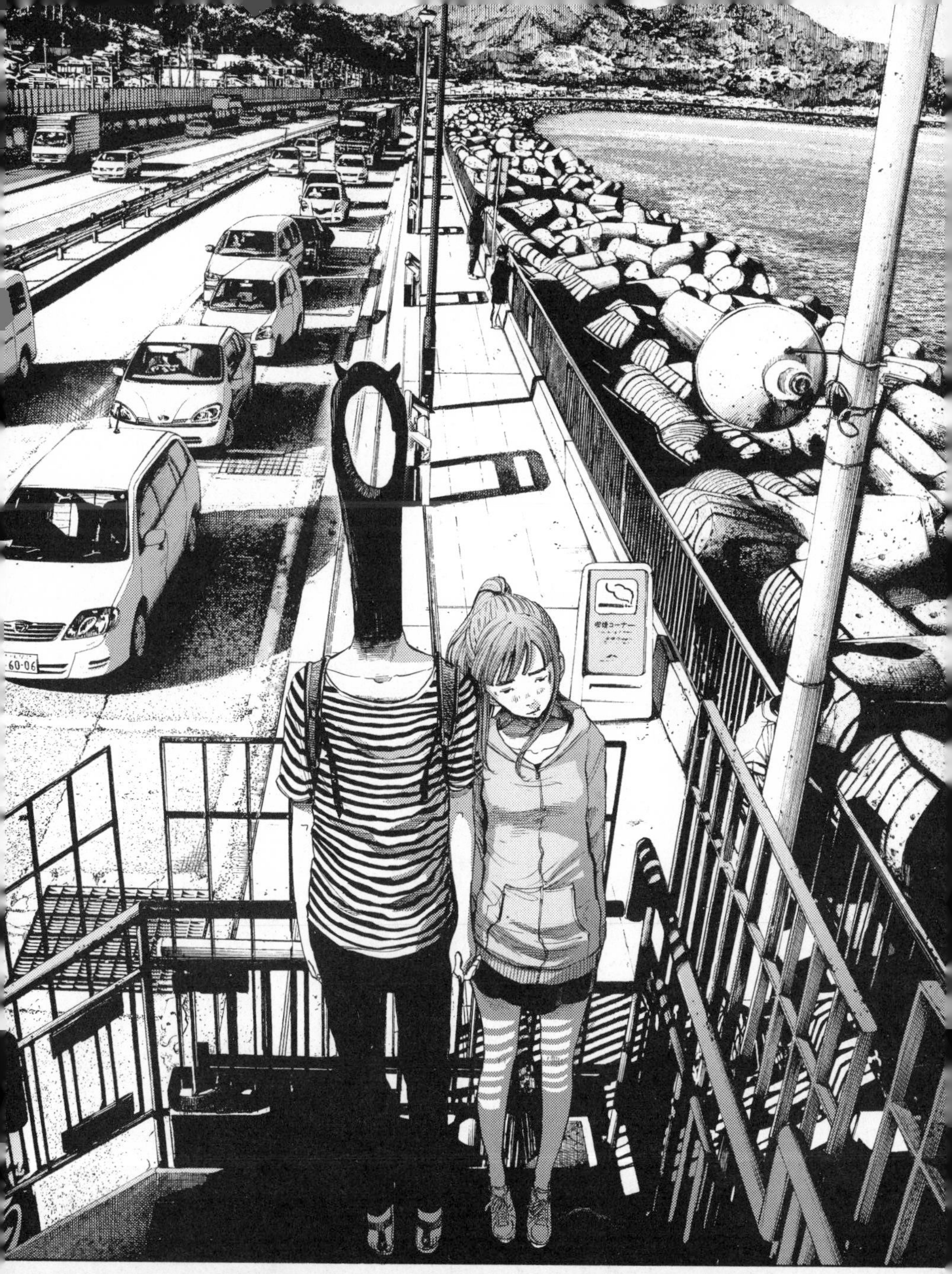
喫煙コーナー
60-06

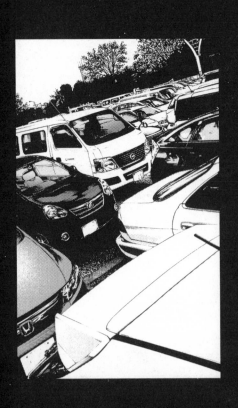

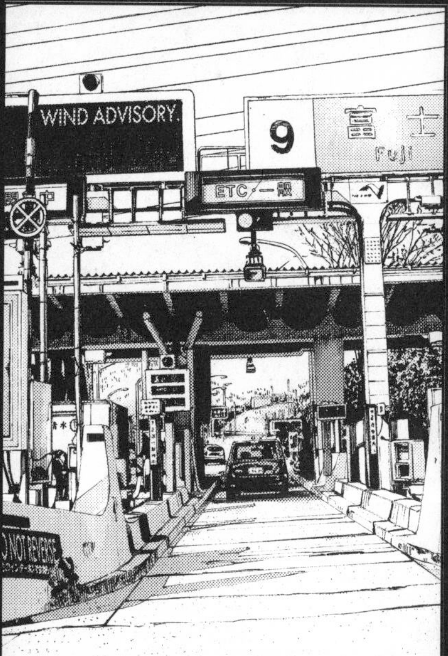
WIND ADVISORY.
9
富士
Fuji
ETC・一般

Chapter 123

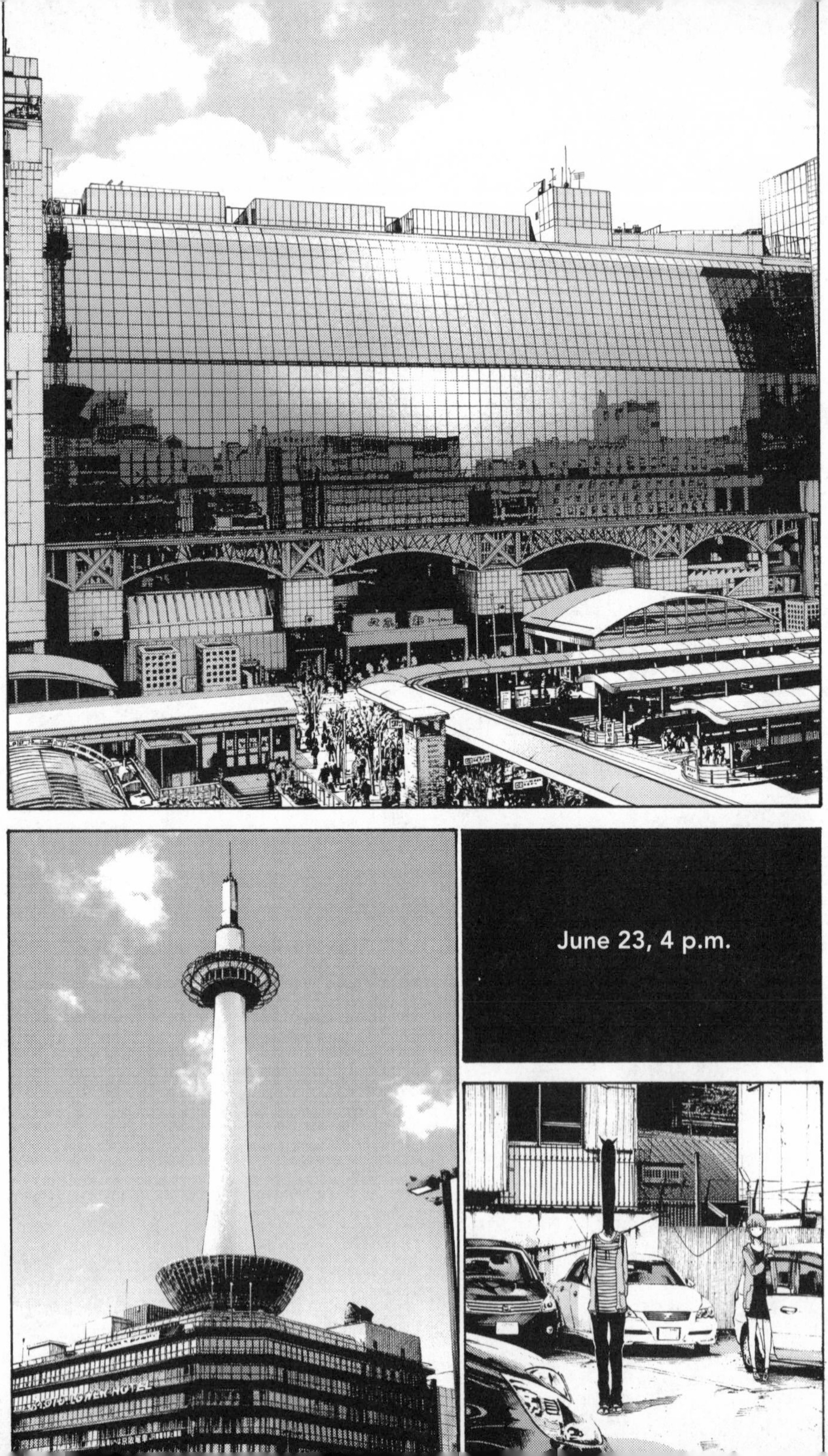
June 23, 4 p.m.
KYOTO TOWER HOTEL

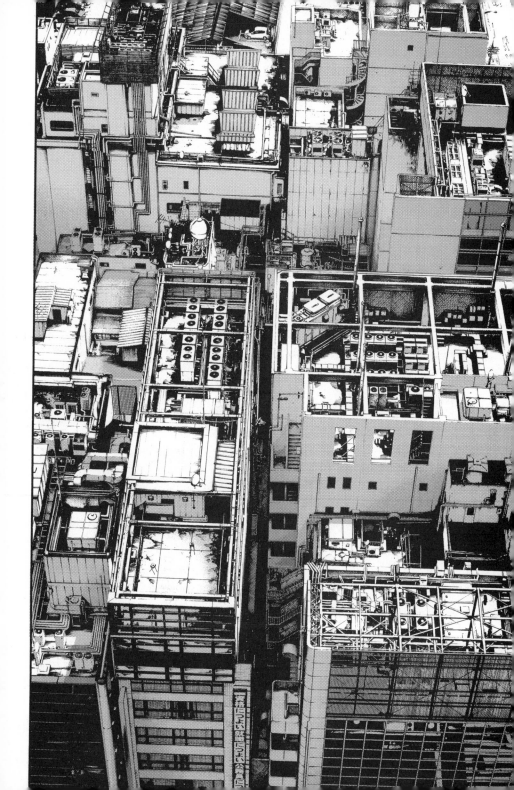

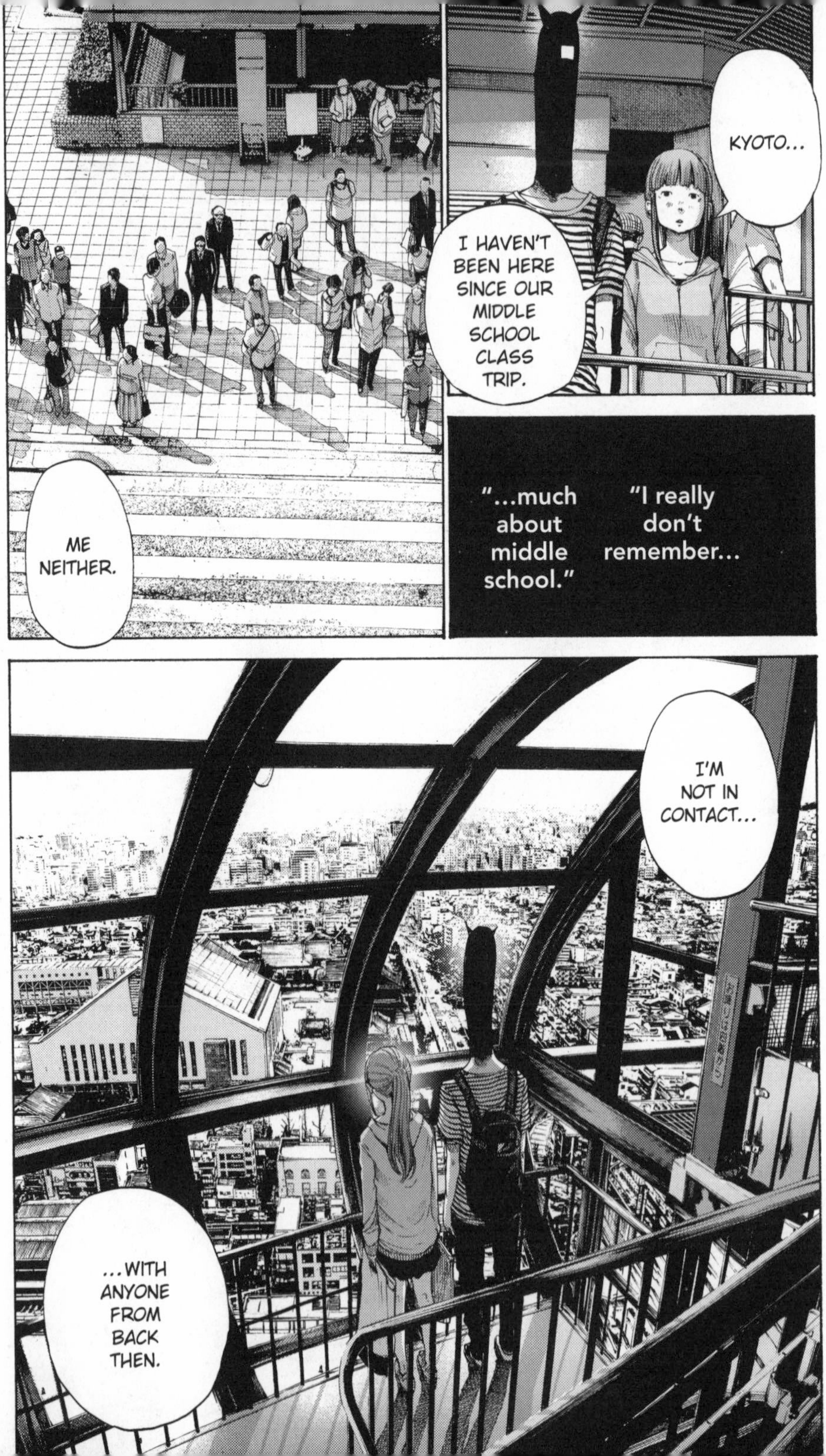
KYOTO...
I HAVEN'T BEEN HERE SINCE OUR MIDDLE SCHOOL CLASS TRIP.
"I really don't remember...
"...much about middle school."
ME NEITHER.
I'M NOT IN CONTACT...
...WITH ANYONE FROM BACK THEN.

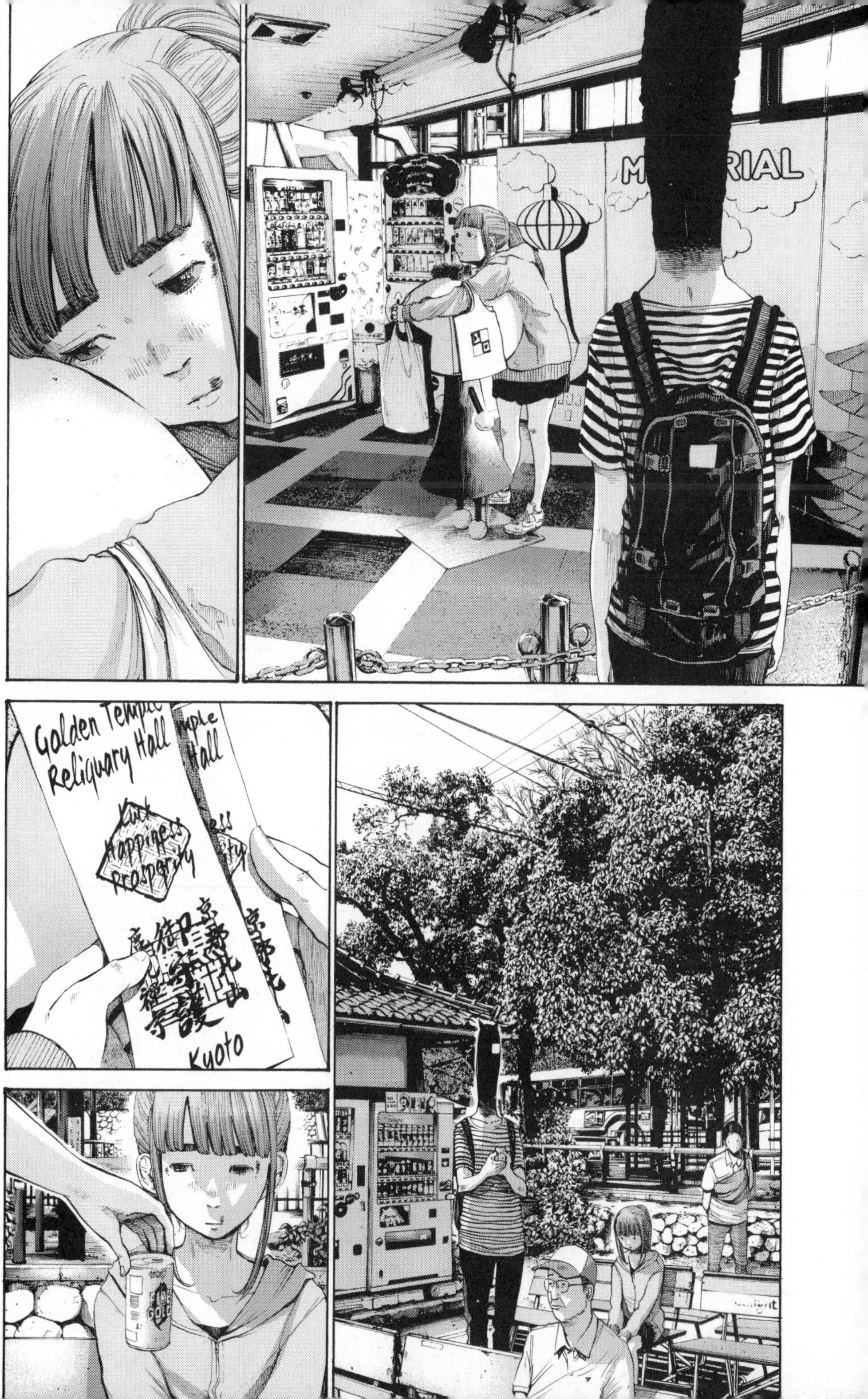
Golden Temple
Reliquary Hall
Luck
Happiness
Prosperity
Kyoto

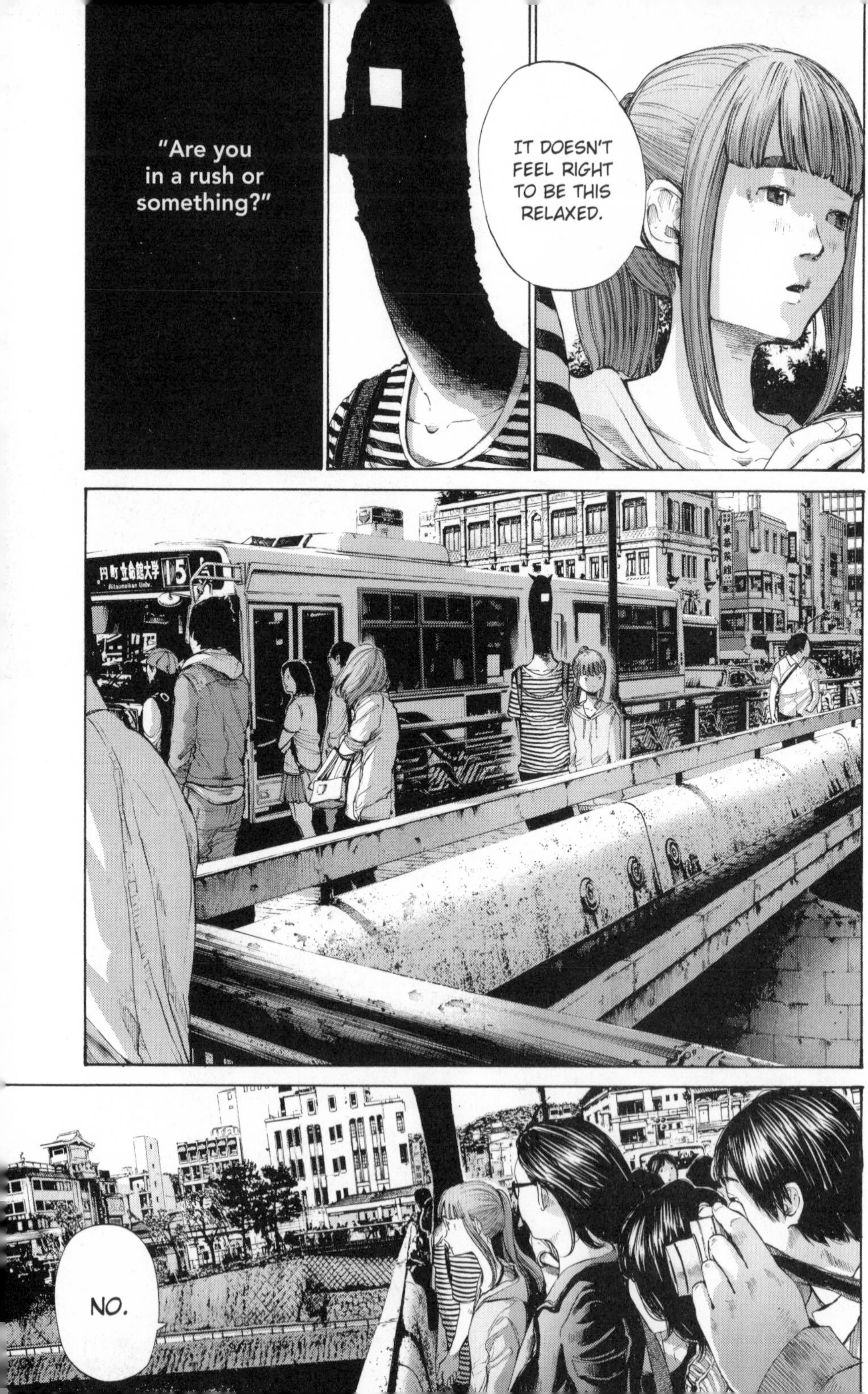
IT DOESN'T FEEL RIGHT TO BE THIS RELAXED.
"Are you in a rush or something?"
NO.

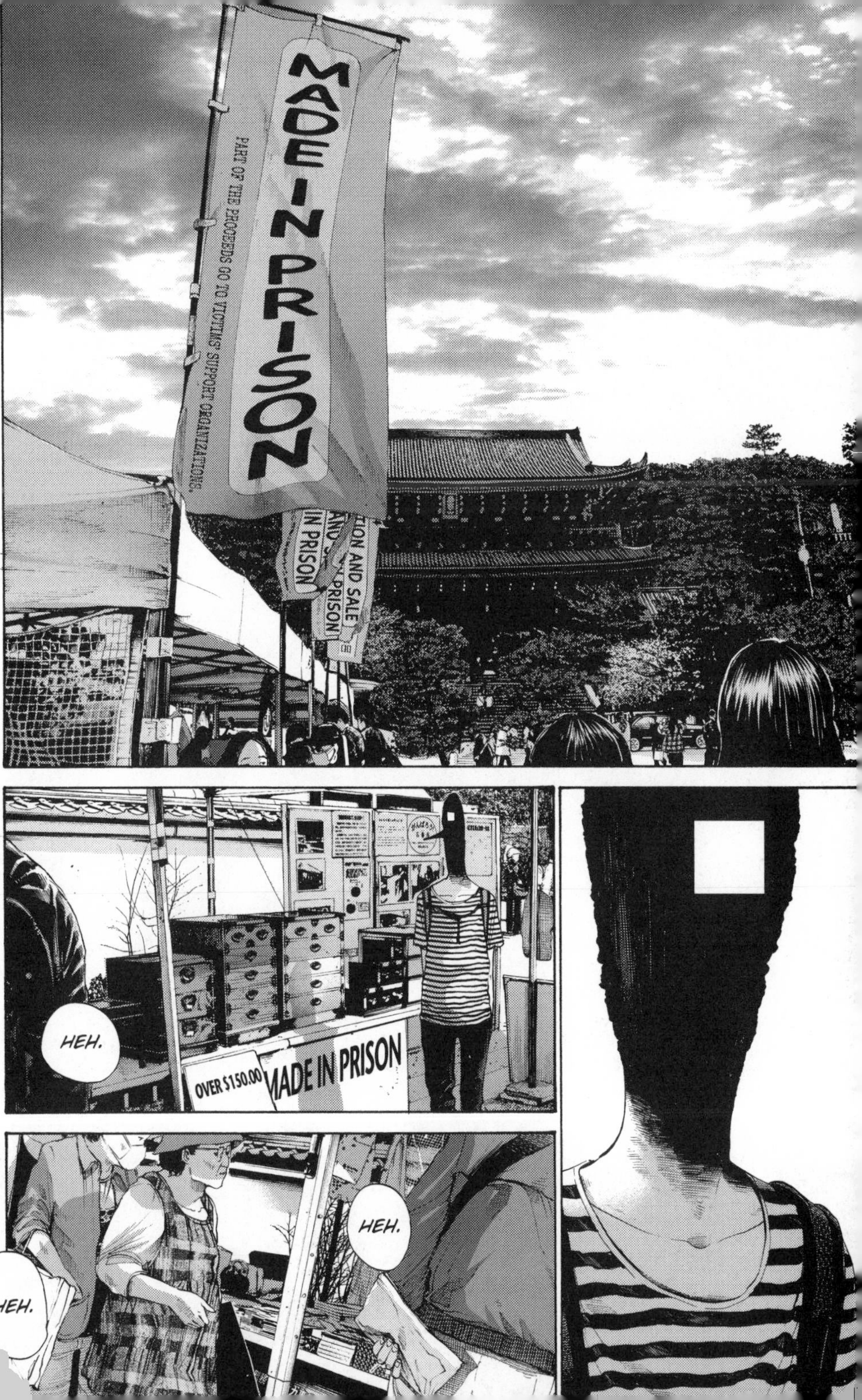
MADE IN PRISON
PART OF THE PROCEEDS GO TO VICTIMS' SUPPORT ORGANIZATIONS.
IN PRISON
HEH.
OVER $150.00
MADE IN PRISON
HEH.
HEH.

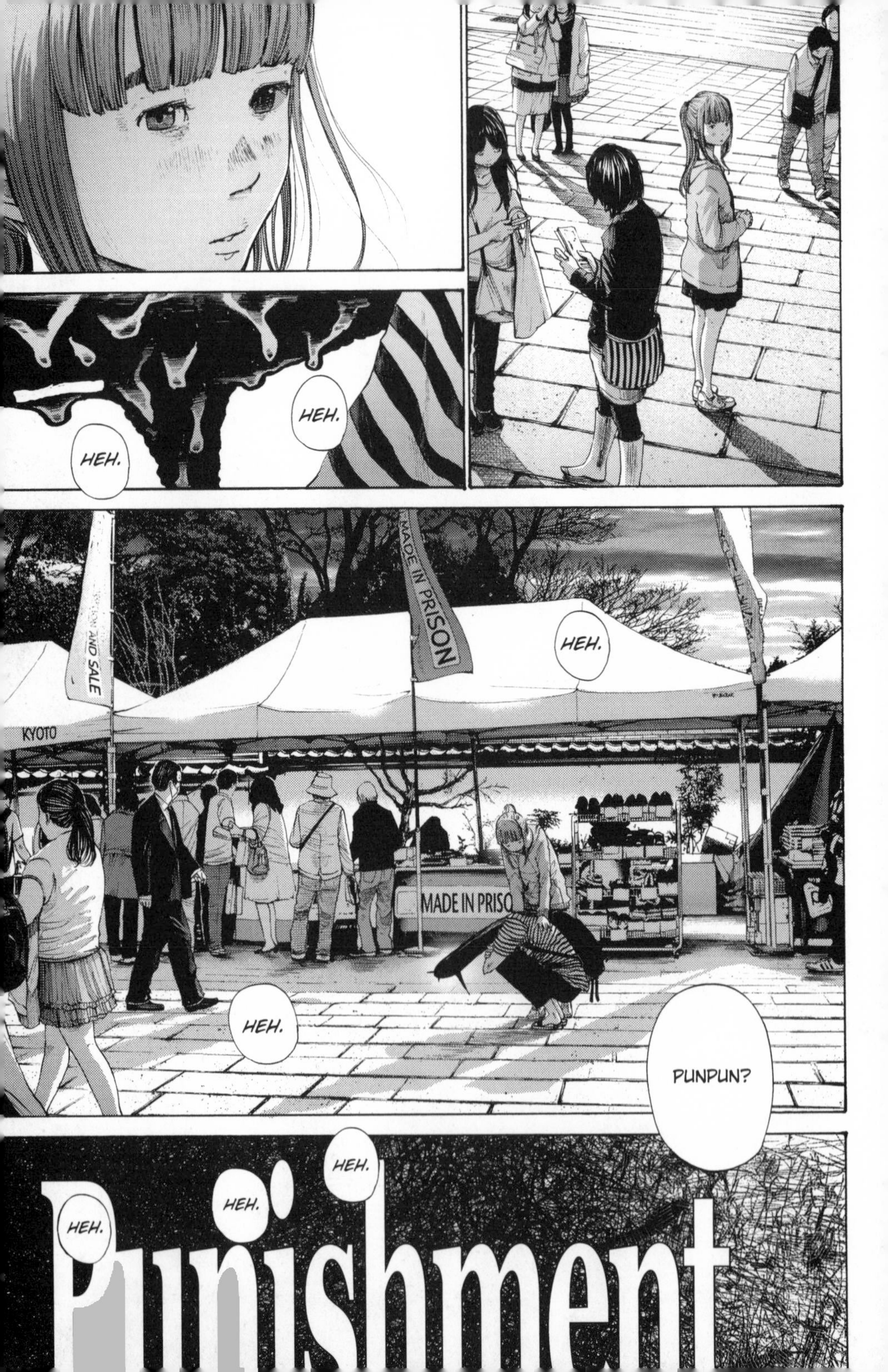
HEH.
HEH.
MADE IN PRISON
AND SALE
KYOTO
MADE IN PRISO
HEH.
PUNPUN?
HEH.
HEH.
HEH.
HEH.
Punishment

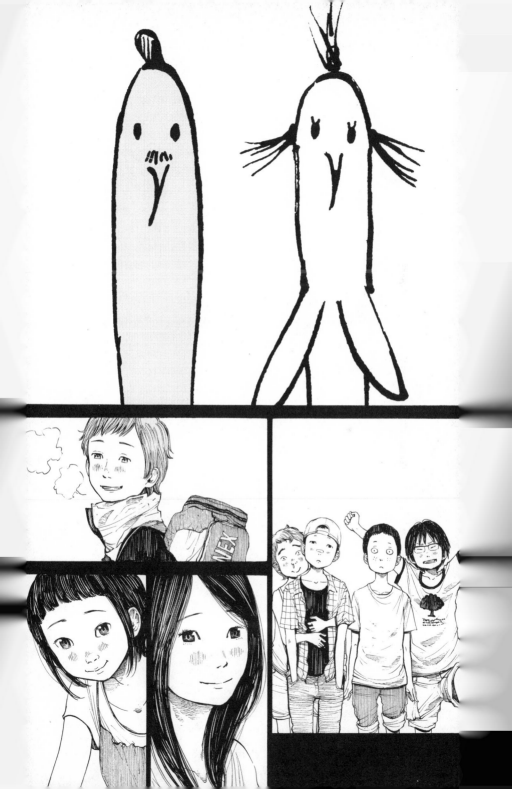

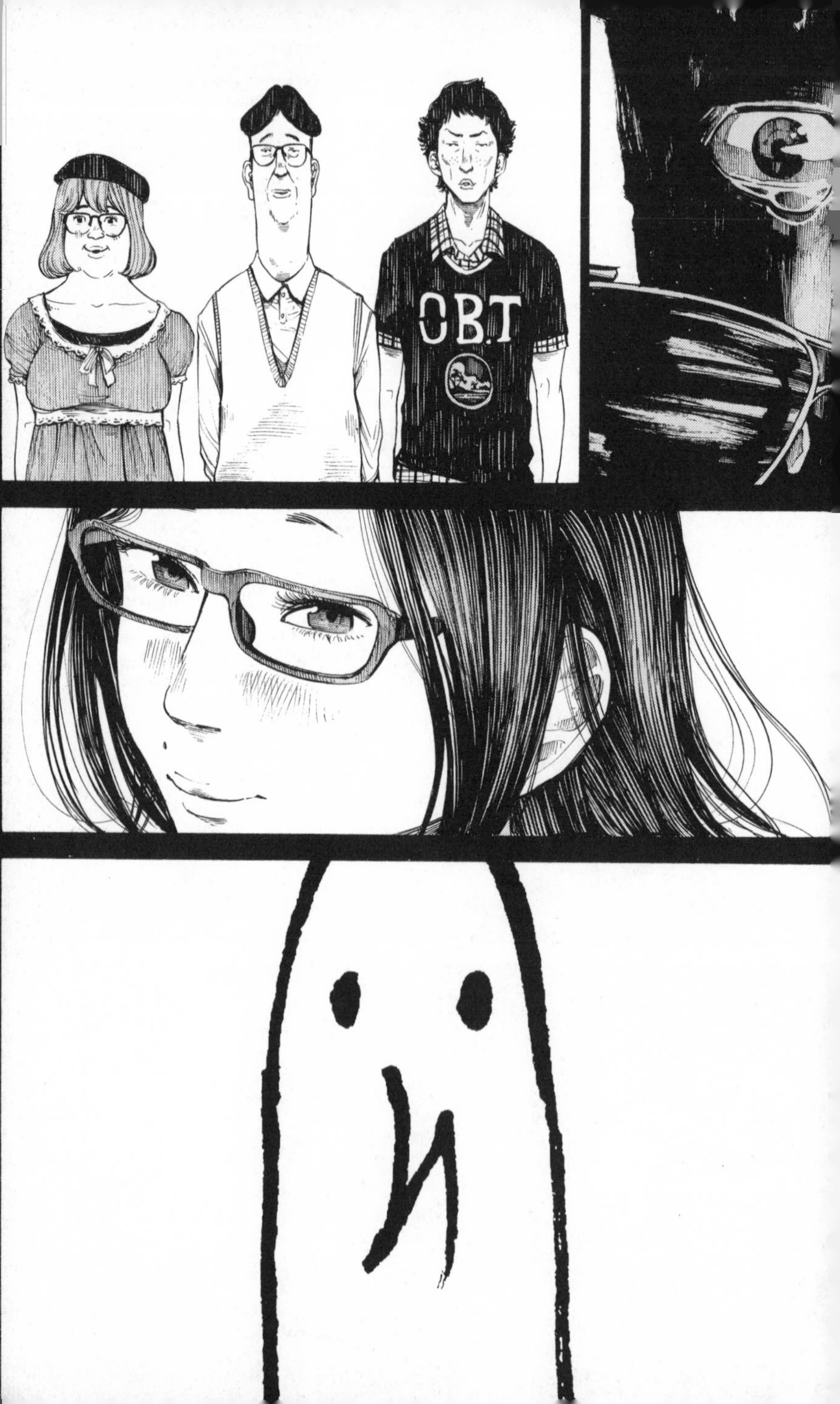
O.B.T

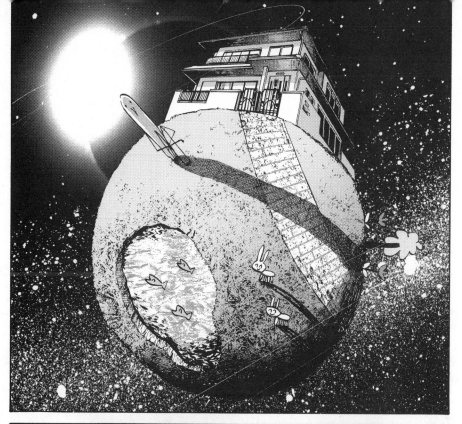

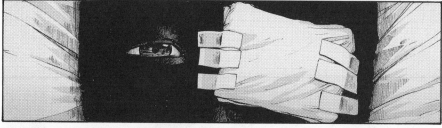

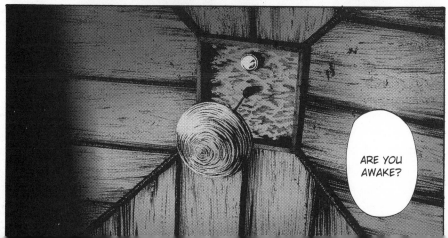

ARE YOU
AWAKE?

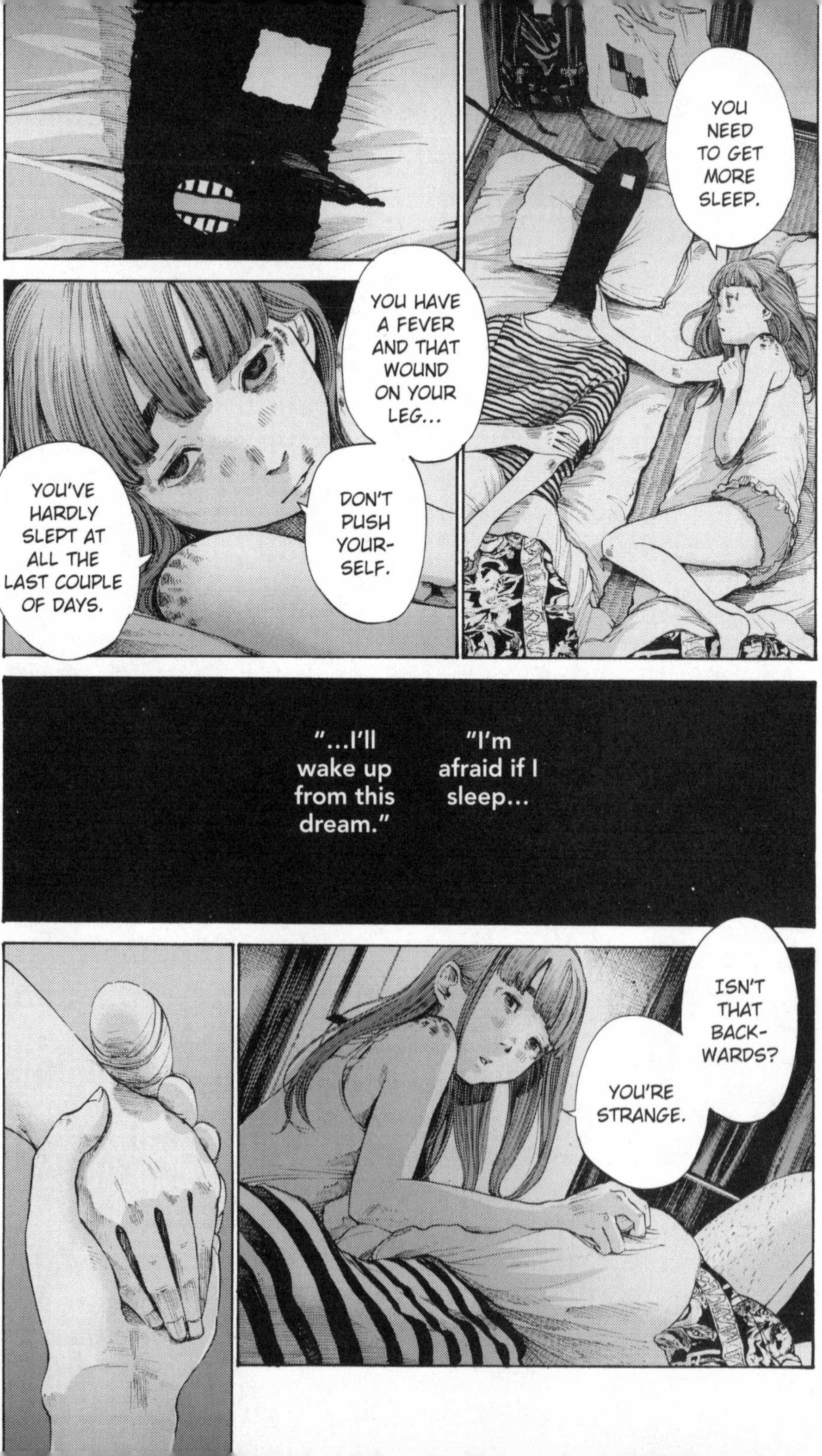
YOU NEED TO GET MORE SLEEP.
YOU HAVE A FEVER AND THAT WOUND ON YOUR LEG...
DON'T PUSH YOURSELF.
YOU'VE HARDLY SLEPT AT ALL THE LAST COUPLE OF DAYS.
"I'm afraid if I sleep...
...I'll wake up from this dream."
ISN'T THAT BACKWARDS?
YOU'RE STRANGE.

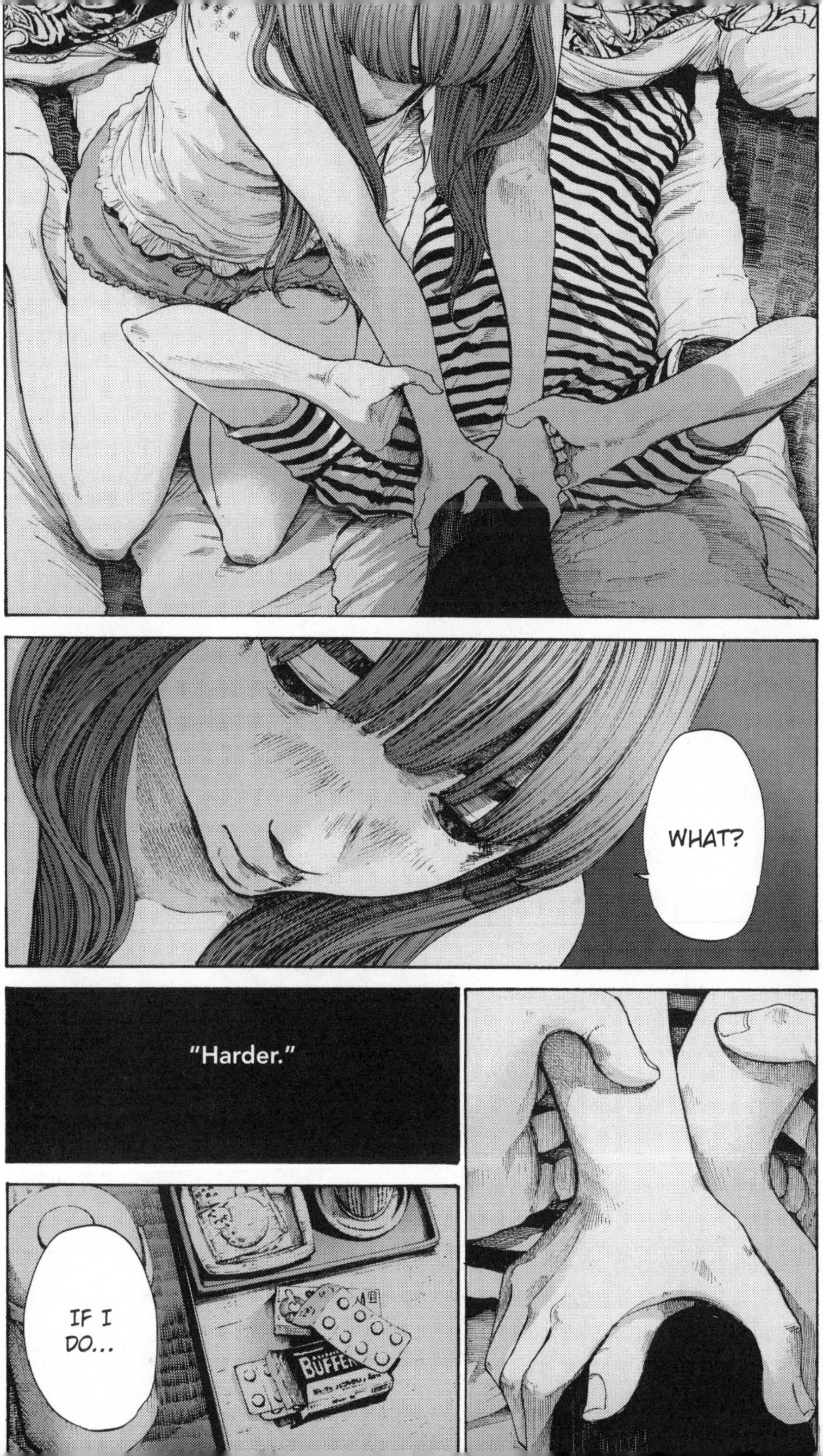
WHAT?
"Harder."
IF I DO...

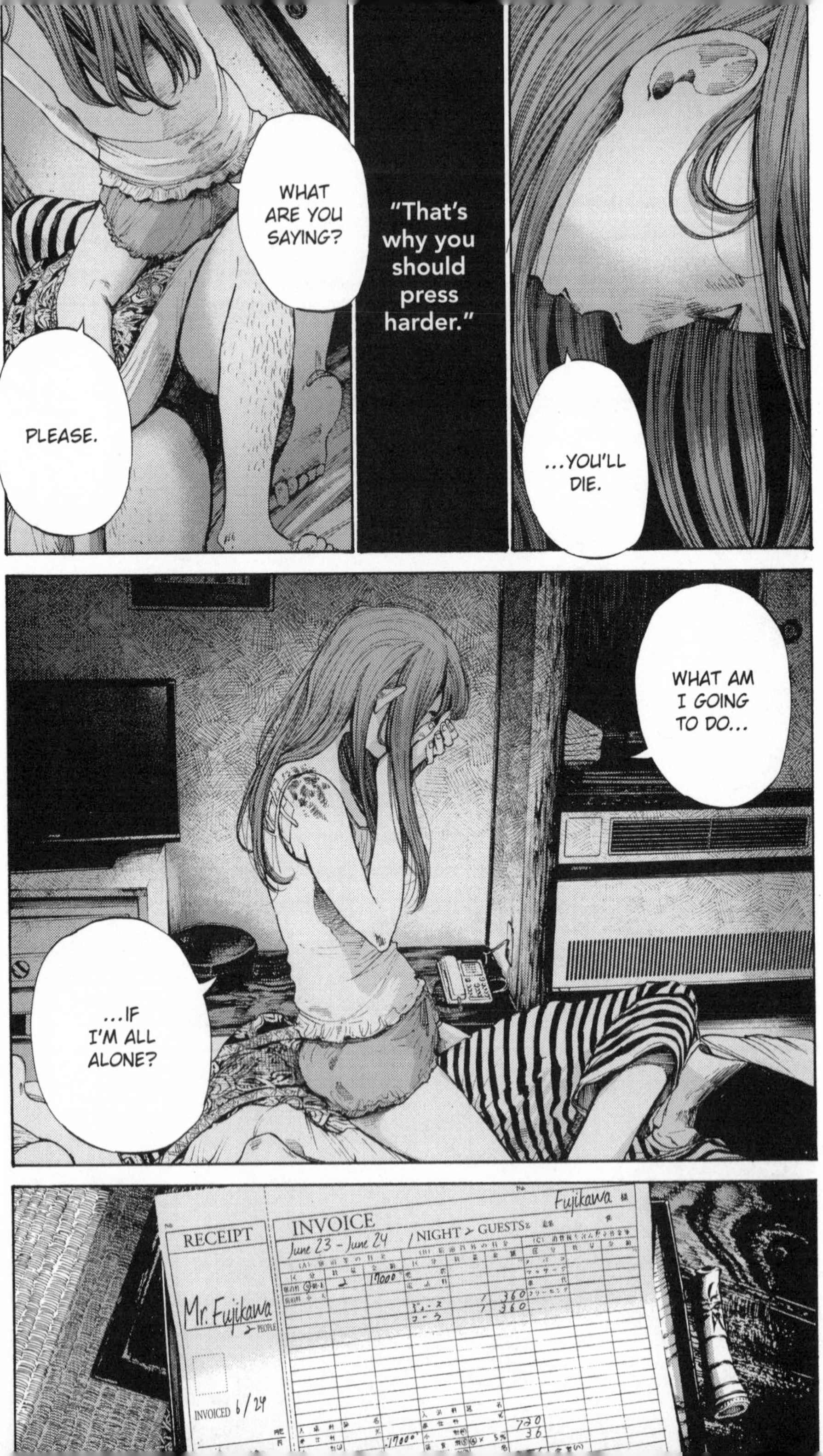
...YOU'LL DIE.
"That's why you should press harder."
WHAT ARE YOU SAYING?
PLEASE.
WHAT AM I GOING TO DO...
...IF I'M ALL ALONE?
Fujikawa
RECEIPT
INVOICE
June 23 – June 24
1 NIGHT 2 GUESTS
Mr. Fujikawa
2 PEOPLE
INVOICED 6/24

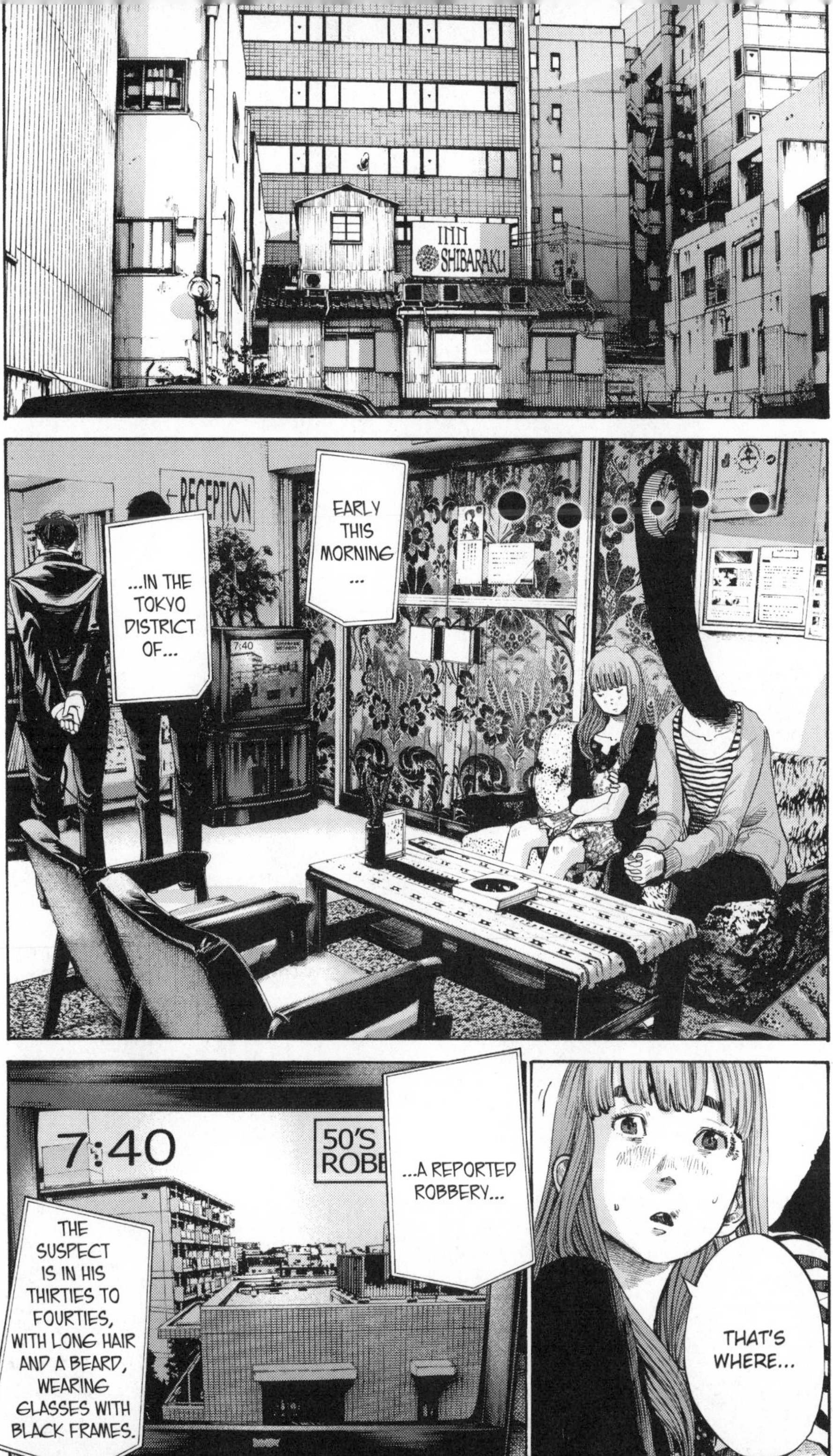
INN SHIBARAKU
EARLY THIS MORNING ...
RECEPTION
...IN THE TOKYO DISTRICT OF...
THAT'S WHERE...
...A REPORTED ROBBERY...
7:40
50'S ROBBE
THE SUSPECT IS IN HIS THIRTIES TO FOURTIES, WITH LONG HAIR AND A BEARD, WEARING GLASSES WITH BLACK FRAMES.

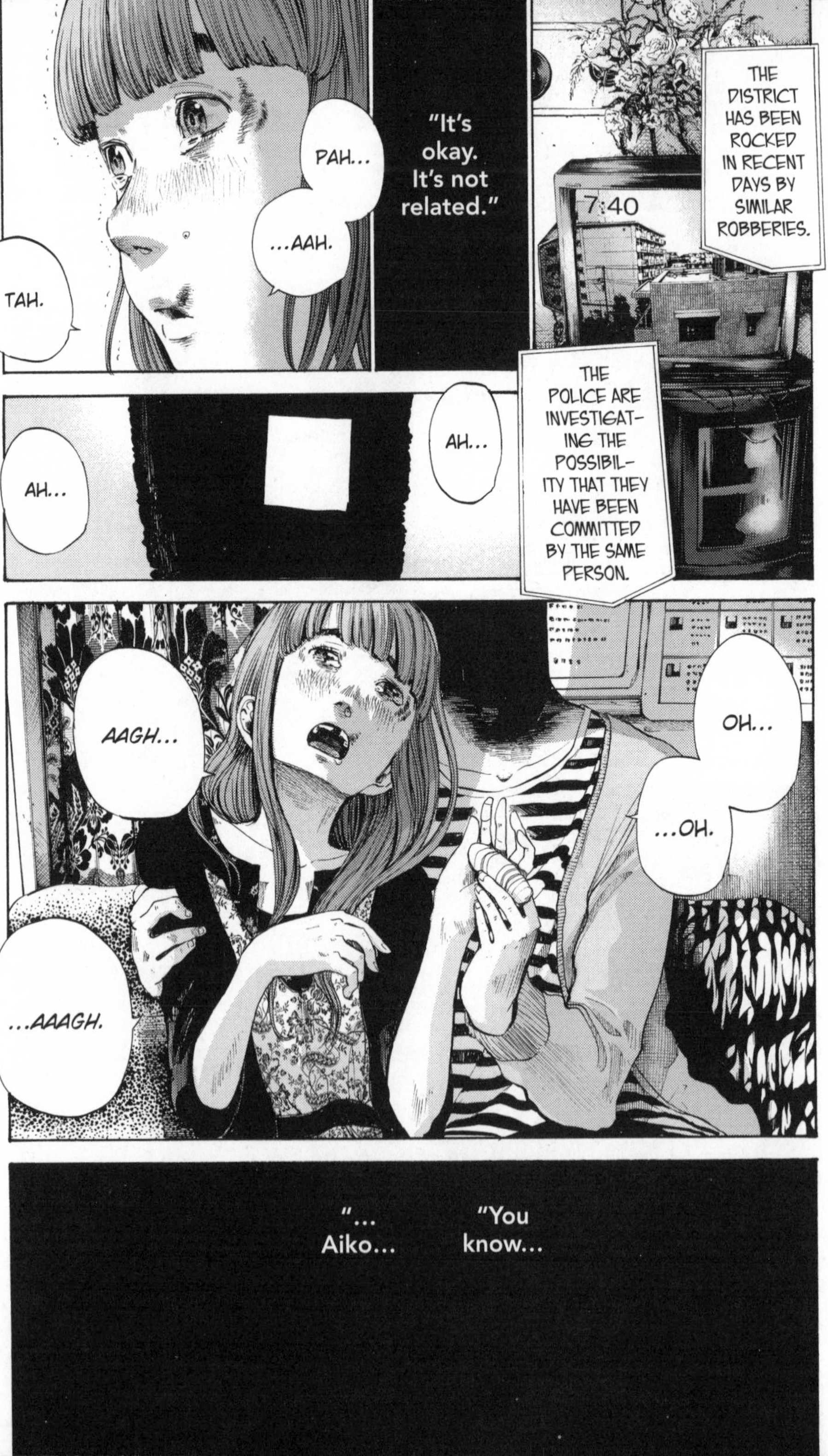
7:40
THE DISTRICT HAS BEEN ROCKED IN RECENT DAYS BY SIMILAR ROBBERIES.
"It's okay. It's not related."
PAH...
...AAH.
TAH.
THE POLICE ARE INVESTIGATING THE POSSIBILITY THAT THEY HAVE BEEN COMMITTED BY THE SAME PERSON.
AH...
AH...
OH...
...OH.
AAGH...
...AAAGH.
"You know...
"... Aiko...

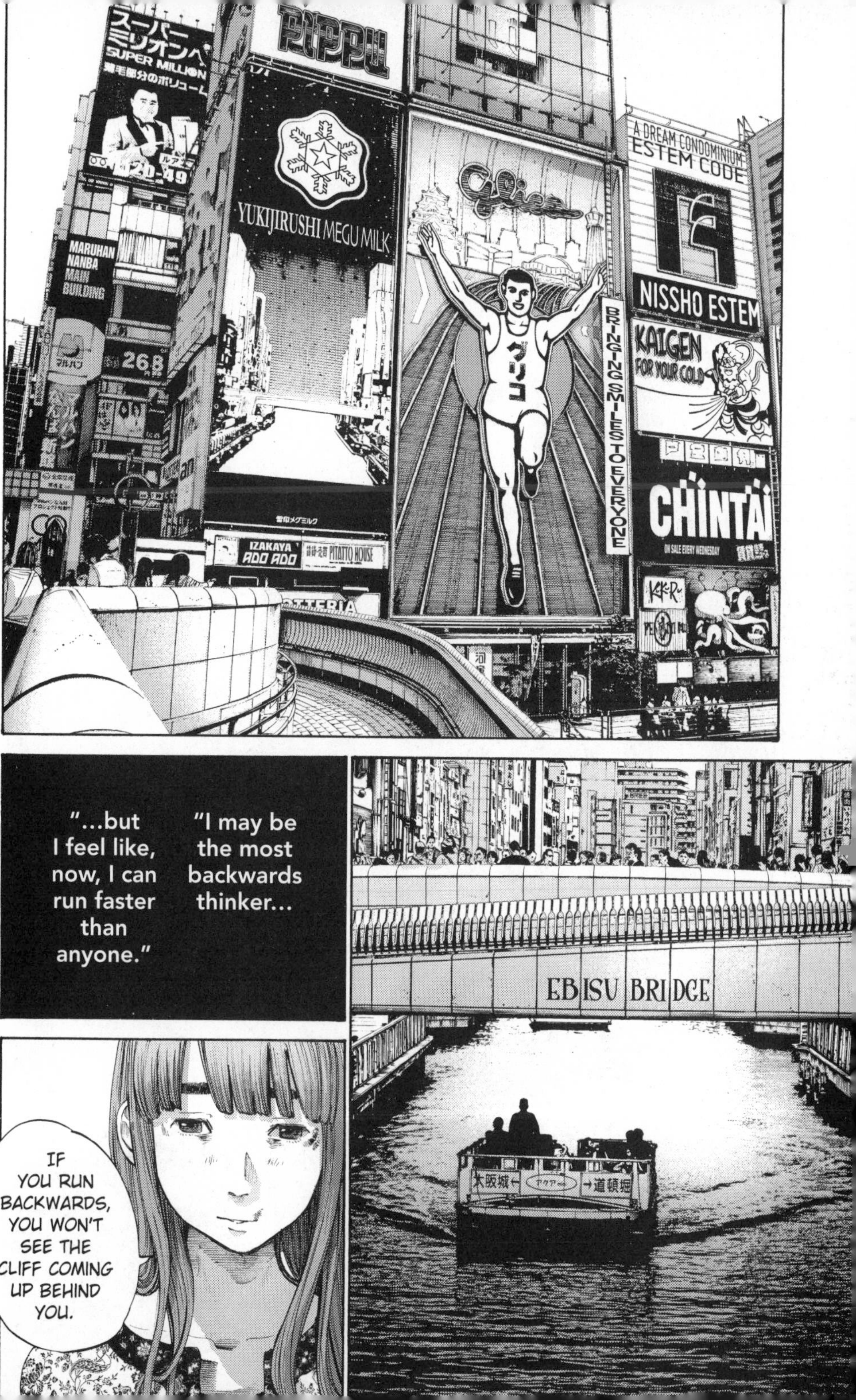

スーパーミリオンヘ
SUPER MILLION
PIPPU
YUKIJIRUSHI MEGU MILK
雪印メグミルク
MARUHAN NANBA MAIN BUILDING
IZAKAYA ADO ADO
PITATTO HOUSE
グリコ
BRINGING SMILES TO EVERYONE
A DREAM CONDOMINIUM ESTEM CODE
NISSHO ESTEM
KAIGEN FOR YOUR COLD
CHINTAI
ON SALE EVERY WEDNESDAY
EBISU BRIDGE
大阪城
道頓堀
"I may be the most backwards thinker...
"...but I feel like, now, I can run faster than anyone."
IF YOU RUN BACKWARDS, YOU WON'T SEE THE CLIFF COMING UP BEHIND YOU.

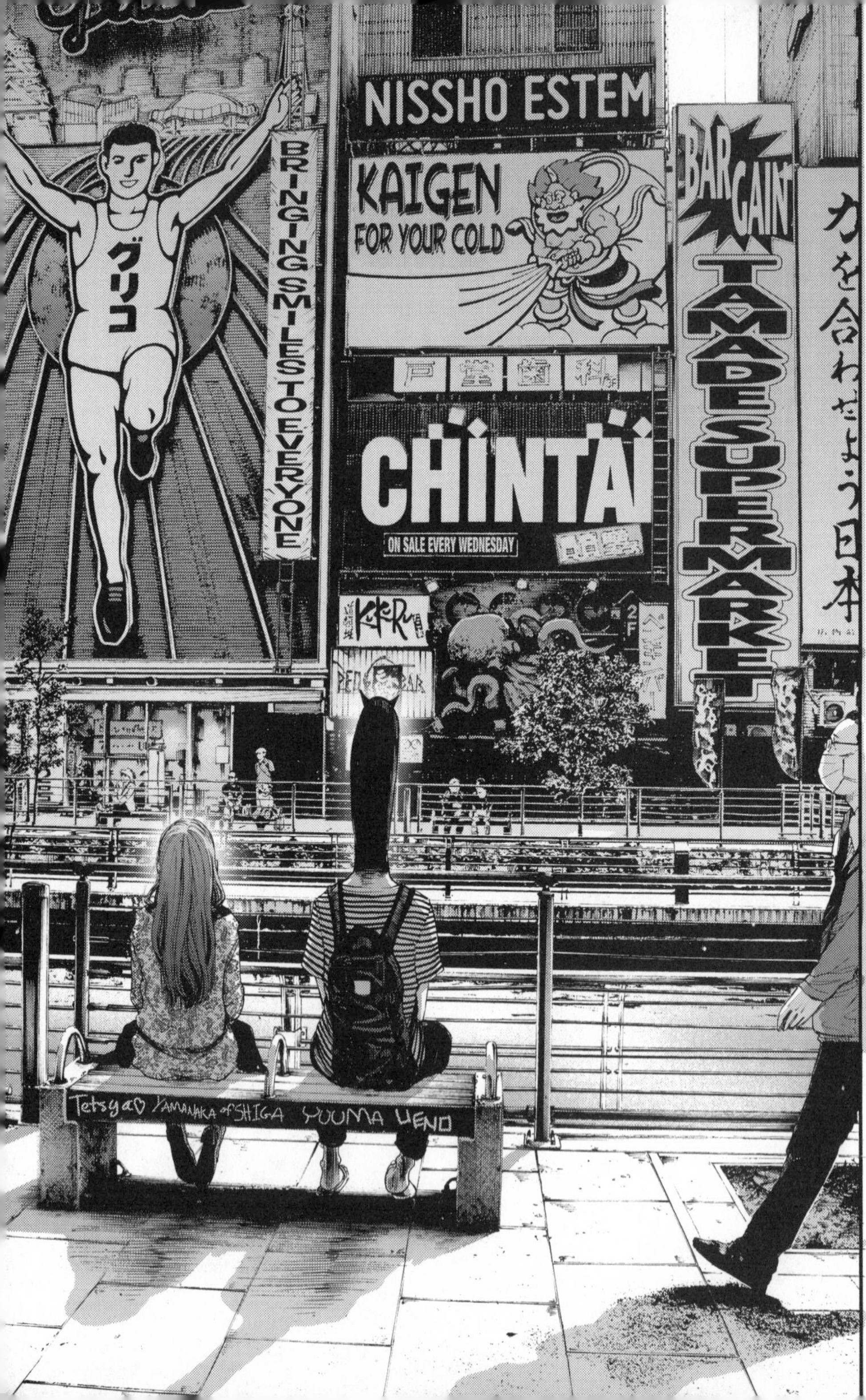
力を合わせよう日本
BARGAIN!
TAMADE SUPERMARKET
NISSHO ESTEM
KAIGEN
FOR YOUR COLD
CHINTAI
ON SALE EVERY WEDNESDAY
BRINGING SMILES TO EVERYONE
グリコ
Tetsya♡ YAMANAKA of SHIGA YUUMA UENO

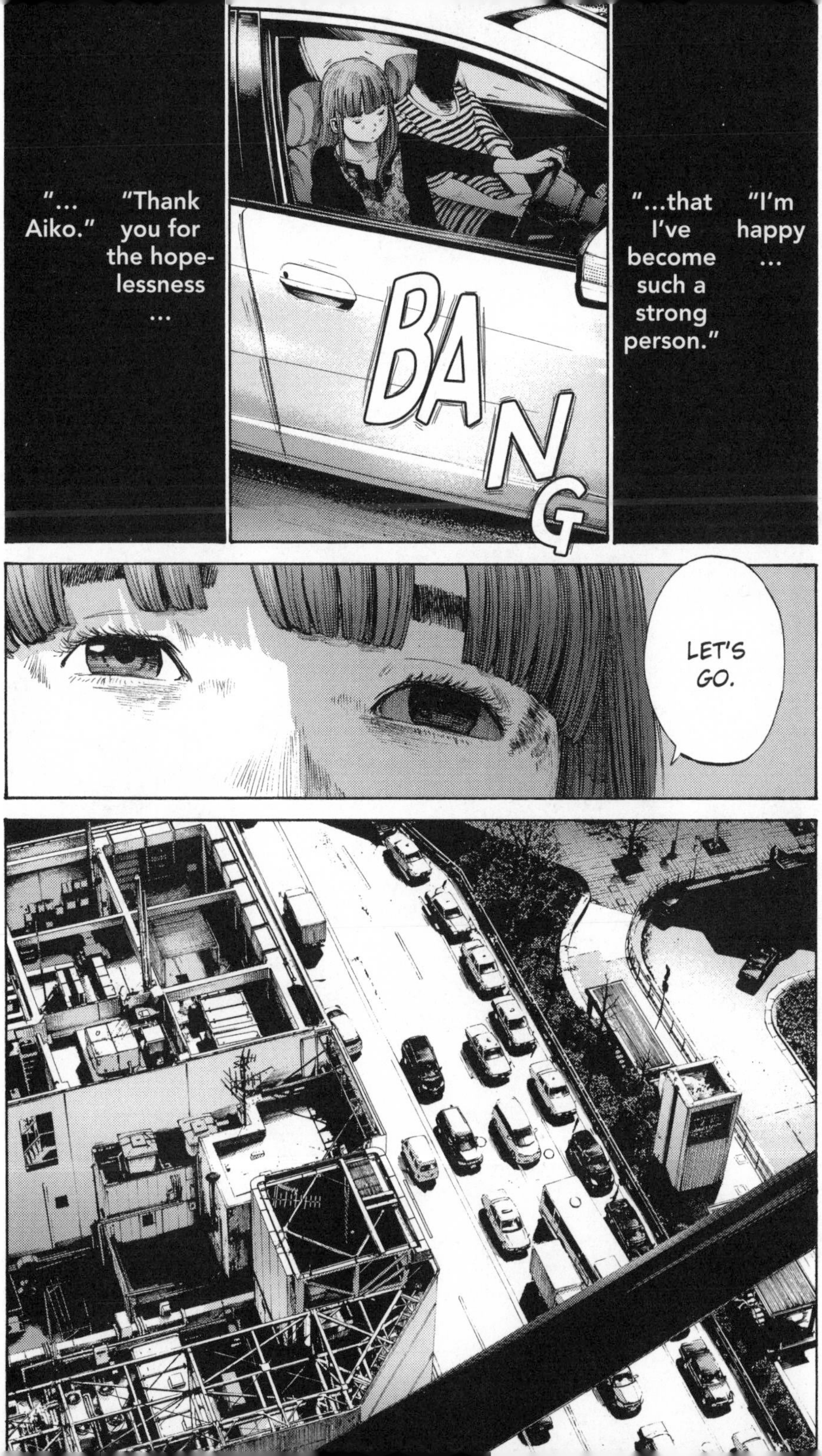
"I'm happy ...
"...that I've become such a strong person."
BANG
"Thank you for the hope-lessness ...
"... Aiko."
LET'S GO.

Chapter 124

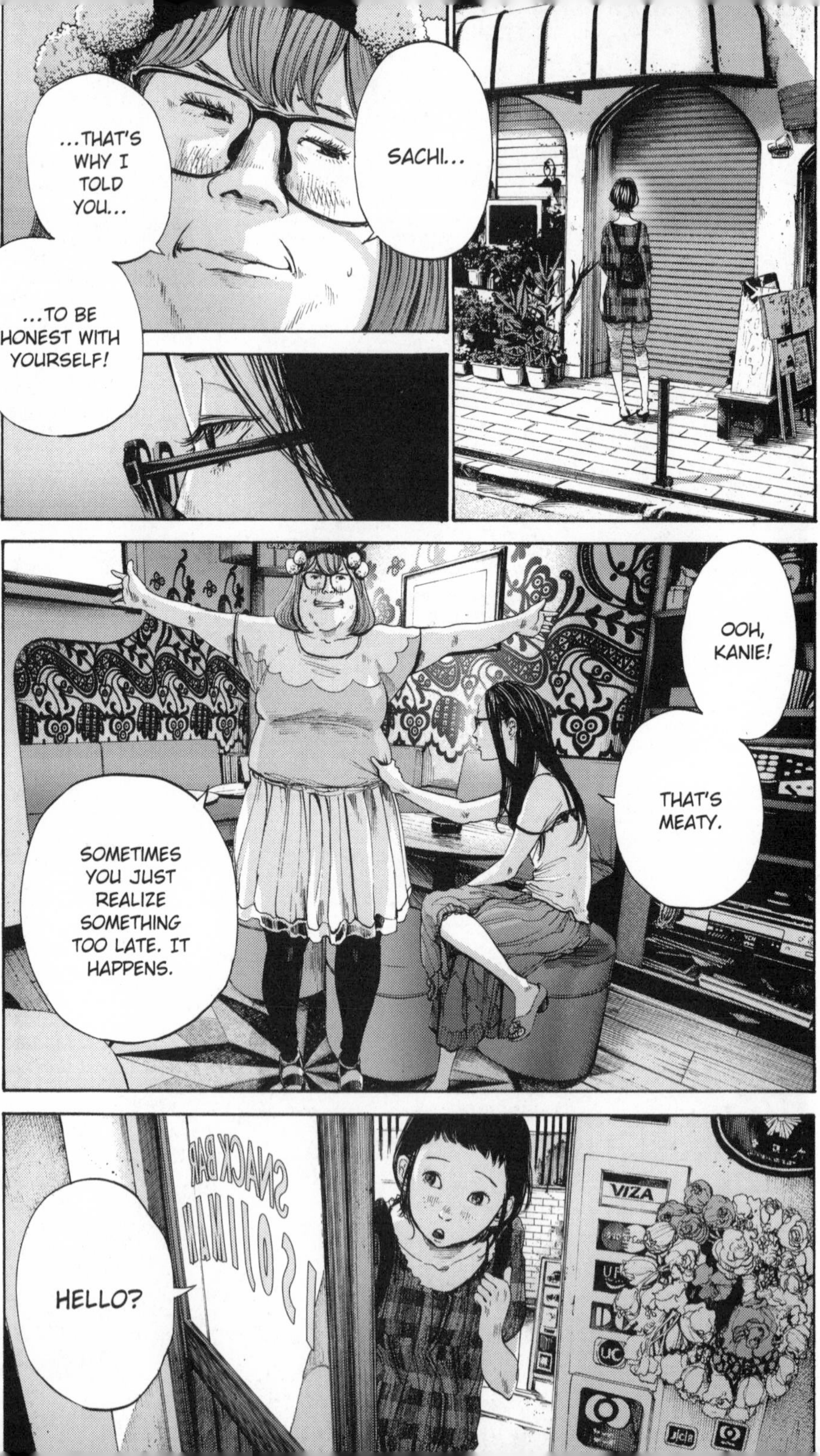
SACHI...
...THAT'S WHY I TOLD YOU...
...TO BE HONEST WITH YOURSELF!
OOH, KANIE!
THAT'S MEATY.
SOMETIMES YOU JUST REALIZE SOMETHING TOO LATE. IT HAPPENS.
VIZA
HELLO?

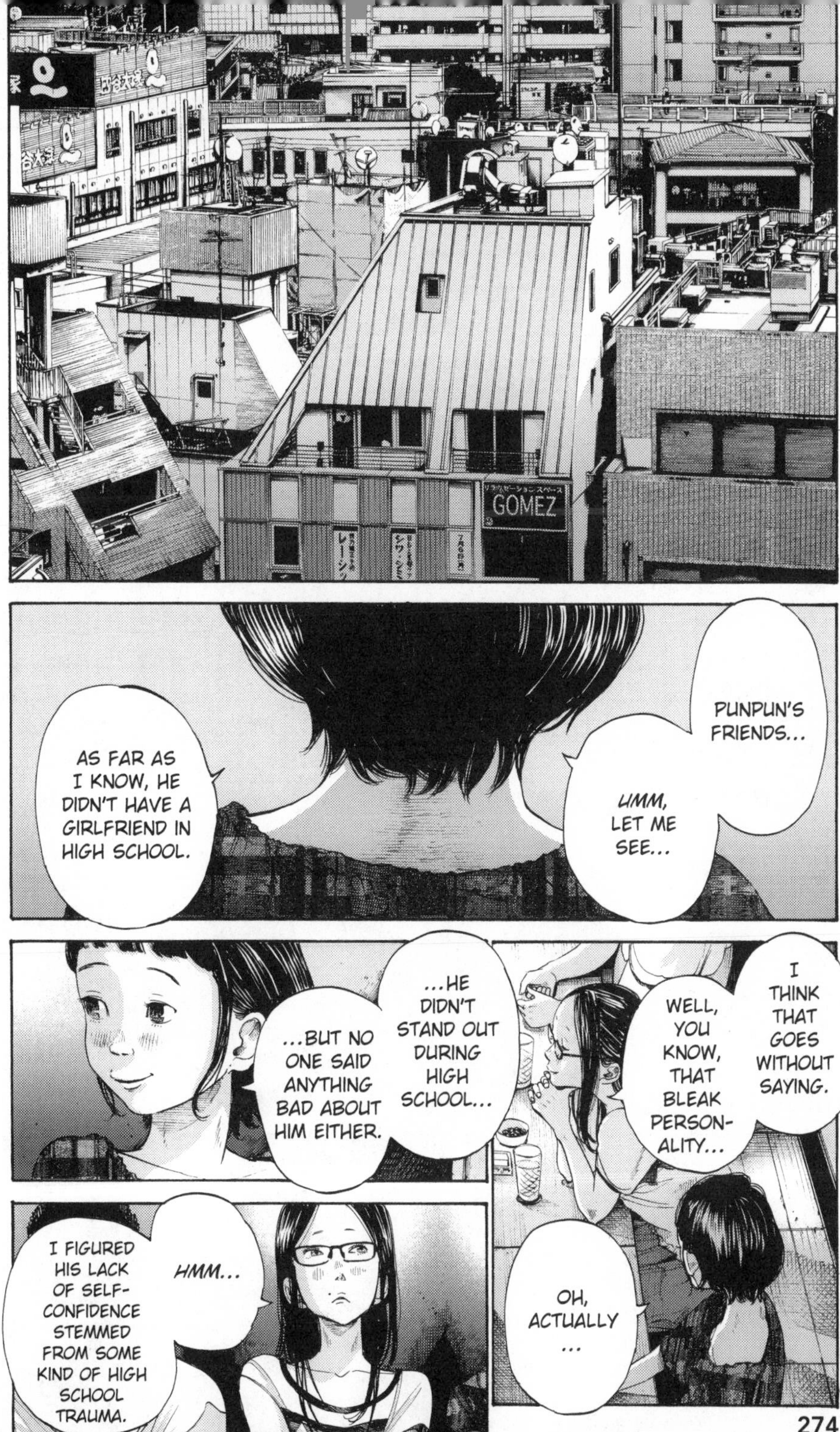
GOMEZ
PUNPUN'S FRIENDS...
UMM, LET ME SEE...
AS FAR AS I KNOW, HE DIDN'T HAVE A GIRLFRIEND IN HIGH SCHOOL.
I THINK THAT GOES WITHOUT SAYING.
WELL, YOU KNOW, THAT BLEAK PERSON-ALITY...
OH, ACTUALLY ...
...HE DIDN'T STAND OUT DURING HIGH SCHOOL...
...BUT NO ONE SAID ANYTHING BAD ABOUT HIM EITHER.
HMM...
I FIGURED HIS LACK OF SELF-CONFIDENCE STEMMED FROM SOME KIND OF HIGH SCHOOL TRAUMA.

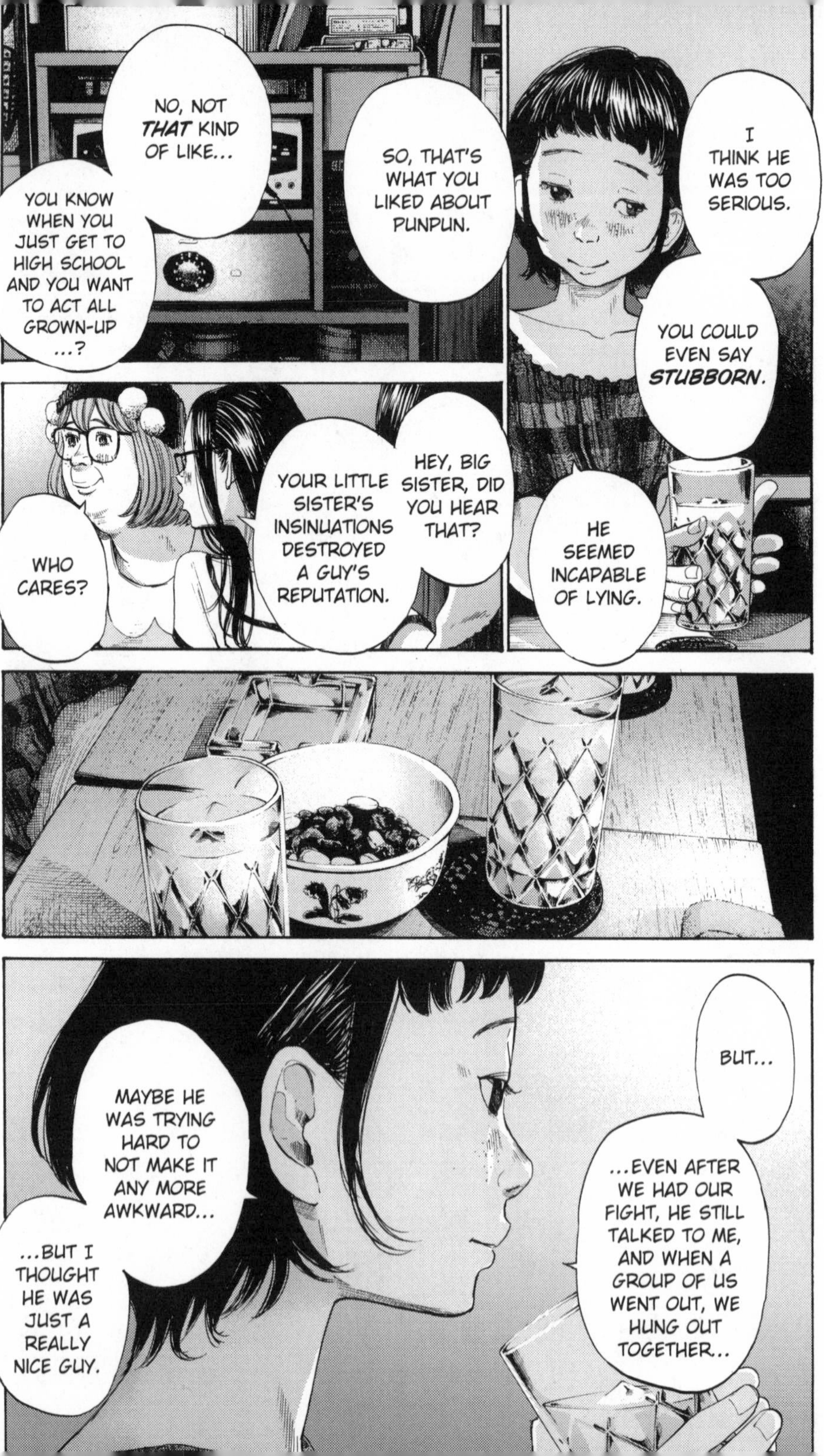
I THINK HE WAS TOO SERIOUS.
YOU COULD EVEN SAY STUBBORN.
HE SEEMED INCAPABLE OF LYING.
SO, THAT'S WHAT YOU LIKED ABOUT PUNPUN.
NO, NOT THAT KIND OF LIKE...
YOU KNOW WHEN YOU JUST GET TO HIGH SCHOOL AND YOU WANT TO ACT ALL GROWN-UP ...?
HEY, BIG SISTER, DID YOU HEAR THAT?
YOUR LITTLE SISTER'S INSINUATIONS DESTROYED A GUY'S REPUTATION.
WHO CARES?
BUT...
...EVEN AFTER WE HAD OUR FIGHT, HE STILL TALKED TO ME, AND WHEN A GROUP OF US WENT OUT, WE HUNG OUT TOGETHER...
MAYBE HE WAS TRYING HARD TO NOT MAKE IT ANY MORE AWKWARD...
...BUT I THOUGHT HE WAS JUST A REALLY NICE GUY.

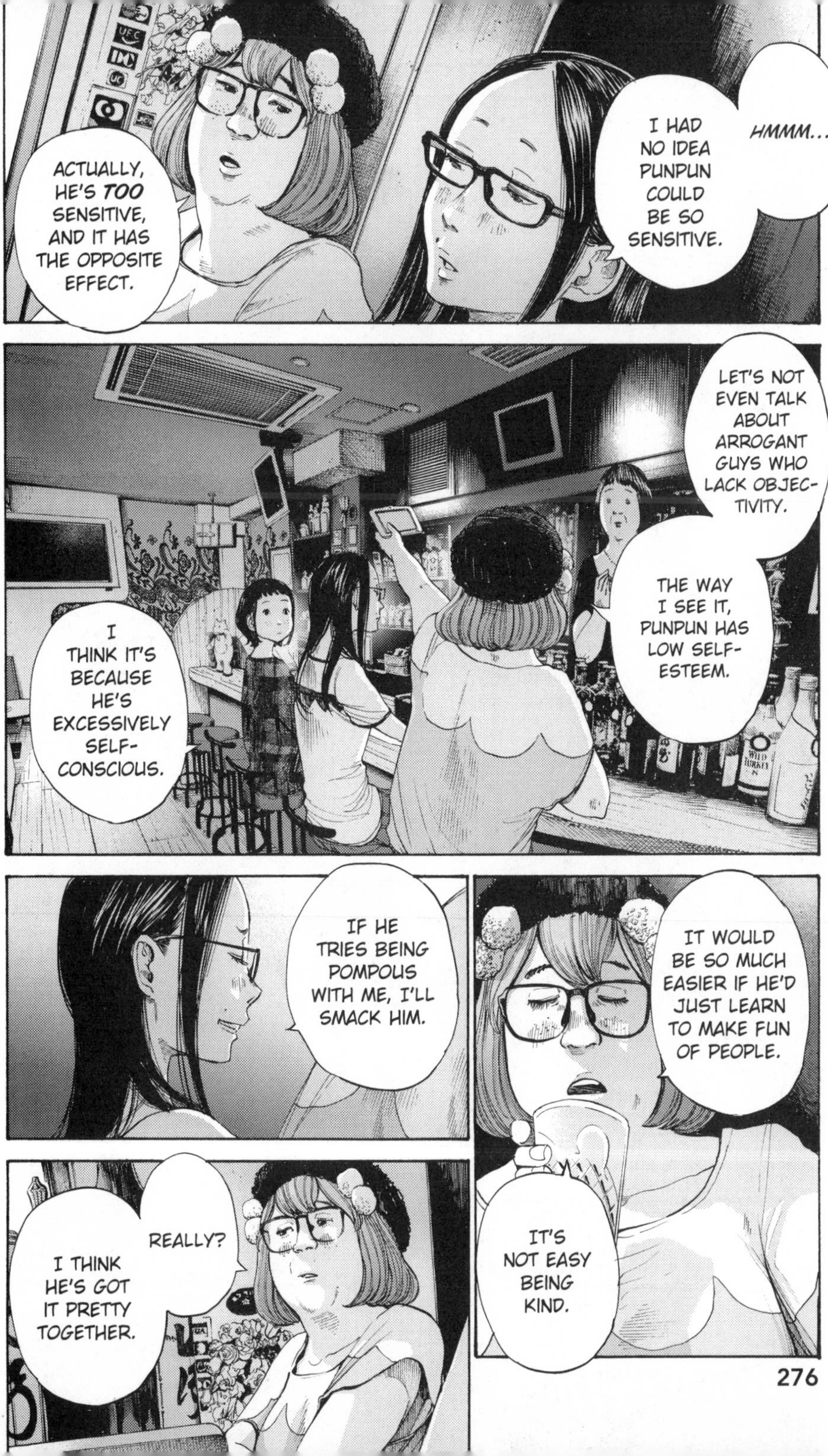
HMMM...
I HAD NO IDEA PUNPUN COULD BE SO SENSITIVE.
ACTUALLY, HE'S *TOO* SENSITIVE, AND IT HAS THE OPPOSITE EFFECT.
LET'S NOT EVEN TALK ABOUT ARROGANT GUYS WHO LACK OBJEC-TIVITY.
THE WAY I SEE IT, PUNPUN HAS LOW SELF-ESTEEM.
I THINK IT'S BECAUSE HE'S EXCESSIVELY SELF-CONSCIOUS.
IT WOULD BE SO MUCH EASIER IF HE'D JUST LEARN TO MAKE FUN OF PEOPLE.
IT'S NOT EASY BEING KIND.
IF HE TRIES BEING POMPOUS WITH ME, I'LL SMACK HIM.
REALLY?
I THINK HE'S GOT IT PRETTY TOGETHER.

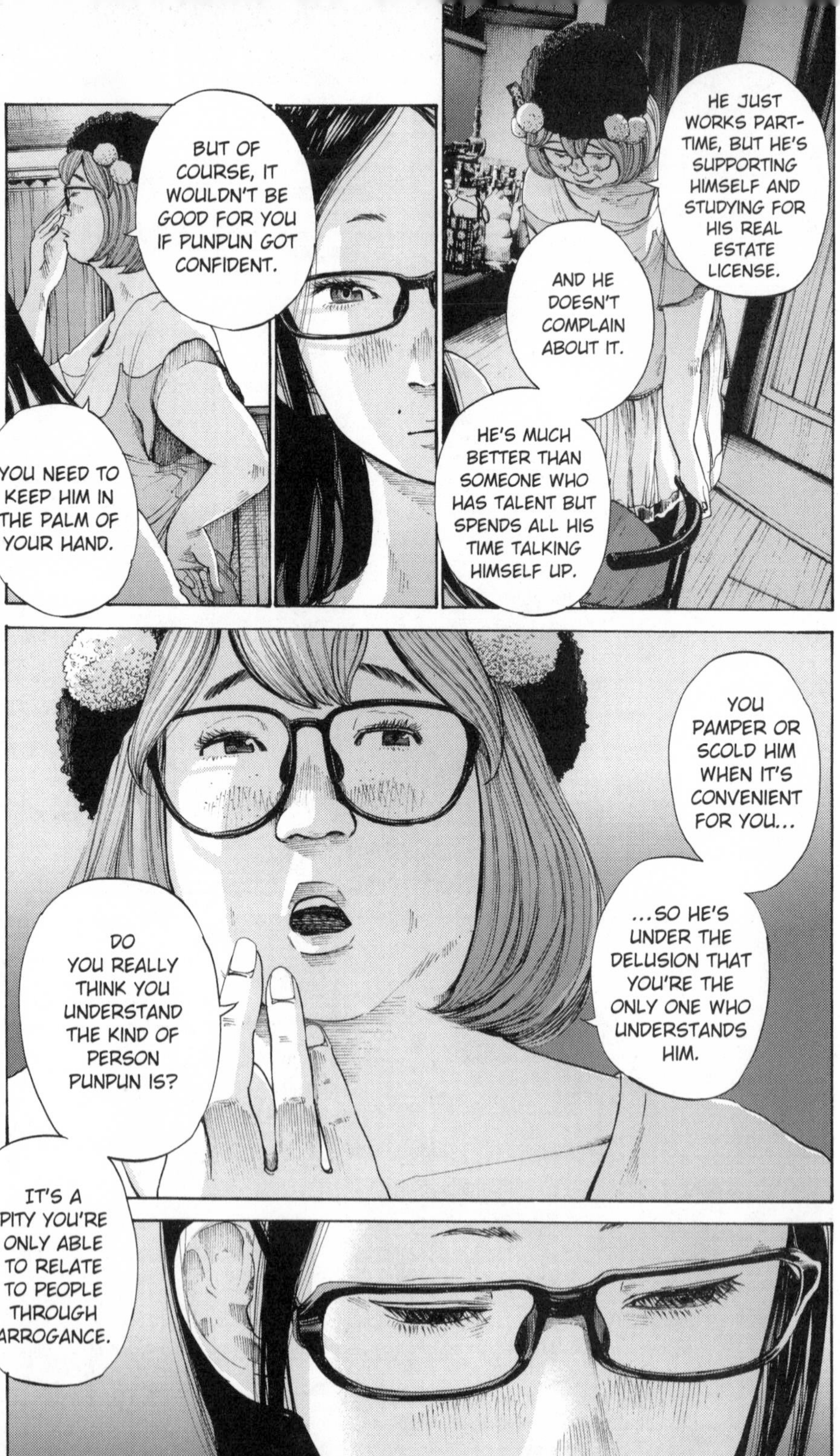
HE JUST WORKS PART-TIME, BUT HE'S SUPPORTING HIMSELF AND STUDYING FOR HIS REAL ESTATE LICENSE.
AND HE DOESN'T COMPLAIN ABOUT IT.
HE'S MUCH BETTER THAN SOMEONE WHO HAS TALENT BUT SPENDS ALL HIS TIME TALKING HIMSELF UP.
BUT OF COURSE, IT WOULDN'T BE GOOD FOR YOU IF PUNPUN GOT CONFIDENT.
YOU NEED TO KEEP HIM IN THE PALM OF YOUR HAND.
YOU PAMPER OR SCOLD HIM WHEN IT'S CONVENIENT FOR YOU...
...SO HE'S UNDER THE DELUSION THAT YOU'RE THE ONLY ONE WHO UNDERSTANDS HIM.
DO YOU REALLY THINK YOU UNDERSTAND THE KIND OF PERSON PUNPUN IS?
IT'S A PITY YOU'RE ONLY ABLE TO RELATE TO PEOPLE THROUGH ARROGANCE.

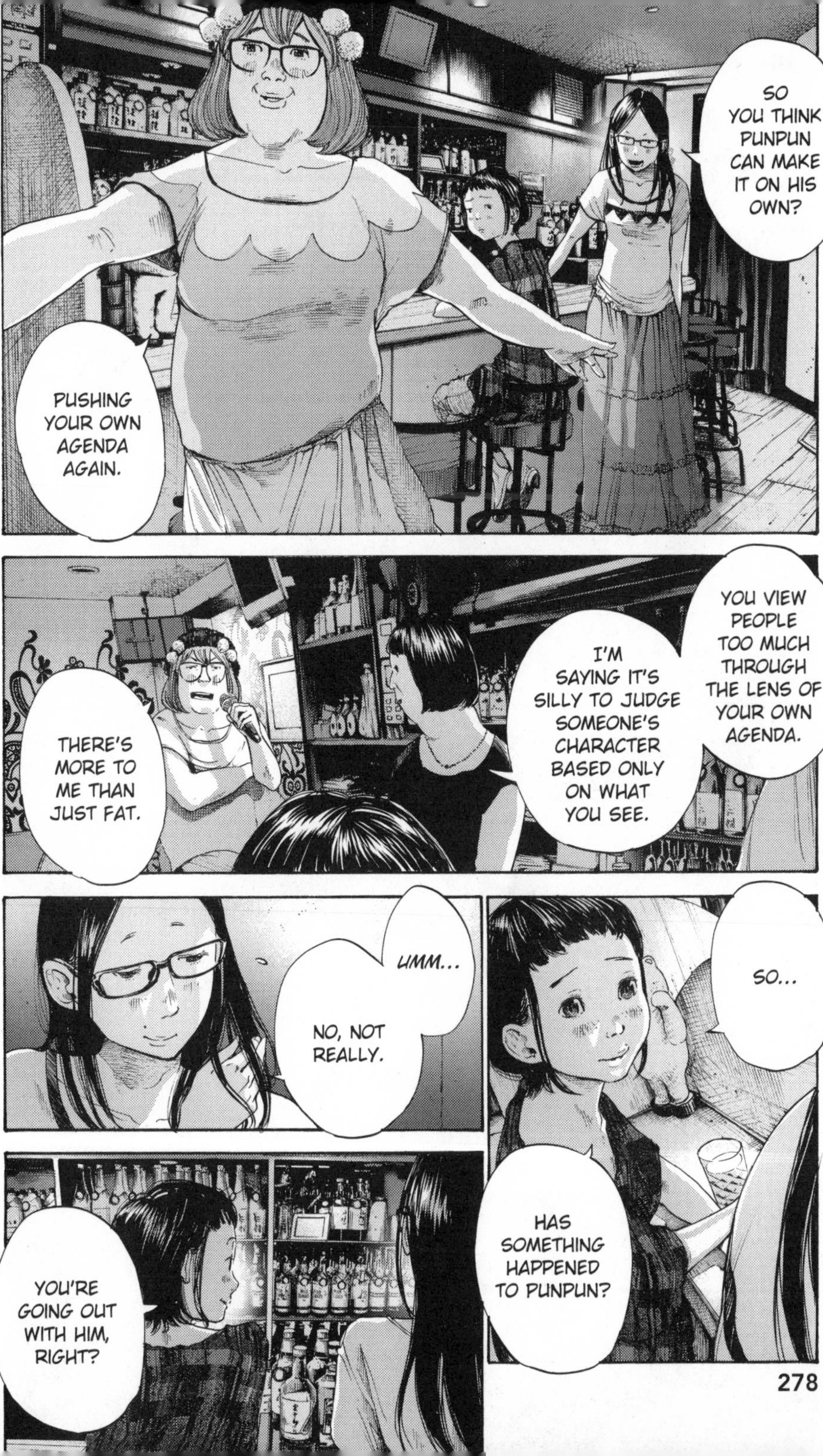
SO YOU THINK PUNPUN CAN MAKE IT ON HIS OWN?
PUSHING YOUR OWN AGENDA AGAIN.
YOU VIEW PEOPLE TOO MUCH THROUGH THE LENS OF YOUR OWN AGENDA.
I'M SAYING IT'S SILLY TO JUDGE SOMEONE'S CHARACTER BASED ONLY ON WHAT YOU SEE.
THERE'S MORE TO ME THAN JUST FAT.
SO...
HAS SOMETHING HAPPENED TO PUNPUN?
UMM...
NO, NOT REALLY.
YOU'RE GOING OUT WITH HIM, RIGHT?

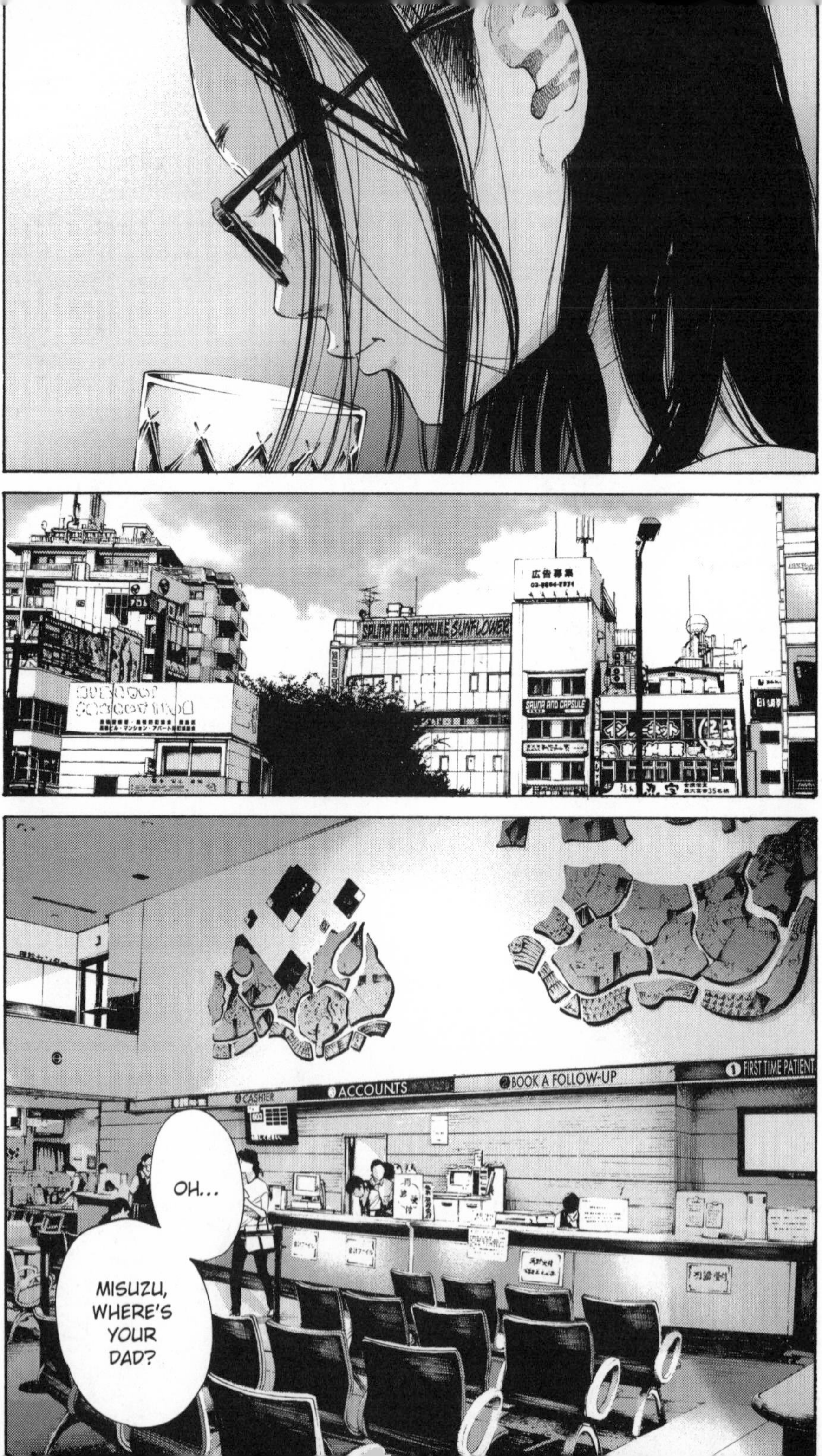
広告募集
SAUNA AND CAPSULE SUNFLOWER
SAUNA AND CAPSULE
1 FIRST TIME PATIENT
2 BOOK A FOLLOW-UP
3 ACCOUNTS
CASHIER
OH...
MISUZU, WHERE'S YOUR DAD?

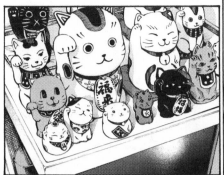

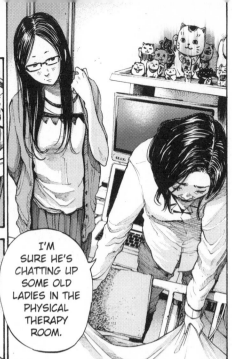

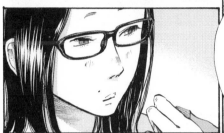

I'M SURE HE'S CHATTING UP SOME OLD LADIES IN THE PHYSICAL THERAPY ROOM.

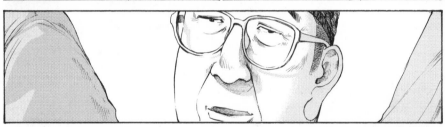

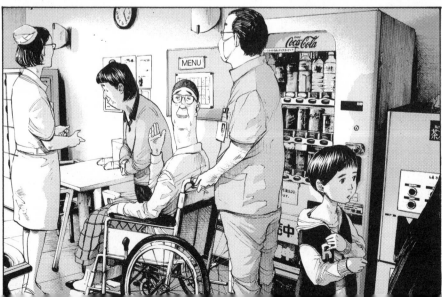

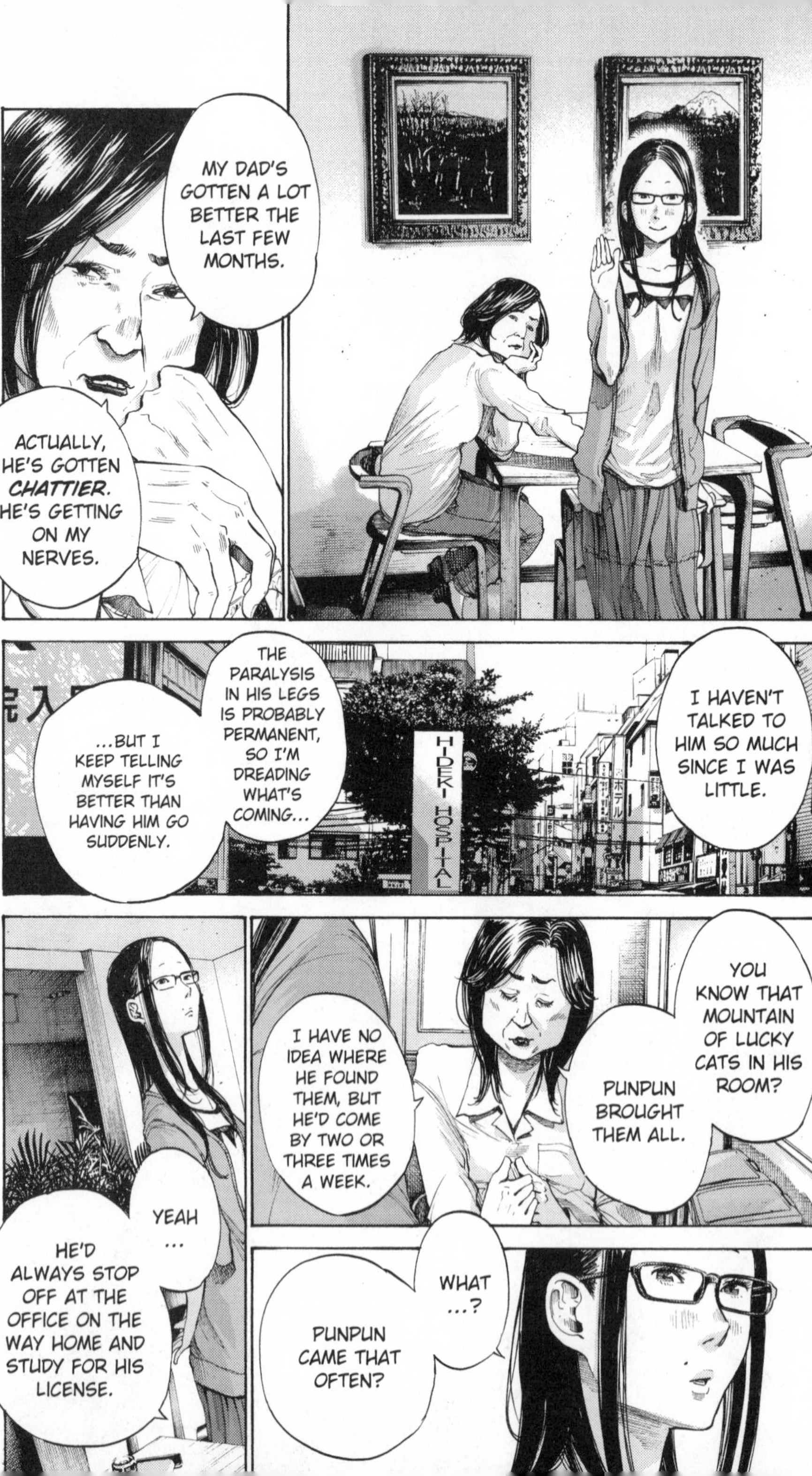

MY DAD'S GOTTEN A LOT BETTER THE LAST FEW MONTHS.
ACTUALLY, HE'S GOTTEN *CHATTIER*. HE'S GETTING ON MY NERVES.
I HAVEN'T TALKED TO HIM SO MUCH SINCE I WAS LITTLE.
HIDEKI HOSPITAL
THE PARALYSIS IN HIS LEGS IS PROBABLY PERMANENT, SO I'M DREADING WHAT'S COMING...
...BUT I KEEP TELLING MYSELF IT'S BETTER THAN HAVING HIM GO SUDDENLY.
YOU KNOW THAT MOUNTAIN OF LUCKY CATS IN HIS ROOM?
PUNPUN BROUGHT THEM ALL.
I HAVE NO IDEA WHERE HE FOUND THEM, BUT HE'D COME BY TWO OR THREE TIMES A WEEK.
WHAT ...?
PUNPUN CAME THAT OFTEN?
YEAH ...
HE'D ALWAYS STOP OFF AT THE OFFICE ON THE WAY HOME AND STUDY FOR HIS LICENSE.

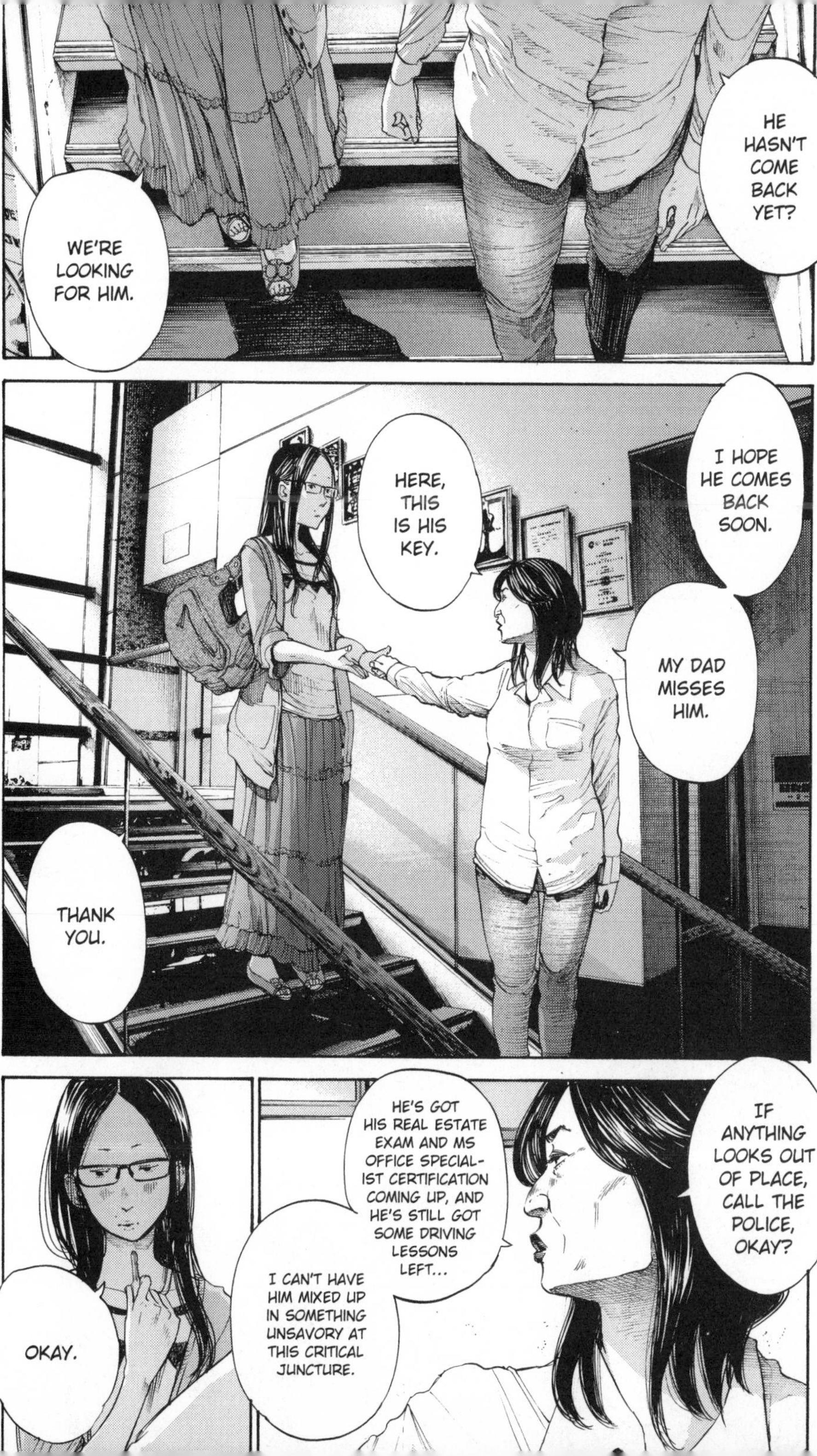
HE HASN'T COME BACK YET?
WE'RE LOOKING FOR HIM.
I HOPE HE COMES BACK SOON.
HERE, THIS IS HIS KEY.
MY DAD MISSES HIM.
THANK YOU.
IF ANYTHING LOOKS OUT OF PLACE, CALL THE POLICE, OKAY?
HE'S GOT HIS REAL ESTATE EXAM AND MS OFFICE SPECIAL-IST CERTIFICATION COMING UP, AND HE'S STILL GOT SOME DRIVING LESSONS LEFT...
I CAN'T HAVE HIM MIXED UP IN SOMETHING UNSAVORY AT THIS CRITICAL JUNCTURE.
OKAY.

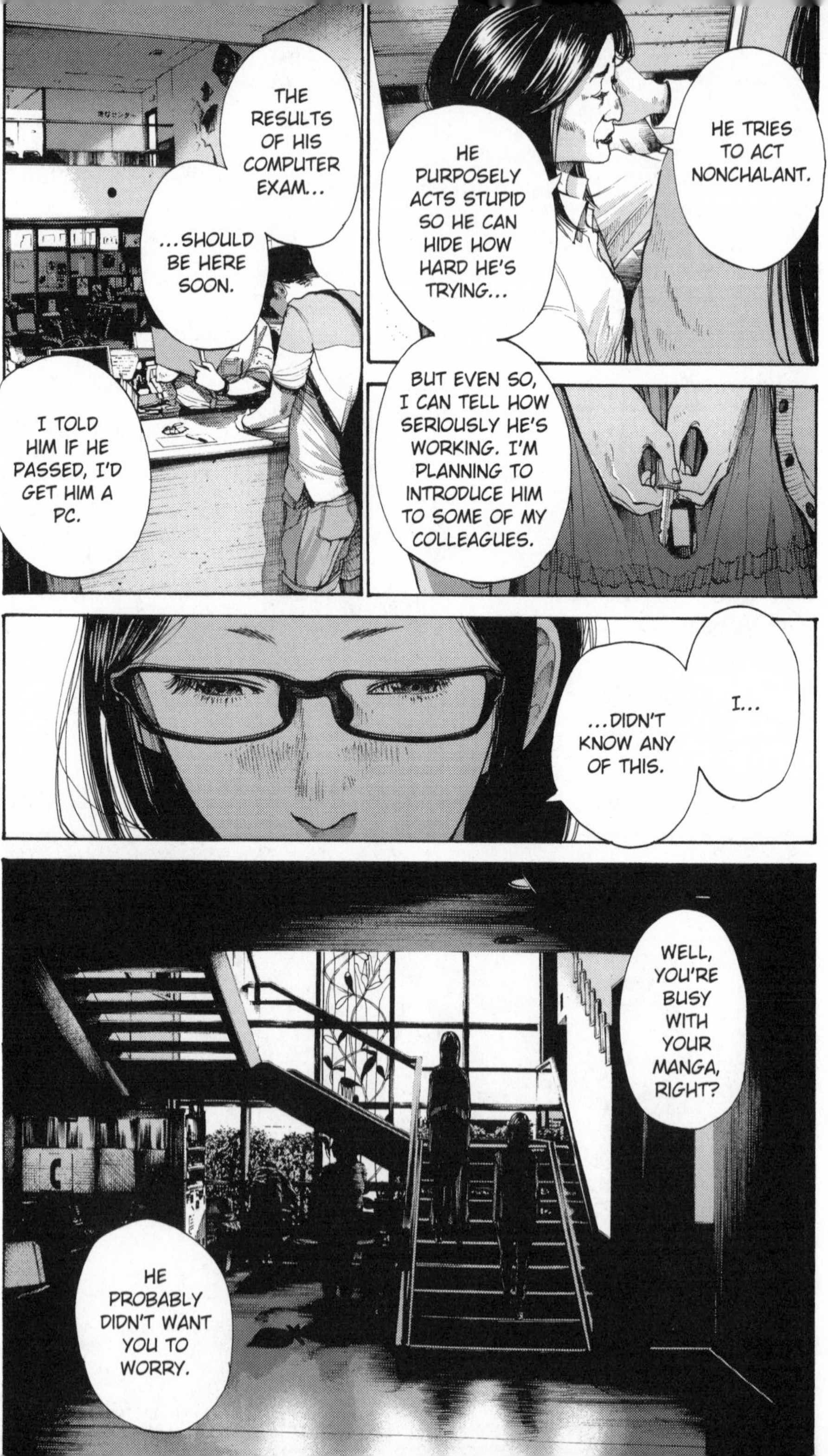
HE TRIES TO ACT NONCHALANT.
HE PURPOSELY ACTS STUPID SO HE CAN HIDE HOW HARD HE'S TRYING...
BUT EVEN SO, I CAN TELL HOW SERIOUSLY HE'S WORKING. I'M PLANNING TO INTRODUCE HIM TO SOME OF MY COLLEAGUES.
THE RESULTS OF HIS COMPUTER EXAM...
...SHOULD BE HERE SOON.
I TOLD HIM IF HE PASSED, I'D GET HIM A PC.
I...
...DIDN'T KNOW ANY OF THIS.
WELL, YOU'RE BUSY WITH YOUR MANGA, RIGHT?
HE PROBABLY DIDN'T WANT YOU TO WORRY.

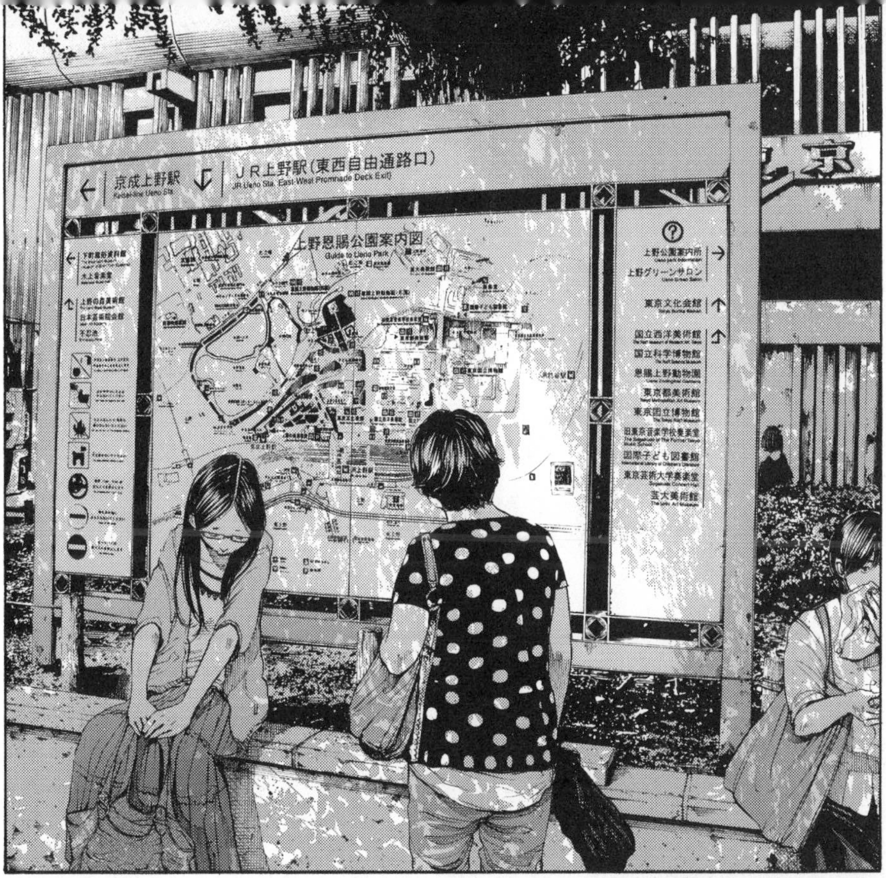
京成上野駅
JR上野駅(東西自由通路口)
JR Ueno Sta. East-West Promnade Deck Exit
上野恩賜公園案内図
Guide to Ueno Park
上野公園案内所
上野グリーンサロン
東京文化会館
国立西洋美術館
国立科学博物館
恩賜上野動物園
東京都美術館
東京国立博物館
旧東京音楽学校奏楽堂
国際子ども図書館
東京芸術大学奏楽堂
芸大美術館
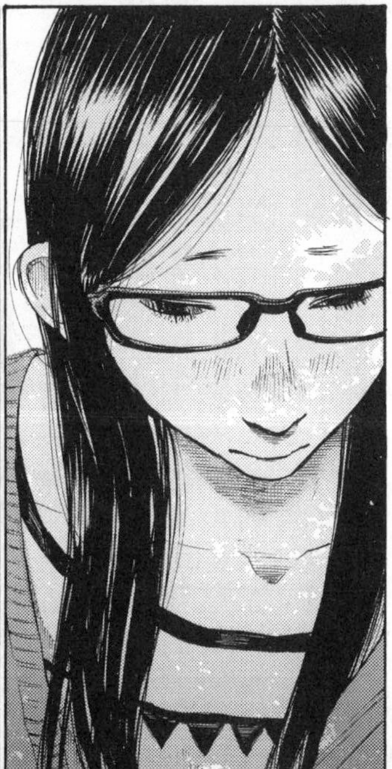
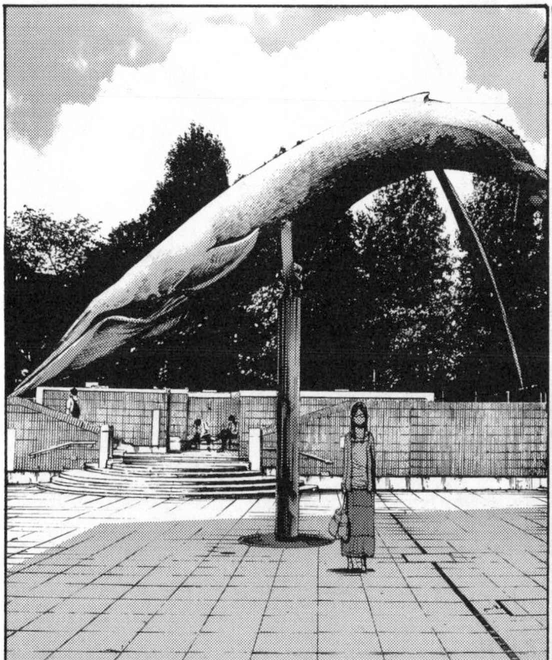

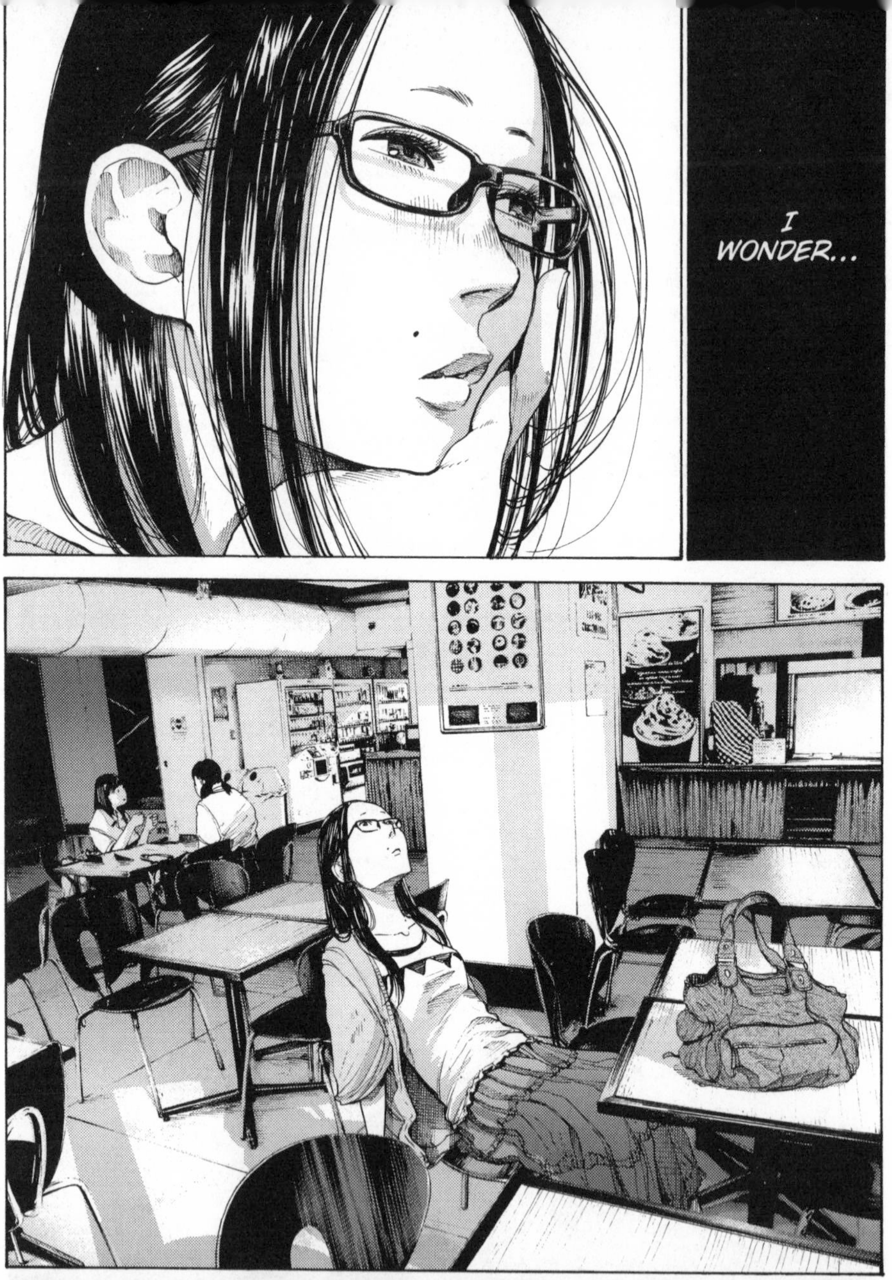
I WONDER...

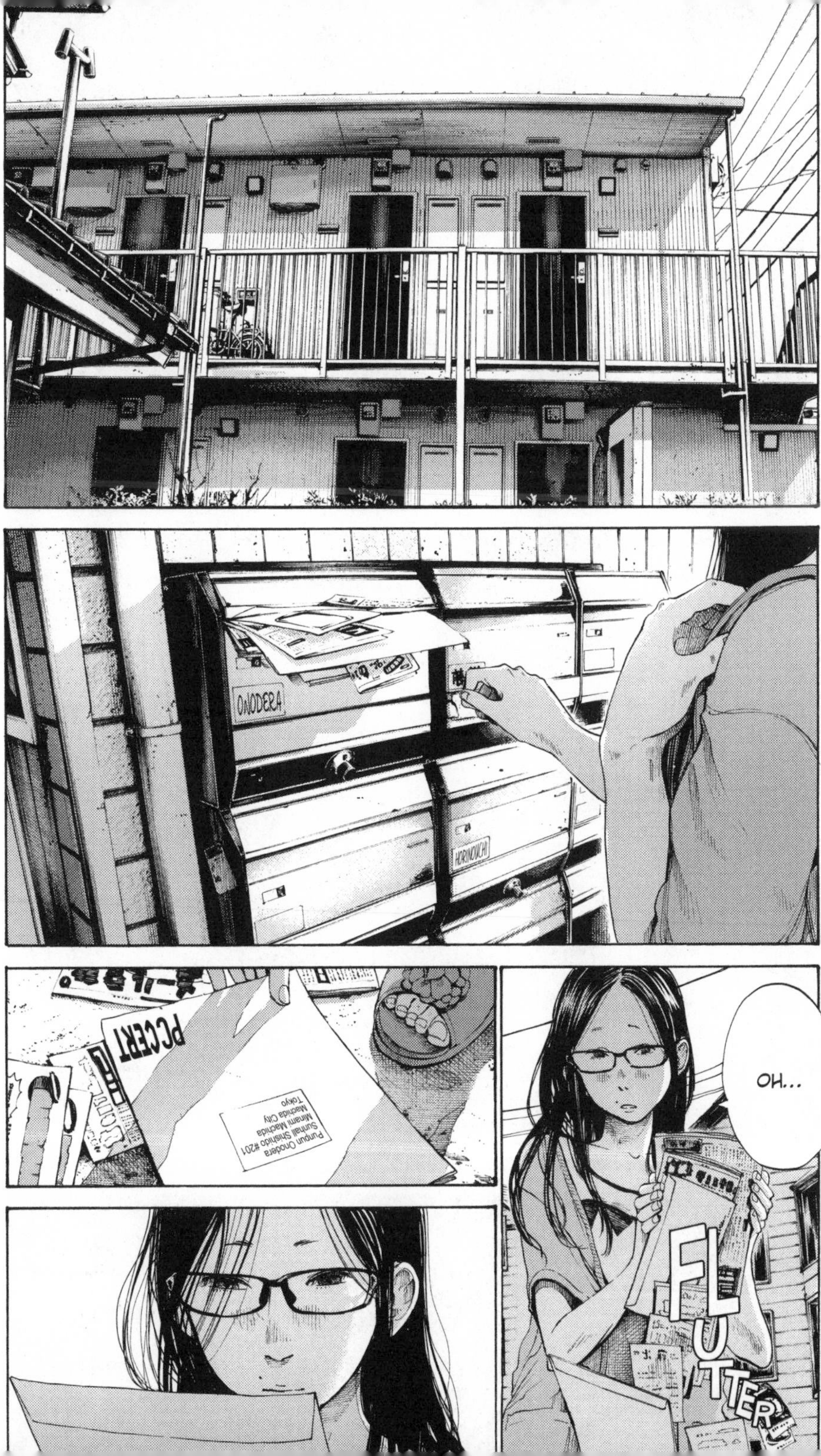
ONODERA
HORINOUCHI
OH...
FLUTTER
PCCERT
Punpun Onodera
Sunhall Shishido #201
Minami Machida
Machida City
Tokyo

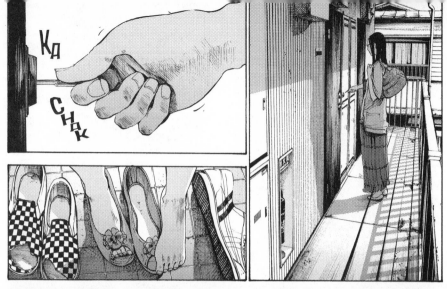

KA
CHAK

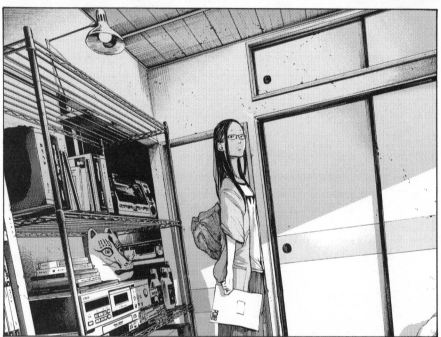

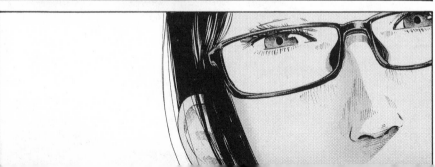

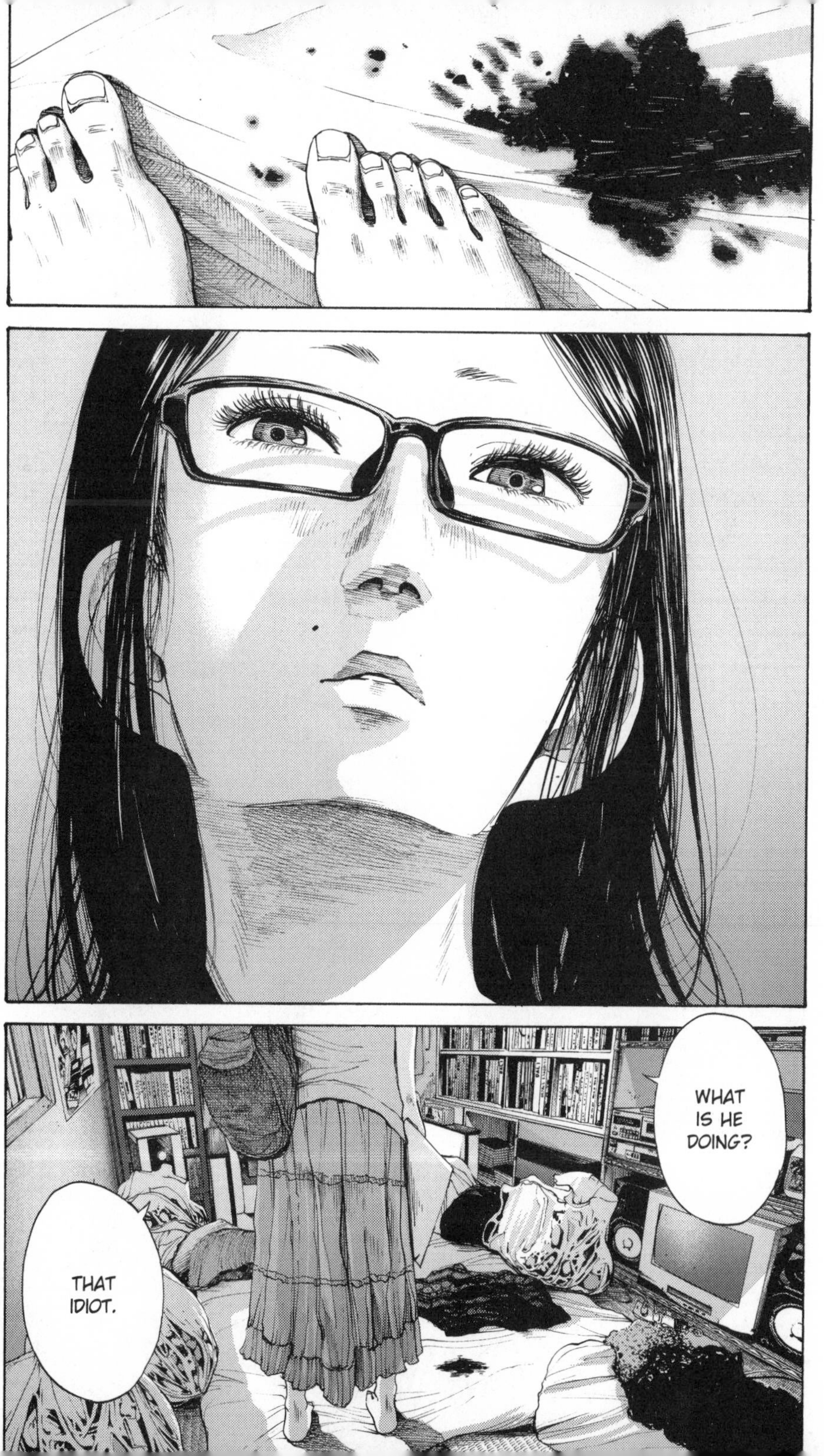
WHAT IS HE DOING?
THAT IDIOT.

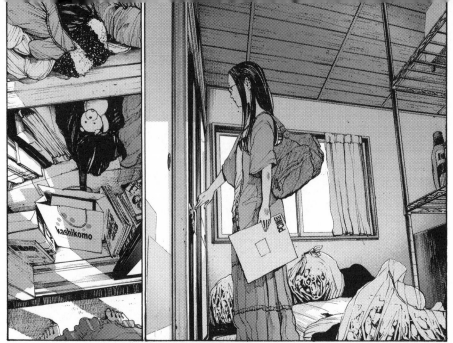

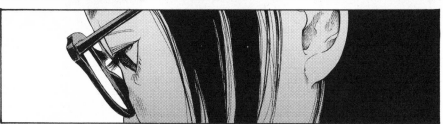

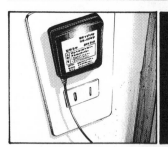

June 24,
6 p.m.

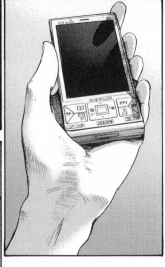

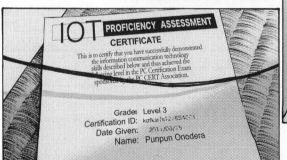

IOT PROFICIENCY ASSESSMENT
CERTIFICATE
This is to certify that you have successfully demonstrated
the information communication technology
skills described below and thus achieved the
following level in the PC Certification Exam
sponsored by the PC CERT Association.

Grade: Level 3
Certification ID: kdfkanb12-654331
Date Given: 2011/06/15
Name: Punpun Onodera

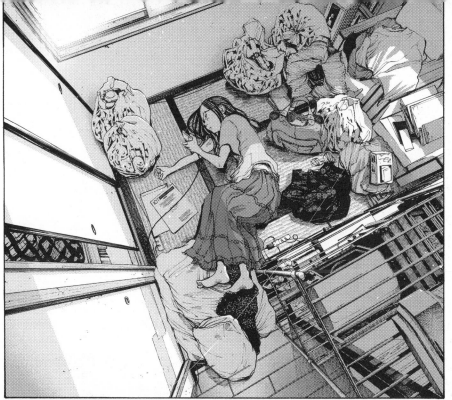

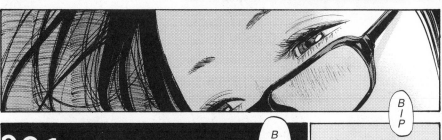

001 MIDORI OKUMA

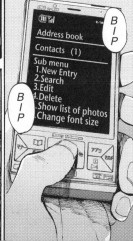

BIP

BIP

BIP

BIP

Address book

Contacts (1)

Sub menu
1. New Entry
2. Search
3. Edit
4. Delete
. Show list of photos
. Change font size

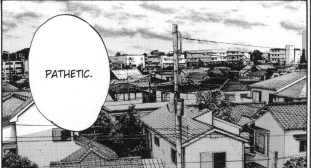

PATHETIC.

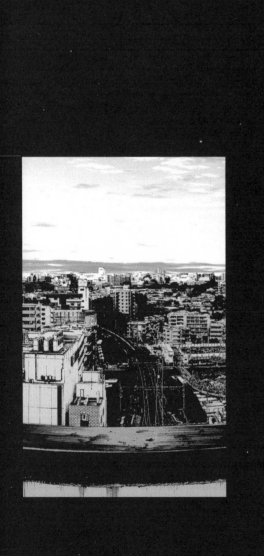

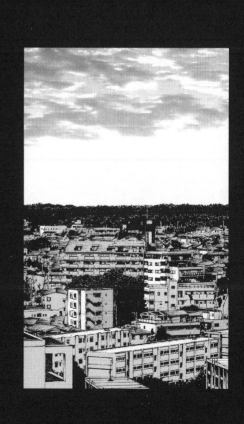

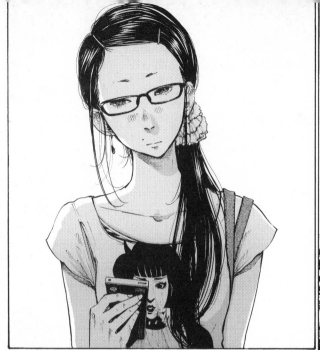

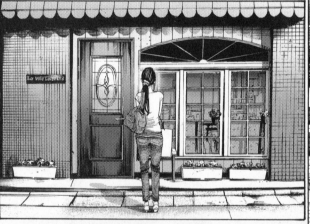

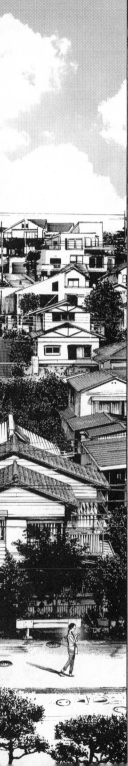

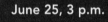

June 25, 3 p.m.

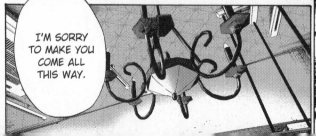

I'M SORRY TO MAKE YOU COME ALL THIS WAY.

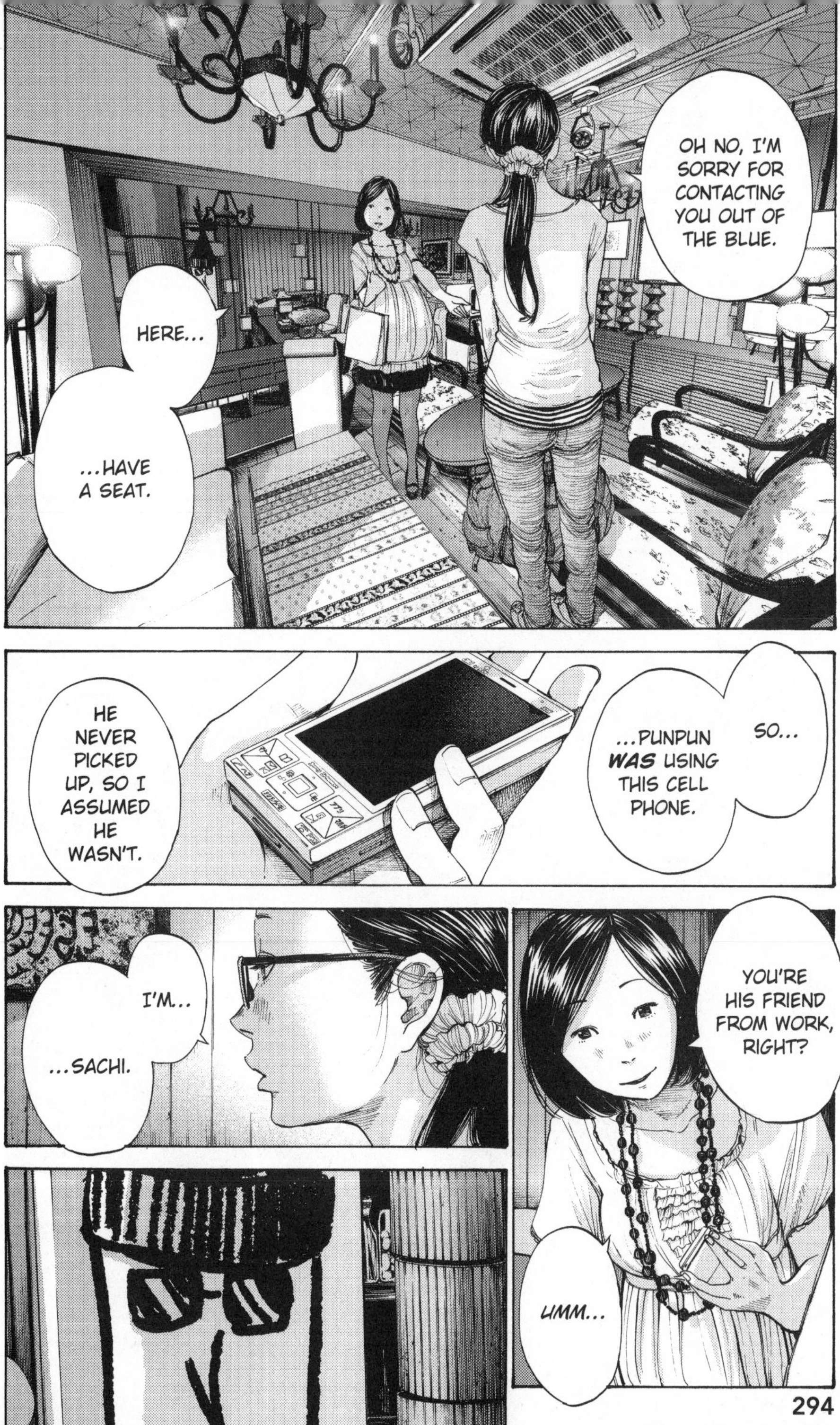
OH NO, I'M SORRY FOR CONTACTING YOU OUT OF THE BLUE.
HERE...
...HAVE A SEAT.
SO...
...PUNPUN **WAS** USING THIS CELL PHONE.
HE NEVER PICKED UP, SO I ASSUMED HE WASN'T.
YOU'RE HIS FRIEND FROM WORK, RIGHT?
UMM...
I'M...
...SACHI.

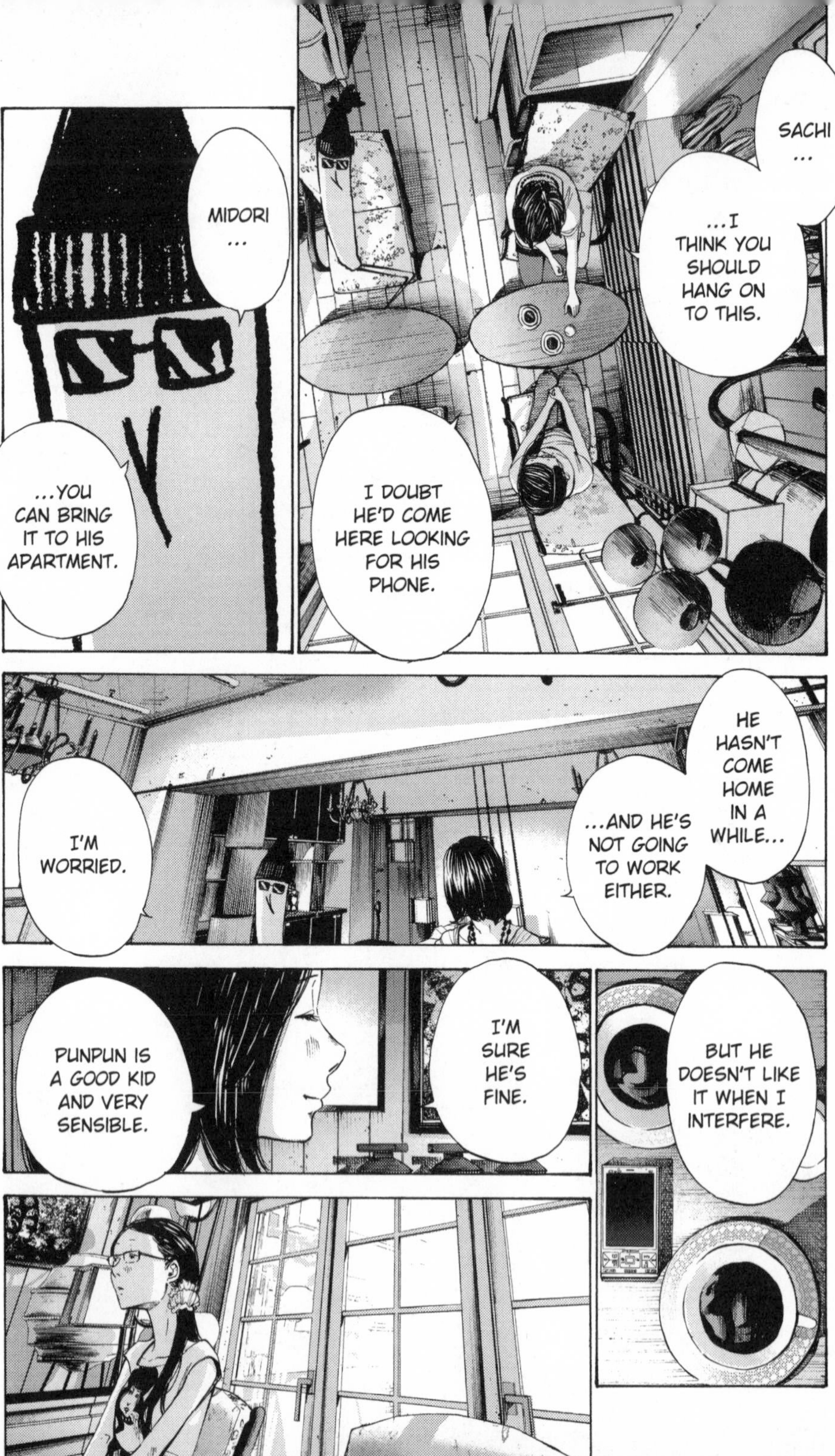
SACHI ...
...I THINK YOU SHOULD HANG ON TO THIS.
I DOUBT HE'D COME HERE LOOKING FOR HIS PHONE.
MIDORI ...
...YOU CAN BRING IT TO HIS APARTMENT.
HE HASN'T COME HOME IN A WHILE...
...AND HE'S NOT GOING TO WORK EITHER.
I'M WORRIED.
BUT HE DOESN'T LIKE IT WHEN I INTERFERE.
I'M SURE HE'S FINE.
PUNPUN IS A GOOD KID AND VERY SENSIBLE.

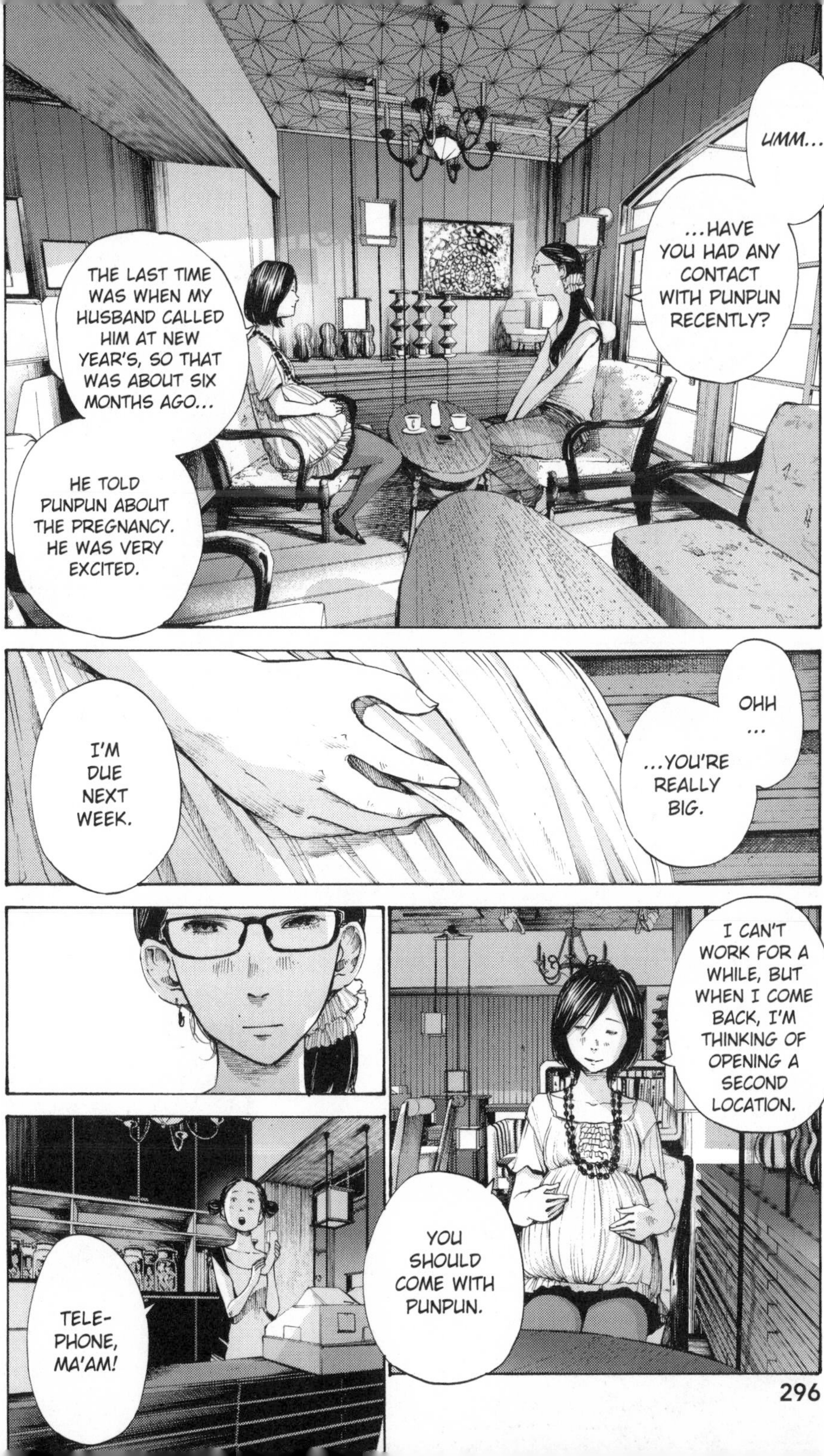
UMM...
...HAVE YOU HAD ANY CONTACT WITH PUNPUN RECENTLY?
THE LAST TIME WAS WHEN MY HUSBAND CALLED HIM AT NEW YEAR'S, SO THAT WAS ABOUT SIX MONTHS AGO...
HE TOLD PUNPUN ABOUT THE PREGNANCY. HE WAS VERY EXCITED.
OHH ...
...YOU'RE REALLY BIG.
I'M DUE NEXT WEEK.
I CAN'T WORK FOR A WHILE, BUT WHEN I COME BACK, I'M THINKING OF OPENING A SECOND LOCATION.
YOU SHOULD COME WITH PUNPUN.
TELE-PHONE, MA'AM!

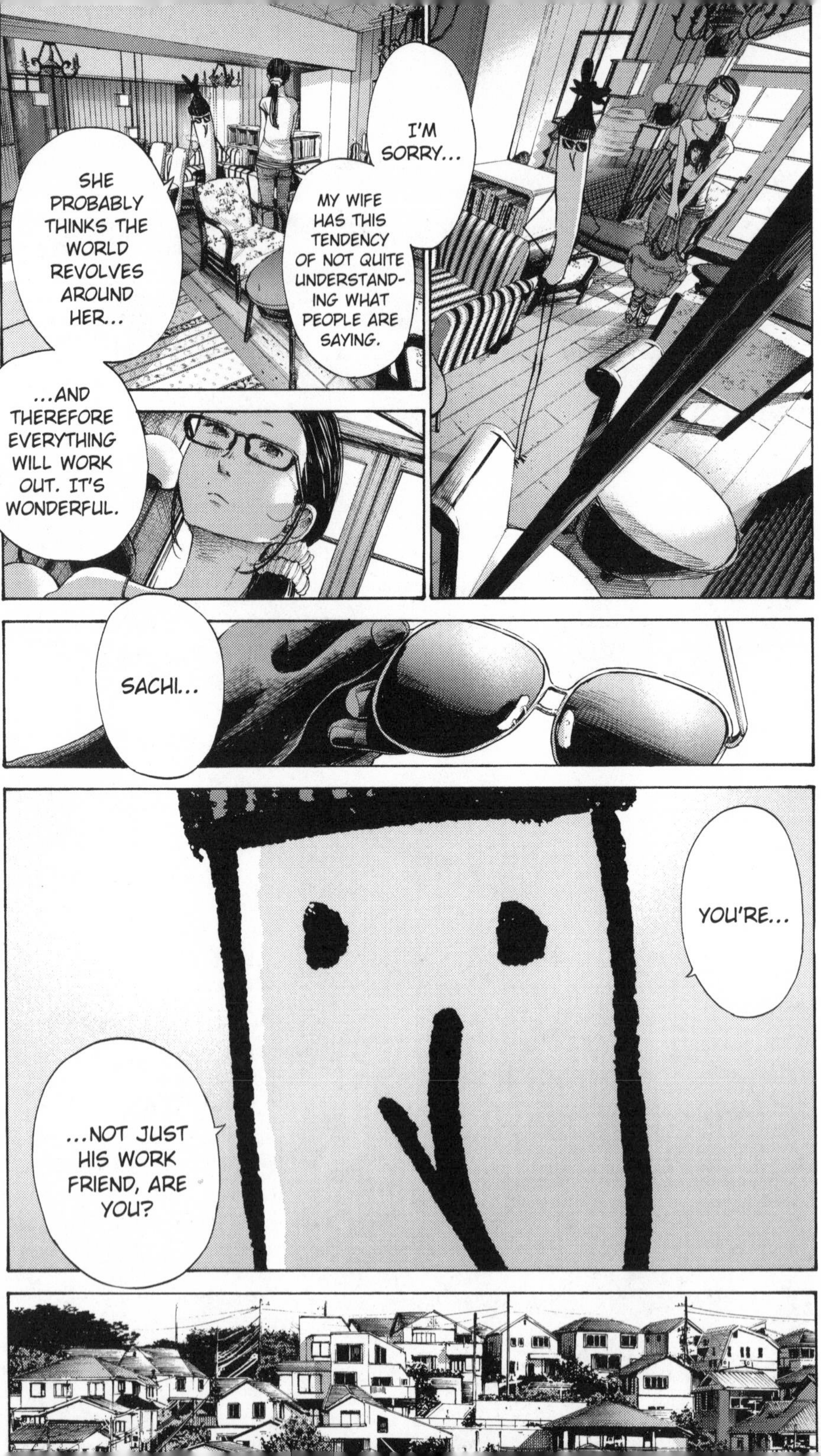
I'M SORRY...
MY WIFE HAS THIS TENDENCY OF NOT QUITE UNDERSTANDING WHAT PEOPLE ARE SAYING.
SHE PROBABLY THINKS THE WORLD REVOLVES AROUND HER...
...AND THEREFORE EVERYTHING WILL WORK OUT. IT'S WONDERFUL.
SACHI...
YOU'RE...
...NOT JUST HIS WORK FRIEND, ARE YOU?

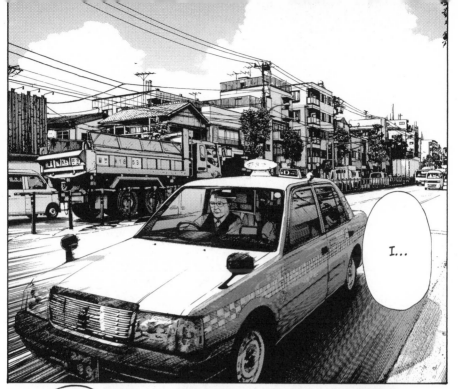

I...

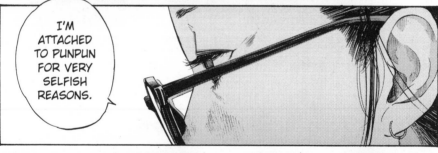

I'M ATTACHED TO PUNPUN FOR VERY SELFISH REASONS.

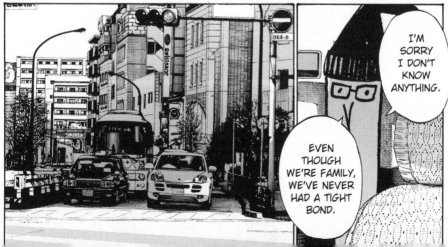

I'M SORRY I DON'T KNOW ANYTHING.

EVEN THOUGH WE'RE FAMILY, WE'VE NEVER HAD A TIGHT BOND.

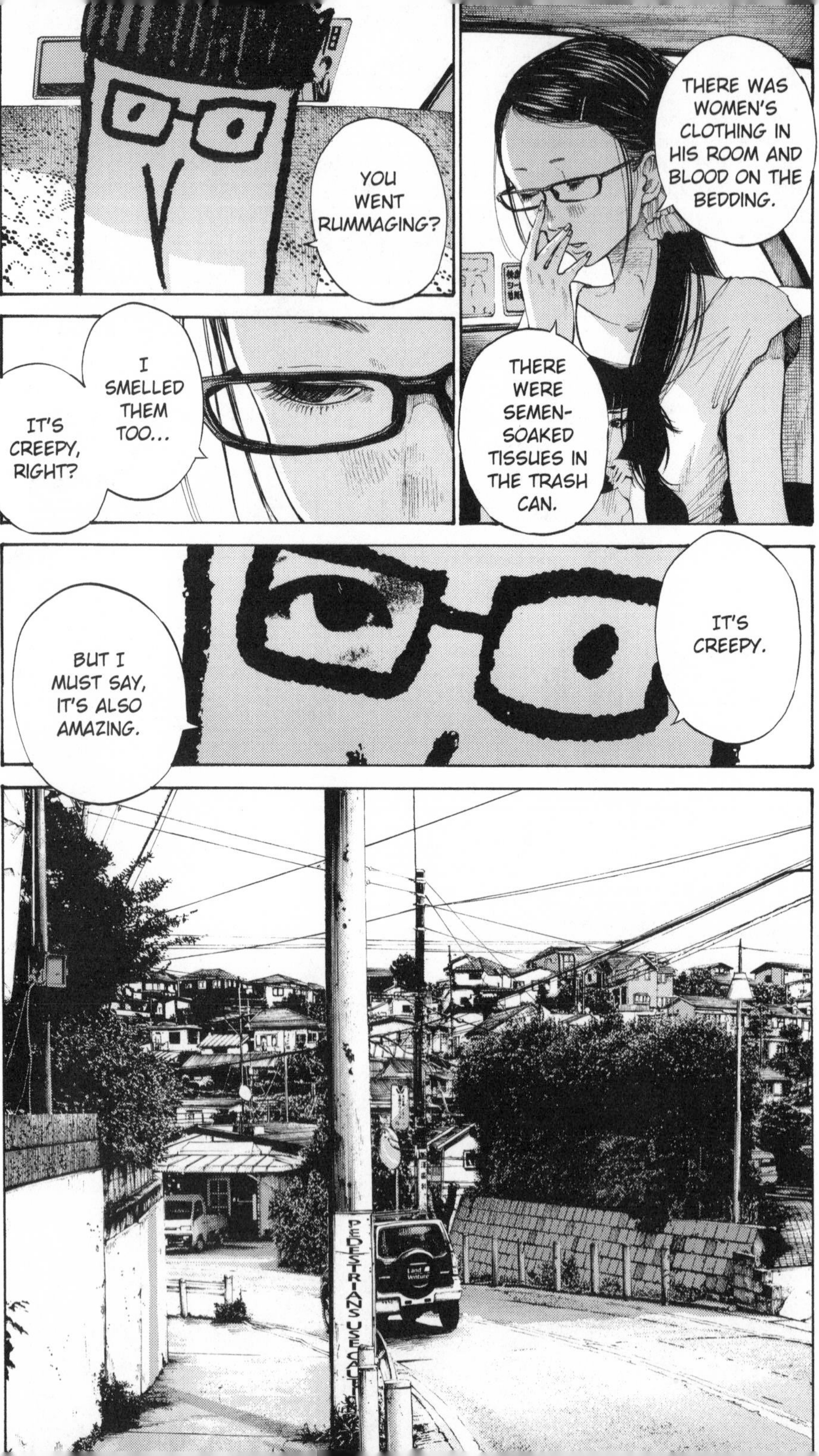
THERE WAS WOMEN'S CLOTHING IN HIS ROOM AND BLOOD ON THE BEDDING.
THERE WERE SEMEN-SOAKED TISSUES IN THE TRASH CAN.
YOU WENT RUMMAGING?
I SMELLED THEM TOO...
IT'S CREEPY, RIGHT?
IT'S CREEPY.
BUT I MUST SAY, IT'S ALSO AMAZING.
PEDESTRIANS USE CAUTI

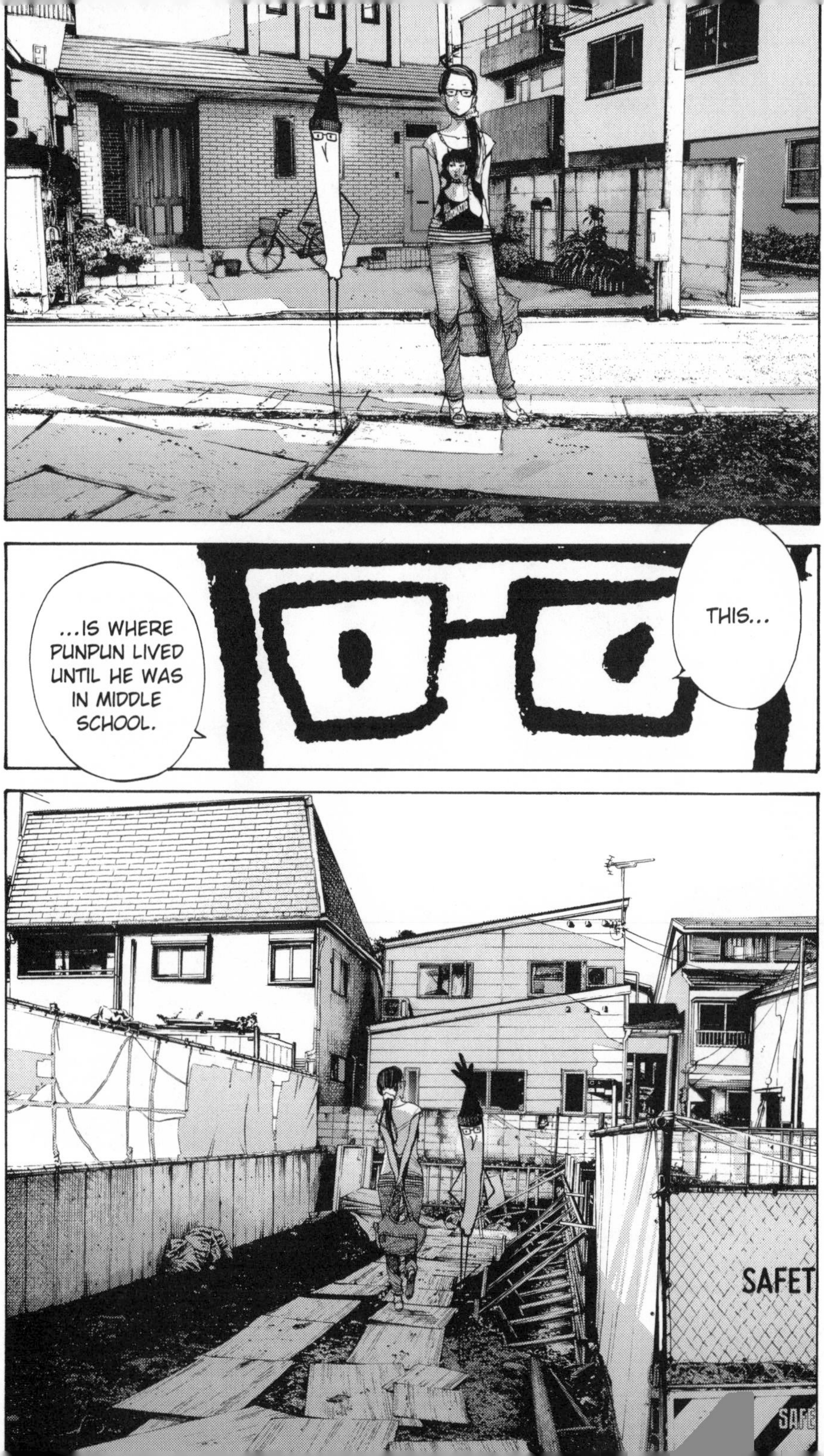
THIS...
...IS WHERE PUNPUN LIVED UNTIL HE WAS IN MIDDLE SCHOOL.
SAFET

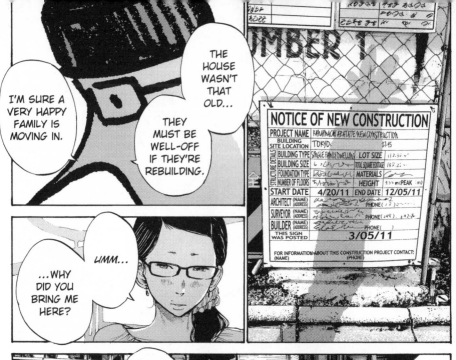

THE HOUSE WASN'T THAT OLD...

I'M SURE A VERY HAPPY FAMILY IS MOVING IN.

THEY MUST BE WELL-OFF IF THEY'RE REBUILDING.

UMM...

...WHY DID YOU BRING ME HERE?

NOTICE OF NEW CONSTRUCTION

PROJECT NAME	KAMIMACHI APATATE NEW CONSTRUCTION			
BUILDING SITE LOCATION	TOKYO,			27-15
BUILDING TYPE	SINGLE FAMILY DWELLING	LOT SIZE	112.32	
BUILDING SIZE	6.09	TOTAL SQUARE FOOTAGE	147.21	
FOUNDATION TYPE		MATERIALS		
NUMBER OF FLOORS		HEIGHT	9.55 m (PEAK m)	
START DATE	4/20/11	END DATE	12/05/11	
ARCHITECT (NAME) (ADDRESS)		PHONE ( )		
SURVEYOR (NAME) (ADDRESS)		PHONE (144) 192-1		
BUILDER (NAME) (ADDRESS)		PHONE ( )		
THIS SIGN WAS POSTED	3/05/11			

FOR INFORMATION ABOUT THIS CONSTRUCTION PROJECT CONTACT:
(NAME)   (PHONE)

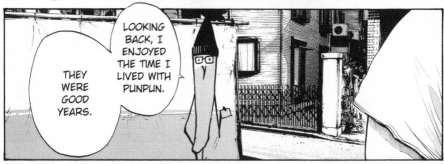

LOOKING BACK, I ENJOYED THE TIME I LIVED WITH PUNPUN.

THEY WERE GOOD YEARS.

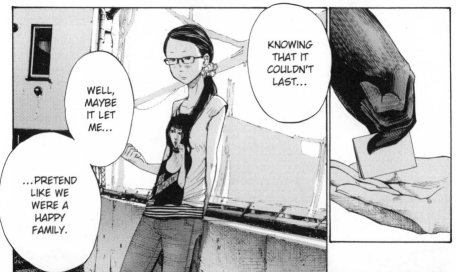

KNOWING THAT IT COULDN'T LAST...

WELL, MAYBE IT LET ME...

...PRETEND LIKE WE WERE A HAPPY FAMILY.

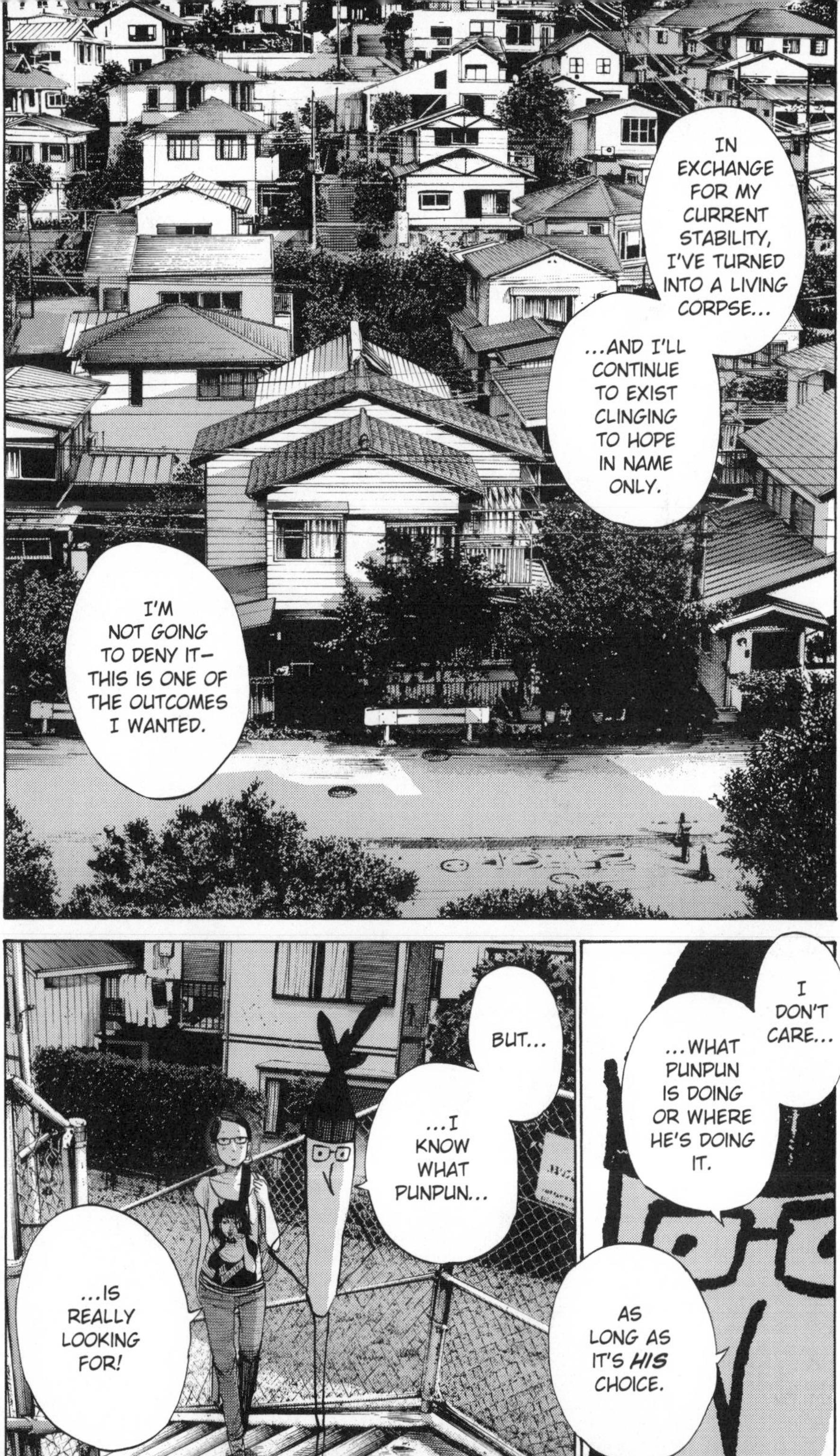
IN EXCHANGE FOR MY CURRENT STABILITY, I'VE TURNED INTO A LIVING CORPSE...
...AND I'LL CONTINUE TO EXIST CLINGING TO HOPE IN NAME ONLY.
I'M NOT GOING TO DENY IT— THIS IS ONE OF THE OUTCOMES I WANTED.
I DON'T CARE...
...WHAT PUNPUN IS DOING OR WHERE HE'S DOING IT.
AS LONG AS IT'S *HIS* CHOICE.
BUT...
...I KNOW WHAT PUNPUN...
...IS REALLY LOOKING FOR!

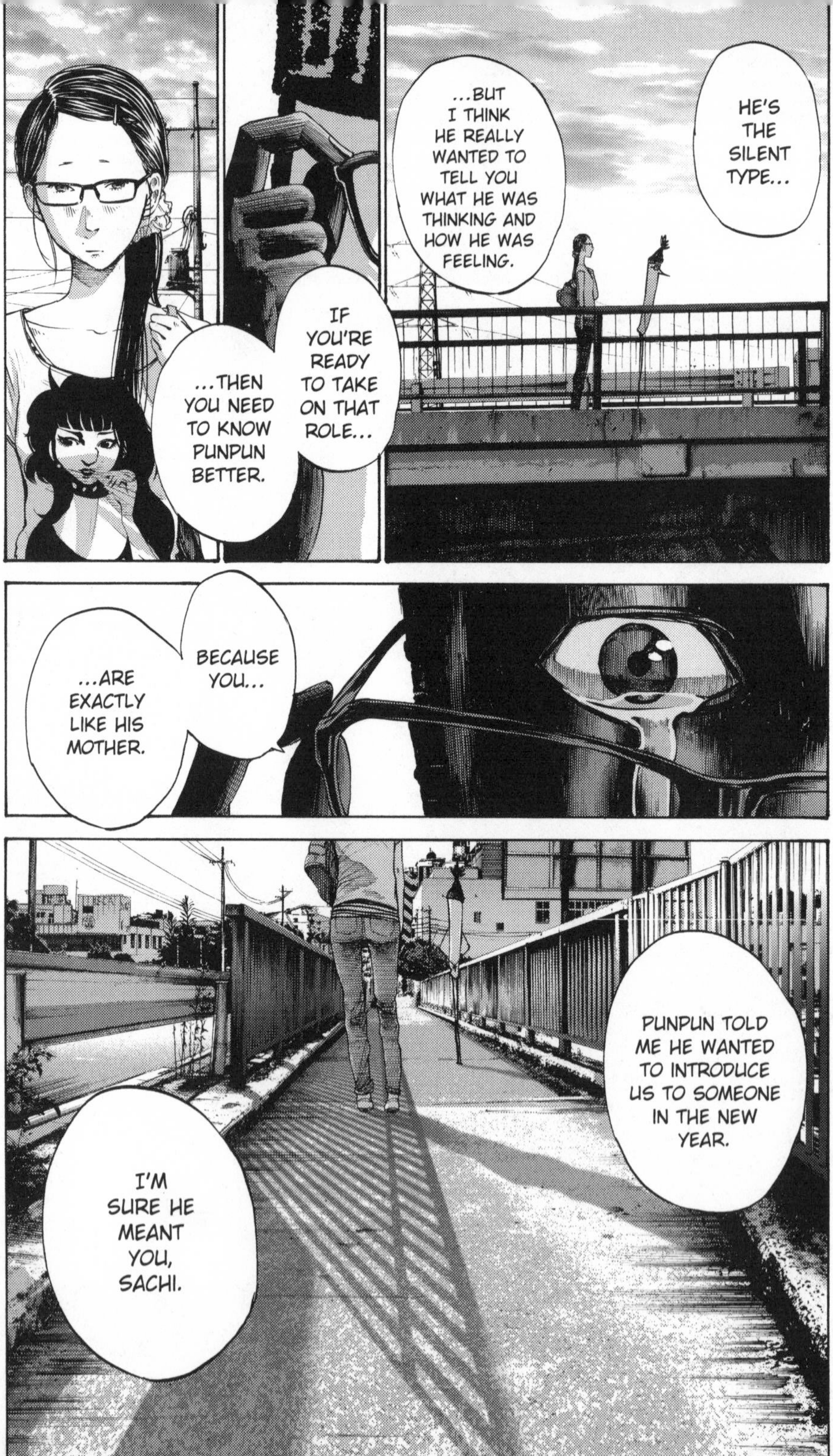
HE'S THE SILENT TYPE...
...BUT I THINK HE REALLY WANTED TO TELL YOU WHAT HE WAS THINKING AND HOW HE WAS FEELING.
IF YOU'RE READY TO TAKE ON THAT ROLE...
...THEN YOU NEED TO KNOW PUNPUN BETTER.
BECAUSE YOU...
...ARE EXACTLY LIKE HIS MOTHER.
PUNPUN TOLD ME HE WANTED TO INTRODUCE US TO SOMEONE IN THE NEW YEAR.
I'M SURE HE MEANT YOU, SACHI.

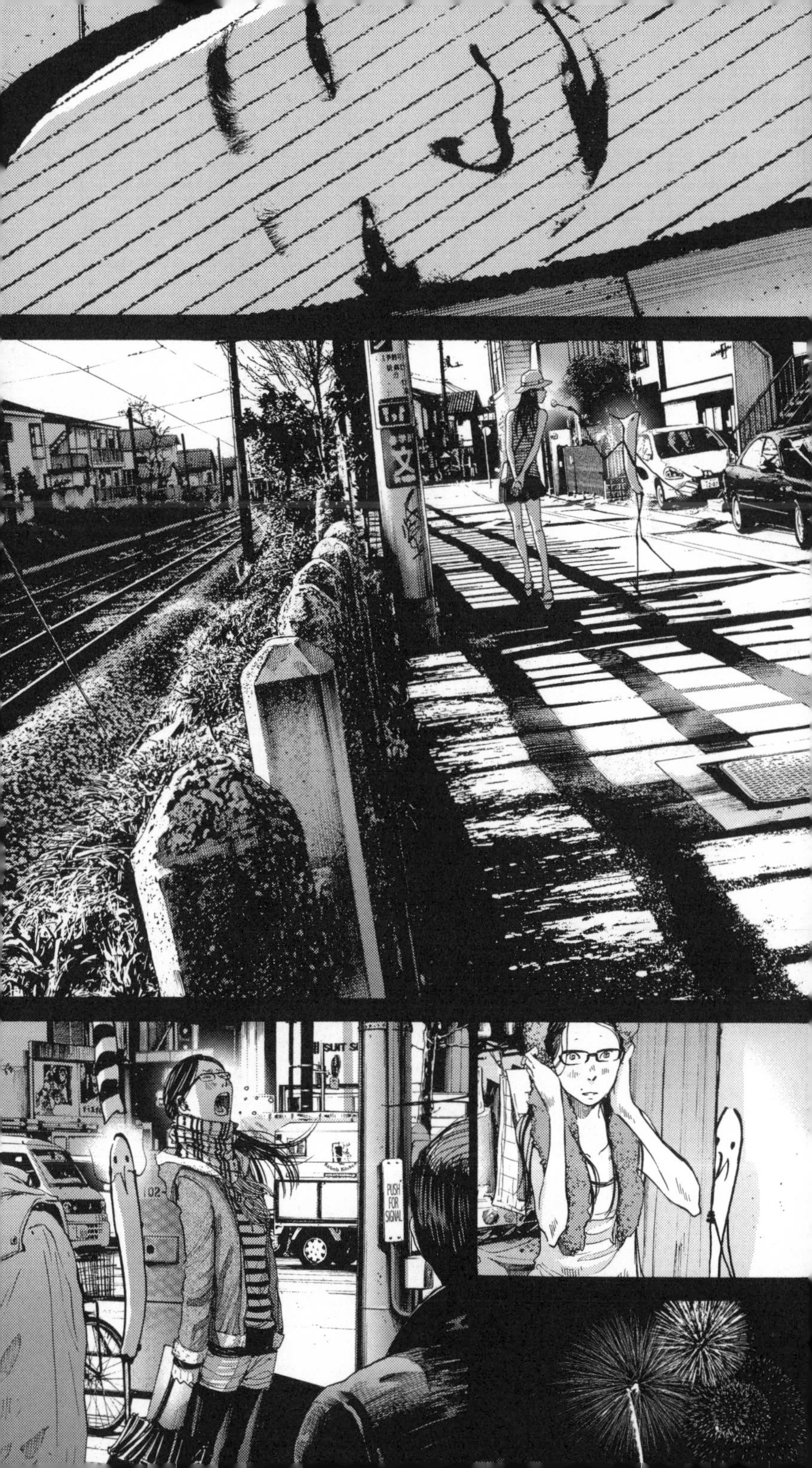
PUSH FOR SIGNAL

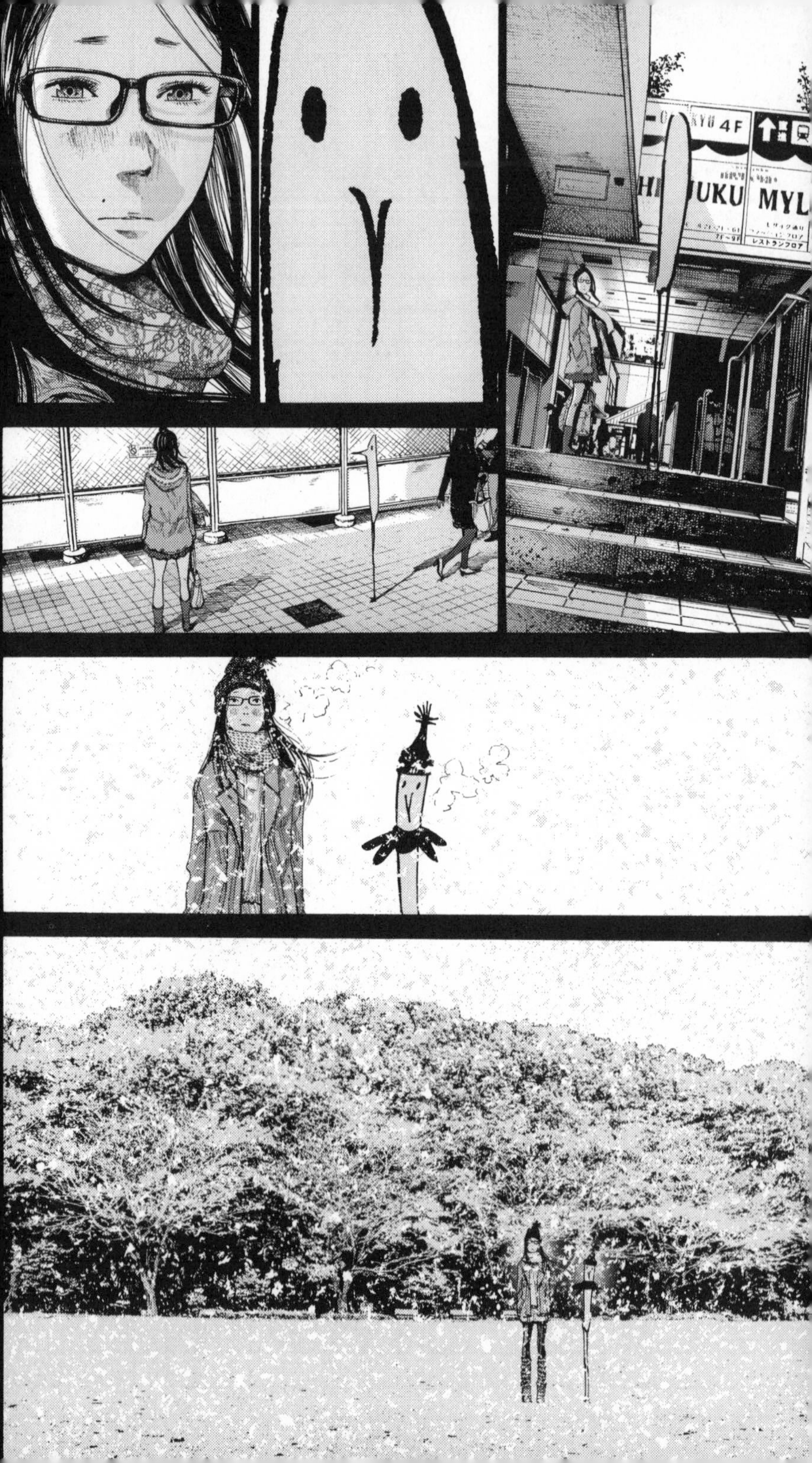

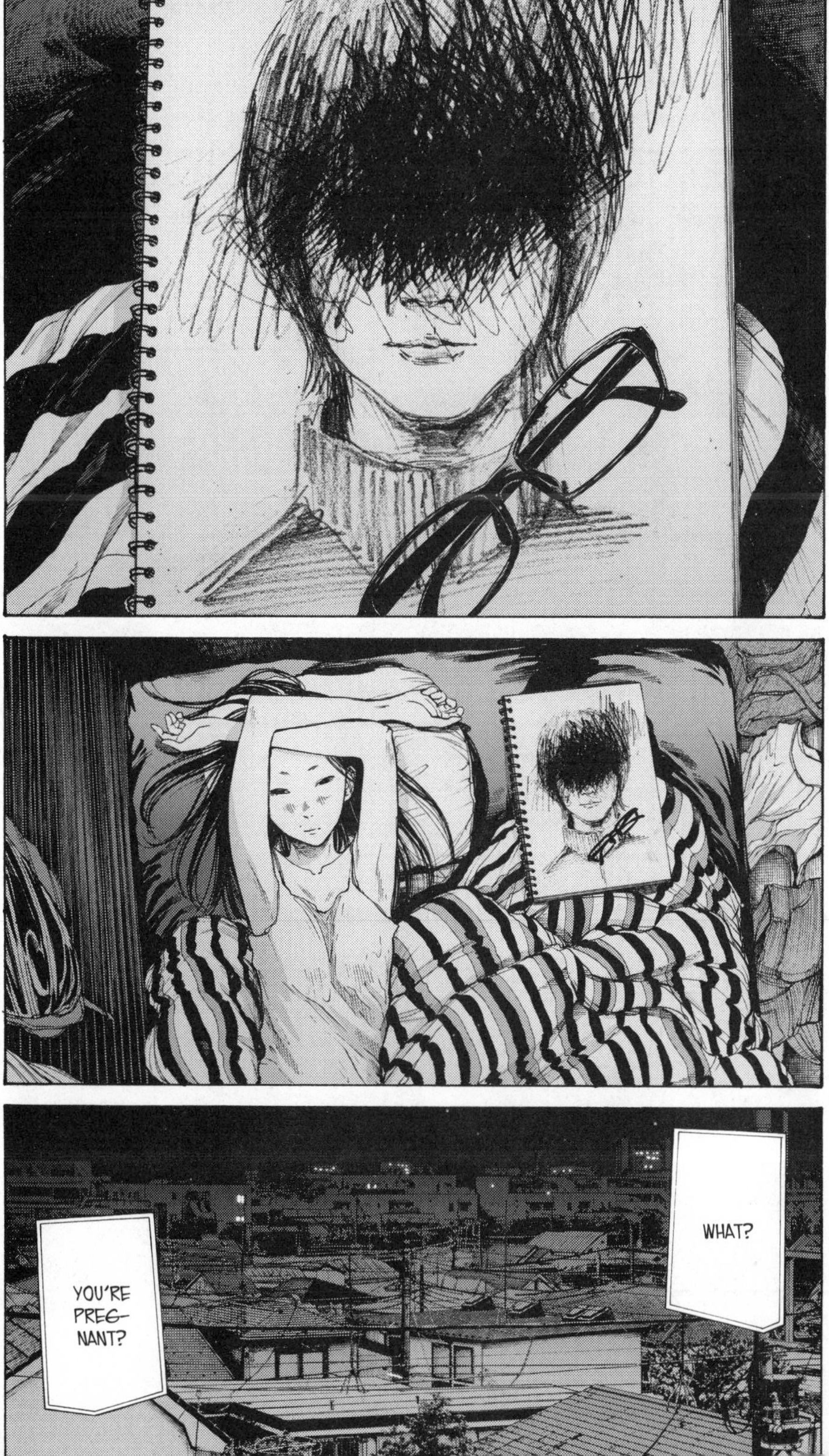
WHAT?
YOU'RE PREG-NANT?

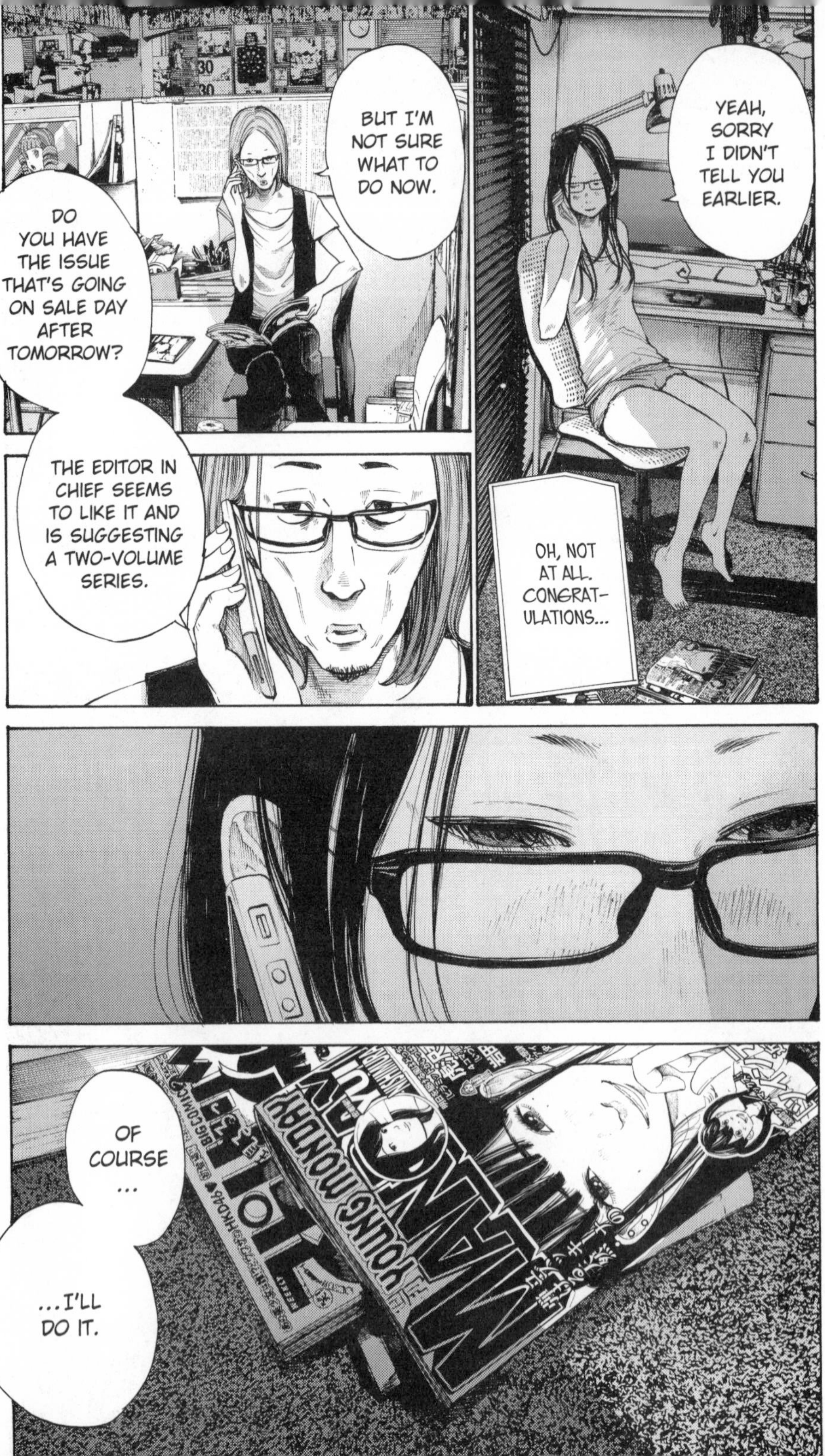
YEAH, SORRY I DIDN'T TELL YOU EARLIER.
OH, NOT AT ALL. CONGRAT-ULATIONS...
BUT I'M NOT SURE WHAT TO DO NOW.
DO YOU HAVE THE ISSUE THAT'S GOING ON SALE DAY AFTER TOMORROW?
THE EDITOR IN CHIEF SEEMS TO LIKE IT AND IS SUGGESTING A TWO-VOLUME SERIES.
OF COURSE ...
...I'LL DO IT.

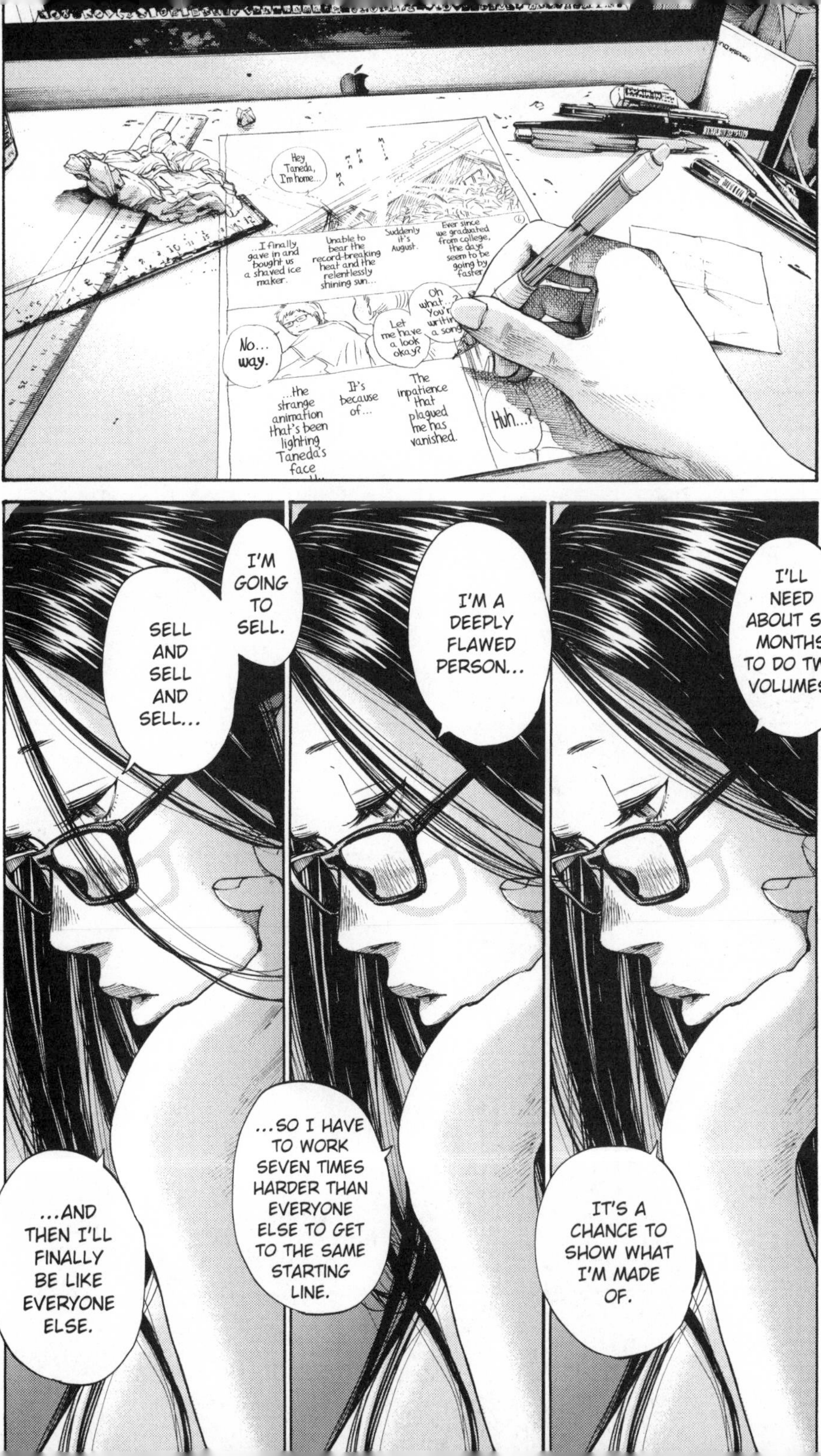

Hey Taneda, I'm home...
Ever since we graduated from college, the days seem to be going by faster
Suddenly it's August.
Unable to bear the record-breaking heat and the relentlessly shining sun...
...I finally gave in and bought us a shaved ice maker.
Oh what...? You'r writin a song
Let me have a look okay?
No... way.
The inpatience that plagued me has vanished.
It's because of...
...the strange animation that's been lighting Taneda's face
Huh...?
I'LL NEED ABOUT SIX MONTHS TO DO TWO VOLUMES.
IT'S A CHANCE TO SHOW WHAT I'M MADE OF.
I'M A DEEPLY FLAWED PERSON...
...SO I HAVE TO WORK SEVEN TIMES HARDER THAN EVERYONE ELSE TO GET TO THE SAME STARTING LINE.
I'M GOING TO SELL.
SELL AND SELL AND SELL...
...AND THEN I'LL FINALLY BE LIKE EVERYONE ELSE.

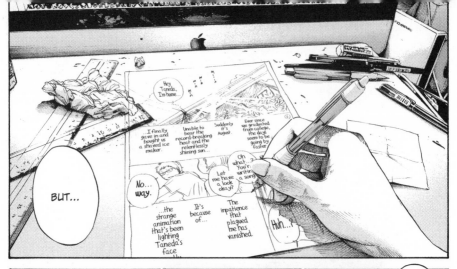

BUT...

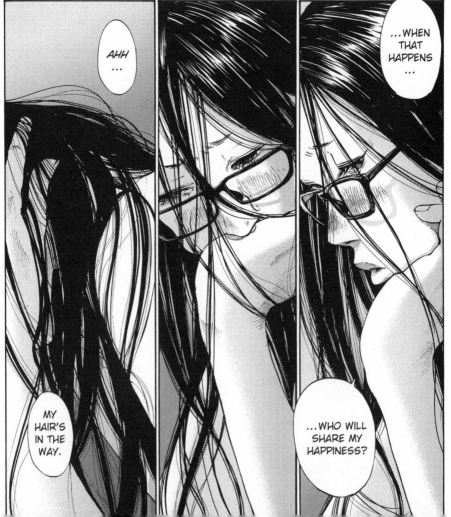

AHH
...

...WHEN
THAT
HAPPENS
...

MY
HAIR'S
IN THE
WAY.

...WHO WILL
SHARE MY
HAPPINESS?

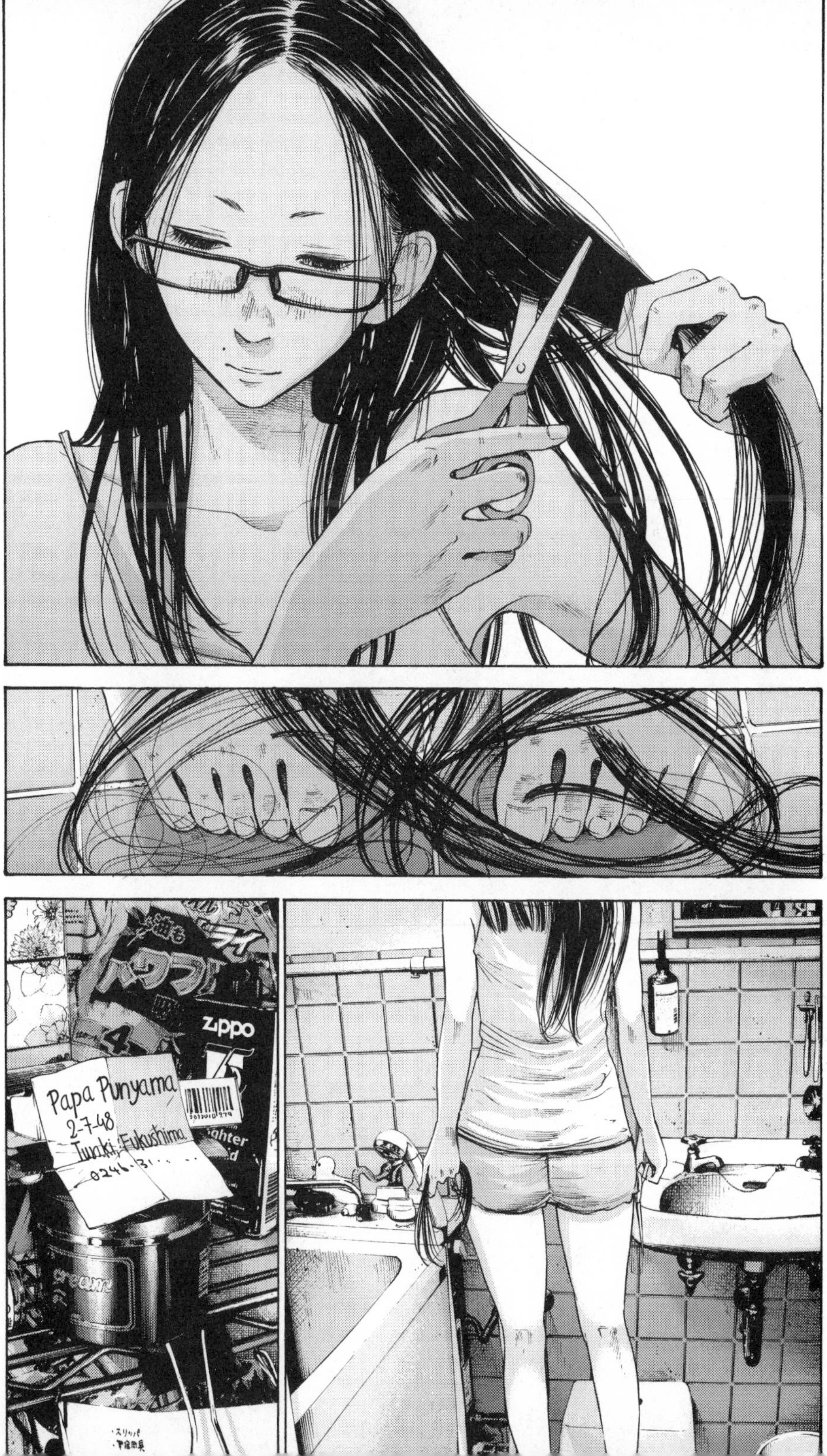

Papa Punyama
2-7-48
Iwaki, Fukushima
0246-31...
ZIPPO

Chapter 126

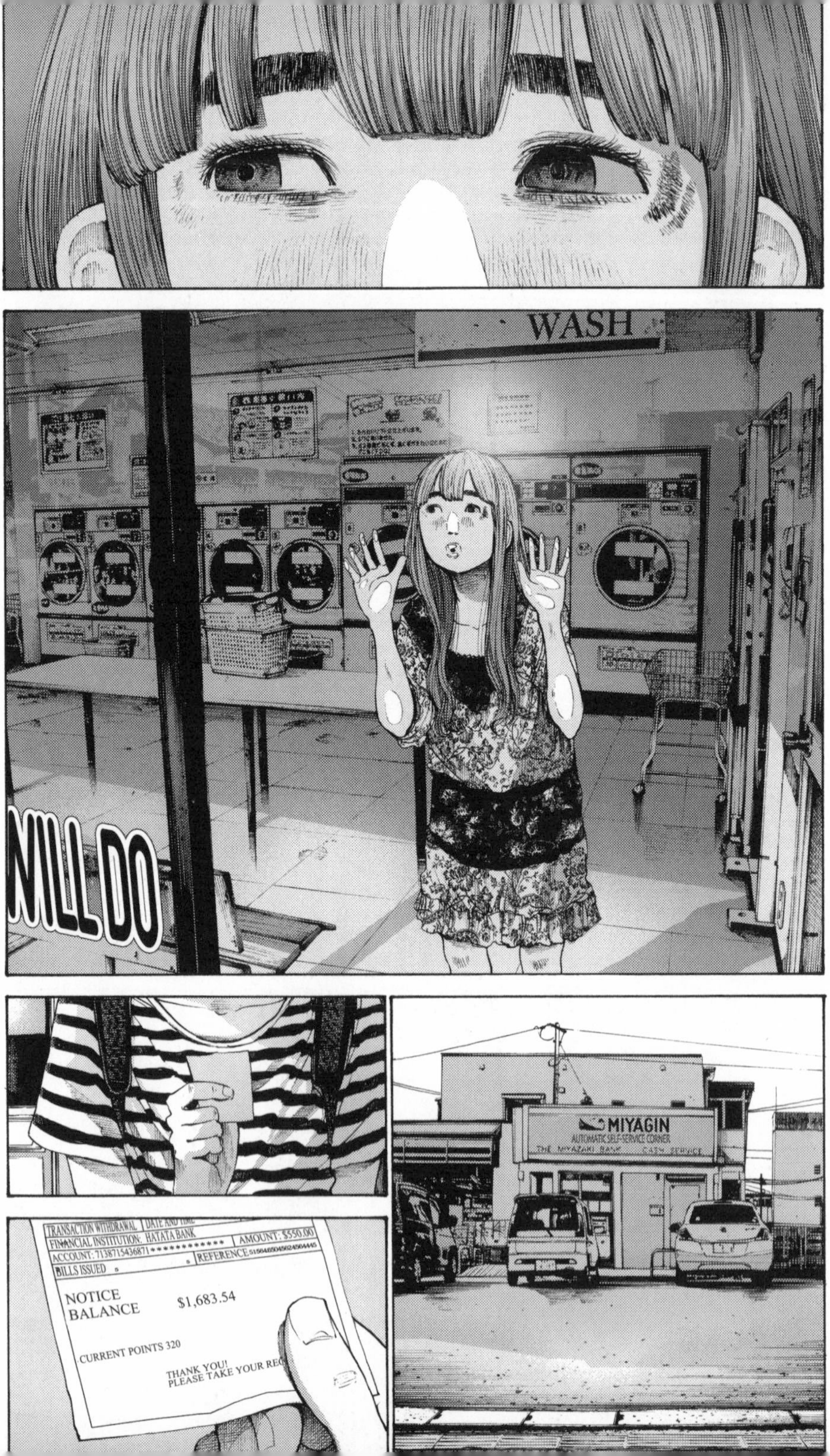
WASH
WILL DO
MIYAGIN
AUTOMATIC SELF-SERVICE CORNER
THE MIYAZAKI BANK CASH SERVICE
TRANSACTION WITHDRAWAL
DATE AND TIME
FINANCIAL INSTITUTION: HATATA BANK
AMOUNT: $550.00
ACCOUNT: 7138715436871 ************
REFERENCE
BILLS ISSUED
NOTICE
BALANCE
$1,683.54
CURRENT POINTS 320
THANK YOU!
PLEASE TAKE YOUR RE

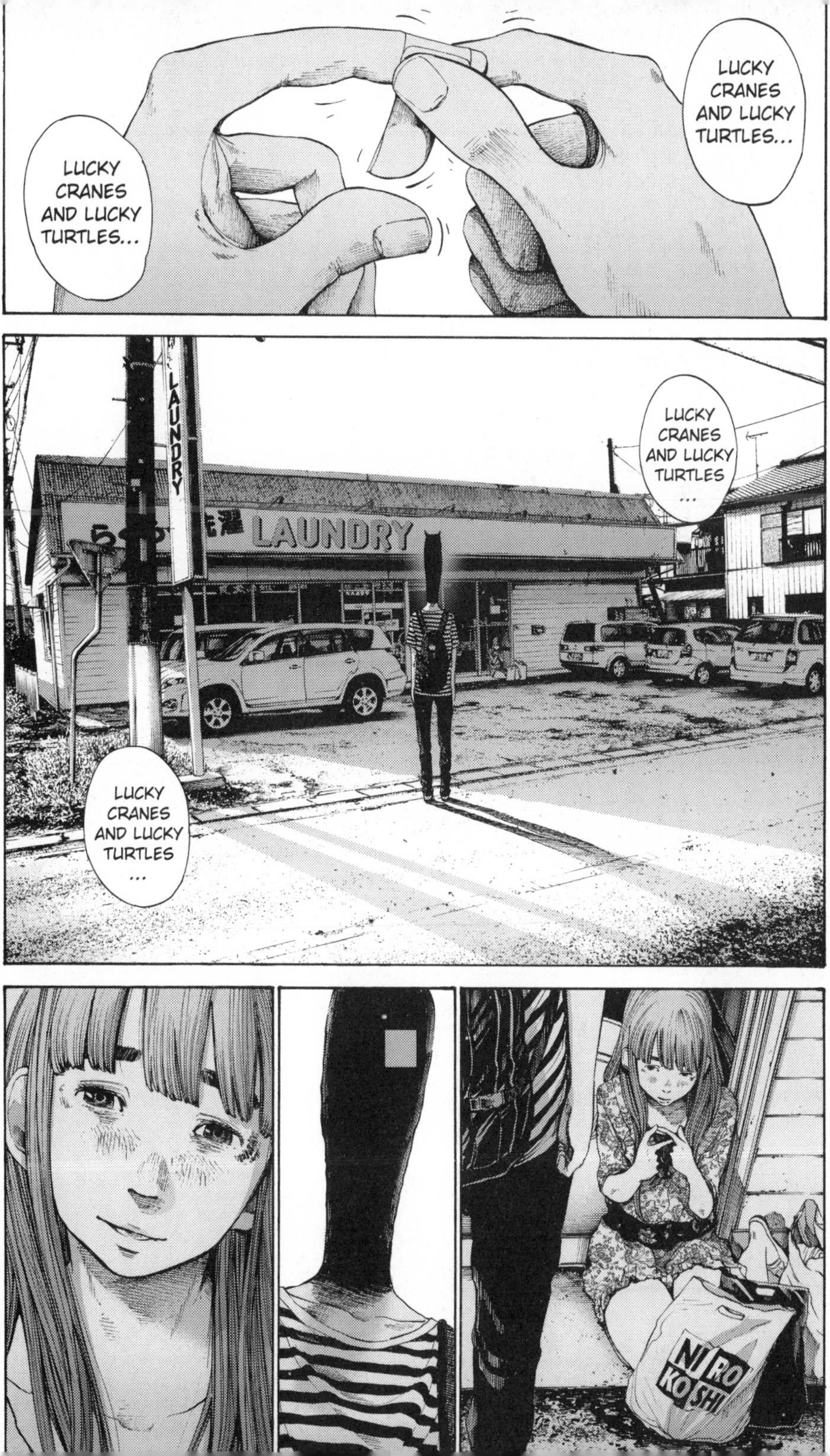
LUCKY CRANES AND LUCKY TURTLES...
LUCKY CRANES AND LUCKY TURTLES...
LUCKY CRANES AND LUCKY TURTLES...
LAUNDRY
LAUNDRY
LUCKY CRANES AND LUCKY TURTLES...
NI RO KO SHI

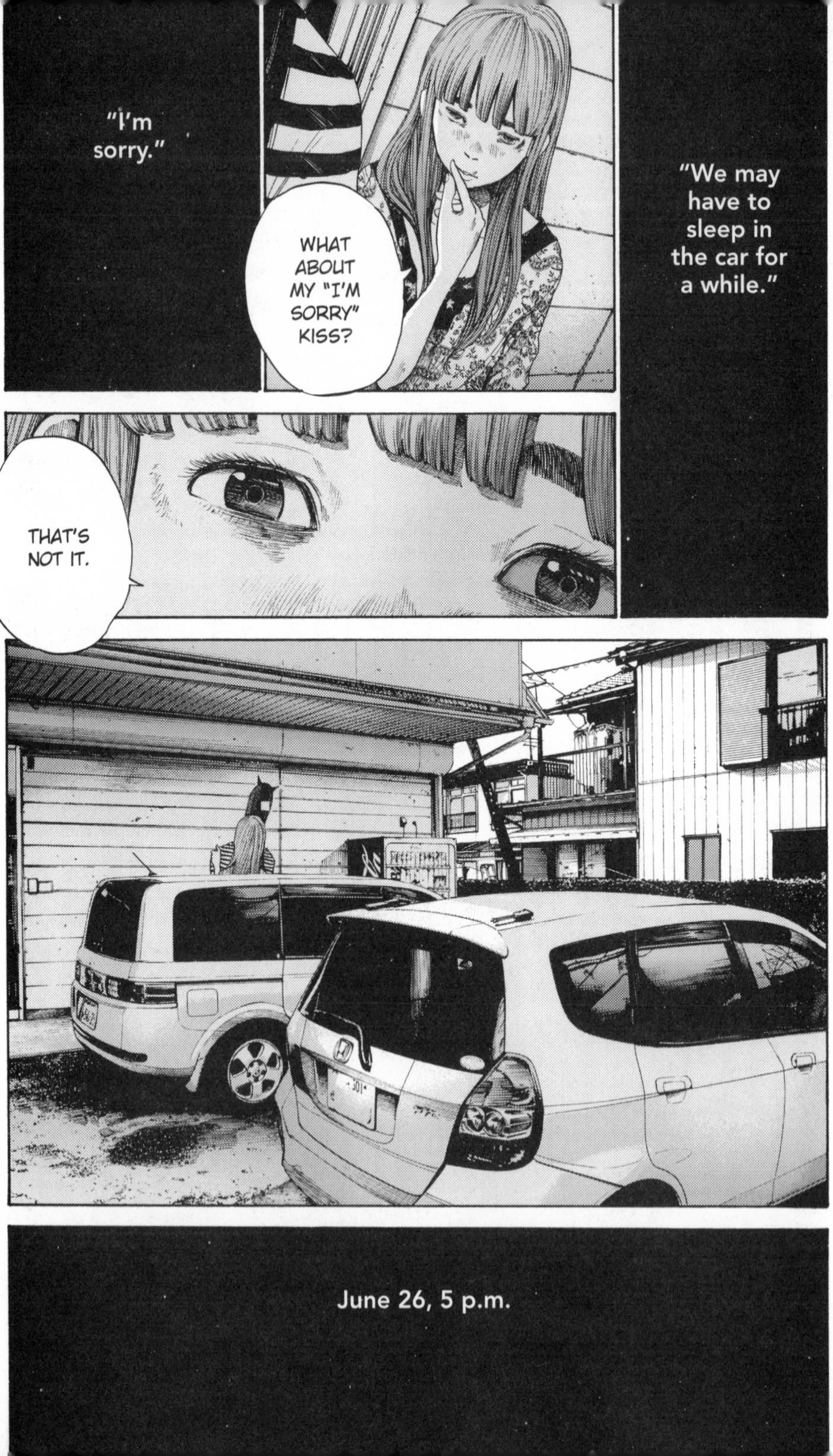
"We may have to sleep in the car for a while."
WHAT ABOUT MY "I'M SORRY" KISS?
"I'm sorry."
THAT'S NOT IT.
June 26, 5 p.m.

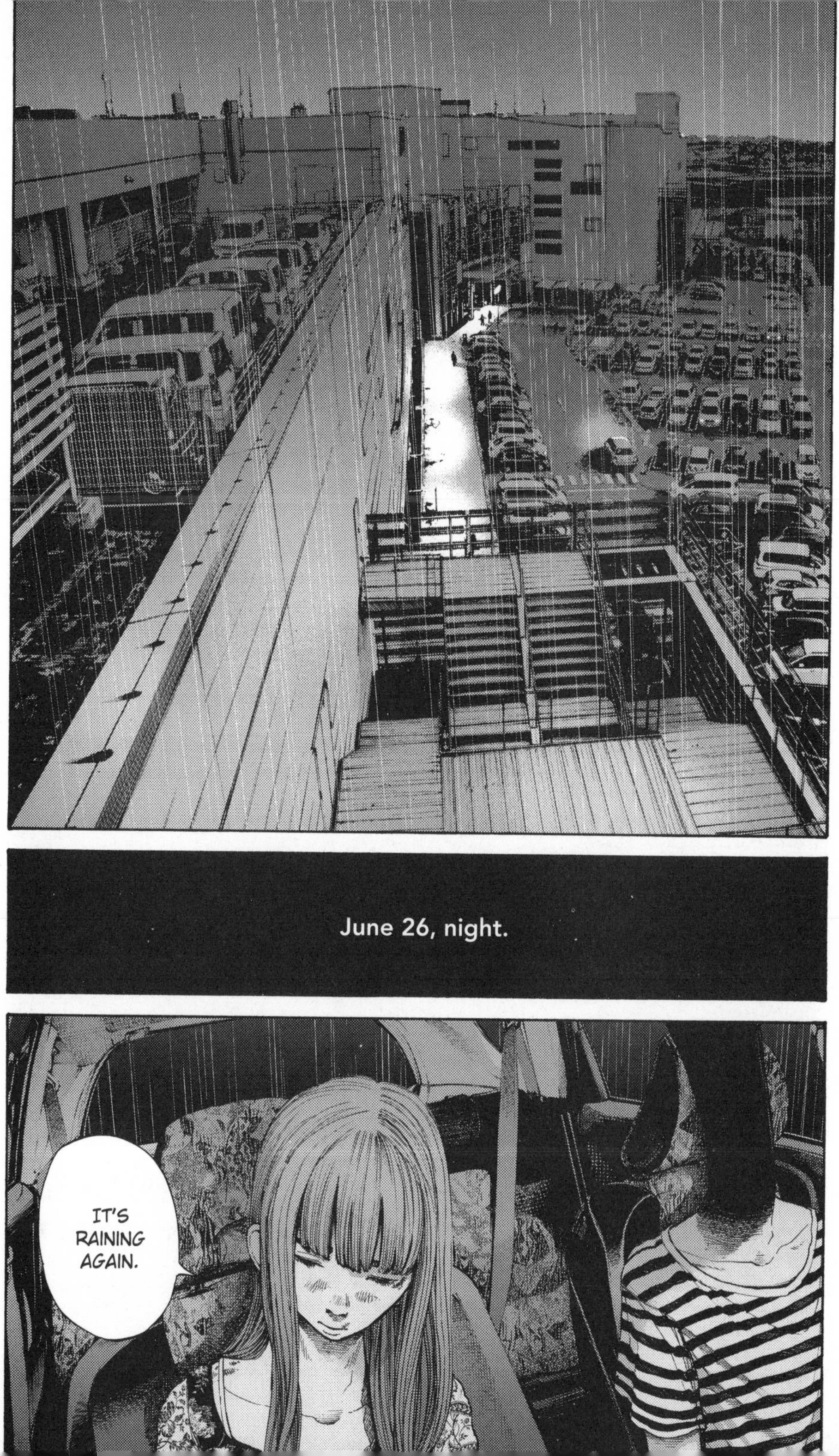
June 26, night.
IT'S RAINING AGAIN.

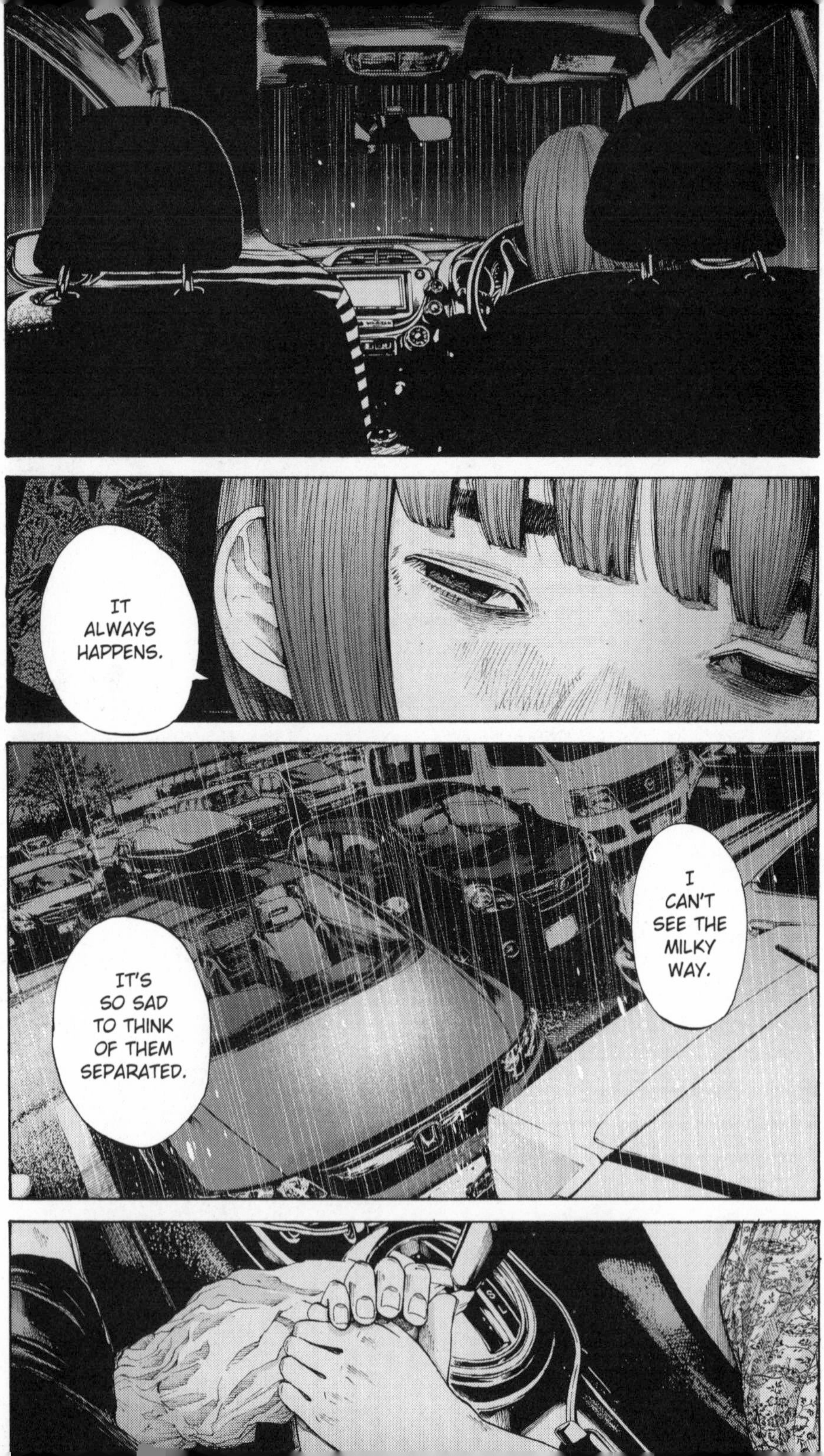
IT ALWAYS HAPPENS.
I CAN'T SEE THE MILKY WAY.
IT'S SO SAD TO THINK OF THEM SEPARATED.

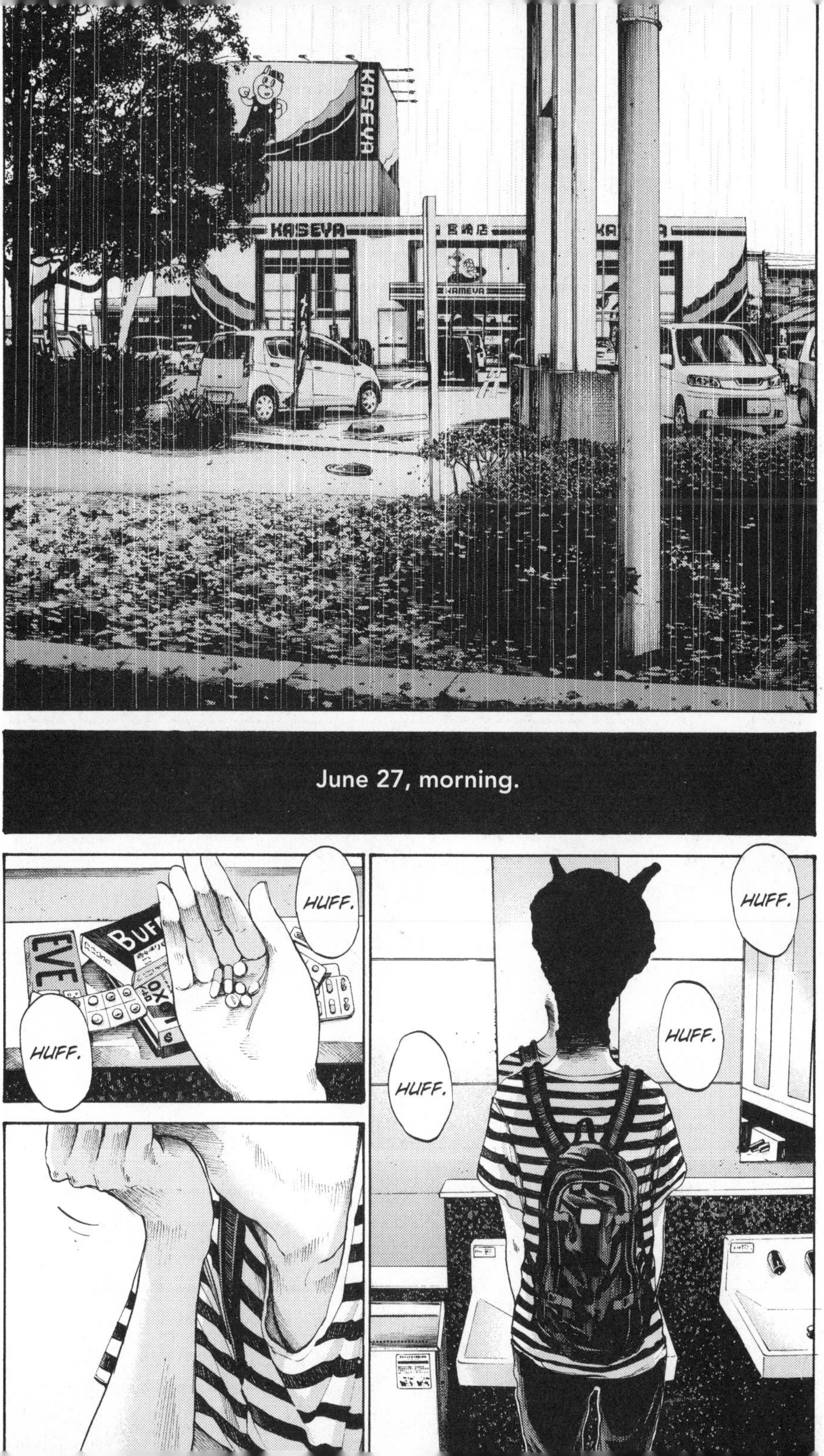
KASEYA
KASEYA
June 27, morning.
HUFF.
HUFF.
HUFF.
HUFF.
EVE
HUFF.

SIGH ...
SIGH ...
SIGH ...
SIGH ...
RESTROOMS
HA HA HA!

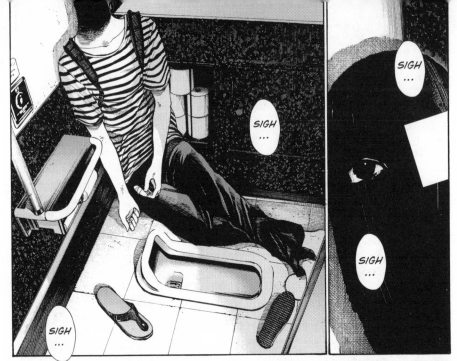

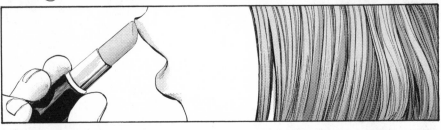

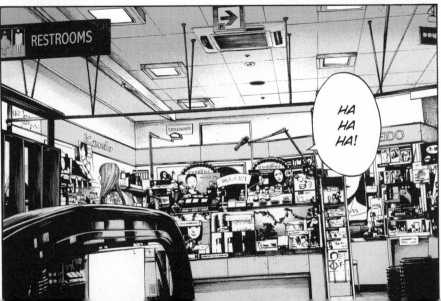

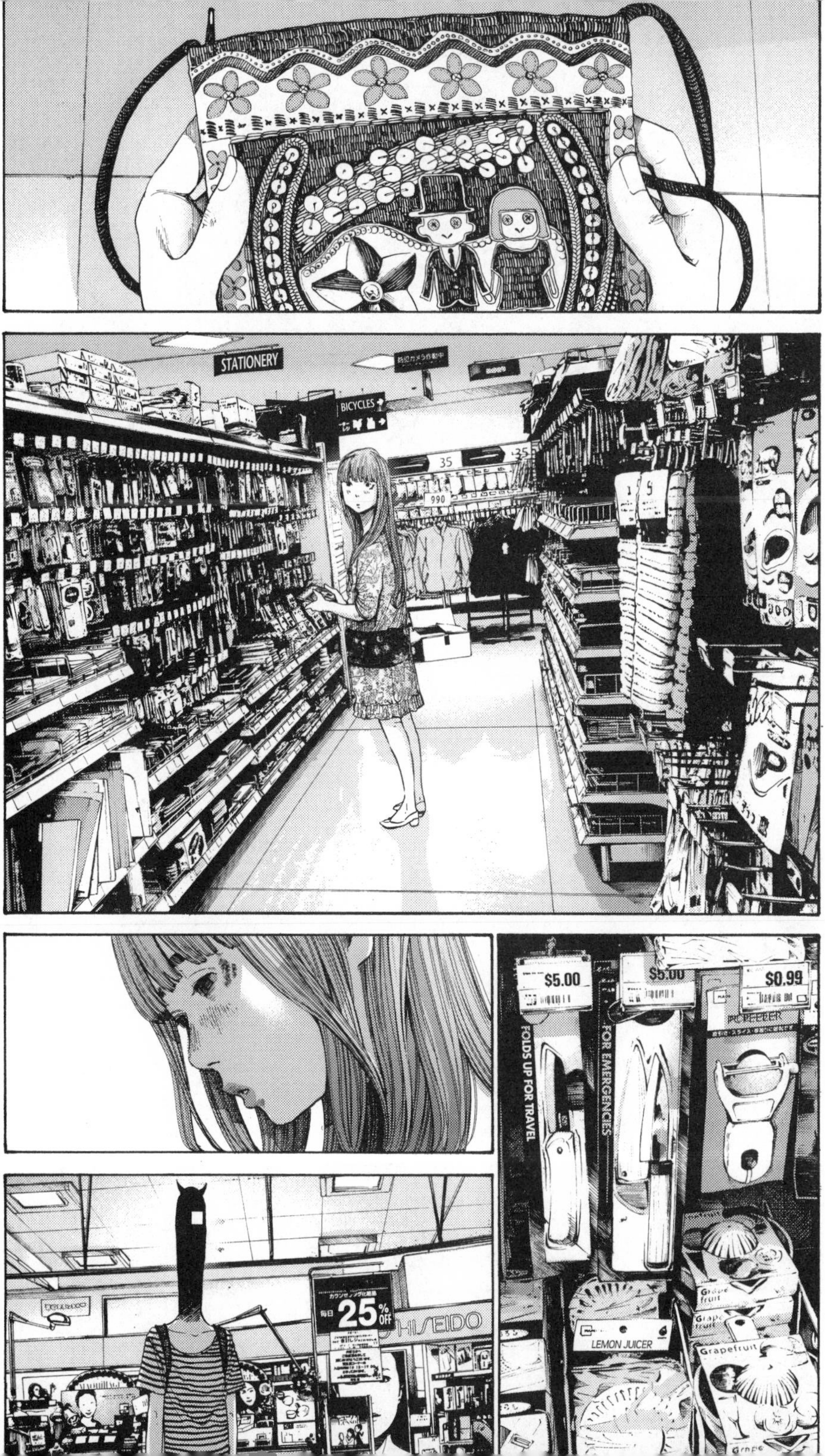
STATIONERY
BICYCLES
35
35
990
$5.00
$5.00
$0.99
FOLDS UP FOR TRAVEL
FOR EMERGENCIES
LEMON JUICER
Grapefruit
毎日 25% OFF
SHISEIDO

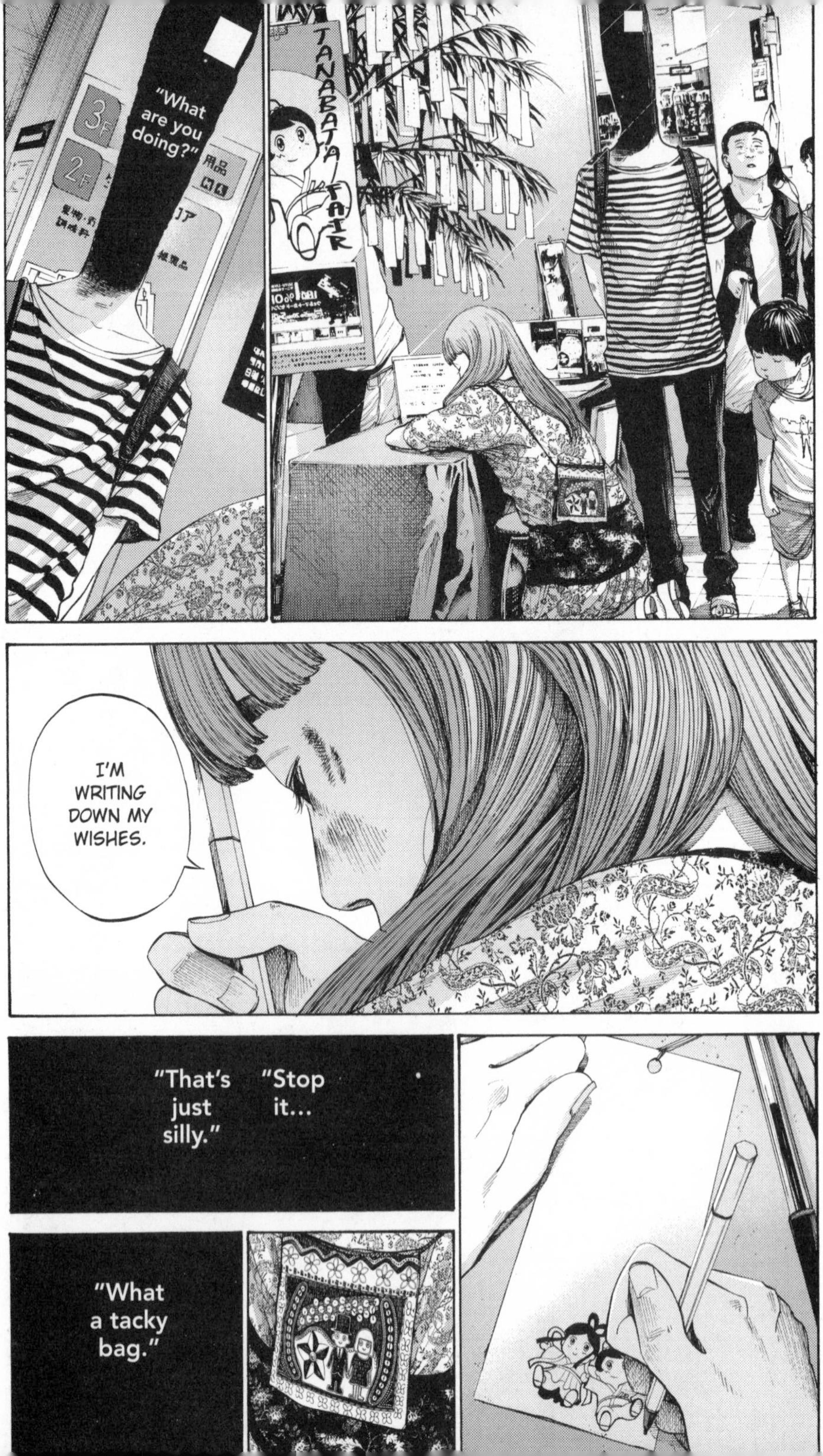
TANABATA FAIR
"What are you doing?"
I'M WRITING DOWN MY WISHES.
"Stop it...
"That's just silly."
"What a tacky bag."

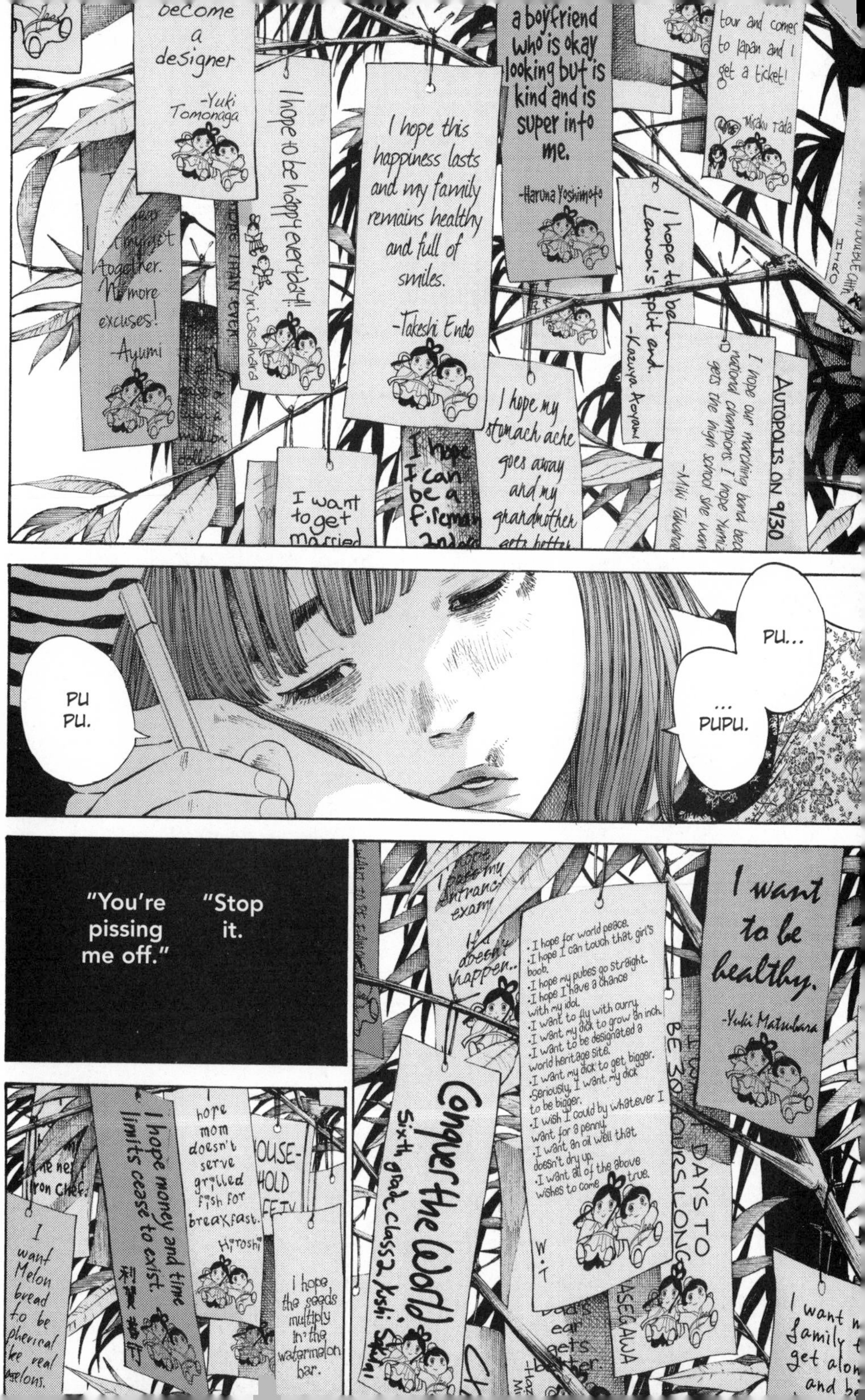
tour and comes to Japan and I get a ticket! Misaki Tada
a boyfriend who is okay looking but is kind and is super into me. -Haruna Yoshimoto
I hope this happiness lasts and my family remains healthy and full of smiles. -Takeshi Endo
I hope to be happy everyday!! -Yuri Sasahara
become a designer -Yuki Tomonaga
together. No more excuses! -Ayumi
AUTOPOLIS ON 9/30
I hope our marching band bec national champions I hope Yumi gets the high school she wan -Miki Takahas
I hope to be Lemon's split end. -Kazuya Aoyam
I hope my stomach ache goes away and my grandmother gets better
I hope I can be a fireman
I want to get married
PU...
...PUPU.
PU PU.
I want to be healthy. -Yuki Matsubara
DAYS TO BE 30 HOURS LONG
·I hope for world peace. ·I hope I can touch that girl's boob. ·I hope my pubes go straight. ·I hope I have a chance with my idol. ·I want to fly with curry. ·I want my dick to grow an inch. ·I want to be designated a world heritage site. ·I want my dick to get bigger. ·Seriously, I want my dick to be bigger. ·I wish I could by whatever I want for a penny. ·I want an oil well that doesn't dry up. ·I want all of the above wishes to come true. W·T
Conquer the World! Sixth grade class 2 Yoshi Sakai
I want my family to get along and be
Dad's ear gets better
doesn't happen...
"Stop it.
"You're pissing me off."
I hope mom doesn't serve grilled fish for breakfast. Hiroshi
I hope money and time limits cease to exist.
I hope the seeds multiply in the watermelon bar.
Iron Chef.
I want Melon bread to be pherical ke real elons.

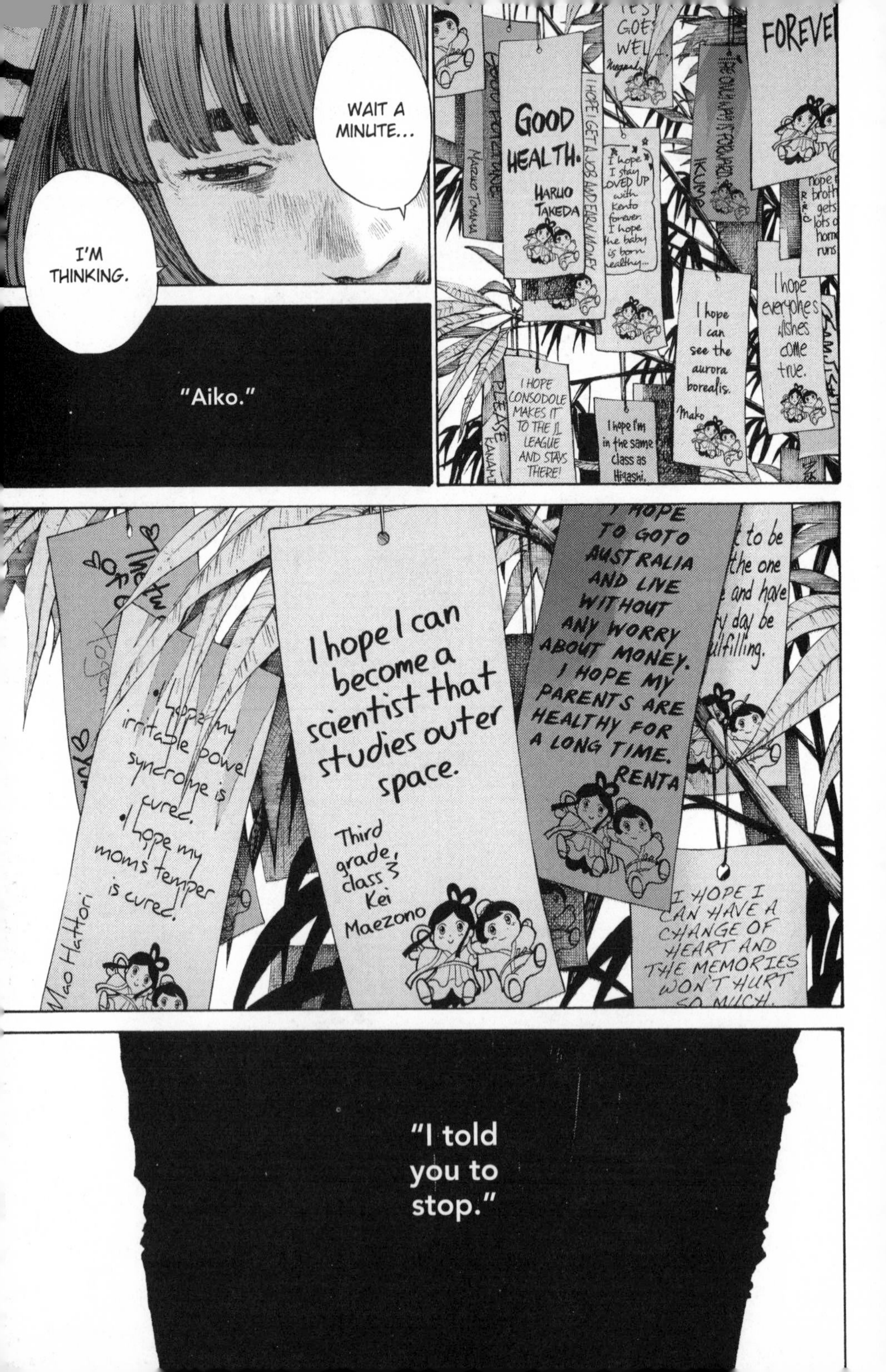
GOOD HEALTH. HARUO TAKEDA
I HOPE I GET A JOB AND EARN MONEY
I hope I stay LOVED UP with Kento forever. I hope the baby is born healthy...
I hope I can see the aurora borealis. Mako
I hope everyone's wishes come true.
I HOPE CONSODOLE MAKES IT TO THE J1 LEAGUE AND STAYS THERE!
I hope I'm in the same class as Higashi.
WAIT A MINUTE...
I'M THINKING.
"Aiko."
TO GOTO AUSTRALIA AND LIVE WITHOUT ANY WORRY ABOUT MONEY. I HOPE MY PARENTS ARE HEALTHY FOR A LONG TIME. RENTA
I hope I can become a scientist that studies outer space. Third grade, class 3 Kei Maezono
irritable bowel syncrome is cured. I hope my moms temper is cured. Mao Hattori
I HOPE I CAN HAVE A CHANGE OF HEART AND THE MEMORIES WON'T HURT
"I told you to stop."

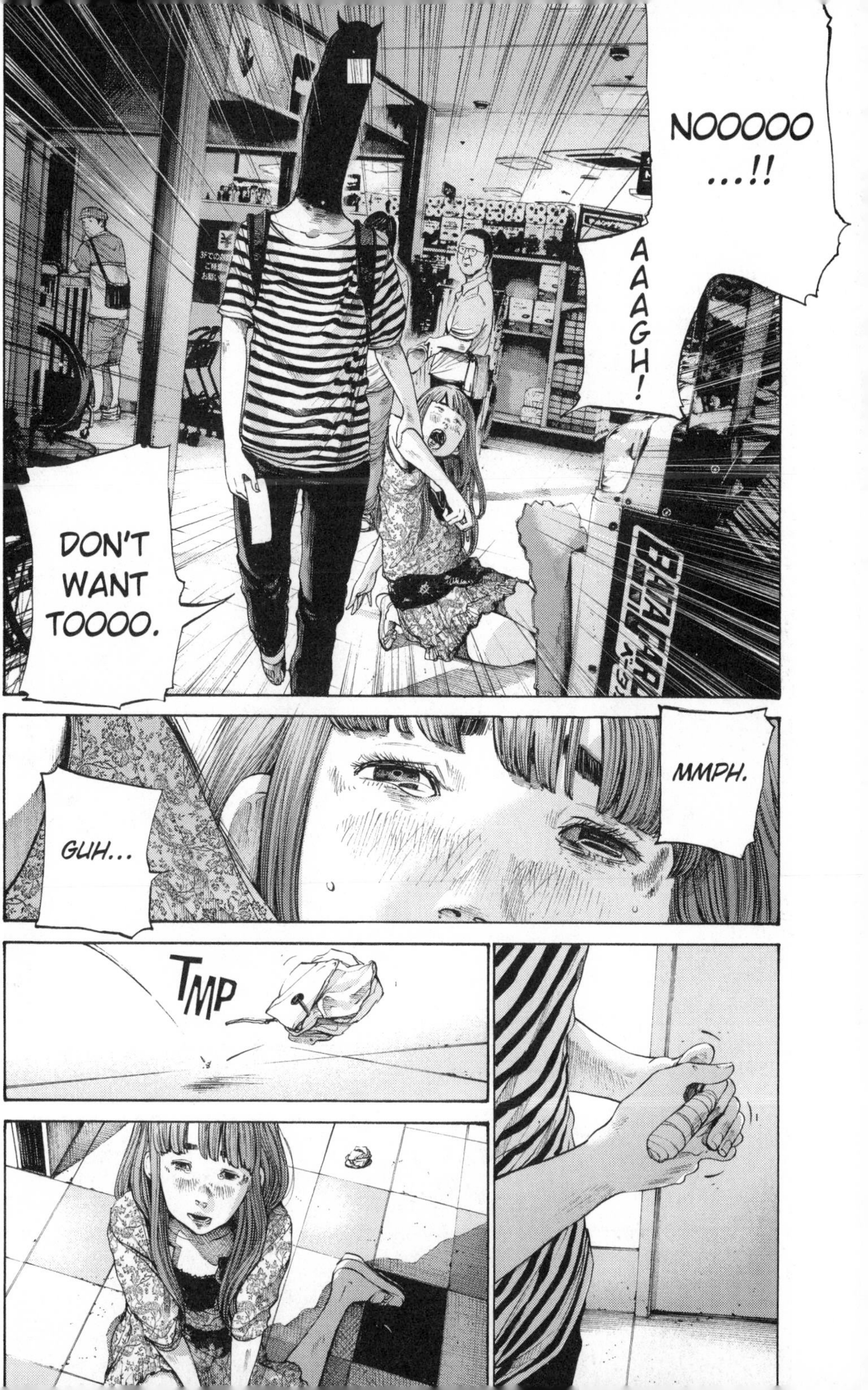
NOOOOO ...!!
AAAAGH!
DON'T WANT TOOOO.
MMPH.
GUH...
TMP

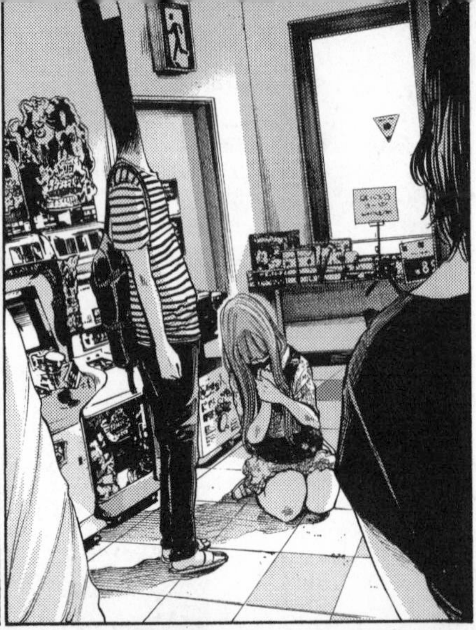

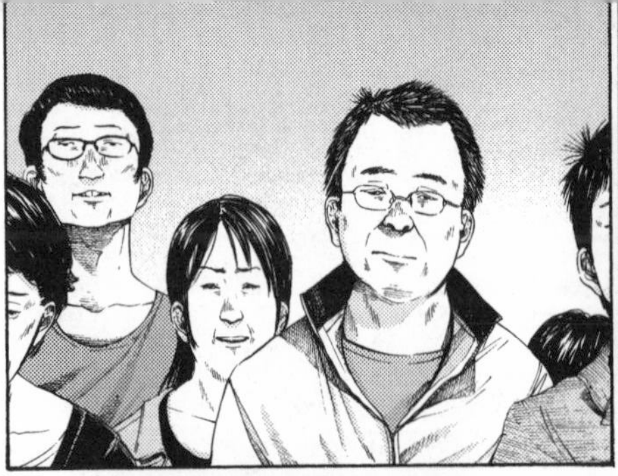

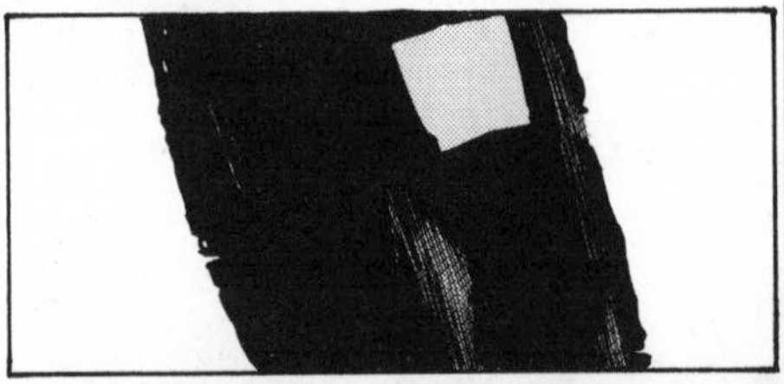

"It's fine...

"Just a lovers' quarrel.

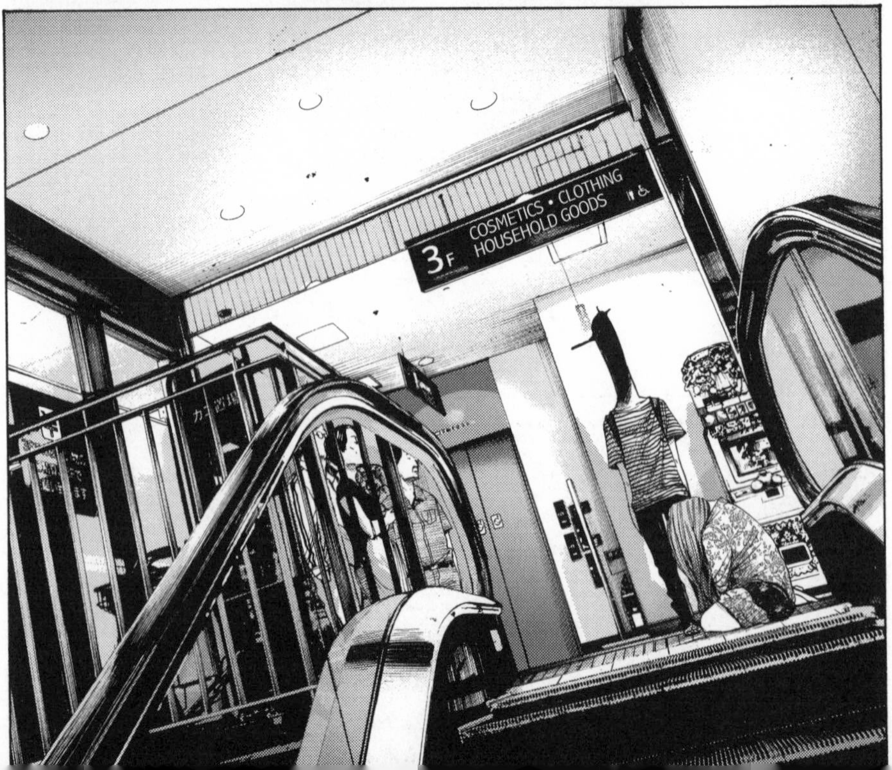
3F
COSMETICS • CLOTHING
HOUSEHOLD GOODS

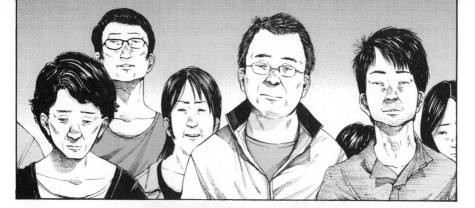

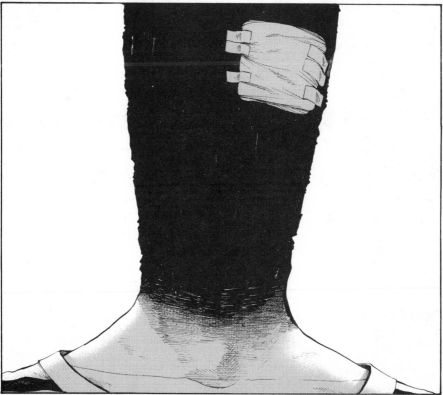

"Quit staring,
you idiots."

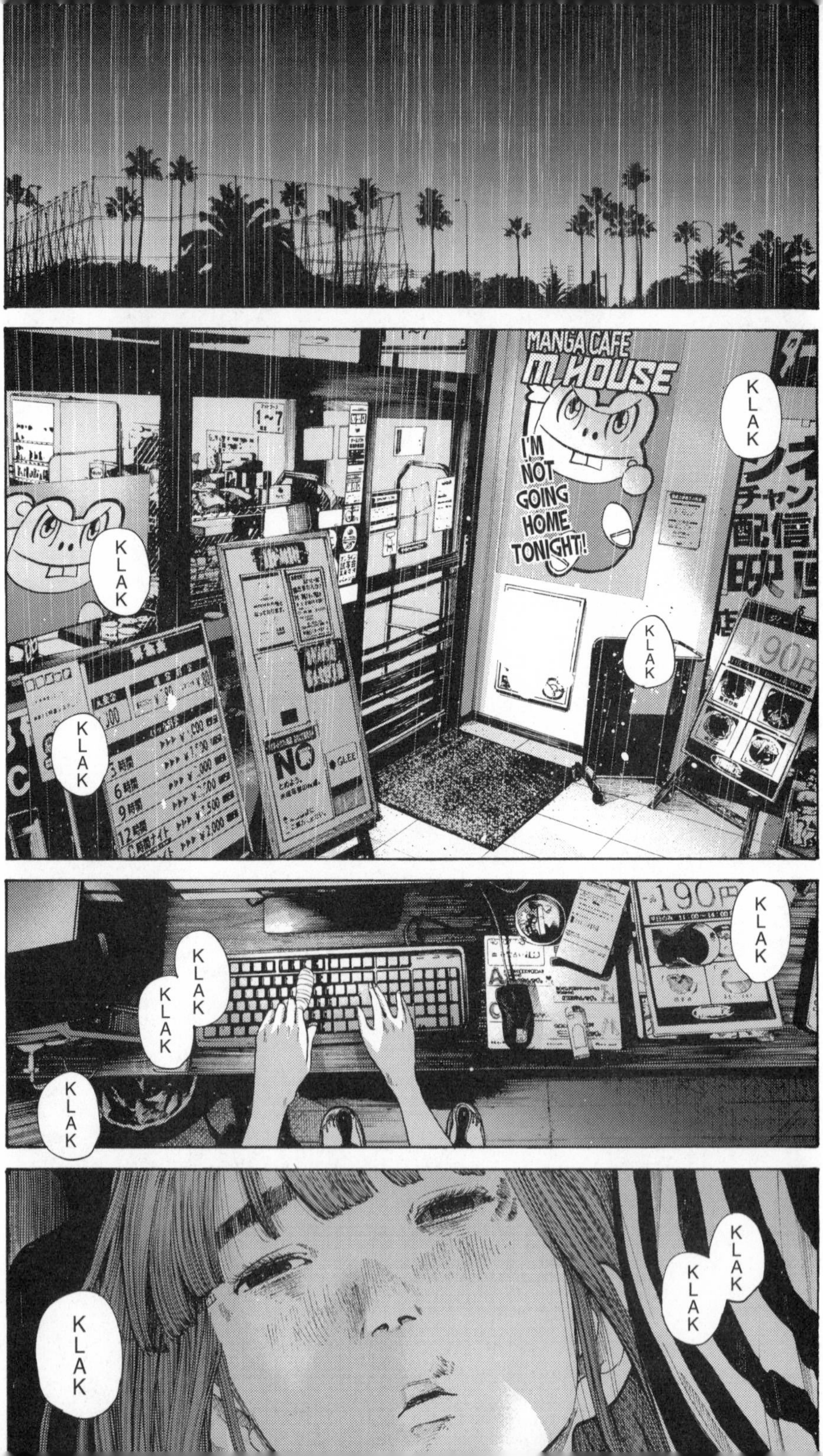
KLAK
MANGA CAFE
M HOUSE
I'M NOT GOING HOME TONIGHT!
KLAK
190円
KLAK
KLAK
NO
KLAK
KLAK
KLAK
KLAK
KLAK
KLAK
KLAK

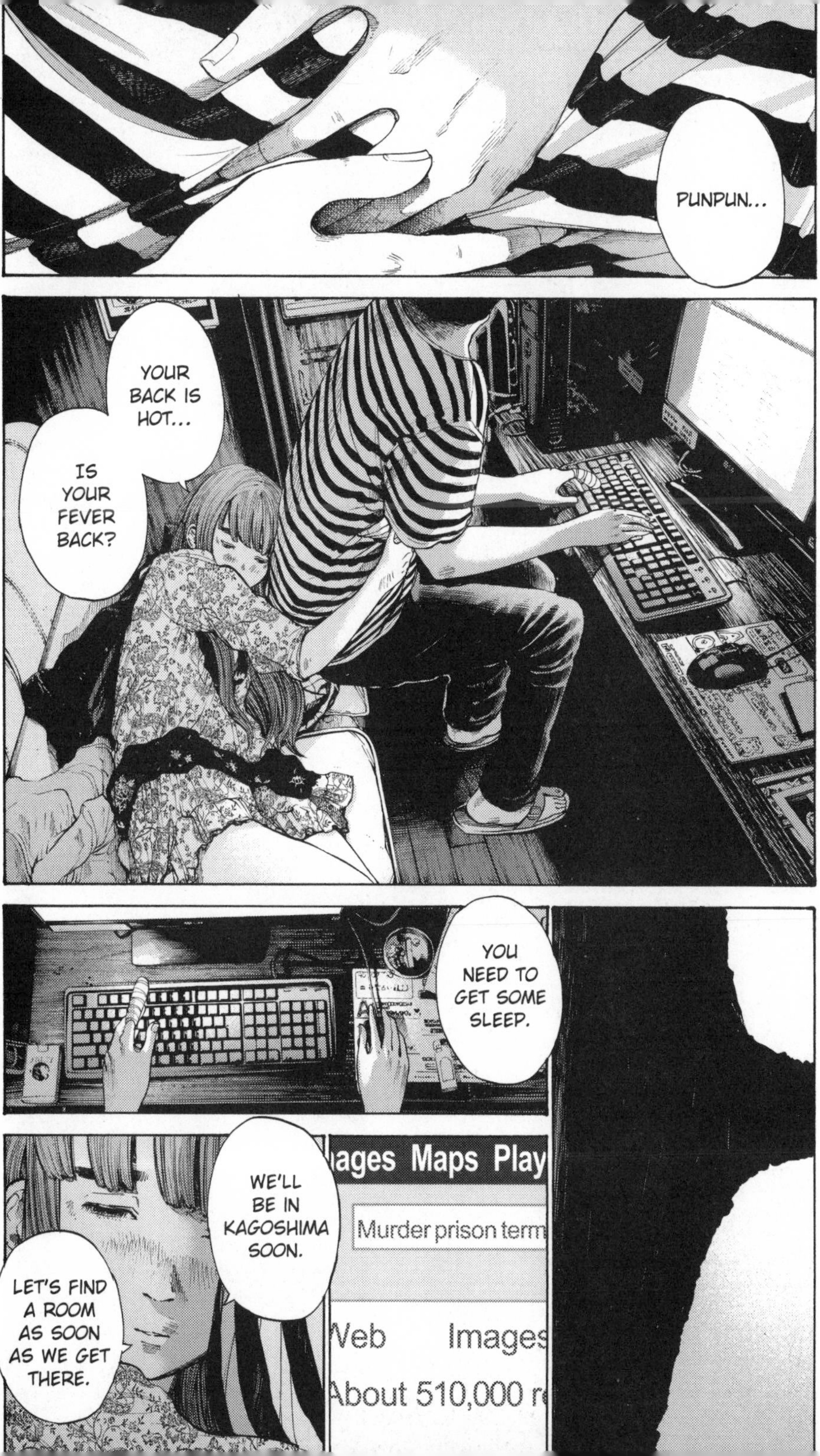
PUNPUN...
YOUR BACK IS HOT...
IS YOUR FEVER BACK?
YOU NEED TO GET SOME SLEEP.
WE'LL BE IN KAGOSHIMA SOON.
ages Maps Play
Murder prison term
Web Images
About 510,000
LET'S FIND A ROOM AS SOON AS WE GET THERE.

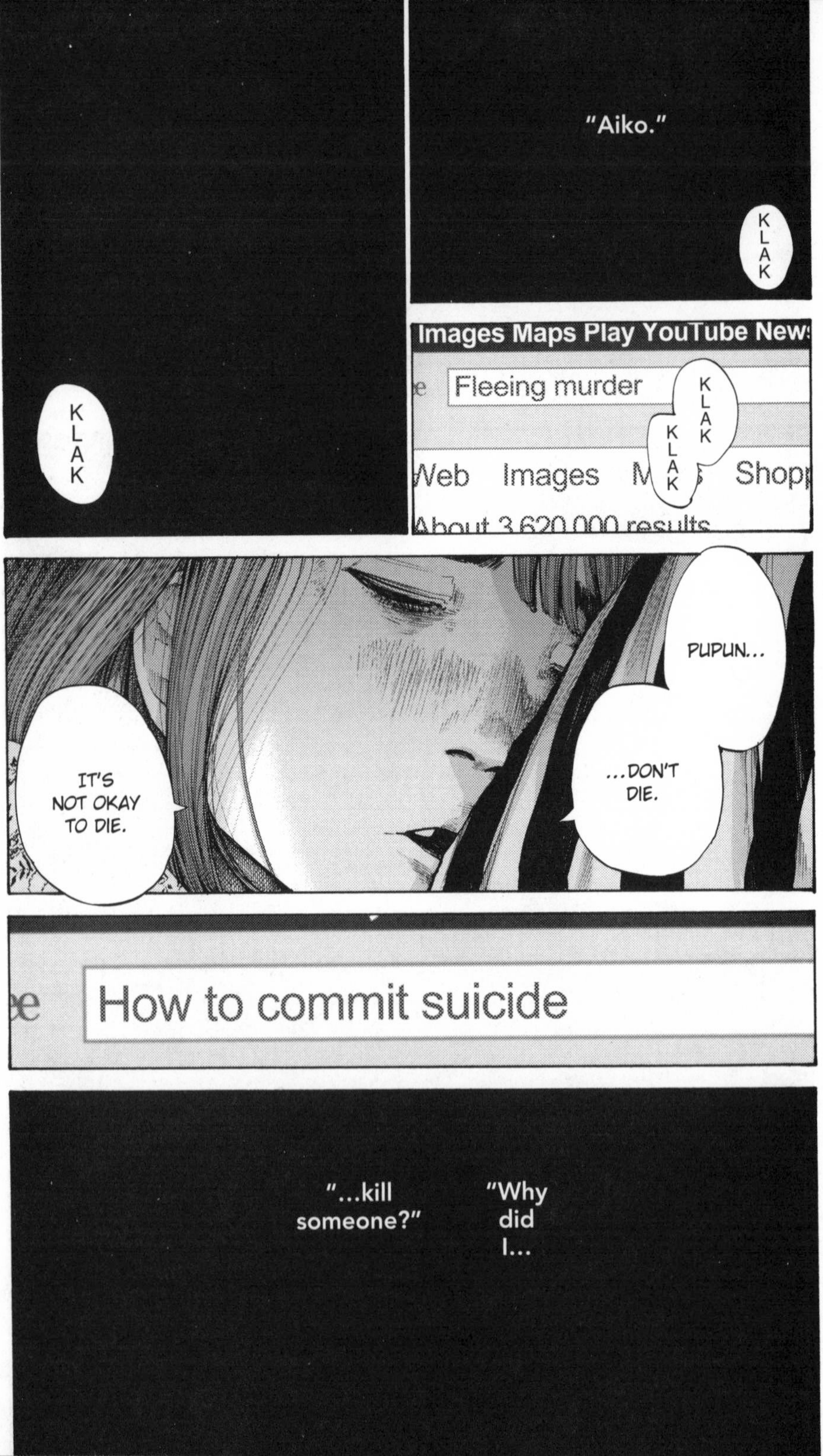
"Aiko."
KLAK
Images Maps Play YouTube New
Fleeing murder
KLAK
KLAK
Web Images Shopp
About 3,620,000 results
KLAK
PUPUN...
...DON'T DIE.
IT'S NOT OKAY TO DIE.
How to commit suicide
"Why did I...
...kill someone?"

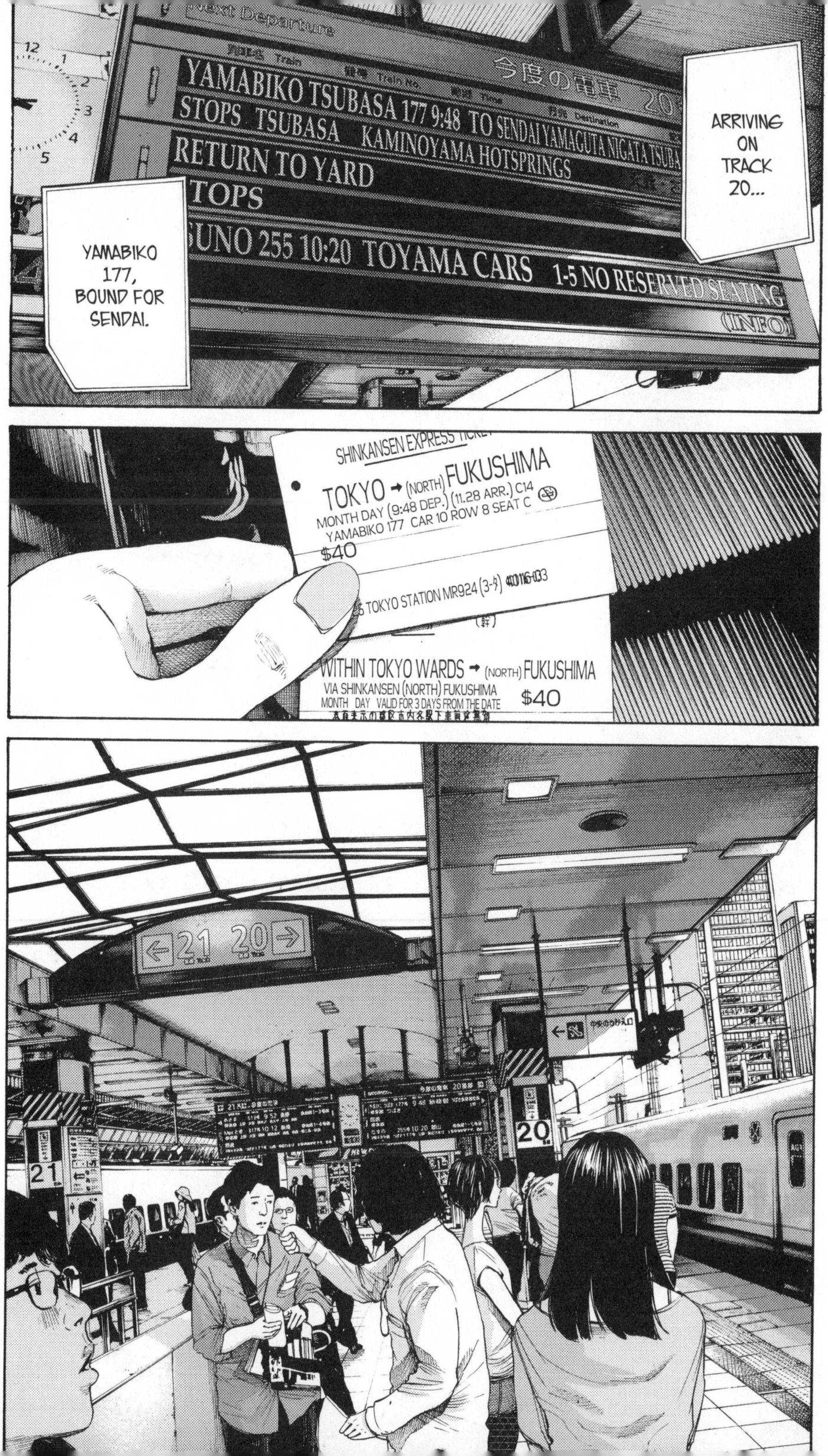
ARRIVING ON TRACK 20...
Next Departure
今度の電車
YAMABIKO TSUBASA 177 9:48 TO SENDAI YAMAGUTA NIGATA TSUBA
STOPS TSUBASA KAMINOYAMA HOTSPRINGS
RETURN TO YARD
TOPS
SUNO 255 10:20 TOYAMA CARS 1-5 NO RESERVED SEATING
(INFO)
YAMABIKO 177, BOUND FOR SENDAI.
SHINKANSEN EXPRESS TICKET
TOKYO → (NORTH) FUKUSHIMA
MONTH DAY (9:48 DEP.) (11.28 ARR.) C14
YAMABIKO 177 CAR 10 ROW 8 SEAT C
$40
TOKYO STATION MR924 (3-タ) 40116-03
WITHIN TOKYO WARDS → (NORTH) FUKUSHIMA
VIA SHINKANSEN (NORTH) FUKUSHIMA
MONTH DAY VALID FOR 3 DAYS FROM THE DATE
$40
21
20
20
21

Chapter 127

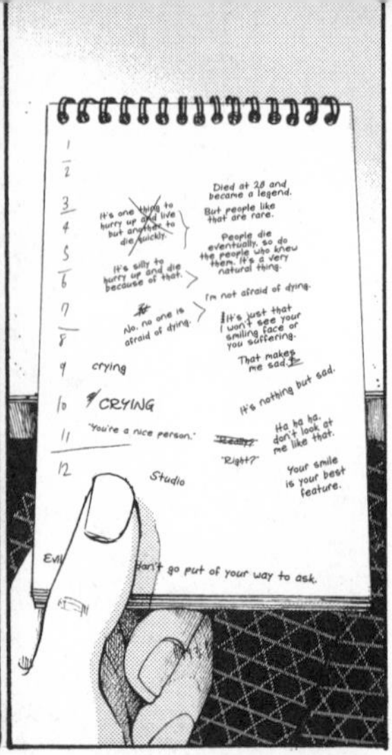
1
2
3
4
5
6
7
8
9
10
11
12
Died at 28 and became a legend.
But people like that are rare.
People die eventually, so do the people who knew them. It's a very natural thing.
It's one thing to hurry up and live but another to die quickly.
It's silly to hurry up and die because of that.
I'm not afraid of dying.
No, no one is afraid of dying.
It's just that I won't see your smiling face or you suffering.
That makes me sad.
crying
CRYING
It's nothing but sad.
"You're a nice person."
Ha ha ha, don't look at me like that.
"Right?"
Studio
Your smile is your best feature.
don't go put of your way to ask.

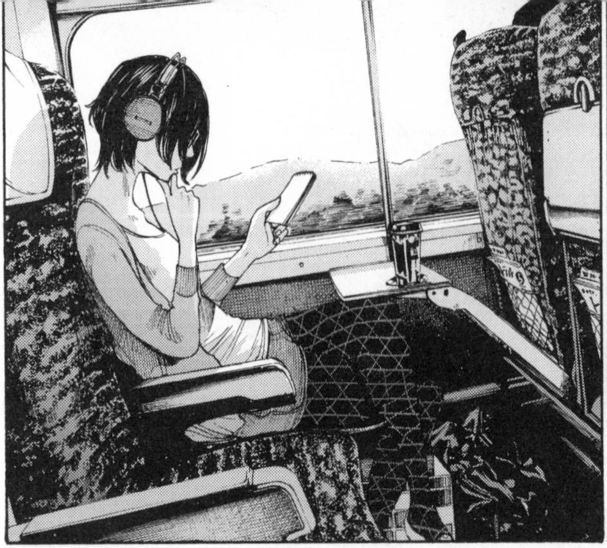

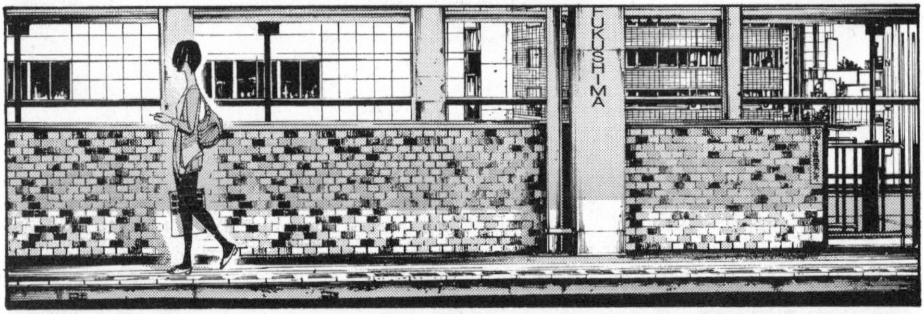
FUKUSHIMA

June 28.

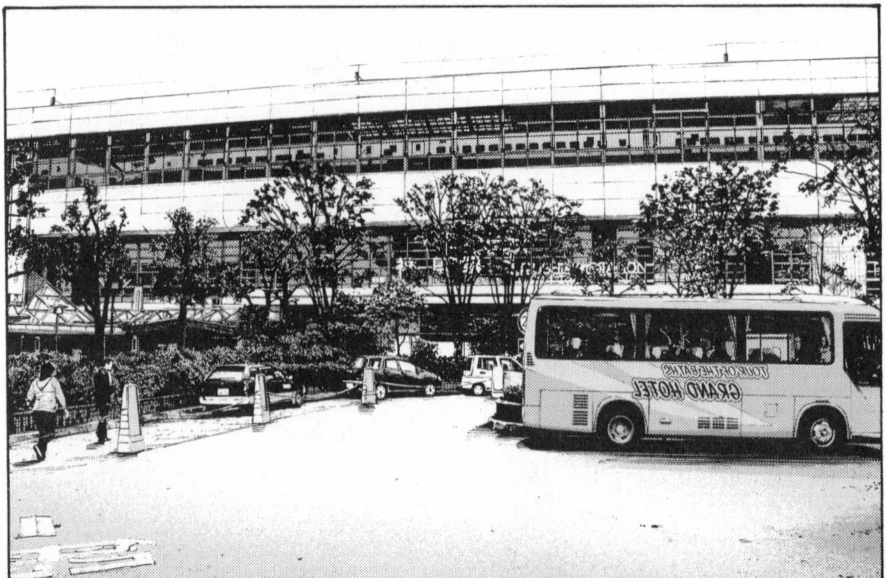

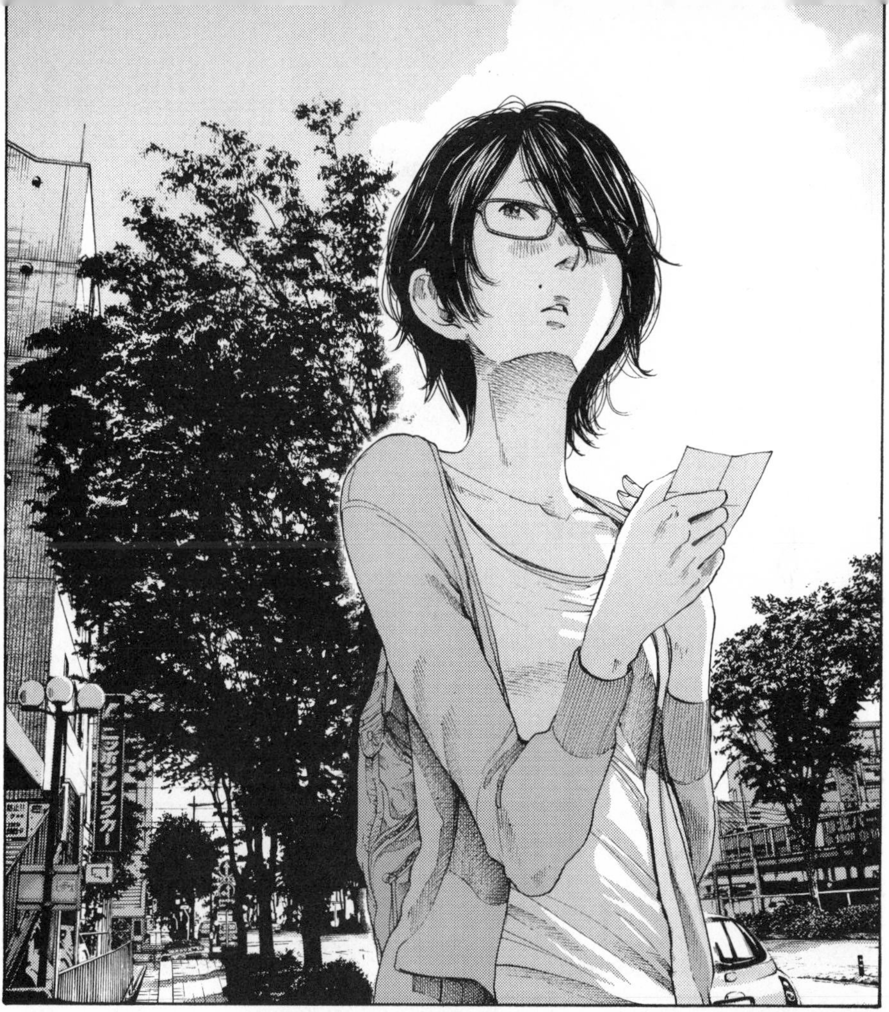
ニッポンレンタカー
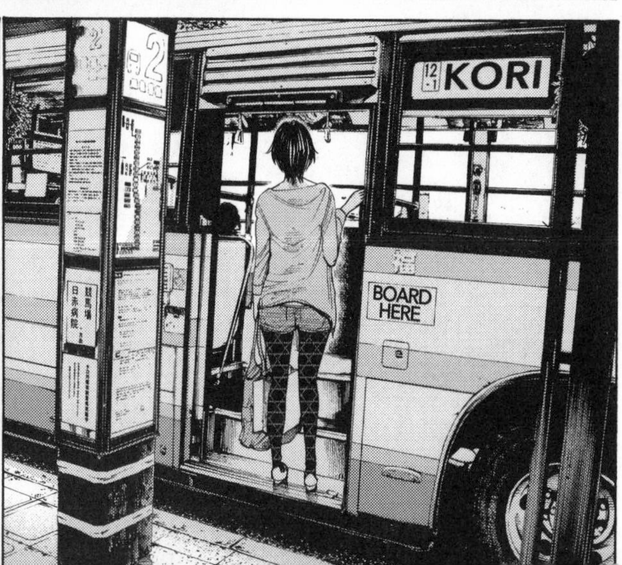
12-1 KORI
BOARD HERE
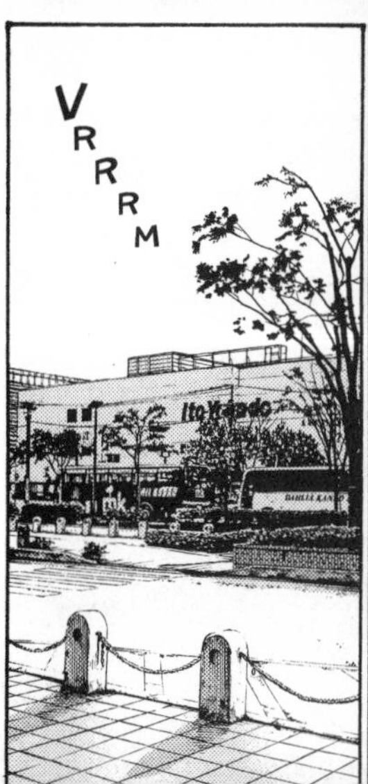
VRRRM

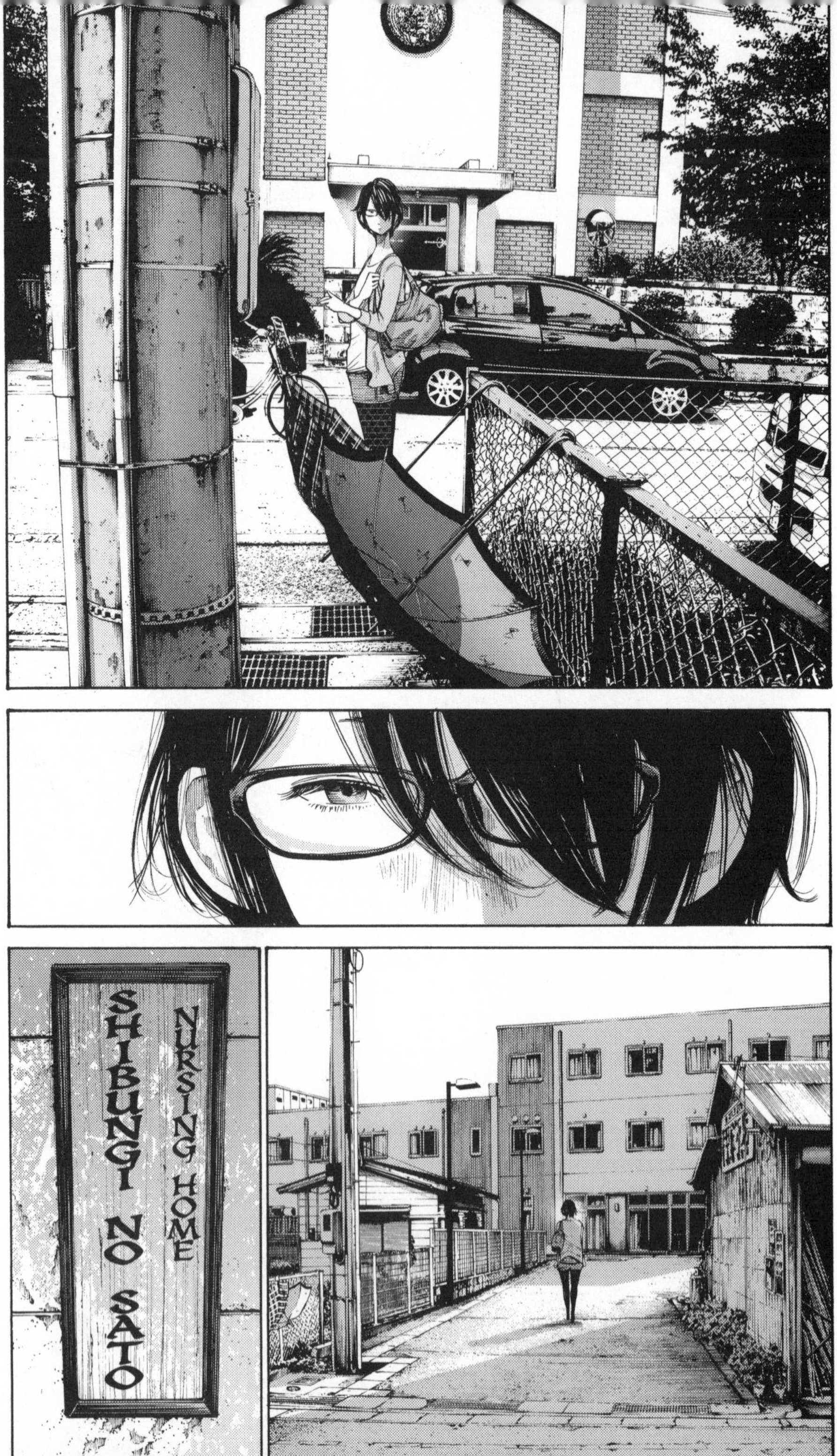
SHIBUNGI NO SATO
NURSING HOME

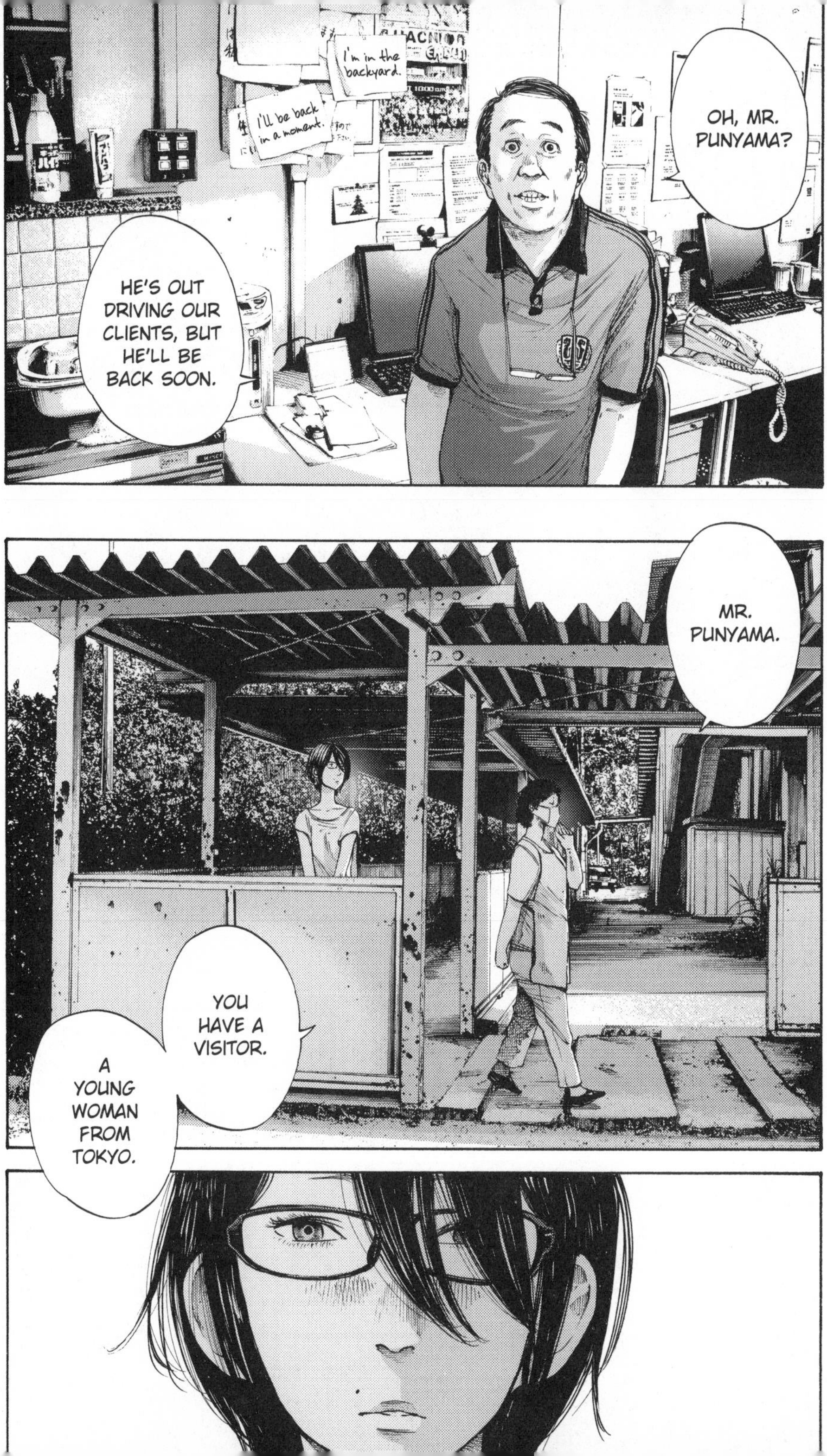
OH, MR. PUNYAMA?
I'm in the backyard.
I'll be back in a moment.
HE'S OUT DRIVING OUR CLIENTS, BUT HE'LL BE BACK SOON.
MR. PUNYAMA.
YOU HAVE A VISITOR.
A YOUNG WOMAN FROM TOKYO.

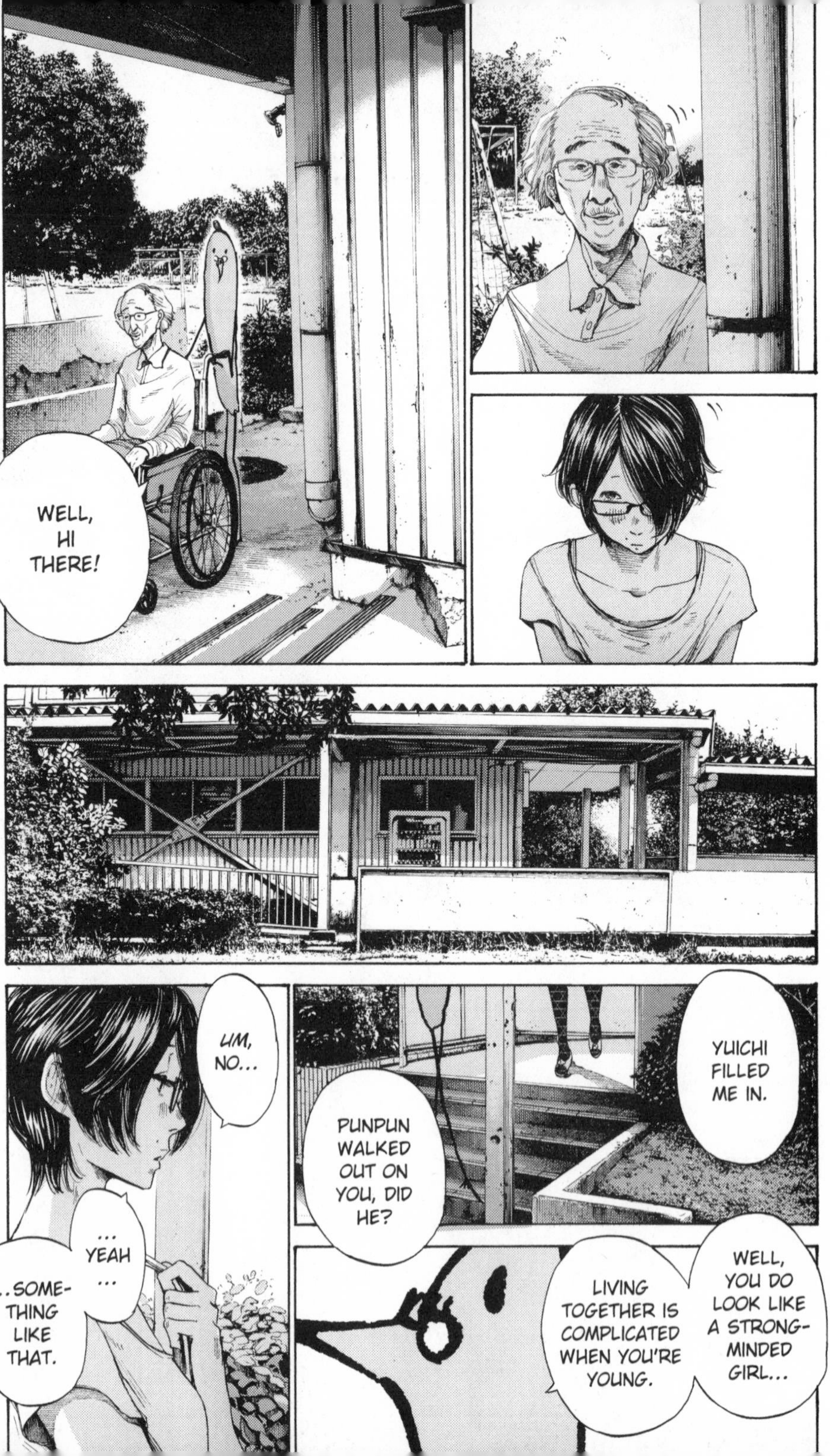
WELL, HI THERE!
YUICHI FILLED ME IN.
PUNPUN WALKED OUT ON YOU, DID HE?
WELL, YOU DO LOOK LIKE A STRONG-MINDED GIRL...
LIVING TOGETHER IS COMPLICATED WHEN YOU'RE YOUNG.
UM, NO...
...YEAH...
...SOME-THING LIKE THAT.

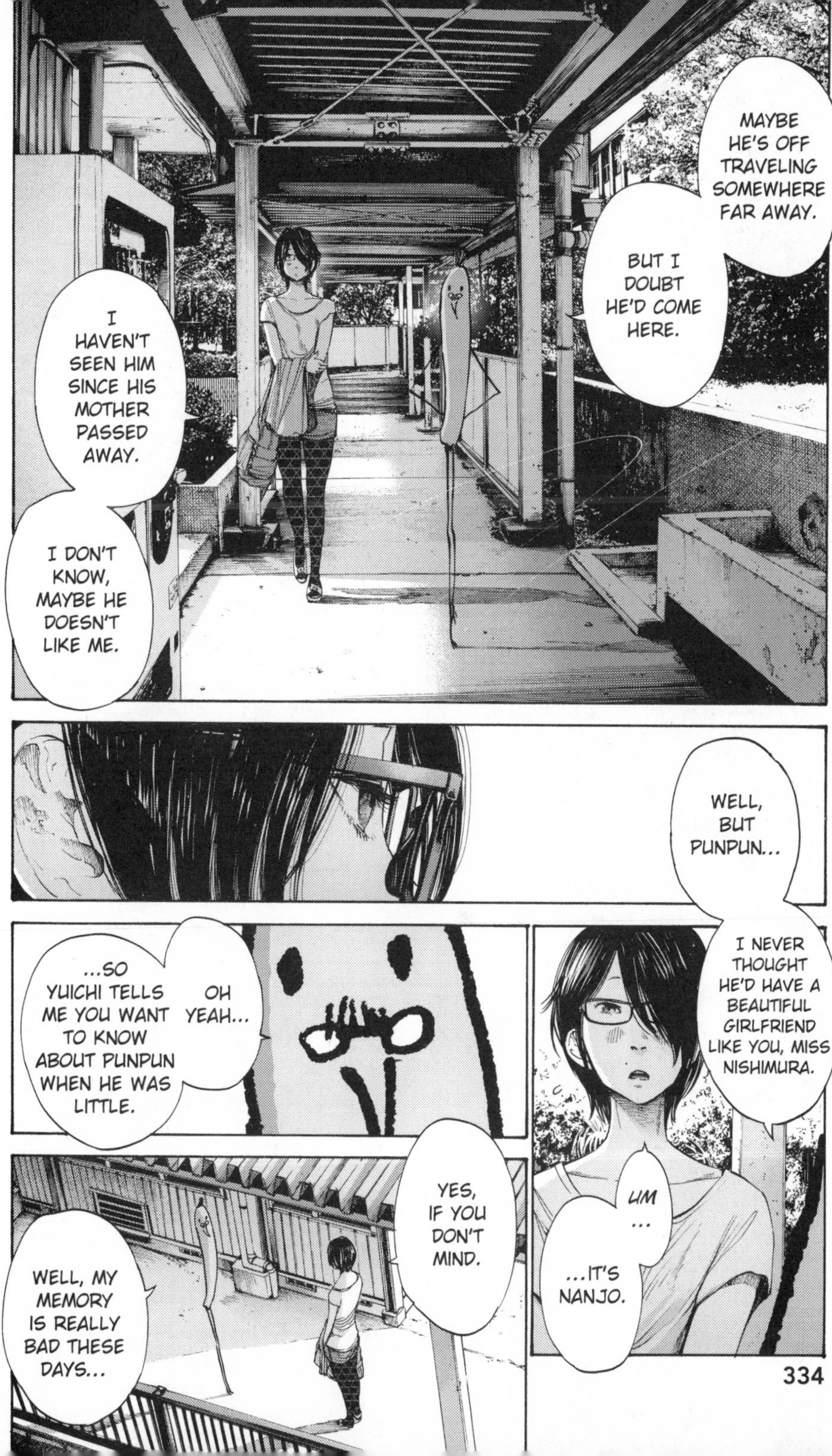

MAYBE HE'S OFF TRAVELING SOMEWHERE FAR AWAY.
BUT I DOUBT HE'D COME HERE.
I HAVEN'T SEEN HIM SINCE HIS MOTHER PASSED AWAY.
I DON'T KNOW, MAYBE HE DOESN'T LIKE ME.
WELL, BUT PUNPUN...
I NEVER THOUGHT HE'D HAVE A BEAUTIFUL GIRLFRIEND LIKE YOU, MISS NISHIMURA.
UM...
...IT'S NANJO.
OH YEAH...
...SO YUICHI TELLS ME YOU WANT TO KNOW ABOUT PUNPUN WHEN HE WAS LITTLE.
YES, IF YOU DON'T MIND.
WELL, MY MEMORY IS REALLY BAD THESE DAYS...

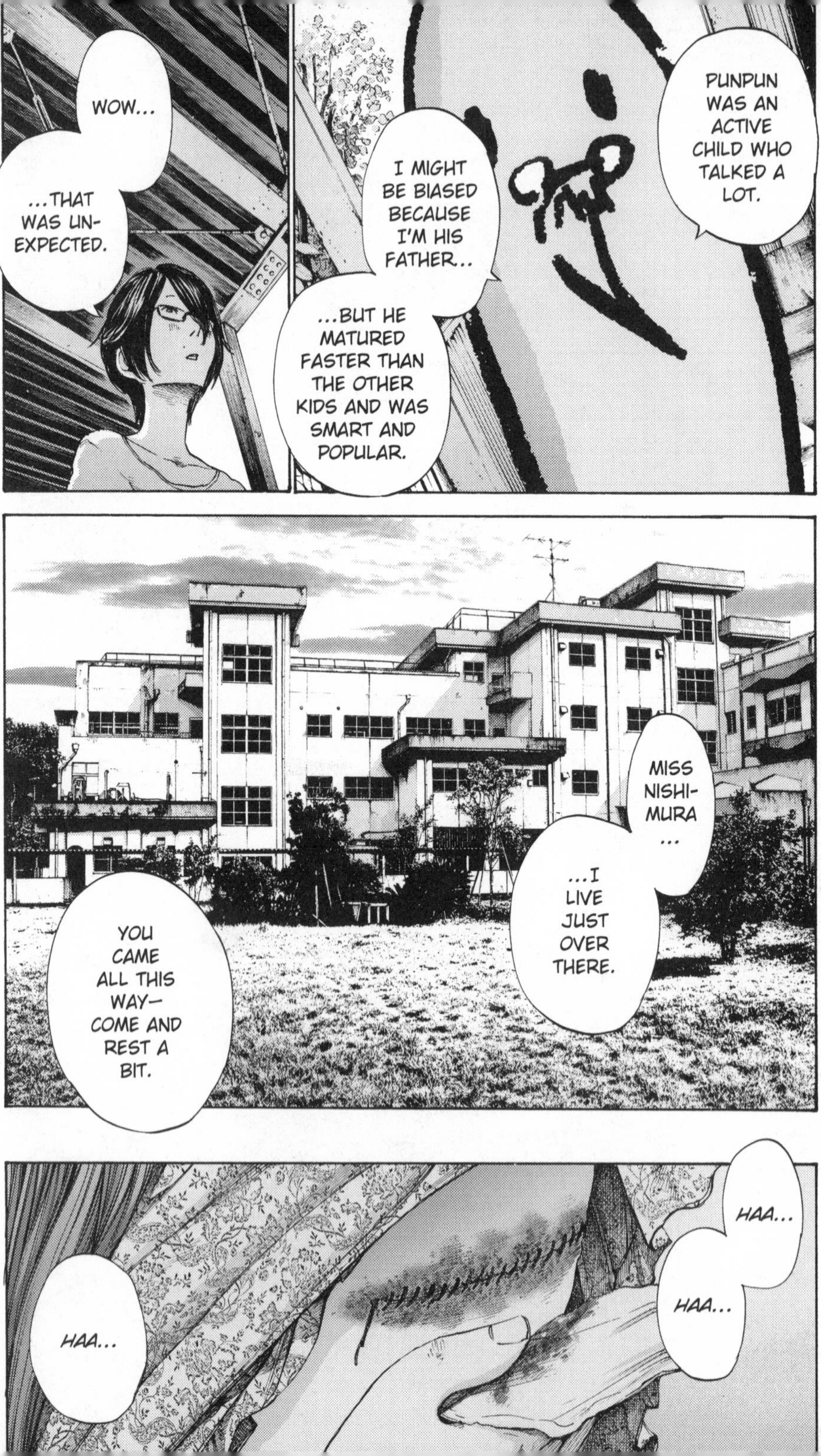
PUNPUN WAS AN ACTIVE CHILD WHO TALKED A LOT.
I MIGHT BE BIASED BECAUSE I'M HIS FATHER...
...BUT HE MATURED FASTER THAN THE OTHER KIDS AND WAS SMART AND POPULAR.
WOW...
...THAT WAS UN-EXPECTED.
MISS NISHI-MURA...
...I LIVE JUST OVER THERE.
YOU CAME ALL THIS WAY—COME AND REST A BIT.
HAA...
HAA...
HAA...

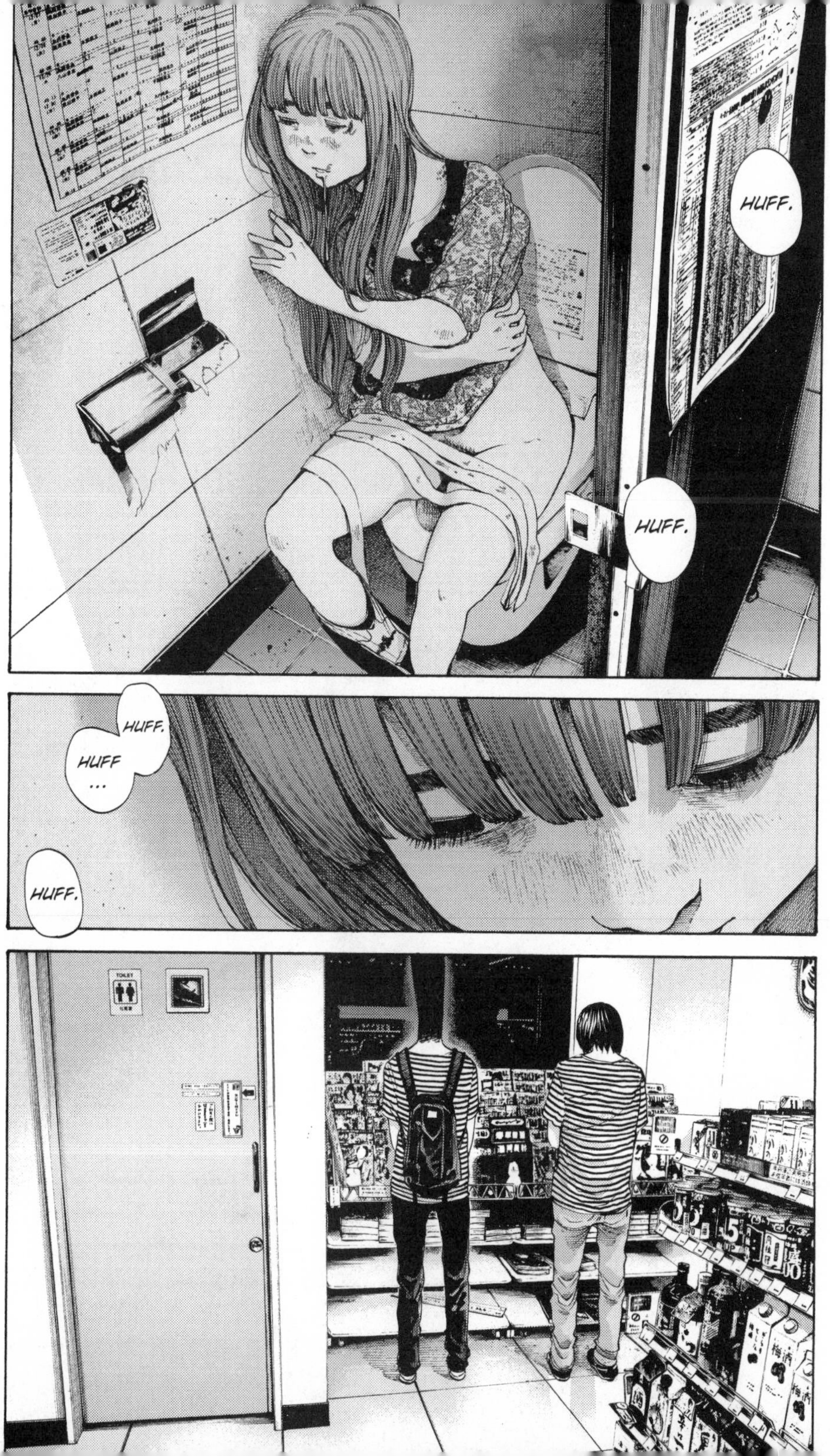
HUFF.
HUFF.
HUFF.
HUFF
...
HUFF.

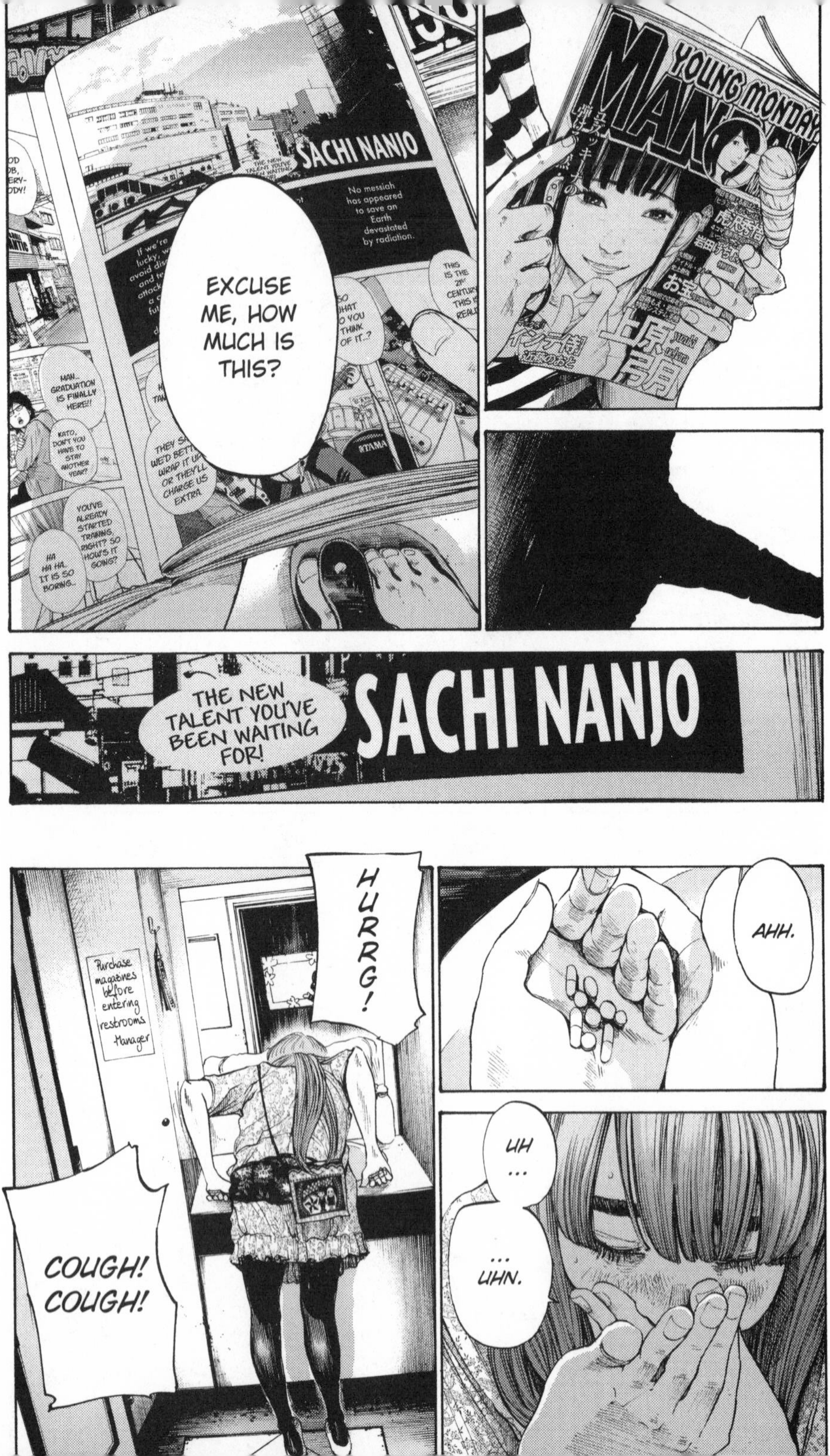
YOUNG MONDAY
SACHI NANJO
No messiah has appeared to save an Earth devastated by radiation.
EXCUSE ME, HOW MUCH IS THIS?
MAN... GRADUATION IS FINALLY HERE!!
KATO, DON'T YOU HAVE TO STAY ANOTHER YEAR?
YOU'VE ALREADY STARTED TRAINING, RIGHT? SO HOW'S IT GOING?
HA HA HA. IT IS SO BORING...
SACHI NANJO
THE NEW TALENT YOU'VE BEEN WAITING FOR!
AHH.
UH ...
... UHN.
HURRG!
Purchase magazines before entering restrooms -Manager
COUGH! COUGH!

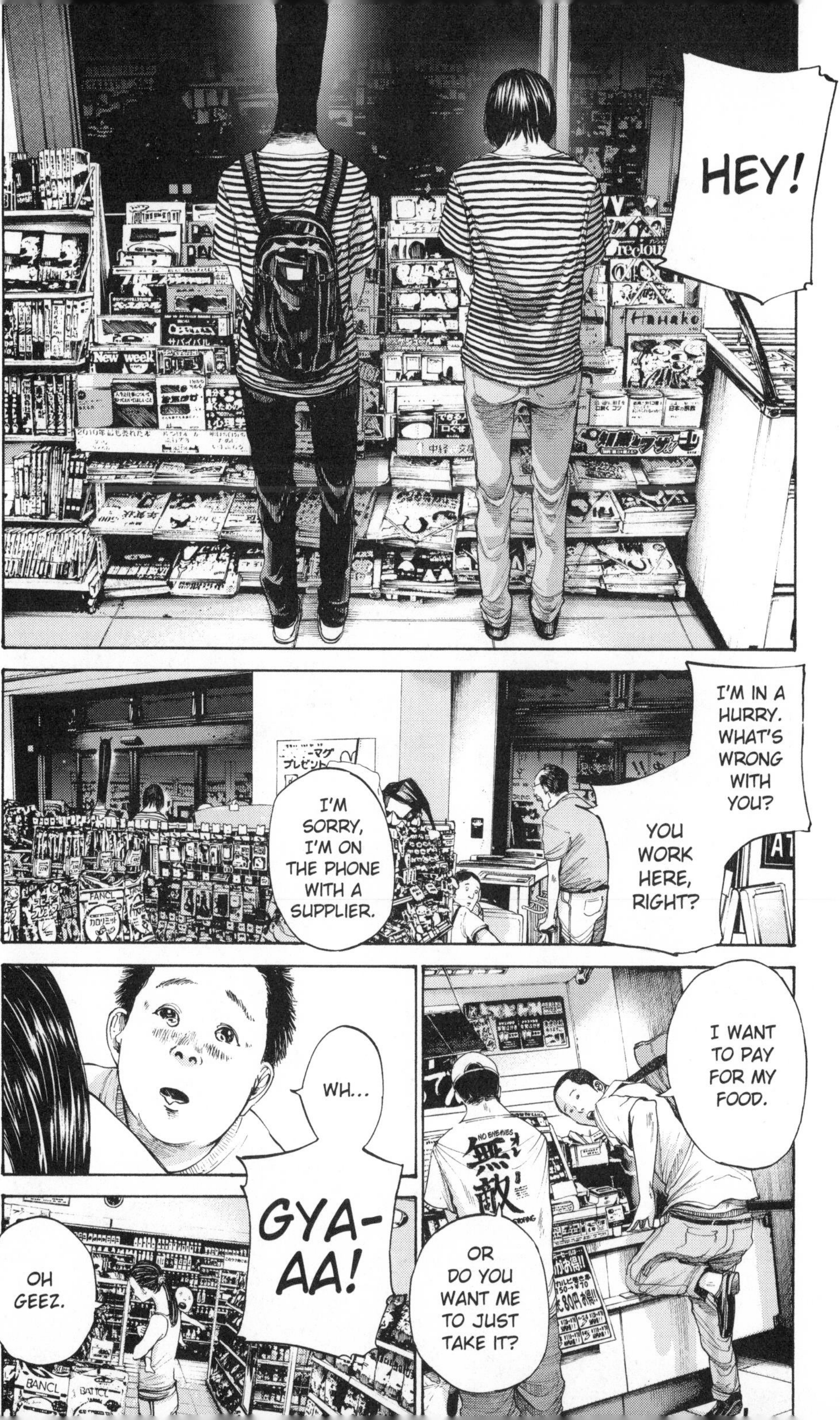
HEY!
I'M IN A HURRY. WHAT'S WRONG WITH YOU?
YOU WORK HERE, RIGHT?
I'M SORRY, I'M ON THE PHONE WITH A SUPPLIER.
I WANT TO PAY FOR MY FOOD.
OR DO YOU WANT ME TO JUST TAKE IT?
WH...
GYA-AA!
OH GEEZ.

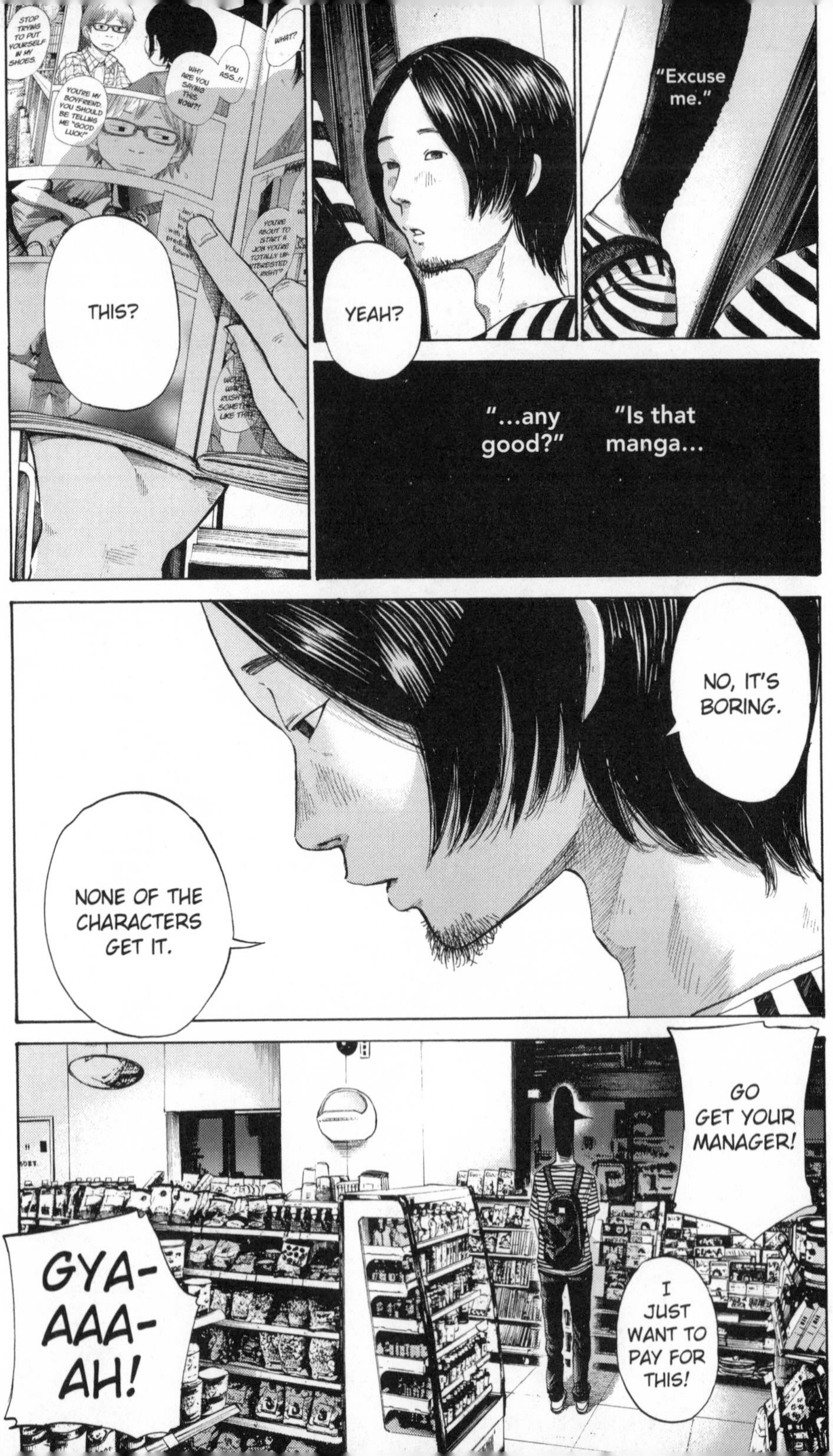
"Excuse me."
YEAH?
"Is that manga...
"...any good?"
WHAT?
YOU ASS..!!
WHY ARE YOU SAYING THIS NOW?!
STOP TRYING TO PUT YOURSELF IN MY SHOES.
YOU'RE MY BOYFRIEND. YOU SHOULD BE TELLING ME "GOOD LUCK!"
THIS?
NO, IT'S BORING.
NONE OF THE CHARACTERS GET IT.
GO GET YOUR MANAGER!
I JUST WANT TO PAY FOR THIS!
GYA-AAA-AH!

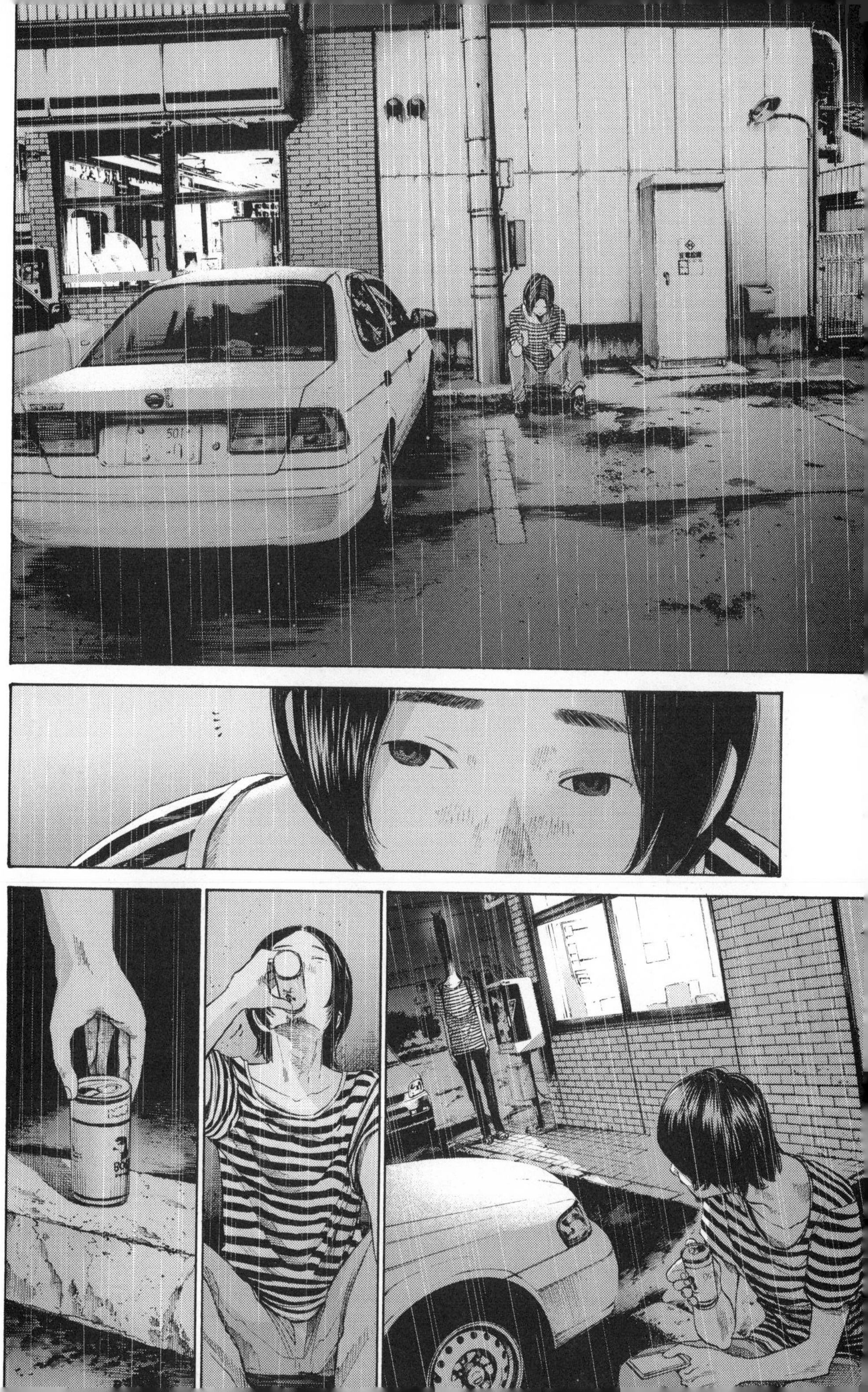

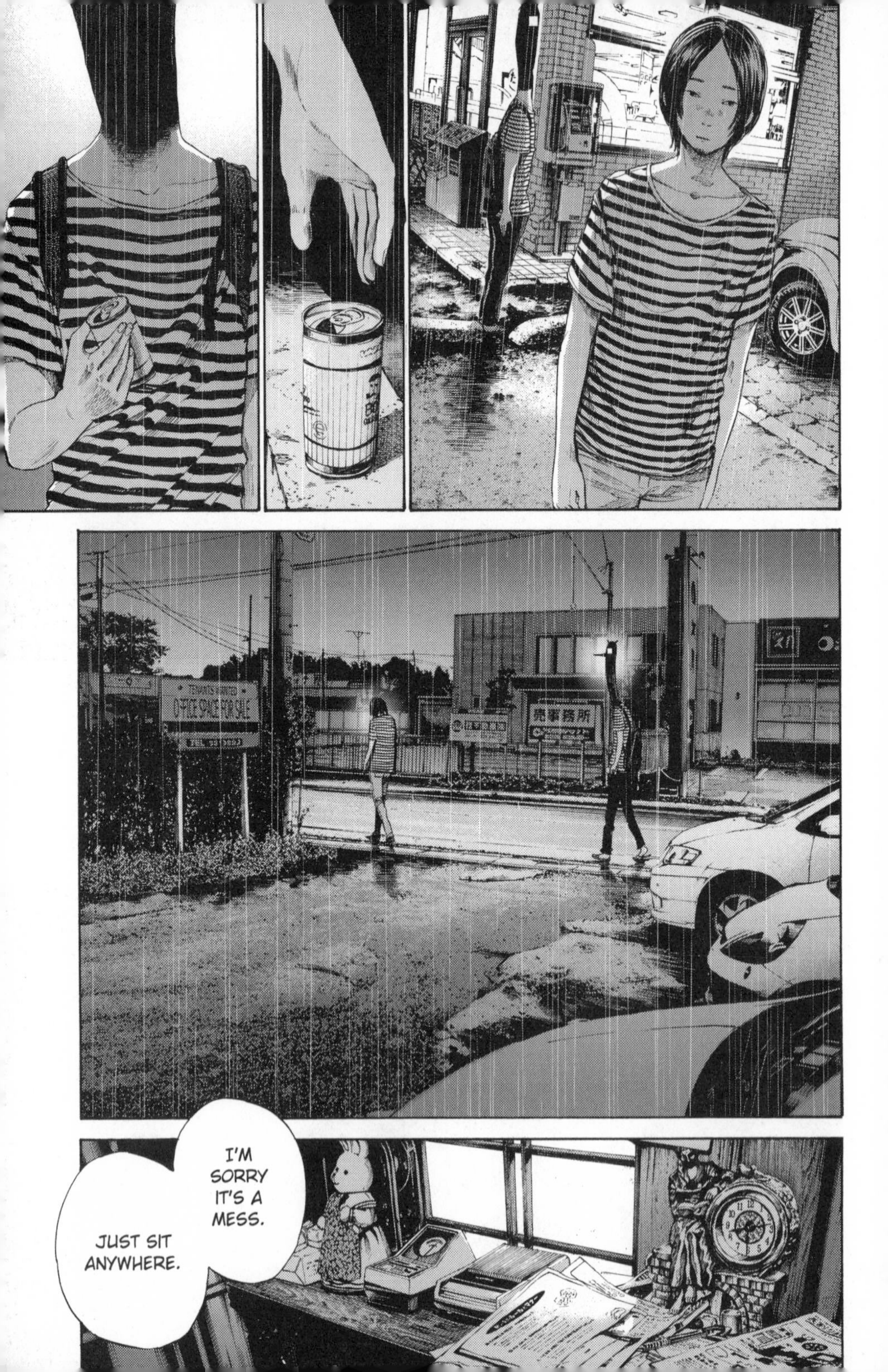
I'M SORRY IT'S A MESS.
JUST SIT ANYWHERE.

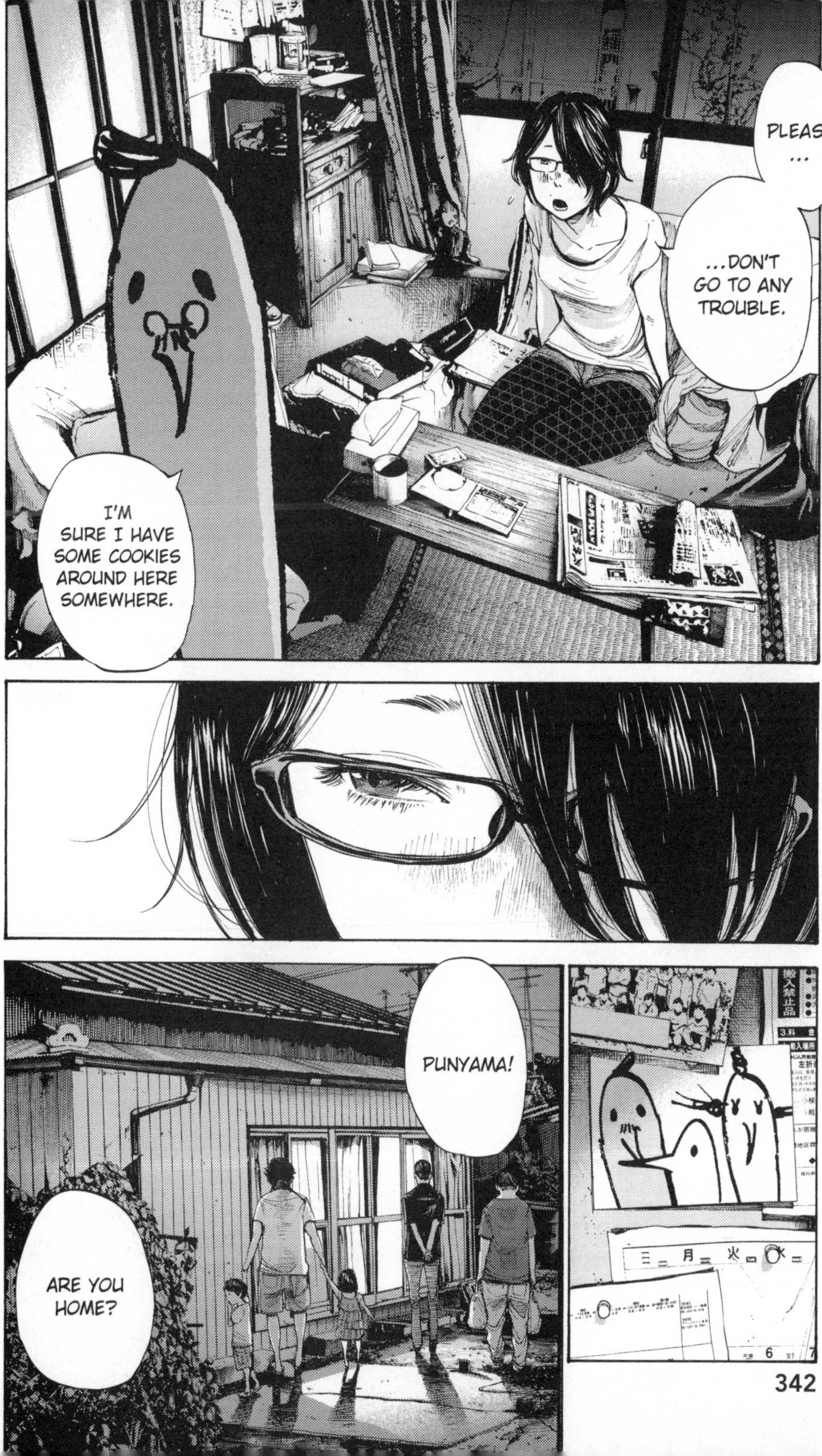
PLEASE ...
...DON'T GO TO ANY TROUBLE.
I'M SURE I HAVE SOME COOKIES AROUND HERE SOMEWHERE.
PUNYAMA!
ARE YOU HOME?

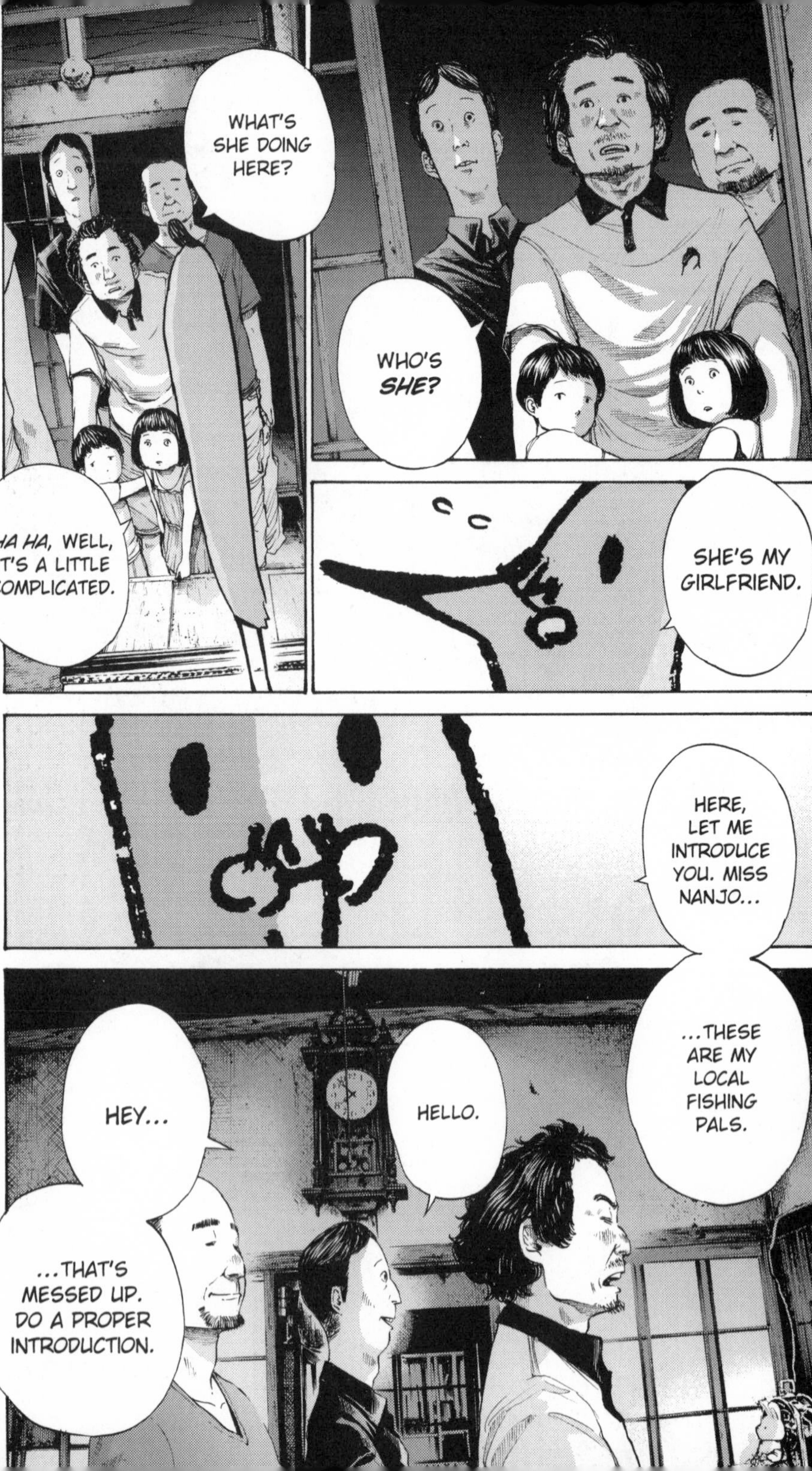
WHO'S *SHE?*
SHE'S MY GIRLFRIEND.
WHAT'S SHE DOING HERE?
HA HA, WELL, IT'S A LITTLE COMPLICATED.
HERE, LET ME INTRODUCE YOU. MISS NANJO...
...THESE ARE MY LOCAL FISHING PALS.
HELLO.
HEY...
...THAT'S MESSED UP. DO A PROPER INTRODUCTION.

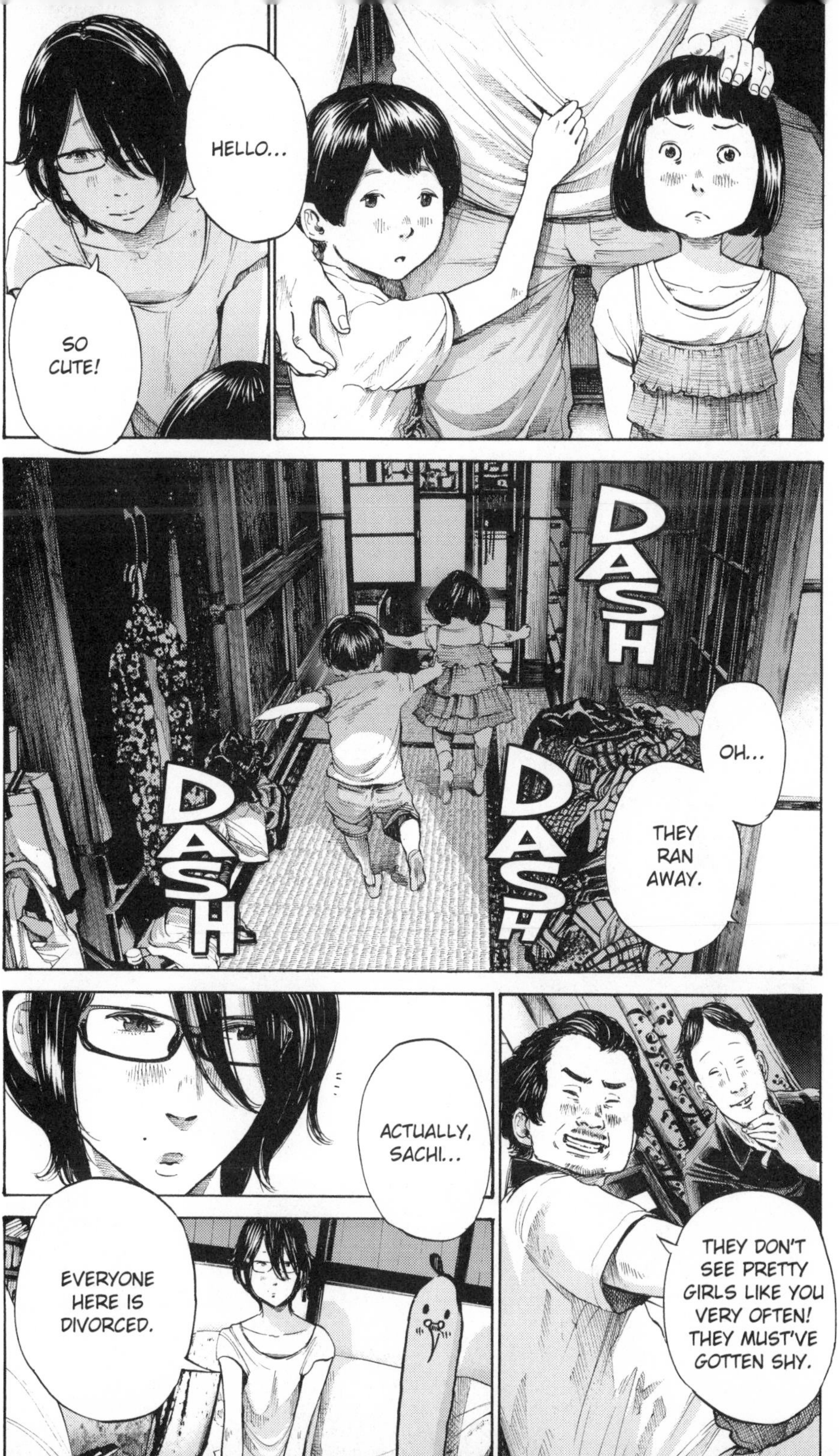

HELLO...
SO CUTE!
DASH
DASH
DASH
OH...
THEY RAN AWAY.
THEY DON'T SEE PRETTY GIRLS LIKE YOU VERY OFTEN! THEY MUST'VE GOTTEN SHY.
ACTUALLY, SACHI...
EVERYONE HERE IS DIVORCED.

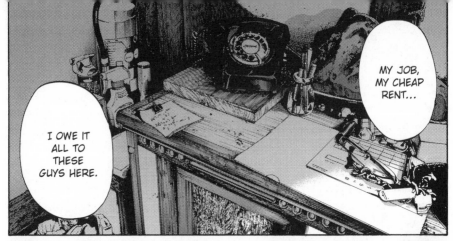

MY JOB, MY CHEAP RENT...

I OWE IT ALL TO THESE GUYS HERE.

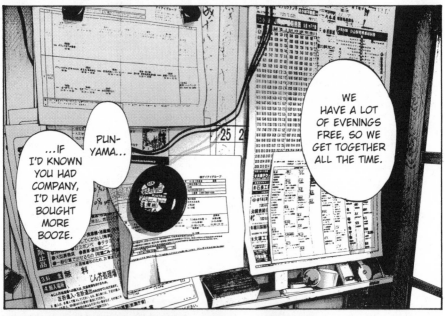

WE HAVE A LOT OF EVENINGS FREE, SO WE GET TOGETHER ALL THE TIME.

PUN-YAMA...

...IF I'D KNOWN YOU HAD COMPANY, I'D HAVE BOUGHT MORE BOOZE.

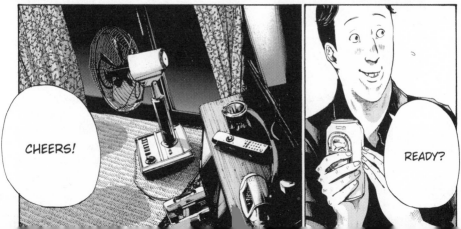

CHEERS!

READY?

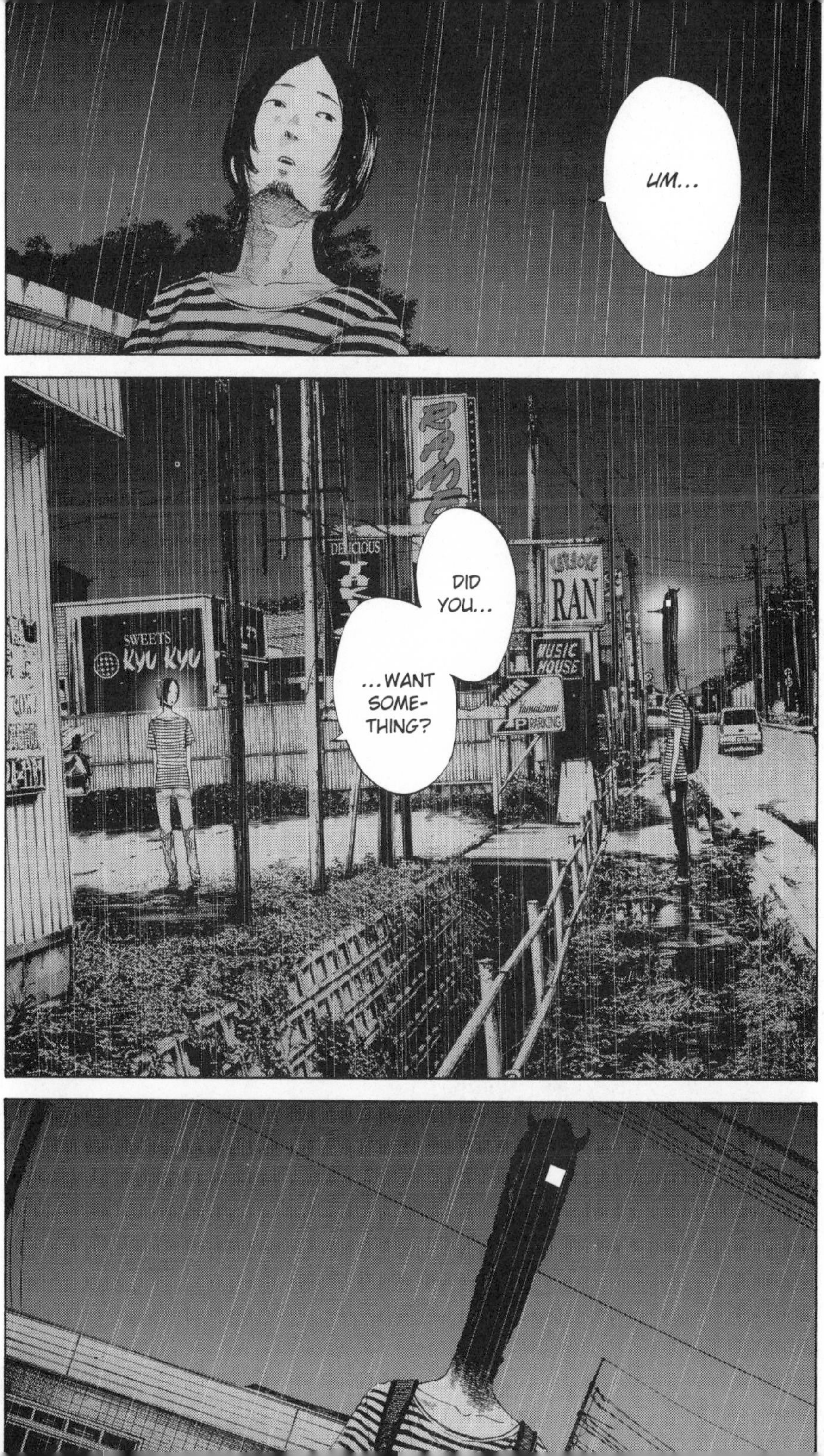
UM...
DID YOU...
...WANT SOMETHING?
RAN
MUSIC HOUSE
PARKING
DELICIOUS
SWEETS
KYU KYU

Chapter 128

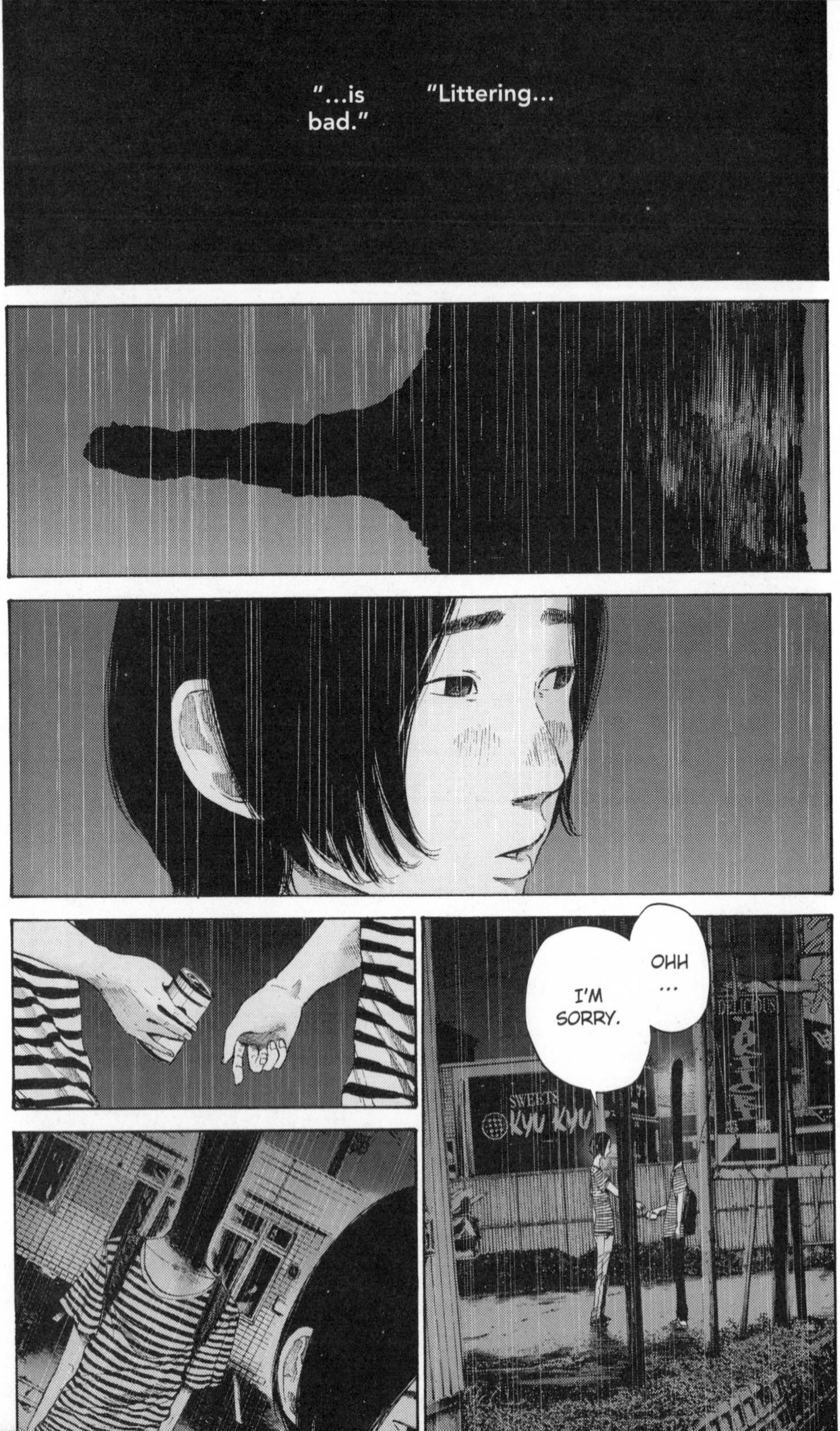
"Littering...
"...is bad."
OHH ...
I'M SORRY.
SWEETS
KYU KYU

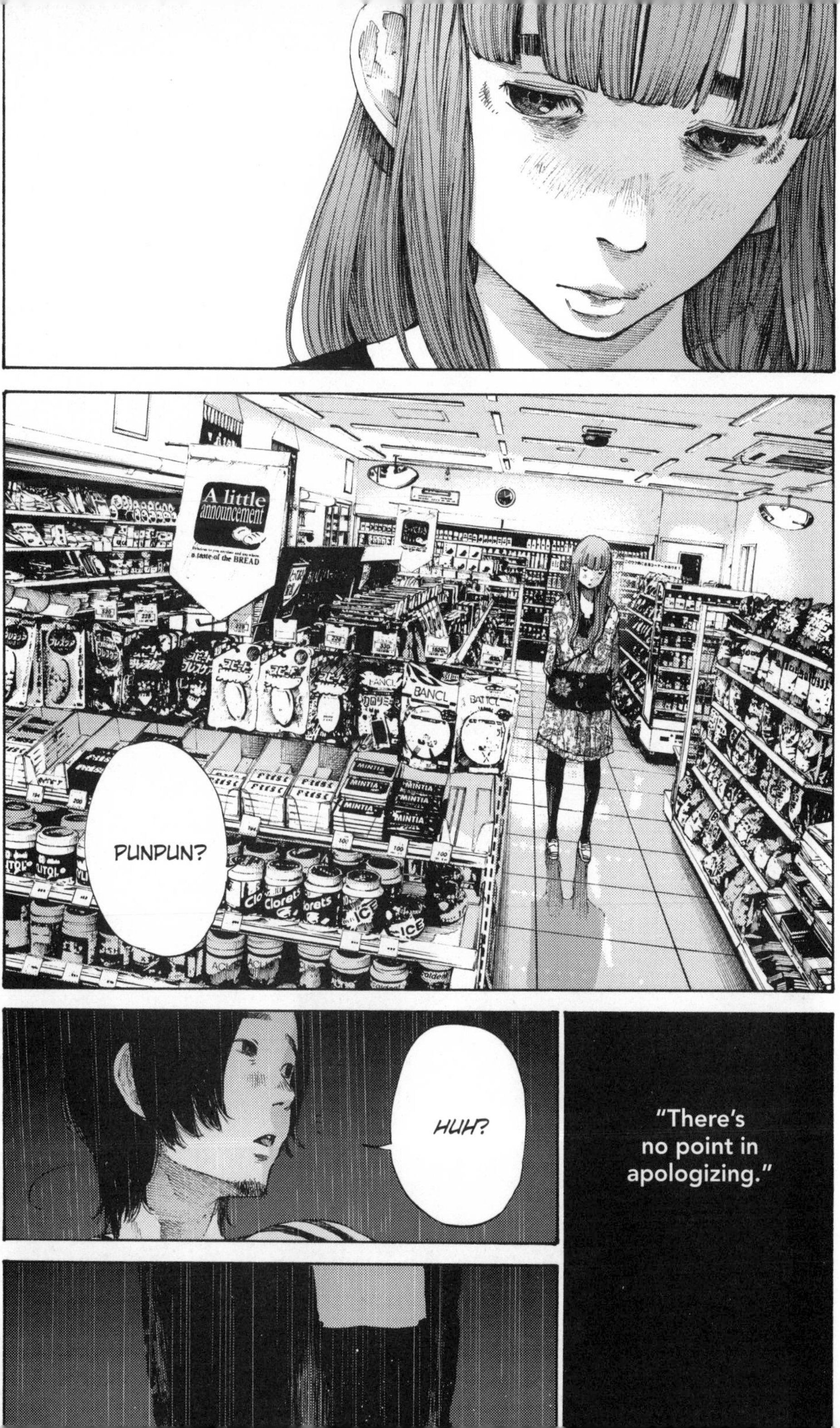
A little announcement
a taste of the BREAD
MINTIA
Clorets
ICE
PUNPUN?
"There's no point in apologizing."
HUH?

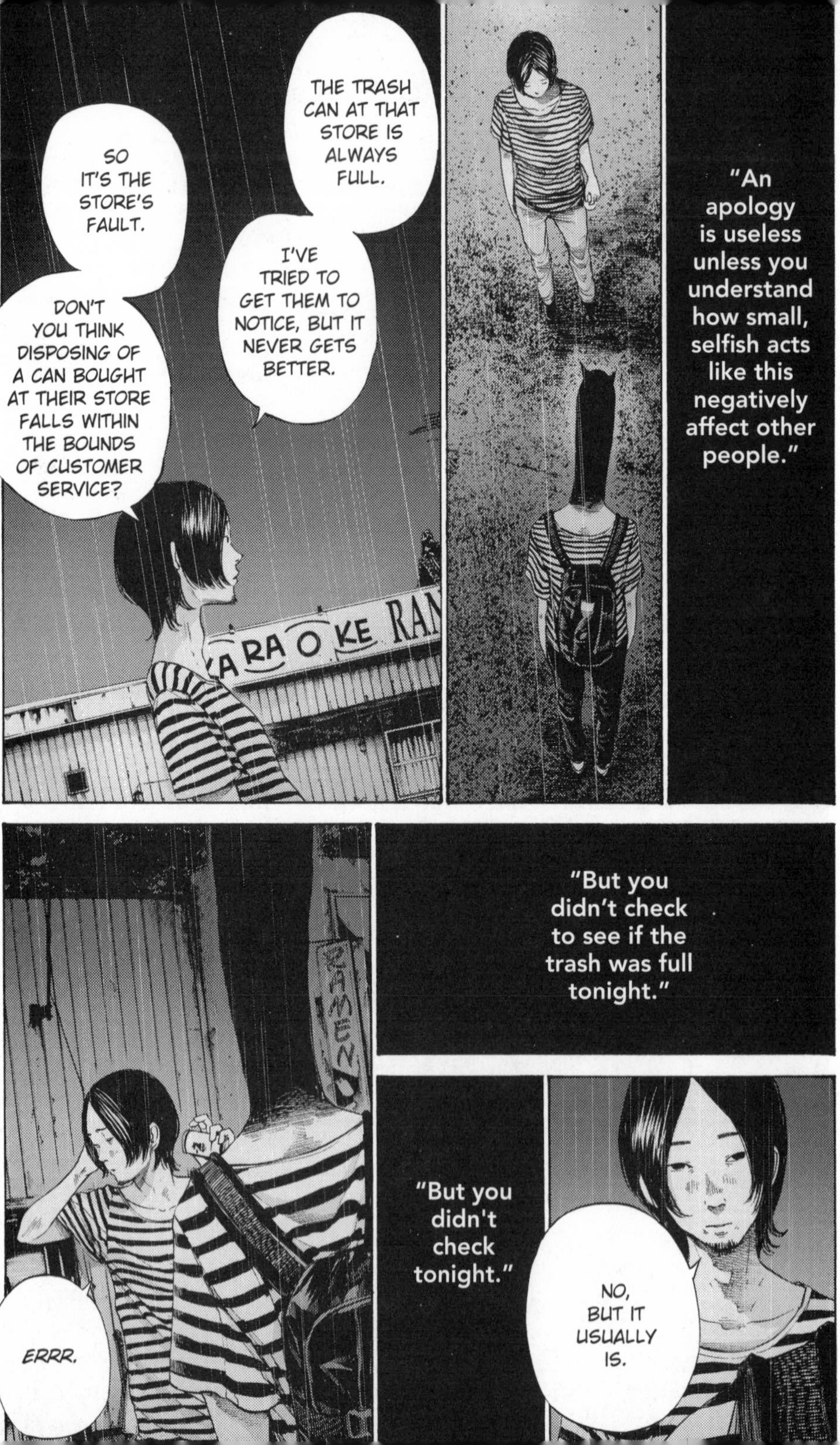
"An apology is useless unless you understand how small, selfish acts like this negatively affect other people."
THE TRASH CAN AT THAT STORE IS ALWAYS FULL.
SO IT'S THE STORE'S FAULT.
I'VE TRIED TO GET THEM TO NOTICE, BUT IT NEVER GETS BETTER.
DON'T YOU THINK DISPOSING OF A CAN BOUGHT AT THEIR STORE FALLS WITHIN THE BOUNDS OF CUSTOMER SERVICE?
KARAOKE
"But you didn't check to see if the trash was full tonight."
NO, BUT IT USUALLY IS.
"But you didn't check tonight."
ERRR.

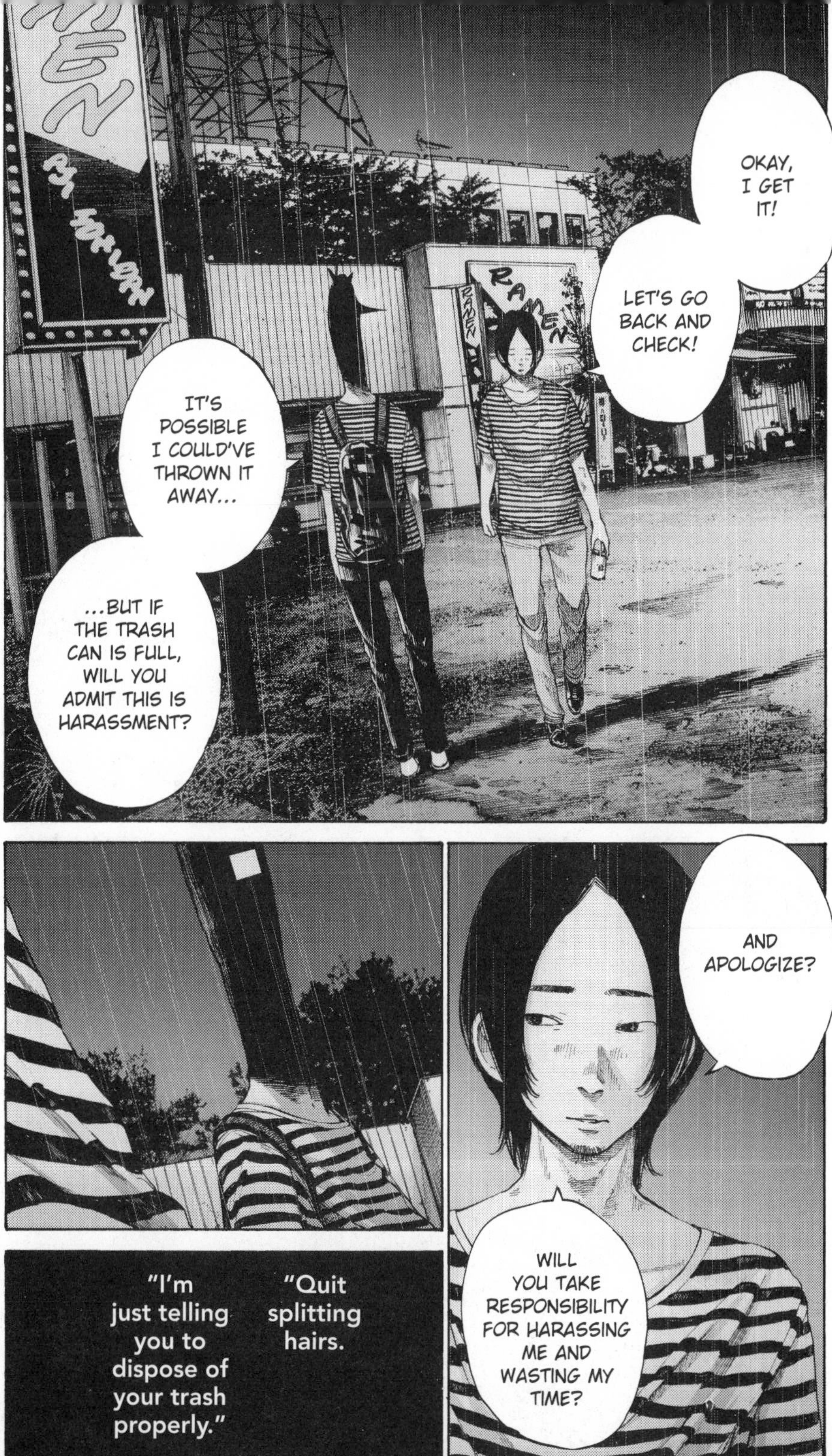
OKAY, I GET IT!
LET'S GO BACK AND CHECK!
RAMEN
IT'S POSSIBLE I COULD'VE THROWN IT AWAY...
...BUT IF THE TRASH CAN IS FULL, WILL YOU ADMIT THIS IS HARASSMENT?
AND APOLOGIZE?
WILL YOU TAKE RESPONSIBILITY FOR HARASSING ME AND WASTING MY TIME?
"Quit splitting hairs.
"I'm just telling you to dispose of your trash properly."

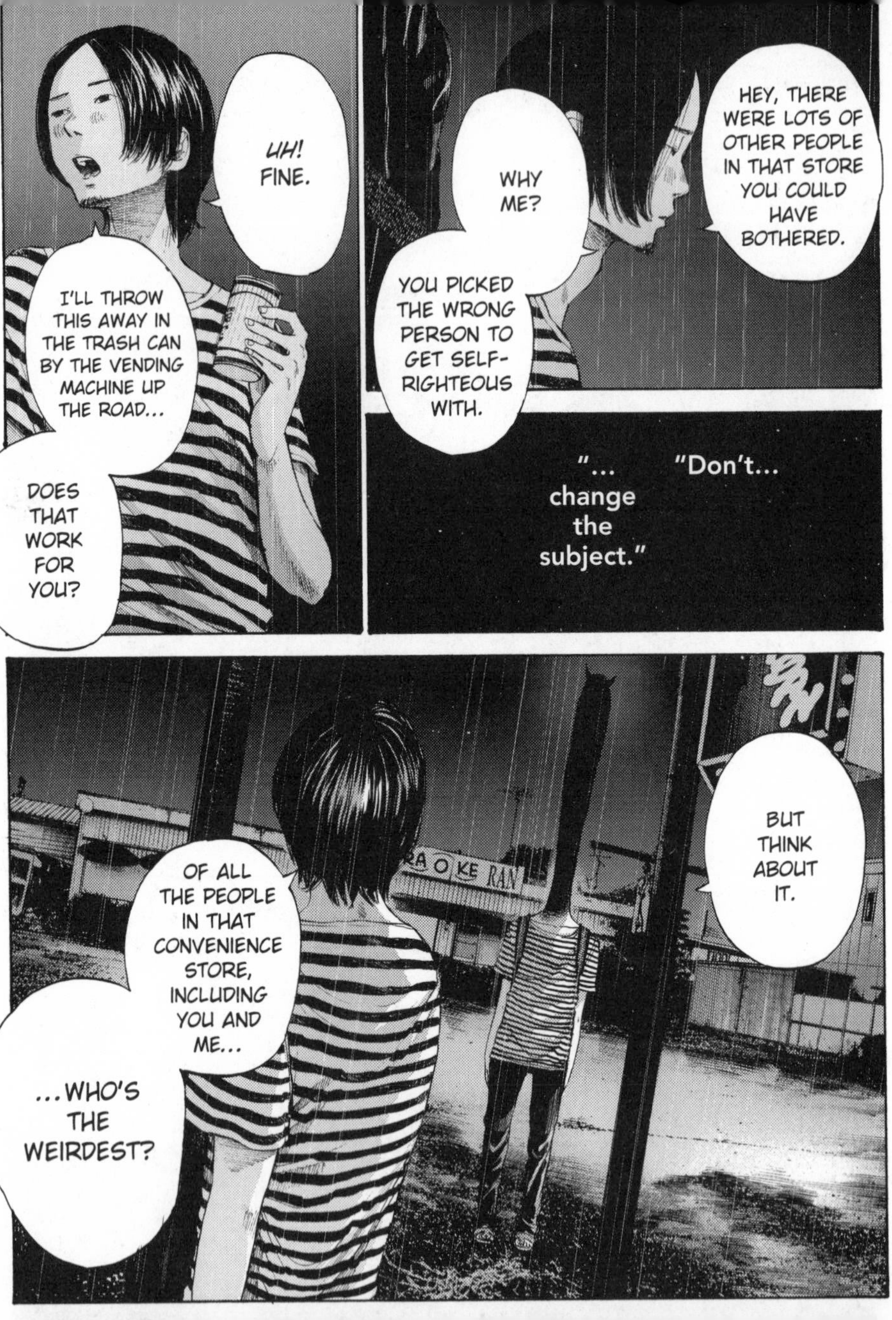
HEY, THERE WERE LOTS OF OTHER PEOPLE IN THAT STORE YOU COULD HAVE BOTHERED.
WHY ME?
YOU PICKED THE WRONG PERSON TO GET SELF-RIGHTEOUS WITH.
"Don't...
"... change the subject."
UH! FINE.
I'LL THROW THIS AWAY IN THE TRASH CAN BY THE VENDING MACHINE UP THE ROAD...
DOES THAT WORK FOR YOU?
BUT THINK ABOUT IT.
OF ALL THE PEOPLE IN THAT CONVENIENCE STORE, INCLUDING YOU AND ME...
...WHO'S THE WEIRDEST?

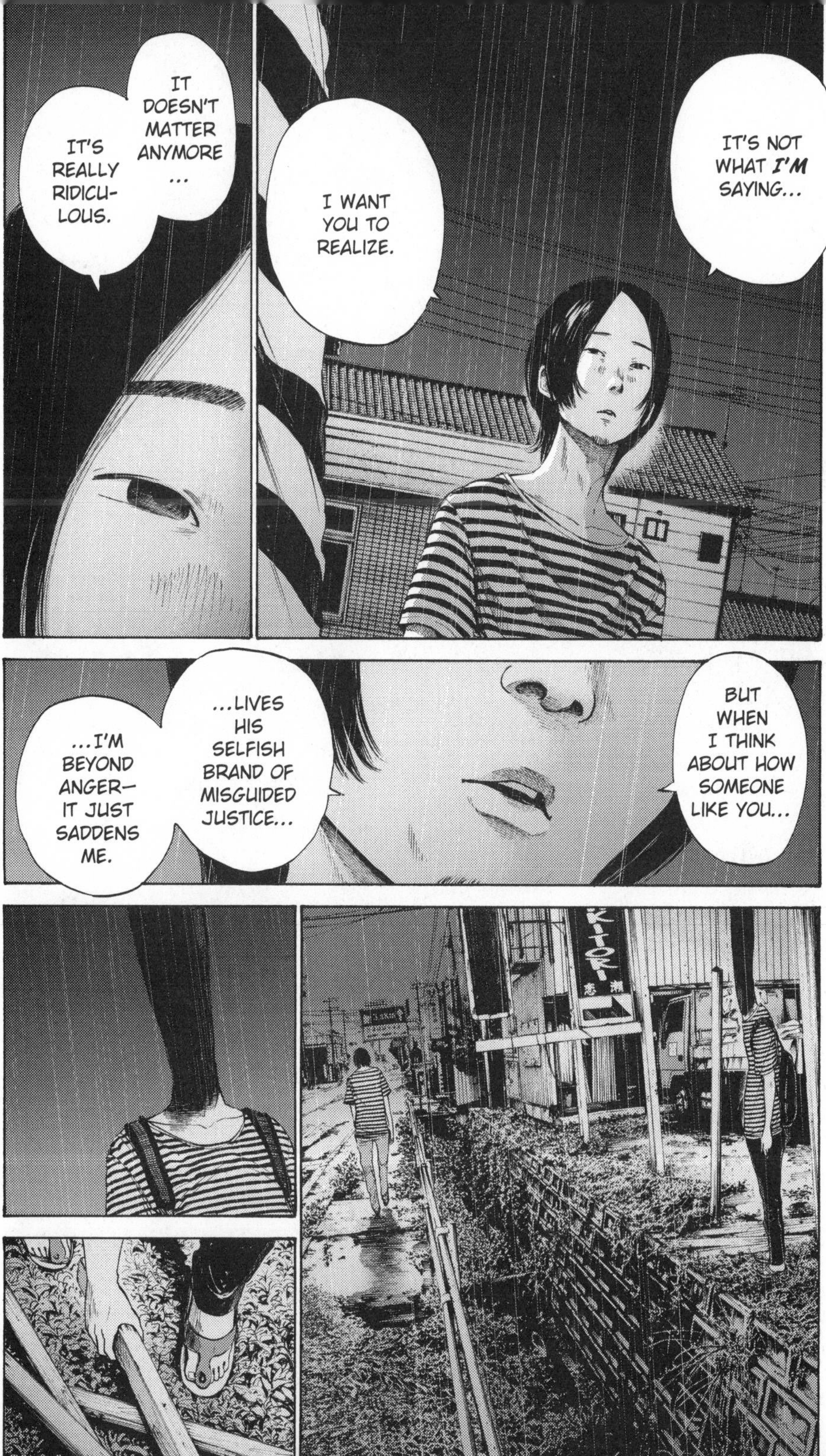
IT'S NOT WHAT *I'M* SAYING...
I WANT YOU TO REALIZE.
IT DOESN'T MATTER ANYMORE...
IT'S REALLY RIDICULOUS.
BUT WHEN I THINK ABOUT HOW SOMEONE LIKE YOU...
...LIVES HIS SELFISH BRAND OF MISGUIDED JUSTICE...
...I'M BEYOND ANGER—IT JUST SADDENS ME.

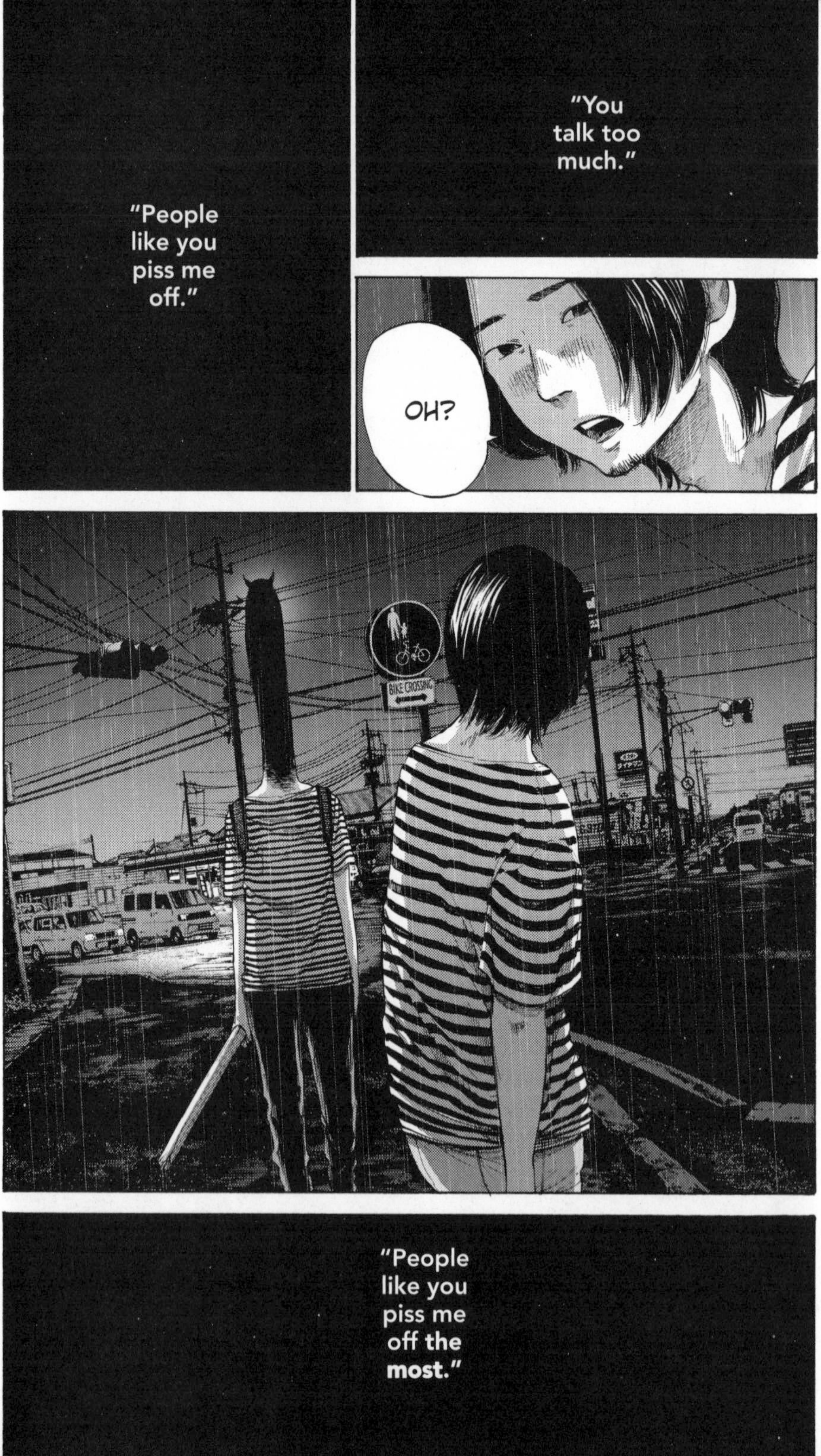
"You talk too much."
OH?
"People like you piss me off."
BIKE CROSSING
"People like you piss me off the **most**."

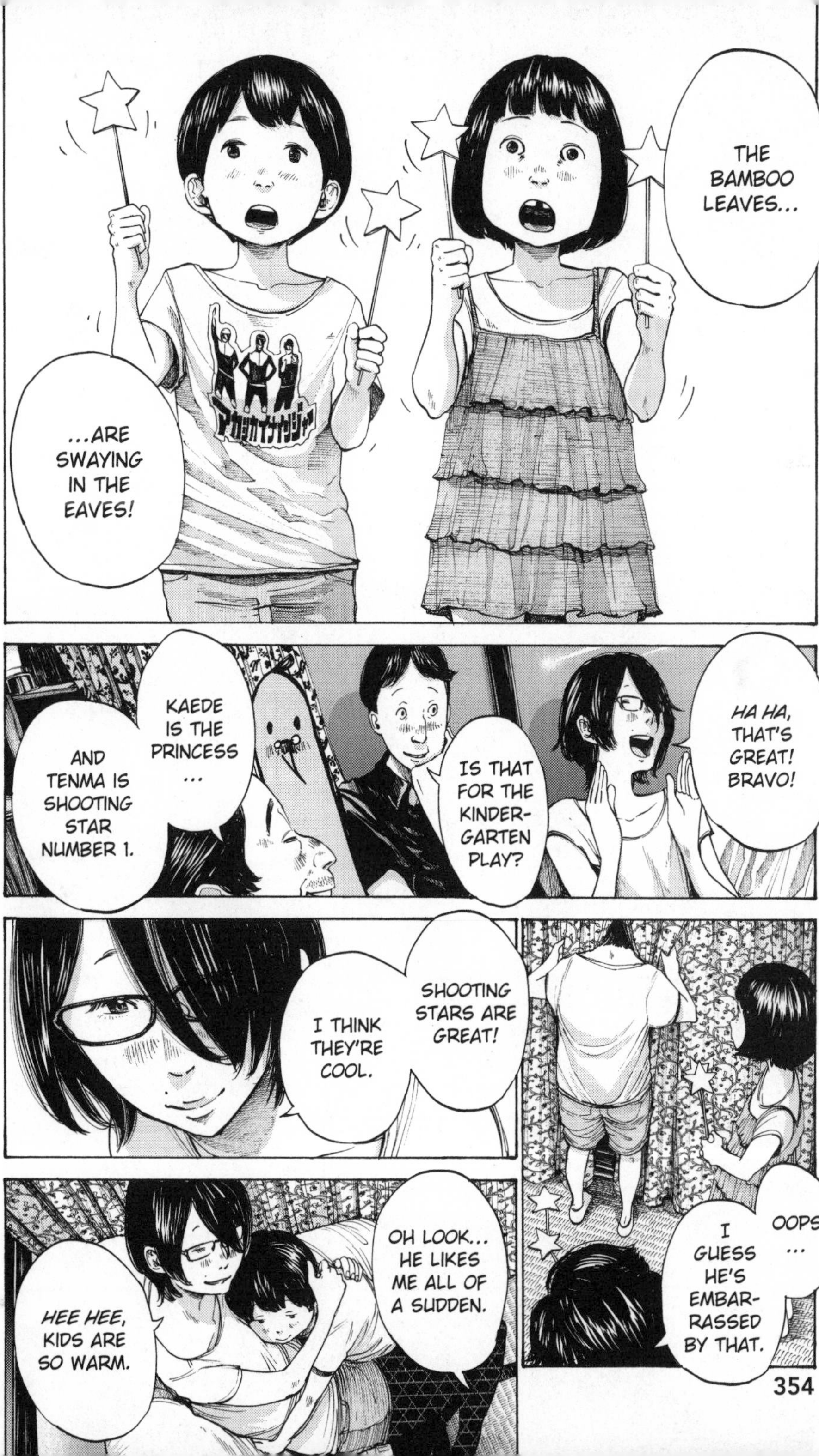
THE BAMBOO LEAVES...
...ARE SWAYING IN THE EAVES!
HA HA, THAT'S GREAT! BRAVO!
IS THAT FOR THE KINDERGARTEN PLAY?
KAEDE IS THE PRINCESS...
AND TENMA IS SHOOTING STAR NUMBER 1.
OOPS...
I GUESS HE'S EMBARRASSED BY THAT.
SHOOTING STARS ARE GREAT!
I THINK THEY'RE COOL.
OH LOOK... HE LIKES ME ALL OF A SUDDEN.
HEE HEE, KIDS ARE SO WARM.

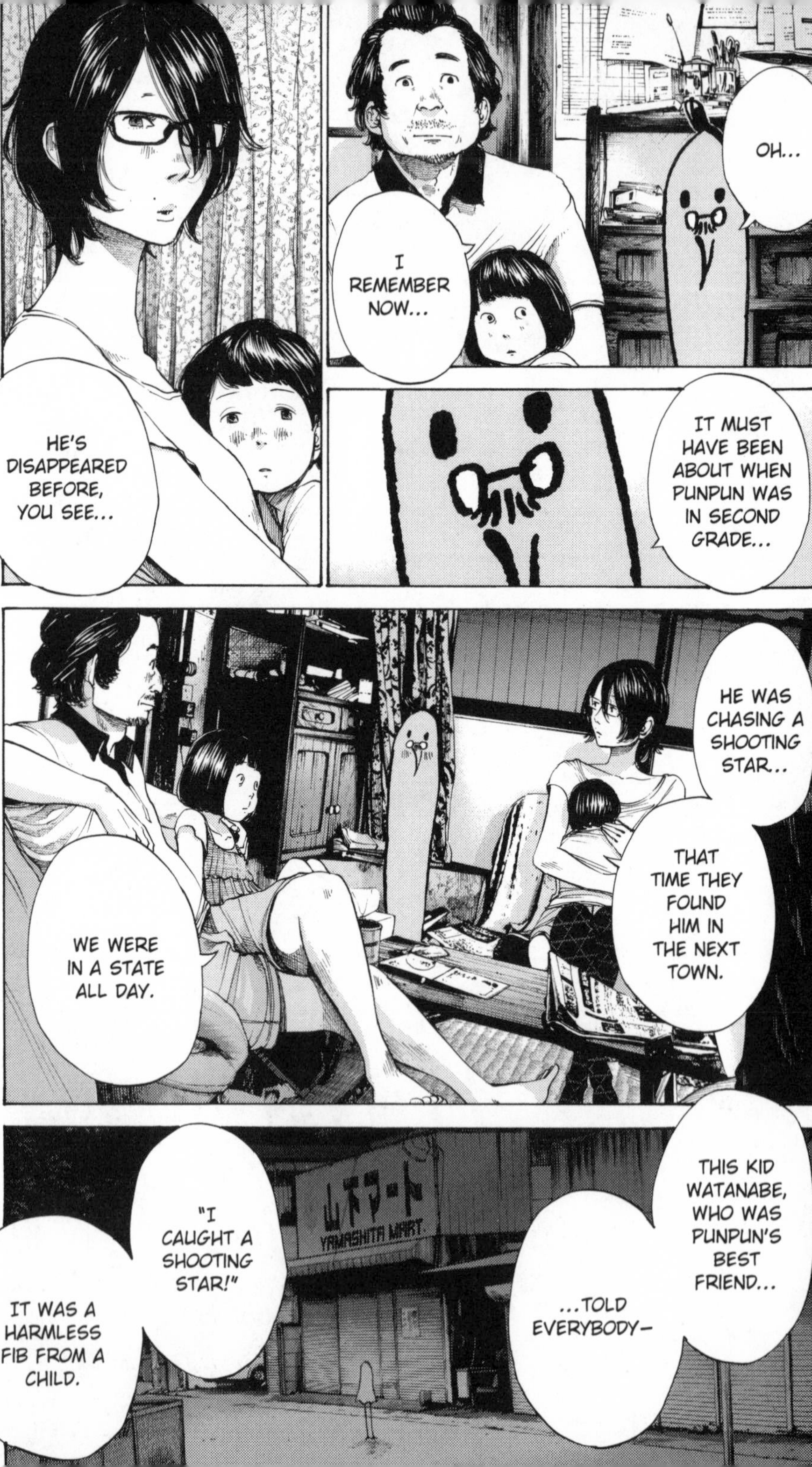
OH...
I REMEMBER NOW...
IT MUST HAVE BEEN ABOUT WHEN PUNPUN WAS IN SECOND GRADE...
HE'S DISAPPEARED BEFORE, YOU SEE...
HE WAS CHASING A SHOOTING STAR...
THAT TIME THEY FOUND HIM IN THE NEXT TOWN.
WE WERE IN A STATE ALL DAY.
THIS KID WATANABE, WHO WAS PUNPUN'S BEST FRIEND...
...TOLD EVERYBODY—
山下マート
YAMASHITA MART
"I CAUGHT A SHOOTING STAR!"
IT WAS A HARMLESS FIB FROM A CHILD.

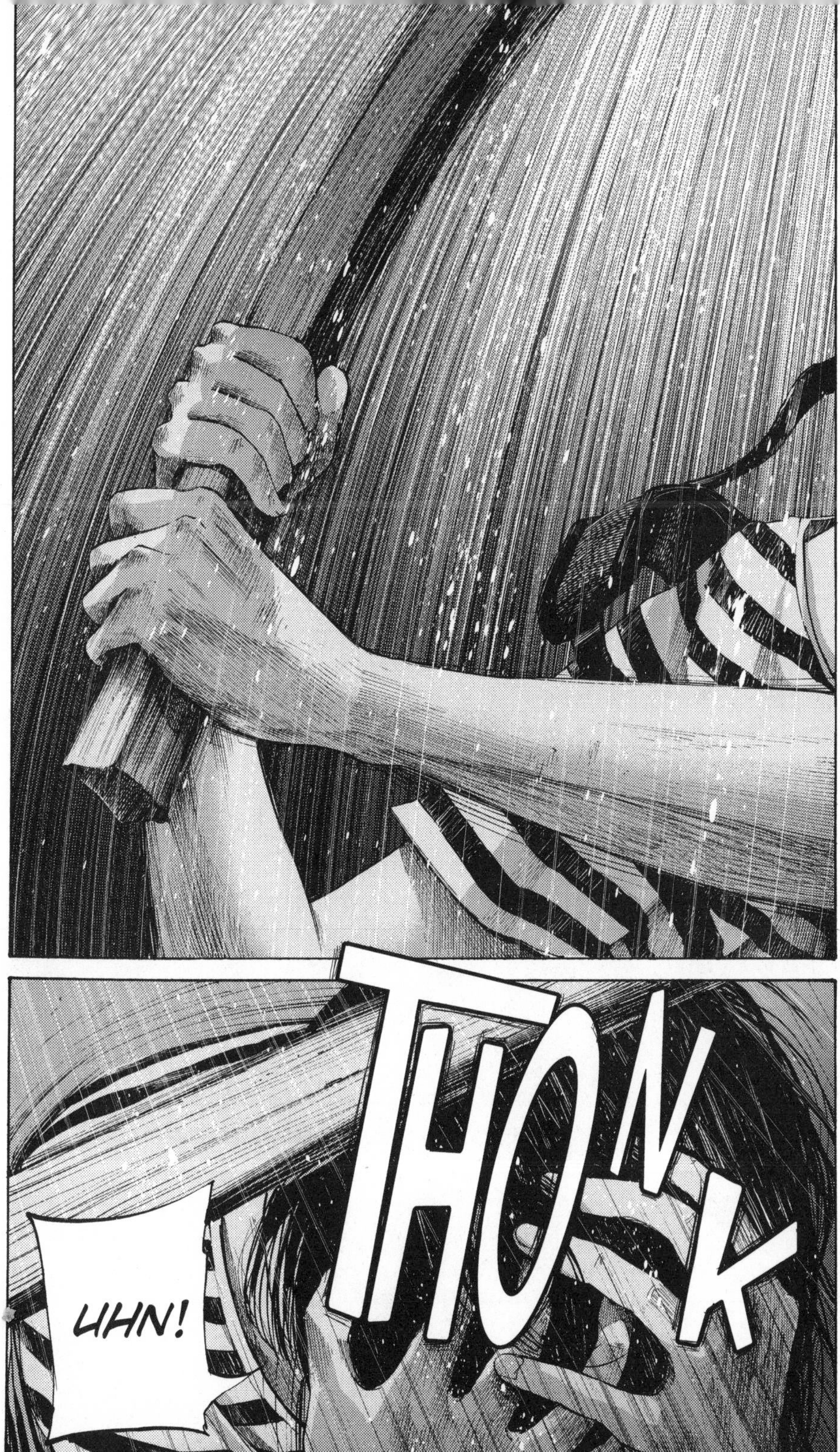
THONK
UHN!

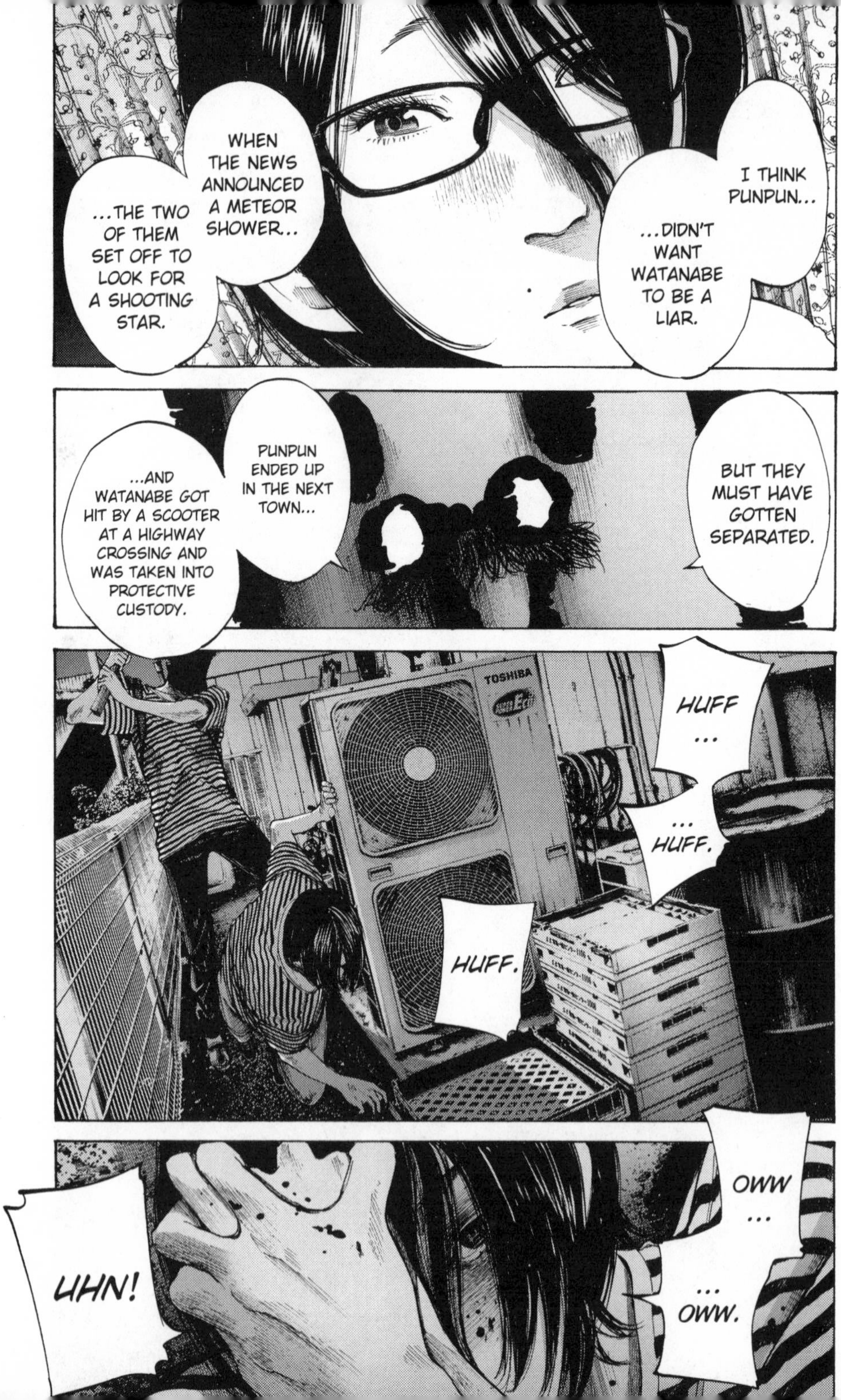
I THINK PUNPUN...
...DIDN'T WANT WATANABE TO BE A LIAR.
WHEN THE NEWS ANNOUNCED A METEOR SHOWER...
...THE TWO OF THEM SET OFF TO LOOK FOR A SHOOTING STAR.
BUT THEY MUST HAVE GOTTEN SEPARATED.
PUNPUN ENDED UP IN THE NEXT TOWN...
...AND WATANABE GOT HIT BY A SCOOTER AT A HIGHWAY CROSSING AND WAS TAKEN INTO PROTECTIVE CUSTODY.
TOSHIBA
HUFF...
...HUFF.
HUFF.
OWW...
...OWW.
UHN!

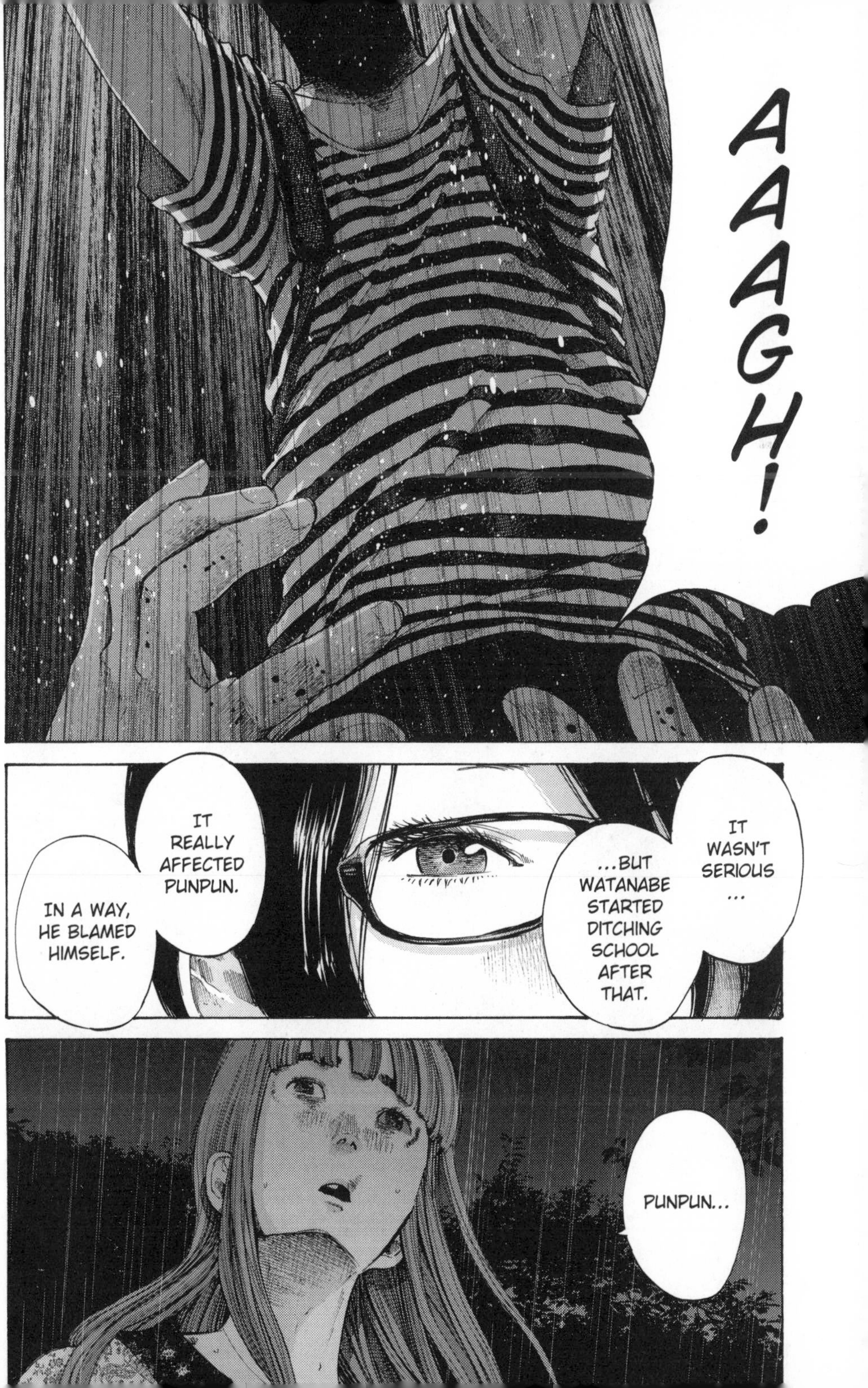
AAAGH!
IT WASN'T SERIOUS...
...BUT WATANABE STARTED DITCHING SCHOOL AFTER THAT.
IT REALLY AFFECTED PUNPUN.
IN A WAY, HE BLAMED HIMSELF.
PUNPUN...

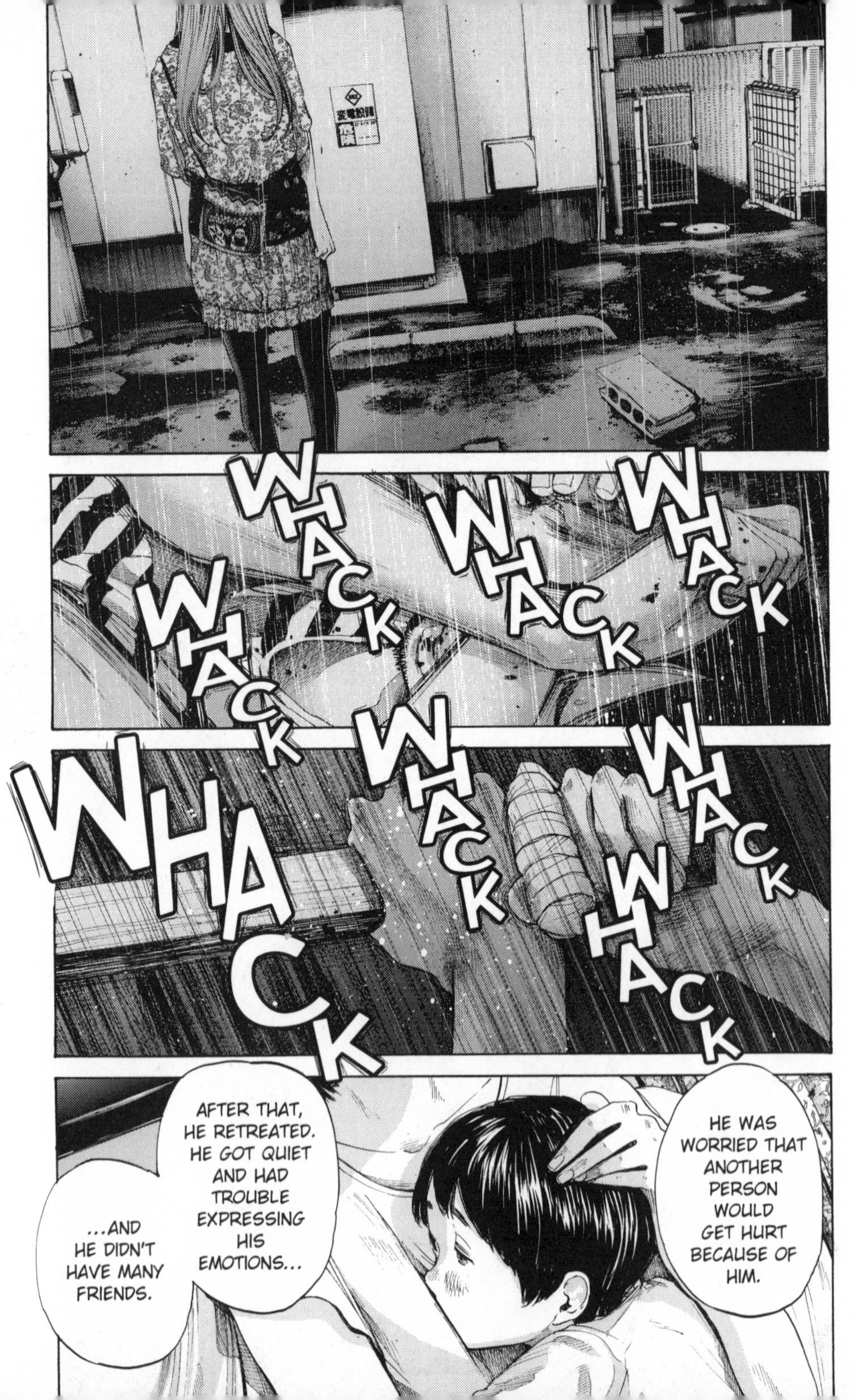

WHACK
WHACK
WHACK
WHACK
WHACK
WHACK
WHACK
WHACK
HE WAS WORRIED THAT ANOTHER PERSON WOULD GET HURT BECAUSE OF HIM.
AFTER THAT, HE RETREATED. HE GOT QUIET AND HAD TROUBLE EXPRESSING HIS EMOTIONS…
…AND HE DIDN'T HAVE MANY FRIENDS.

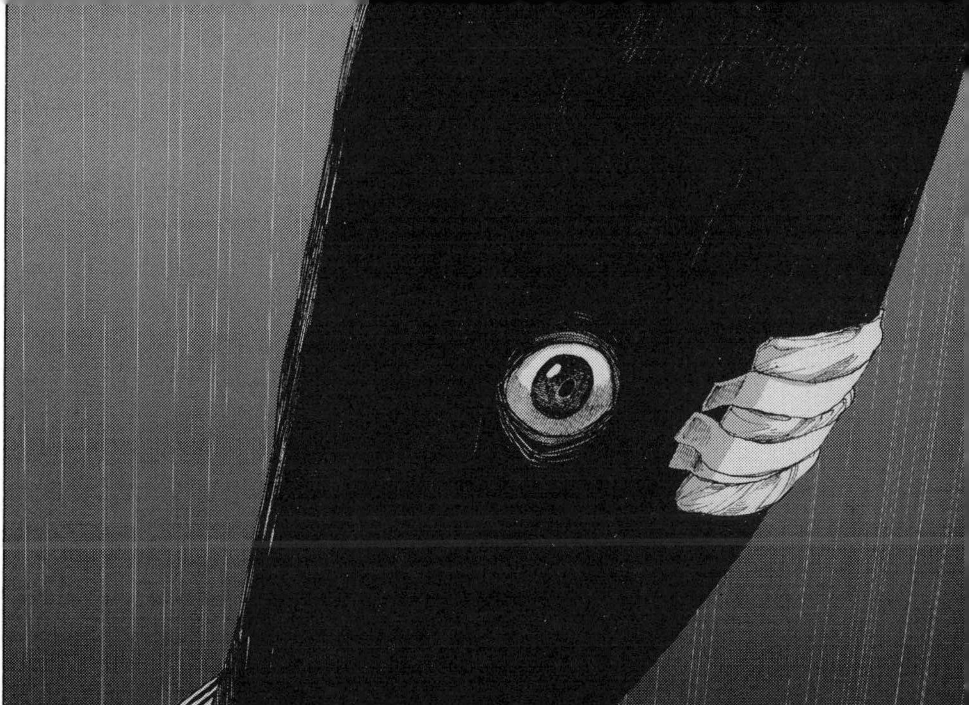

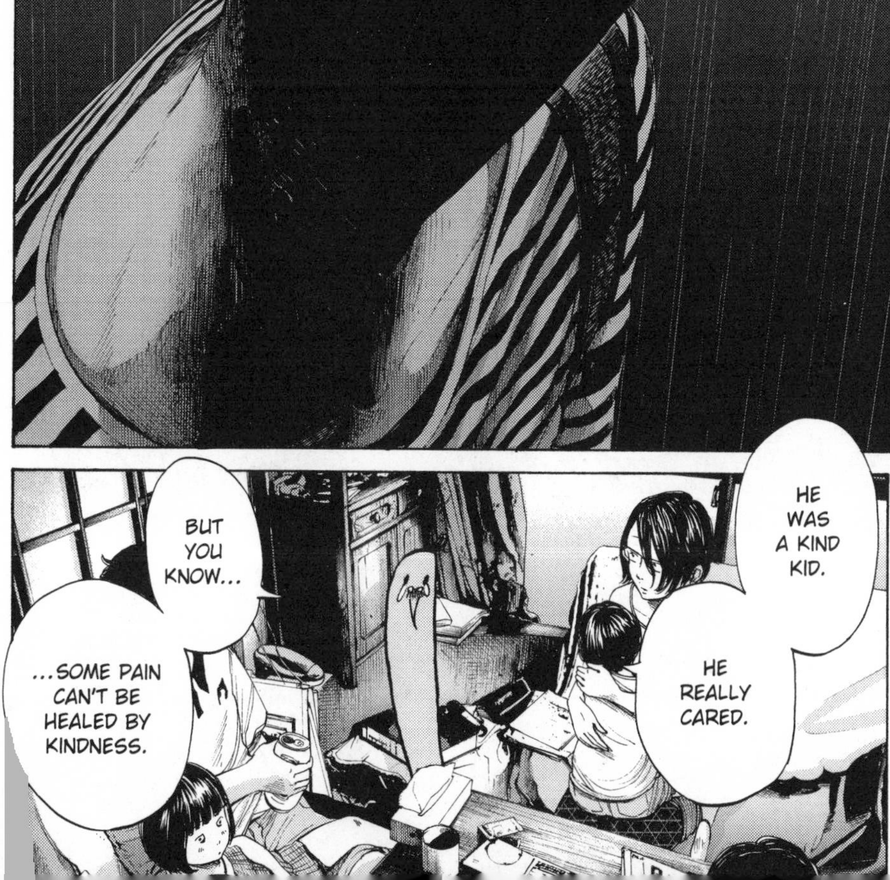
HE WAS A KIND KID.
HE REALLY CARED.
BUT YOU KNOW...
...SOME PAIN CAN'T BE HEALED BY KINDNESS.

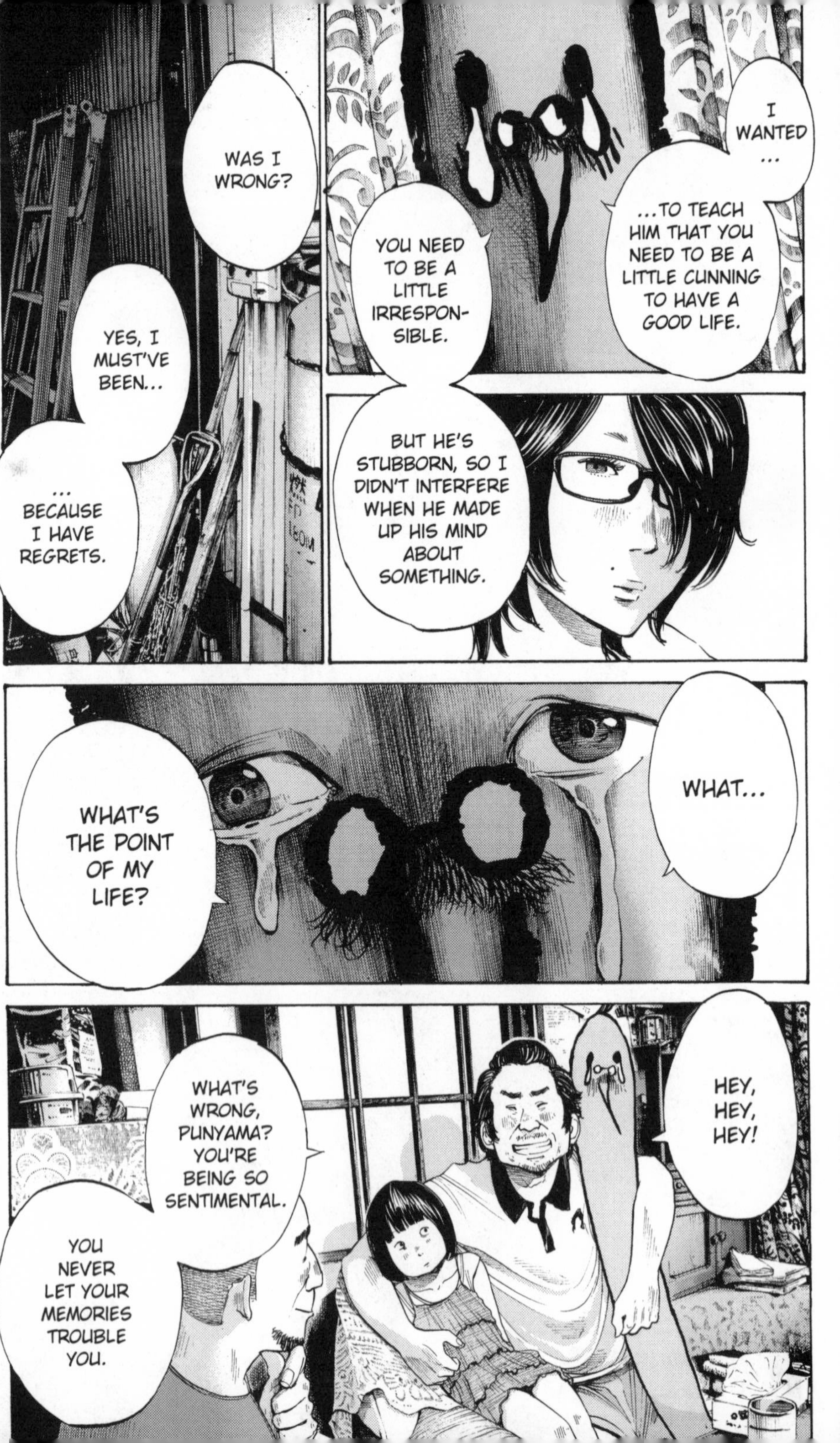
I WANTED...
...TO TEACH HIM THAT YOU NEED TO BE A LITTLE CUNNING TO HAVE A GOOD LIFE.
YOU NEED TO BE A LITTLE IRRESPON-SIBLE.
BUT HE'S STUBBORN, SO I DIDN'T INTERFERE WHEN HE MADE UP HIS MIND ABOUT SOMETHING.
WAS I WRONG?
YES, I MUST'VE BEEN...
...BECAUSE I HAVE REGRETS.
WHAT...
WHAT'S THE POINT OF MY LIFE?
HEY, HEY, HEY!
WHAT'S WRONG, PUNYAMA? YOU'RE BEING SO SENTIMENTAL.
YOU NEVER LET YOUR MEMORIES TROUBLE YOU.

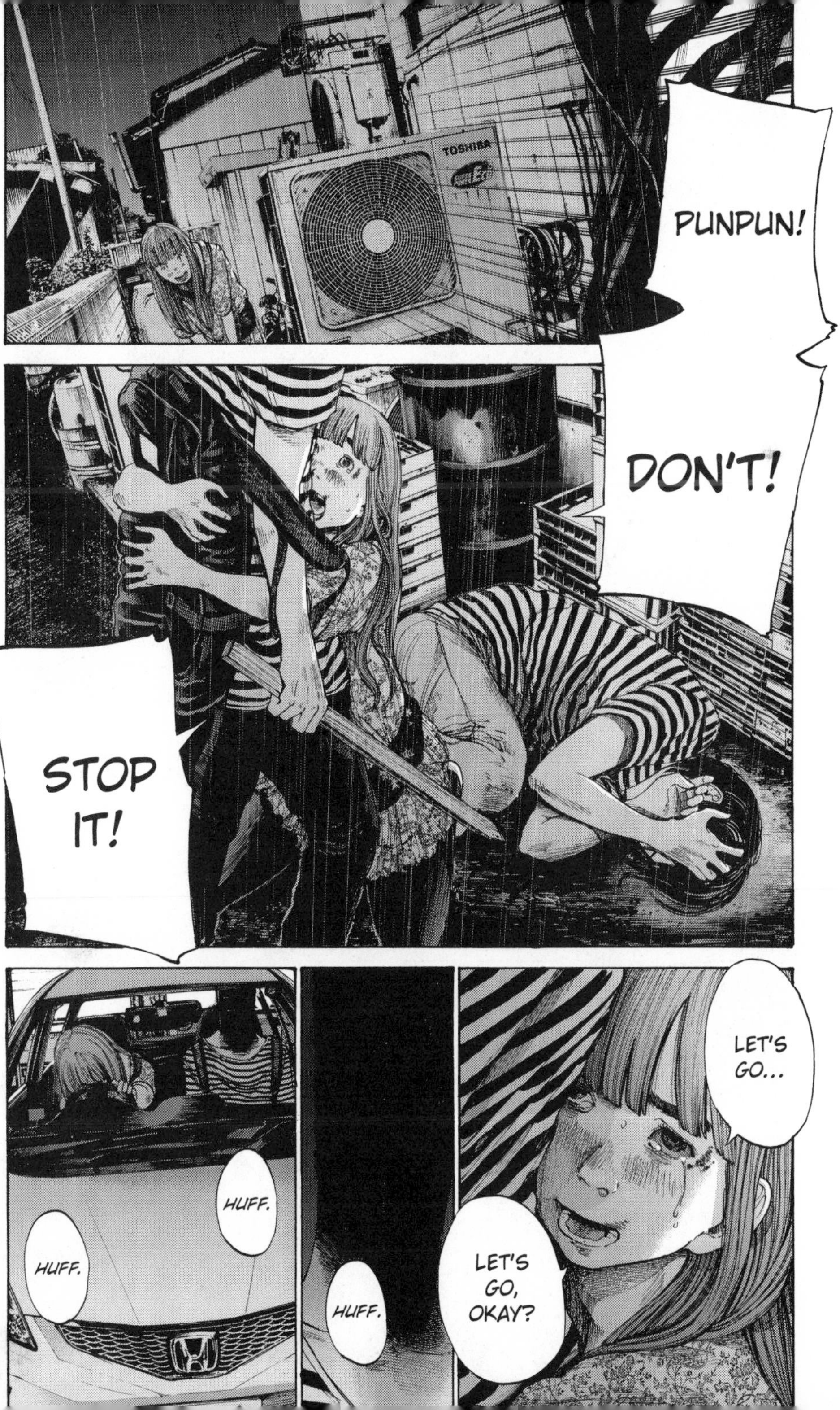
PUNPUN!
DON'T!
STOP IT!
LET'S GO...
LET'S GO, OKAY?
HUFF.
HUFF.
HUFF.

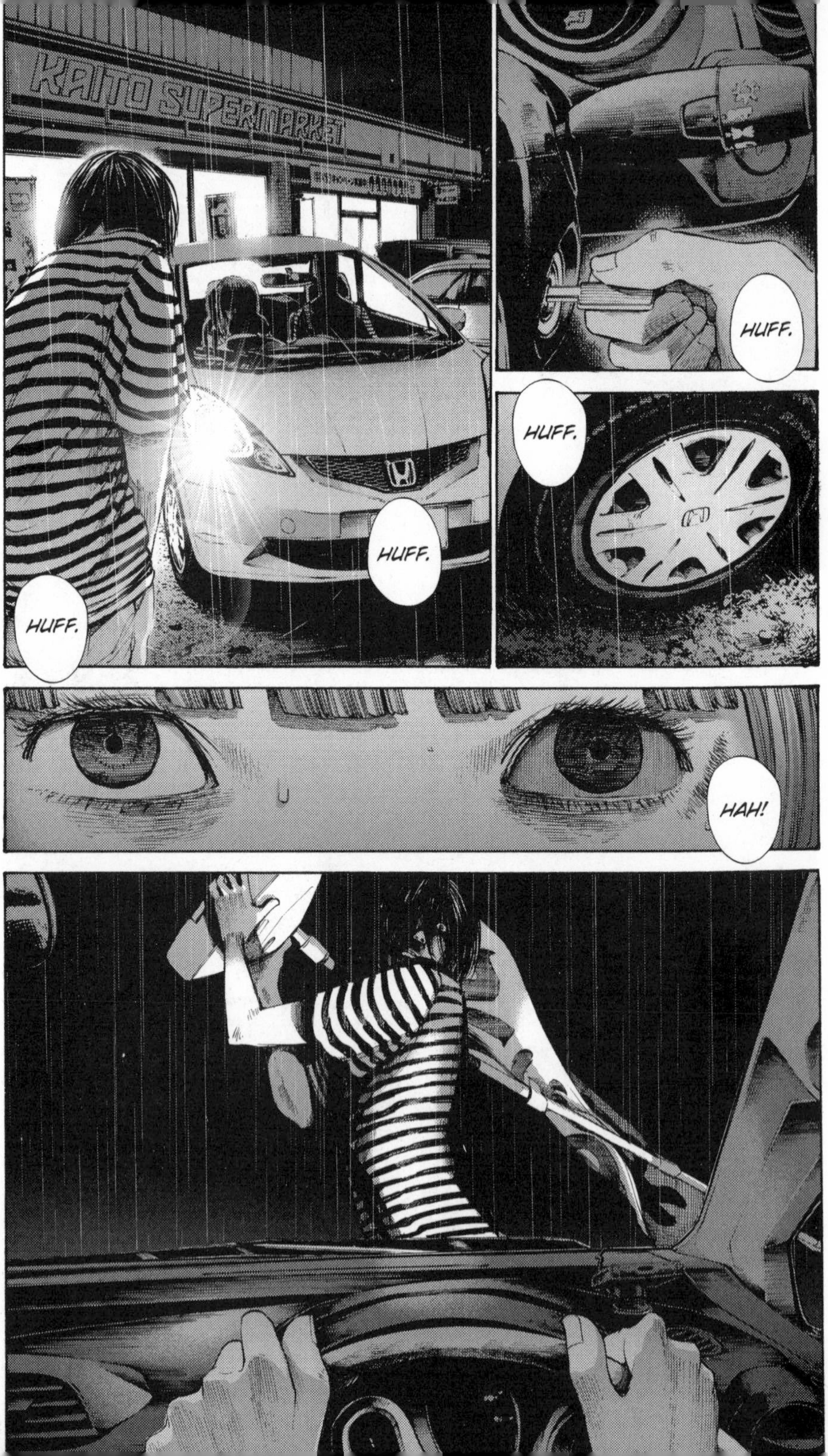
HUFF.
HUFF.
KAITO SUPERMARKET
HUFF.
HUFF.
HAH!

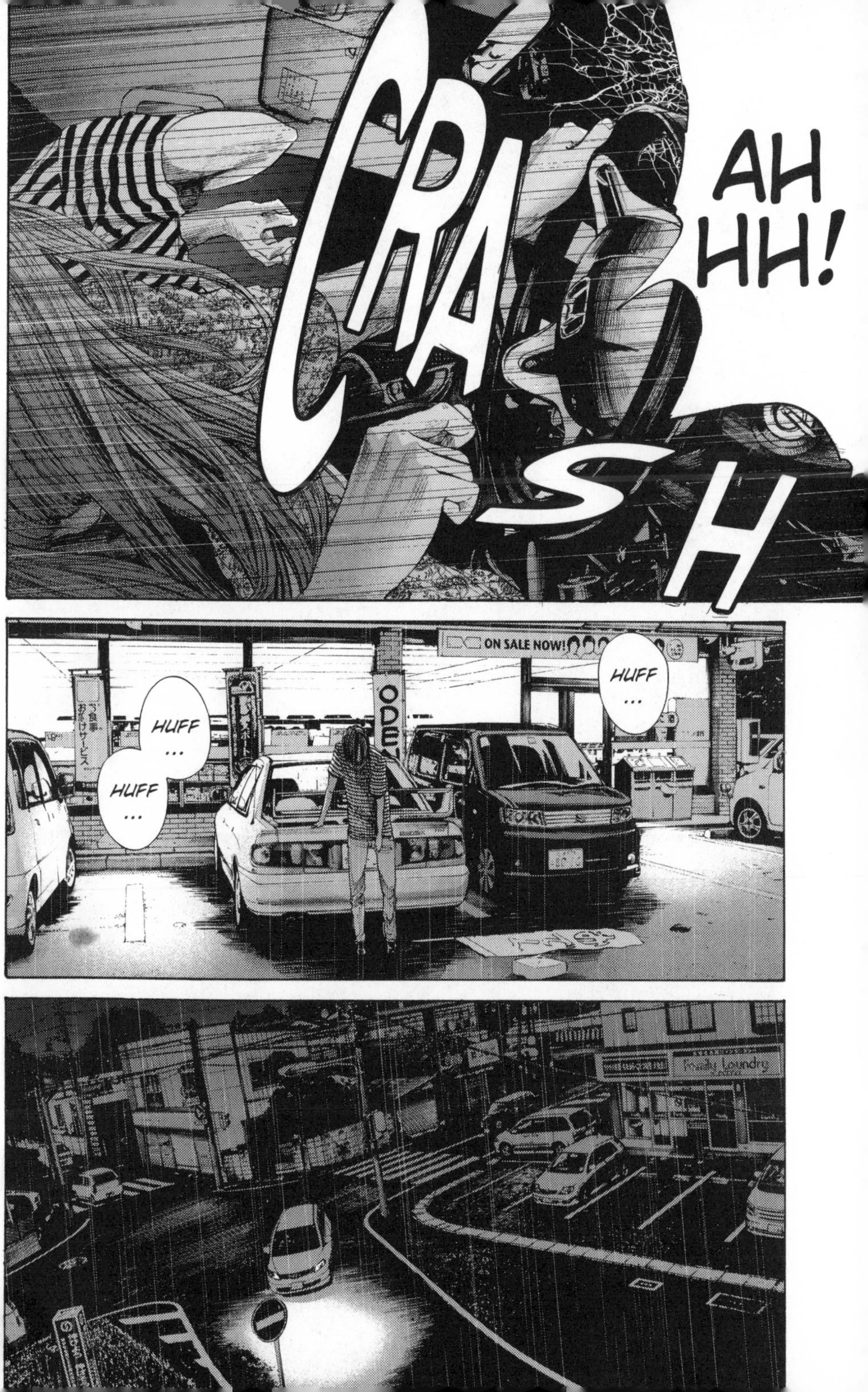
AHHH!
CRASH
ON SALE NOW!
HUFF...
ODEN
HUFF...
HUFF...
Family Laundry

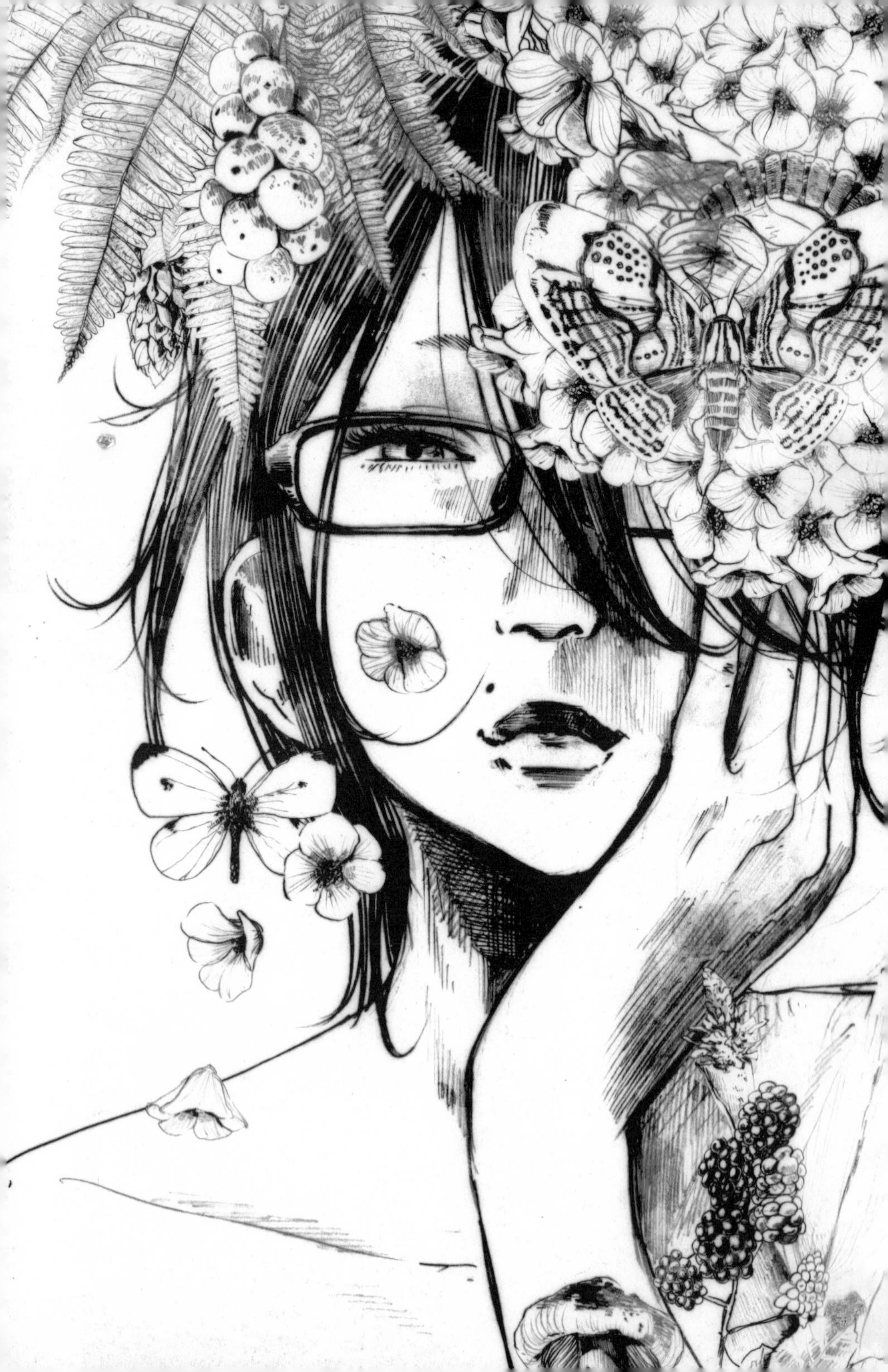

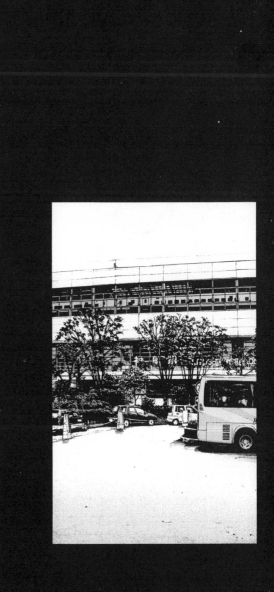

Chapter 129

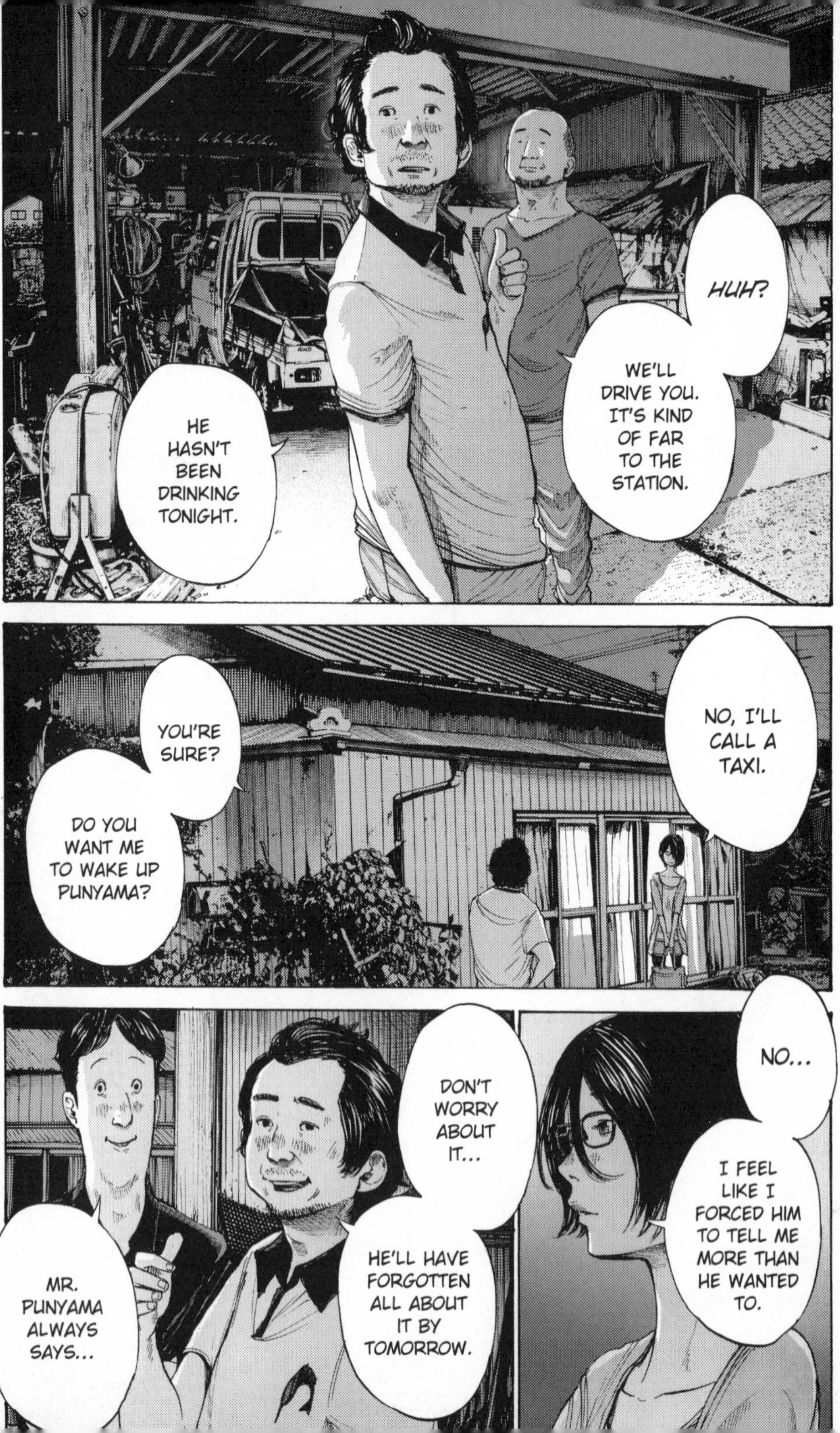
HUH?
WE'LL DRIVE YOU. IT'S KIND OF FAR TO THE STATION.
HE HASN'T BEEN DRINKING TONIGHT.
NO, I'LL CALL A TAXI.
YOU'RE SURE?
DO YOU WANT ME TO WAKE UP PUNYAMA?
NO...
I FEEL LIKE I FORCED HIM TO TELL ME MORE THAN HE WANTED TO.
DON'T WORRY ABOUT IT...
HE'LL HAVE FORGOTTEN ALL ABOUT IT BY TOMORROW.
MR. PUNYAMA ALWAYS SAYS...

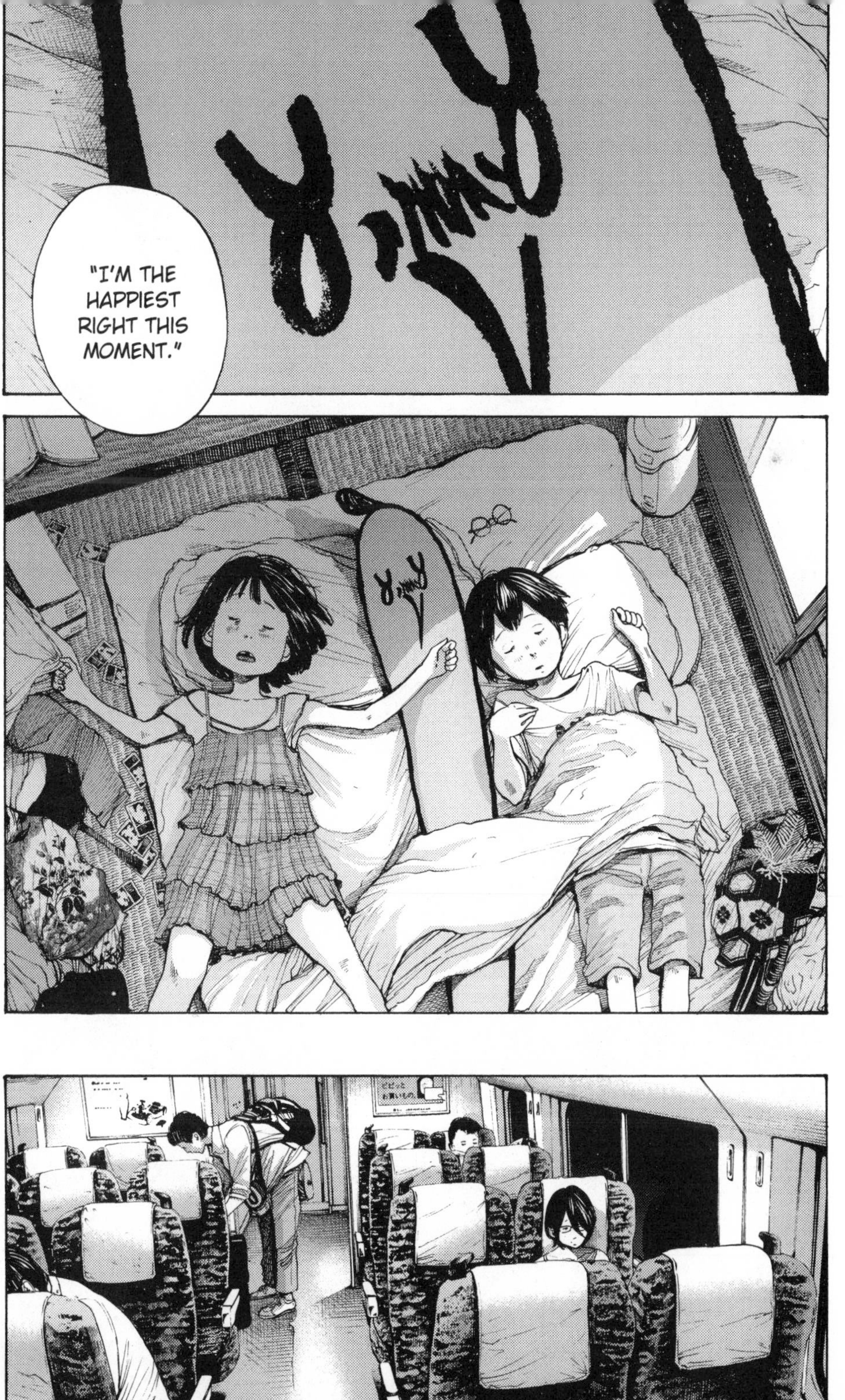
"I'M THE HAPPIEST RIGHT THIS MOMENT."

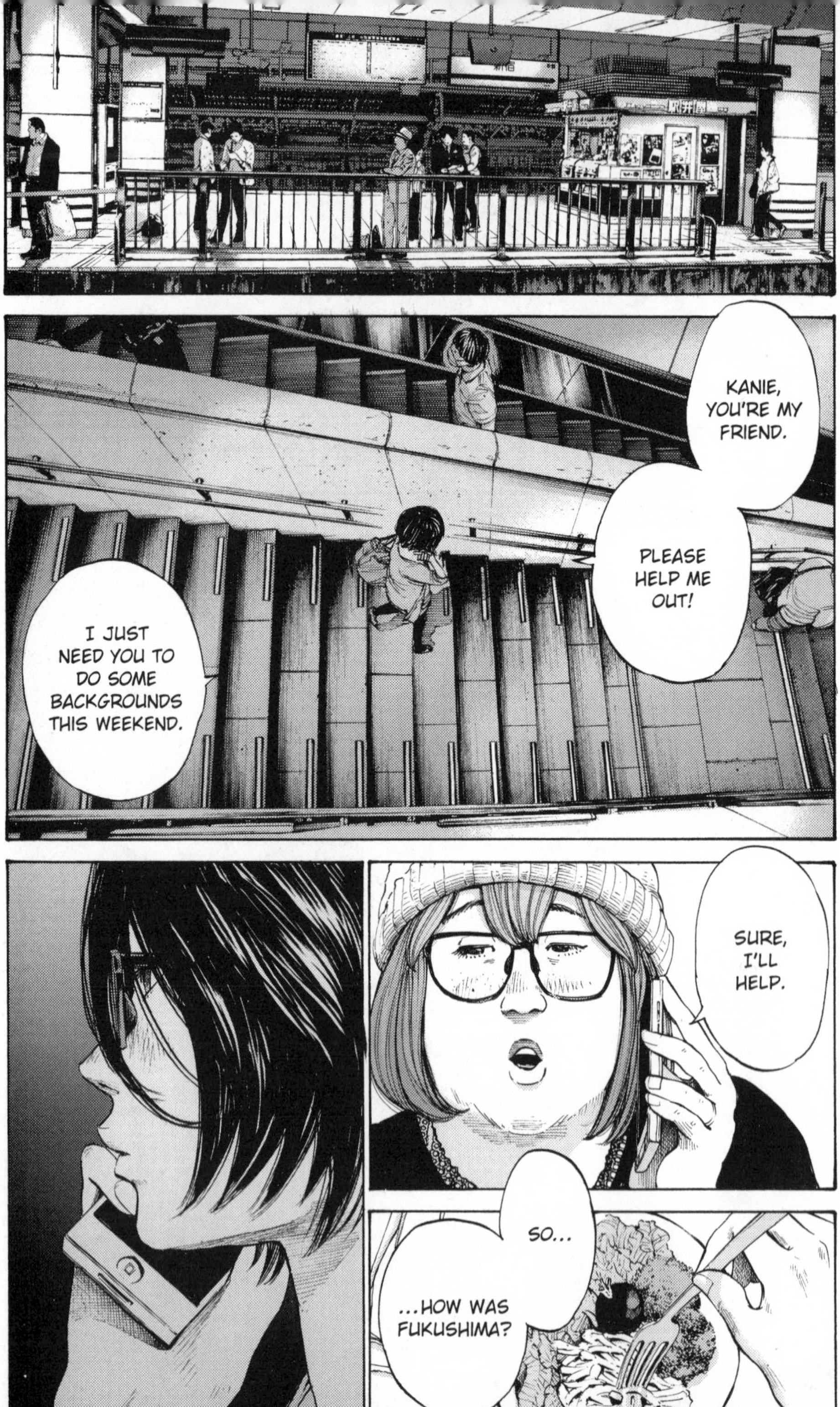
KANIE, YOU'RE MY FRIEND.
PLEASE HELP ME OUT!
I JUST NEED YOU TO DO SOME BACKGROUNDS THIS WEEKEND.
SURE, I'LL HELP.
SO...
...HOW WAS FUKUSHIMA?

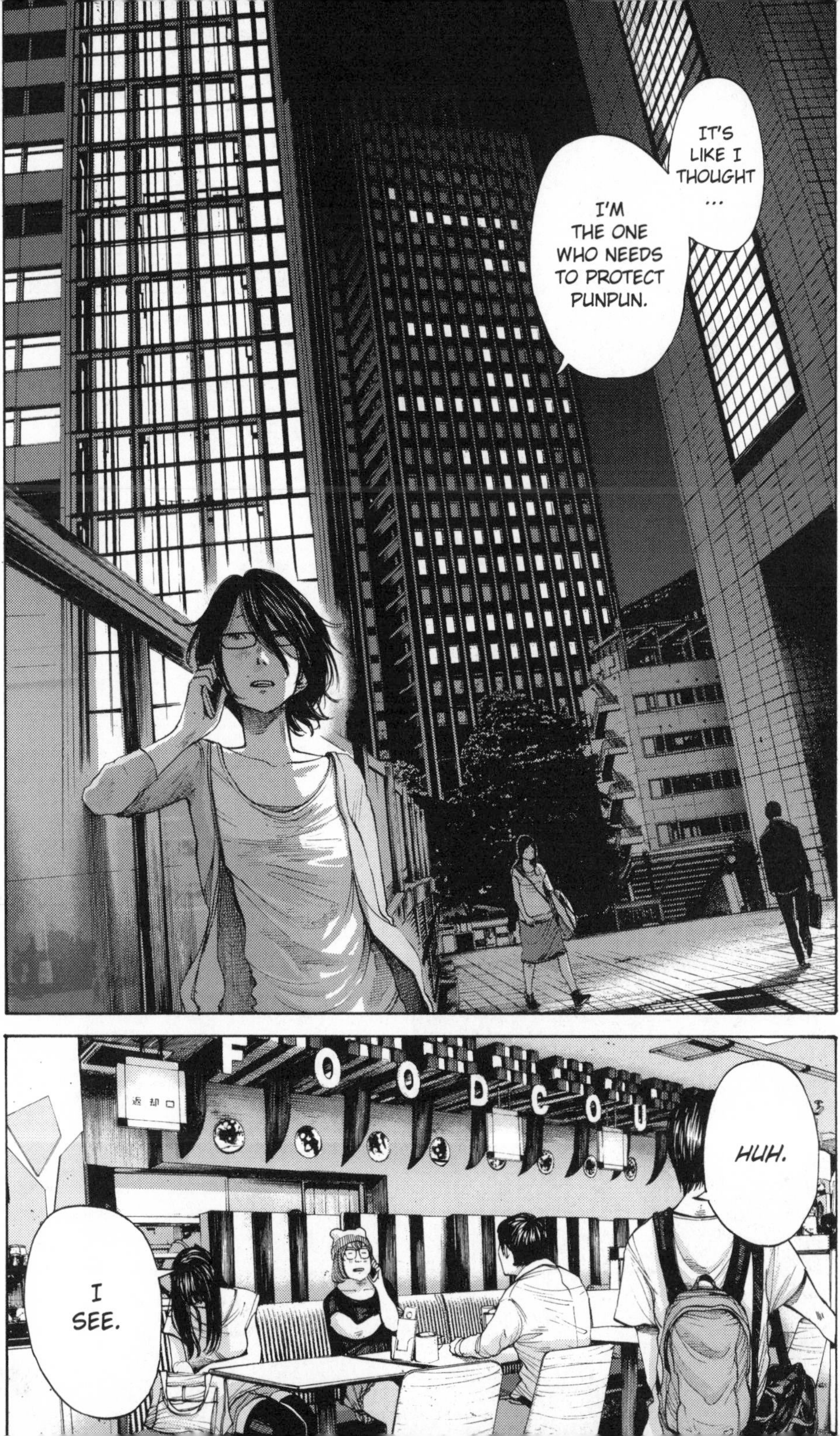
IT'S LIKE I THOUGHT ...
I'M THE ONE WHO NEEDS TO PROTECT PUNPUN.
HUH.
FOOD COU
返却口
I SEE.

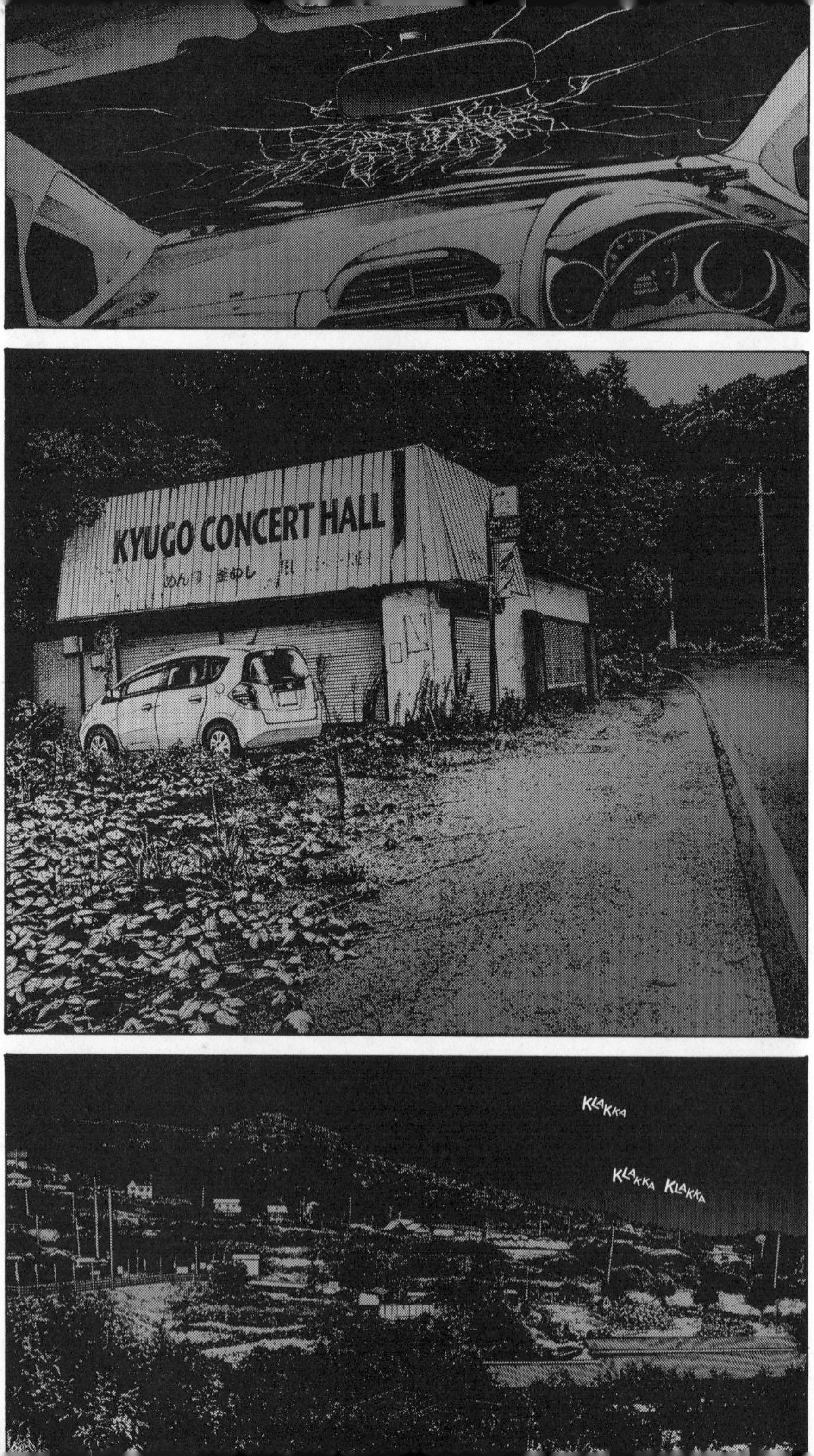
KYUGO CONCERT HALL
KLAKKA
KLAKKA KLAKKA

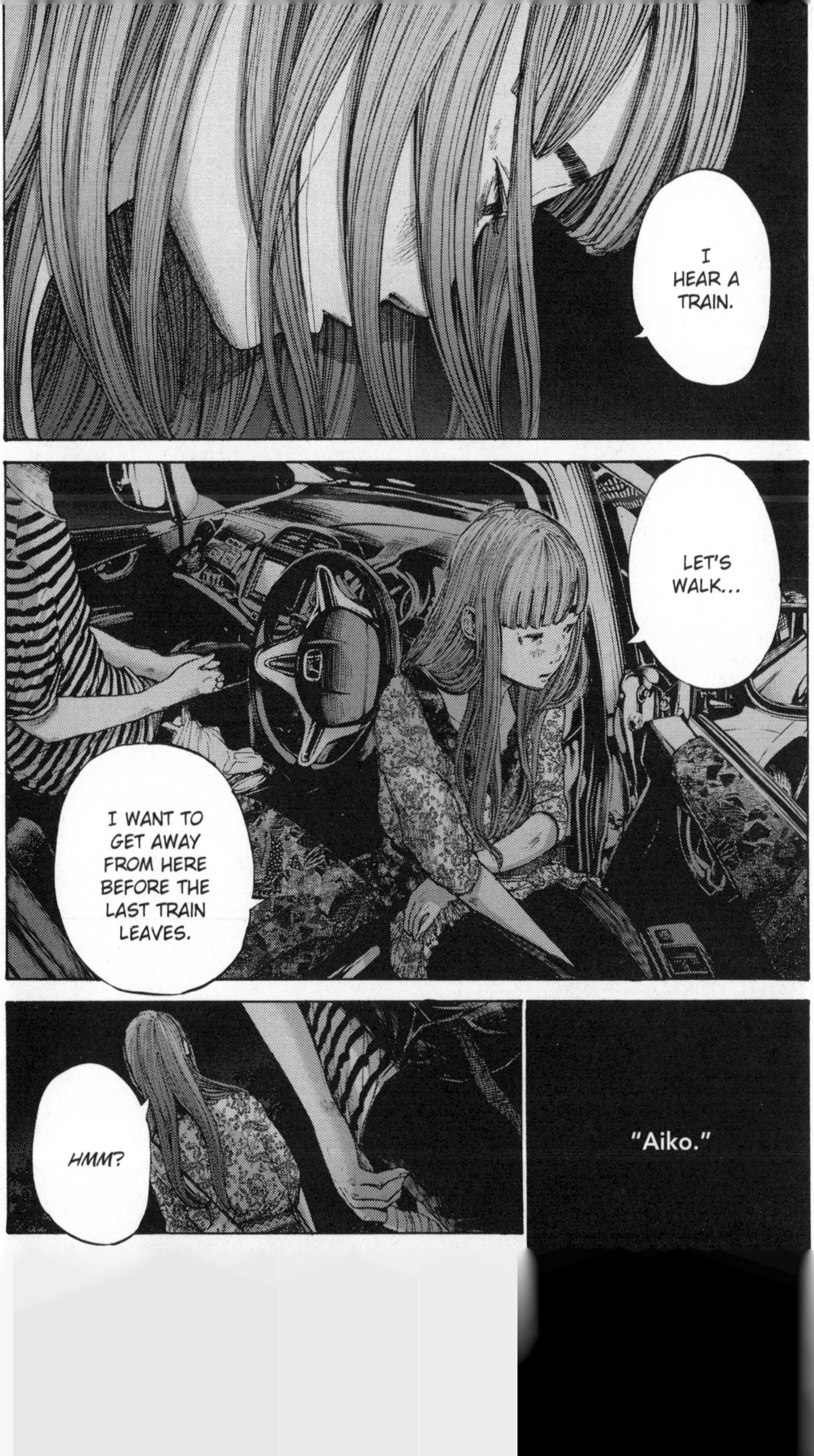
I HEAR A TRAIN.
LET'S WALK...
I WANT TO GET AWAY FROM HERE BEFORE THE LAST TRAIN LEAVES.
"Aiko."
HMM?

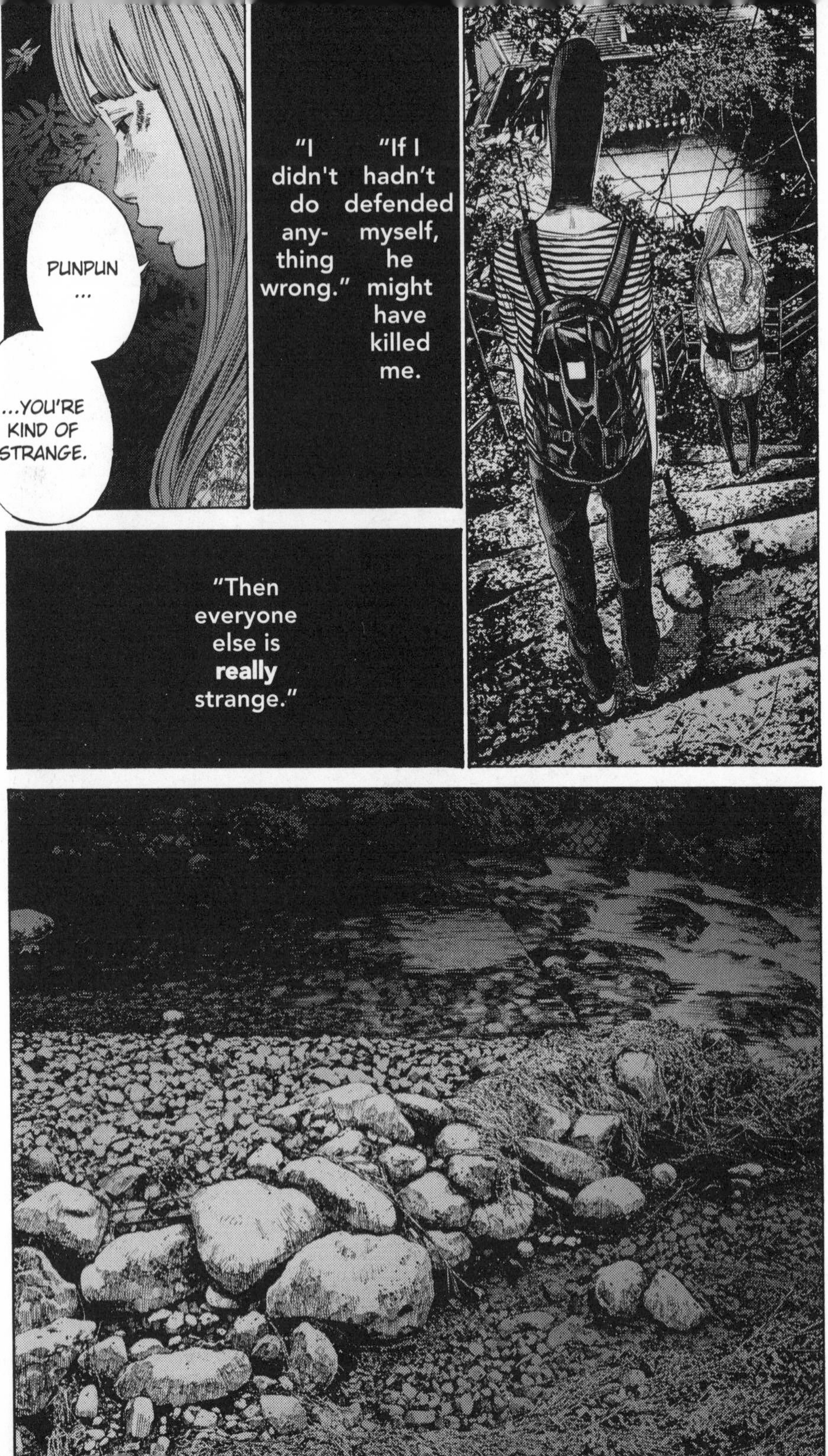
"If I hadn't defended myself, he might have killed me.
"I didn't do any-thing wrong."
PUNPUN ...
...YOU'RE KIND OF STRANGE.
"Then everyone else is **really** strange."

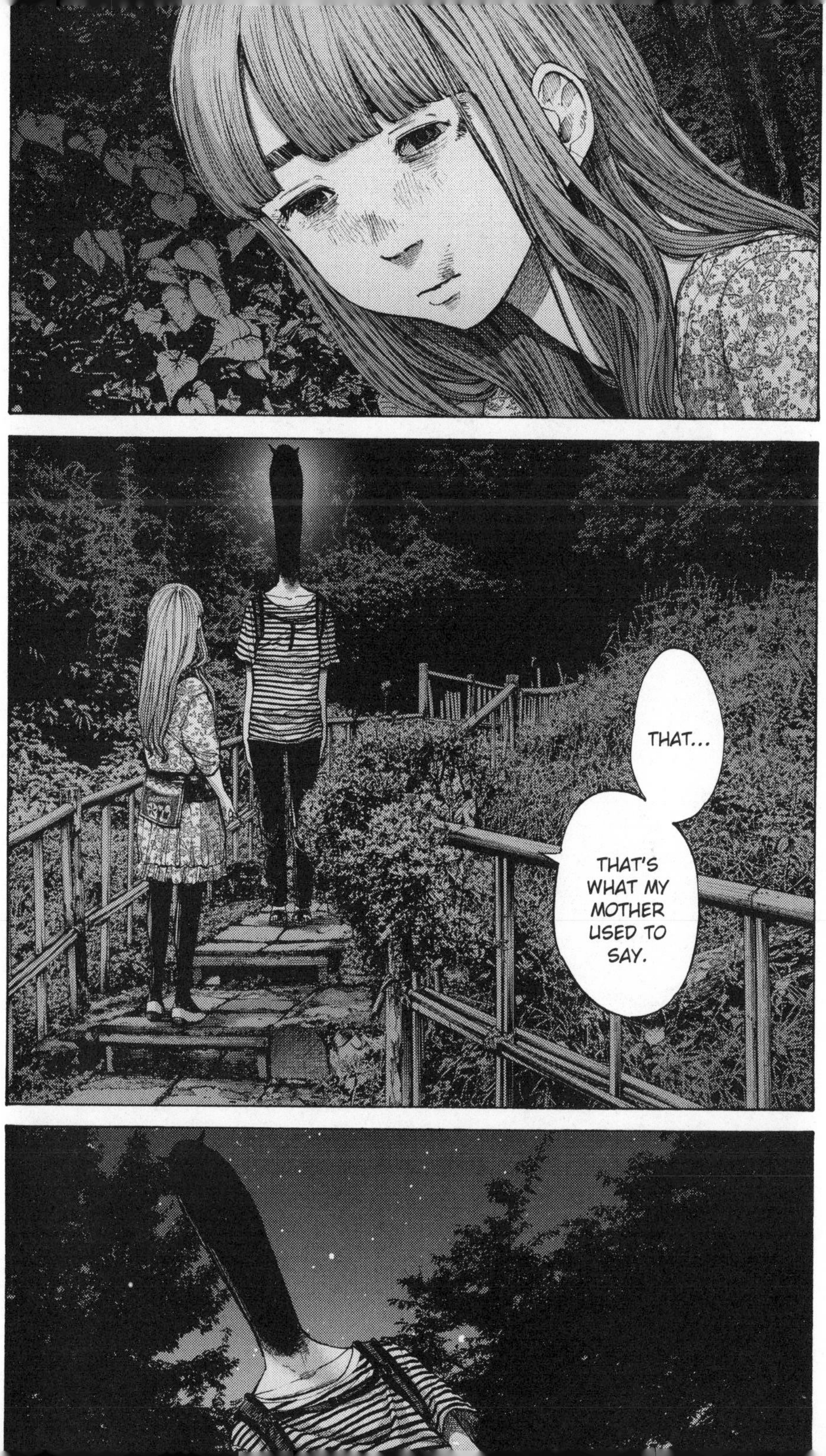
THAT...
THAT'S WHAT MY MOTHER USED TO SAY.

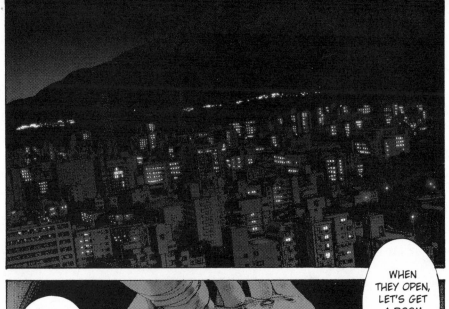

WHEN THEY OPEN, LET'S GET A ROOM IMMEDIATELY...

I WANT TO SLEEP AND CHANGE MY CLOTHES.

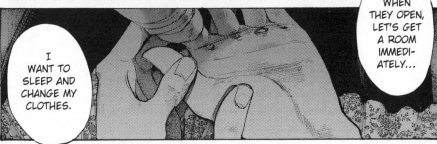

I'M TIRED.

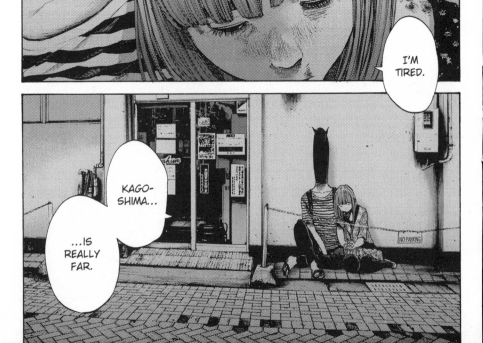

KAGOSHIMA...

...IS REALLY FAR.

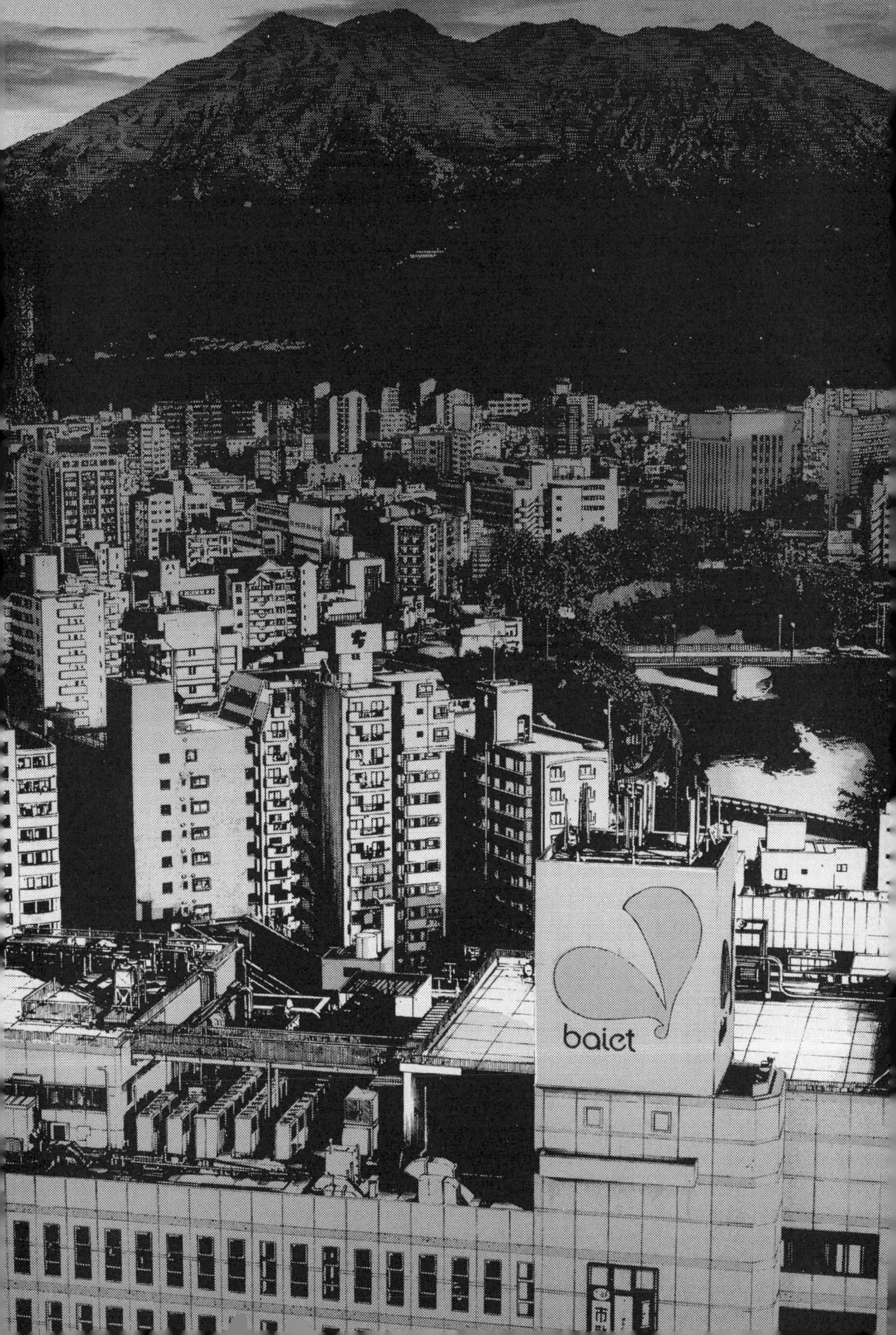
baiet

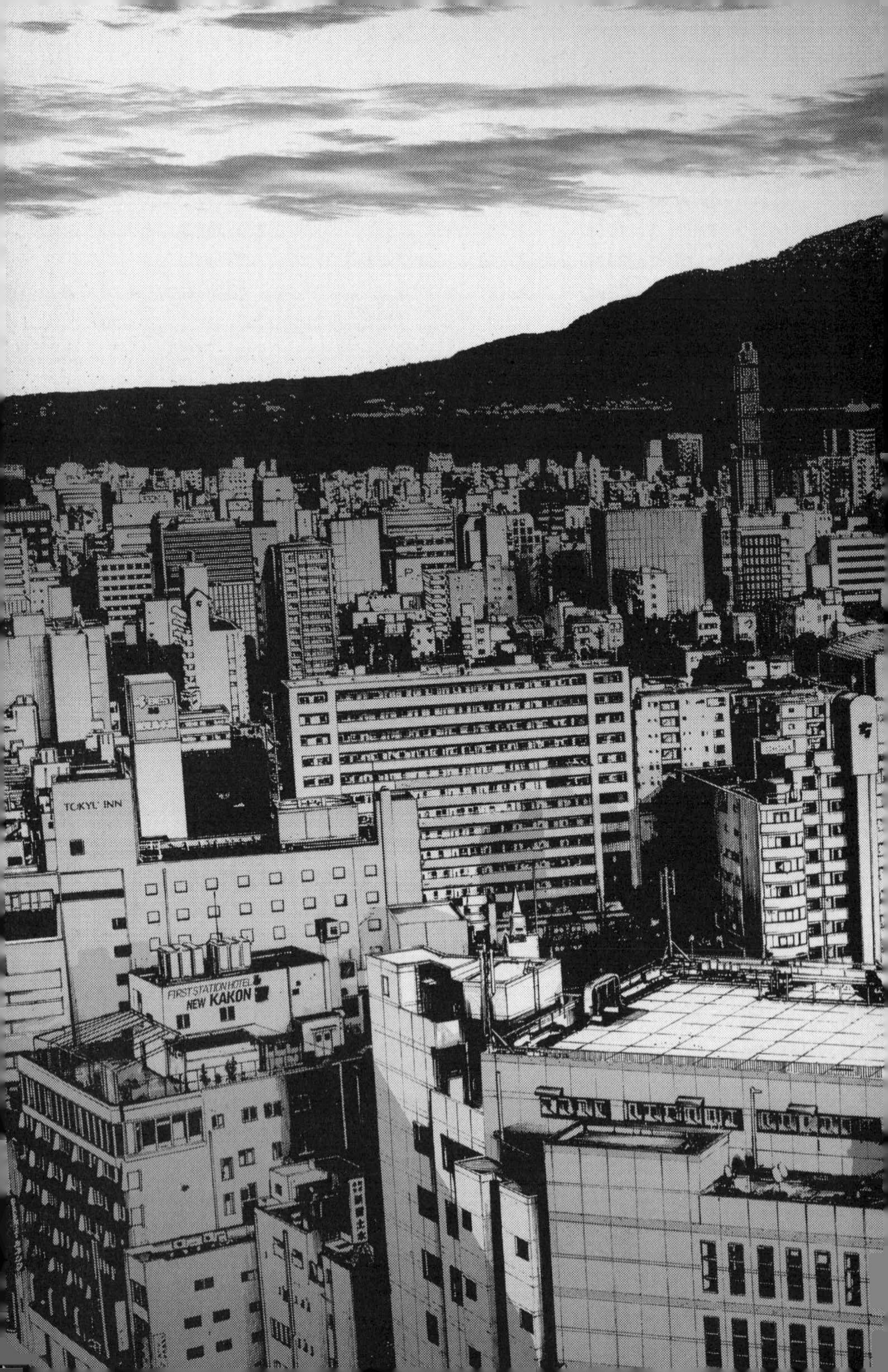
TOKYU INN
FIRST STATION HOTEL
NEW KAKON

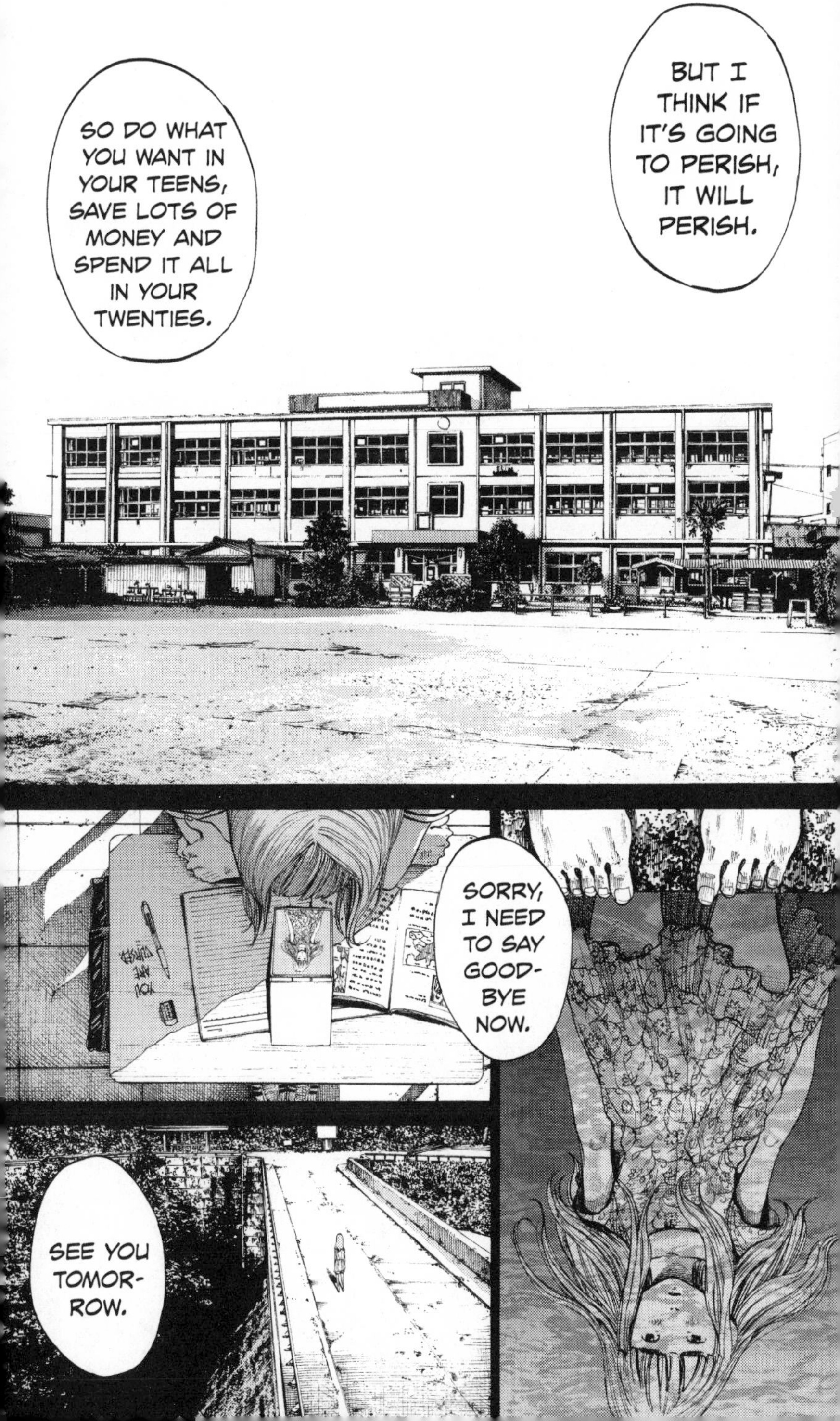
BUT I THINK IF IT'S GOING TO PERISH, IT WILL PERISH.
SO DO WHAT YOU WANT IN YOUR TEENS, SAVE LOTS OF MONEY AND SPEND IT ALL IN YOUR TWENTIES.
SORRY, I NEED TO SAY GOOD-BYE NOW.
SEE YOU TOMOR-ROW.

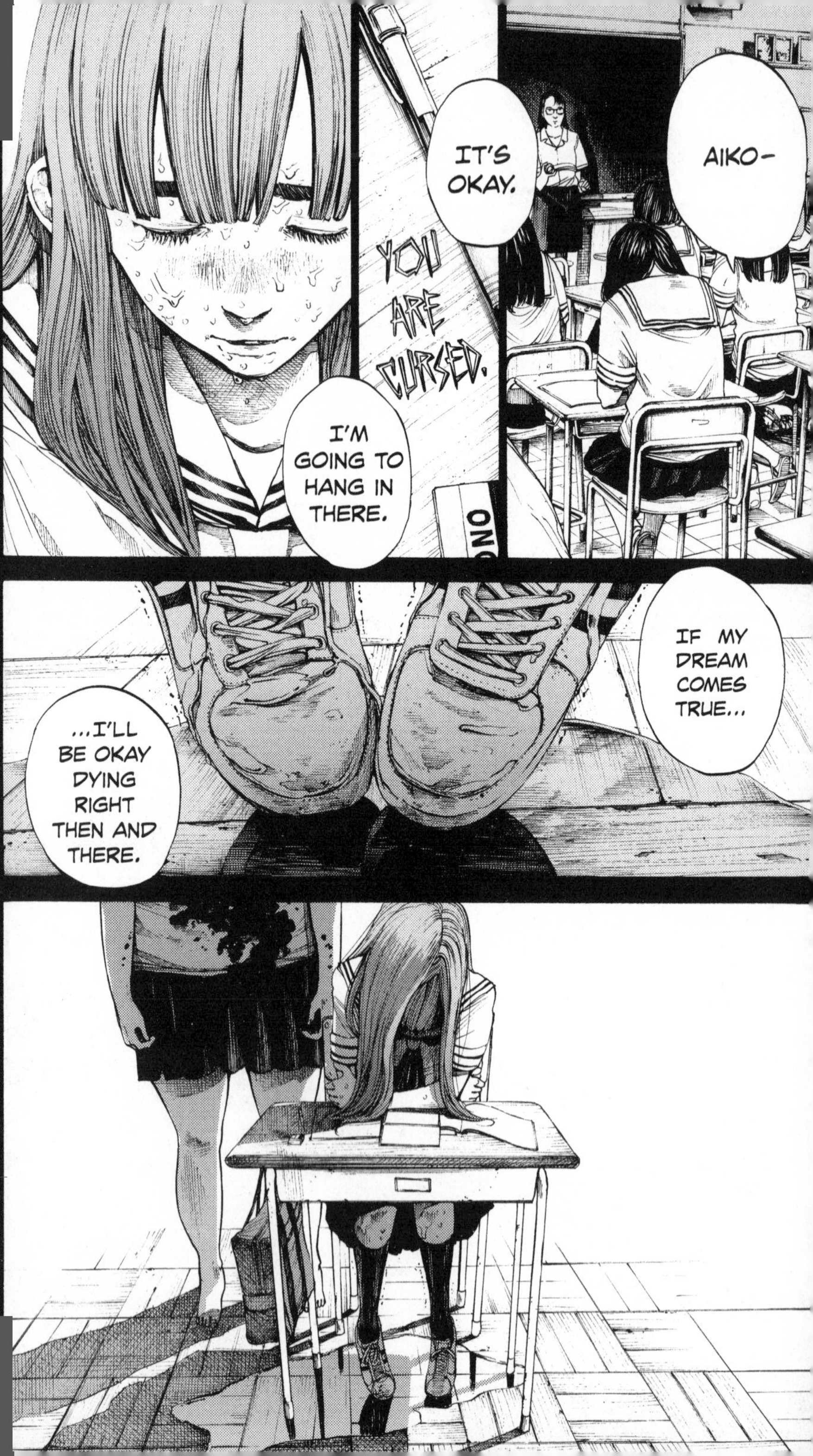
AIKO-
IT'S OKAY.
YOU ARE CURSED.
ONO
I'M GOING TO HANG IN THERE.
IF MY DREAM COMES TRUE...
...I'LL BE OKAY DYING RIGHT THEN AND THERE.

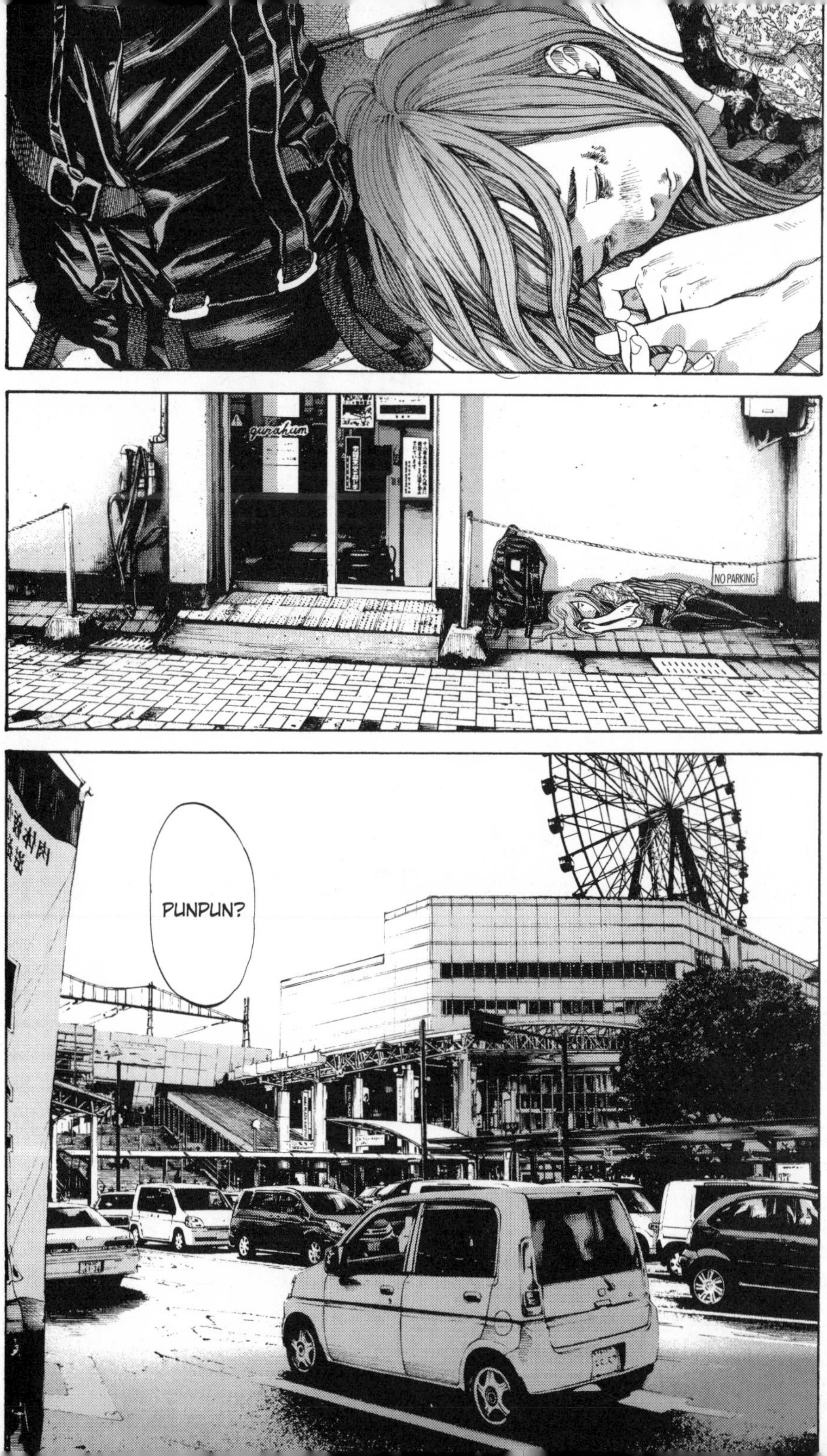
NO PARKING
PUNPUN?

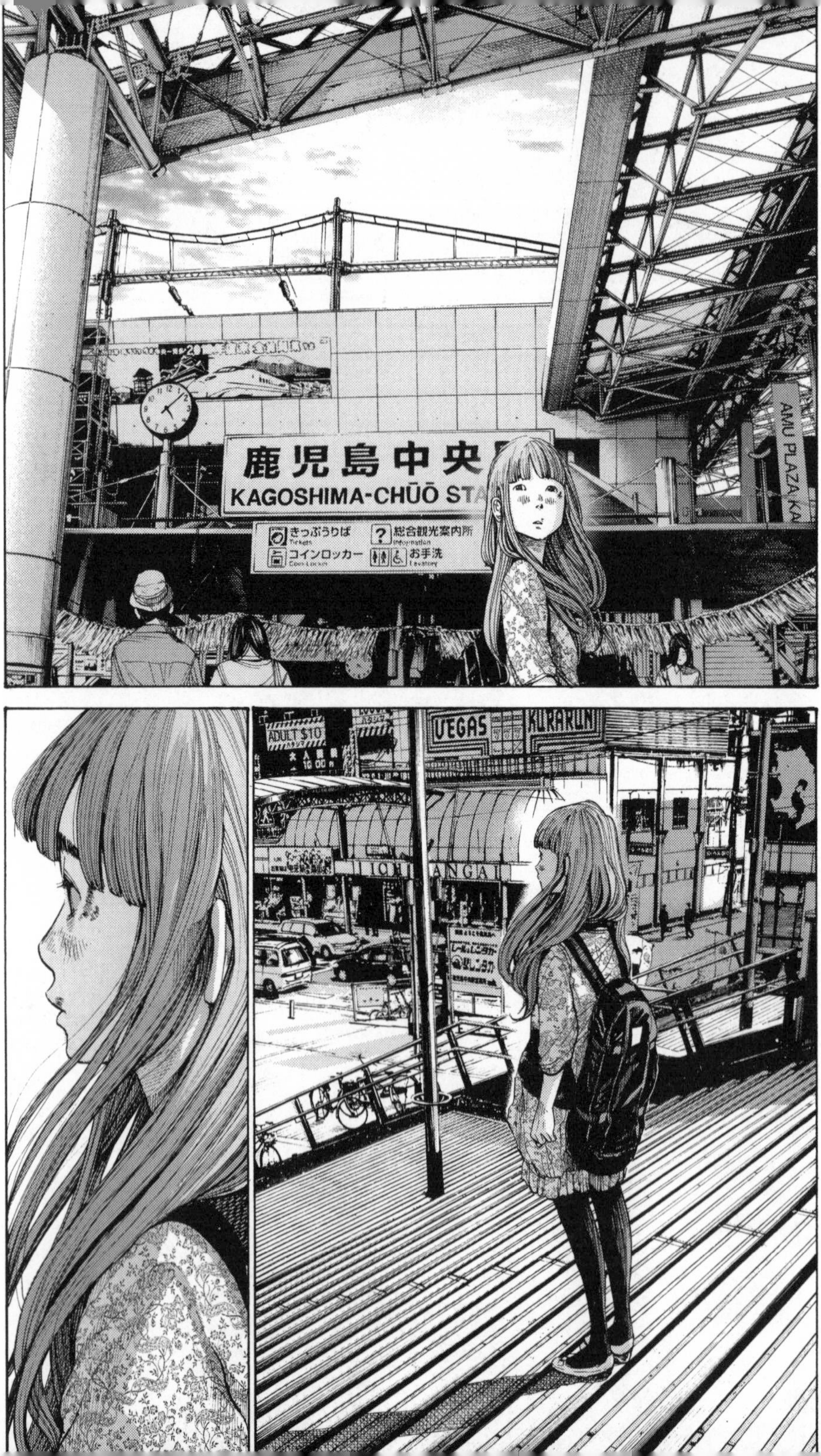
鹿児島中央
KAGOSHIMA-CHŪO STA
きっぷうりば
Tickets
総合観光案内所
Information
コインロッカー
お手洗
AMU PLAZA KA
VEGAS
KURARUN
ADULT $10

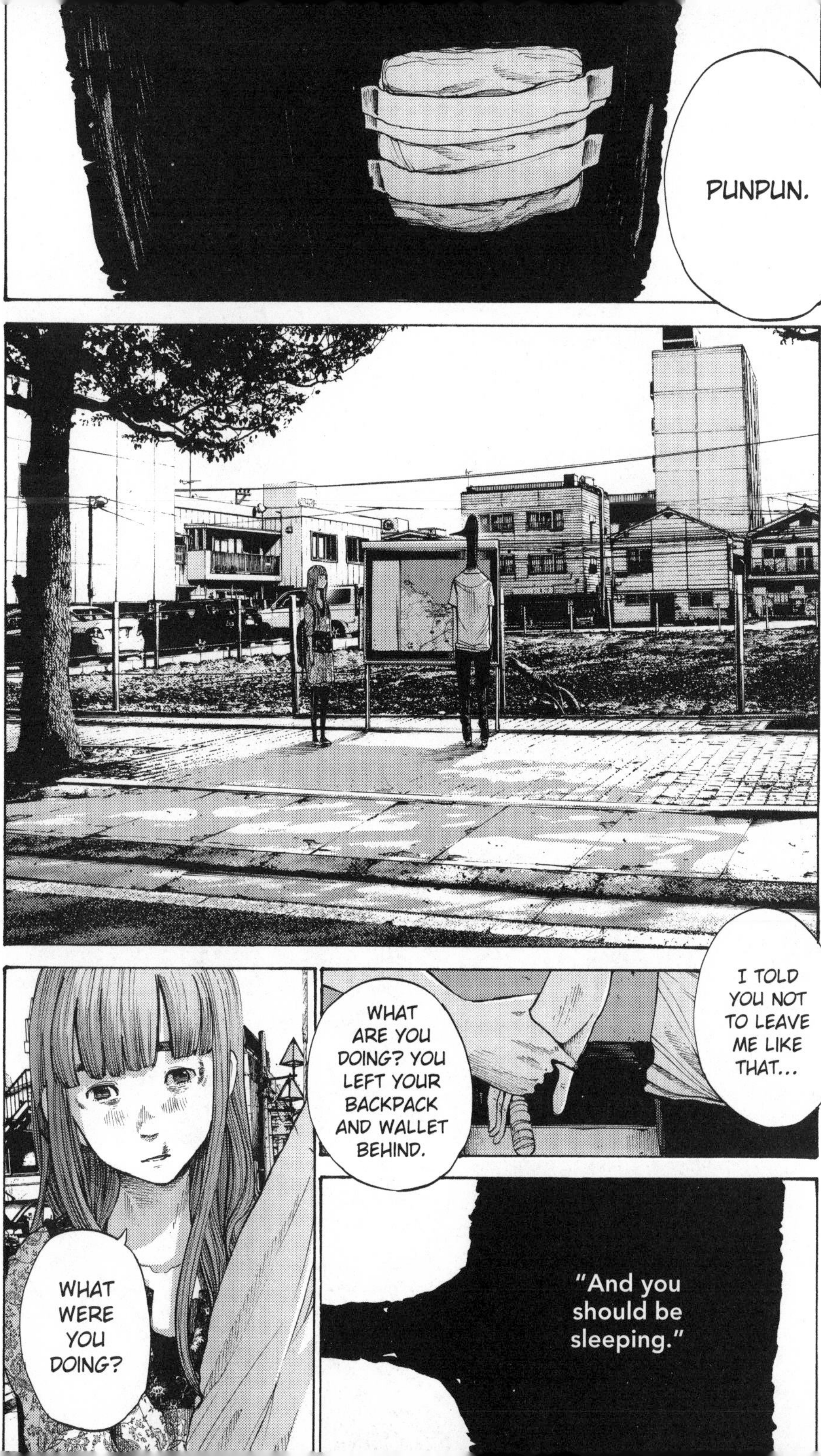
PUNPUN.
I TOLD YOU NOT TO LEAVE ME LIKE THAT...
WHAT ARE YOU DOING? YOU LEFT YOUR BACKPACK AND WALLET BEHIND.
"And you should be sleeping."
WHAT WERE YOU DOING?

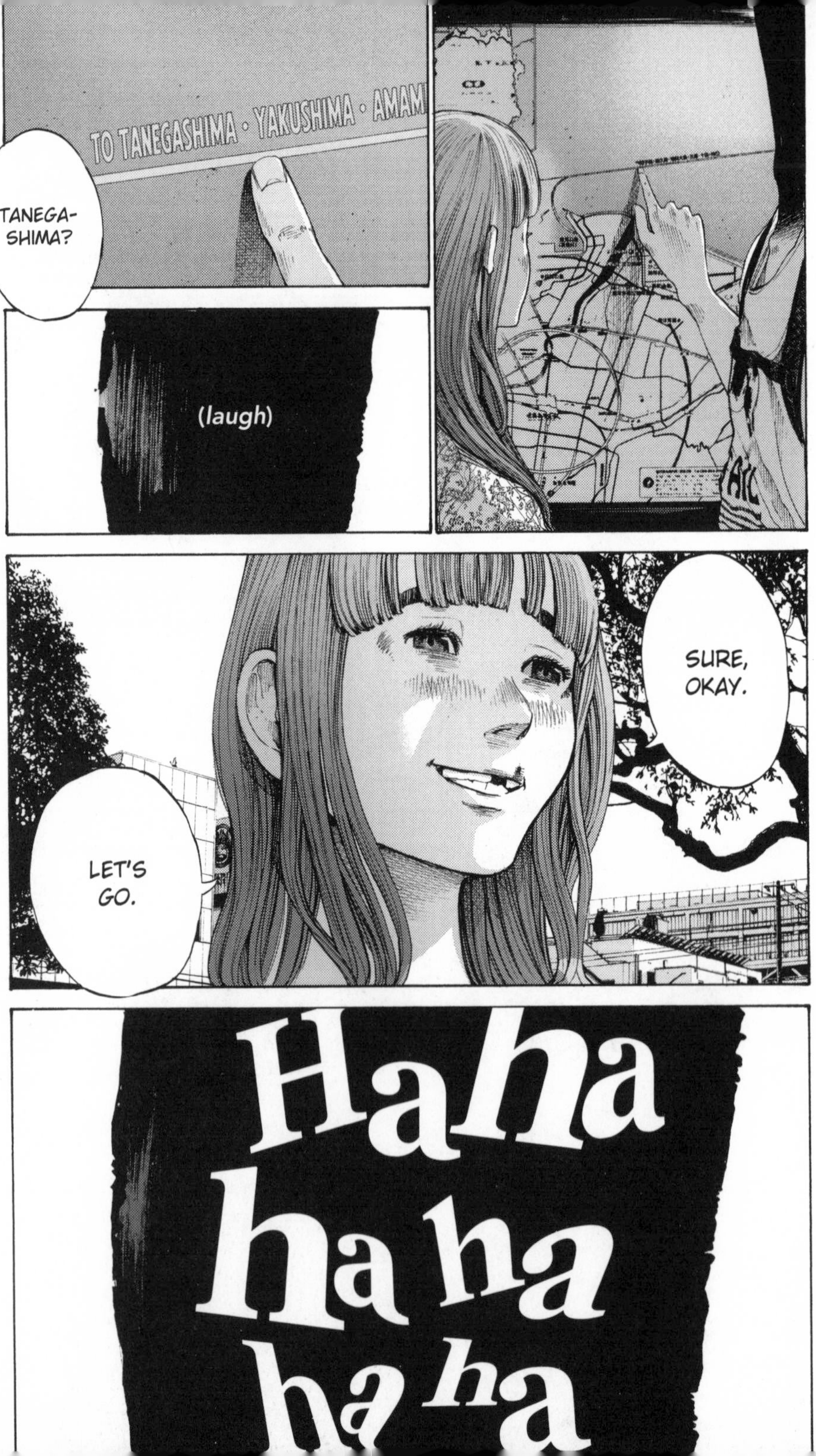
TO TANEGASHIMA · YAKUSHIMA · AMAMI
TANEGA-SHIMA?
(laugh)
SURE, OKAY.
LET'S GO.
Hahahahahaha

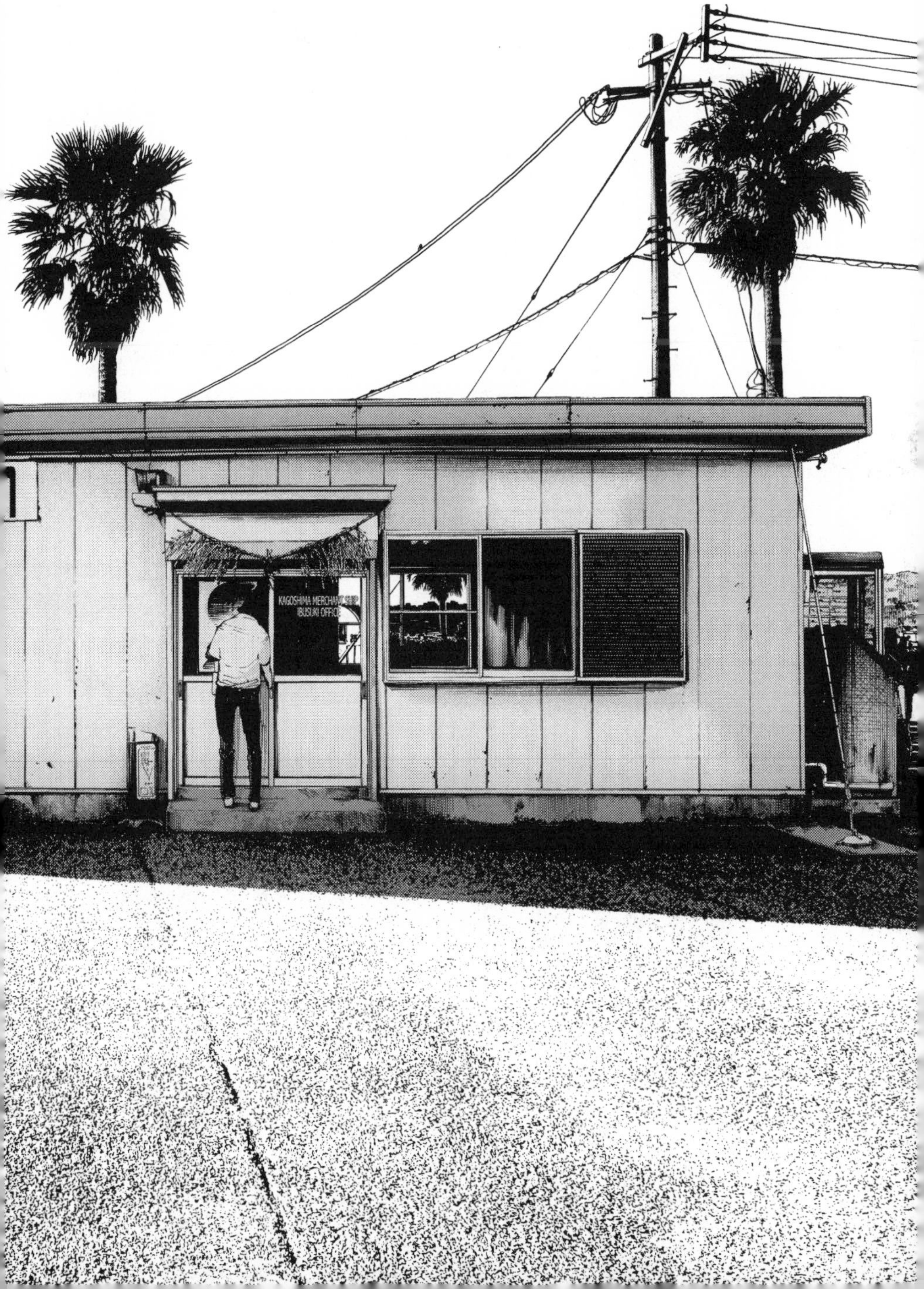
KAGOSHIMA MERCHANT SHIP
IBUSUKI OFFICE

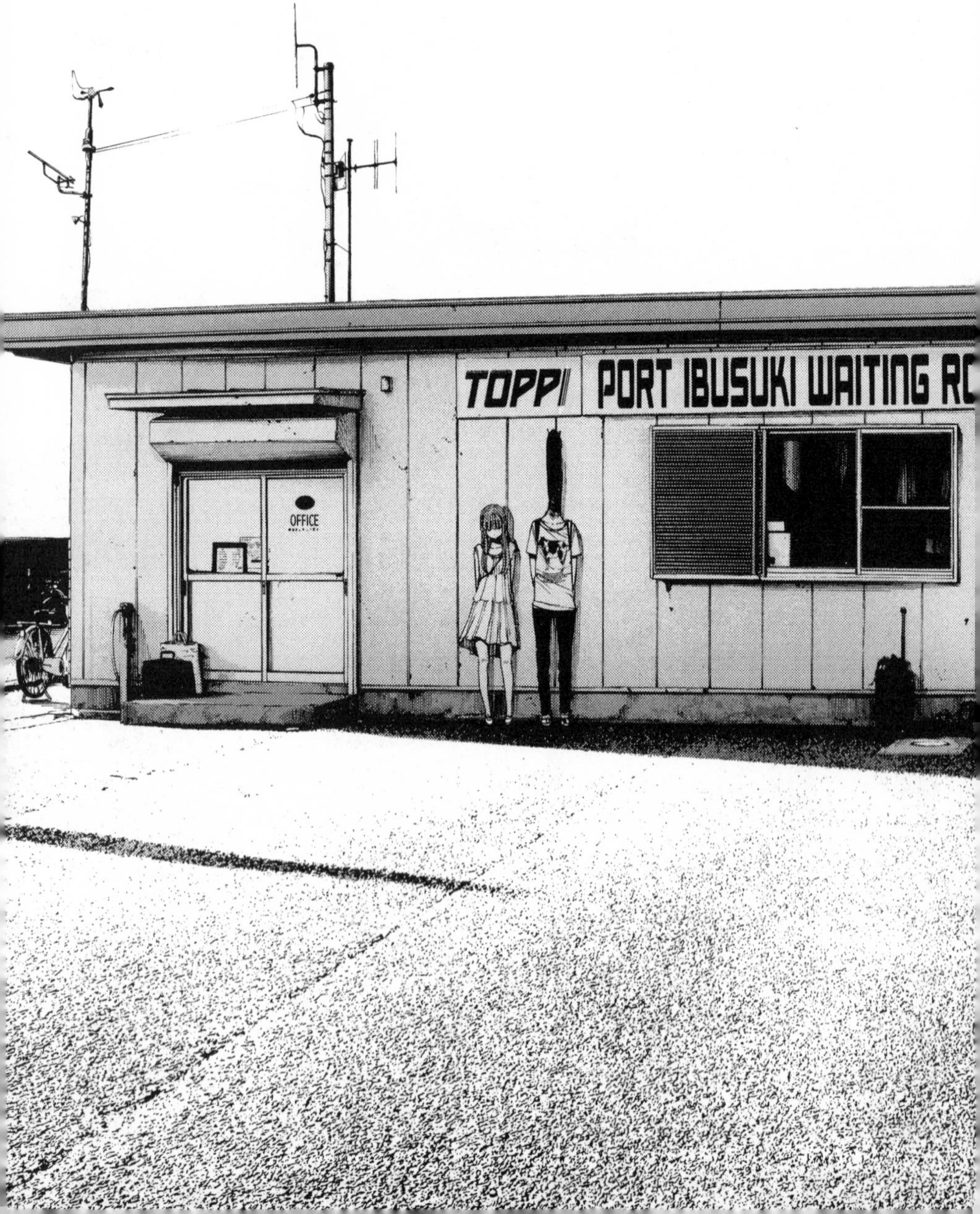
PORT IBUSUKI WAITING RO
OFFICE

TIMETABLE
KAGOSHIMA MERCHANT SHIP
FARES
TOPPI
INFORMATION

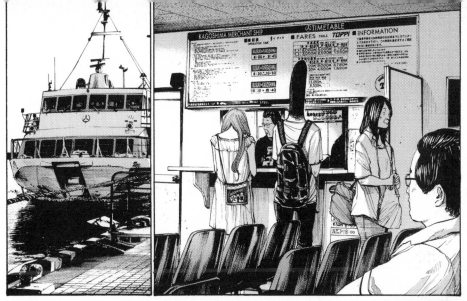

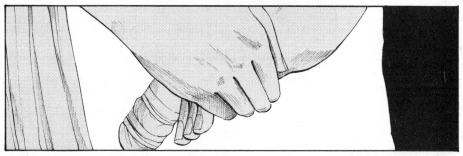

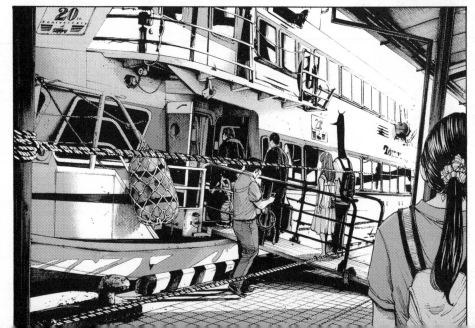

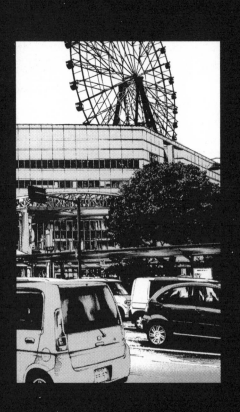

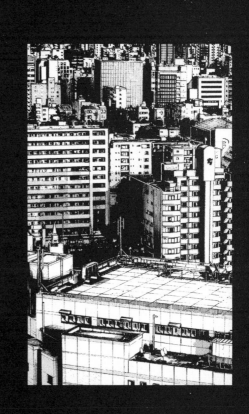

Chapter 130

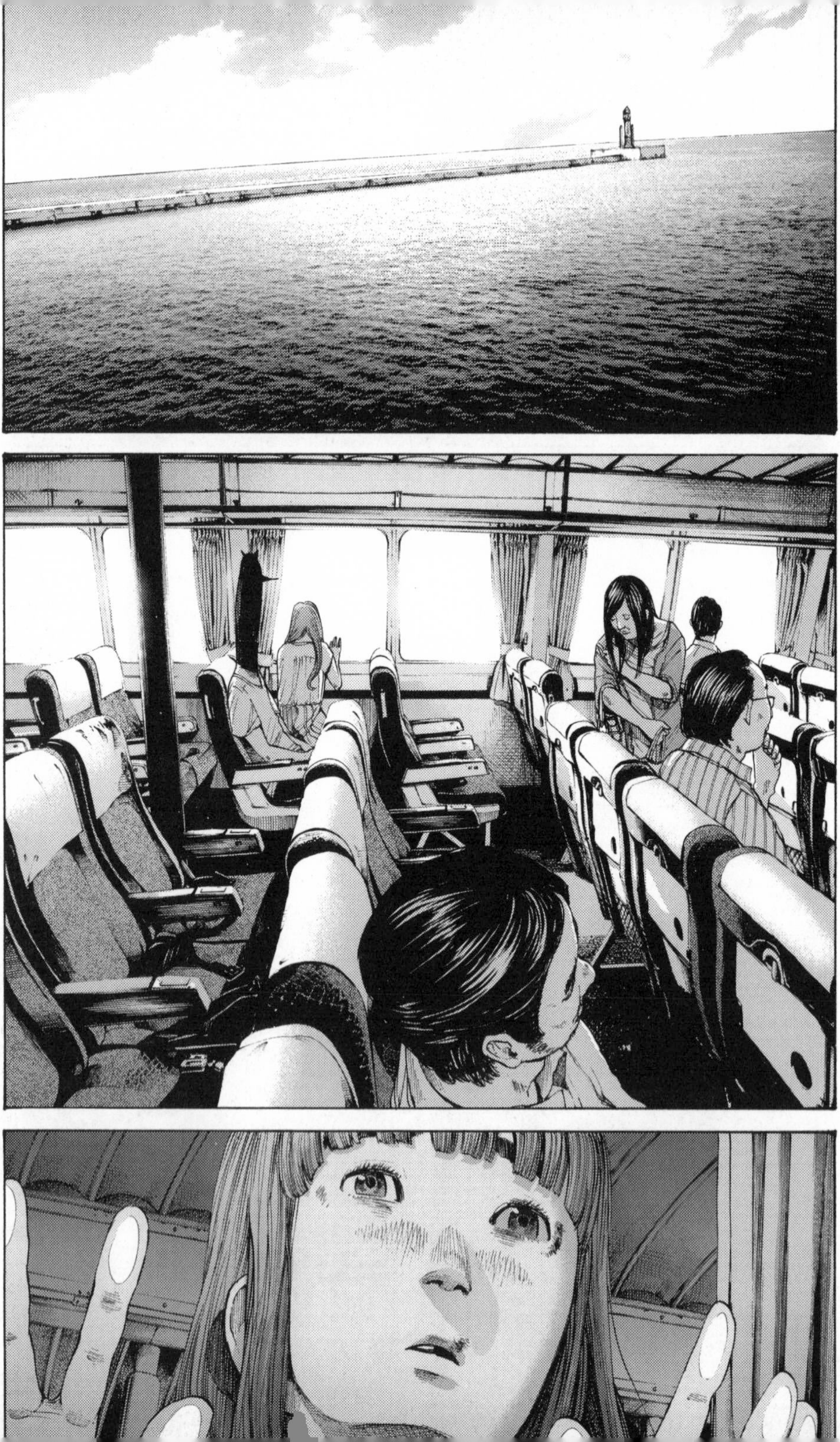

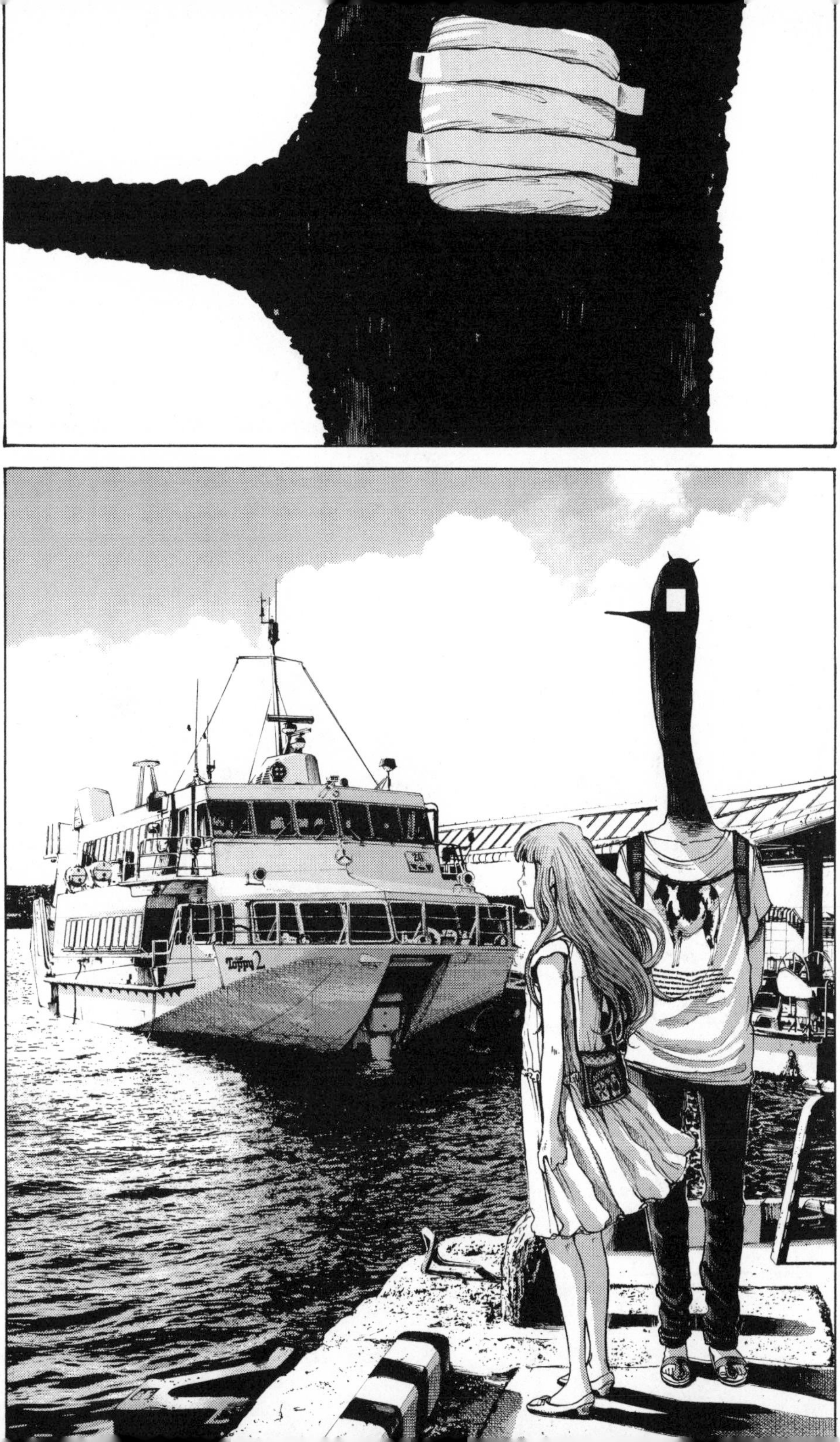
Toppy 2

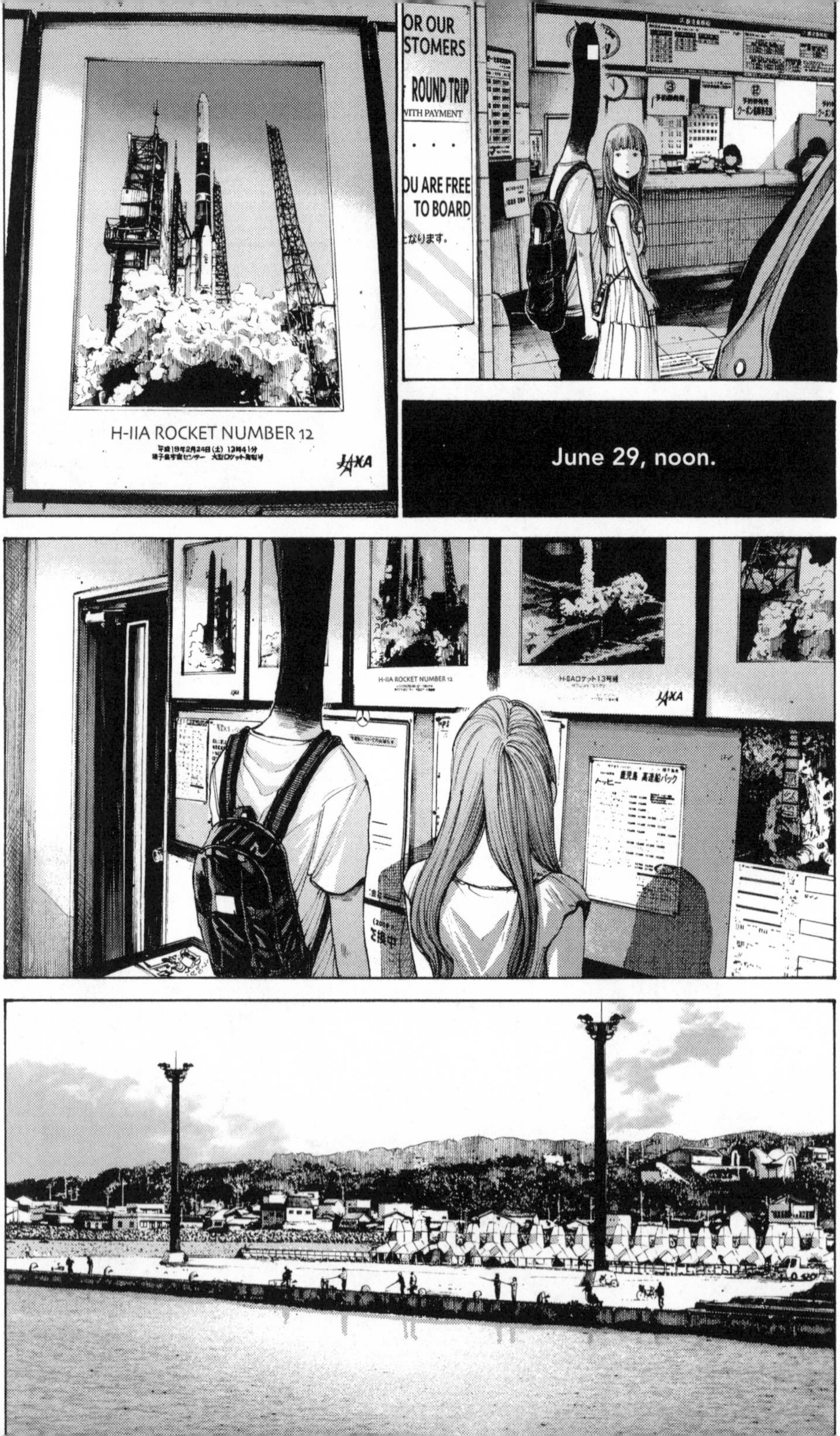

OR OUR
STOMERS
ROUND TRIP
WITH PAYMENT
OU ARE FREE
TO BOARD
となります。
June 29, noon.
H-IIA ROCKET NUMBER 12
JAXA
H-IIA ROCKET NUMBER 12
H-IIAロケット13号機
JAXA
鹿児島 高速船パック
トッピー

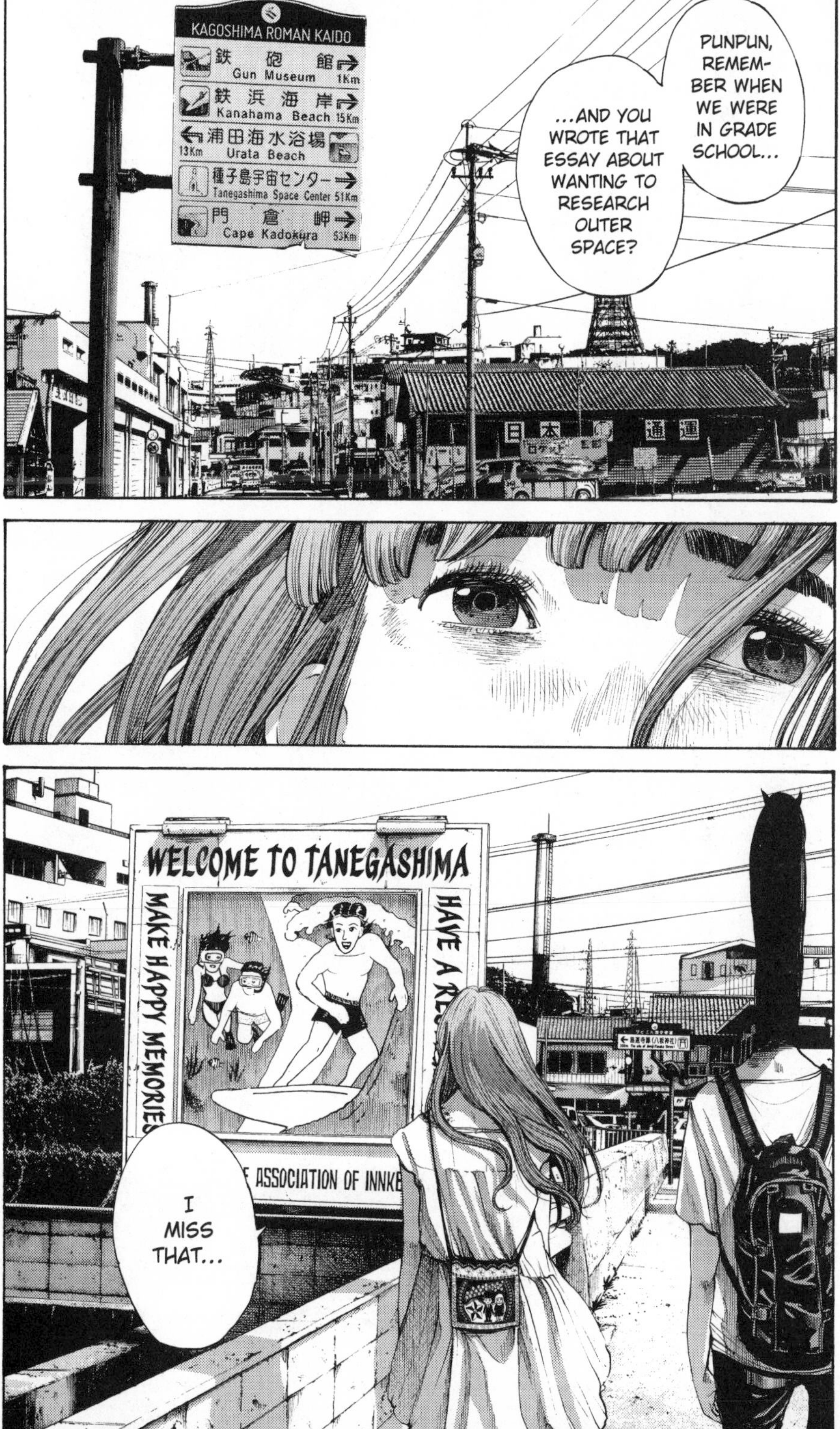
PUNPUN, REMEMBER WHEN WE WERE IN GRADE SCHOOL...
...AND YOU WROTE THAT ESSAY ABOUT WANTING TO RESEARCH OUTER SPACE?
KAGOSHIMA ROMAN KAIDO
鉄砲館 Gun Museum 1Km
鉄浜海岸 Kanahama Beach 15Km
浦田海水浴場 13Km Urata Beach
種子島宇宙センター Tanegashima Space Center 51Km
門倉岬 Cape Kadokura 53Km
WELCOME TO TANEGASHIMA
MAKE HAPPY MEMORIES
I MISS THAT...

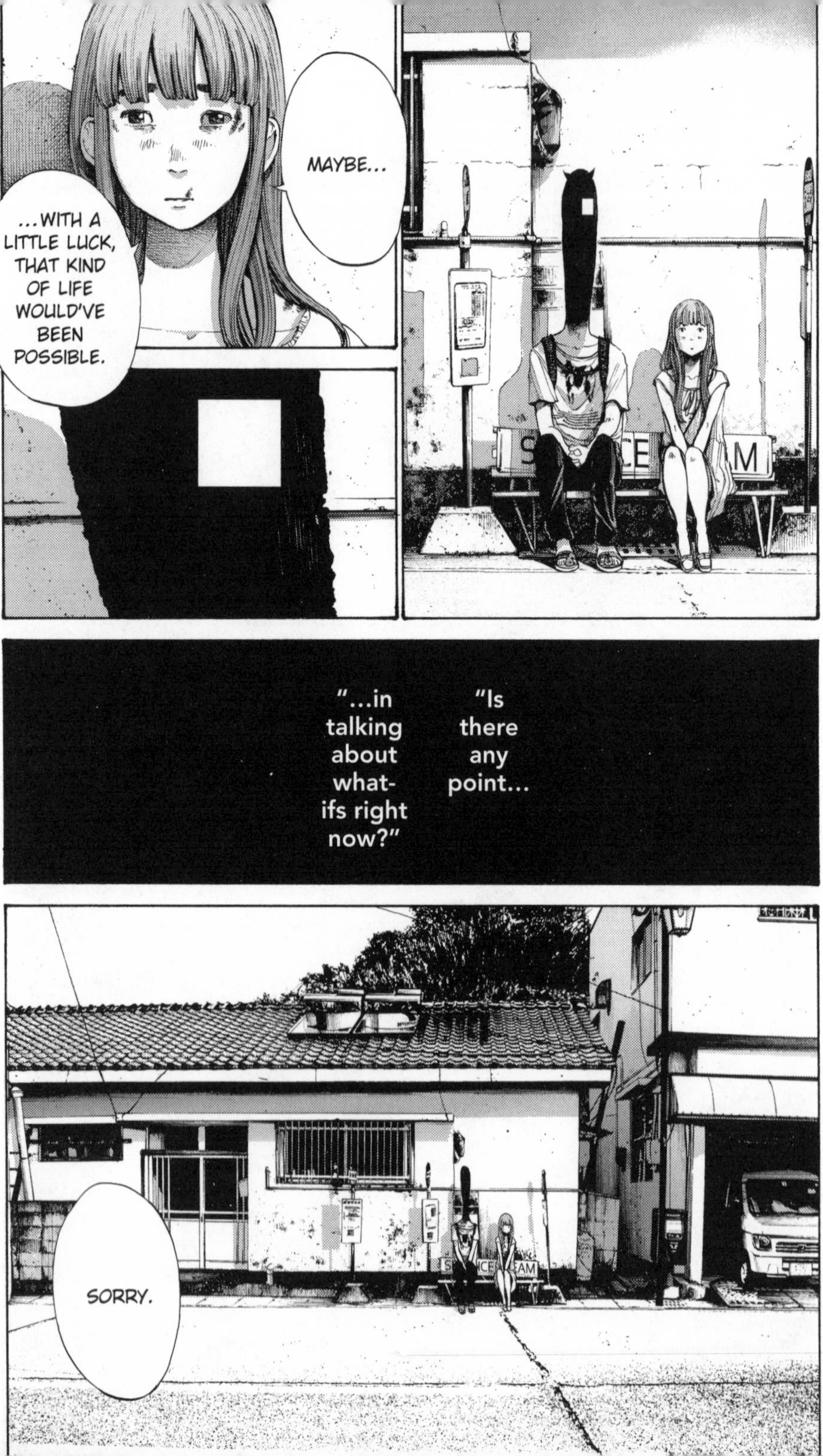
MAYBE...
...WITH A LITTLE LUCK, THAT KIND OF LIFE WOULD'VE BEEN POSSIBLE.
"Is there any point...
...in talking about what-ifs right now?"
SORRY.

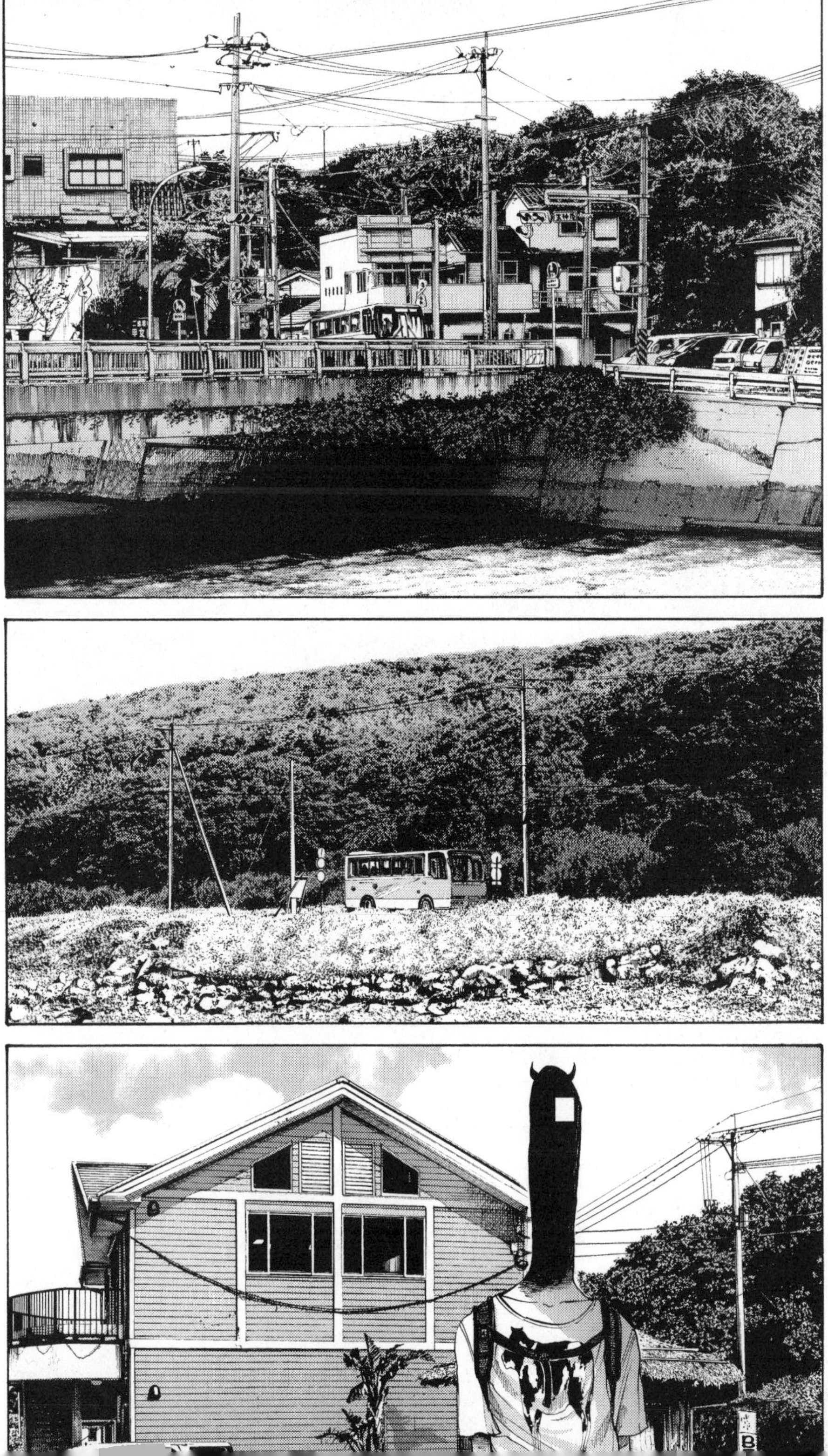

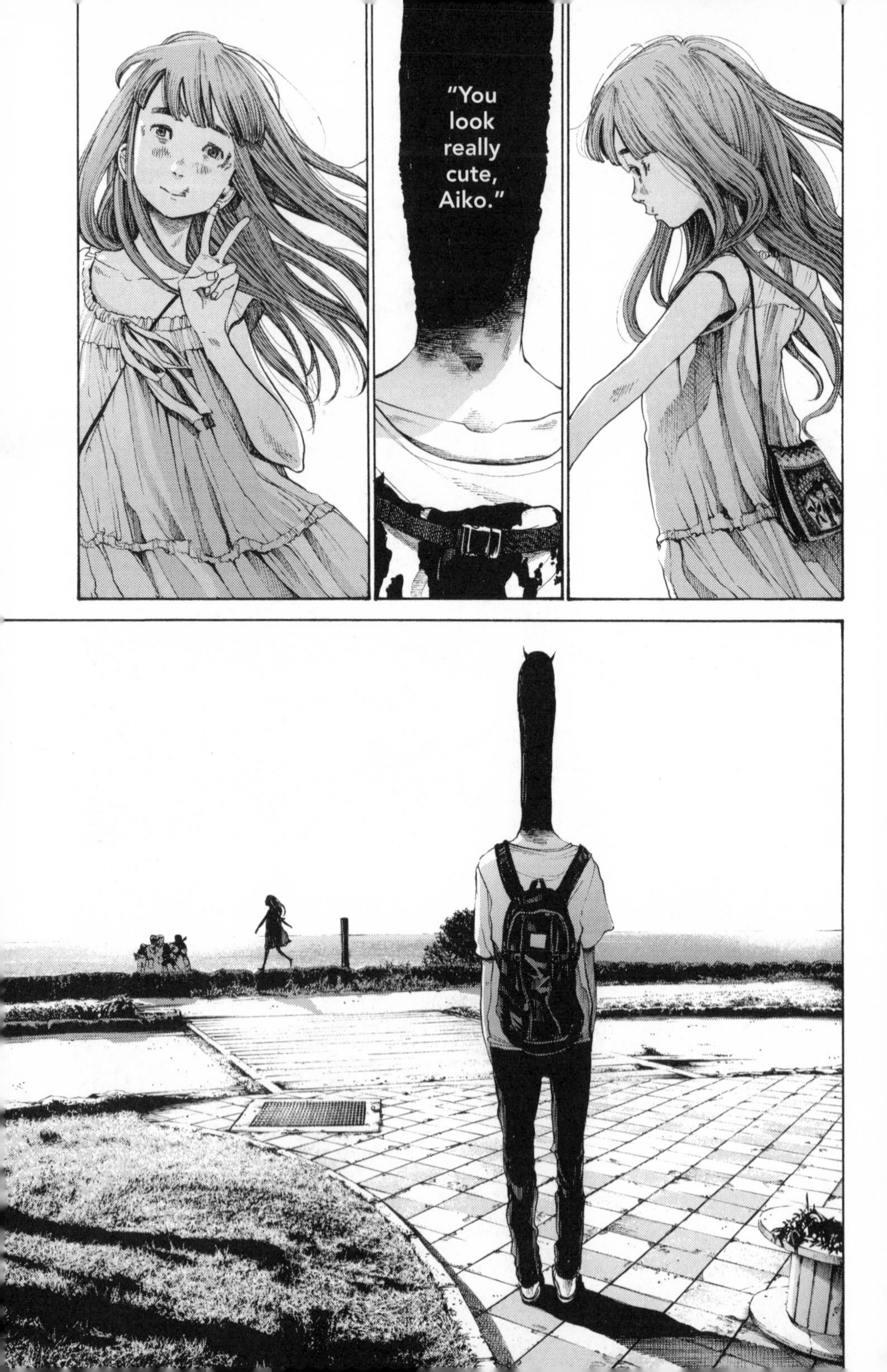
"You look really cute, Aiko."

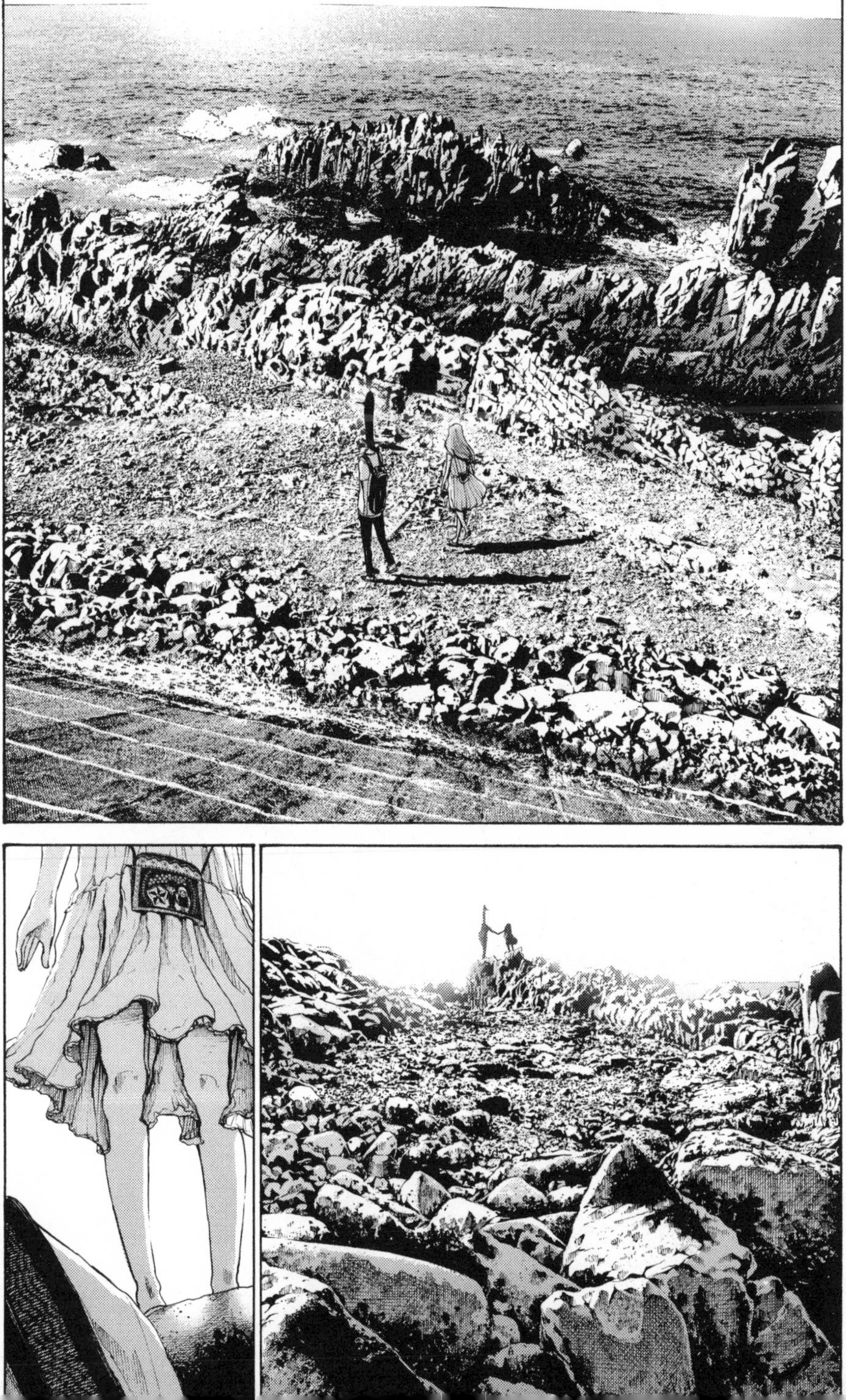

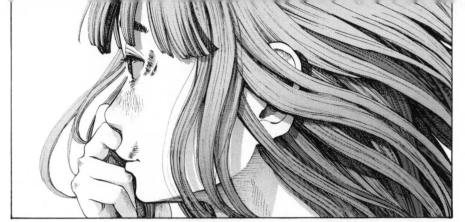

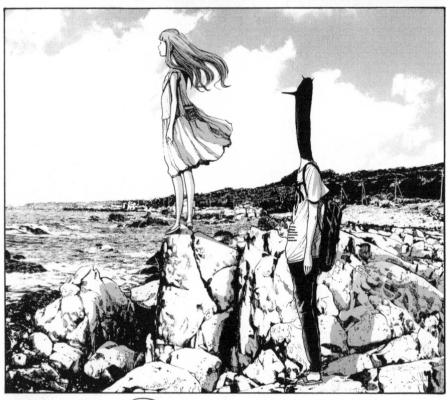

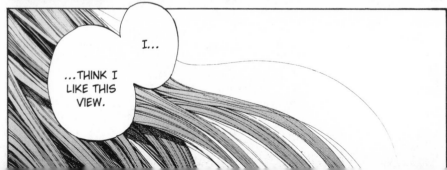

I...

...THINK I LIKE THIS VIEW.

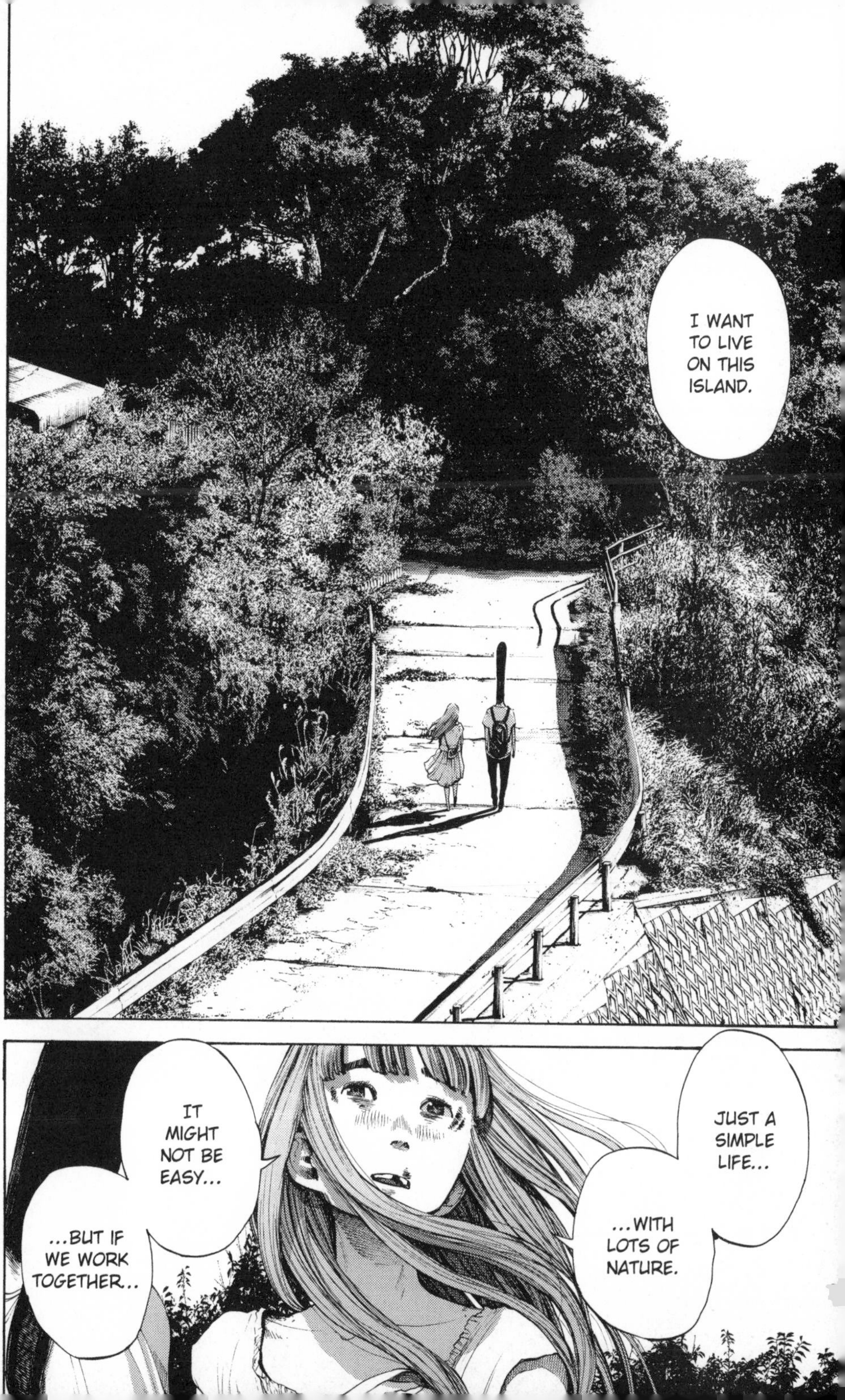
I WANT TO LIVE ON THIS ISLAND.
JUST A SIMPLE LIFE...
...WITH LOTS OF NATURE.
IT MIGHT NOT BE EASY...
...BUT IF WE WORK TOGETHER...

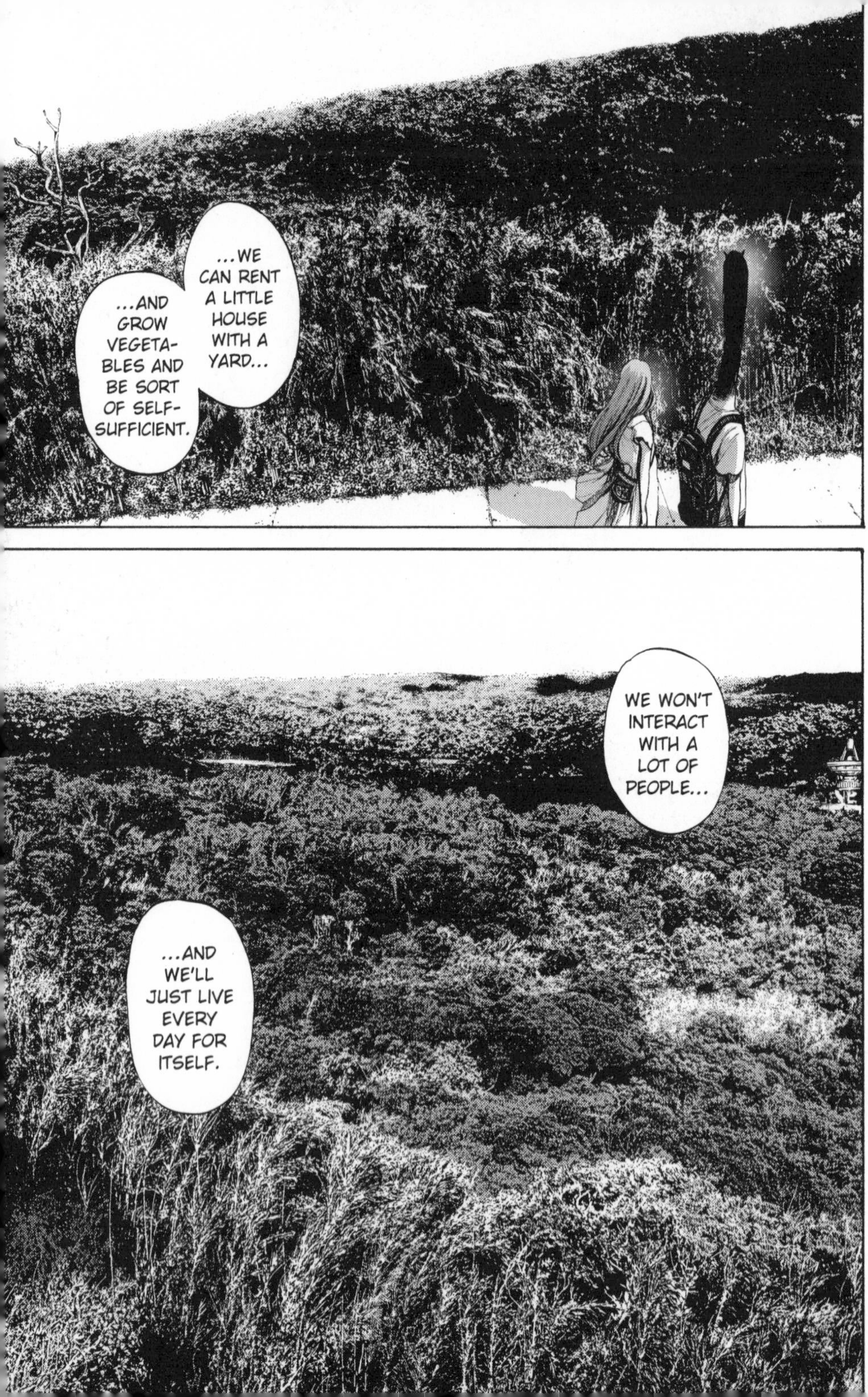
...WE CAN RENT A LITTLE HOUSE WITH A YARD...
...AND GROW VEGETA-BLES AND BE SORT OF SELF-SUFFICIENT.
WE WON'T INTERACT WITH A LOT OF PEOPLE...
...AND WE'LL JUST LIVE EVERY DAY FOR ITSELF.

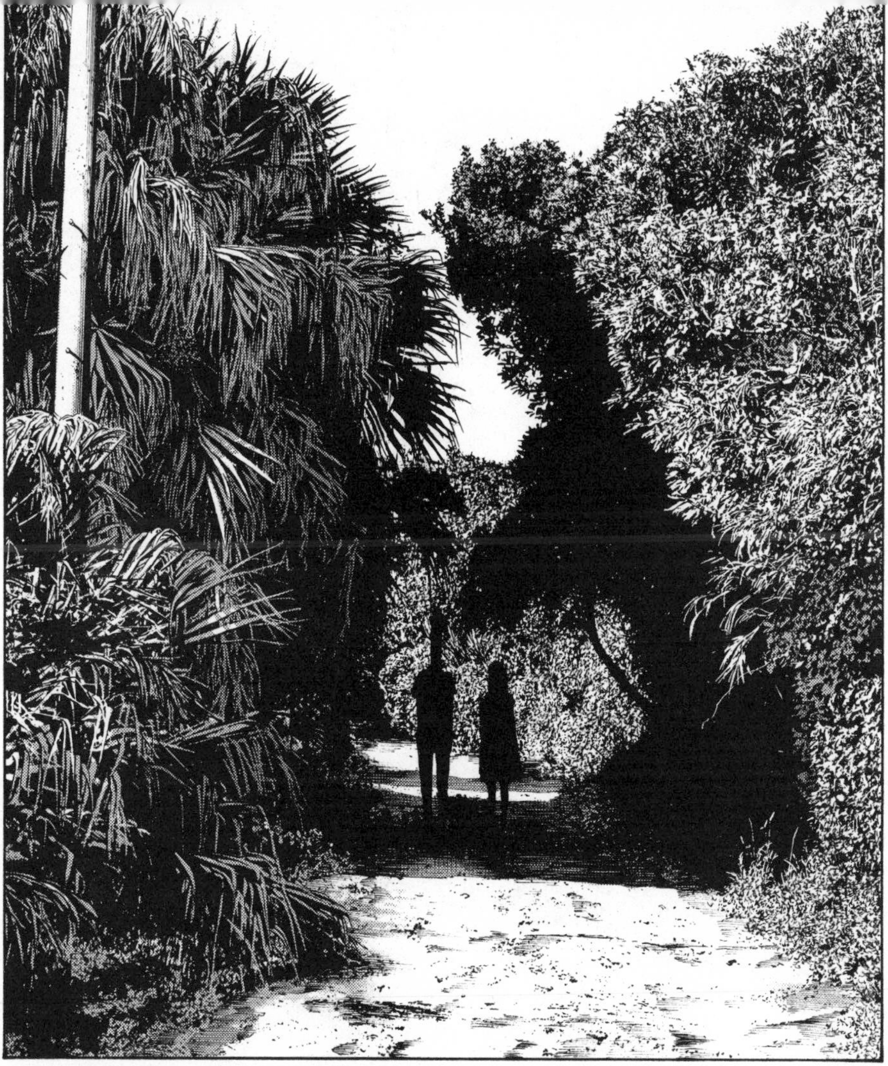
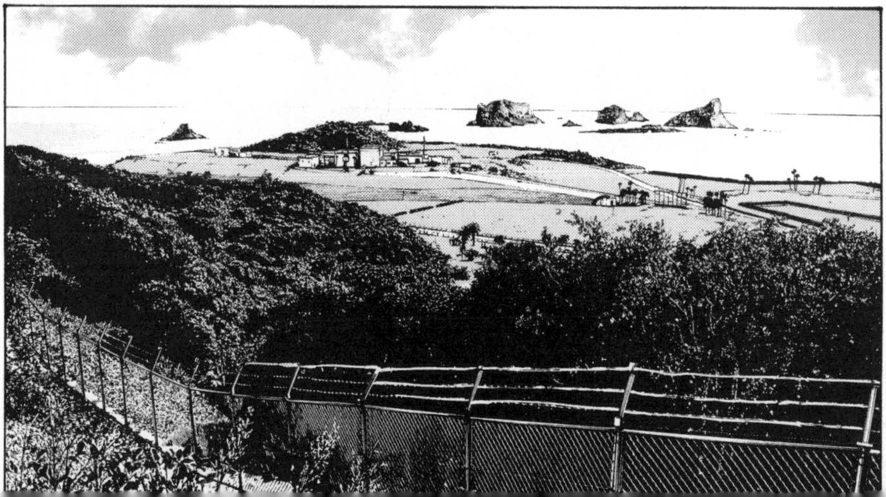

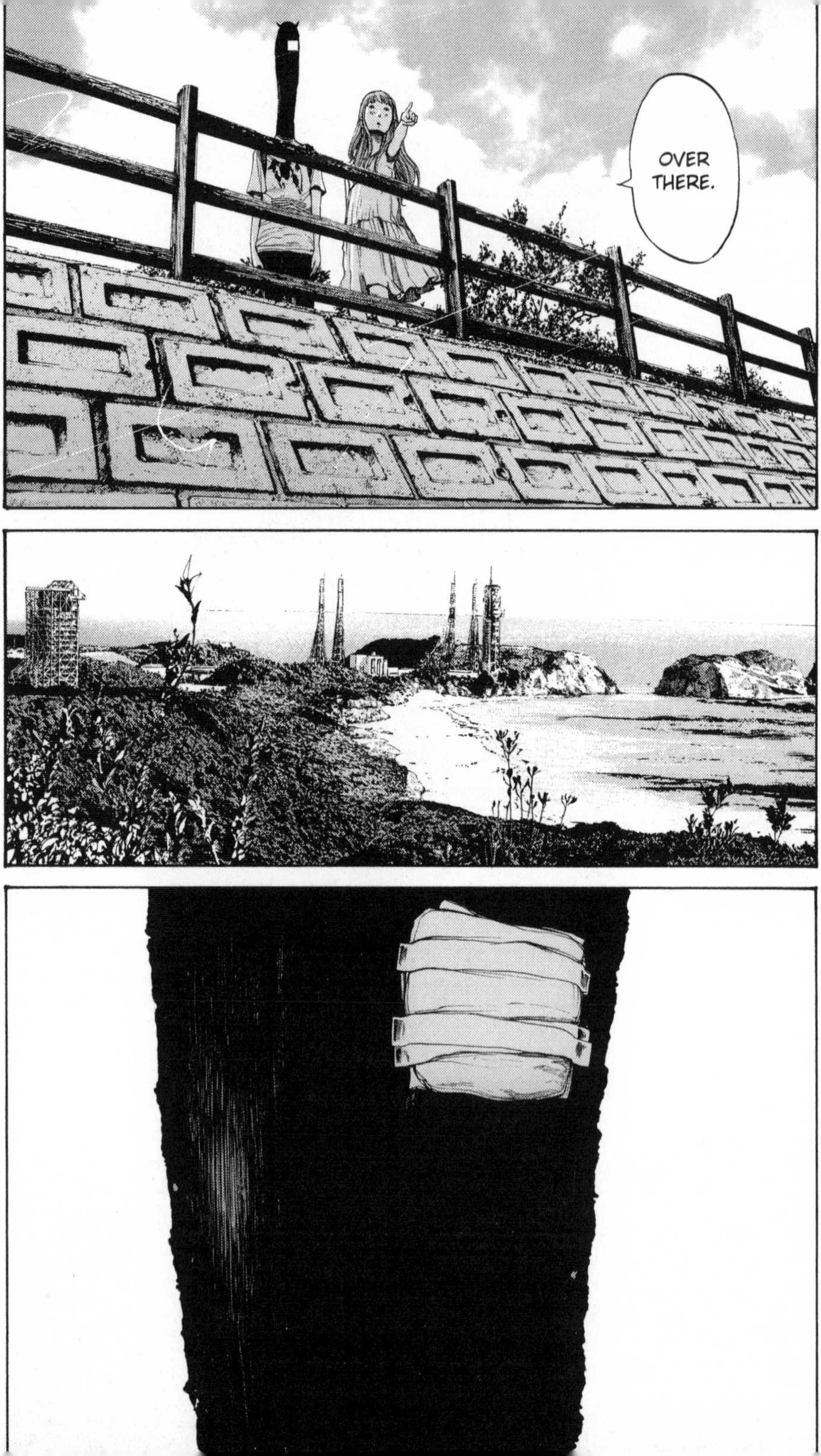
OVER THERE.

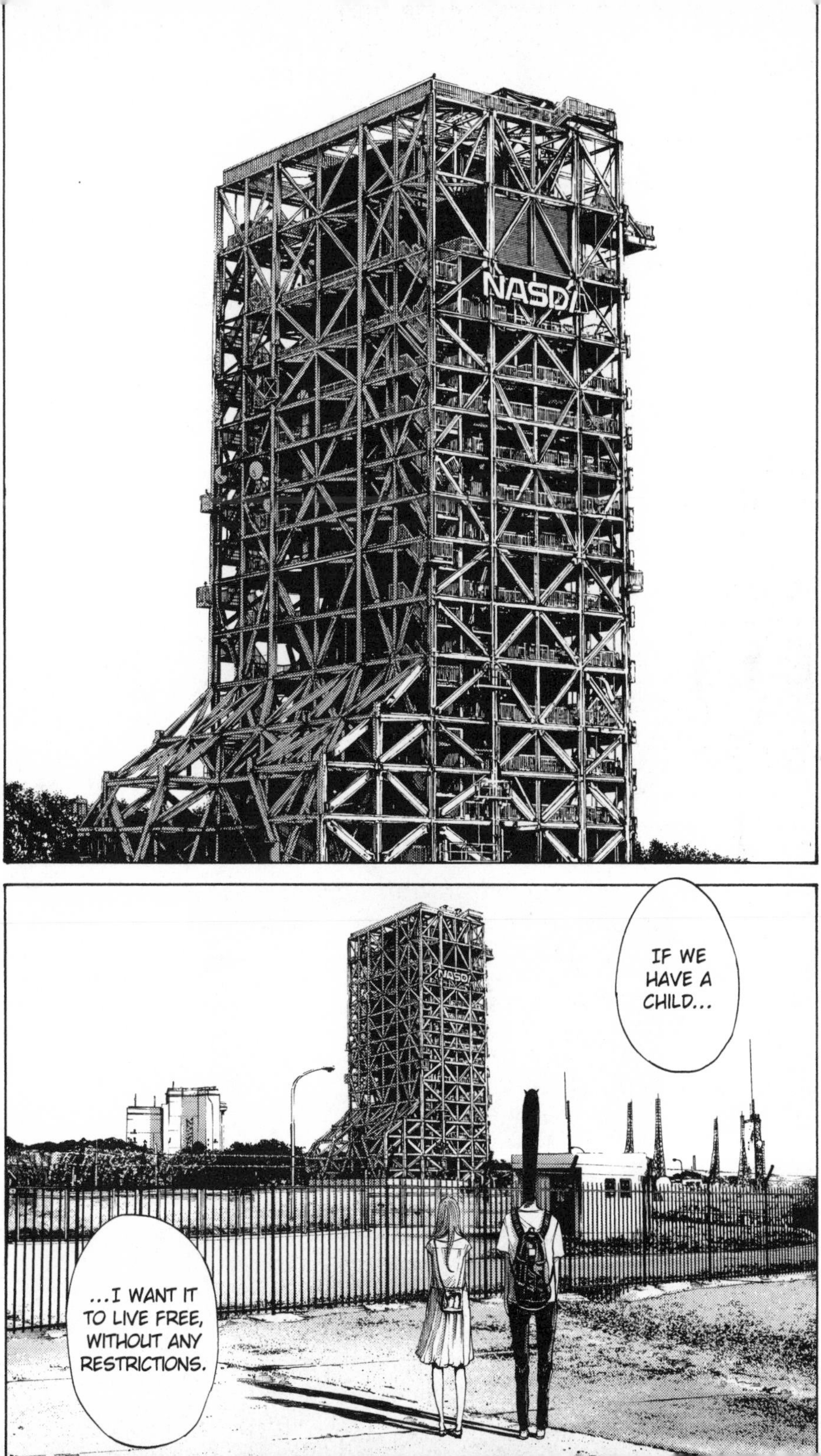
IF WE HAVE A CHILD...
...I WANT IT TO LIVE FREE, WITHOUT ANY RESTRICTIONS.

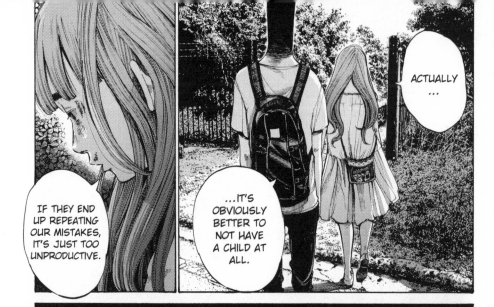

ACTUALLY ...
...IT'S OBVIOUSLY BETTER TO NOT HAVE A CHILD AT ALL.
IF THEY END UP REPEATING OUR MISTAKES, IT'S JUST TOO UNPRODUCTIVE.
"That's why...
"...I think what-ifs are meaningless."
SORRY.

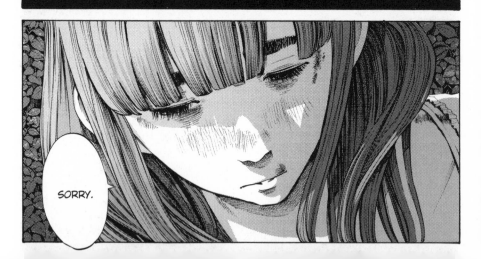

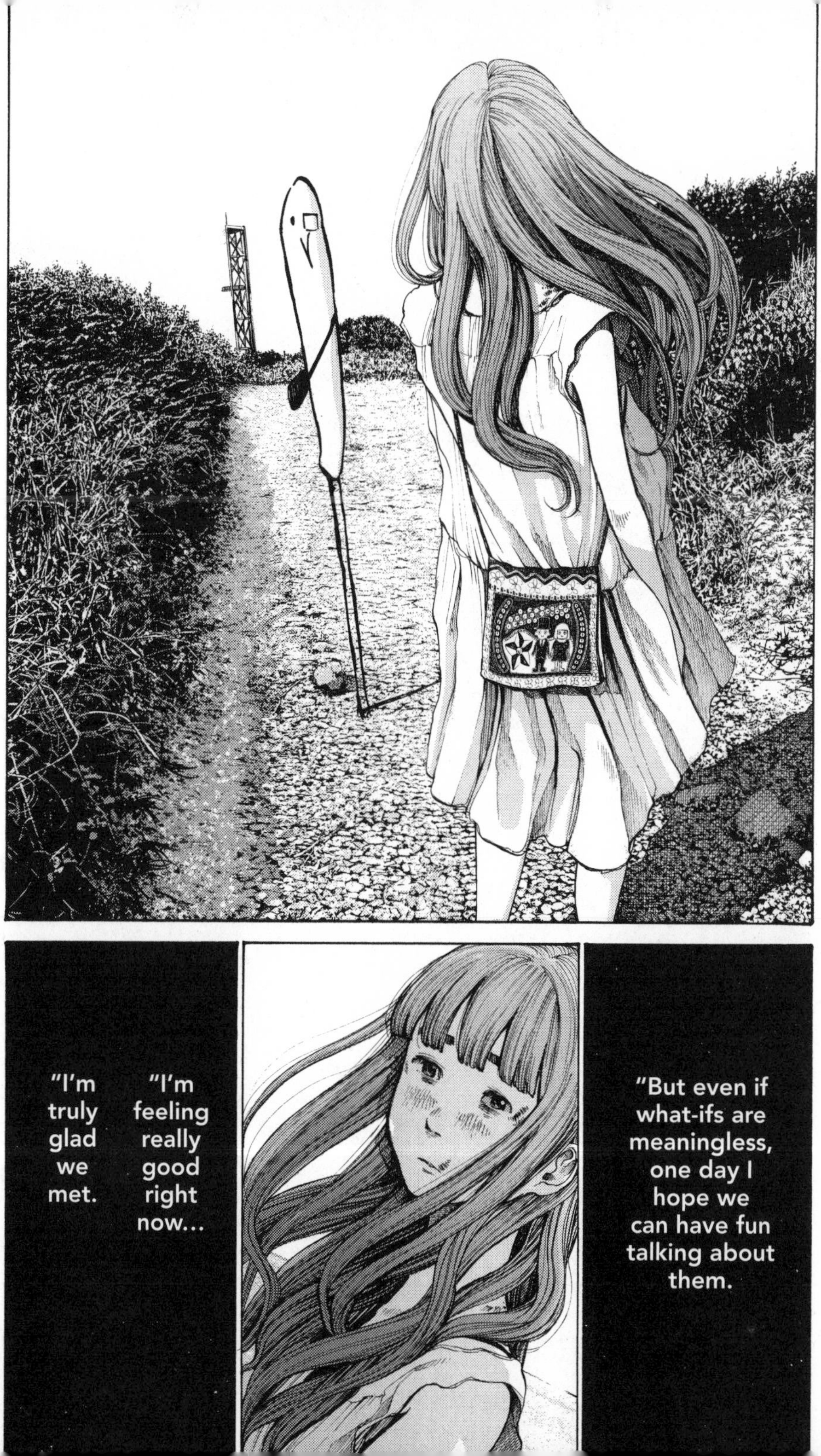
"But even if what-ifs are meaningless, one day I hope we can have fun talking about them.
"I'm feeling really good right now...
"I'm truly glad we met.

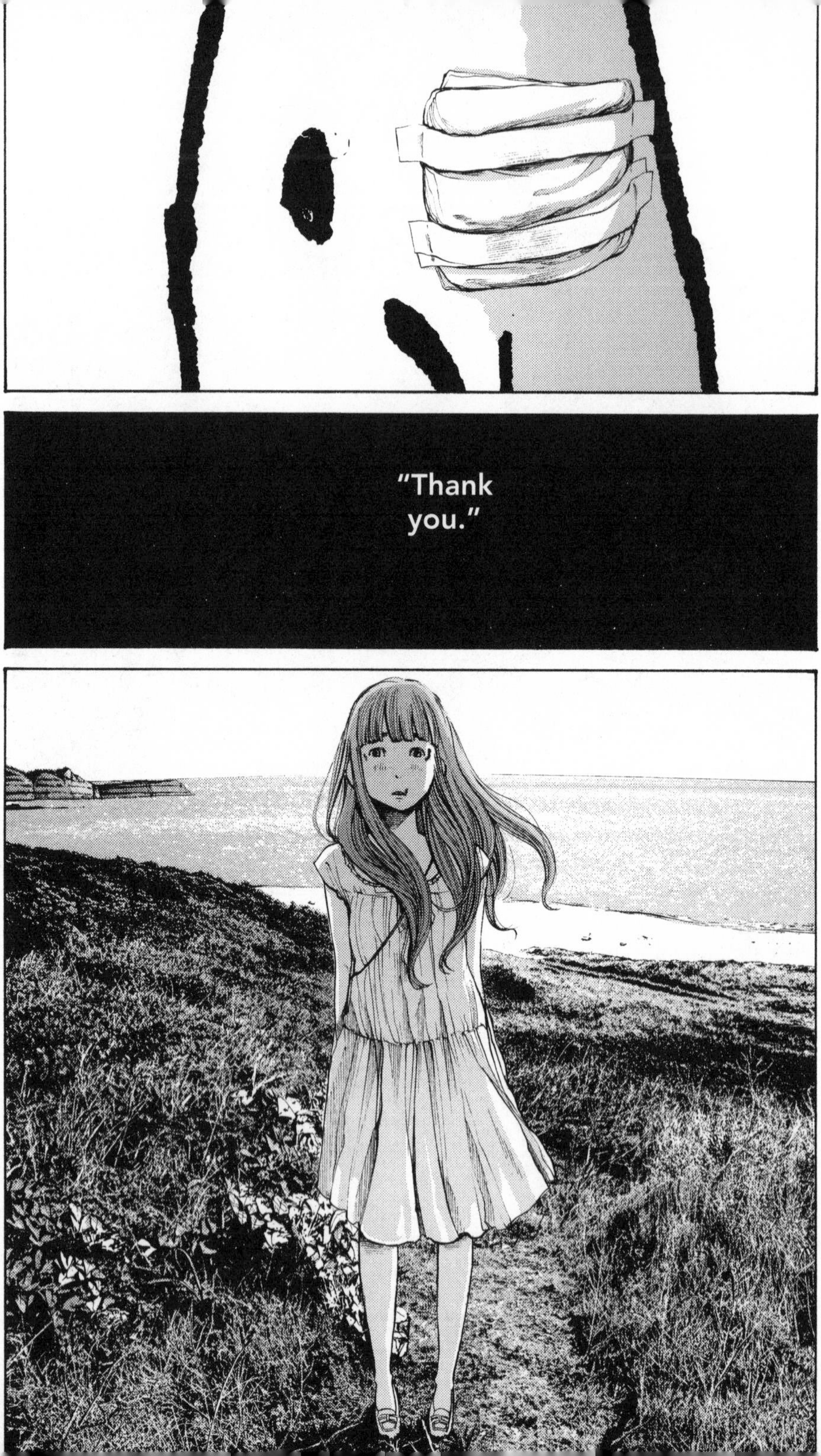
"Thank you."

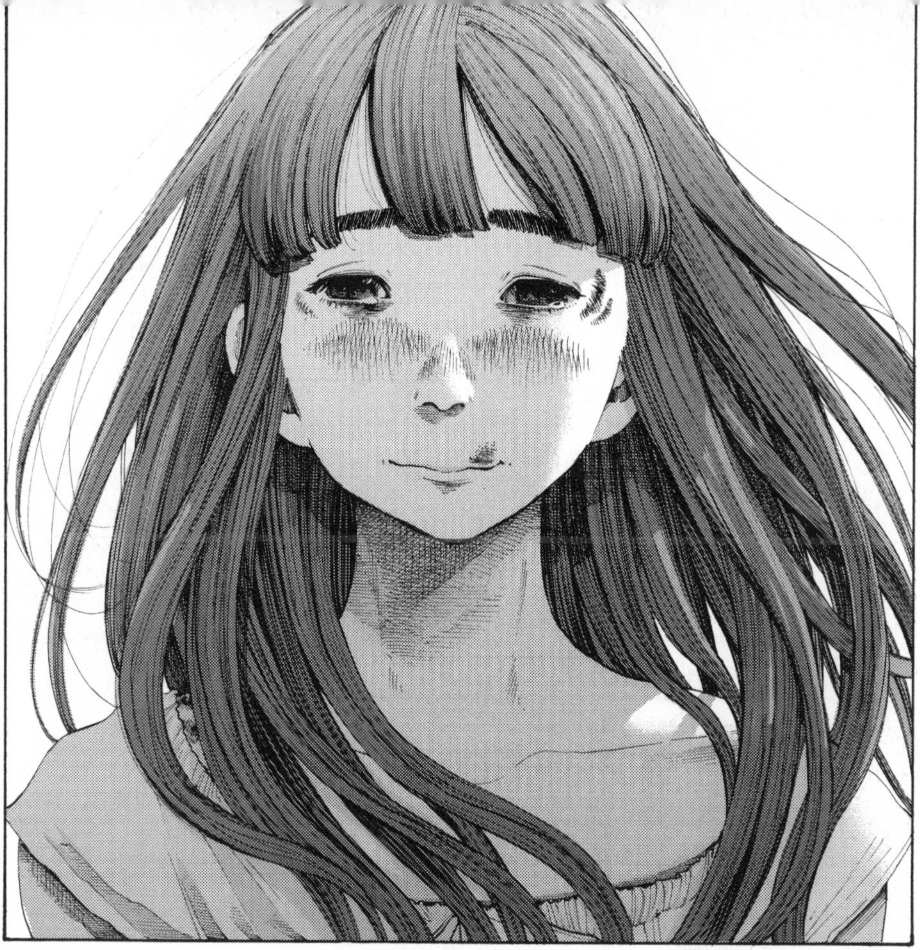
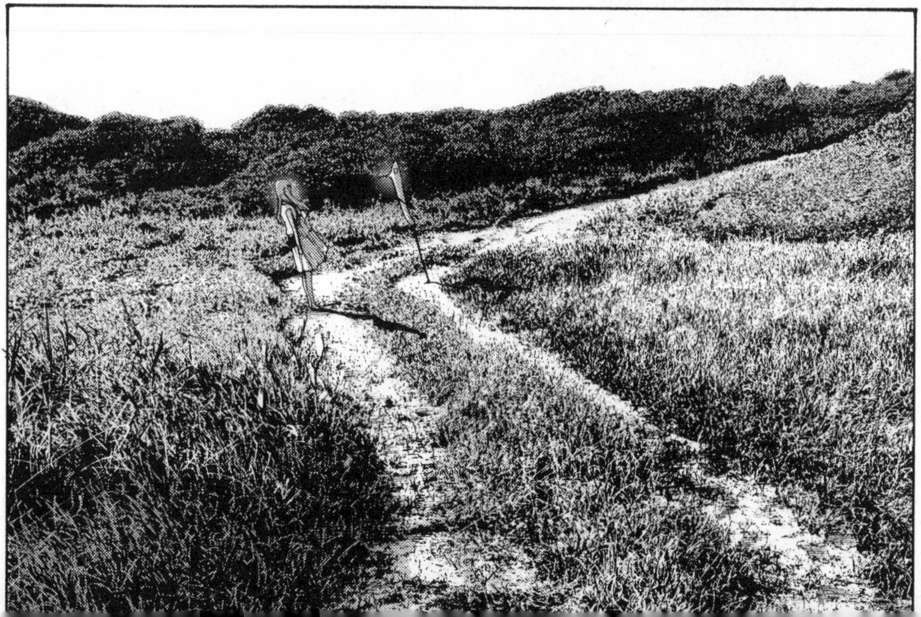

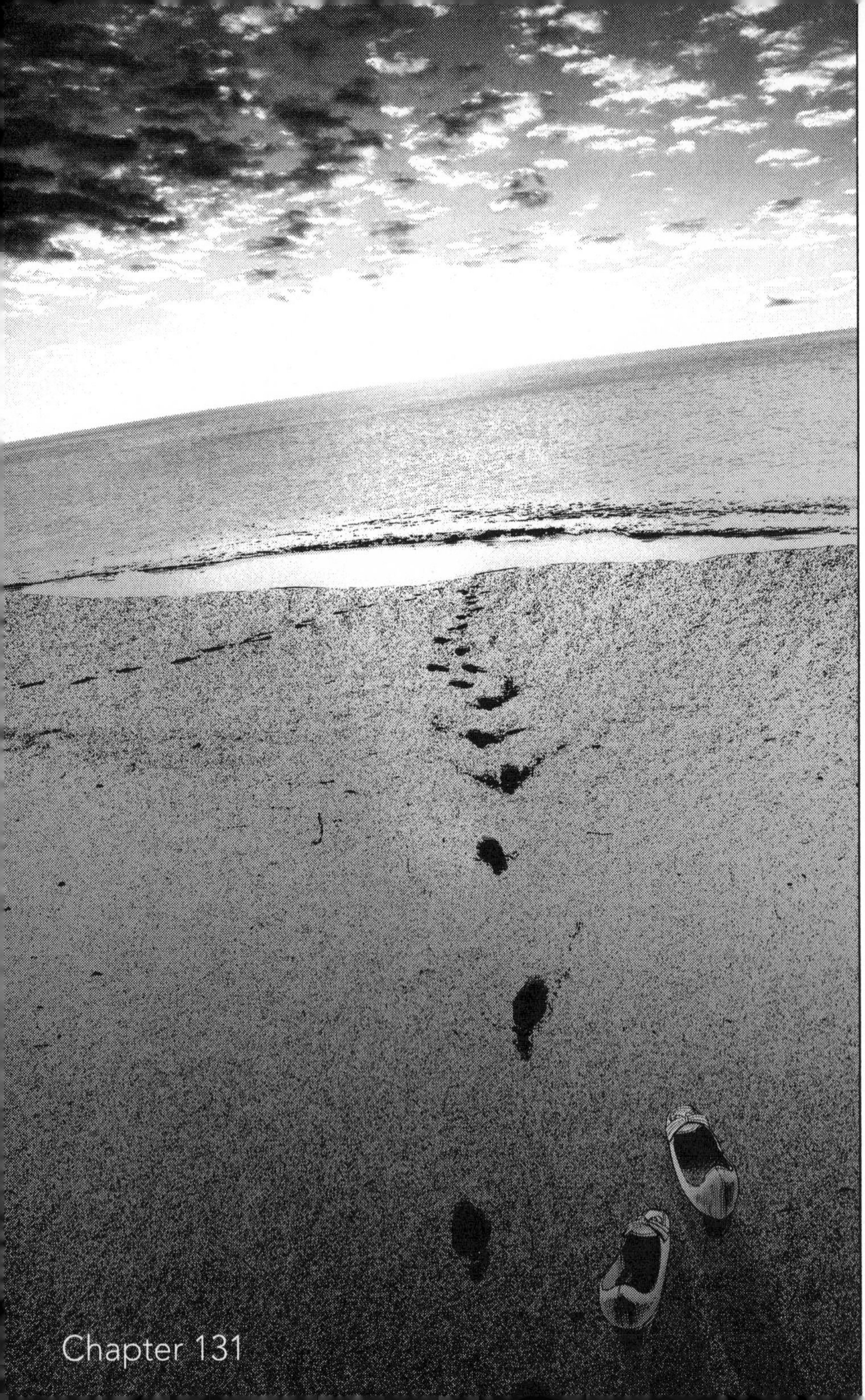

Chapter 131

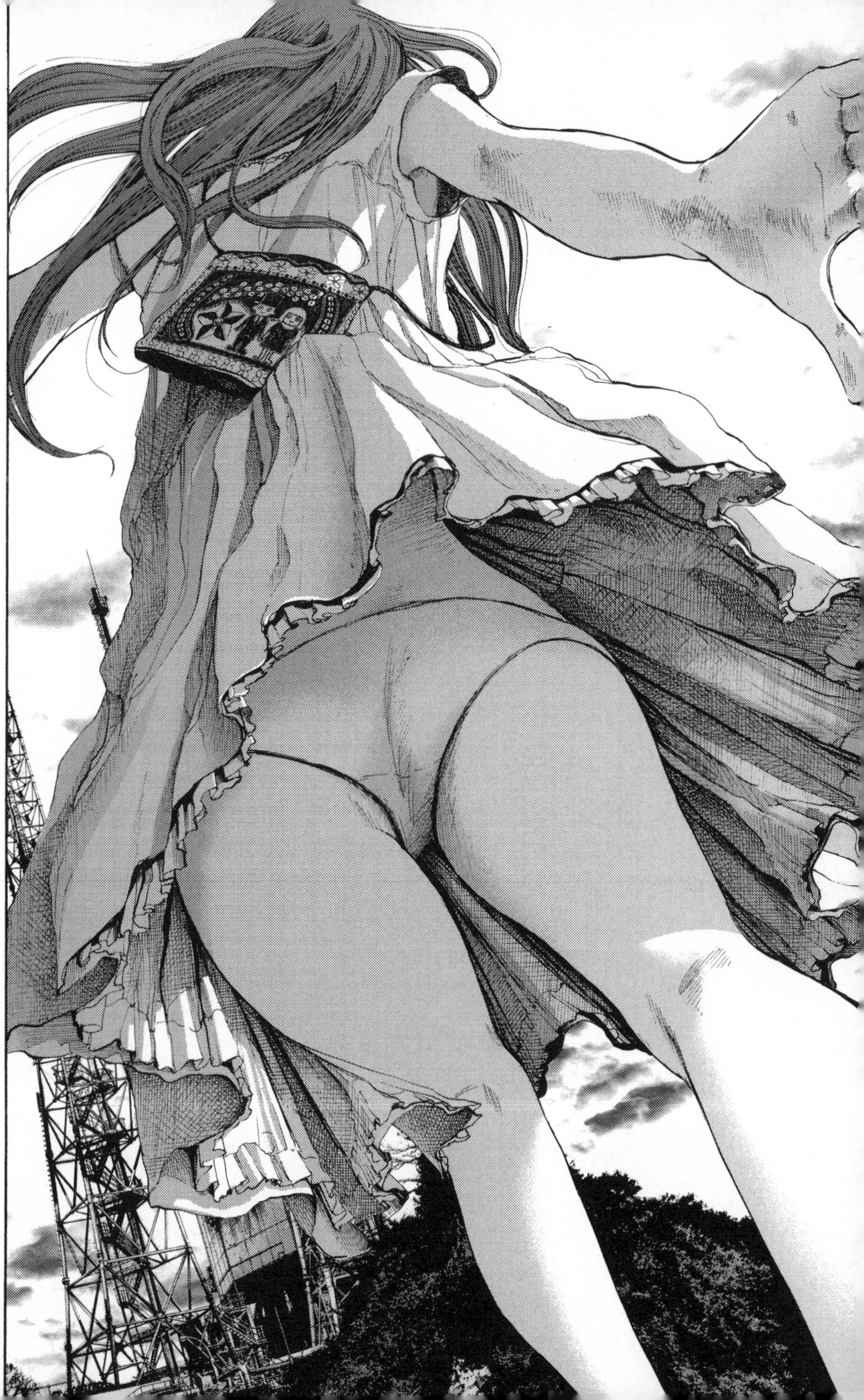

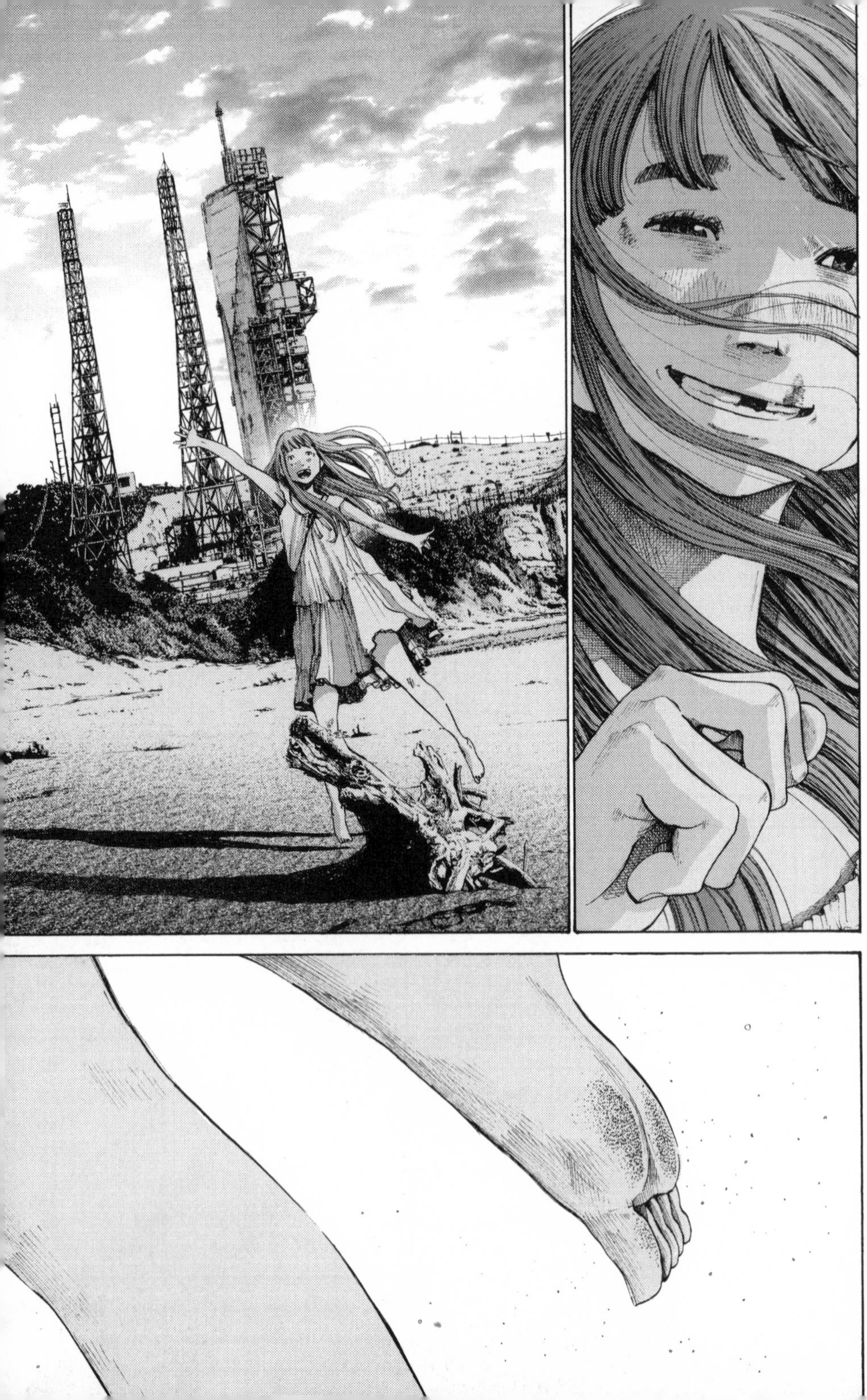

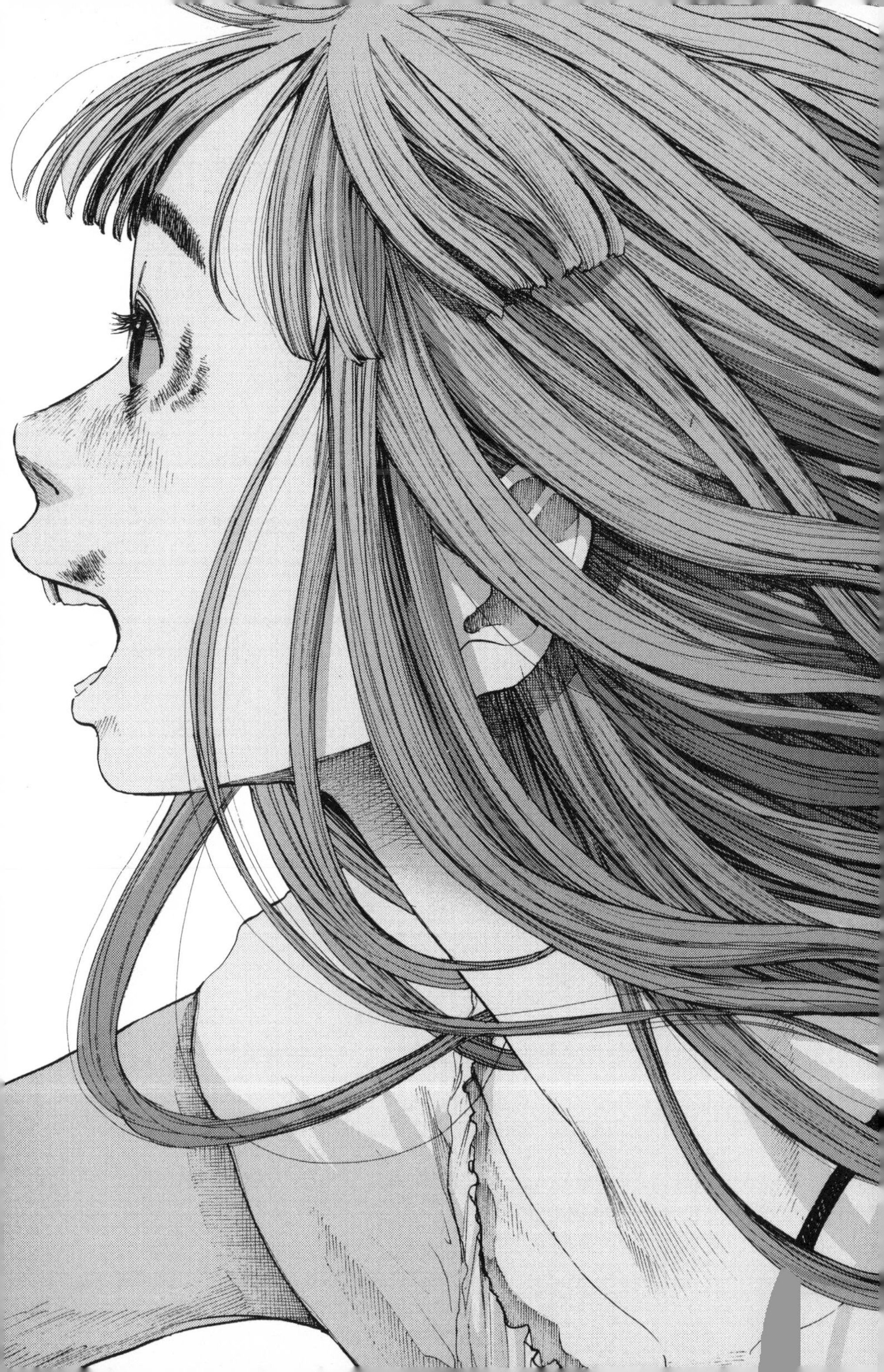

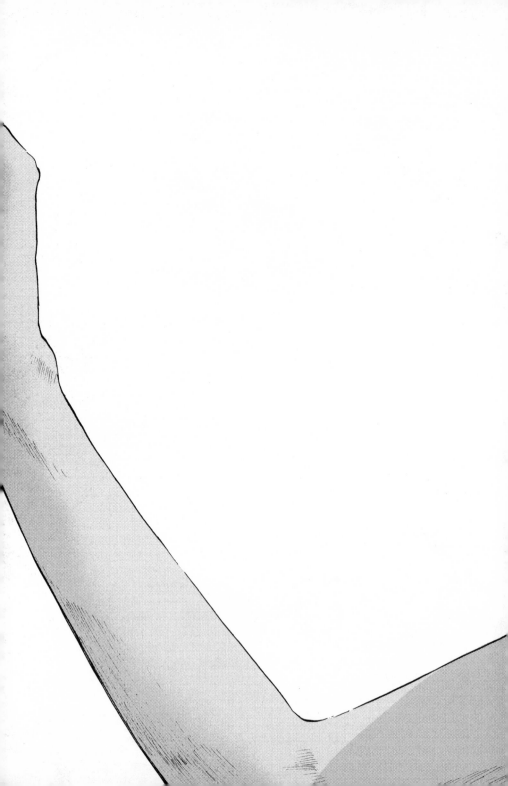

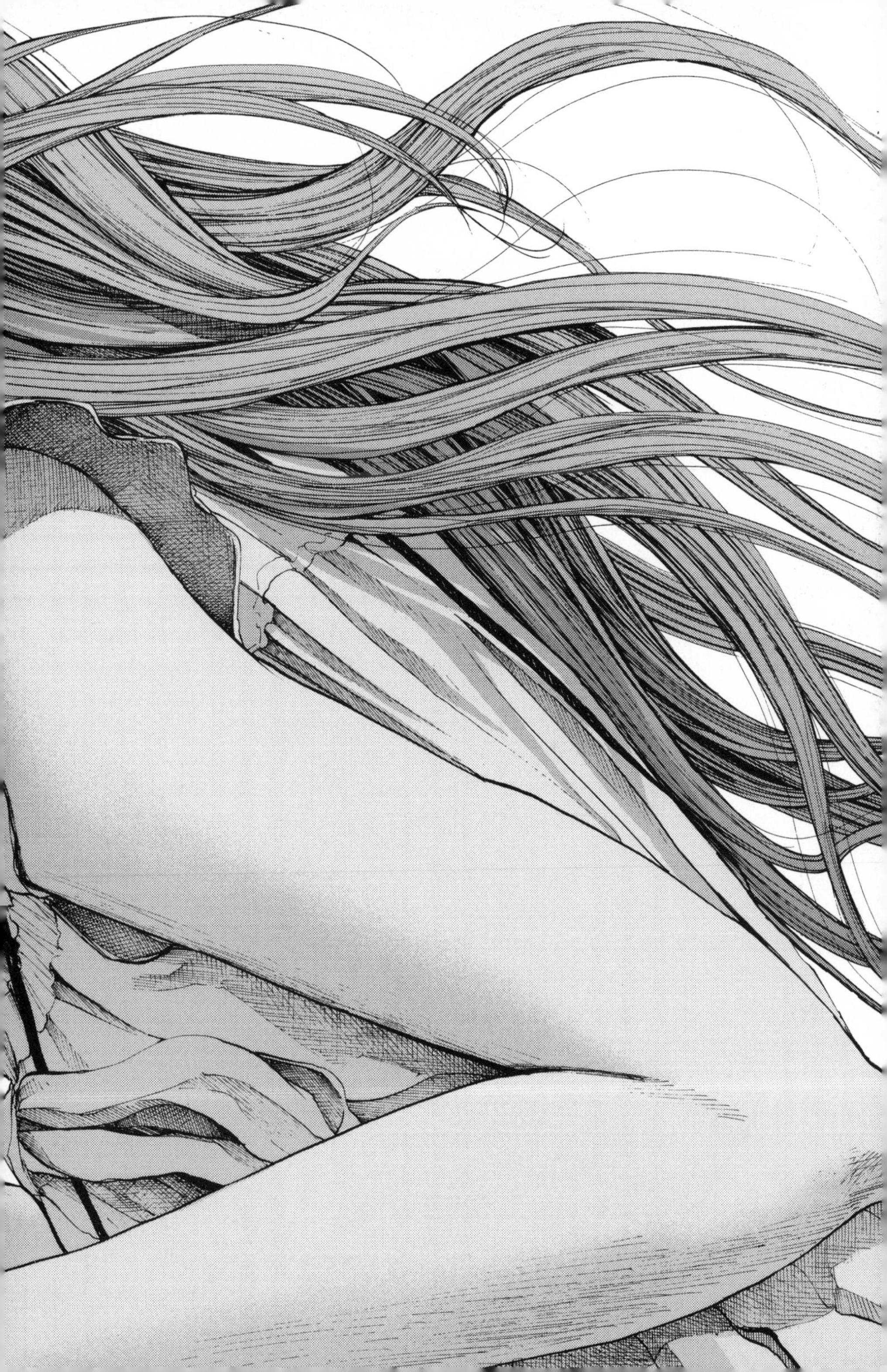

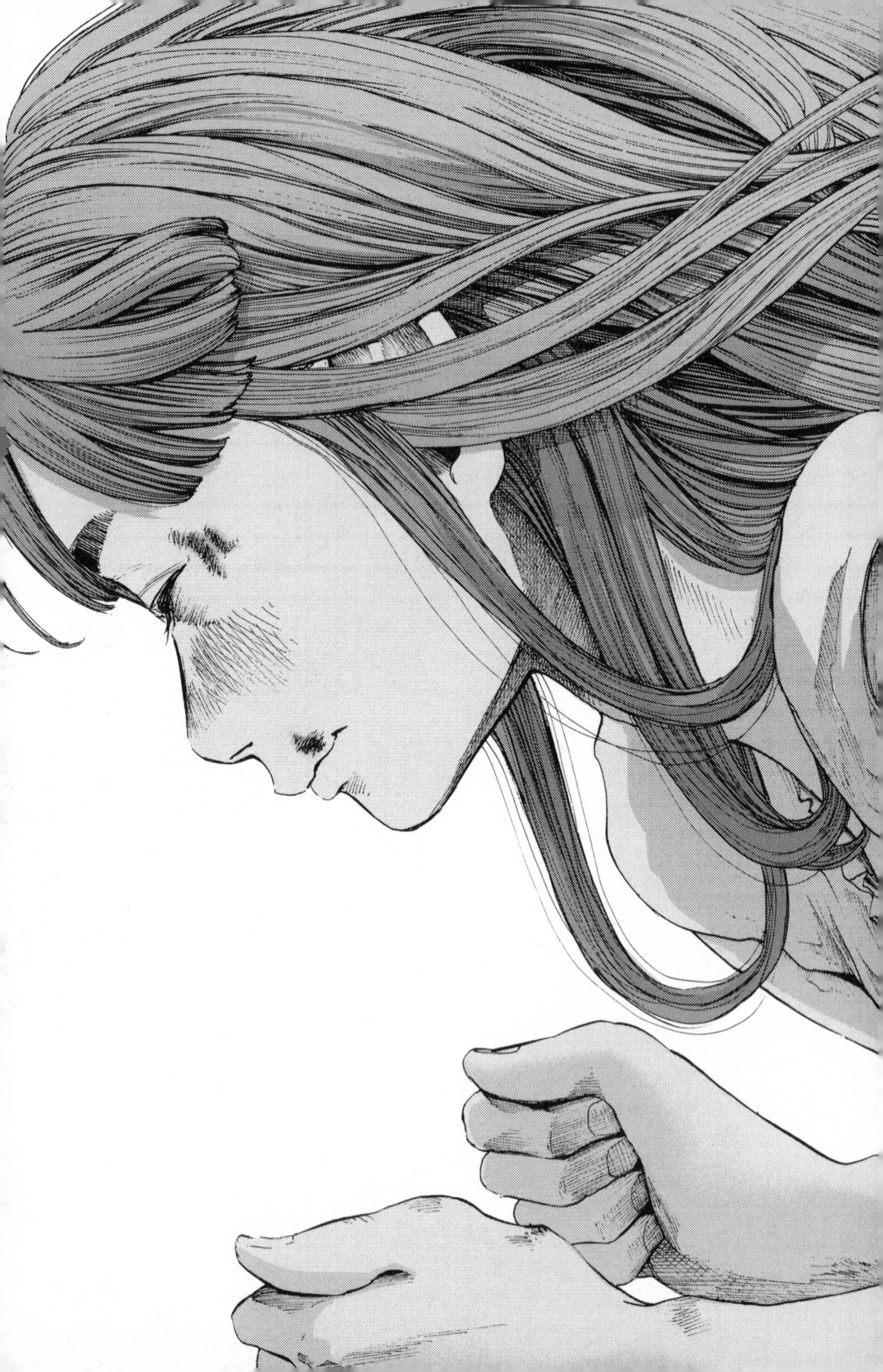

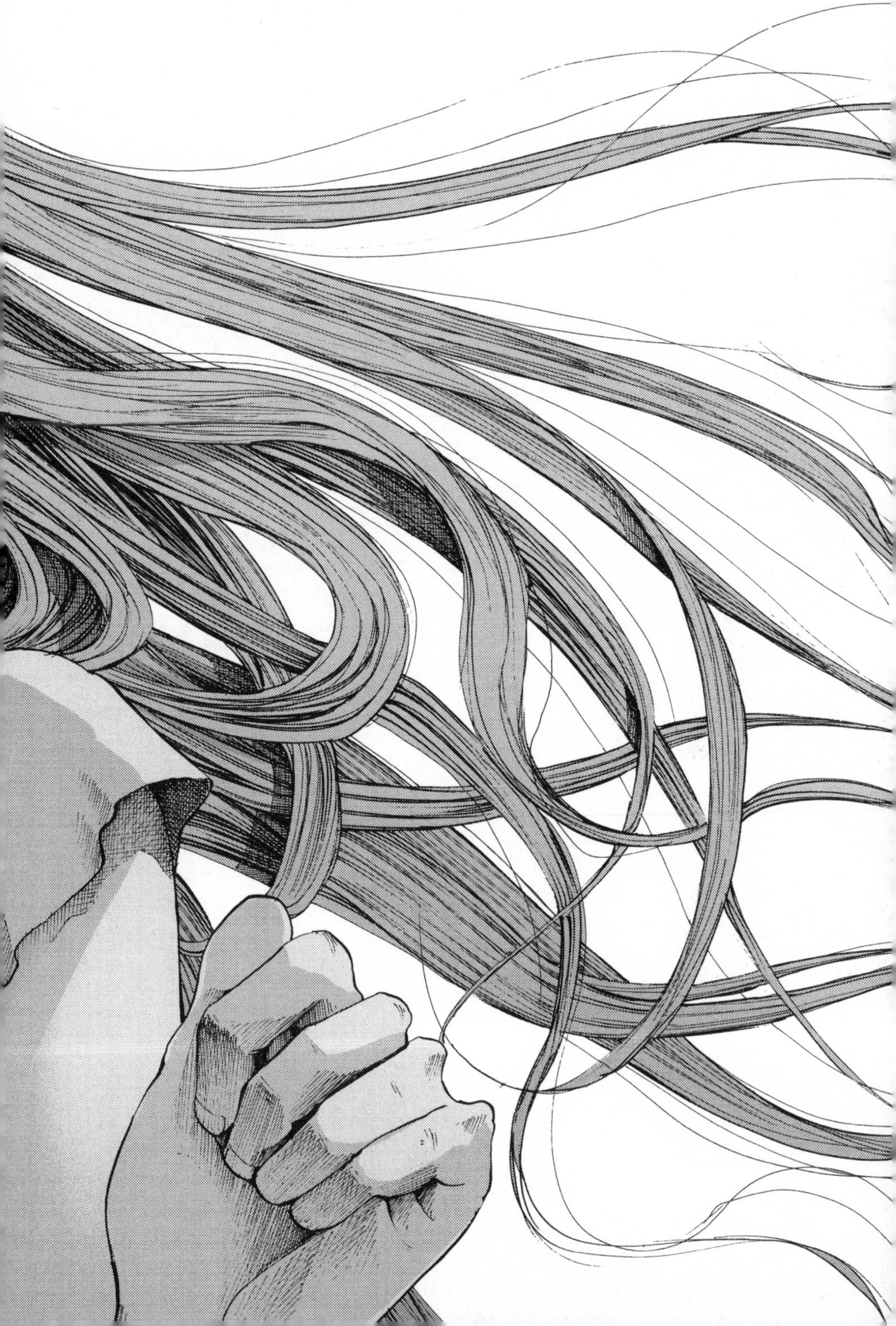

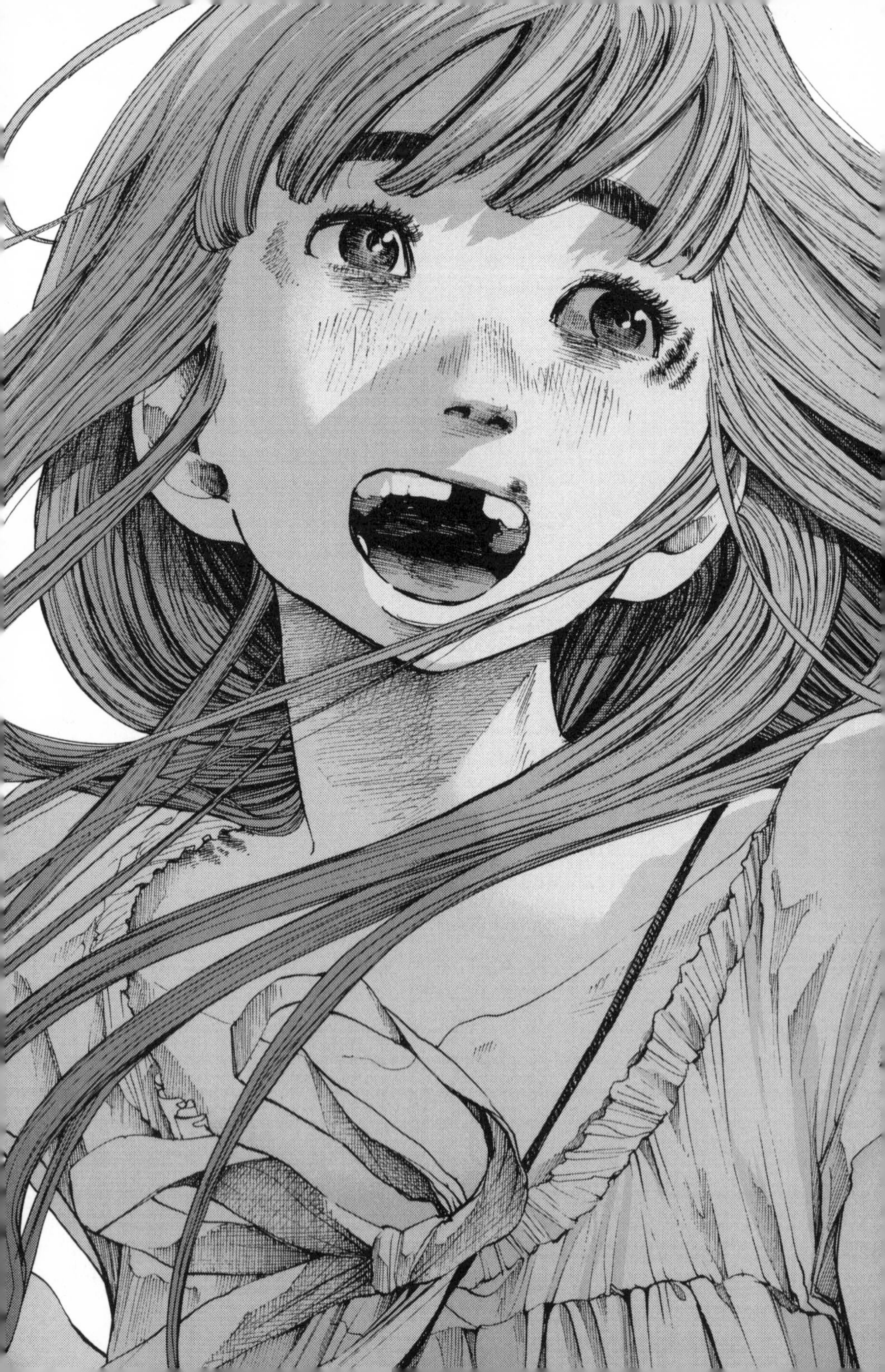

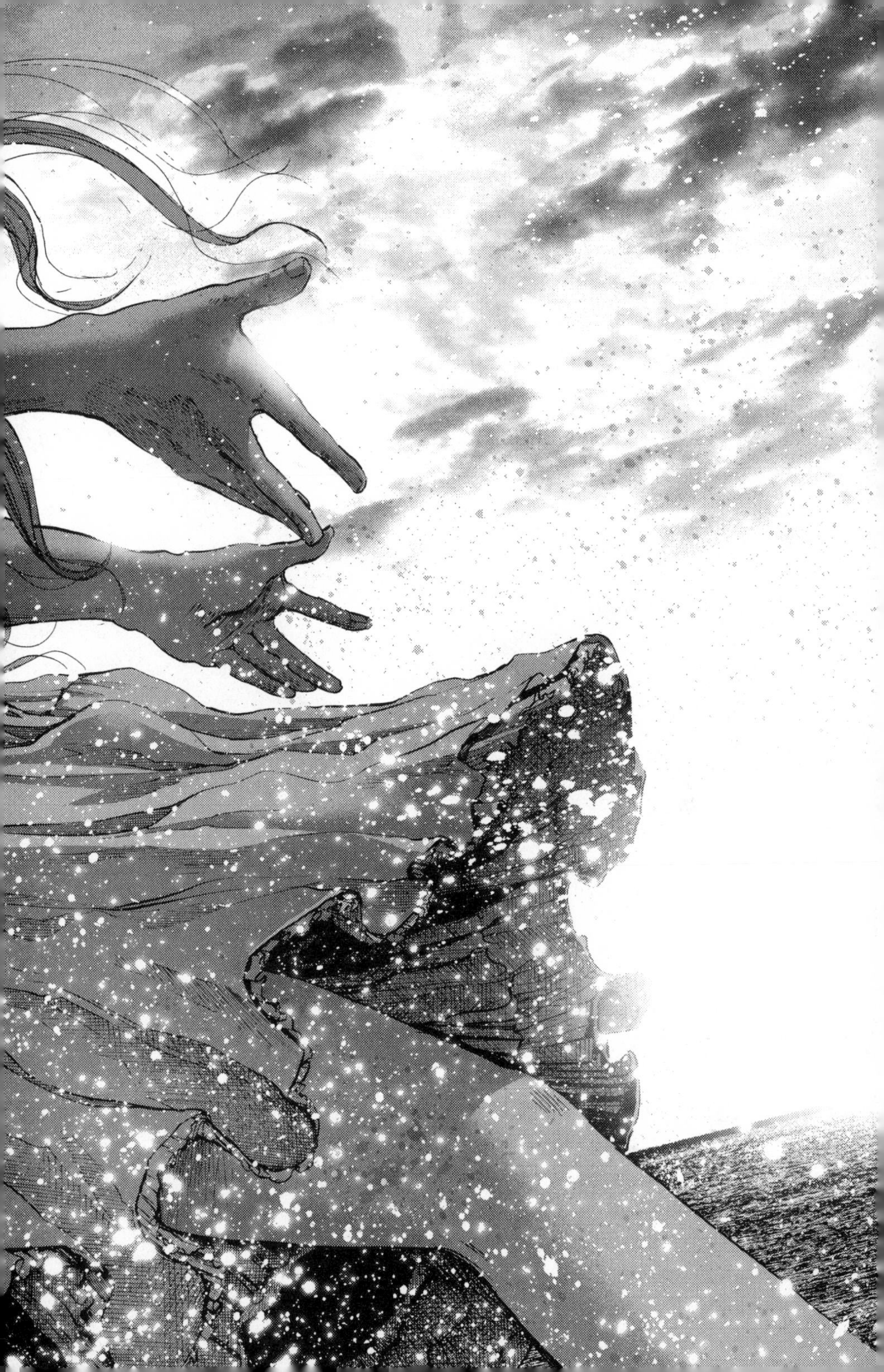

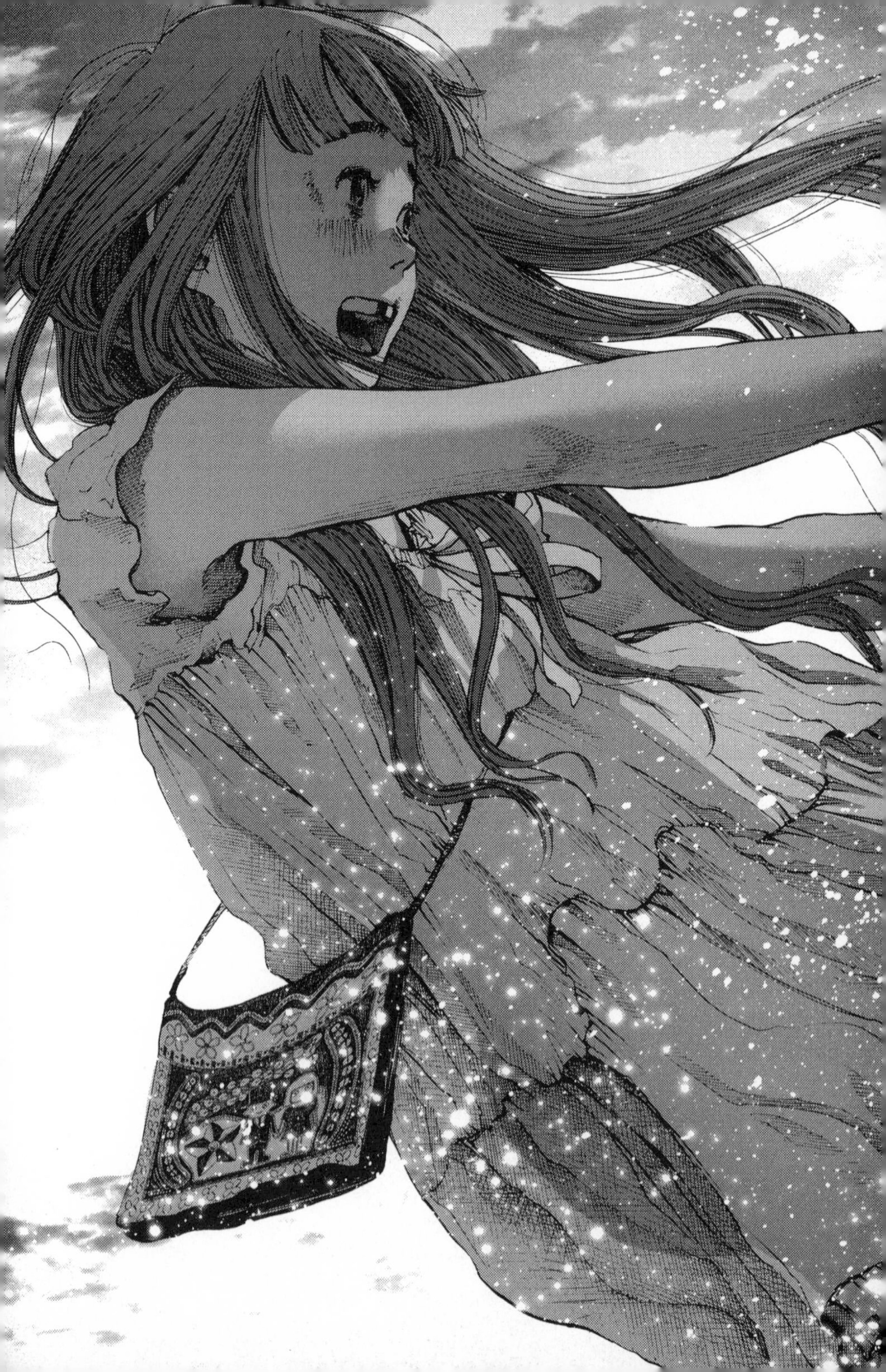

GOODNIGHT PUNPUN

Part Twelve

INIO ASANO

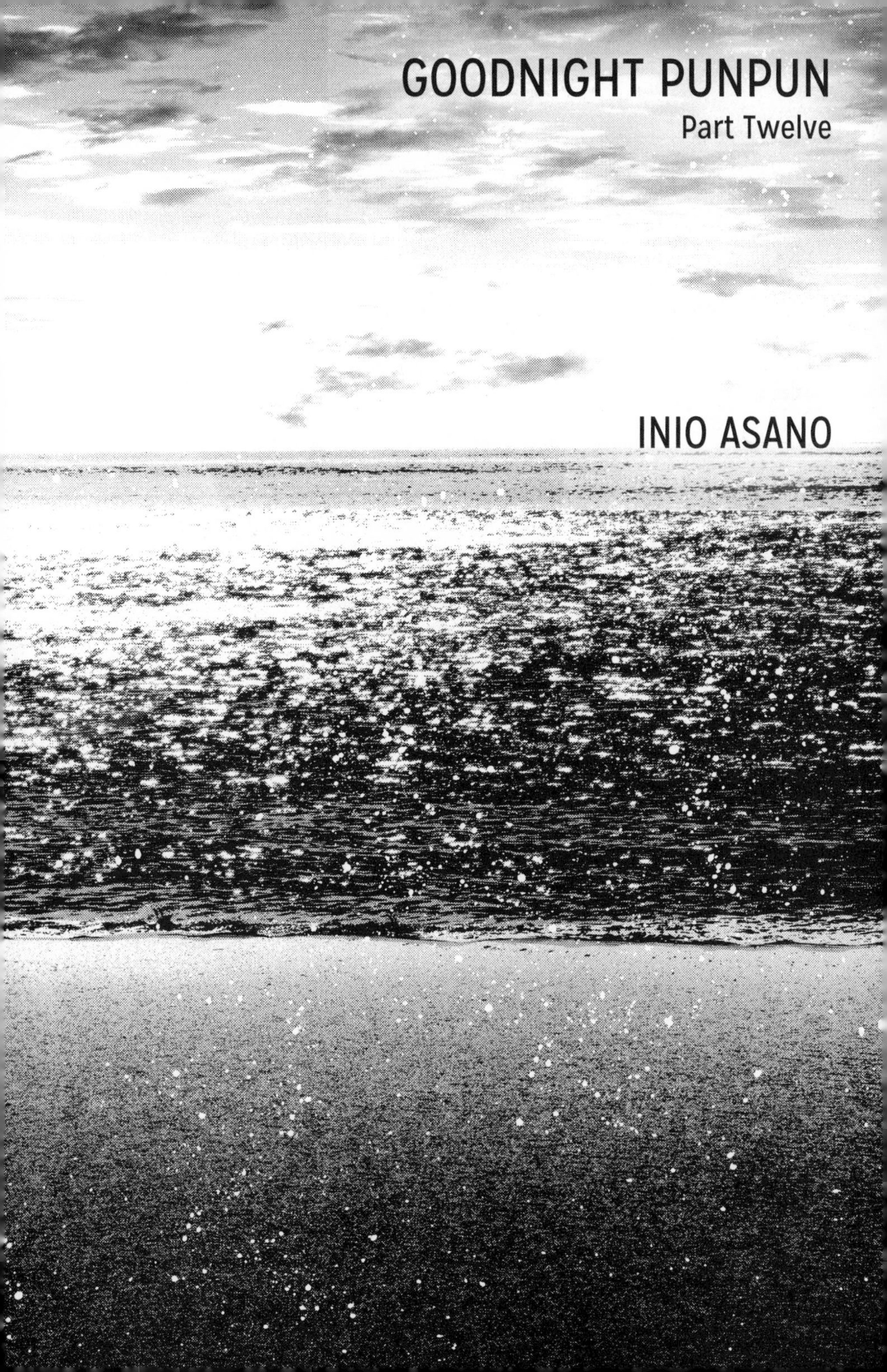

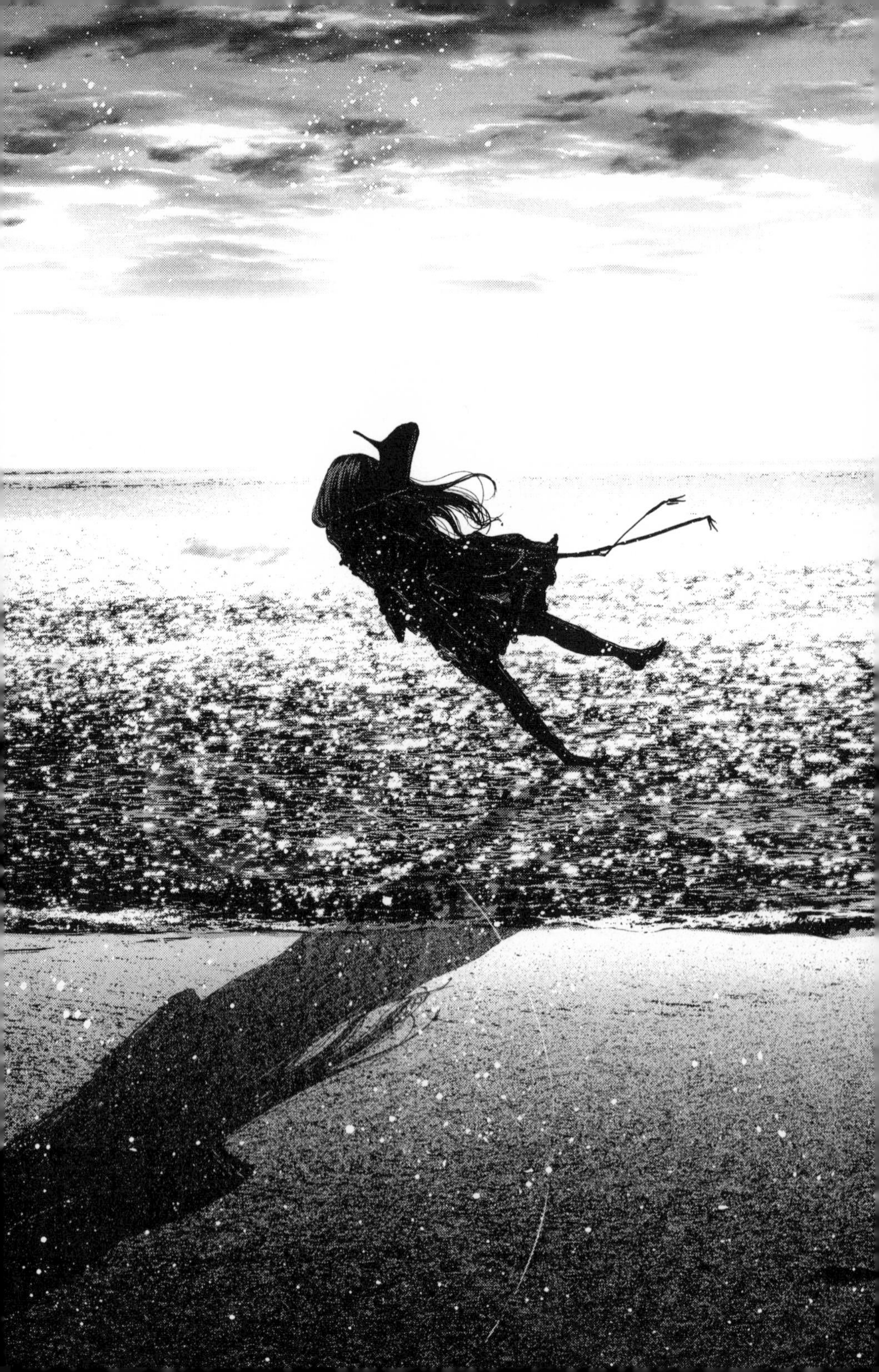

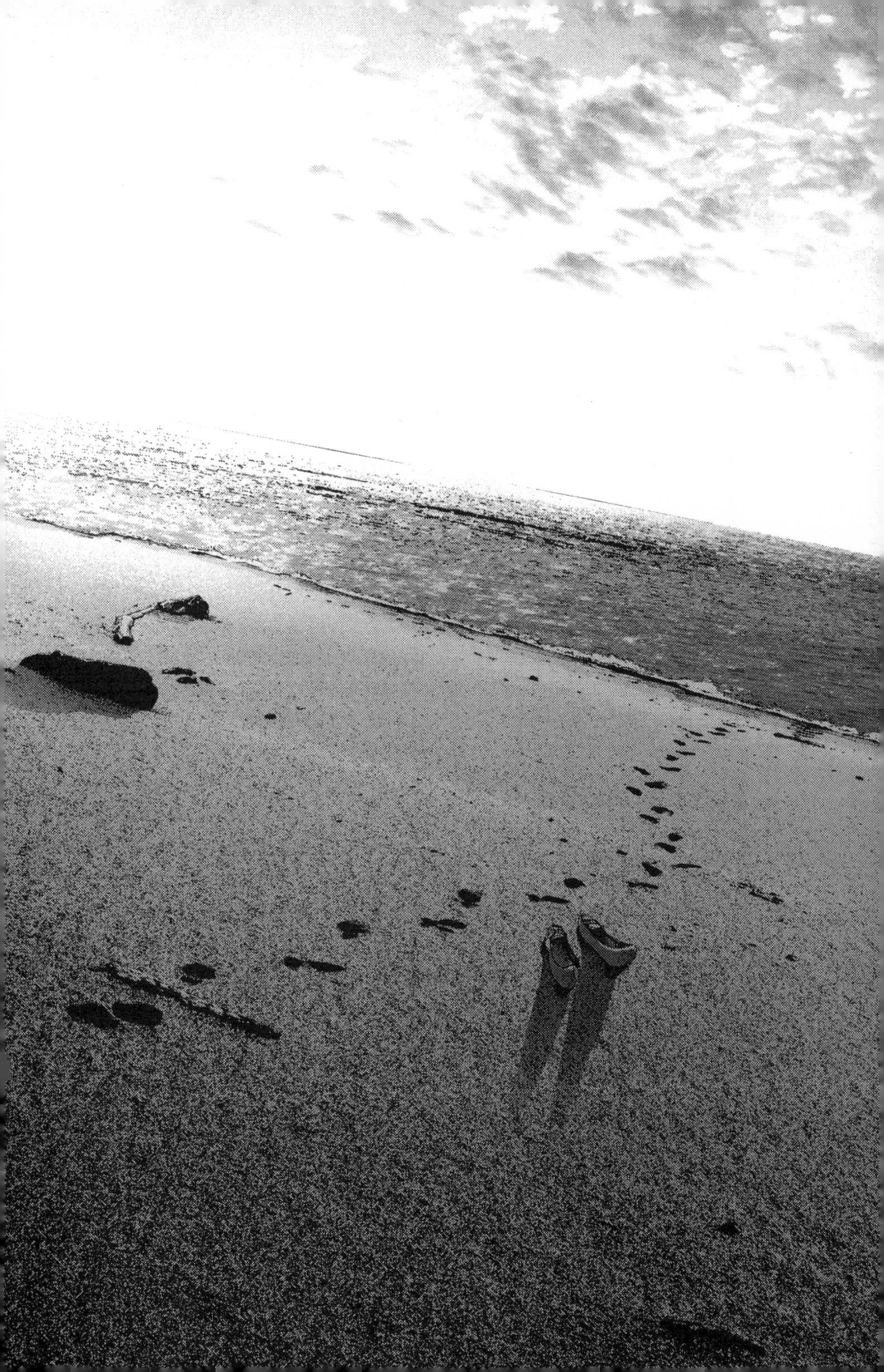

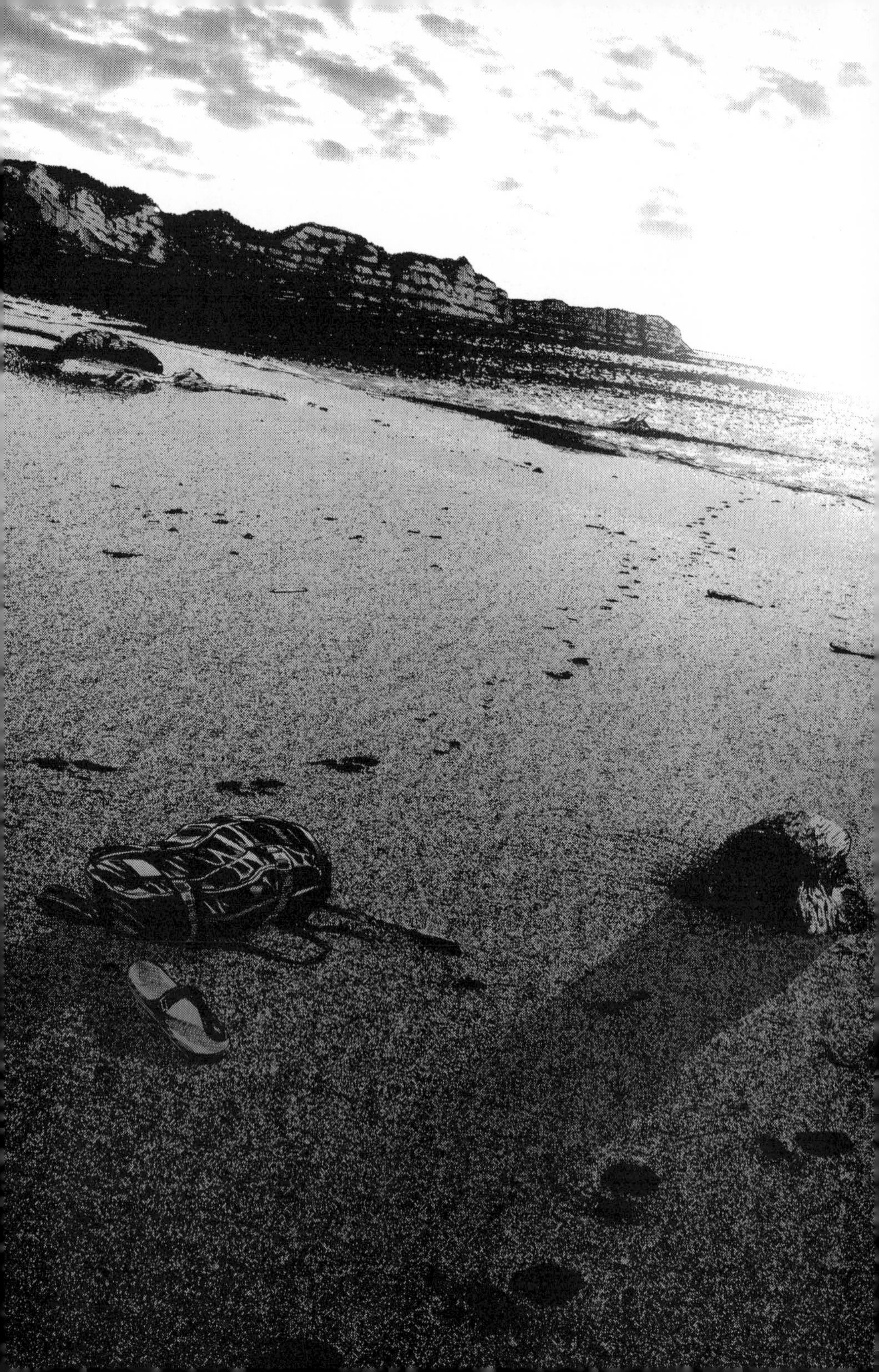

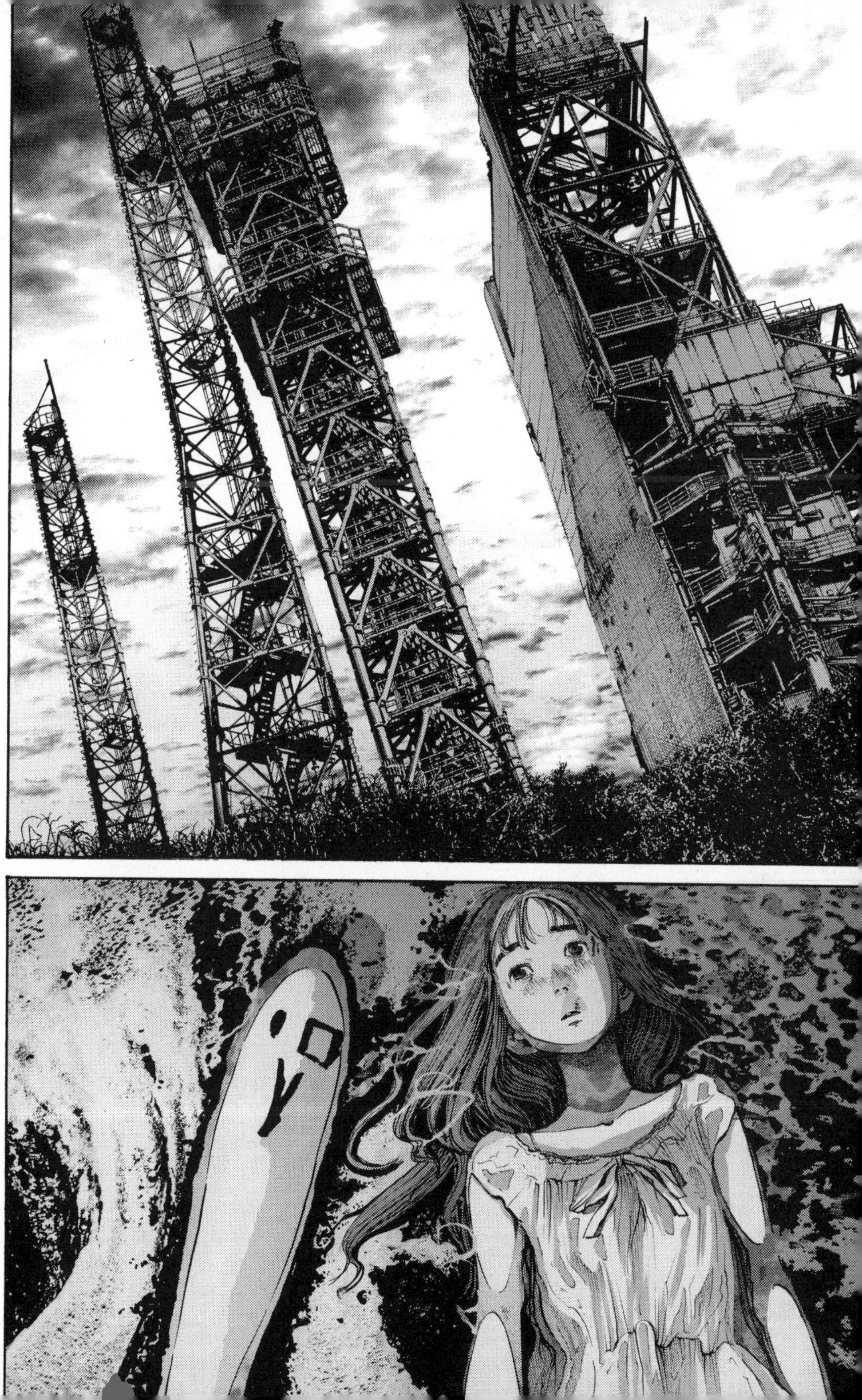

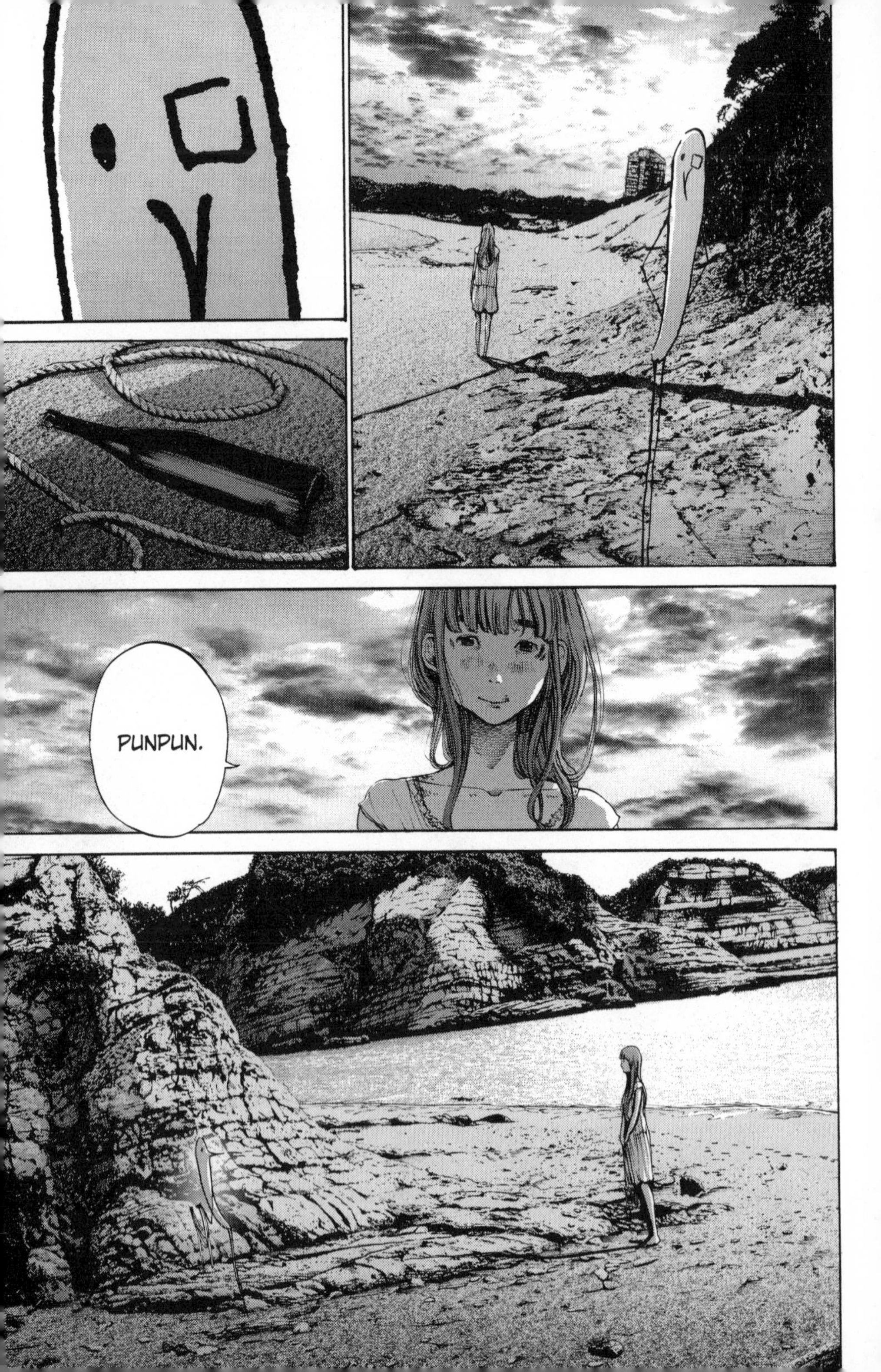
PUNPUN.

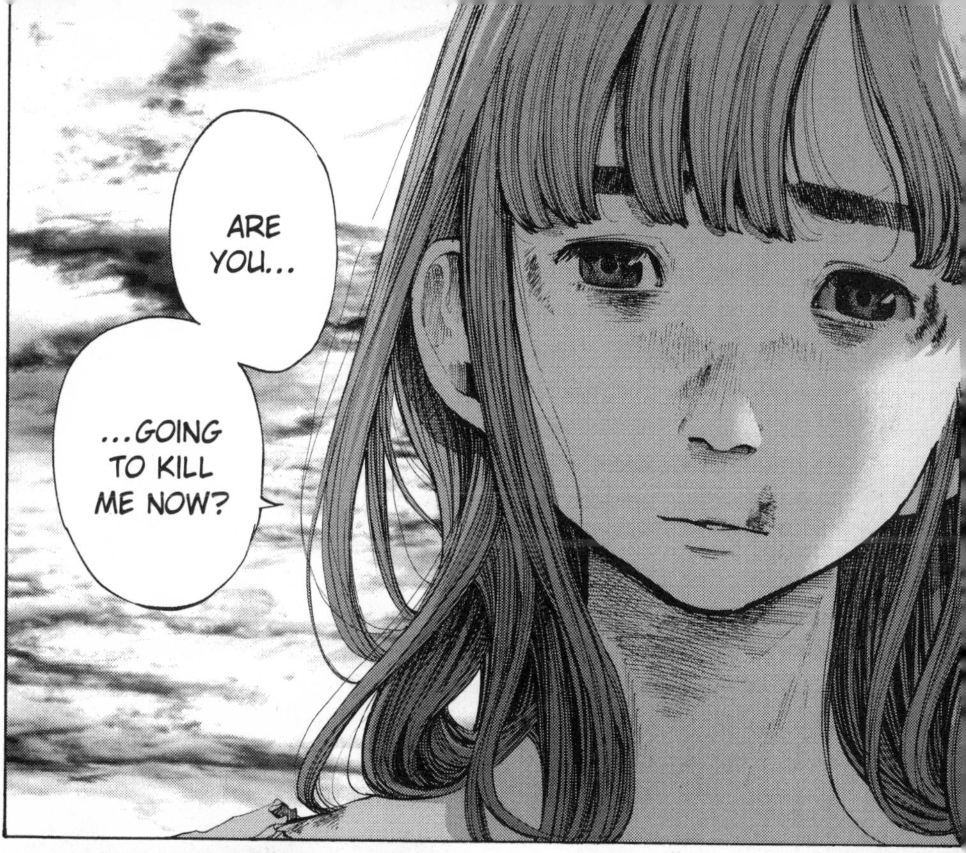
ARE YOU...
...GOING TO KILL ME NOW?
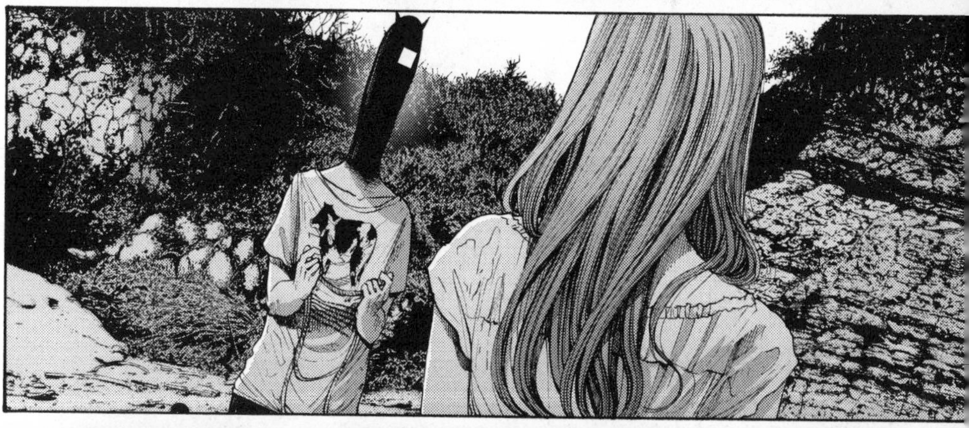

Chapter 132

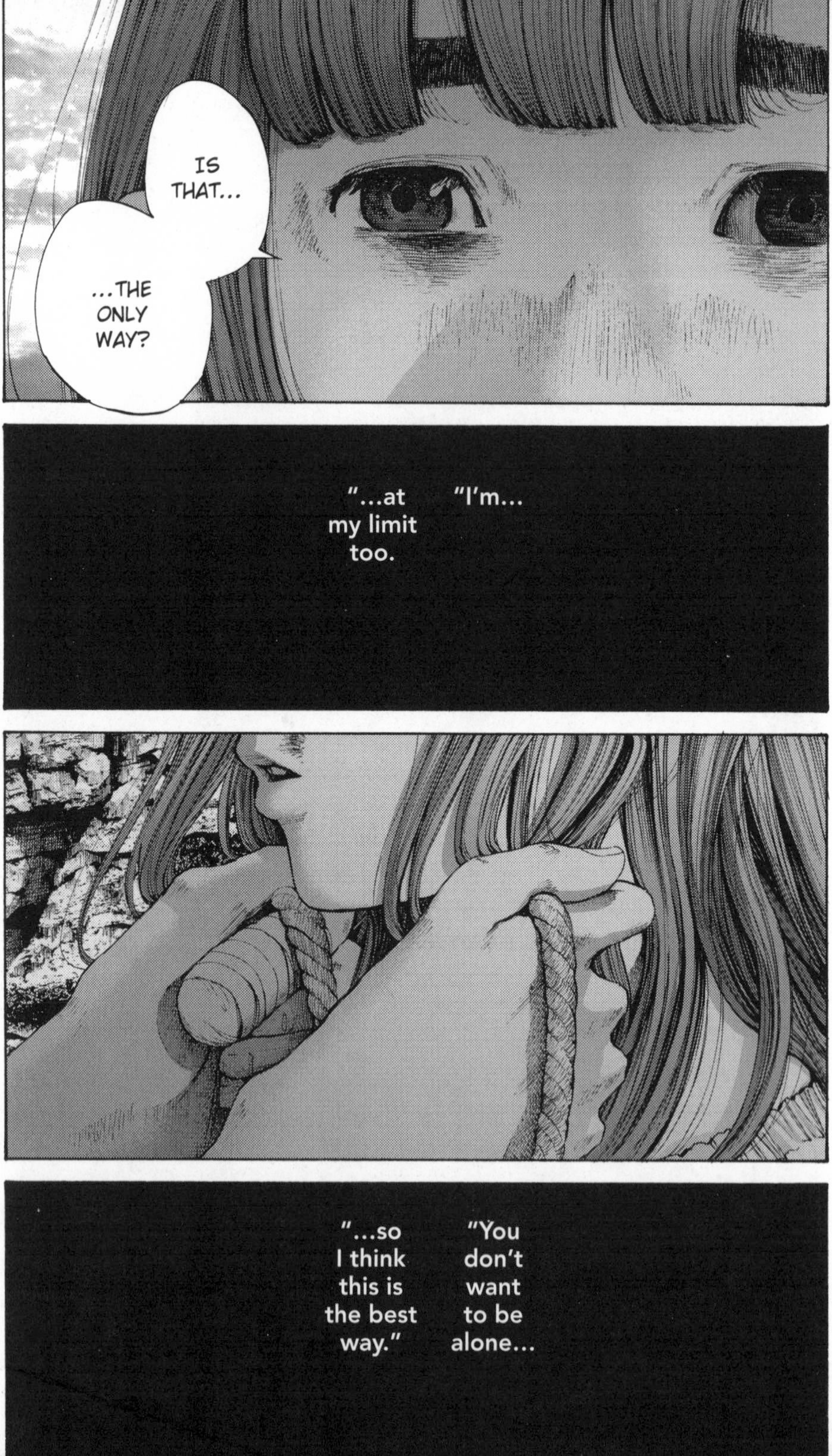
IS THAT...
...THE ONLY WAY?
"I'm...
"...at my limit too.
"You don't want to be alone...
"...so I think this is the best way."

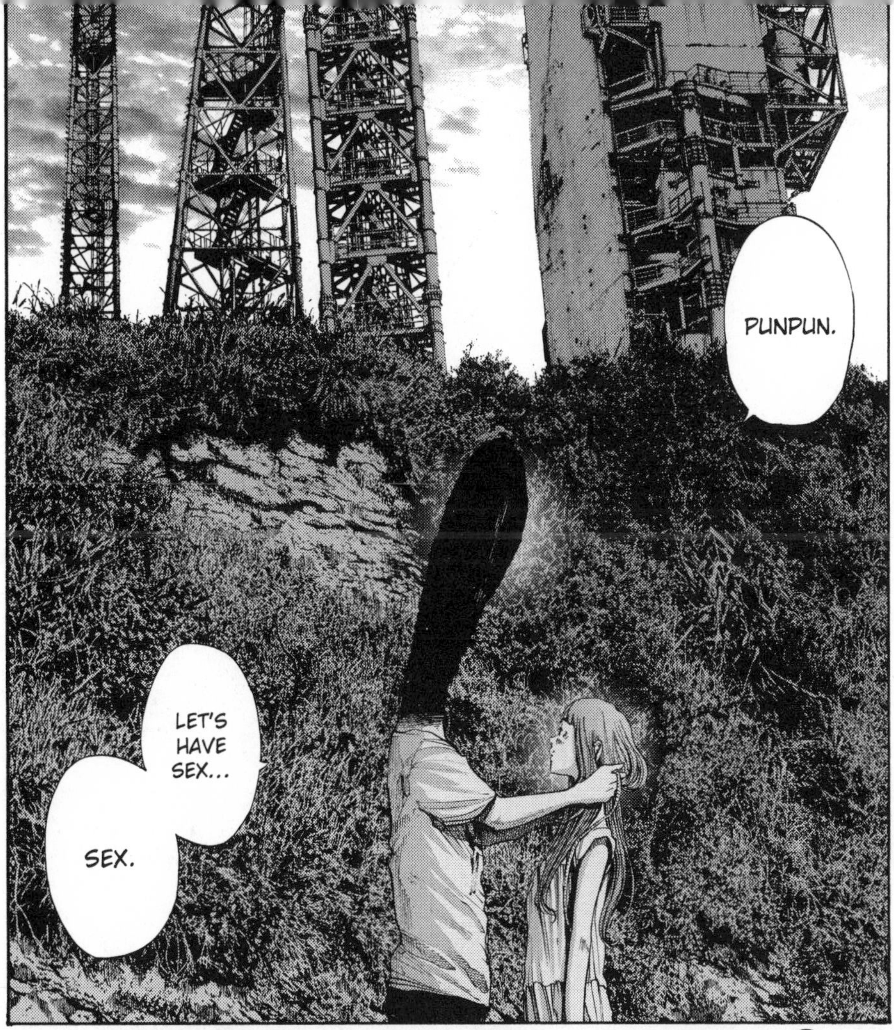
PUNPUN.
LET'S HAVE SEX...
SEX.

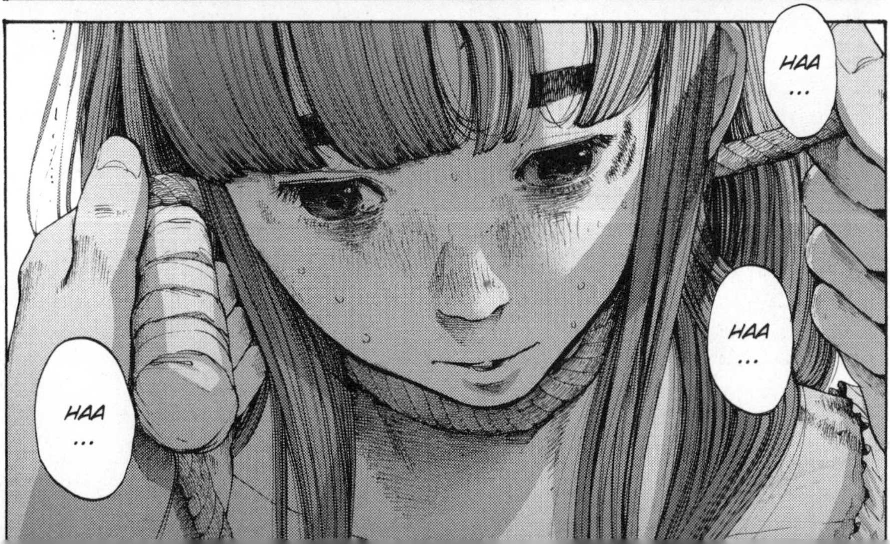
HAA ...
HAA ...
HAA ...

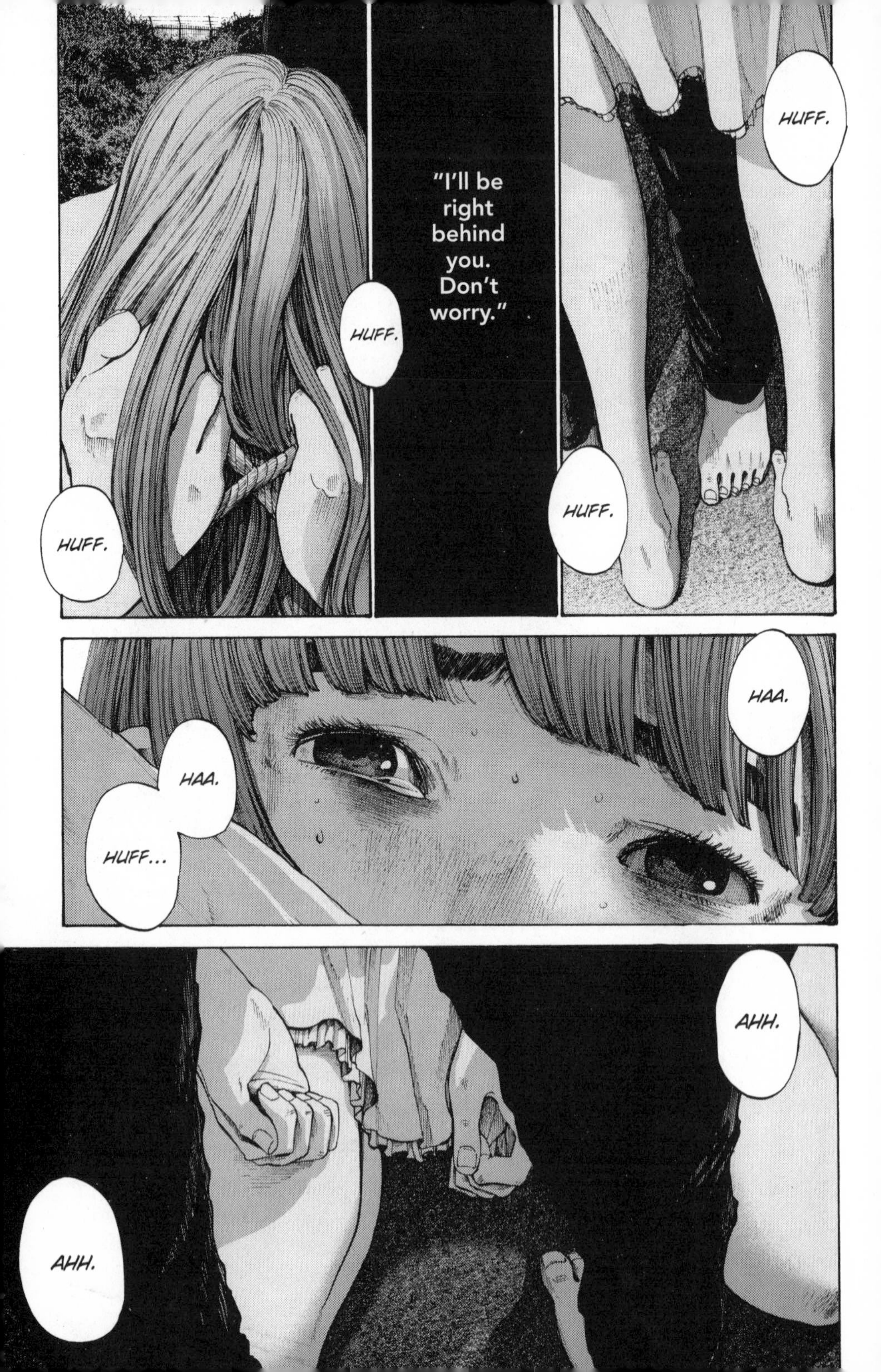
HUFF.
HUFF.
"I'll be right behind you. Don't worry."
HUFF.
HUFF.
HAA.
HAA.
HUFF...
AHH.
AHH.

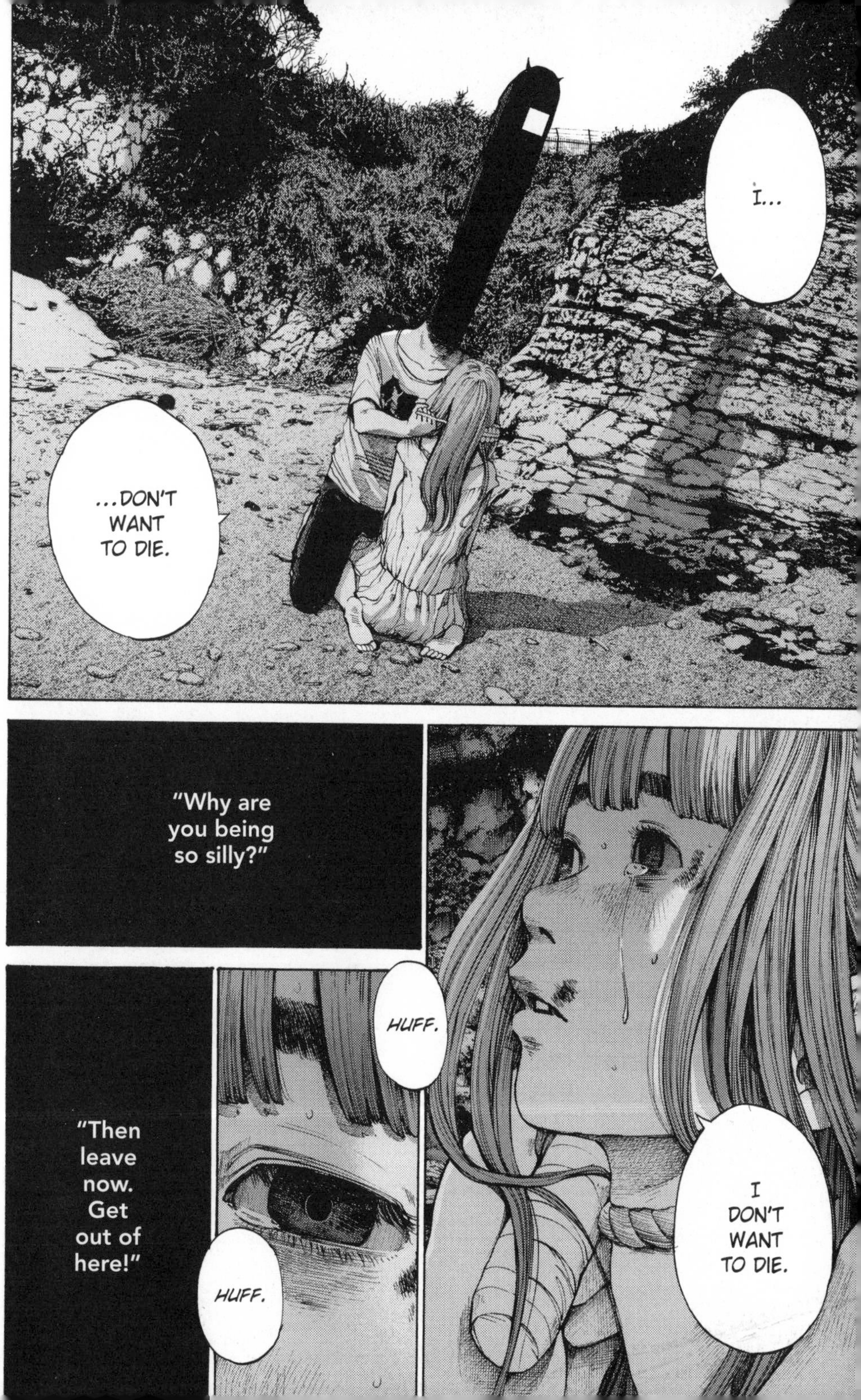
I...
...DON'T WANT TO DIE.
HUFF.
I DON'T WANT TO DIE.
"Why are you being so silly?"
HUFF.
"Then leave now. Get out of here!"

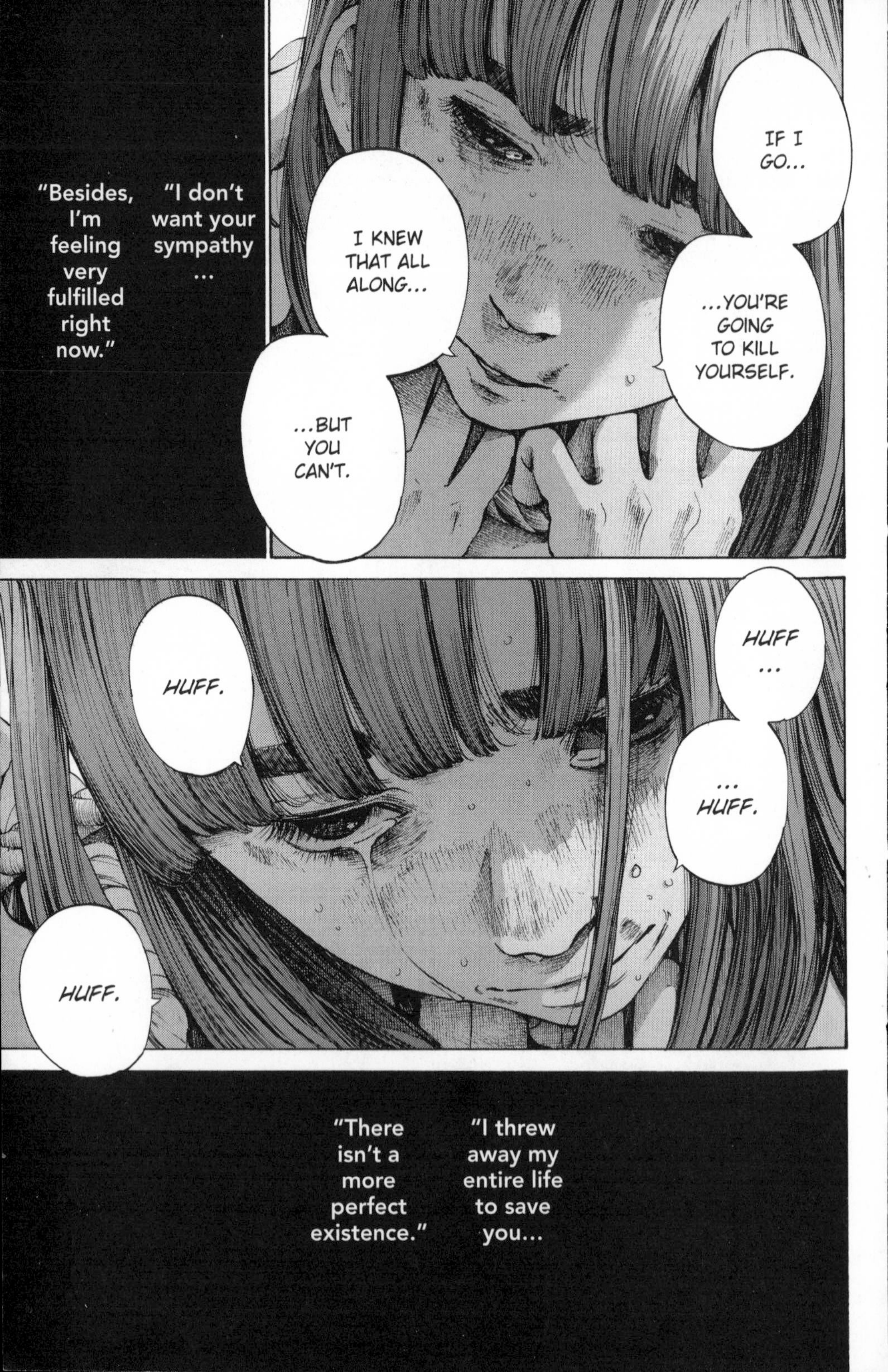
IF I GO...
...YOU'RE GOING TO KILL YOURSELF.
I KNEW THAT ALL ALONG...
...BUT YOU CAN'T.
"I don't want your sympathy...
"Besides, I'm feeling very fulfilled right now."
HUFF...
...HUFF.
HUFF.
HUFF.
"I threw away my entire life to save you...
"There isn't a more perfect existence."

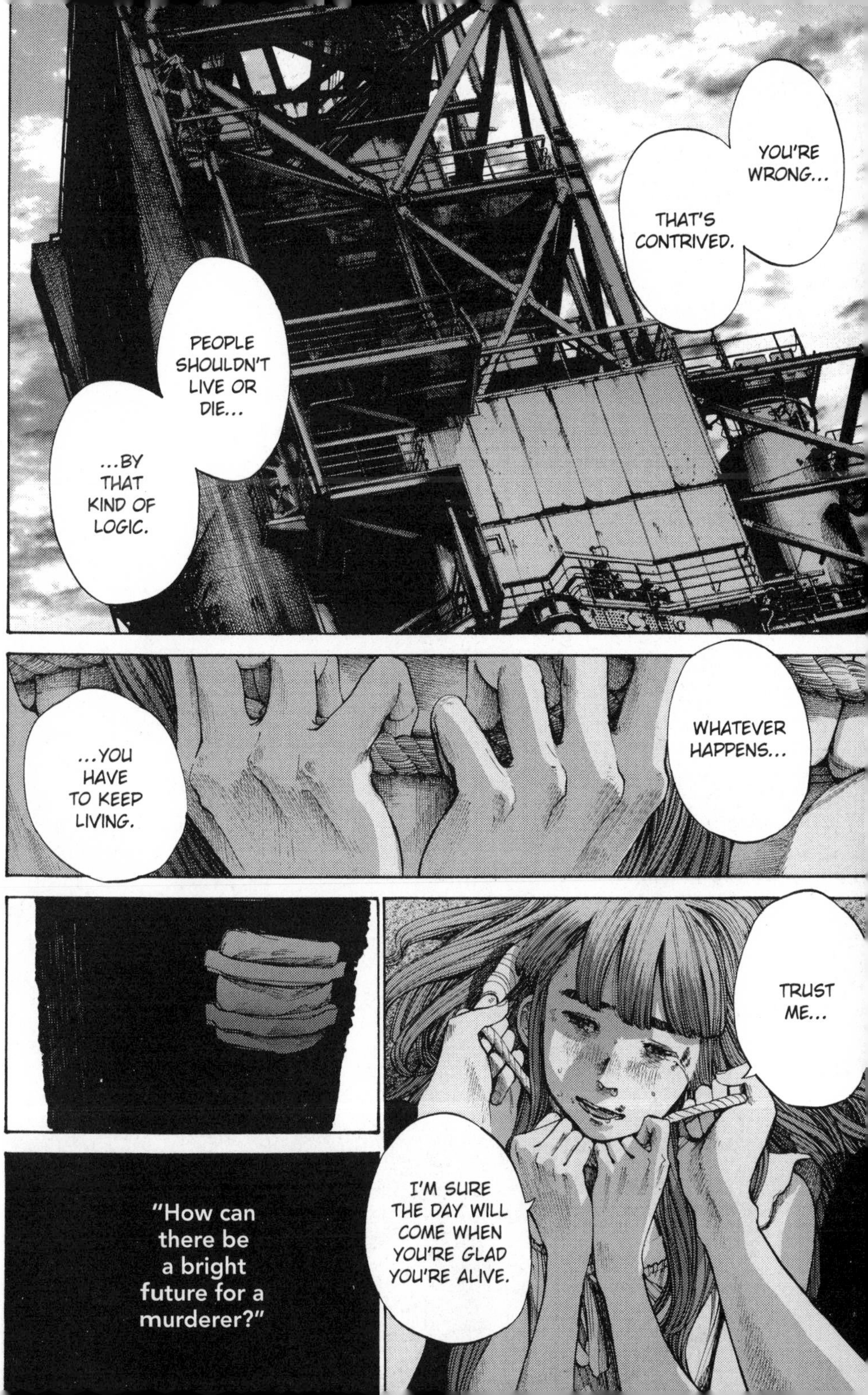
YOU'RE WRONG...
THAT'S CONTRIVED.
PEOPLE SHOULDN'T LIVE OR DIE...
...BY THAT KIND OF LOGIC.
WHATEVER HAPPENS...
...YOU HAVE TO KEEP LIVING.
TRUST ME...
I'M SURE THE DAY WILL COME WHEN YOU'RE GLAD YOU'RE ALIVE.
"How can there be a bright future for a murderer?"

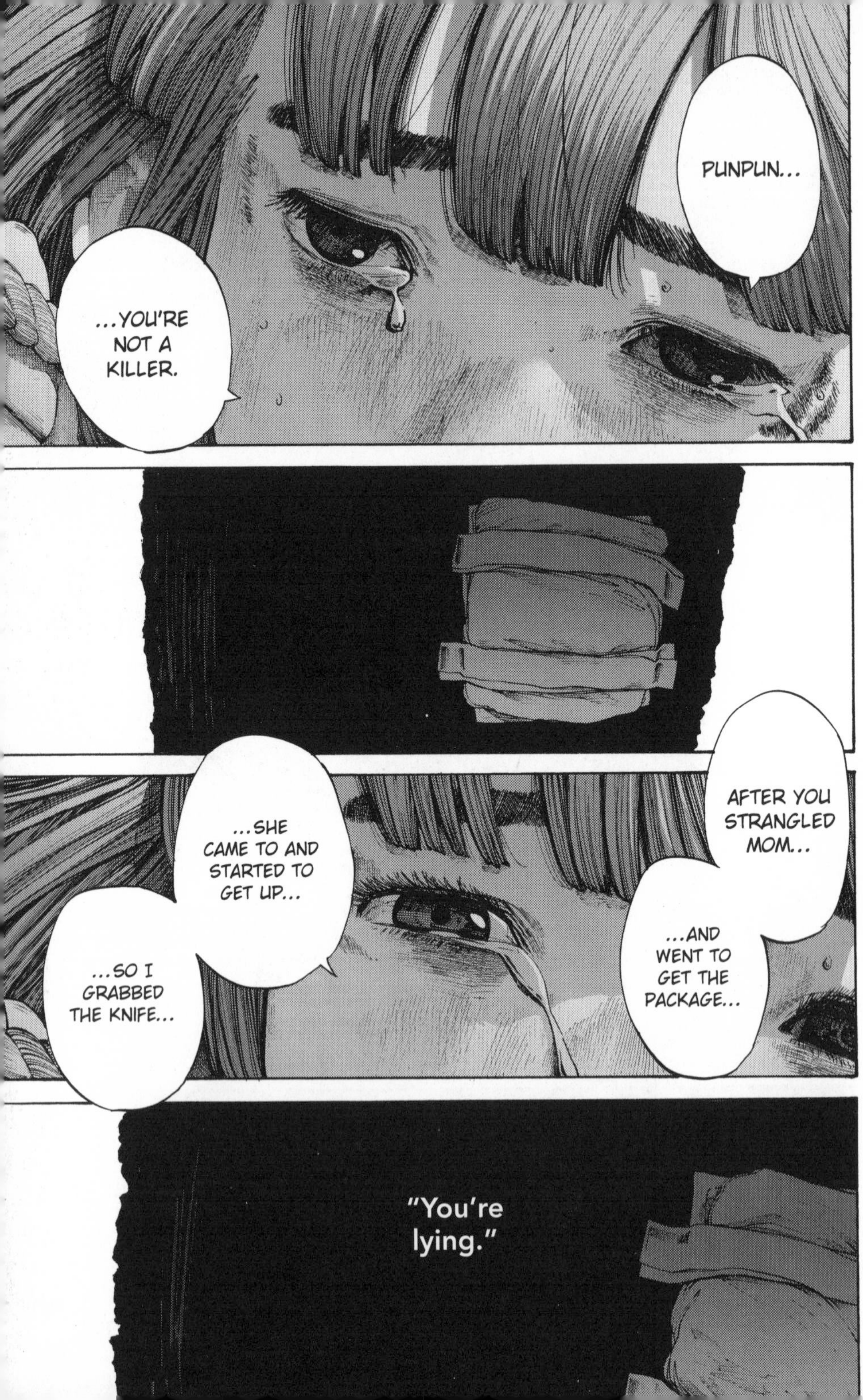
PUNPUN...
...YOU'RE NOT A KILLER.
AFTER YOU STRANGLED MOM...
...AND WENT TO GET THE PACKAGE...
...SHE CAME TO AND STARTED TO GET UP...
...SO I GRABBED THE KNIFE...
"You're lying."

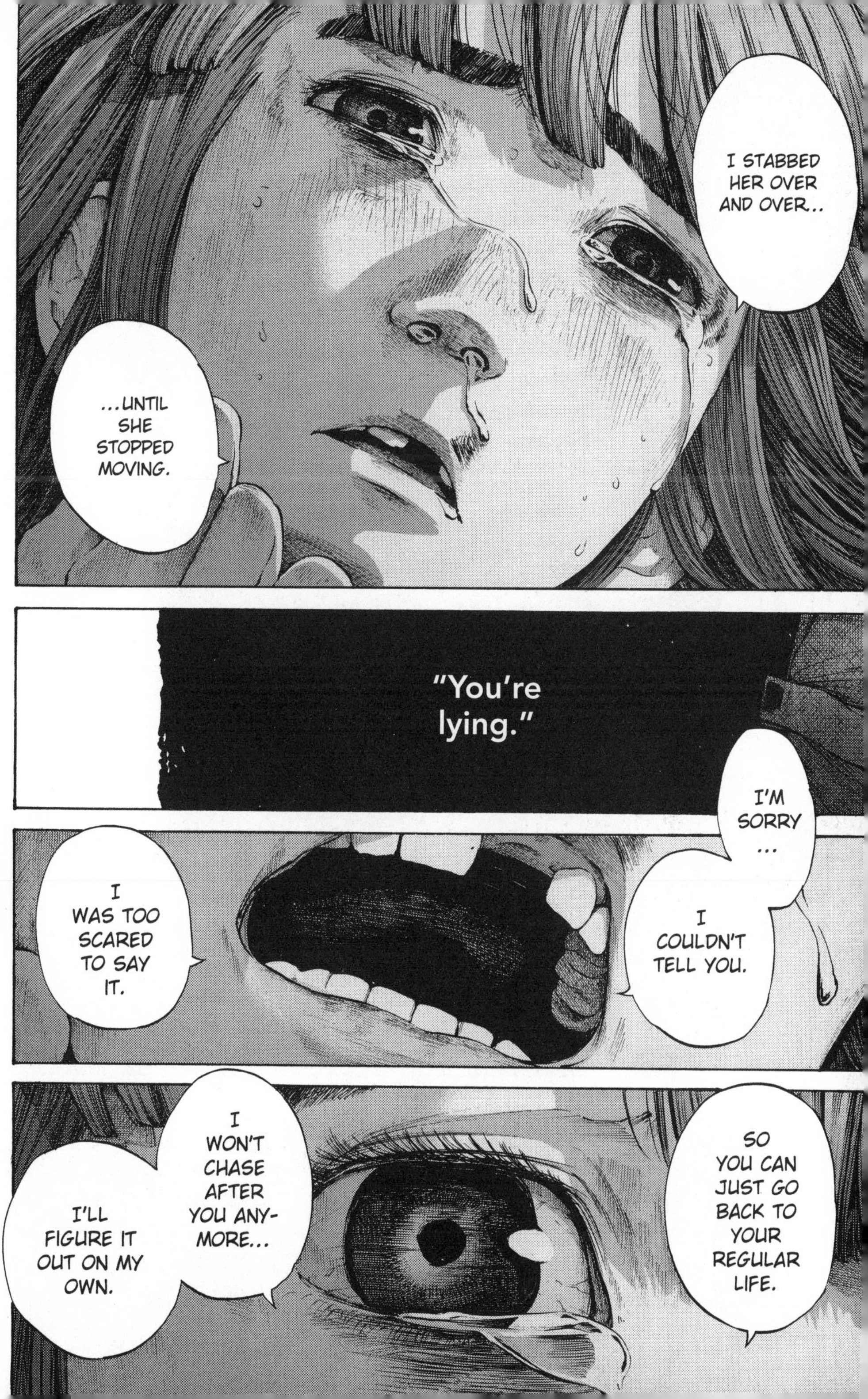
I STABBED HER OVER AND OVER...
...UNTIL SHE STOPPED MOVING.
"You're lying."
I'M SORRY...
I COULDN'T TELL YOU.
I WAS TOO SCARED TO SAY IT.
SO YOU CAN JUST GO BACK TO YOUR REGULAR LIFE.
I WON'T CHASE AFTER YOU ANY-MORE...
I'LL FIGURE IT OUT ON MY OWN.

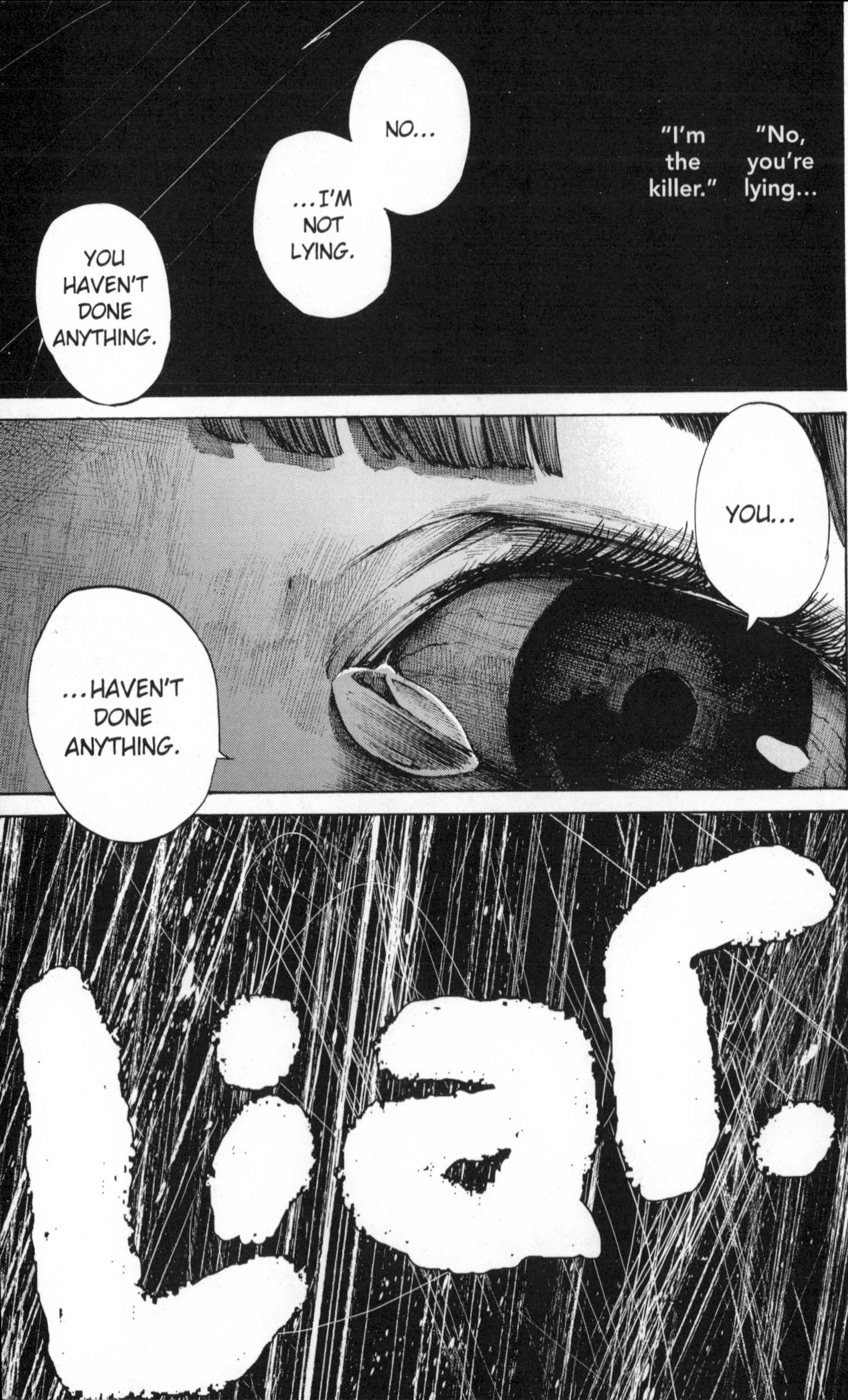
"No, you're lying...
"I'm the killer."
NO...
...I'M NOT LYING.
YOU HAVEN'T DONE ANYTHING.
YOU...
...HAVEN'T DONE ANYTHING.
Liar.

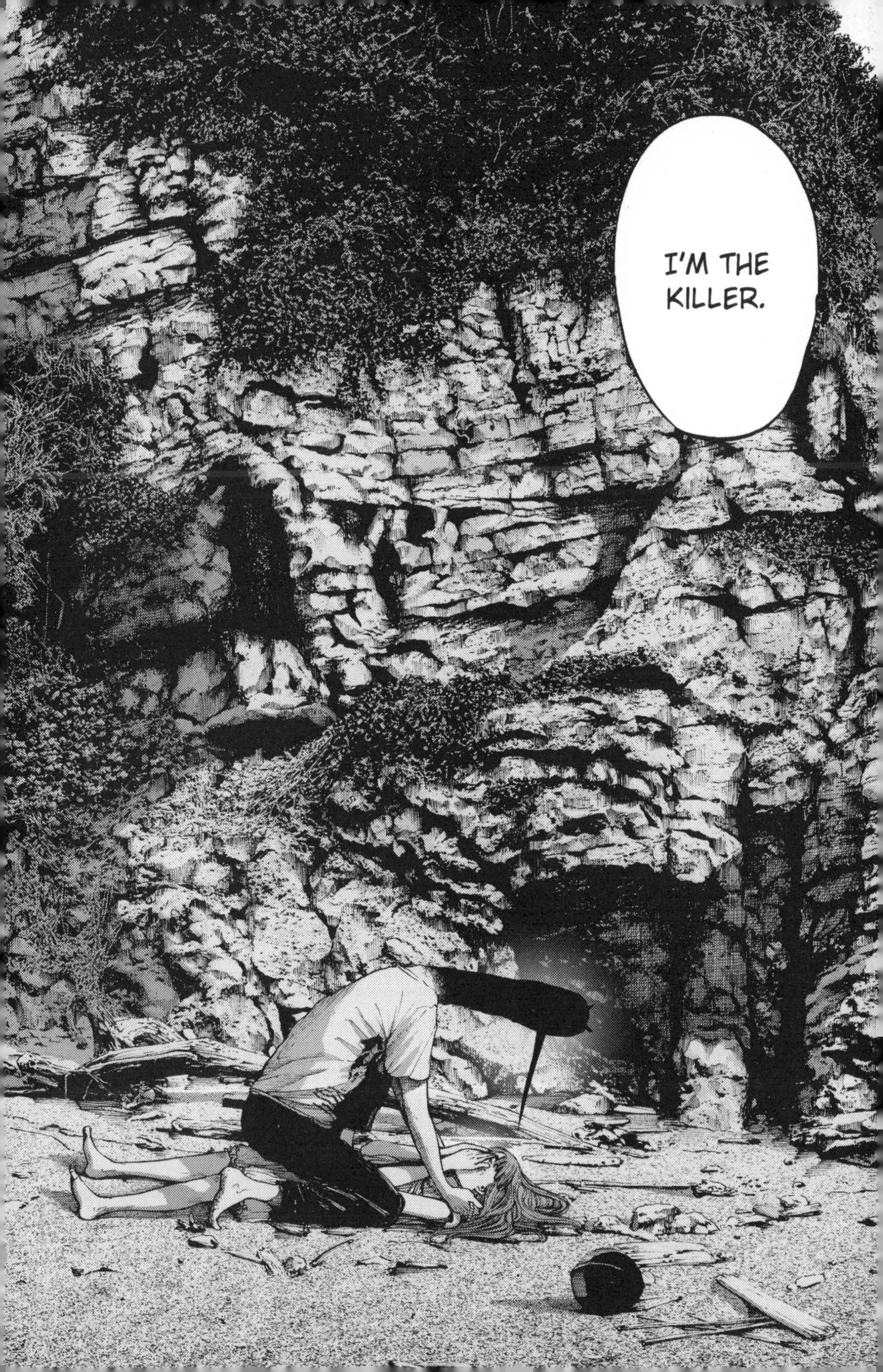
I'M THE KILLER.

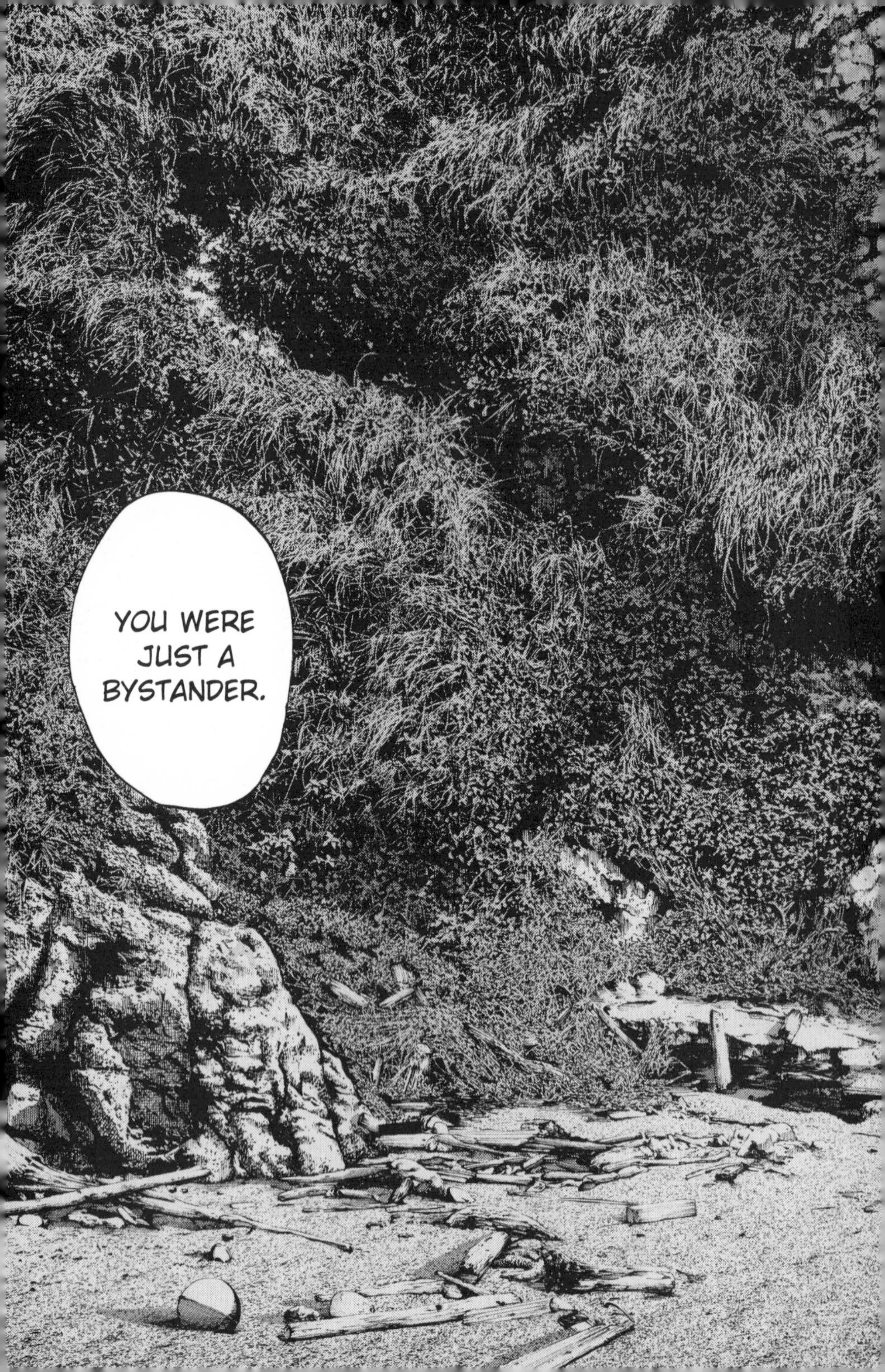
YOU WERE JUST A BYSTANDER.

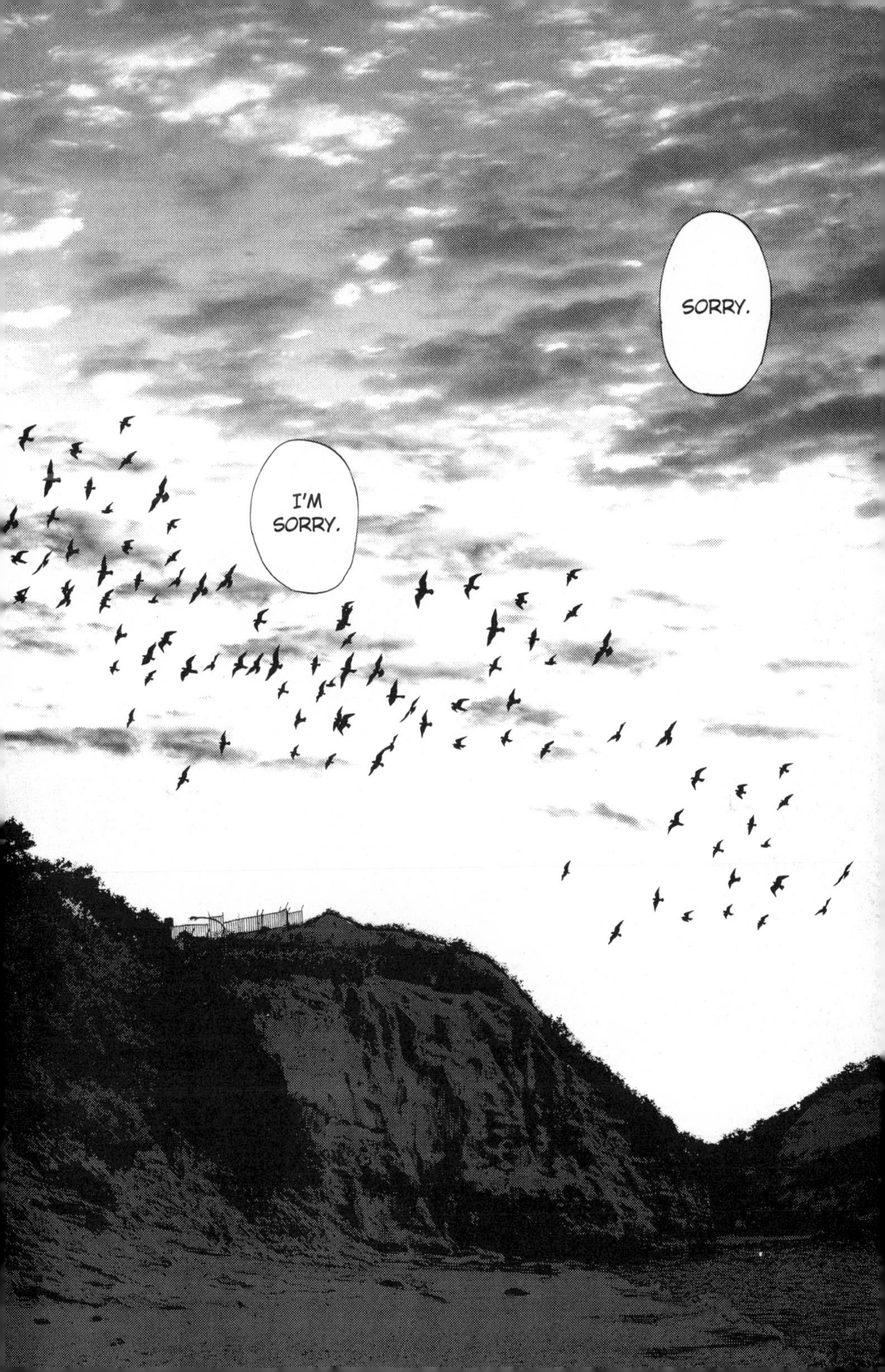
SORRY.
I'M SORRY.

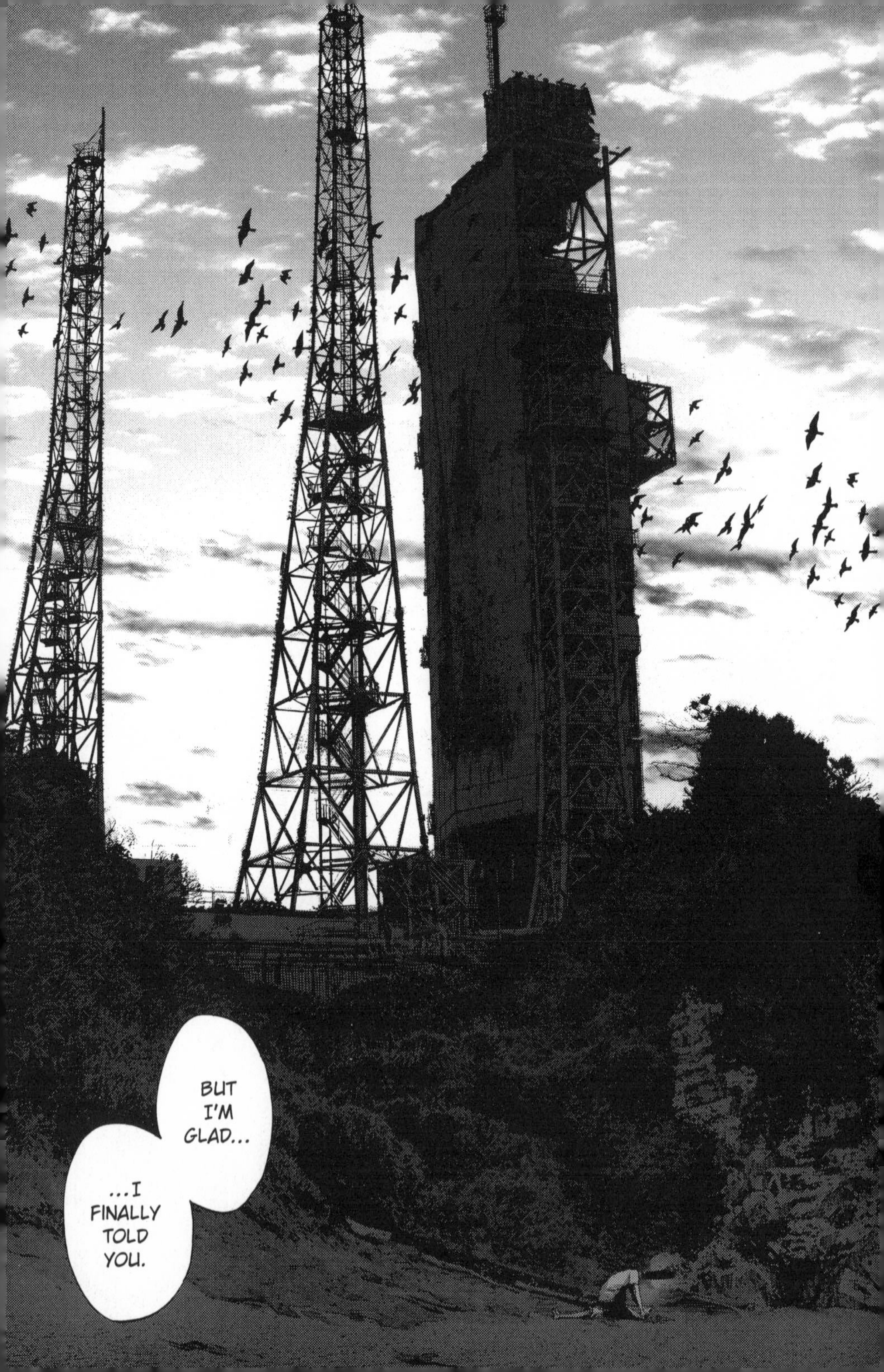
BUT I'M GLAD...
...I FINALLY TOLD YOU.

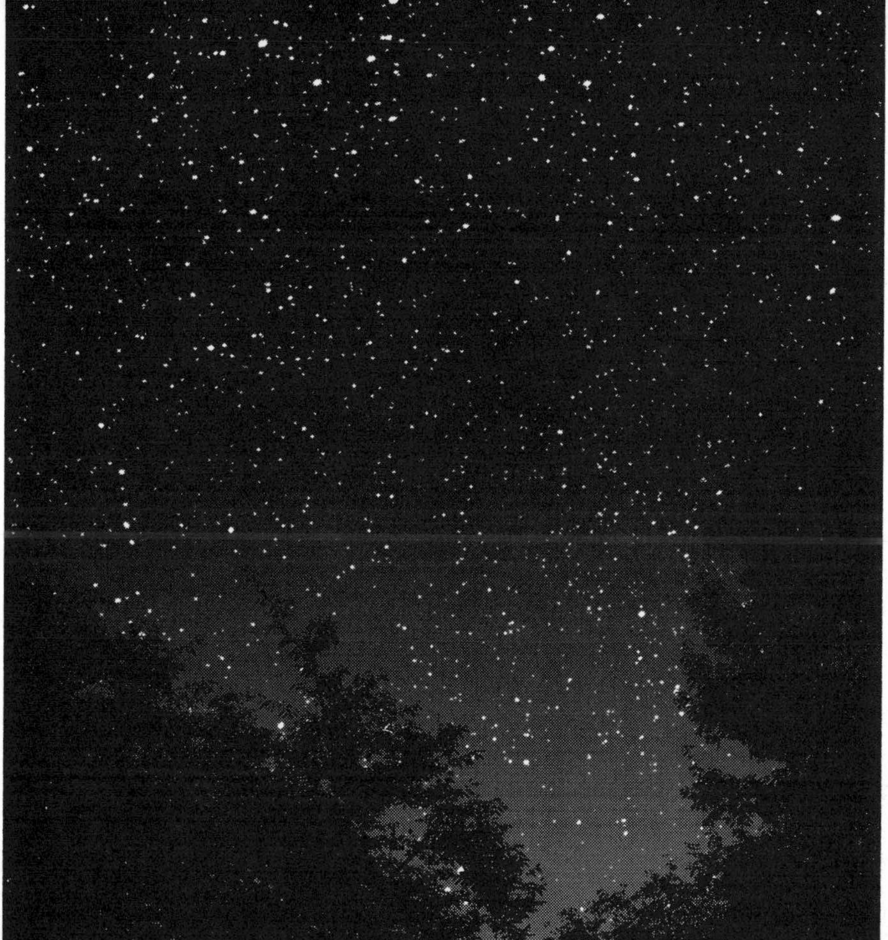
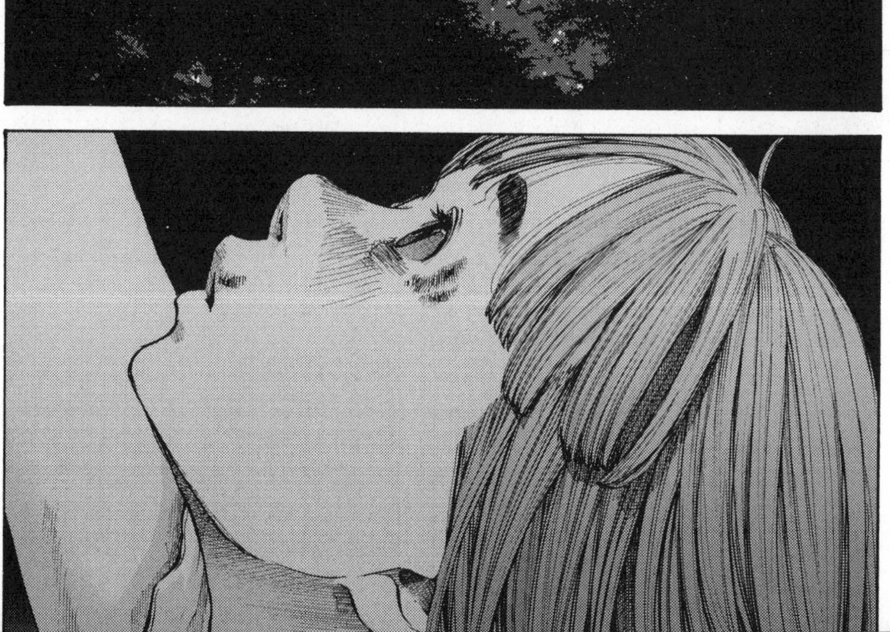

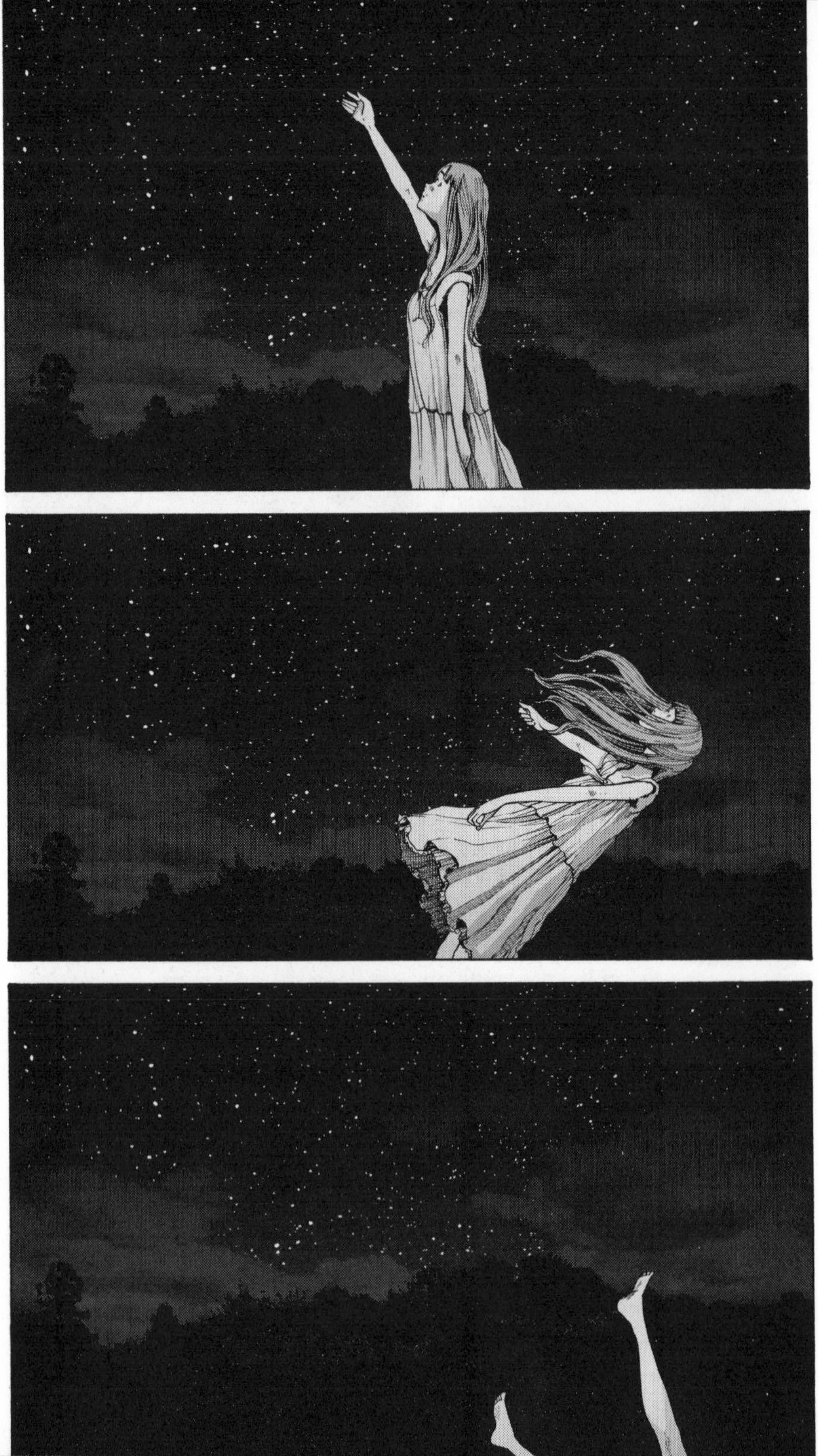

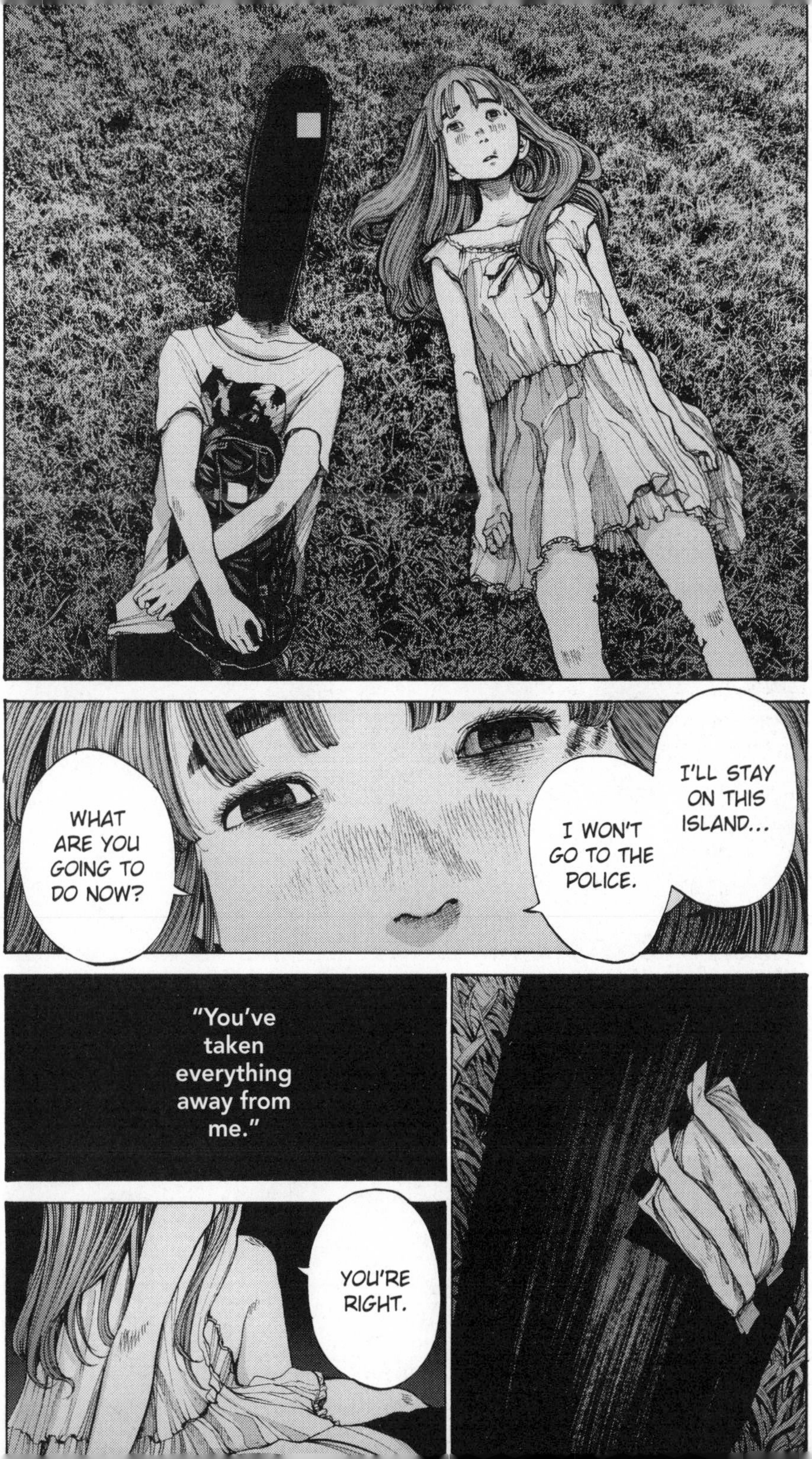
I'LL STAY ON THIS ISLAND...
I WON'T GO TO THE POLICE.
WHAT ARE YOU GOING TO DO NOW?
"You've taken everything away from me."
YOU'RE RIGHT.

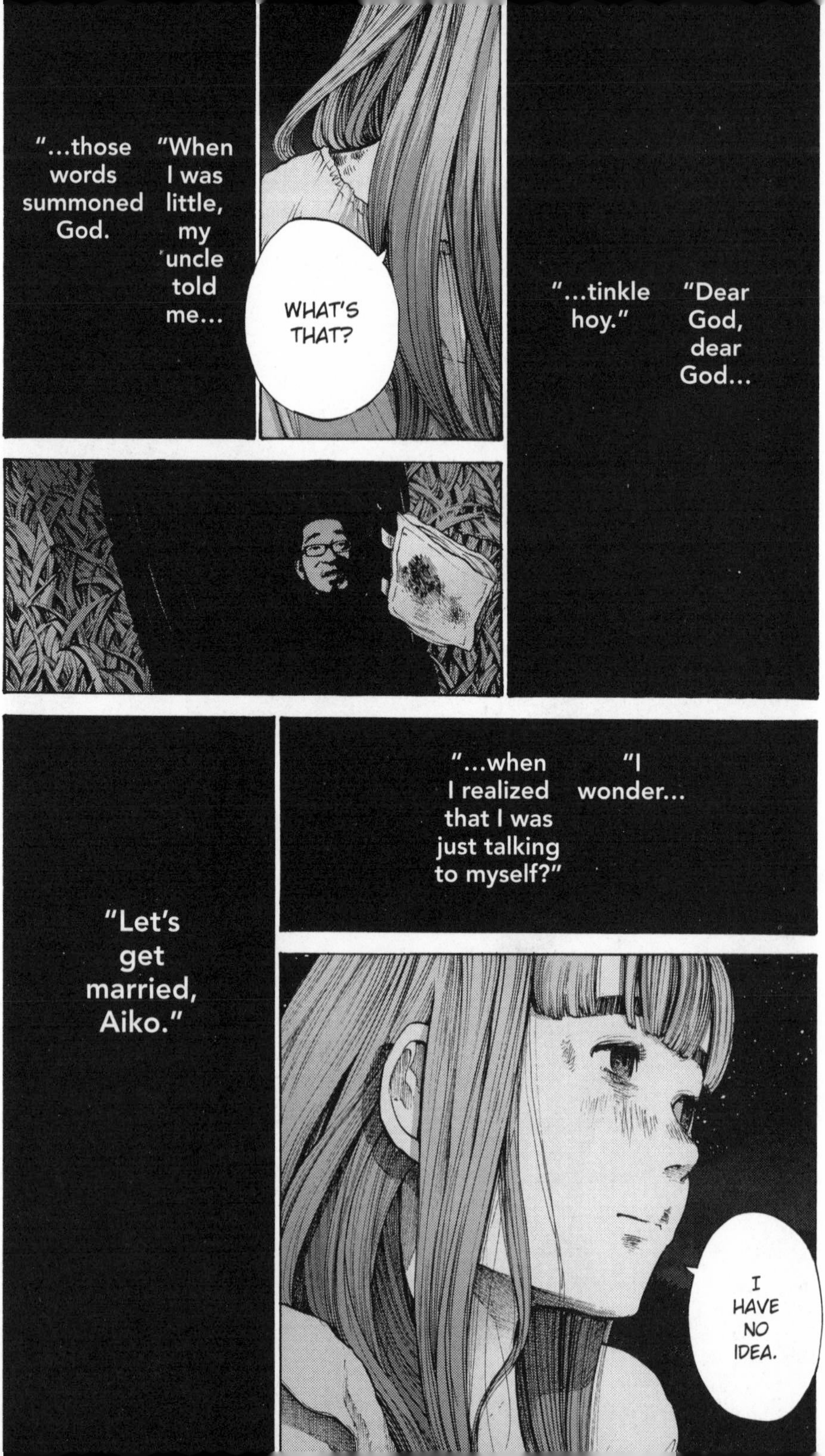
"Dear God, dear God...
"...tinkle hoy."
WHAT'S THAT?
"When I was little, my uncle told me...
"...those words summoned God.
"I wonder...
"...when I realized that I was just talking to myself?"
I HAVE NO IDEA.
"Let's get married, Aiko."

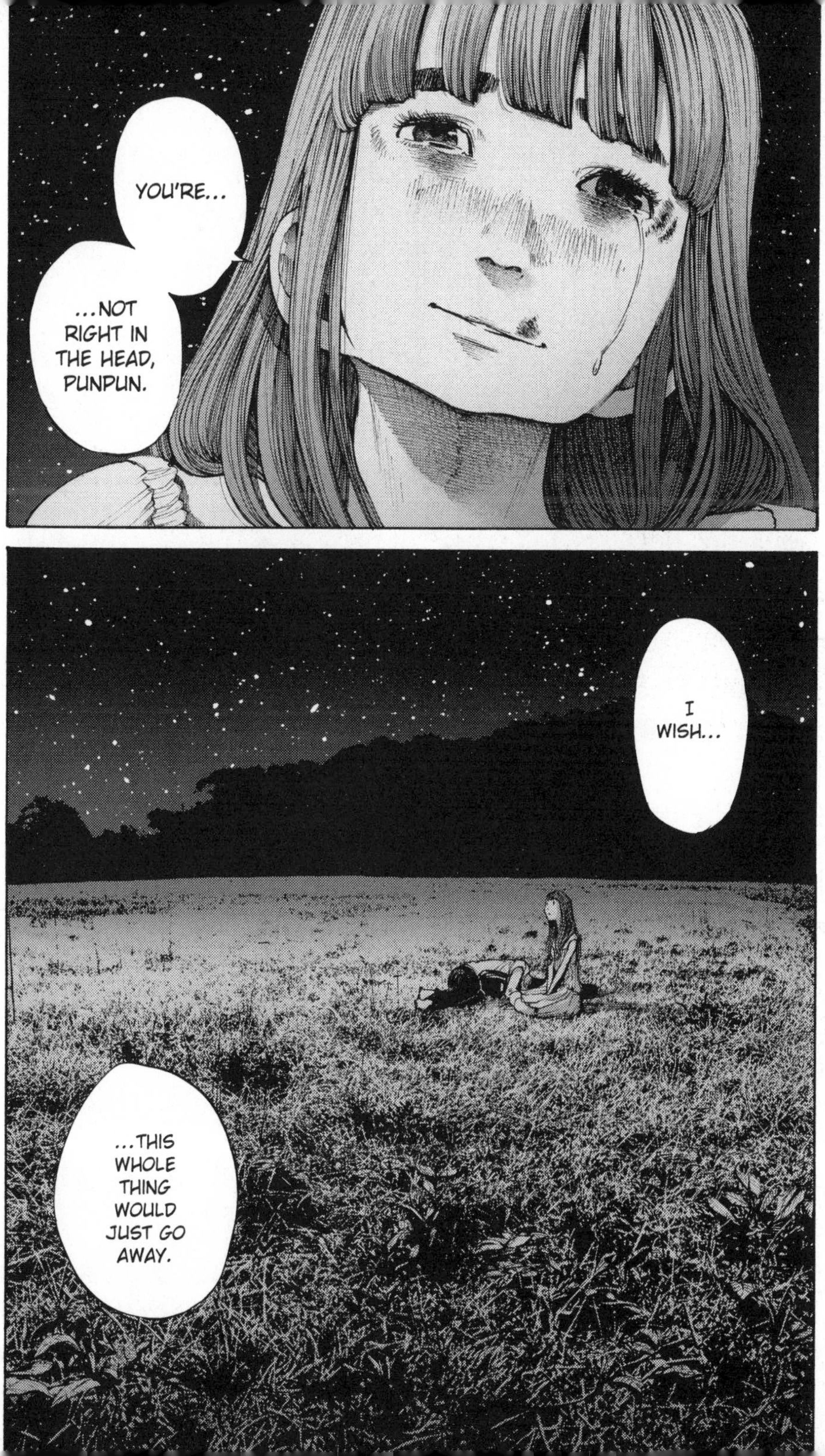
YOU'RE...
...NOT RIGHT IN THE HEAD, PUNPUN.
I WISH...
...THIS WHOLE THING WOULD JUST GO AWAY.

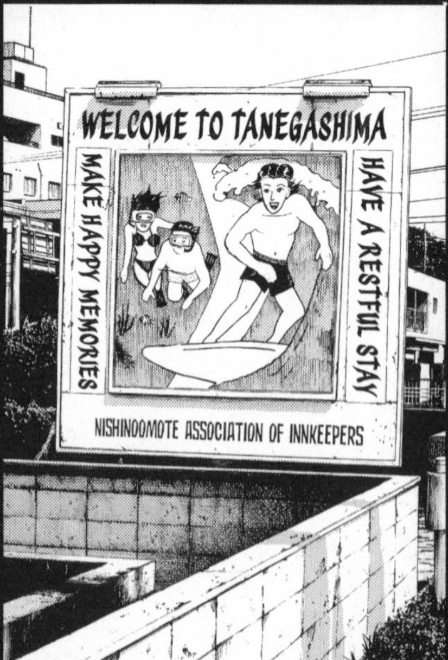
WELCOME TO TANEGASHIMA
MAKE HAPPY MEMORIES
HAVE A RESTFUL STAY
NISHINOOMOTE ASSOCIATION OF INNKEEPERS

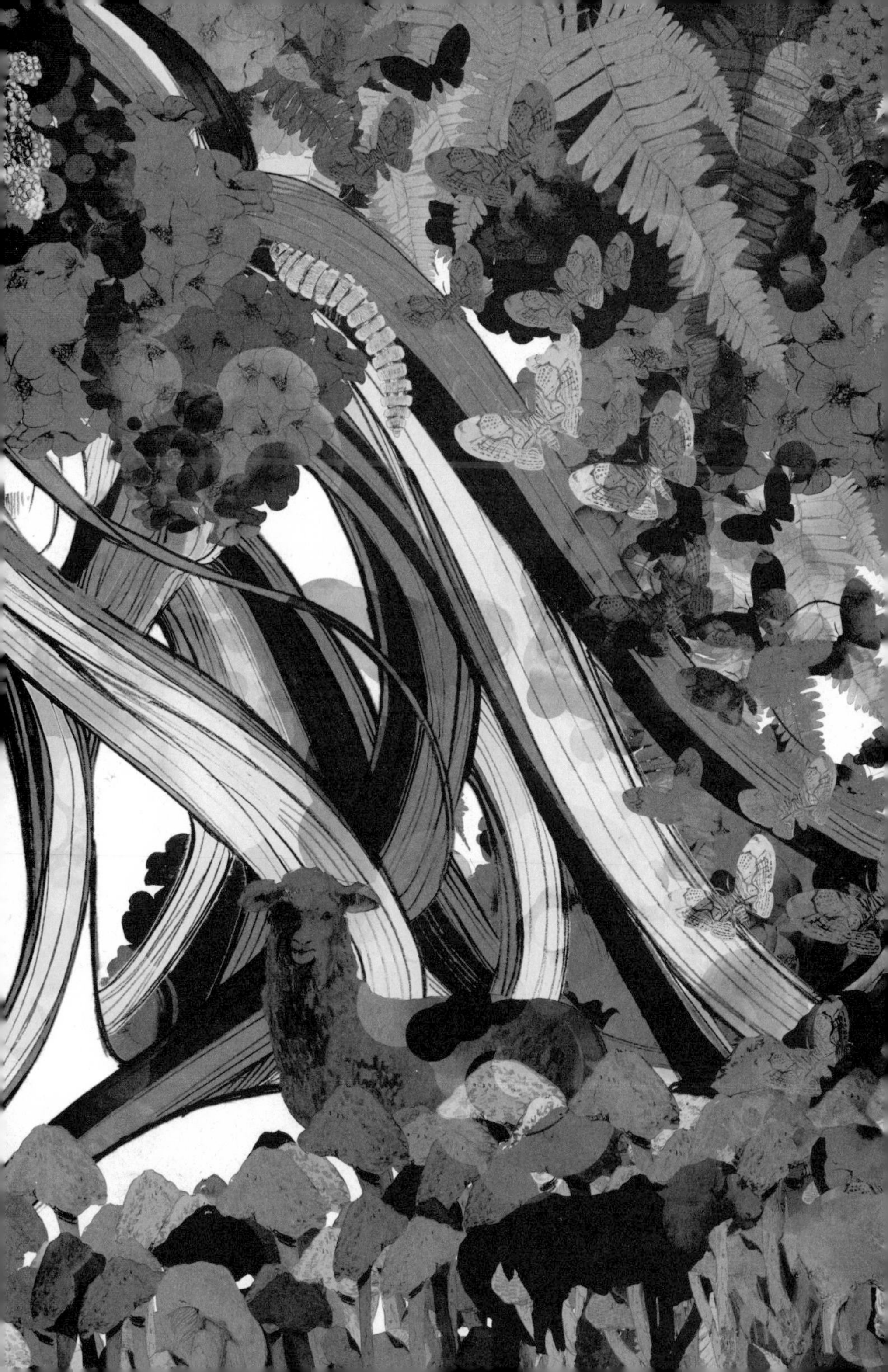

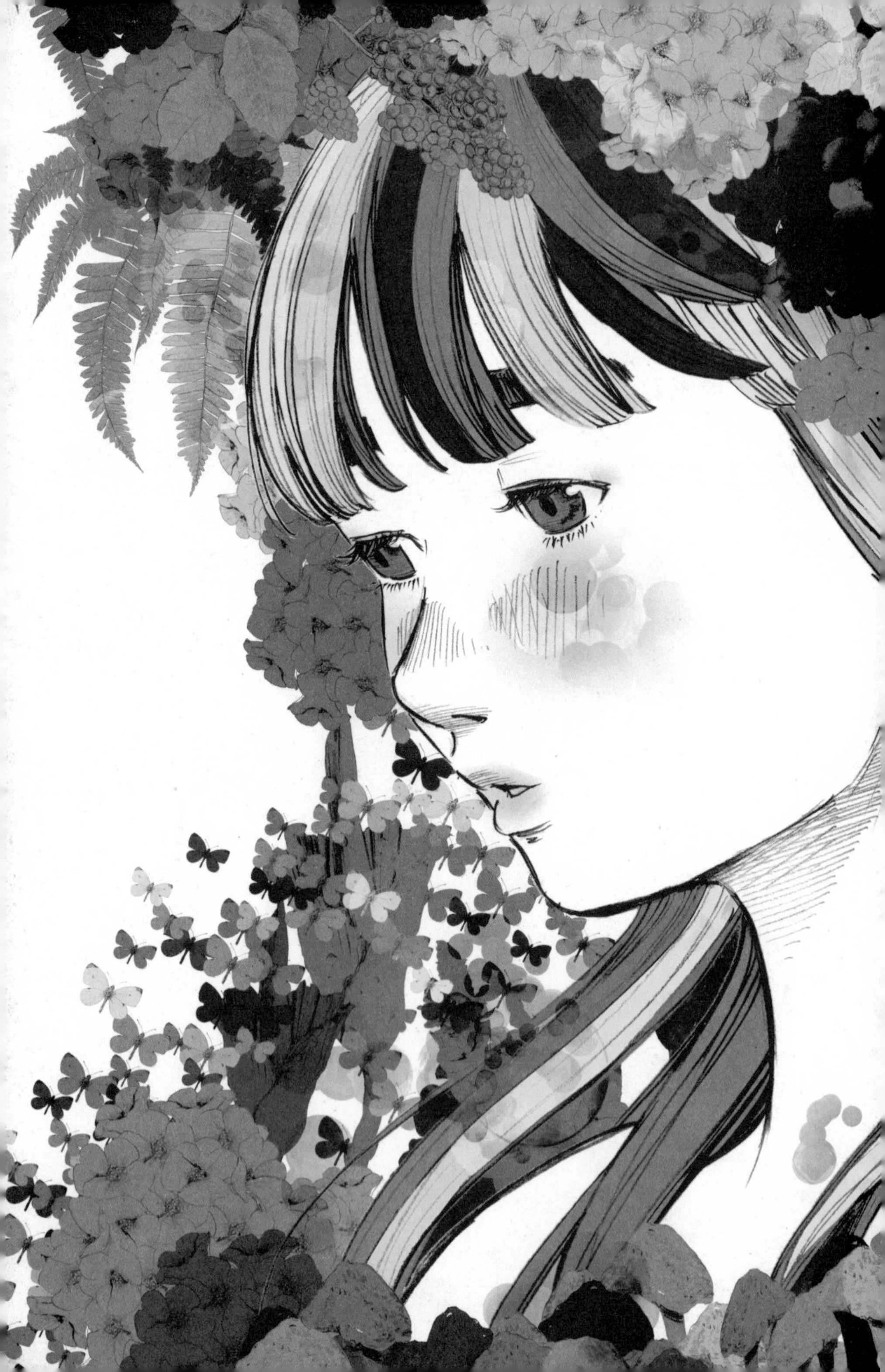

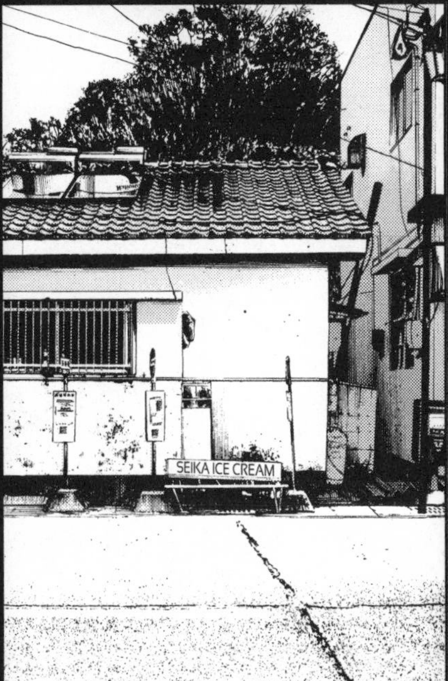
SEIKA ICE CREAM

Chapter 133

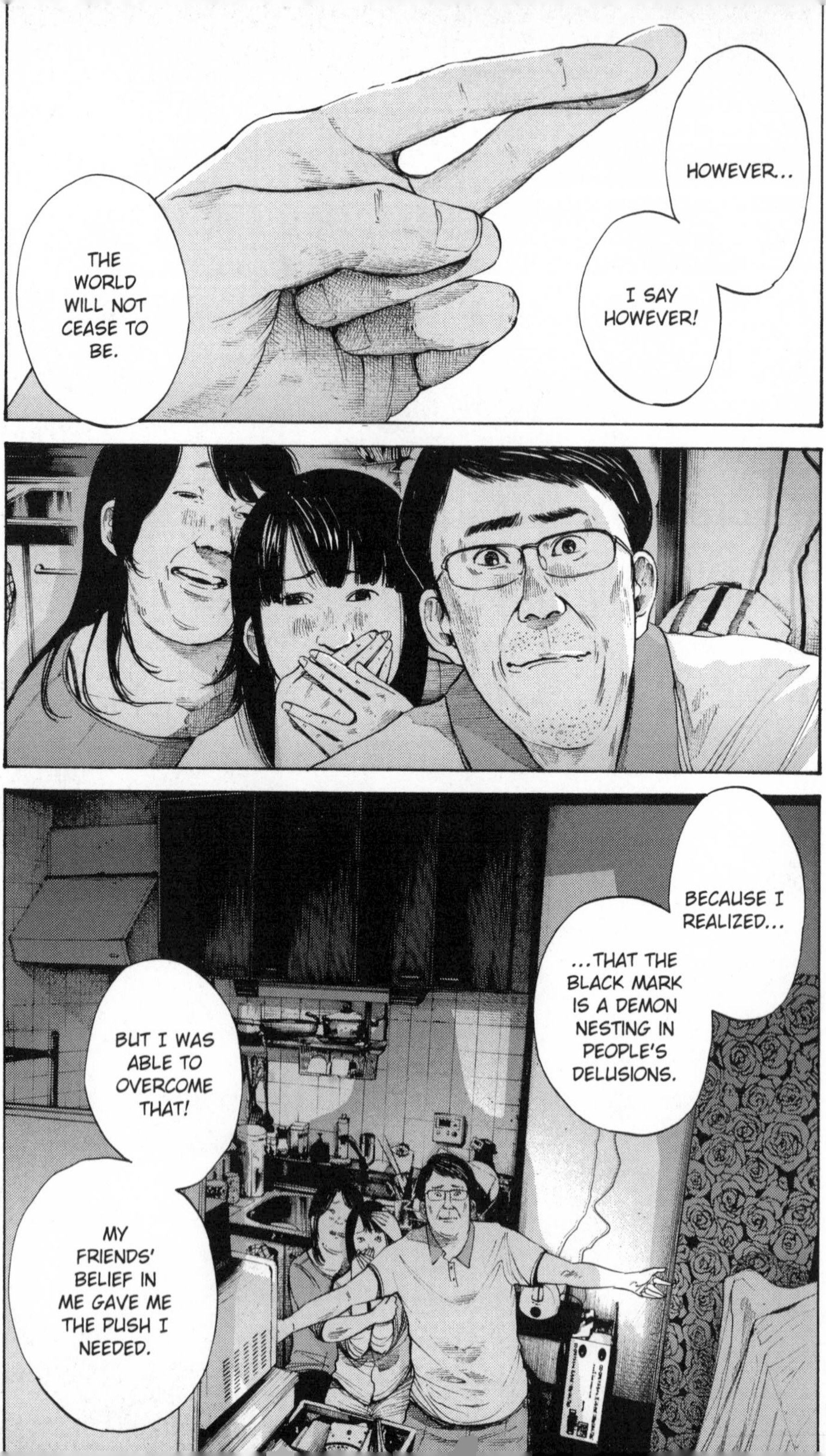
HOWEVER...
I SAY HOWEVER!
THE WORLD WILL NOT CEASE TO BE.
BECAUSE I REALIZED...
...THAT THE BLACK MARK IS A DEMON NESTING IN PEOPLE'S DELUSIONS.
BUT I WAS ABLE TO OVERCOME THAT!
MY FRIENDS' BELIEF IN ME GAVE ME THE PUSH I NEEDED.

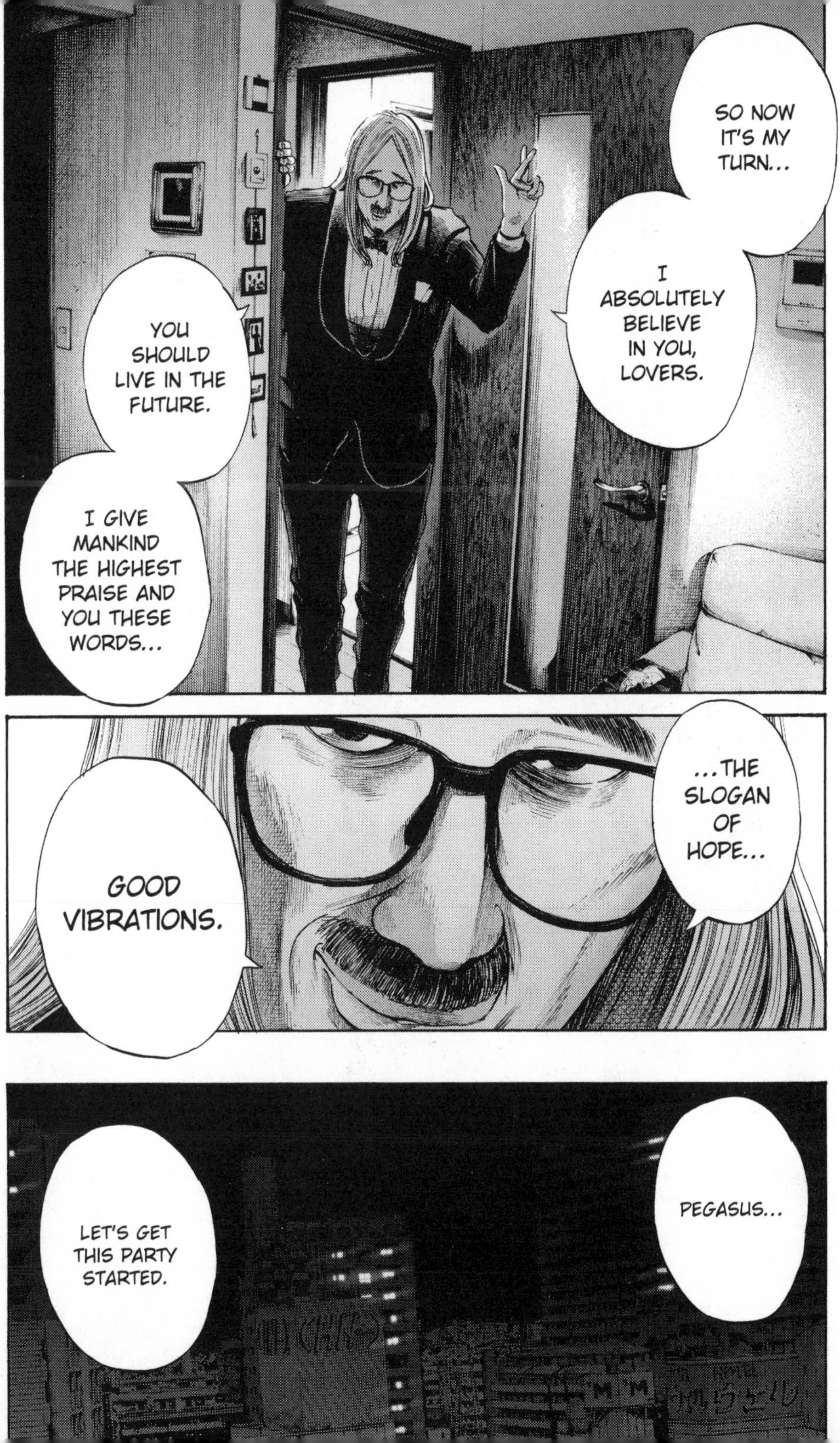
SO NOW IT'S MY TURN...
I ABSOLUTELY BELIEVE IN YOU, LOVERS.
YOU SHOULD LIVE IN THE FUTURE.
I GIVE MANKIND THE HIGHEST PRAISE AND YOU THESE WORDS...
...THE SLOGAN OF HOPE...
GOOD VIBRATIONS.
PEGASUS...
LET'S GET THIS PARTY STARTED.

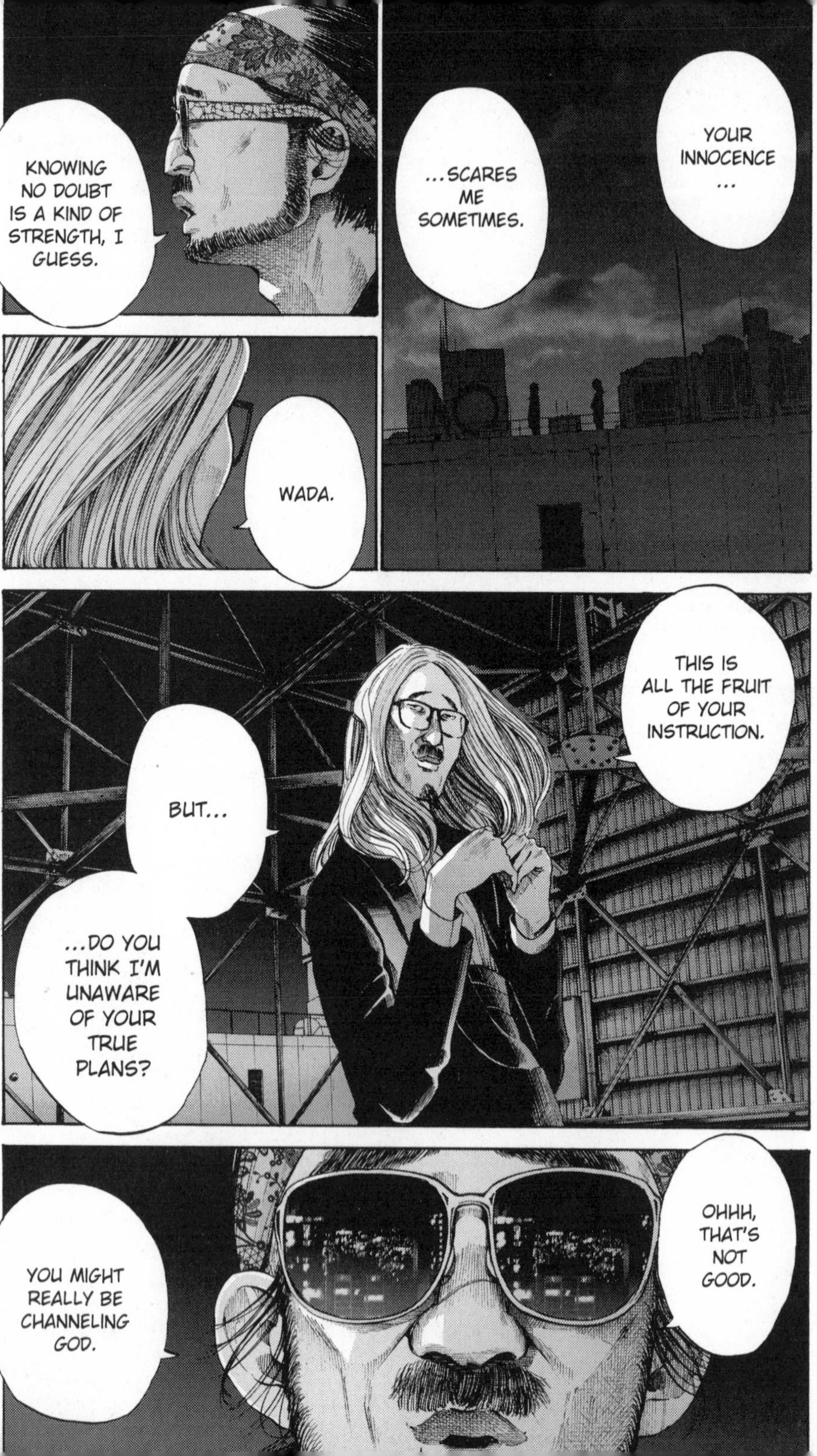
YOUR INNOCENCE...
...SCARES ME SOMETIMES.
KNOWING NO DOUBT IS A KIND OF STRENGTH, I GUESS.
WADA.
THIS IS ALL THE FRUIT OF YOUR INSTRUCTION.
BUT...
...DO YOU THINK I'M UNAWARE OF YOUR TRUE PLANS?
OHHH, THAT'S NOT GOOD.
YOU MIGHT REALLY BE CHANNELING GOD.

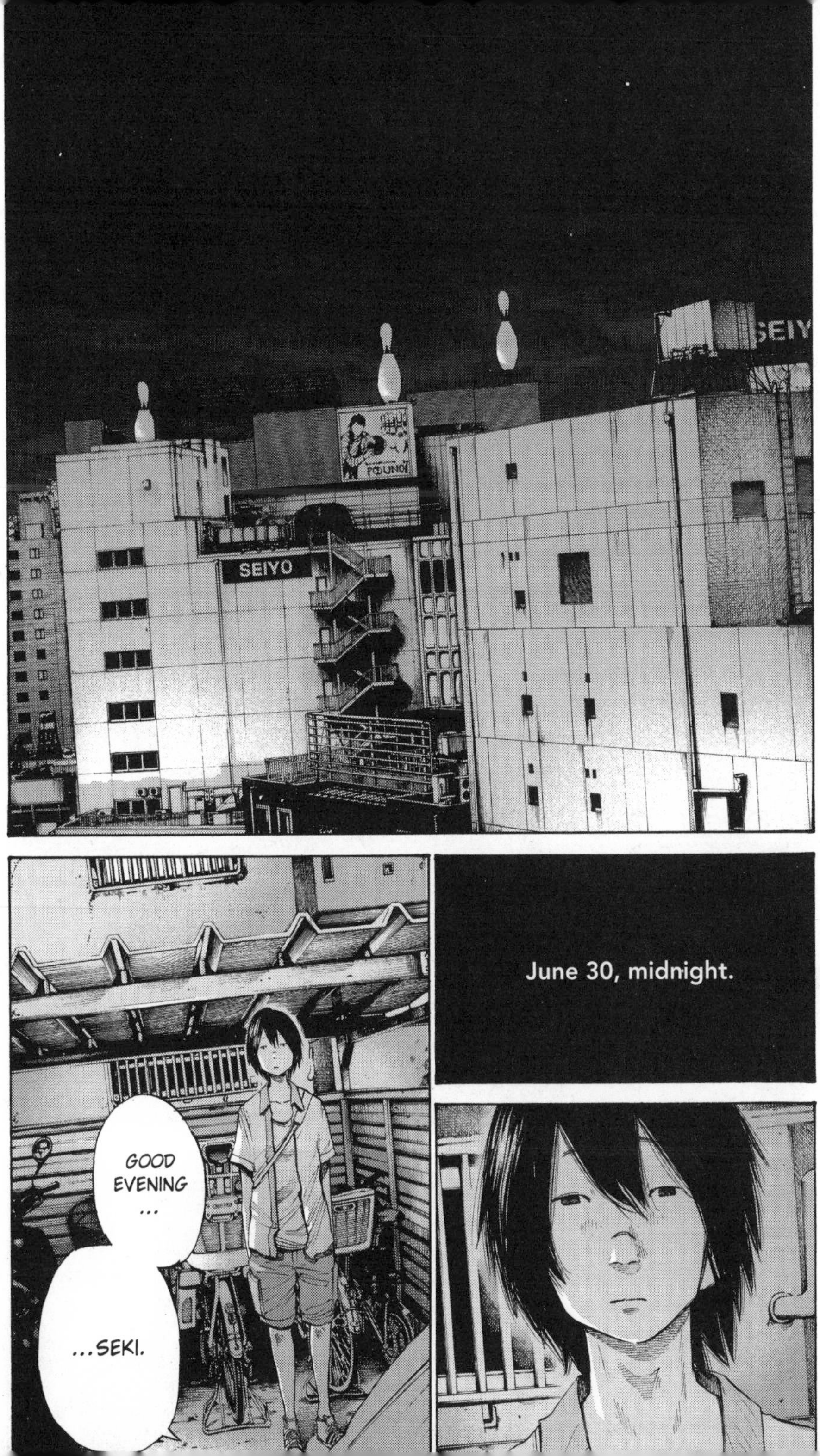
SEIYO
June 30, midnight.
GOOD EVENING ...
...SEKI.

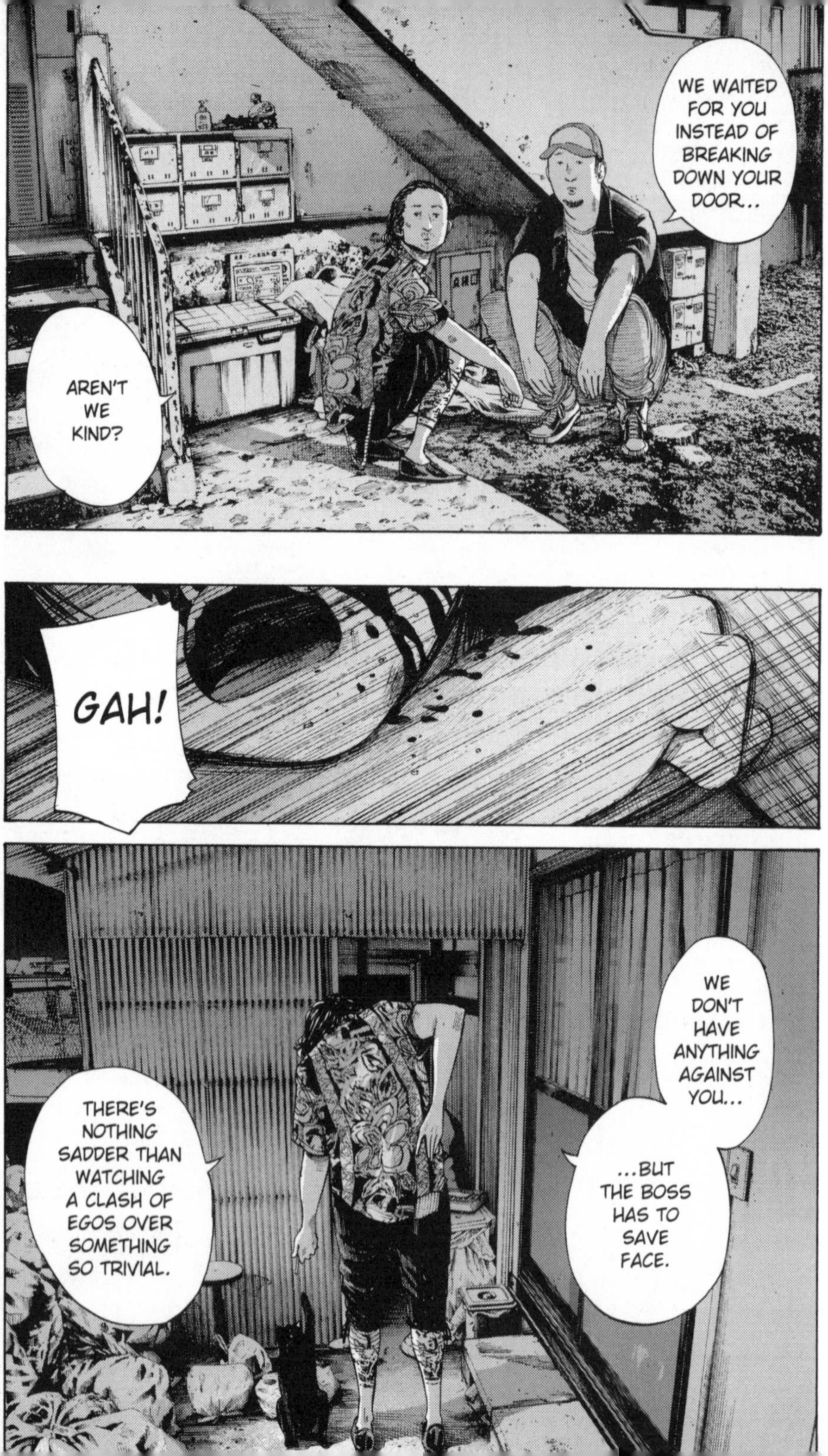
WE WAITED FOR YOU INSTEAD OF BREAKING DOWN YOUR DOOR...
AREN'T WE KIND?
GAH!
WE DON'T HAVE ANYTHING AGAINST YOU...
...BUT THE BOSS HAS TO SAVE FACE.
THERE'S NOTHING SADDER THAN WATCHING A CLASH OF EGOS OVER SOMETHING SO TRIVIAL.

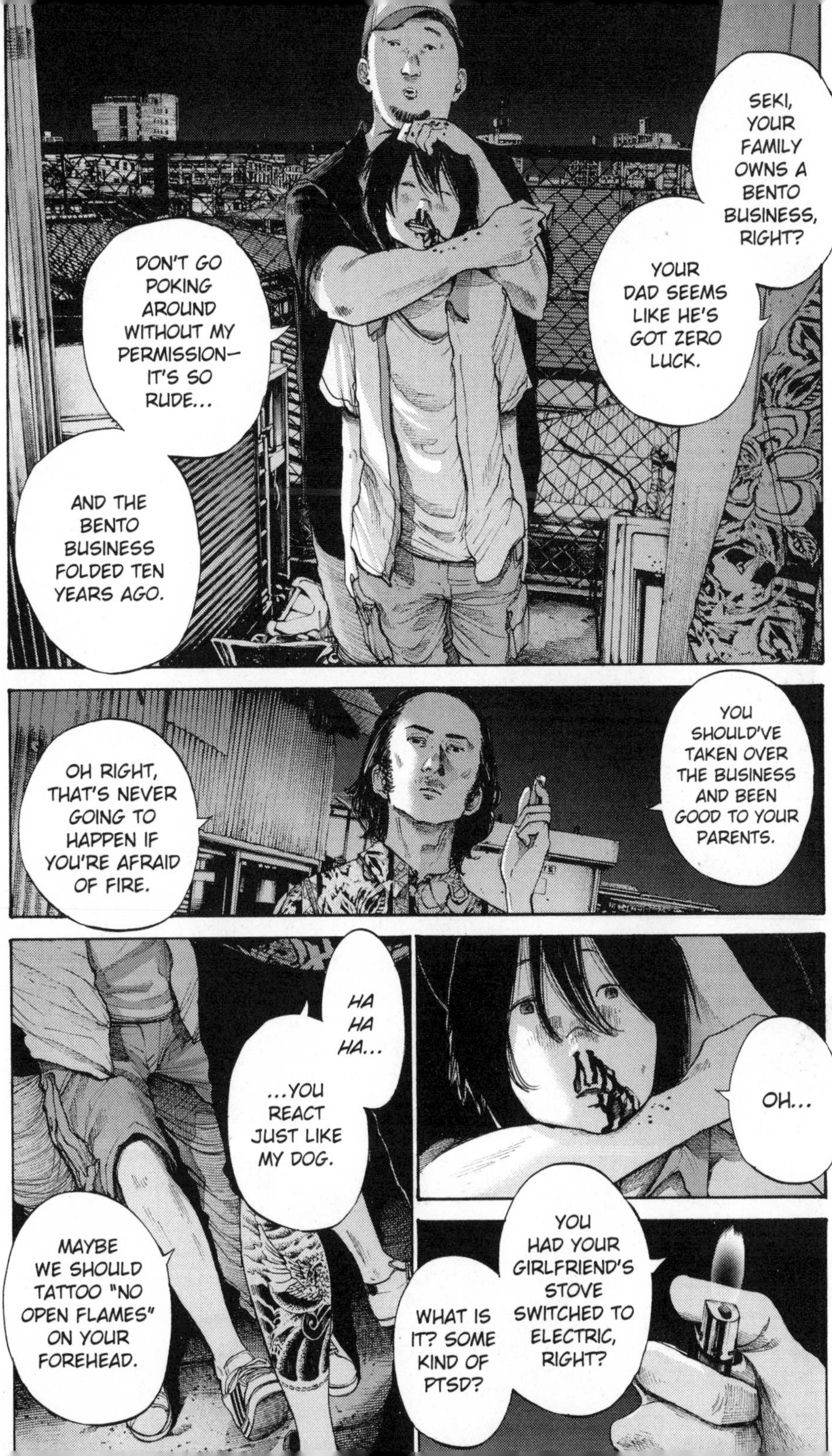
SEKI, YOUR FAMILY OWNS A BENTO BUSINESS, RIGHT?
YOUR DAD SEEMS LIKE HE'S GOT ZERO LUCK.
DON'T GO POKING AROUND WITHOUT MY PERMISSION— IT'S SO RUDE...
AND THE BENTO BUSINESS FOLDED TEN YEARS AGO.
YOU SHOULD'VE TAKEN OVER THE BUSINESS AND BEEN GOOD TO YOUR PARENTS.
OH RIGHT, THAT'S NEVER GOING TO HAPPEN IF YOU'RE AFRAID OF FIRE.
OH...
YOU HAD YOUR GIRLFRIEND'S STOVE SWITCHED TO ELECTRIC, RIGHT?
WHAT IS IT? SOME KIND OF PTSD?
HA HA HA...
...YOU REACT JUST LIKE MY DOG.
MAYBE WE SHOULD TATTOO "NO OPEN FLAMES" ON YOUR FOREHEAD.

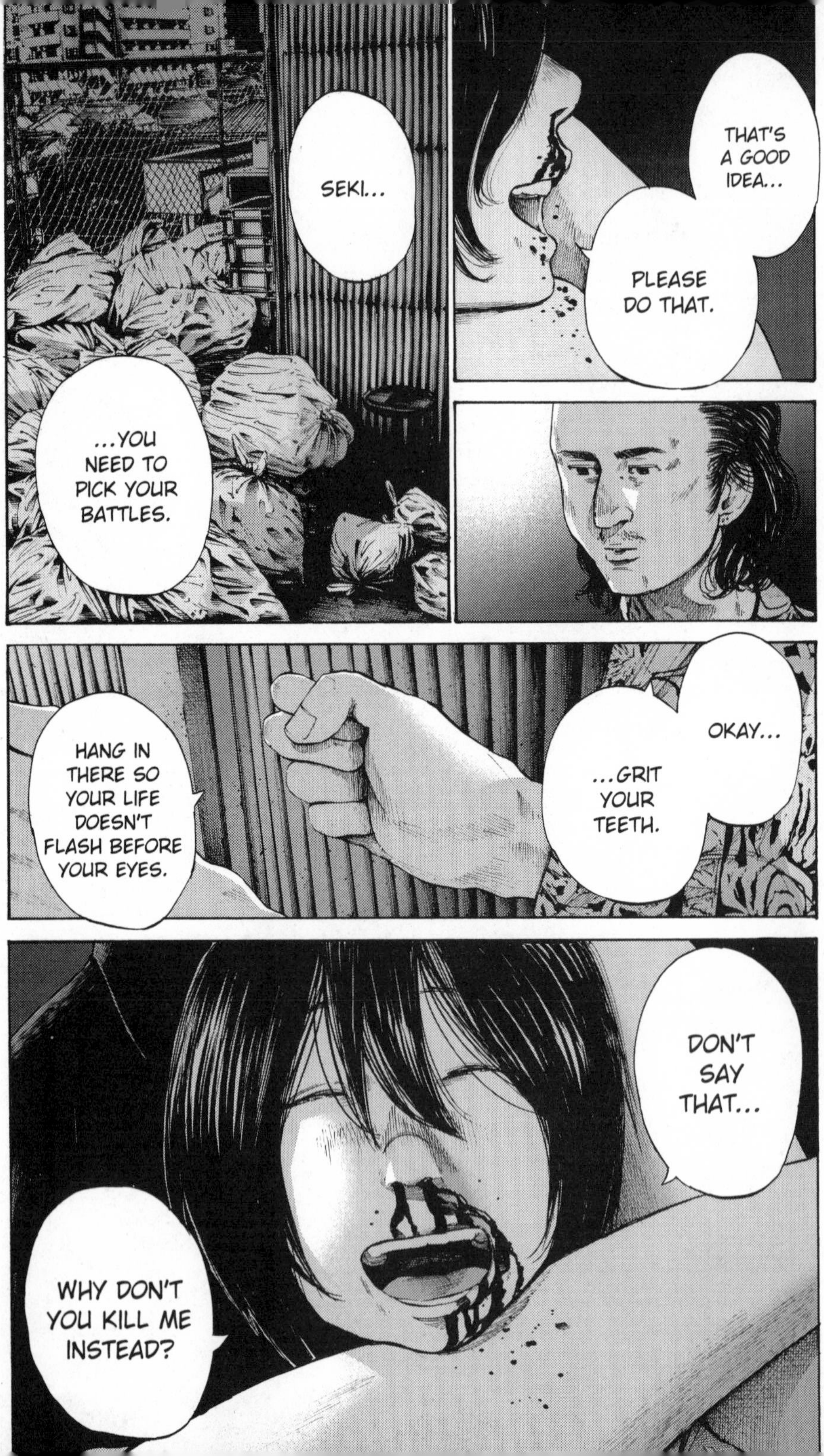
THAT'S A GOOD IDEA...
PLEASE DO THAT.
SEKI...
...YOU NEED TO PICK YOUR BATTLES.
OKAY...
...GRIT YOUR TEETH.
HANG IN THERE SO YOUR LIFE DOESN'T FLASH BEFORE YOUR EYES.
DON'T SAY THAT...
WHY DON'T YOU KILL ME INSTEAD?

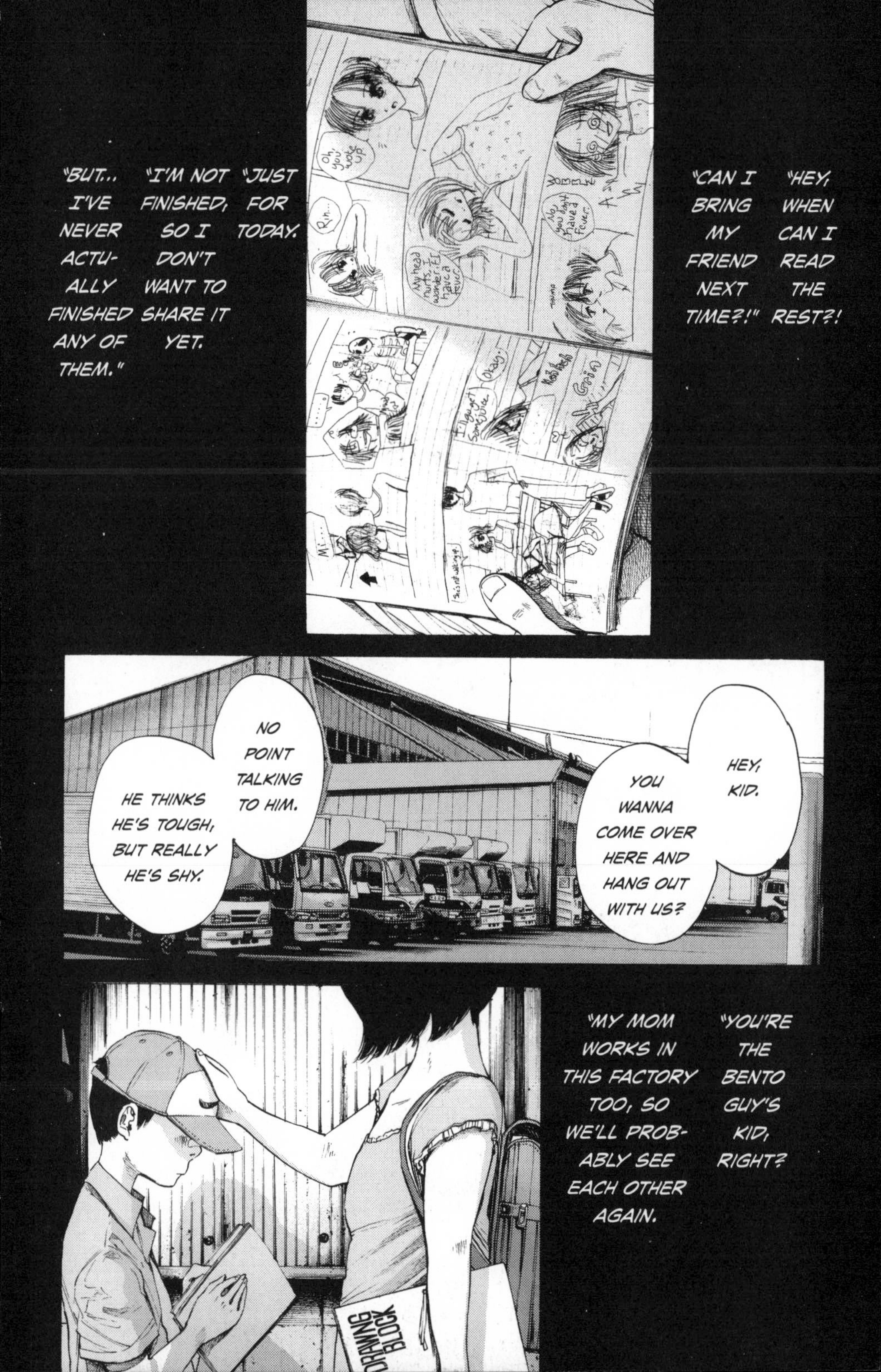
"HEY, WHEN CAN I READ THE REST?!
"CAN I BRING MY FRIEND NEXT TIME?!"
"JUST FOR TODAY.
"I'M NOT FINISHED, SO I DON'T WANT TO SHARE IT YET.
"BUT... I'VE NEVER ACTUALLY FINISHED ANY OF THEM."
HEY, KID. YOU WANNA COME OVER HERE AND HANG OUT WITH US?
NO POINT TALKING TO HIM.
HE THINKS HE'S TOUGH, BUT REALLY HE'S SHY.
"YOU'RE THE BENTO GUY'S KID, RIGHT?
"MY MOM WORKS IN THIS FACTORY TOO, SO WE'LL PROBABLY SEE EACH OTHER AGAIN.
DRAWING BLOCK

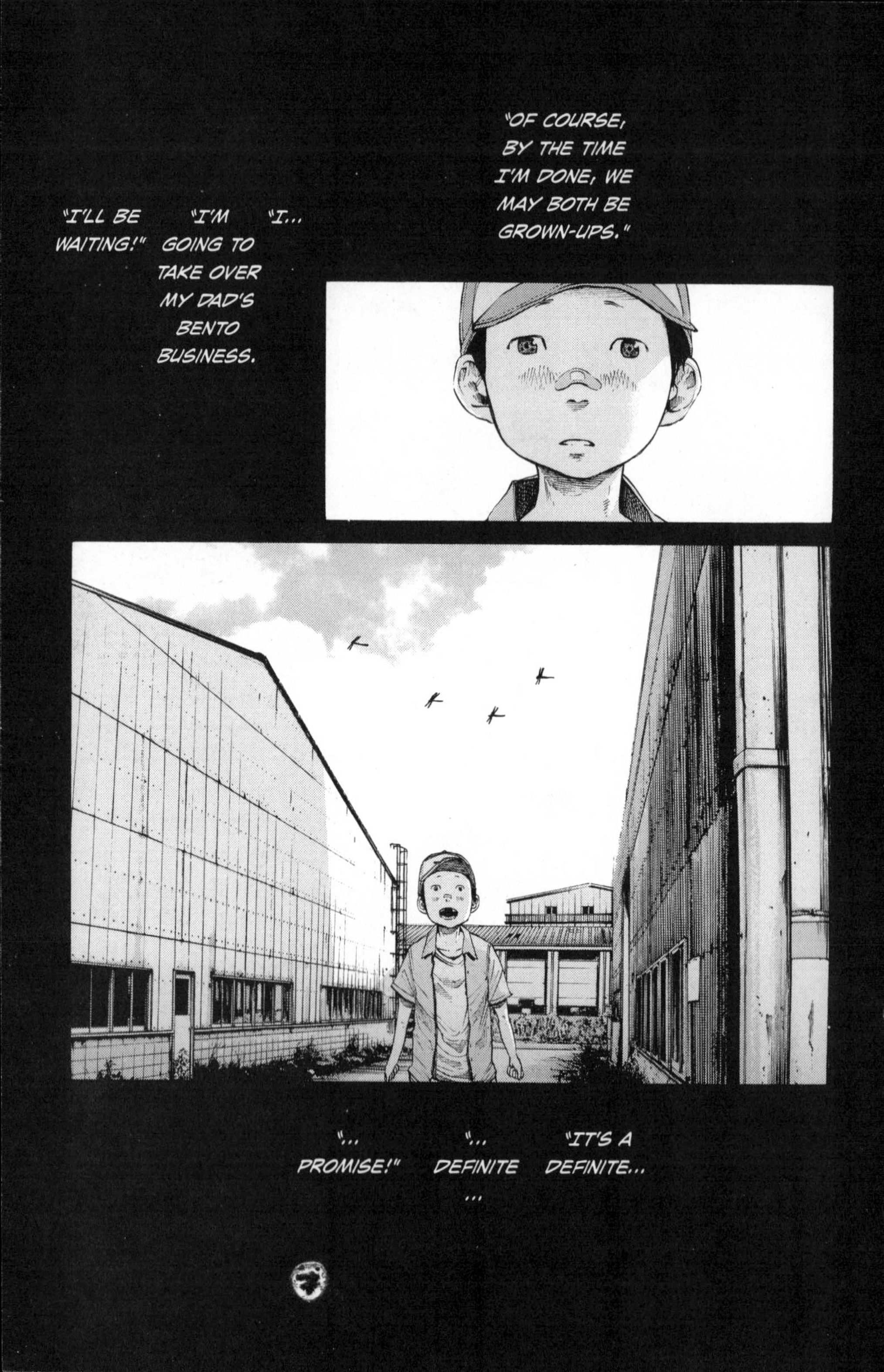
"I...
"I'M GOING TO TAKE OVER MY DAD'S BENTO BUSINESS.
"OF COURSE, BY THE TIME I'M DONE, WE MAY BOTH BE GROWN-UPS."
"I'LL BE WAITING!"
"IT'S A DEFINITE...
"... DEFINITE ...
"... PROMISE!"

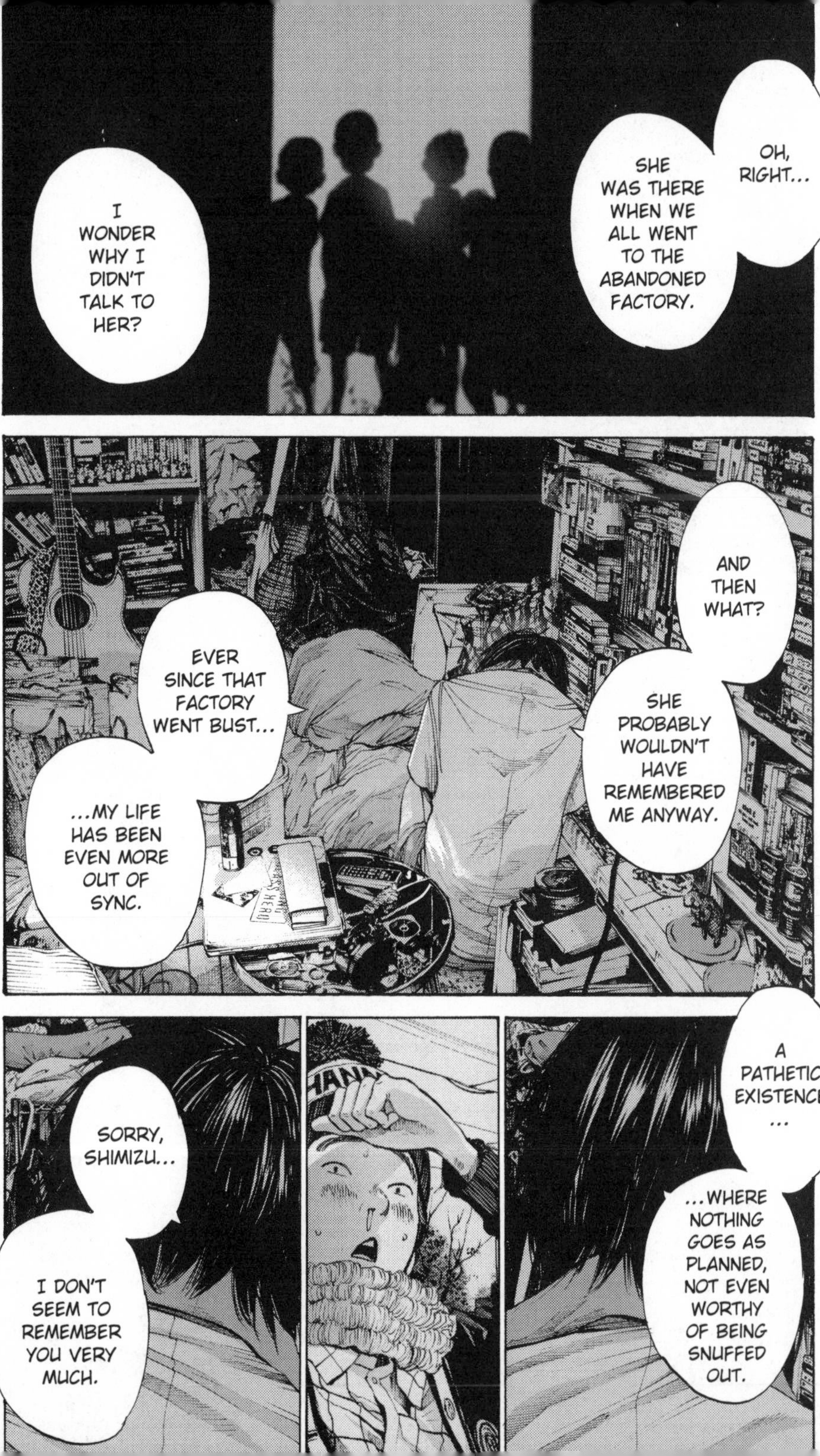
OH, RIGHT...
SHE WAS THERE WHEN WE ALL WENT TO THE ABANDONED FACTORY.
I WONDER WHY I DIDN'T TALK TO HER?
AND THEN WHAT?
SHE PROBABLY WOULDN'T HAVE REMEMBERED ME ANYWAY.
EVER SINCE THAT FACTORY WENT BUST...
...MY LIFE HAS BEEN EVEN MORE OUT OF SYNC.
A PATHETIC EXISTENCE ...
...WHERE NOTHING GOES AS PLANNED, NOT EVEN WORTHY OF BEING SNUFFED OUT.
SORRY, SHIMIZU...
I DON'T SEEM TO REMEMBER YOU VERY MUCH.

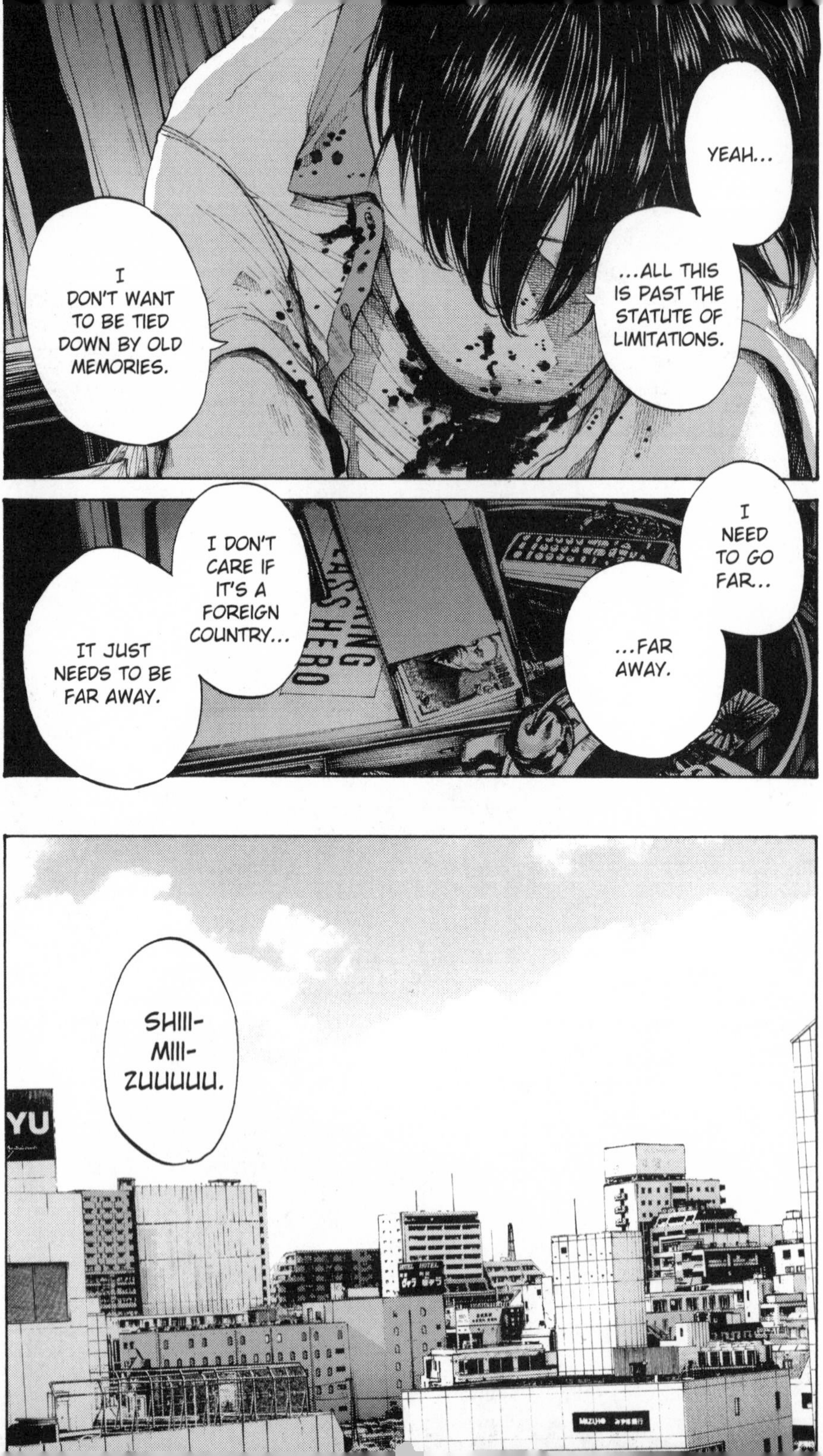
YEAH...
...ALL THIS IS PAST THE STATUTE OF LIMITATIONS.
I DON'T WANT TO BE TIED DOWN BY OLD MEMORIES.
I NEED TO GO FAR...
...FAR AWAY.
I DON'T CARE IF IT'S A FOREIGN COUNTRY...
IT JUST NEEDS TO BE FAR AWAY.
SHIII-MIII-ZUUUUU.

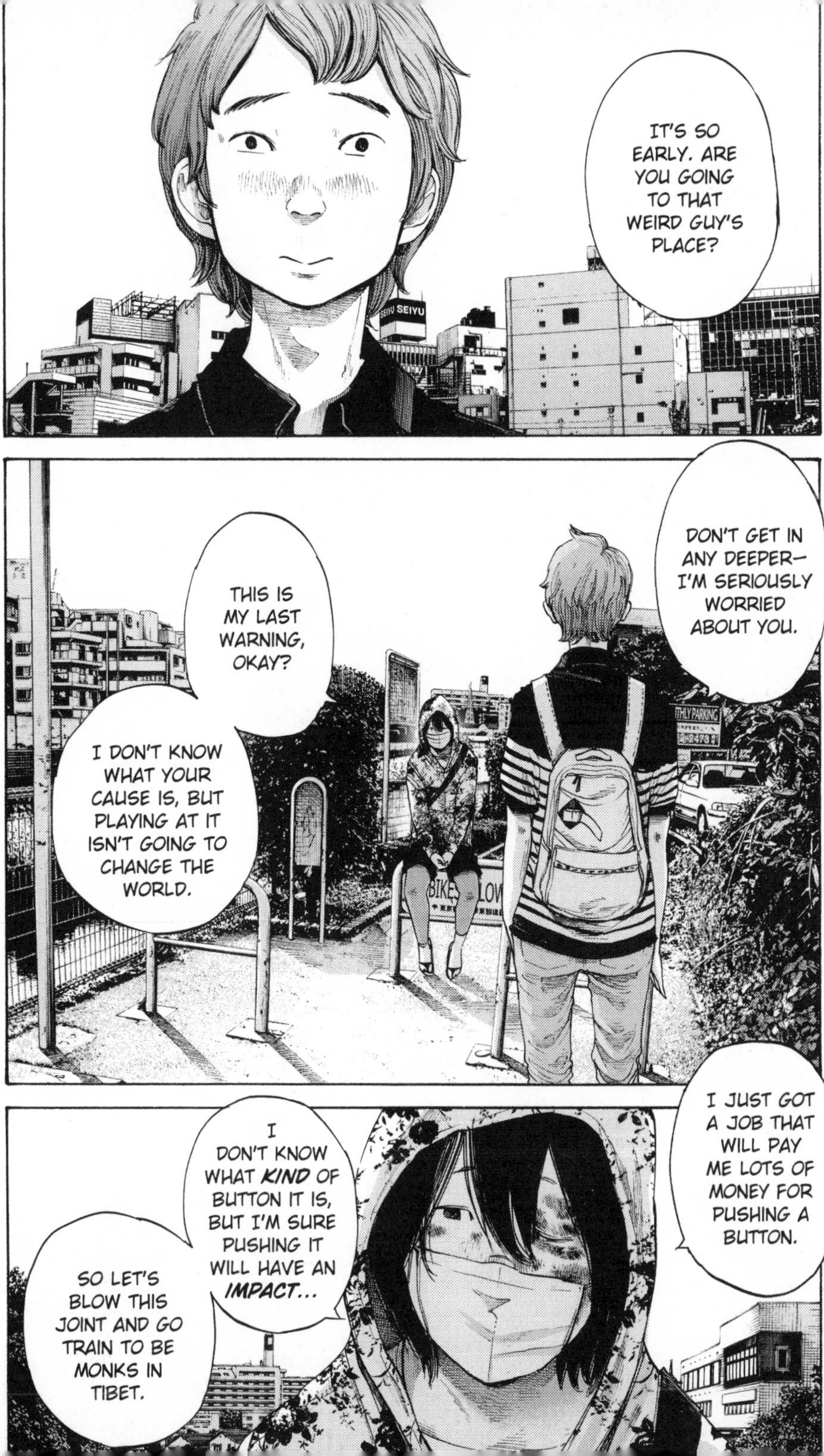
IT'S SO EARLY. ARE YOU GOING TO THAT WEIRD GUY'S PLACE?
SEIYU SEIYU
DON'T GET IN ANY DEEPER— I'M SERIOUSLY WORRIED ABOUT YOU.
THIS IS MY LAST WARNING, OKAY?
I DON'T KNOW WHAT YOUR CAUSE IS, BUT PLAYING AT IT ISN'T GOING TO CHANGE THE WORLD.
I JUST GOT A JOB THAT WILL PAY ME LOTS OF MONEY FOR PUSHING A BUTTON.
I DON'T KNOW WHAT *KIND* OF BUTTON IT IS, BUT I'M SURE PUSHING IT WILL HAVE AN *IMPACT*...
SO LET'S BLOW THIS JOINT AND GO TRAIN TO BE MONKS IN TIBET.

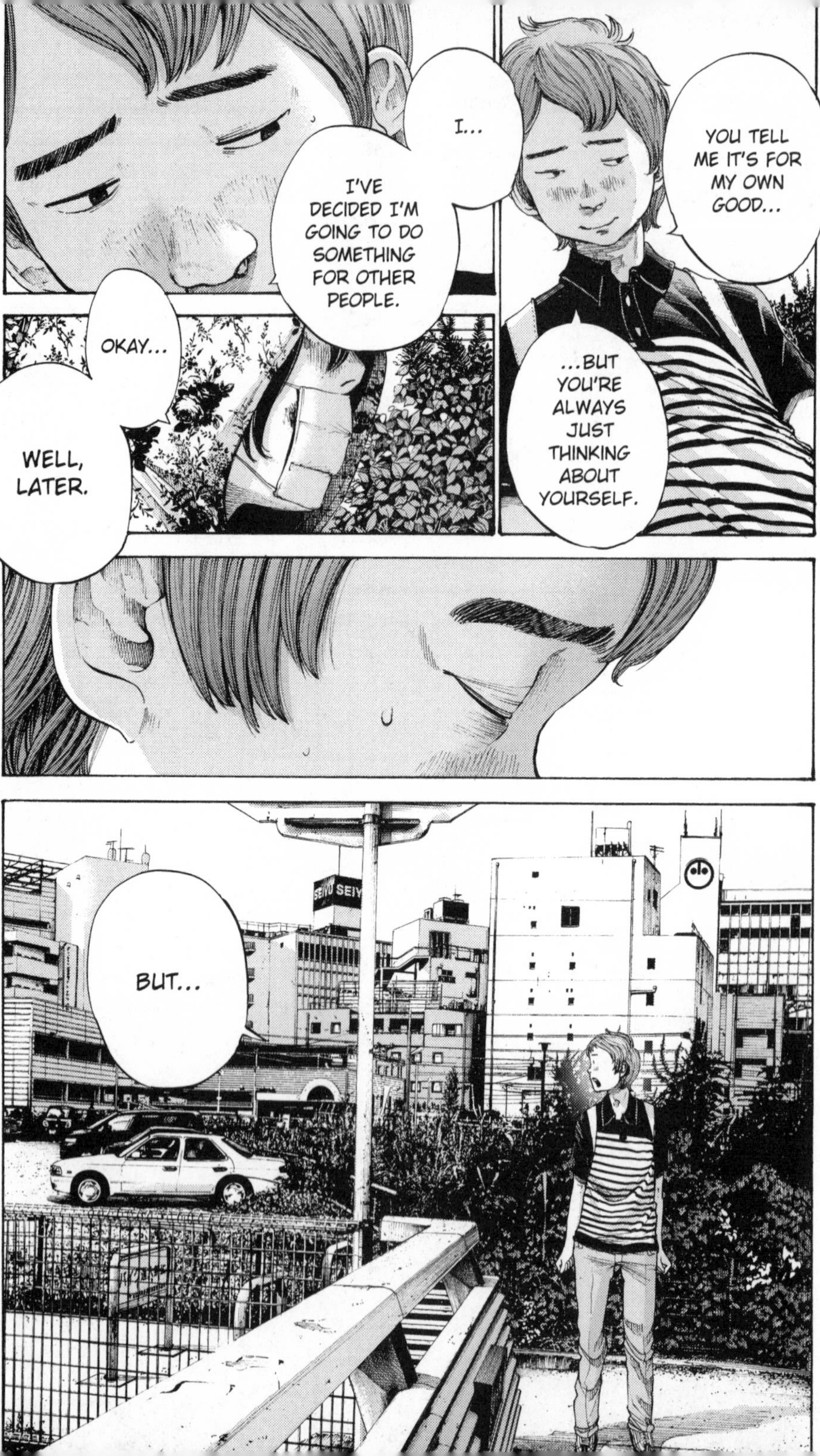
YOU TELL ME IT'S FOR MY OWN GOOD...
...BUT YOU'RE ALWAYS JUST THINKING ABOUT YOURSELF.
I...
I'VE DECIDED I'M GOING TO DO SOMETHING FOR OTHER PEOPLE.
OKAY...
WELL, LATER.
BUT...
SEIYU

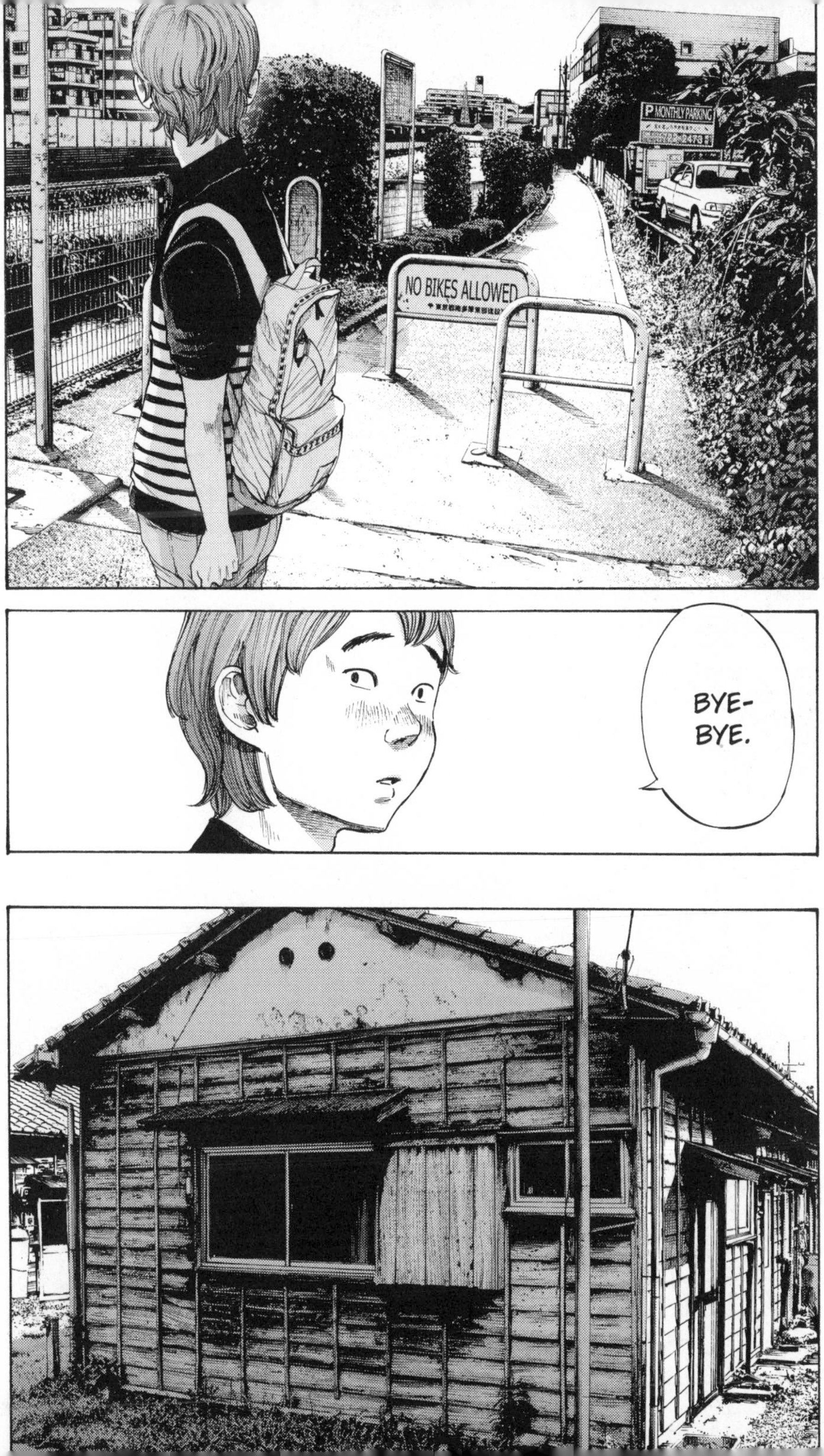
P MONTHLY PARKING
NO BIKES ALLOWED
BYE-BYE.

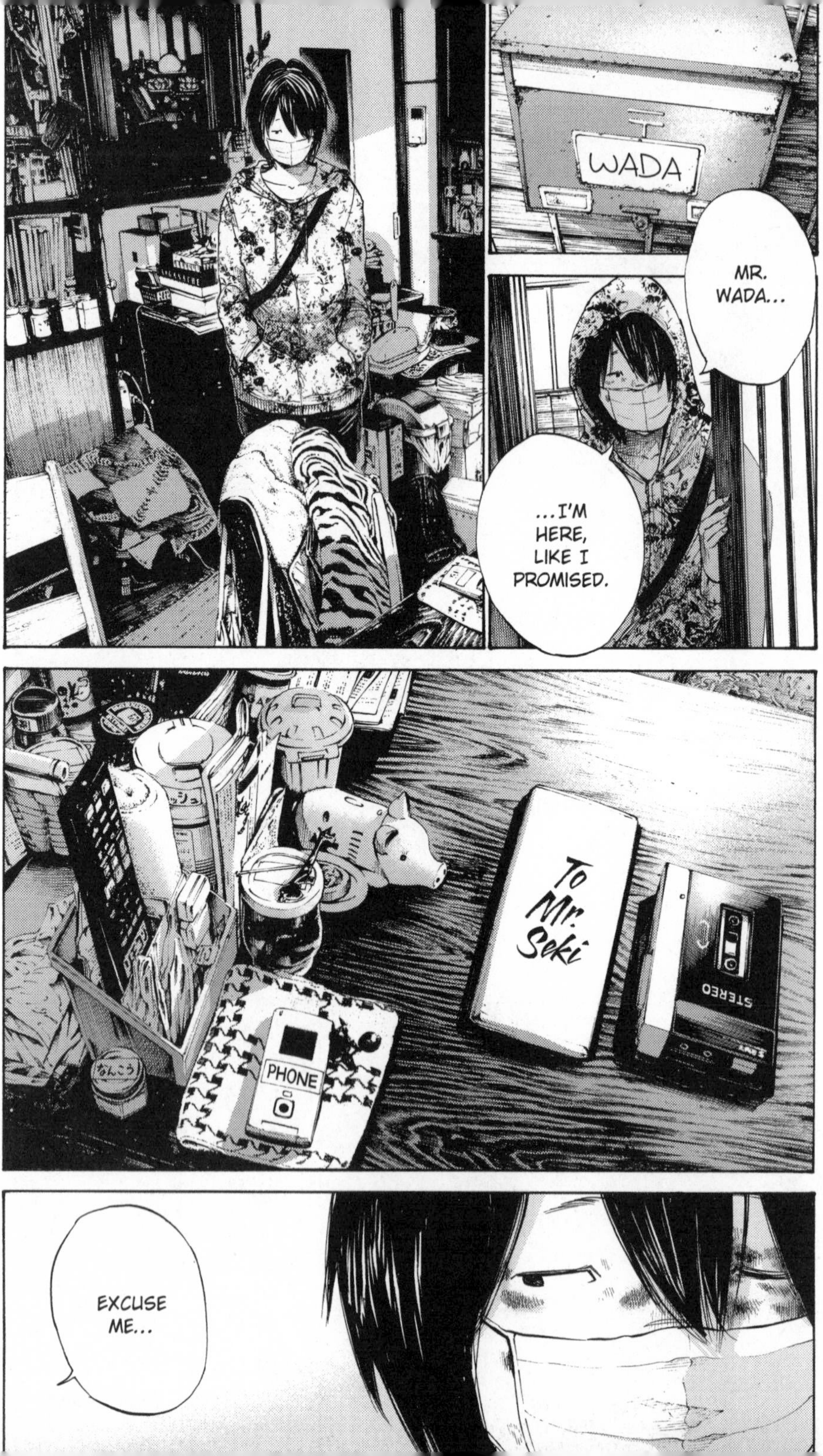
WADA
MR. WADA...
...I'M HERE, LIKE I PROMISED.
To Mr. Seki
STEREO
PHONE
なんこう
EXCUSE ME...

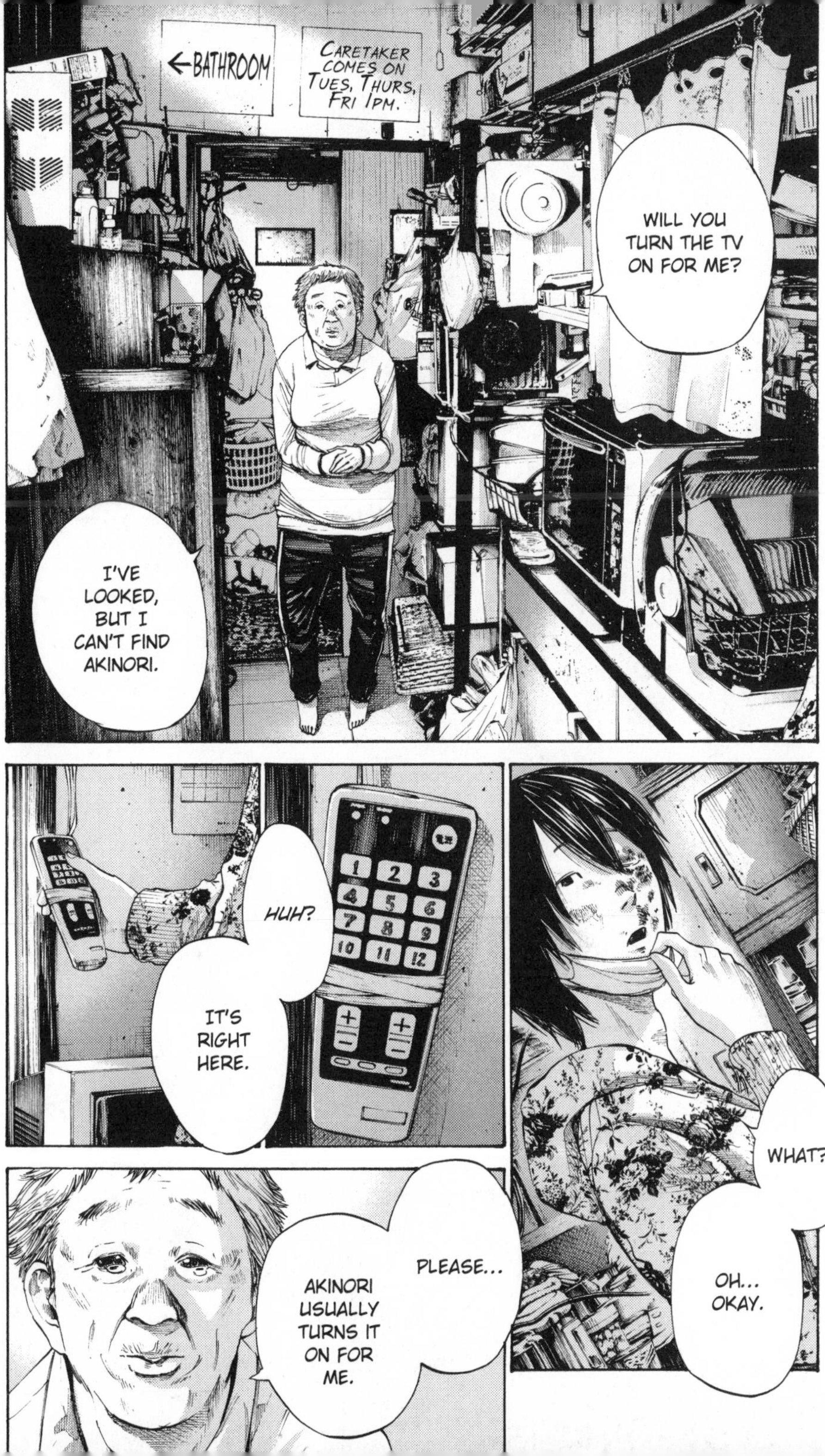
←BATHROOM
CARETAKER COMES ON TUES, THURS, FRI 1PM.
WILL YOU TURN THE TV ON FOR ME?
I'VE LOOKED, BUT I CAN'T FIND AKINORI.
HUH?
IT'S RIGHT HERE.
WHAT?
PLEASE...
AKINORI USUALLY TURNS IT ON FOR ME.
OH... OKAY.

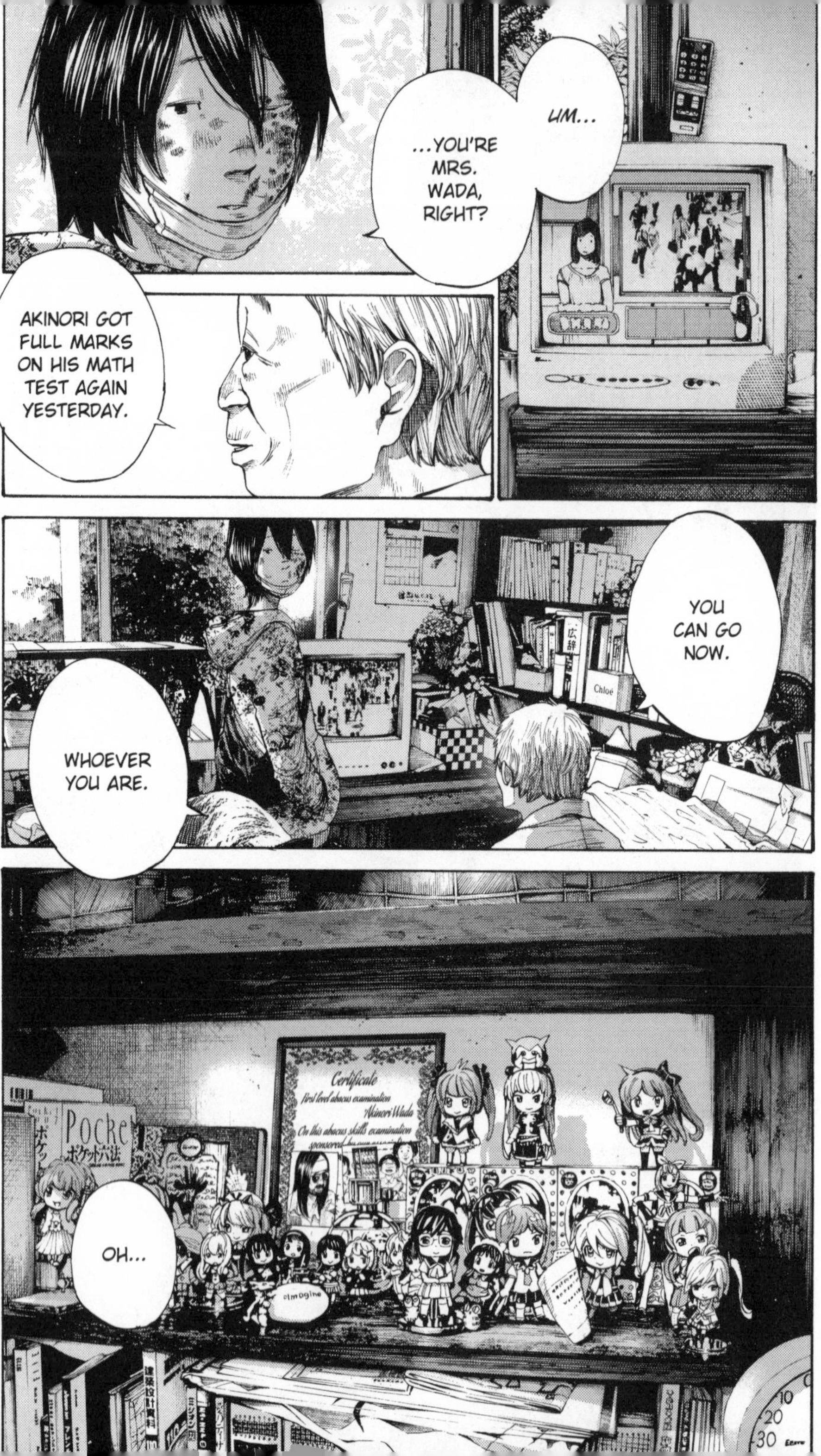
UM...
...YOU'RE MRS. WADA, RIGHT?
AKINORI GOT FULL MARKS ON HIS MATH TEST AGAIN YESTERDAY.
YOU CAN GO NOW.
Chloé
WHOEVER YOU ARE.
Certificate
First level abacus examination
Akinori Wada
On this abacus skills examination
Pocke
ポケット六法
OH...
Imagine

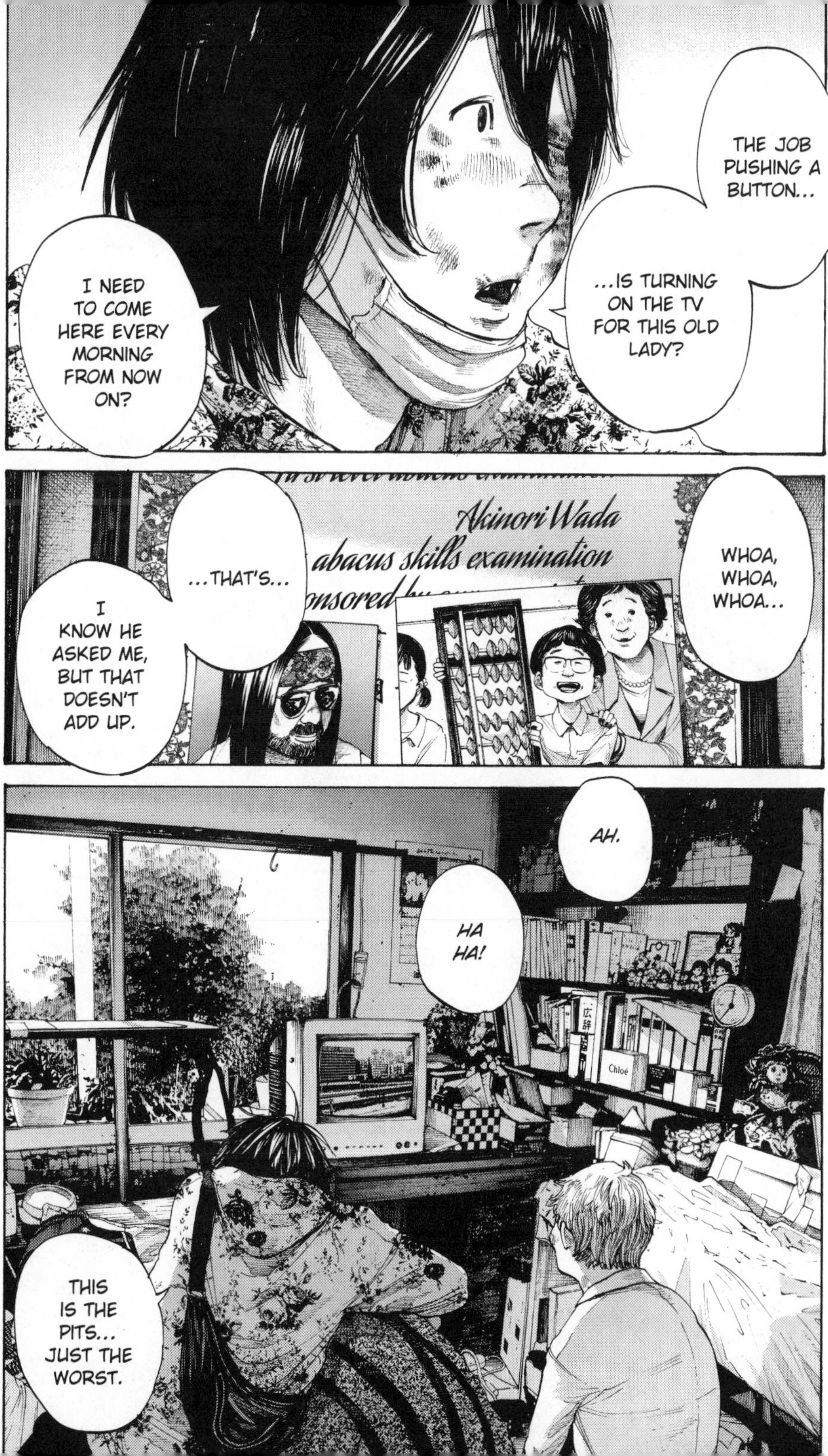
THE JOB PUSHING A BUTTON...
...IS TURNING ON THE TV FOR THIS OLD LADY?
I NEED TO COME HERE EVERY MORNING FROM NOW ON?
WHOA, WHOA, WHOA...
Akinori Wada
abacus skills examination
...THAT'S...
I KNOW HE ASKED ME, BUT THAT DOESN'T ADD UP.
AH.
HA HA!
広辞
Chloé
THIS IS THE PITS... JUST THE WORST.

Chapter 134

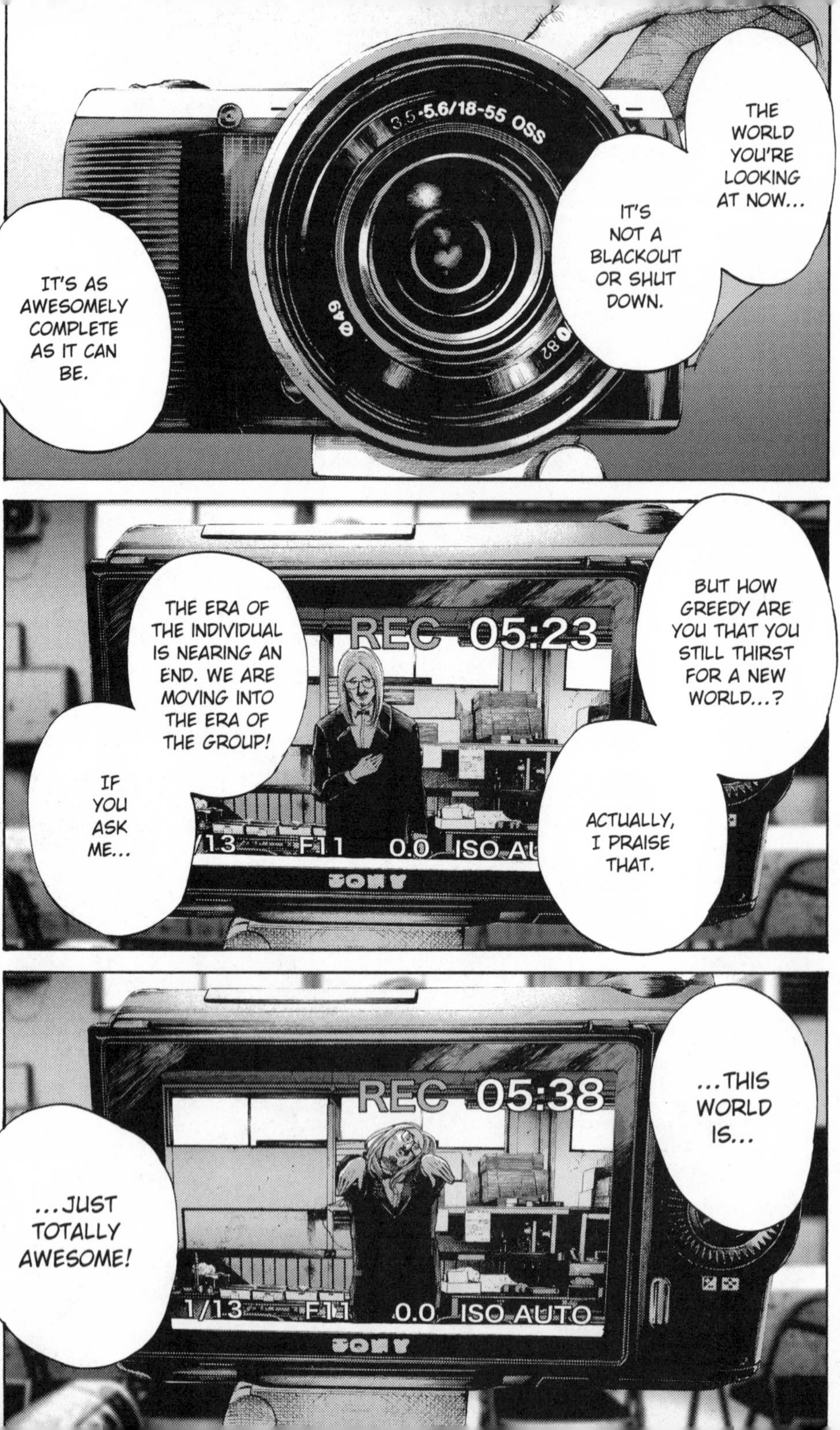
THE WORLD YOU'RE LOOKING AT NOW...
IT'S NOT A BLACKOUT OR SHUT DOWN.
IT'S AS AWESOMELY COMPLETE AS IT CAN BE.
BUT HOW GREEDY ARE YOU THAT YOU STILL THIRST FOR A NEW WORLD...?
ACTUALLY, I PRAISE THAT.
REC 05:23
THE ERA OF THE INDIVIDUAL IS NEARING AN END. WE ARE MOVING INTO THE ERA OF THE GROUP!
IF YOU ASK ME...
...THIS WORLD IS...
REC 05:38
1/13 F11 0.0 ISO AUTO
...JUST TOTALLY AWESOME!

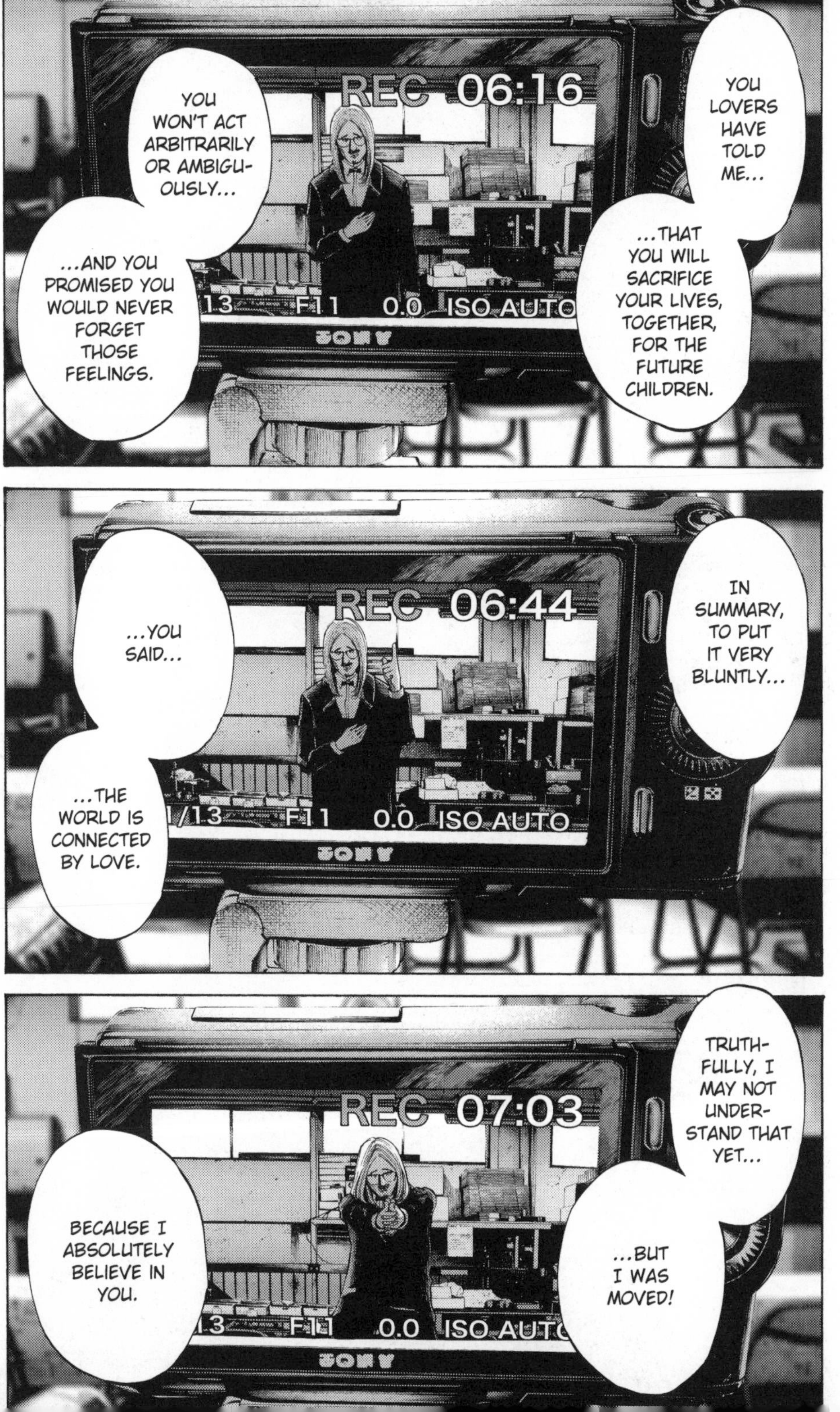
REC 06:16
YOU LOVERS HAVE TOLD ME...
...THAT YOU WILL SACRIFICE YOUR LIVES, TOGETHER, FOR THE FUTURE CHILDREN.
YOU WON'T ACT ARBITRARILY OR AMBIGU-OUSLY...
...AND YOU PROMISED YOU WOULD NEVER FORGET THOSE FEELINGS.
13 F11 0.0 ISO AUTO
REC 06:44
IN SUMMARY, TO PUT IT VERY BLUNTLY...
...YOU SAID...
...THE WORLD IS CONNECTED BY LOVE.
1/13 F11 0.0 ISO AUTO
REC 07:03
TRUTH-FULLY, I MAY NOT UNDER-STAND THAT YET...
...BUT I WAS MOVED!
BECAUSE I ABSOLUTELY BELIEVE IN YOU.
13 F11 0.0 ISO AUTO

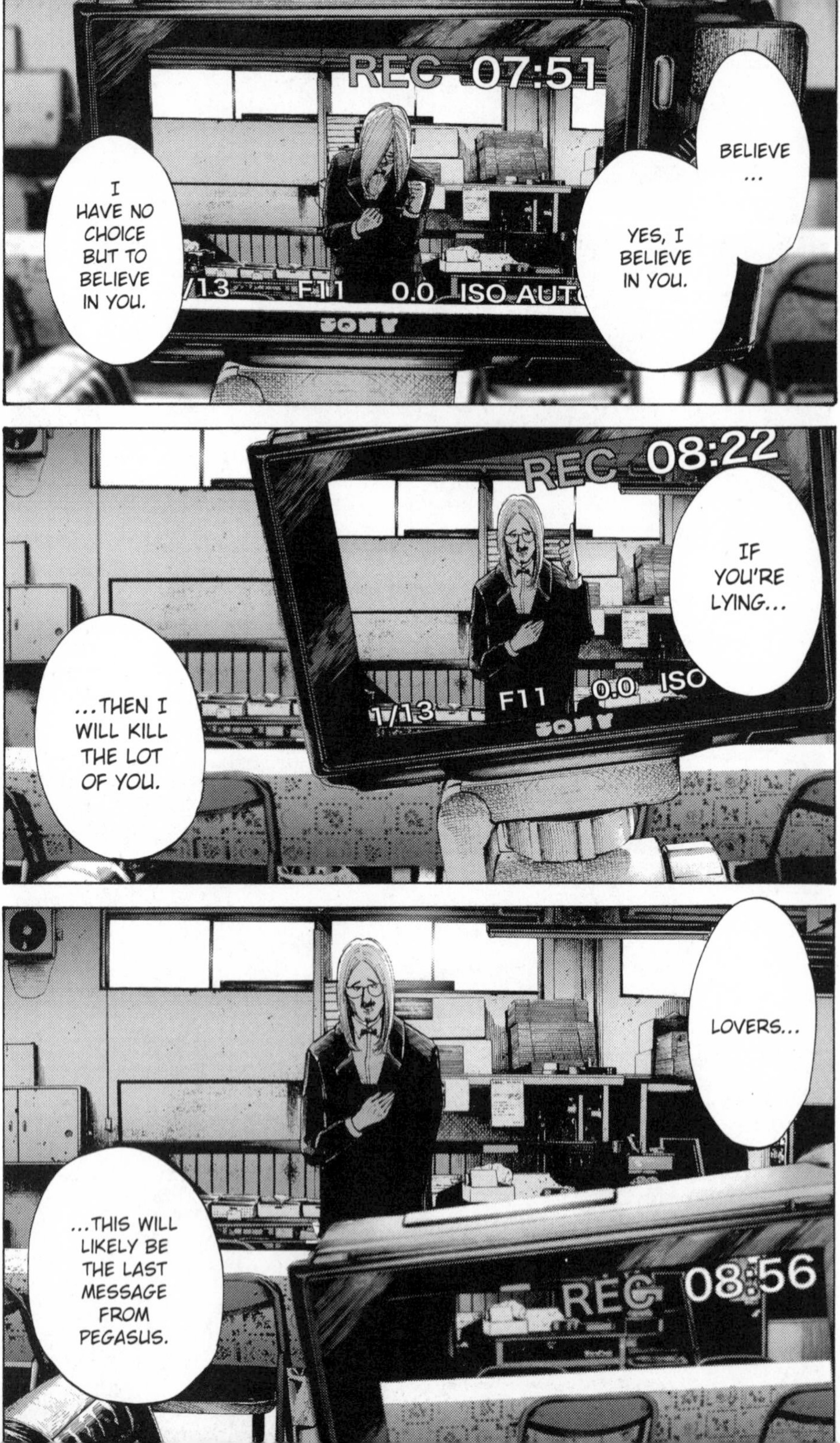
REC 07:51
BELIEVE ...
YES, I BELIEVE IN YOU.
I HAVE NO CHOICE BUT TO BELIEVE IN YOU.
F11 0.0
REC 08:22
IF YOU'RE LYING...
...THEN I WILL KILL THE LOT OF YOU.
1/13 F11 0.0 ISO
LOVERS...
...THIS WILL LIKELY BE THE LAST MESSAGE FROM PEGASUS.
REC 08:56

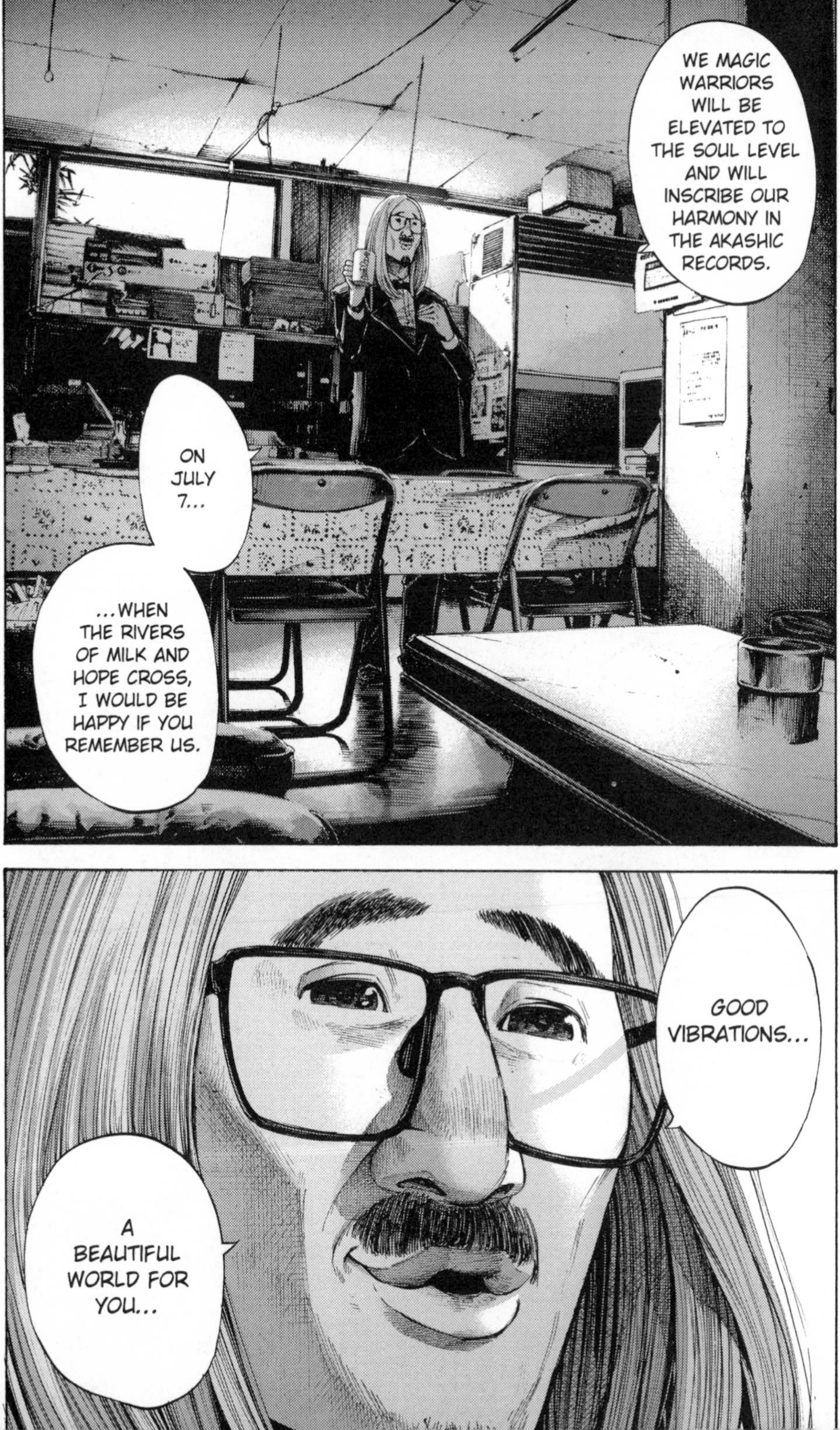
WE MAGIC WARRIORS WILL BE ELEVATED TO THE SOUL LEVEL AND WILL INSCRIBE OUR HARMONY IN THE AKASHIC RECORDS.
ON JULY 7...
...WHEN THE RIVERS OF MILK AND HOPE CROSS, I WOULD BE HAPPY IF YOU REMEMBER US.
GOOD VIBRATIONS...
A BEAUTIFUL WORLD FOR YOU...

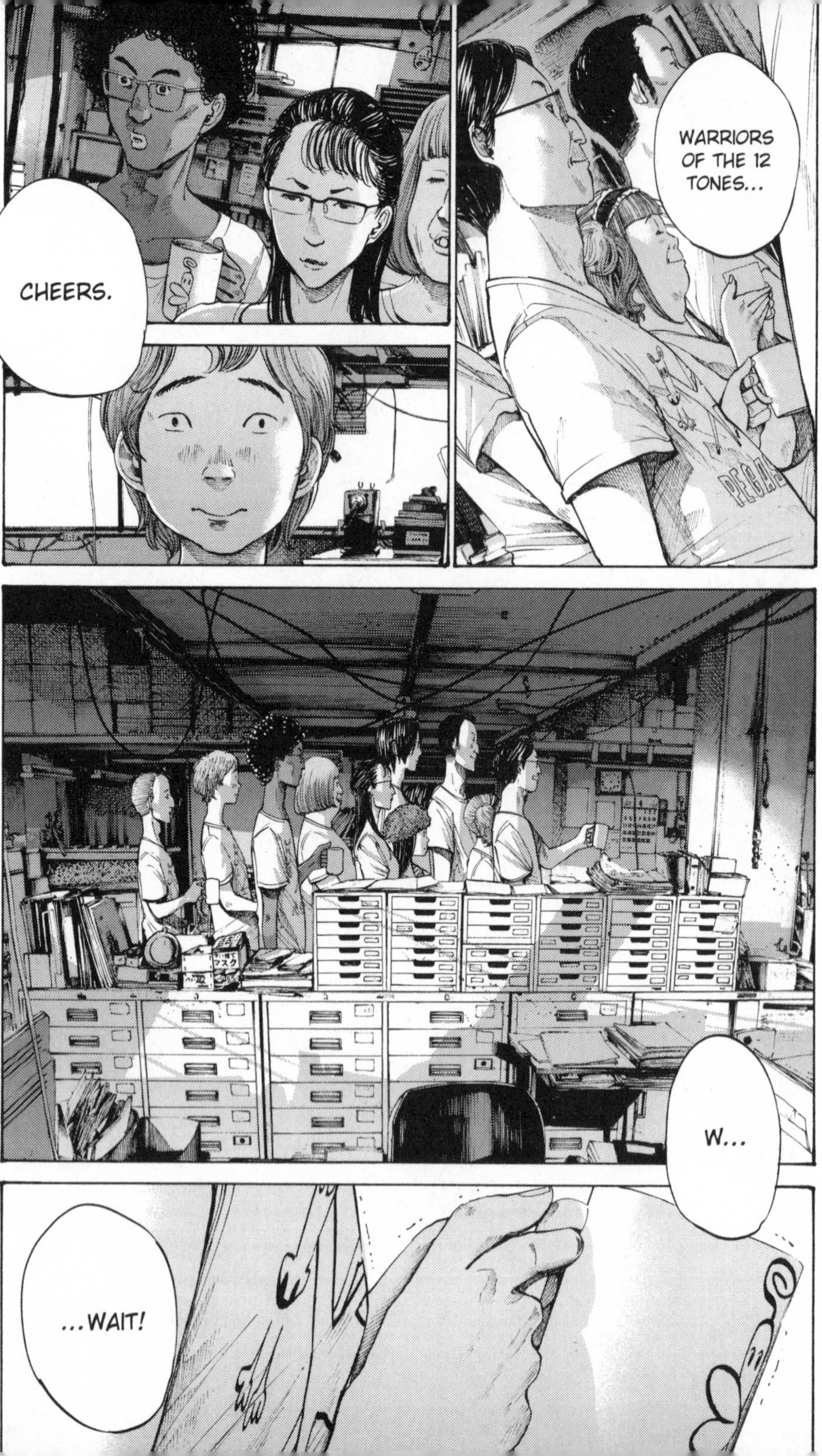
WARRIORS OF THE 12 TONES...
CHEERS.
W...
...WAIT!

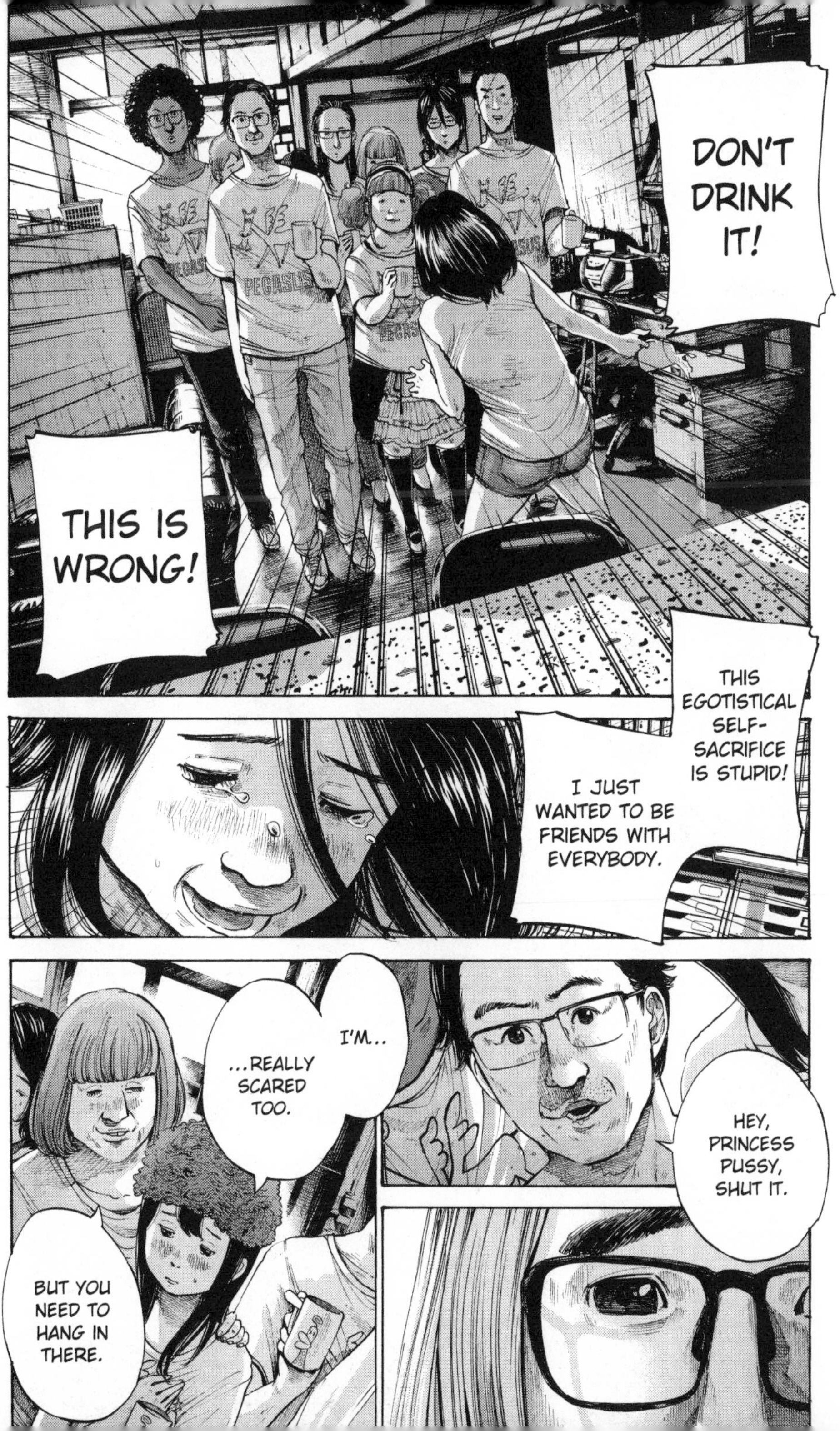
DON'T DRINK IT!
THIS IS WRONG!
THIS EGOTISTICAL SELF-SACRIFICE IS STUPID!
I JUST WANTED TO BE FRIENDS WITH EVERYBODY.
HEY, PRINCESS PUSSY, SHUT IT.
I'M...
...REALLY SCARED TOO.
BUT YOU NEED TO HANG IN THERE.

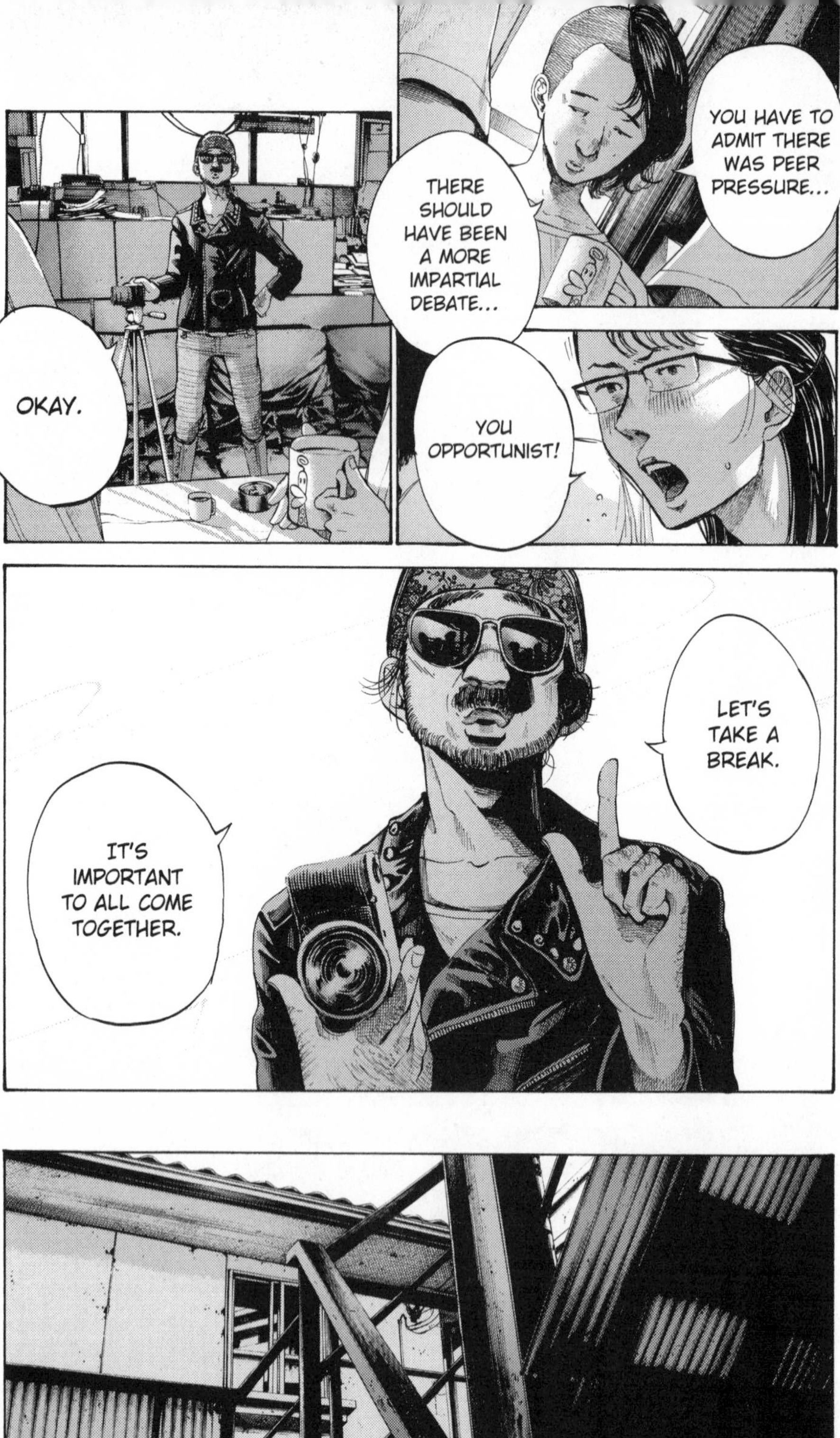
YOU HAVE TO ADMIT THERE WAS PEER PRESSURE...
THERE SHOULD HAVE BEEN A MORE IMPARTIAL DEBATE...
YOU OPPORTUNIST!
OKAY.
LET'S TAKE A BREAK.
IT'S IMPORTANT TO ALL COME TOGETHER.

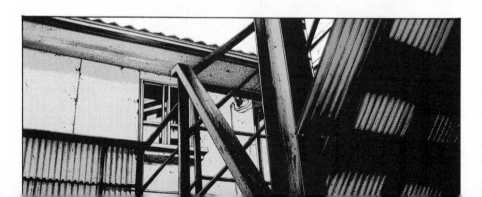

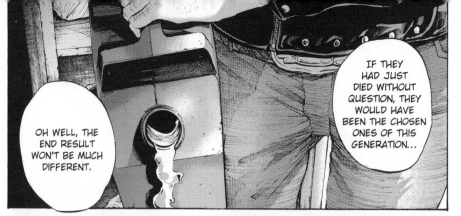

IF THEY HAD JUST DIED WITHOUT QUESTION, THEY WOULD HAVE BEEN THE CHOSEN ONES OF THIS GENERATION...

OH WELL, THE END RESULT WON'T BE MUCH DIFFERENT.

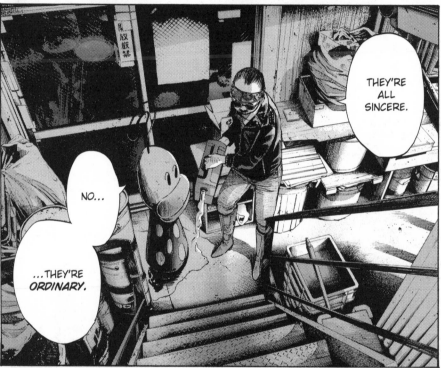

THEY'RE ALL SINCERE.

NO...

...THEY'RE *ORDINARY.*

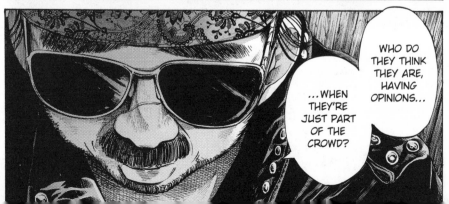

WHO DO THEY THINK THEY ARE, HAVING OPINIONS...

...WHEN THEY'RE JUST PART OF THE CROWD?

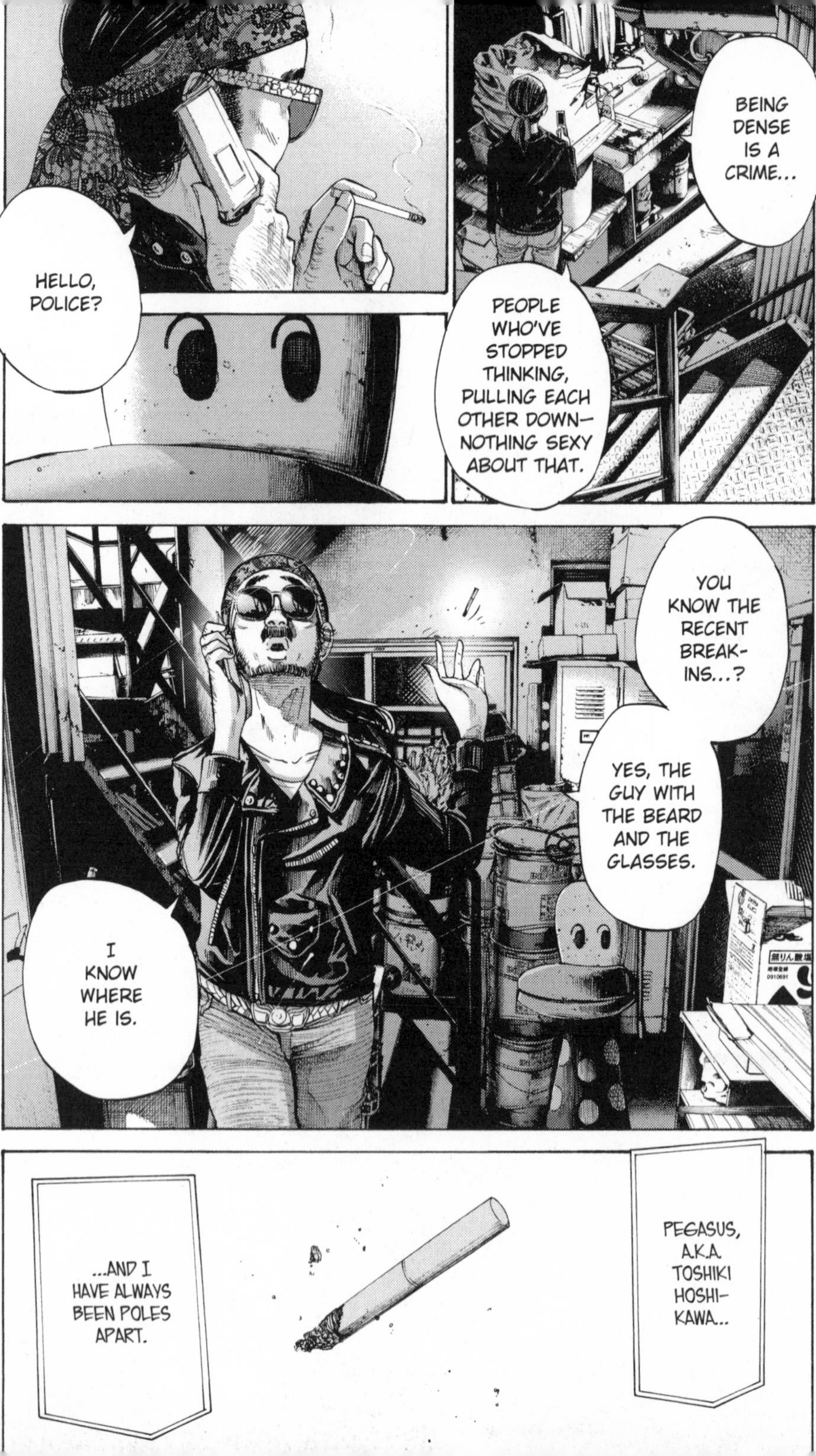
BEING DENSE IS A CRIME...
PEOPLE WHO'VE STOPPED THINKING, PULLING EACH OTHER DOWN—NOTHING SEXY ABOUT THAT.
HELLO, POLICE?
YOU KNOW THE RECENT BREAK-INS...?
YES, THE GUY WITH THE BEARD AND THE GLASSES.
I KNOW WHERE HE IS.
PEGASUS, A.K.A. TOSHIKI HOSHIKAWA...
...AND I HAVE ALWAYS BEEN POLES APART.

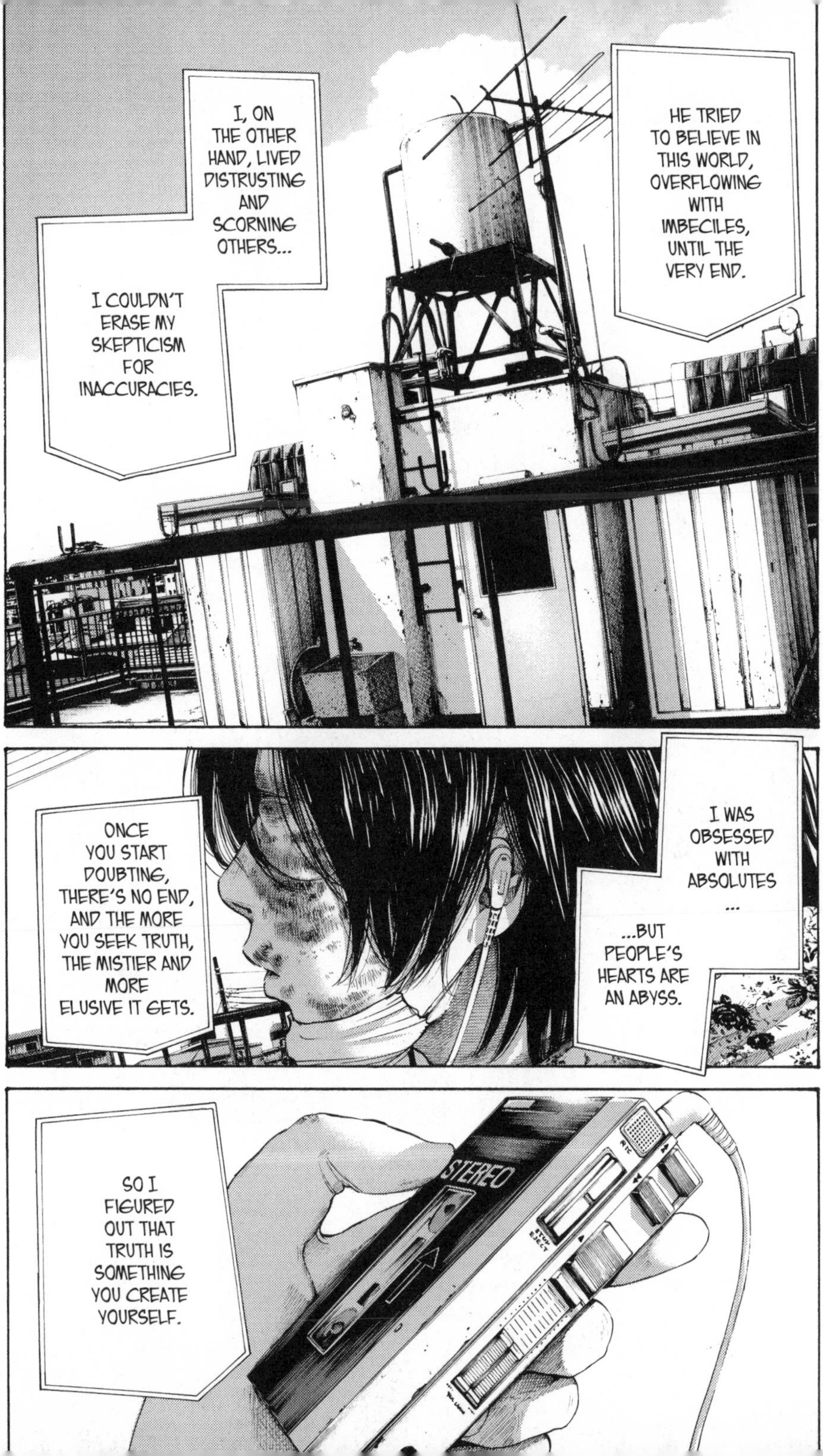
HE TRIED TO BELIEVE IN THIS WORLD, OVERFLOWING WITH IMBECILES, UNTIL THE VERY END.
I, ON THE OTHER HAND, LIVED DISTRUSTING AND SCORNING OTHERS...
I COULDN'T ERASE MY SKEPTICISM FOR INACCURACIES.
I WAS OBSESSED WITH ABSOLUTES ...
...BUT PEOPLE'S HEARTS ARE AN ABYSS.
ONCE YOU START DOUBTING, THERE'S NO END, AND THE MORE YOU SEEK TRUTH, THE MISTIER AND MORE ELUSIVE IT GETS.
SO I FIGURED OUT THAT TRUTH IS SOMETHING YOU CREATE YOURSELF.
STEREO

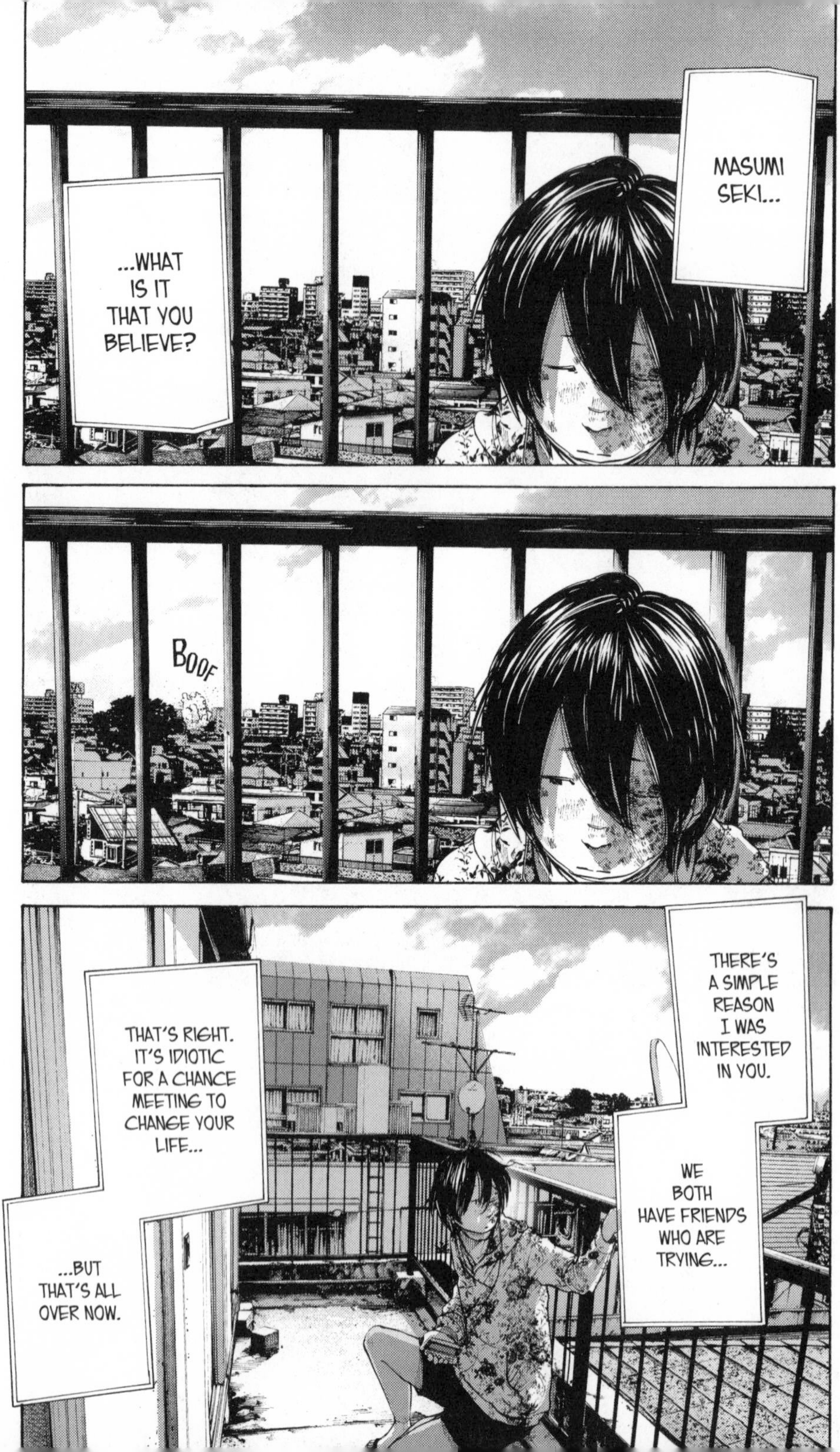
MASUMI SEKI...
...WHAT IS IT THAT YOU BELIEVE?
BOOF
THERE'S A SIMPLE REASON I WAS INTERESTED IN YOU.
WE BOTH HAVE FRIENDS WHO ARE TRYING...
THAT'S RIGHT. IT'S IDIOTIC FOR A CHANCE MEETING TO CHANGE YOUR LIFE...
...BUT THAT'S ALL OVER NOW.

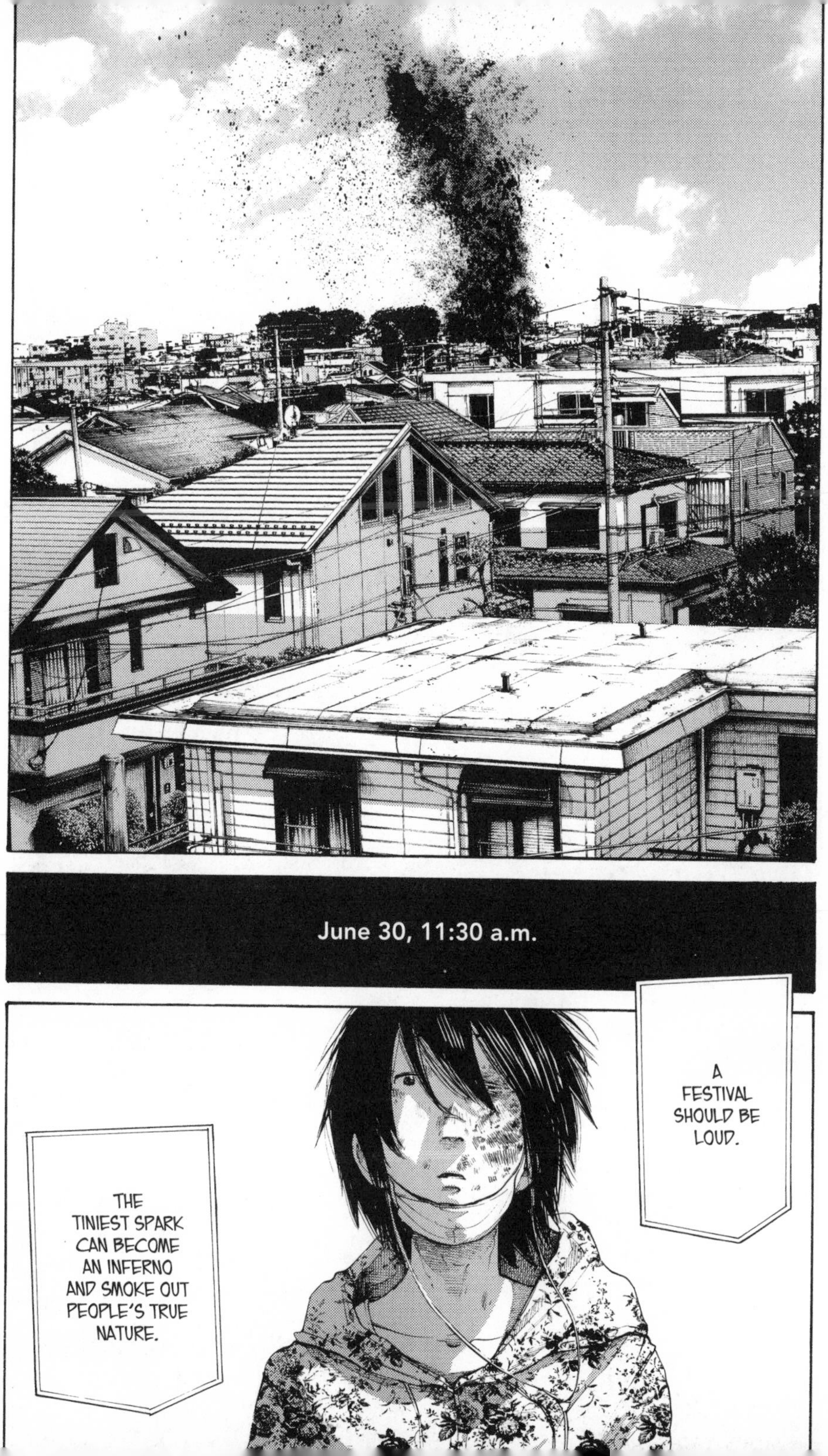
June 30, 11:30 a.m.
A FESTIVAL SHOULD BE LOUD.
THE TINIEST SPARK CAN BECOME AN INFERNO AND SMOKE OUT PEOPLE'S TRUE NATURE.

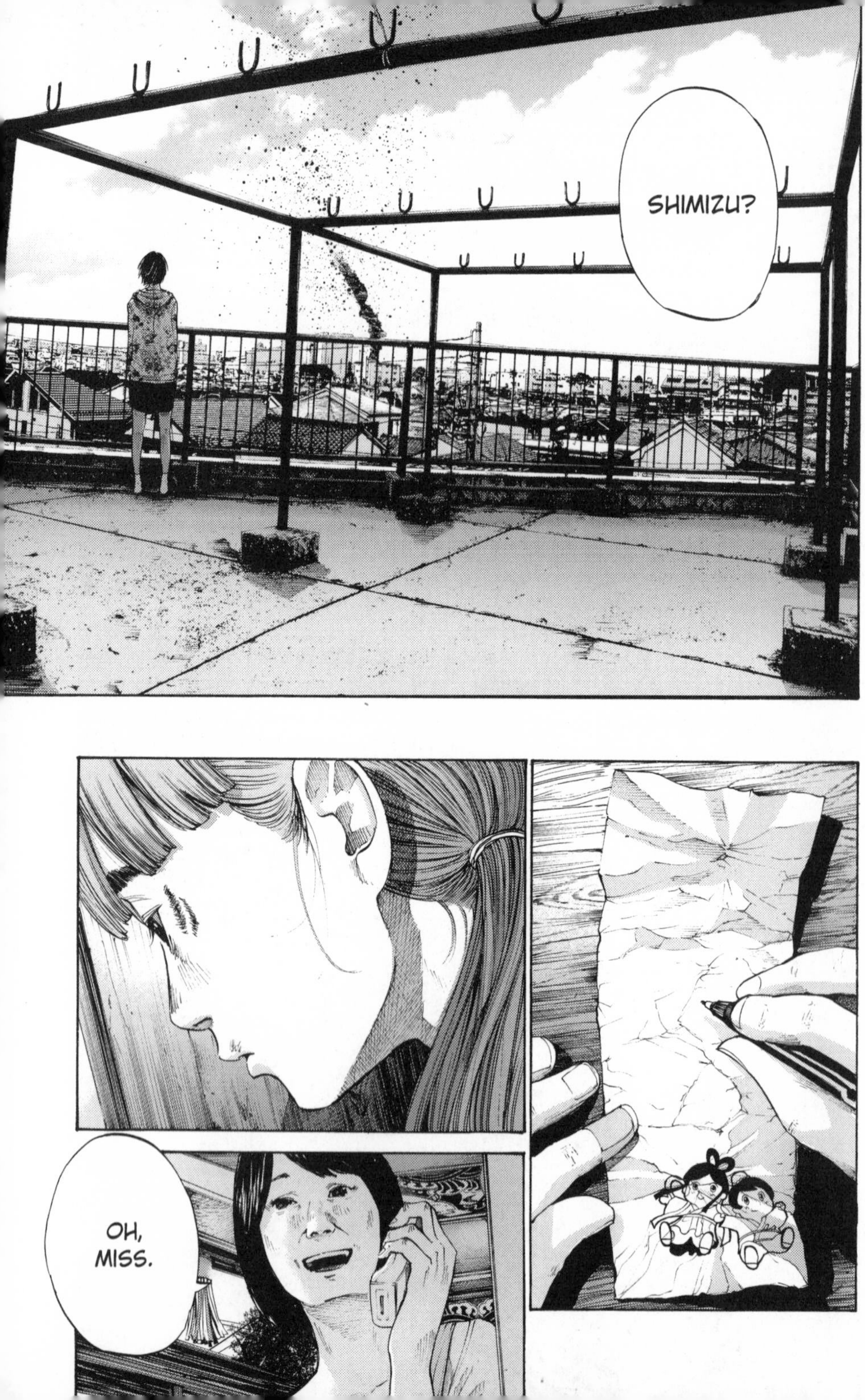
SHIMIZU?
OH, MISS.

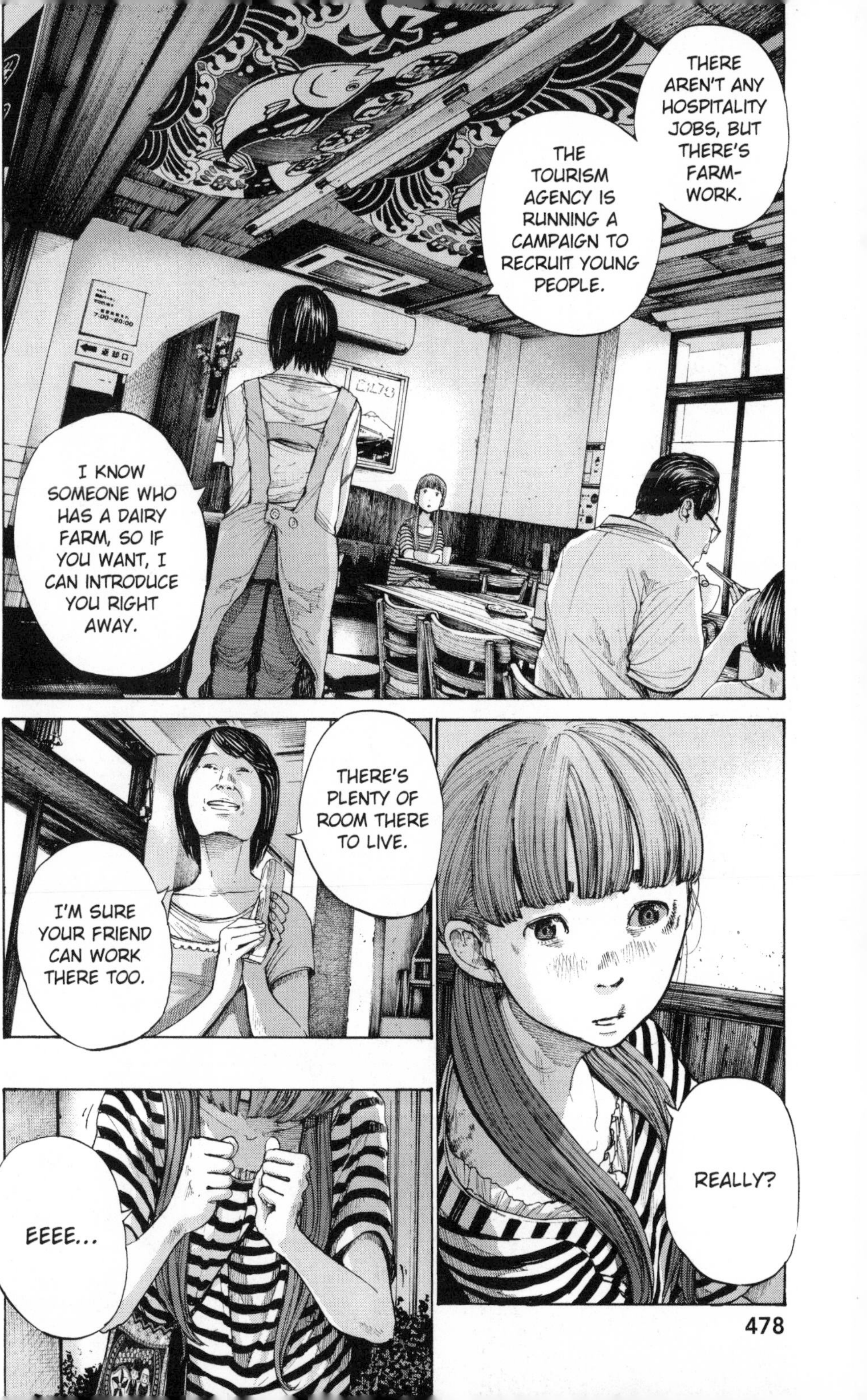
THERE AREN'T ANY HOSPITALITY JOBS, BUT THERE'S FARM-WORK.
THE TOURISM AGENCY IS RUNNING A CAMPAIGN TO RECRUIT YOUNG PEOPLE.
I KNOW SOMEONE WHO HAS A DAIRY FARM, SO IF YOU WANT, I CAN INTRODUCE YOU RIGHT AWAY.
REALLY?
THERE'S PLENTY OF ROOM THERE TO LIVE.
I'M SURE YOUR FRIEND CAN WORK THERE TOO.
EEEE...

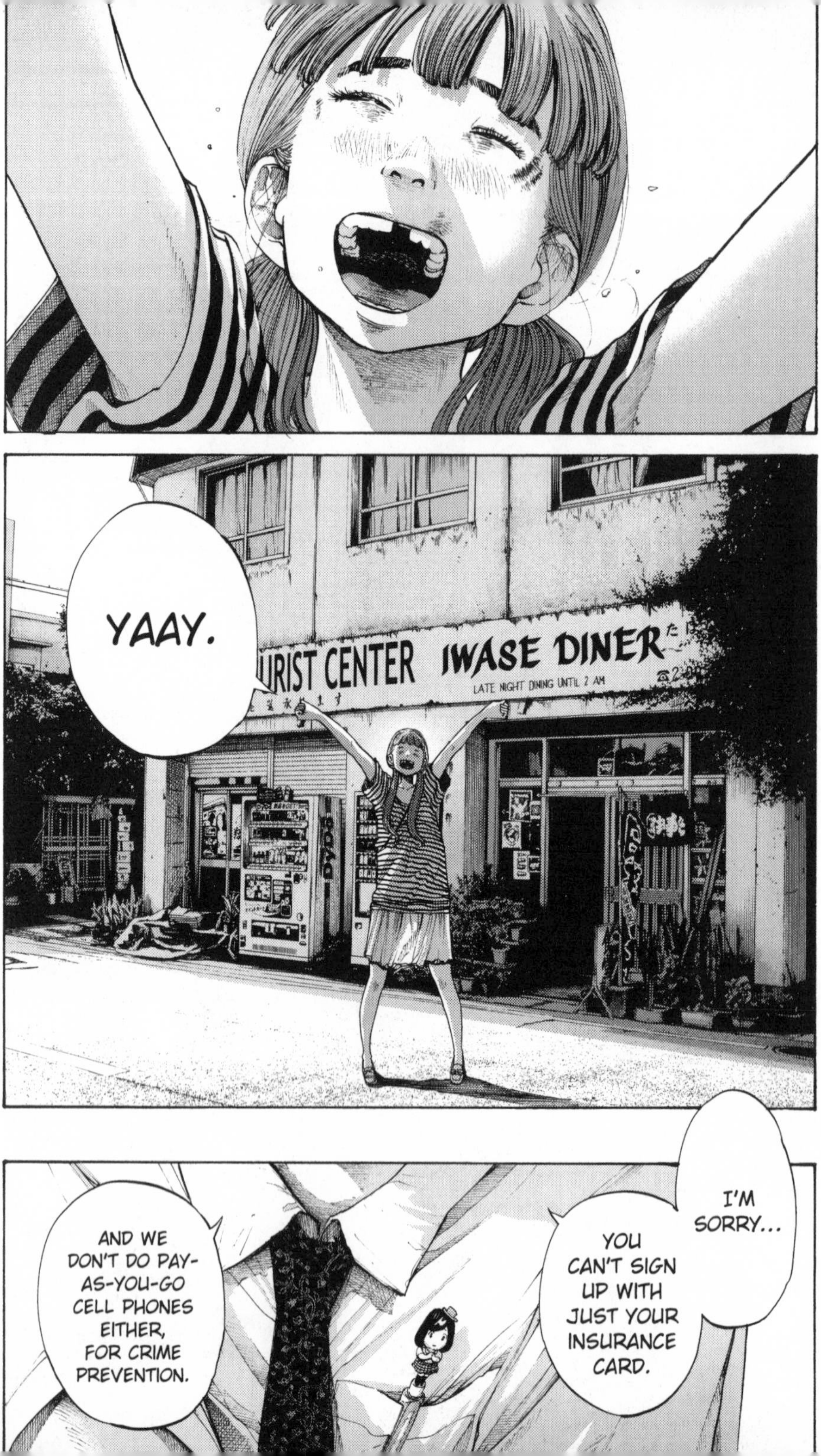
YAAY.
URIST CENTER
IWASE DINER
LATE NIGHT DINING UNTIL 2 AM
I'M SORRY...
YOU CAN'T SIGN UP WITH JUST YOUR INSURANCE CARD.
AND WE DON'T DO PAY-AS-YOU-GO CELL PHONES EITHER, FOR CRIME PREVENTION.

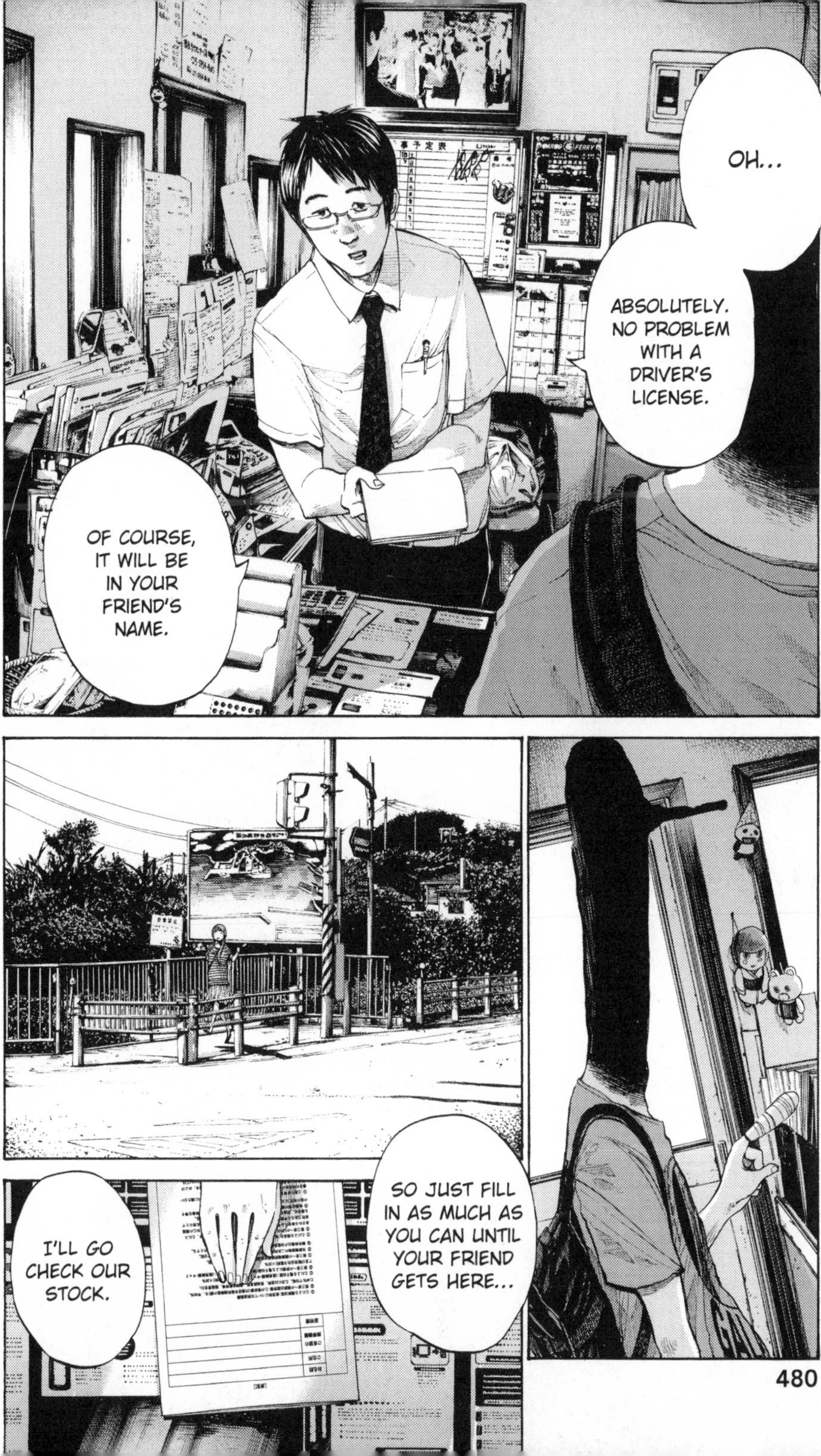
OH...
ABSOLUTELY. NO PROBLEM WITH A DRIVER'S LICENSE.
OF COURSE, IT WILL BE IN YOUR FRIEND'S NAME.
SO JUST FILL IN AS MUCH AS YOU CAN UNTIL YOUR FRIEND GETS HERE...
I'LL GO CHECK OUR STOCK.

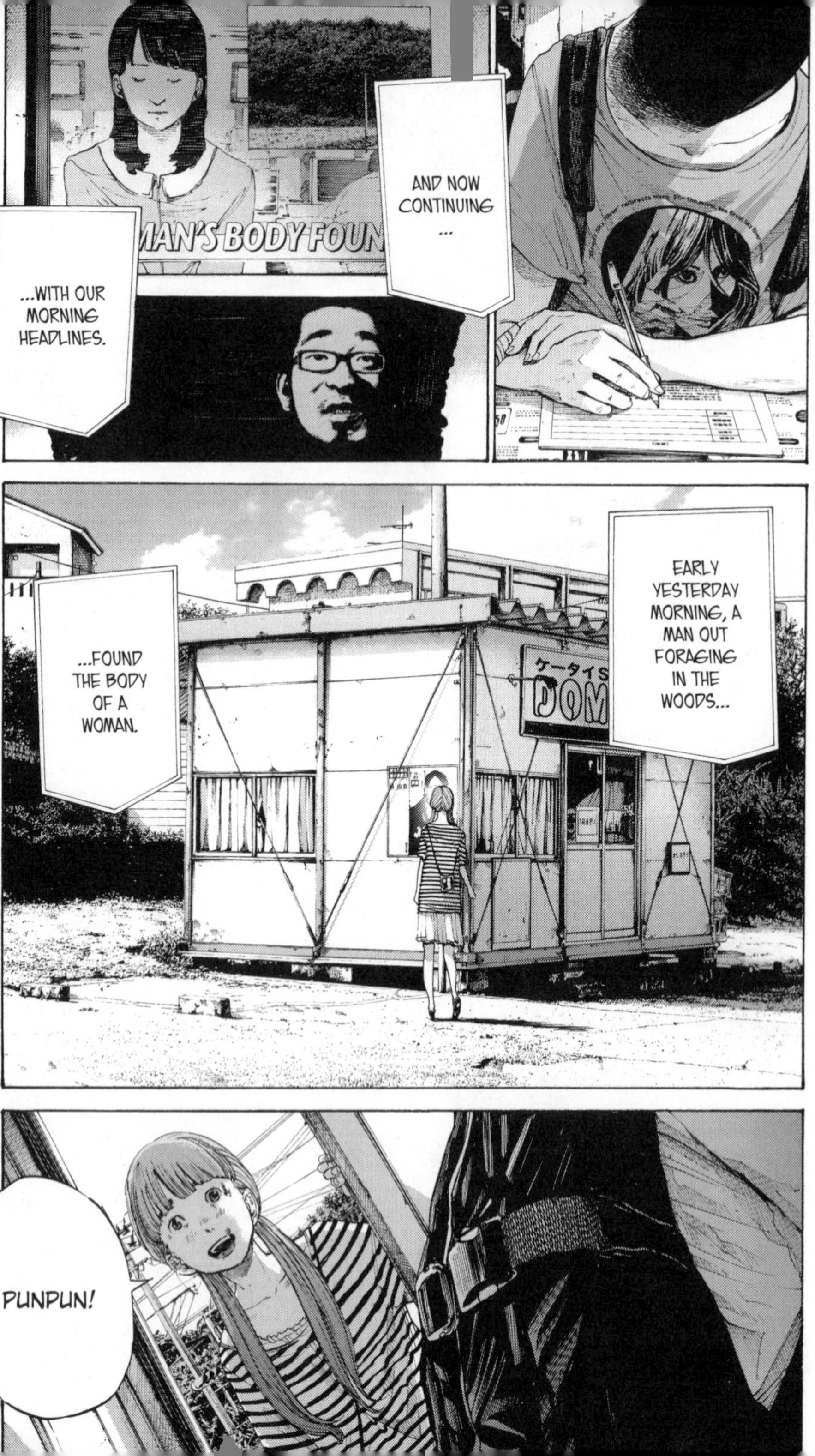
AND NOW CONTINUING ...
MAN'S BODY FOUN
...WITH OUR MORNING HEADLINES.
EARLY YESTERDAY MORNING, A MAN OUT FORAGING IN THE WOODS...
ケータイS
DOM
...FOUND THE BODY OF A WOMAN.
PUNPUN!

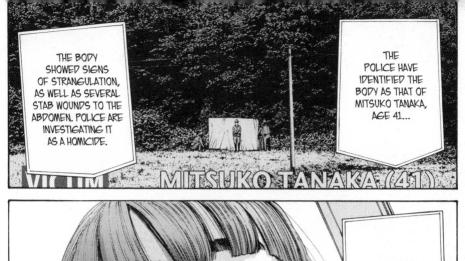

THE BODY SHOWED SIGNS OF STRANGULATION, AS WELL AS SEVERAL STAB WOUNDS TO THE ABDOMEN. POLICE ARE INVESTIGATING IT AS A HOMICIDE.

THE POLICE HAVE IDENTIFIED THE BODY AS THAT OF MITSUKO TANAKA, AGE 41...

[VICTIM] MITSUKO TANAKA (41)

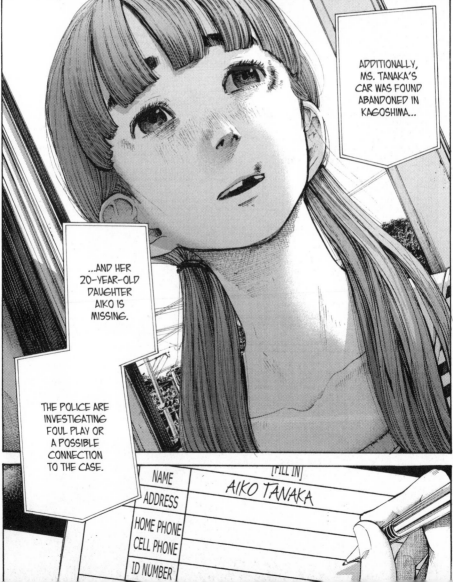

ADDITIONALLY, MS. TANAKA'S CAR WAS FOUND ABANDONED IN KAGOSHIMA...

...AND HER 20-YEAR-OLD DAUGHTER AIKO IS MISSING.

THE POLICE ARE INVESTIGATING FOUL PLAY OR A POSSIBLE CONNECTION TO THE CASE.

	[FILL IN]
NAME	AIKO TANAKA
ADDRESS	
HOME PHONE	
CELL PHONE	
ID NUMBER	

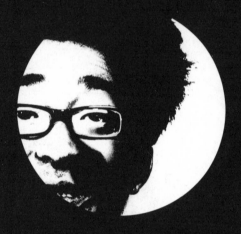

GOODNIGHT PUNPUN   INIO ASANO
Part Twelve

BACKGROUND ASSISTANTS: Satsuki Sato
Hiro Kashiwaba
Ran Atsumori
COOPERATION: Kumatsuto
Yu Uehara

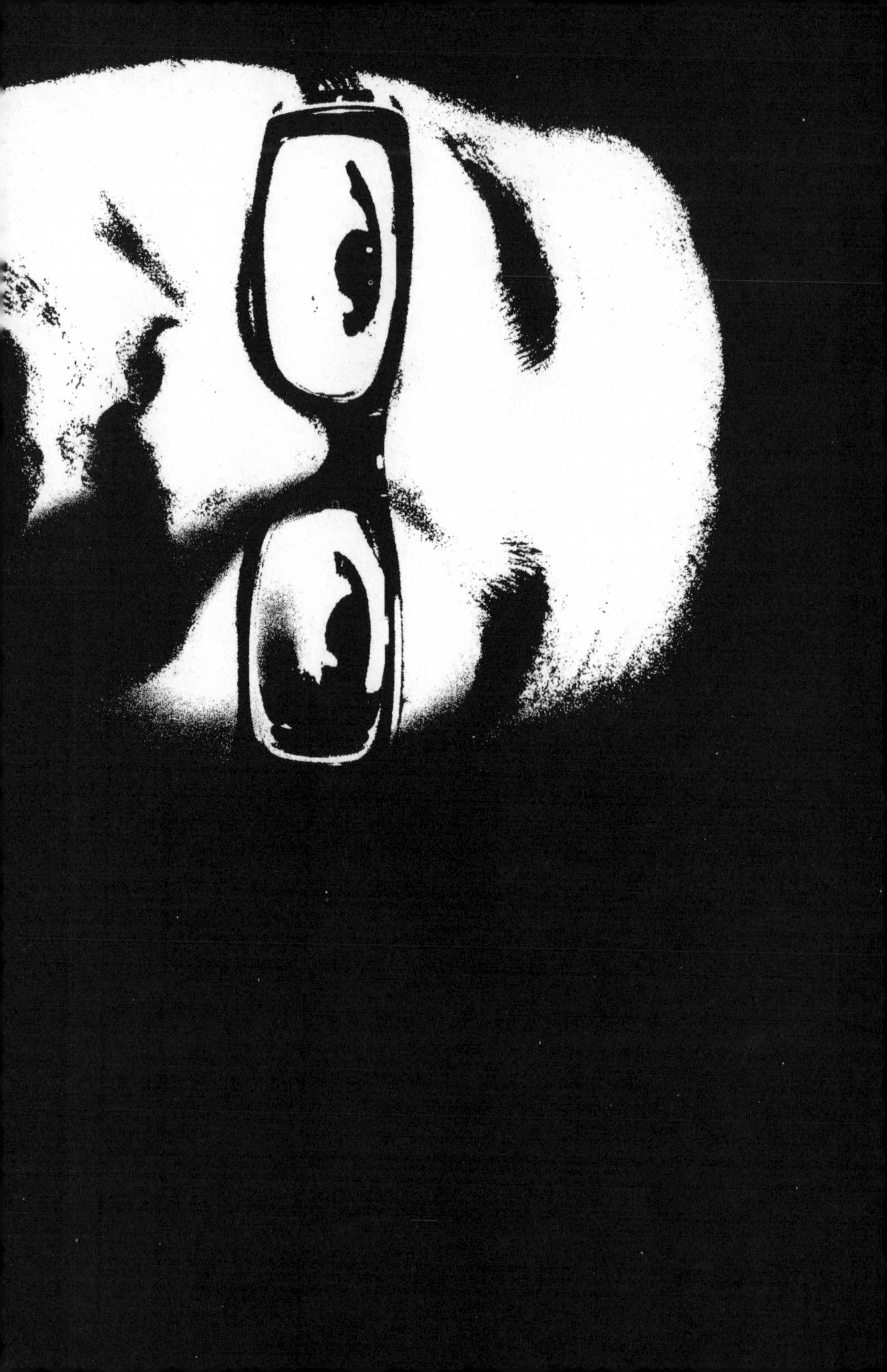

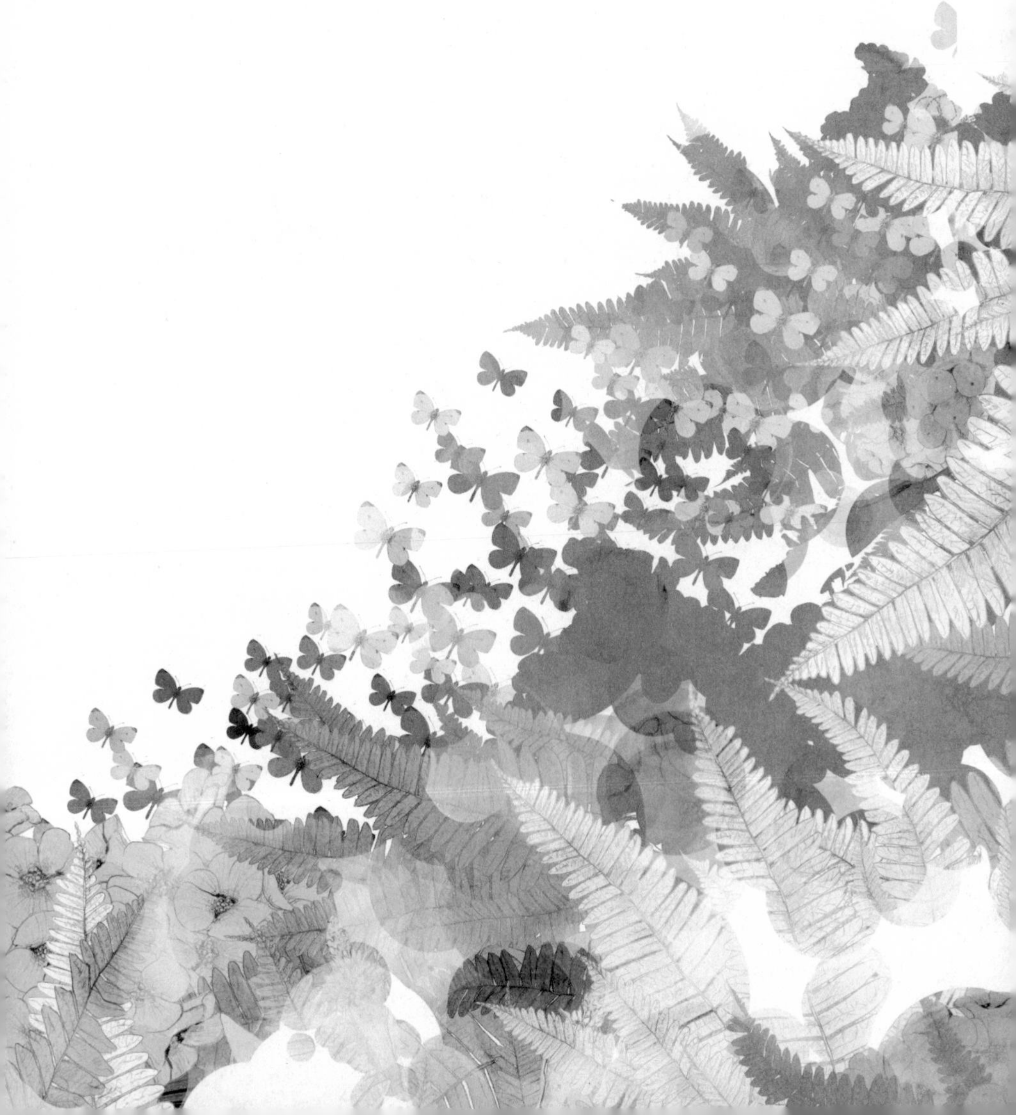

THE END IS COMING.

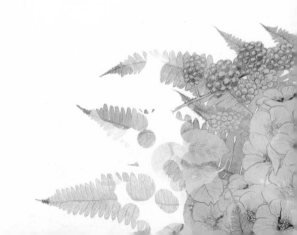

INIO ASANO, a bona fide earthling, was born in Ibaraki, Japan, in 1980. In 2001, his short story "Uchu kara Konnichiwa" (Hello from Outer Space) won the first Sunday GX Rookie Prize. Later, GX published his series *Subarashi Sekai*, available in English from VIZ Media as *What a Wonderful World!* His other works include *Hikari no Machi* (City of Light), *Nijigahara Holograph* and *Umibe no Onna no Ko* (A Girl on the Shore), as well as *solanin*, also available from VIZ Media.

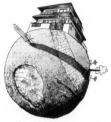

GOODNIGHT PUNPUN

Volume 6
VIZ Signature Edition

Story and Art by INIO ASANO

OYASUMI PUNPUN Vol. 11, 12
by Inio ASANO
© 2007 Inio ASANO
All rights reserved.
Original Japanese edition published by SHOGAKUKAN.
English translation rights in the United States of America,
Canada, the United Kingdom and Ireland arranged with
SHOGAKUKAN.

Translation ☆ JN PRODUCTIONS
Touch-Up Art & Lettering ✮ ANNALIESE CHRISTMAN
Design ✦ IZUMI EVERS, FAWN LAU
Editor ✪ PANCHA DIAZ

Printed in Canada

Published by VIZ Media, LLC
P.O. Box 77010
San Francisco, CA 94107

10 9 8 7 6 5 4 3 2 1
First printing, June 2017

www.viz.com *VIZ SIGNATURE*

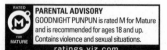

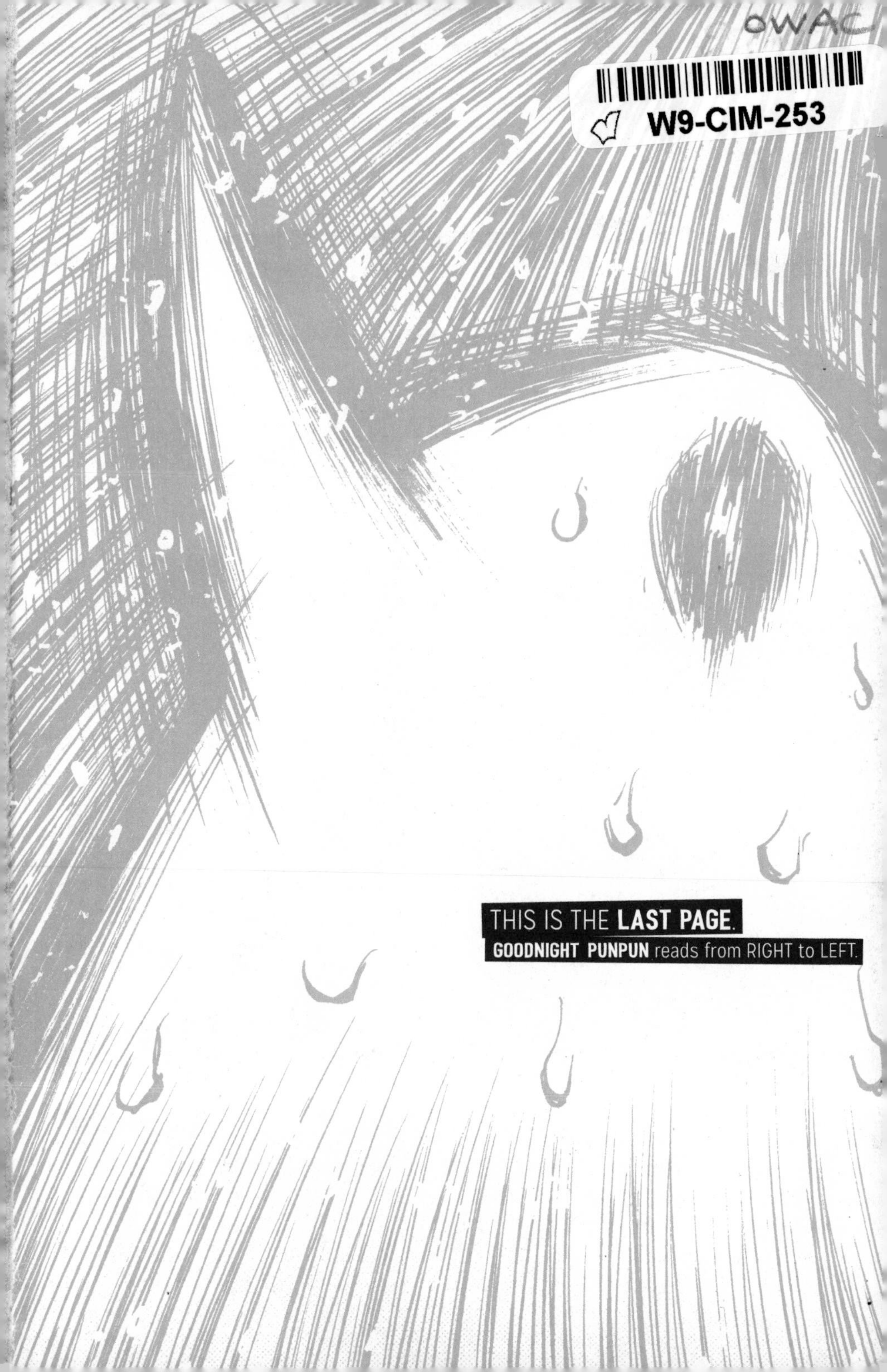

THIS IS THE **LAST PAGE**.

GOODNIGHT PUNPUN reads from RIGHT to LEFT.